A HISTORY OF SOVIET RUSSIA

A HISTORY OF SOVIET RUSSIA

FIFTH REVISED EDITION

by Georg von Rauch

Translated by Peter and Annette Jacobsohn

FREDERICK A. PRAEGER, Publishers
New York · Washington · London

FREDERICK A. PRAEGER, *Publishers*
111 Fourth Avenue, New York, N.Y. 10003, U.S.A.
5, Cromwell Place, London S.W. 7, England

Published in the United States of America in 1967
by Frederick A. Praeger, Inc., Publishers

Third printing, 1969

This is the fifth revised edition of the book
first published in 1957 by Frederick A. Praeger, Inc.
The second edition was published in 1958;
the third edition in 1962; the fourth edition in 1964.

Library of Congress Catalog Card Number: 67-20493

This book is Number 9 in the series
Praeger Publications in Russian History and World Communism

Printed in the United States of America

PREFACE

A History of Soviet Russia is intended to be a generally understandable and clearly-organized outline of Russia's history since 1917.

The existing works on this period usually stress the evolution of the Marxist ideology. A number of important general histories emphasize the foreign policy of the Soviet Union or even its foreign trade policies. In some other works, events revolve around the lives of Lenin or Stalin. English and American authors have provided us with excellent decriptions of the Russian Revolution. The already published volumes of more extensive works offer a wealth of valuable material, although at times the official pronouncements of the Party Congresses or the Communist press are followed too religiously, with too much importance attached to ideological and tactical argumentation.

What has so far not been available is a summarized survey of the events of the years 1917-1963, described in chronological order. There was need for a guide book which, without being shallow, did not bog down in a discussion of the problems or neglect the actual events sometimes lost in the rhetoric of Party leaders. What was needed was a work for easy reference for the student, the teacher, the truly concerned.

I have not based my book on theories but on the actual Russian background of the October Revolution—the revolutionary trends of the 19th and early 20th century. The revolution itself is depicted as the product of the interaction of many factors—too innumerable to be perceived in their totality by their contemporaries. Lenin's central role must not, of course, be overlooked here. However, any objective observer will also consider all the other revolutionary figures and trends even if they did not finally prevail. The influence of the Mensheviks and of the Social Revolutionaries, which could be felt until 1921, as well as Trotsky's pre-eminent role in the Rev-

v

olution and the civil war, must not be obscured by adopting the Stalinist viewpoint.

I am entirely opposed to the view that Russia's evolution toward Bolshevism was in any way predetermined. I do not hold that present conditions are a natural consequence of a Russian predisposition for autocratic, despotic forms of government. The centralist and autocratic Muscovite state was by no means the only possible form in which the spirit of the Russian people could manifest itself. There have long existed indigenous and democratic elements in Russia; the struggle for the liberation of the people did not, inevitably, have to result in the Stalinist dictatorship with all its consequences.

Viewed thus, Bolshevism is a social structure which owes its origin to a curious amalgam of rational Western Marxism and the secularized Messianic bent of Russian political thought. It is by no means the only possible realization of the social concept on Russian soil. Primitive slogans and equations such as "Stalin: the Red Czar," or "Bolshevist imperialism: the legitimate successor of Czarist expansionism," merely serve to confuse. Despite periods of isolation and alienation, there has been an indissoluble bond between the culture of Russia and that of the West since the days of Vladimir the Saint and Yaroslav the Wise. The European cultural heritage would be truncated without the contributions of Pushkin, Dostoevsky and Tolstoy, Tchaikovsky, Stravinsky and others. Occidental Christianity would be poorer without the Eastern Church as its third branch.

The dominant role of the Russian people in the history of the East European regions inhabited by Eastern slavic tribes is undisputed. It is stressed by the official historiography of Russia's present rulers, even if differently accented. Nevertheless, the Eurasian region is multi-national in character. In spite of bloody persecutions of many nationalities, in spite of the forced transplantation and Russification of entire peoples, the Soviet Union today is clearly a multinational state. The Soviet system uses the federalist structure only as a barren shrine for the centralist party doctrine.

Even though the historian must take these facts into account, he should not look upon Russia as a kind of orange which divides neatly into its national components. Even the Ukraine, the largest of the East Slavic but non-Russian nations, is joined to the Great Russian people by many ties reaching far back into a common past. The situation is more different where non-Slavic nations, during an almost thousand-year-old history, have absorbed so much of the Occident that their annexation or re-annexation by Soviet Russia can only be considered rapine.

The polarity of nationalism and internationalism, which began with the debates about the peace of Brest-Litovsk and became unmistakable in the thirties, is of great importance in understanding the Soviet era. It is the basis for the fight against oppositional trends, for the phenomenon of Soviet patriotism and the excessive chauvinism of the recent past. It is also the basis for a Soviet foreign policy weaving between ideological rigidity and realistic flexibility. The divergence between theory and practice runs like a scarlet thread through the forty years of the Bolshevik experiment; it is chiefly this contrast which makes of it one of the greatest mockeries of world history. Nothing demonstrates this more clearly than a detailed analysis of the present social structure and governmental practice of a state which smothered the cry for freedom under the sway of a party oligarchy.

This formulation also indicates the position I have taken. My aim, however, is to relate the history of Soviet Russia, from 1917 to the present, *sine ira et studio*. While Soviet historiography opposes a "formalistic objectivism" and party dogma requires an ideologically correct history, I have tried to be faithful to Western scientific tradition.

The use of source materials, especially original Russian materials, presented certain difficulties. Nevertheless, I had recourse to them whenever possible. The excellent English work on Russian foreign policy under the editorship of Jane Degras, and E. M. Carroll's and F. T. Epstein's collection of documents on the history of Russian-German relations, were of invaluable assistance. I am particularly indebted to a number of authors for the stimulation and instruction received from their works, even though we have occasional or basic differences of interpretation and evaluation. Among these are the works and articles of E. H. Carr, W. H. Chamberlin, I. Deutscher and W. Gurian; of Max Beloff, I. M. Bochenski, Franz Borkenau, David J. Dallin, Louis Fischer, V. Gitermann, E. Hanisch; of Sidney Hook, N. Jasny, Boris Meissner, K. Mehnert, Boris Nicolaevsky, H. Seton-Watson, David Shub, Fedor Stepun, Alexander Weissberg-Cybulski, G. A. Wetter, and Bertram D. Wolfe. Apart from official Soviet organs, the periodicals "American Review of the Soviet Union", "Soviet Studies", "Ostprobleme" and "Osteuropa", offered a considerable source of material.

I am particularly grateful to my friend Boris Meissner for his many helpful suggestion in the preparation of this book. Thanks are also due to the American publisher Frederick A. Praeger who has facilitated the work in every way, particularly by making available new publications and other material, and to Peter and Annette Jacobsohn for translating the manuscript and for editorial assistance.

Georg von Rauch

TABLE OF CONTENTS

CHAPTER 2

THE CIVIL WAR

CHAPTER 3

THE ERA OF THE NEW ECONOMIC POLICY (NEP)

CHAPTER 9

THE END OF THE STALIN ERA

CHAPTER 10

KHRUSHCHEV AND AFTER

A History of Soviet Russia

PROLOGUE

The Awakening of Political Thought in Russia

Where are the roots of Bolshevik Russia to be found? Is Russian Marxism a phenomenon that belongs to the great waves of Western influence or does it grow out of the Russian past? Was Stalin justified in ranking himself with Ivan the Terrible and Peter the Great? Or was his a spiritually alien regime, as radical as that of the Tatar yoke, which extends its dominion beyond the political sphere into that of the mind? And may one hope that this time, too, the Russian and the other East European nations will be liberated—just as the Tatar rule was broken from within—by the Russian people?

The great Russian philosopher, Nikolai Berdyaev, views Bolshevism as a divine punishment, an inescapable fate for the Russian people which they must bear with dignity. However, he believes that Russia will experience a change of heart which will receive its decisive impetus from a purified Greek Orthodox Church.

This determinist view—that Bolshevism is the inescapable destiny of Russia—contains the great danger of accusing the Russian people of a predisposition for this way of life. There is no doubt that the history of the Soviet Union cannot be explained solely in terms of Marxist ideology, nor solely in terms of the Russian heritage. The Marxist ideology was exposed to strong influences from the Russian environment. The Stalin era in particular clearly demonstrated the interaction between doctrine and environment. But the belief that the country's development tends irrevocably towards Bolshevism is a misinterpretation of the forces evolving in the course of Russian history. Without going too far back into Russian history, the nineteenth century alone reveals the whole gamut of possibilities that were available for the solution of national and social problems.

The Bolshevik solution was, no doubt, one of them. However, the results of forty years of Soviet rule entitle us to regard the other solutions not only as happier but also as more suitable to the Russian character.

3

The Napoleonic wars and the problematic relationship between Russia and Europe led to the development of a Russian national consciousness. The beginning of historical thought in Russia produced contrasting reactions to the question of Russia's own contribution to world history; the answer was either negative and pessimistic, or romantic and messianic. The political realities of the reign of Nicholas I provoked criticism and it was but a short step from historical thinking to political discussion—discussion not only of the national but of the liberal problem as well. The enlightenment had brought the first breeze of liberal ideas. The European ideal of liberty, thus established, was strengthened by the common people's anarchical and inarticulate thirst for freedom. The Russian language differentiates not without reason between *volya* and *svoboda:* the one expressing the elementary chaotic urge as it had appeared in the revolts of a Razin and Pugachev; the other signifying aspirations reaching back to ancient Russian forms of a period older than that of the Muscovite contralist autocracy, but also related to West European impulses as expressed by Rousseau and Schiller. The first eruption of this pent up thirst for freedom, heightened by French rationalism and German idealism, was the so-called "Decembrist" revolt launched by officers of the Guard in 1825. It was a thrust into the void; the people did not echo it, since they set little store by political freedom, looking upon the omnipotent Czar and his autocracy as their only guarantee against the arbitrary power of the nobles. It was not long, however, until a particular, specifically Russian, social class began to form a broader basis for political aspirations and ideas. It was the so-called intelligentsia, the class—difficult to define—between officialdom and army on the one side and the peasant masses on the other. It was held together by the use of education as a weapon in its opposition to Czarism, and by its role in the battle for social justice. In this respect the intelligentsia took over the function of a third estate which did not exist in Russia in so pronounced a form. Its most prominent members were often followers of Hegel; from him they often passed to materialism, and politically its radical wing soon came under the influence of socialist ideas.

Of the greatest importance for the development of political thinking on a broader basis was the reform era of Alexander II. Whatever the many defects of the reforms, they did set free the tremendous energies of the people and brought about a sudden advance of social and intellectual life. The door was opened wide to the technical skill of the West which led to the triumph of capitalist economic forms and the birth of a bourgeoisie which in this shape had been unknown in Russia. The entrepreneur appeared beside the merchant of the old Russian type, the industrial worker detached himself from the peasantry, a host of new professions began to evolve and increasing interest was shown in intellectual pursuits.

The Populists

The many discussions on social, economic, political and ethical questions centered on the relationship to the people, the great masses of the still largely uneducated and politically unorganized workers and peasants. The intelligentsia was seized by a mystical faith in the simple Russian people, especially the Russian peasant, a faith which formed the basis of the Russian nationalism of the 1860's and 1870's with its Messianic accents. It was also the basis of the socio-political movement of those years, the *Narodnichestvo*, the movement of the populists.

"To go to the people" became the watchword for thousands of young men and women, especially students. As yet their aim was not political propaganda, but merely enlightenment and education, their efforts being imbued with much selfless idealism.

The belief in the simple Russian was closely tied to the hopes placed in the peasant village community, the *mir*. It was hailed as the long-incubating germ of a coming socialist society; and one believed that for the West too, it pointed the way to a regeneration of social relationships. Russia could thus apparently reach the goal of socialism without having to pass through the stage of Western bourgeois capitalism. One of the adherents of this view was Alexander Herzen, the great radical of the Russian intelligentsia, who since the 1840's had strongly influenced Russian public opinion through his "Bell", which he published in London. Out of his disillusionment with the Western bourgeoisie he concluded that Russia needed not a bourgeois revolution but a socialist one. Even Karl Marx conceded—in answer to an enquiry from the Russian revolutionary, Vera Zasulich—that under certain conditions the village community might enable Russia to pass directly from feudalism to socialism.

But the *narodniki* suffered a fiasco. The peasants did not overcome their inherited distrust of the educated classes nor could their clerically-inspired loyalty to the Czarist autocracy be shaken. Herzen's hope for a peaceful evolutionary transition to socialism put a great deal of strain on the patience of those involved. The slogans of another radical emigrant—Michael Bakunin—seemed to promise more speedy attainment of the ultimate goal. Bakunin, strongly influenced by Proudhon, carried his anarchism to extremes; he wanted to overthrow the state by violent revolution. The words of his Prague appeal to the Slavs of 1848 were macabre but hopeful: "From a sea of flames and blood the Revolution's star will rise in Moscow, high and wondrous, becoming the lodestar of happiness for all mankind." Bakunin, too, hoped for the liberation of Russia from the autocratic yoke by a great revolt of the peasants; with his appeals and pronunciamentos, he, like Herzen, acted as a goad to the *Narodniki* movement. But his demoniac destructiveness was basic to the terrorist trends which first appeared in the 1860's.

Russian terrorism evolved simultaneously with the *Narodnichestvo;* occasionally there were personal and intellectual ties. The attempts on the lives of Alexander II and his high officials from 1866 to 1881, were testimony of the iron determination of small groups of conspirators, frequently led by women. The great trials gave the terrorists and their lawyers opportunity for fiery public confessions full of idealism and laced with biting attacks on the regime. But within these groups sinister crimes were often committed demonstrating a frighteningly consistent negation of all ethics, as for example the Nechaev case.[1] It was also characteristic of the terrorists that the ideal of equality far out-weighed that of freedom. Their hatred for the upper classes almost exceeded their loathing for the government, and the trends leading to a levelling and collectivization of the people were unmistakable.

These circles had long ceased to be inspired by Herzen and Bakunin and were now chiefly influenced by N. G. Chernyshevsky. For him too, the village community was the basis of the socialist society but, going far beyond the mild utopianism of the French socialists, he called for concrete revolutionary action. The youth of that time was lastingly influenced by the image of the iron-willed professional revolutionary whom he extolled in a programmatic novel which also portrayed the communist state of the future.

During the 1870's Peter Tkachev developed a genuine theory of revolution. He judged the time ripe for an uprising in Russia. He differed from Bakunin in maintaining that the power apparatus of the state should not be destroyed. It was rather to be conquered through conspiracy and a *coup d'état* and then used to further the revolution. In order to transform society radically it would for some time be necessary to use coercion against the adherents of the status quo. The revolutionaries could only attain their goal by means of tight party discipline and with a centralized power apparatus at their disposal. Tkachev also rejected mass organization of the workers for Russia, primarily because the Russian industrial proletariat was as yet infinitesimal. A revolution could only be carried out by a small elite, inspired by revolutionary *élan*. He argued that just because Russia did not yet have a bourgeoisie in the Western sense, and capitalism was in its embryonic stage, the prospects of a successful revolution were far more favorable. A mass rising of the peasants from below, a *coup d'état* of the revolutionaries from above, would suffice to overthrow the Czar's regime.

The long overdue emancipation of the serfs, carried out somewhat precipitately by Alexander II in 1861, granted personal freedom to the bulk of the peasant population. But it did not guarantee them sufficient economic freedom. This had important consequences. Land allotments, made by the village community, usually resulted in too small and widely scattered parcels and the tax burden was too great. The peasants were far from being independent farmers, free to use their own initiative. As things stood, the many discontents among the rural proletariat provided ideal material for revolutionary propaganda.

In 1876 radical *narodniki* founded an organization, "Land and Freedom" *(zemlya i volya)*. The program envisaged different forms of agitation among peasants, workers and students. A special shock troop was to liquidate traitors and disorganize the government's power apparatus. Further steps were to be agreed upon at a secret revolutionary congress at Voronezh in 1879. The question of the use of terror led to a split. A minority rejected political terror as senseless and withdrew their support; the advocates of terror formed a new organization, "People's Will" *(narodnaya volya)*, and a group of moderate *narodniki*, primarily advocating agitation among the peasants, founded the "Black Repartition" *(chernyi peredel)*, an organization with agrarian-socialist aims.

The active functions of the "People's Will" were assigned to an Executive Committee, which planned the last attempts on the life of Alexander II. They succeeded in March 1881, a few days before the draft of a quasi-constitution, already approved by the Czar, was to be made public.

Although this constitution, like that planned by Alexander I in 1819-1820, envisaged only an Advisory Assembly and fulfilled only part of the demands of the liberals, it could yet claim to pave the way for further political reforms. Those connected with the Zemstvo (the county or provincial elective assembly), which had been created in the 1860's, regarded it as a kind of academy for liberal politicians and hoped that in time all classes would be entitled to participate in the self-administration of the country. Reactionary circles held to the comfortable but dangerous thesis that every attempt to introduce Western parliamentary forms in Russia was doomed to failure and that the downfall of the Czarist regime could only be followed by Communism![2] To consider Russian liberalism *a priori* as a still-born child was certainly incorrect. It was by no means clear why Russian democratic and liberal thought should be confined to Western parliamentary forms since a genuine democratic tradition had respectable ancestors in Russia itself.

Following the death of Alexander II a reactionary trend was initiated under Alexander III by Pobedonostsev who not only smothered all attempts at democracy but also banished the revolutionary movement from the political scene. However, it continued to smolder underground, soon to burst forth anew in Marxist guise.

The Beginnings of Marxism in Russia

Chernyshevsky, Tkachev and the thousands of "Friends of the People", including the radical terrorist wing, had one trait in common. They all believed that the Russian people were pre-destined to realize socialism in a special way, different from that advocated in Western Europe. They looked upon the peasantry, whom they idealized, as the foundation of the future social order. "Admittedly our people are very uneducated," Tkachev wrote, "but they are saturated with the idea of communal ownership. They are, so to speak, instinctively, traditionally communistic." In his opinion the Russian people were thus far closer to socialism than the peoples of the West.

However, these men generally ignored the fact that the much vaunted village community, the core of the Communist community of the future, was already disintegrating. Upon the liberation of the serfs it was incapable of meeting the varied demands of the modern agricultural economy, unable to compete with the farms and crownlands run on capitalist lines. The first Russian socialist who broke with the romanticism of the *mir* was Plekhanov. With him the proletariat became the focal point of revolutionary discussion.

Georgi Valentinovich Plekhanov (1857-1918) is the founder of Marxism in Russia. He was a member of the Central Russian landed gentry. As a twenty year old student in St. Petersburg he made a revolutionary speech at one of the earliest workers' demonstrations where the Red Flag was hoisted for the first time. At an early age he had become familiar with the thinking of Karl Marx. When, at the Voronezh Conference in 1879, he rejected terror as a political weapon, his arguments already echoed the Marxist theory that the evolution of each people proceeds according to economic conditions and cannot, therefore, be hastened arbitrarily by the removal of individual representatives of the regime. After the split in the "Land and Freedom" movement, the opponents of the terror gathered around him. In 1880 he emigrated to Switzerland where he completed his education.

Outwardly too, Plekhanov was the highly educated, well-mannered scholar. In his speeches he maintained a high standard and his writings must be considered important contributions to the theory of history and economics. He lacked, however, the gift of establishing direct contact with the working classes. He was no agitator and his thinking about the social situation in Russia and the question of revolution was never free of theoretical pallor. At first he attempted to gather around him in Switzerland a number of Russian socialists of Marxist persuasion. Among them was Vera Zasulich whose trial in 1878 had been headline news and who, in an exchange of letters in 1881, had induced Karl Marx to define his position regarding the *mir*. In the following year she published in Geneva a Russian translation of the Communist Manifesto with a preface by Marx and Engels.

In 1883 Plekhanov founded in Geneva the first Russian Marxist group, the "Liberation of Labor." Plekhanov developed his ideas concerning developments in Russia in the group's organ and in an extensive book. He attempted to expose as utopian the belief that Russia could directly attain a socialist order by further developing the village community and by-passing the capitalist stage. Plekhanov considered the Russian peasantry as an inarticulate, conservative mass which would gradually be absorbed by the proletariat on the one hand and the bourgeoisie on the other; as an independent factor it had to be ruled out. He pinned his hopes on the liberal bourgeoisie and the industrial proletariat, which were to unite

for the overthrow of the regime. While in the West the time
was ripe for proletarian revolution, in Russia only a bourgeois revolution was feasible at this point. For this reason the proletariat was
to support the efforts of the liberals, in order to gain freedom for
the middle classes. Only after the fall of the autocracy could the
fight for a socialist revolution begin. The proletariat would take
over after the bourgeoisie had dug its own grave.

An essay published in 1895, entitled "The Question of the Evolution of the Monistic Theory of History," finally disposed of the
narodniki and stressed the importance of the industrial proletariat
for the future.

The Russian working class was just growing at that time. The
number of factory workers in 1865 was given as 380,000; only the
forced industrialization at the end of the century brought a sudden
rise in numbers which, in 1898, reached 3 million. In the 1880's
the public became strongly aware of the growing number of strike
movements. The most important of these was the great textile
workers' strike in the Morozov works in Orekhovo-Suyevo in 1885
in which 8,000 workers took part. But the 1880's also saw the first
modest attempts at factory legislation—initiated by the Minister of
Finance and Economy, Bunge—which removed the worst excesses
of women and child labor. In 1886 a comprehensive factory law
extended factory inspection. However, the opposition of the industrialists resulted in the dismissal of the Minister a year later and the
lax application of most of the factory laws under his successor,
Vyshnegradsky.

The workers had no right of association. The first illegal organizations, partly based on the ideas of the *narodniki,* had been formed
in the 1870's. At the end of the 1880's small Social Democrat societies appeared which furthered a more intensive study of the
works of Marx and Engels. Among them were not only Russian,
but also Polish, Jewish and other groups. They were not really
effective and mostly of ephemeral importance. Plekhanov's group
in Geneva was too far removed to influence the organizational aspects of the revolutionary task to any extent.

Plekhanov had the concept of a concurrent development in the
West and in Russia based on the working class. But what other
possibilities existed for a solution of social and economic problems
more appropriate to the specific structure of Russian society?

V. P. Vorontsov, in his "Fate of Capitalism in Russia," published in 1882, held out little hope for capitalism. Limited buying

power within the country precluded any considerable increase in sales and Russian capitalism was in no position to compete with the older industrial powers in foreign markets. From this Vorontsov concluded that capitalism would remain a stranger in Russia with little influence on the structure of society. He believed that there was no universally valid pattern of historical development and that Russia would have to find its own way. This way, according to Vorontsov, lay in the direction of production co-operatives *(artels)* whose members work merely to meet their own needs, not in order to increase their private capital. These ideas, based on the *Narodnichestvo,* passed beyond the narrow agrarian viewpoint of the admirers of the village community and placed beside it a structural form which also stemmed from an old Russian tradition. They were further developed in the writings of N. Danielson and S. Yushakov in 1893 and 1894. Both these writers thought it possible to introduce the mechanics of capitalism without its class structure, believing that Russian communal forms could be further developed without falling victim to the disintegrating effects of capitalism.

Lenin's Rise

The spread of Marxist ideas in Russia was furthered by the wave of industrialization that began in 1892. It was the energetic Minister of Finance and Economy, S. J. Witte, who succeeded in considerably improving the state's economic position by ending the long customs war with Germany, by introducing the gold standard, by the forced export of grain and the conclusion of new trade agreements. A disproportionately high share of government income came from the national liquor monopoly; the demoralizing effects of this monopoly were among the most important grievances of radical circles.

Soon foreign capital, especially from French, English and Belgian sources, came into the country to produce a much more intensive exploitation of its mineral wealth. Coal production rose from 1,800,000 tons in 1877 to 16 million in 1900, iron ore from 377,000 to 2,800,000 tons, oil from 213,000 to 9,830,000 tons. Heavy industry and textile manufacture experienced an equally rapid rise, ship yards and harbors were built in large numbers, the railroad network was enlarged, and the great Trans-Siberian Railroad begun.

Living conditions of the industrial proletariat, however, did not keep pace with this rapid rise. Merciless exploitation was still the order of the day. As the labor laws concerning women and children had been disregarded, children worked in the factories from the age of six up, the older ones also on the night shifts, while women were even used for heavy labor in the iron processing industry. The only concession consisted in the limitation in 1897 of the work day to eleven and a half hours!

Intensified agitation found a ready audience. In 1895 the "Union of Struggle for the Liberation of the Working Class" was founded in St. Petersburg. It was to be the cornerstone of the Marxist movement in Russia.

Lenin's appearance heralded, unrecognized by his contemporaries, a new era in world history. To call him the greatest figure in recent history, dwarfing all other protagonists, may be overstating the case. But with him a new political person enters the stage of history, a person combining the features of the false prophet with that of the *terrible simplificateur*. That this may be a man of towering intellect and iron will power does not alter the verdict. In him the element of simplification produces an anti-humanist, stunted ethical code, leading him to reject not only every religious belief, but also all moral philosophies, so that he may combine the highest personal integrity with absolute political unscrupulousness. Lenin— the short man with faintly mongoloid features, the small goatee, the skull of a Socrates and the glimmer in the small, shrewd eyes—was not the utopian and philanthropic social reformer with roots in the spiritual heritage of antiquity or Christian Europe. A sovereign contempt for the individual was the starting point for a demoniac hunger for power which operated within the framework of the Marxist messianic belief in the future. Lenin felt justified in all his actions by the belief that he was the executor of a predetermined logic of history.

Lenin was born Vladimir Ilyich Ulyanov, the son of a civil servant of the petite bourgeoisie who had attained the rank of elementary school inspector in the school system of Simbirsk (now Ulyanovsk) on the Volga, and the patent of nobility that went with his rank. The Ulyanovs came originally from Astrakhan, and it is possible that Tartar or Kalmuck ancestors are responsible for Lenin's features.[4] Lenin's mother, Maria Alexandrovna, née Blank, was the daughter of a physician who had left his daughter a small estate near Simbirsk. She may have been of German extraction, although the name can be interpreted variously; that she was descended from Protestant Volga Germans cannot be entirely proved. Nor, of course, can it be proved that her son inherited, from her, a pietistic heritage of love for order and method and a Puritan attitude to work, as well as a sectarian fanaticism.[5]

Lenin's father, Ilya Nikolaevich Ulyanov, was a loyal Czarist, a civil servant of moderately liberal views. The children—Vladimir had two brothers and three sisters—grew up in a settled, middle-class atmosphere. Like many other young people of the time the older brother, Alexander, as a student in the eighties, became involved with radical, revolutionary groups in St. Petersburg. Alexander III's reactionary regime made short shrift of him and his kind; in 1887 he was sentenced to death and executed as a terrorist. The affect this had on the young Vladimir, just turned seventeen, was never to be overcome. He finished high school in Simbirsk with distinction and began to study law at Kazan. But soon he was arrested for taking part in student demonstrations and exiled to a rural district. There he gained some idea of the living conditions of the peasants. When the university refused to readmit him, he moved to Samara. He plunged into a study of the writings of Marx and Engels and soon founded a Marxist group. His first article, dealing with the situation of the peasants in Russia, proved the extent to which capitalist trends even then influenced agriculture to the detriment of the peasants.

Eventually he was permitted to complete his final state examination as a day student, and was admitted to the bar. He was, however, not attracted by a bourgeois career. Moving to St. Petersburg for good in 1893 he sedulously preached the Marxist gospel to various illegal groups of the capital. Here, as well as at meetings in Moscow he crossed swords with representatives of the *narodniki*. He considered their teaching the chief obstacle to the spread of Marxist ideas. In his opinion the *narodniki* indulged in romantic illusions instead of facing economic and social realities. In his pamphlet, "Who are the Friends of the People?", he demolished the allegedly petit bourgeois notions of the *narodniki*. For the first time he demanded that the Russian workers and peasants combine to overthrow the autocracy and wrest political power from the bourgeoisie. Here he deviated from the point of view of Plekhanov who, looking upon the Russian peasants as a backward, counter-revolutionary element, advocated collaboration of the proletariat with the liberal bourgeoisie. Lenin did not regard the peasantry as socially homogeneous and pinned his hopes on the agricultural proletariat. This alone added a new note to Marxist doctrine; by including the peasants in the revolutionary program one nourished the hope that contrary to the general view, the revolution could also break out in an economically backward country.

First, however, the St. Petersburg workers had to be organized. In the winter of 1895 Lenin consolidated the existing secret groups in a "Union of Struggle for the Liberation of the Working Class." In the meantime industrialization made rapid progress in the capital too. The number of workers increased and it became important to awaken their class consciousness and stir their interest in political questions.

His first journey abroad, in 1895, took Lenin to Berlin and Switzerland. In Geneva he met Plekhanov and his group. They welcomed him as a representative of the Russian Socialists with whom they had been able to maintain only loose contacts. Lenin showed respect for Plekhanov who was fourteen years his senior, but the outlines of later differences of opinion became apparant even then. They were as one, however, in their rejection of the *narodniki*.

After his return from abroad, the police were alerted to Lenin just as he was about to publish an illegal paper. He was arrested in December, 1895, and, after fourteen months' imprisonment, exiled for three years to Yeniseisk Province in eastern Siberia. He had used his imprisonment for intensive studies and wrote a pamphlet, *Tasks of Russian Social Democracy*, as well as several articles in which he opposed the *narodniki* and every "opportunistic" concession to the bourgeoisie as well. In 1899 Lenin's great work, *The Development of Capitalism in Russia*, for which he had gathered material for many years, was published legally under a pseudonym. His thesis was that Russia already showed all the symptoms of capitalism as described by Marx. As the peasantry still comprised 80% of the total population and the industrial sector was as yet very small, agricultural conditions deserved particular attention, precisely because of Russia's future social development. With the aid of exact statistical analyses he disclosed the population structure in detail. The distinction between village bourgeoisie and village proletariat he felt to be of the utmost importance. He saw possibilities of rousing the proletariat and the peasants to a common revolution.

However, he believed that the leading role in this revolution should fall to the industrial proletariat. The workers should not be satisfied with an improvement of their economic position; they were to make political as well as social demands, they were to aim at political power. Here Lenin outlined his view of what the party of Russian revolutionaries would be like—not a party of like-minded friends loosely bound together, but a conspiratorial organization of trained and disciplined professional revolutionaries. Only in this form would it be equal to its task of being the general staff of the coming revolution.

Lenin borrowed the concept of the small qualified elite party from Tkachev; so too he borrowed the idea of using the existing state power after conquering it, not destroying it. In this he differed from the anarchist program and from Marx as well. Marx undoubtedly put greater stress on the transitory character of the withering state than did Lenin. The latter's attitude toward power almost seems to smack of Pareto's influence. Berdyaev, who at that time also tended toward Marxism, considered Tkachev— because of the frequent agreement between Tkachev's and Lenin's ideas—as the actual ancestor of Bolshevism, while he looked upon Marx and Engels much more as prophets of the Mensheviks.[6]

While Lenin was in Siberia, the Russian Social Democrats held their first congress in Minsk in March, 1898. This congress led to the merger of all Social Democratic groups in a "Russian Social Democratic Labor Party" which represented an important milestone in the revolutionary movement. The congress charged Peter Struve, one of the outstanding Russian intellectuals who had been attracted by Marxism, with the composition of the Party manifesto, a kind of party program.

When Lenin, Martov, and Potresov returned from exile in 1900, they were determined to emigrate to the West to create a permanent organ there since it was impossible to do an effective job in Russia. After some discussion, agreement was reached with Plekhanov and his group in Geneva, and publication of the paper *Iskra* ("The Spark") decided upon. Apart from Lenin and Plekhanov, Vera Zasulich, P. B. Axelrod, Julius Martov-Tsederbaum and Potresov made up the editorial staff. The paper was printed first in Leipzig, later in Munich and Stuttgart. Following the pattern of *Iskra*, which was smuggled under great precautions into Russia, a number of similar illegal papers of limited, provincial significance sprang up in Russia. One of these was *Brdzola* ("The Struggle"), published in Tiflis as the organ of the Georgian Social Democratic group with Stalin as one of the editors.

Iskra provided Lenin with abundant opportunity to make his ideas more widely known. He was especially severe and intolerant in his attacks on left-wing bourgeois liberalism which gained adherents particularly among student groups. Rejecting any common action between socialists and bourgeois liberals, he renewed his advocacy of the party as a small group of self-renouncing professional revolutionaries and demanded strict leadership, a "strong, directing core."

He summarized his opinions of the nature and goals of the party in a book entitled "What is to be done?" which contains the directives of the revolutionary tactics which the Bolsheviks were soon to follow. Lenin's opinions were not shared by all his party comrades. Violent differences of opinion were threshed out in the editorial offices of *Iskra*. There was a good deal of support for copying the example of the West European Social Democrats as closely as possible, and Lenin's emphasis on the pecularities of the Russian situation, the radicalism of his program, and the impatience with which he wanted to speed up things met with criticism.

In these first years of the new century, the omens of a coming crisis in Russia multiplied. The prosperity of the industrial boom was followed by a depression. Many factories closed down; the number of unemployed rose; the country suffered a wave of strikes against low wages and poor working conditions. But behind the economic demands, Socialist and political slogans began to emerge more and more openly. Occasionally the demonstrations led to bloody conflicts with the police. From 1902 on, peasant riots were also on the increase for, after a bad harvest, their debts would often become insufferable.

The Social Democrats pressed on with their work. In August, 1903, a Party Congress, after a few sessions in Brussels, had to be transferred to London. 43 delegates attended. Apart from the *Iskra* group, some other organizations were represented, among them the "General Jewish Workers' Alliance in Lithuania, Poland and Russia" (founded in 1897) and a more moderate "Union of Russian Social Democrats."

The Congress had to vote the draft of a Party program agreed on by Lenin and Plekhanov; it consisted of a maximum and a minimum program. The former referred to the final goals of the party, to the Socialist revolution and the dictatorship of the proletariat. Plekhanov, although he had included it in his original draft, strenuously resisted the inclusion of the latter phrase, which had been taken over from the Communist Manifesto but was not part of the program of the West European Social Democrats. But he finally yielded to Lenin's pressure. The minimum program outlined the more immediate tasks of the party. The list of socioeconomic demands was headed by the introduction of the eight-hour day for the workers and the return of the land taken from the peasants at the time of their emancipation. The paramount political demands were the overthrow of the Czarist regime and the establishment of a democratic republic.

Equal in importance to the party program were the party statutes. Here it was more difficult to bring about unanimity. Article 1, dealing with the membership, was the touchstone for the two alternatives—mass party or elite party. Lenin wanted the elite party; the party was to be a homogeneous avant-garde of the working class. Julius Martov, Pavel Axelrod and Leon Trotsky pointed out, however, that so rigid a party structure would limit opportunities for party development. The more liberal view won the day with 28 against 22 votes.

Another question of utmost importance was that of the national structure of the party, which was raised by the Jewish Bund. Lenin was sharply opposed to a party organized along ethnic lines; he feared this would impair the striking power of the entire party. He carried his point, whereupon seven delegates walked out of the meeting in protest. Henceforth Lenin's supporters were in the majority, and were eventually called Bolsheviks, supporters of the majority, as against the Mensheviks, the supporters of the minority.

This distribution of forces played a decisive role when the congress finally came to choose the staff of the party organ. On Lenin's request there were to be only three editors instead of six; Plekhanov and Martov and himself. Martov did not accept. In the Central Committee of the party all three seats went to the Leninists. Thus the rift was complete, although both sides continued for some years to cling to the fiction of a united Social Democratic Party.

Plekhanov found himself in a difficult position. In an effort to re-establish party unity he tried to bring about a reconciliation with the Mensheviks. He managed to get Martov back on the editorial staff of *Iskra* and attempted to have the three earlier members reinstated by co-optation. Now it was Lenin's turn to quit. *Iskra* became a purely Menshevik paper. Plekhanov opposed Lenin more and more until the break between the two was unmistakable.

In the summer of 1904 Lenin attacked his former comrades with the publication of his book, "One Step Forward, Two Steps Back." Reviewing the London Party Congress, he again said that the Menshevik course could only further the aims of the bourgeoisie in Russia; that this course was unable to utilize the revolutionary strength of the working class and the peasants. In essence, he tried to justify centralism and a disciplined party bureaucracy; he felt that autonomistic and democratic tendencies contained the seeds of anarchism.

With the fuctionaries who had remained loyal to him he established a bureau as well as a new paper, *Vperyod* ("Forward"), which he edited together with Lunacharsky and Vorovsky.

Lenin's contemporaries doubtless did not realize the significance of the developments initiated by the London party congress. Many considered the differences of opinion irrelevant, the necessity of joint action far more urgent. Lenin himself, however, quite consciously widened the breach with the above mentioned pamphlet. In that year of 1904 no one foresaw more clearly where the course chosen by Lenin would lead than his opponent—but later his comrade-in-arms—Leon Trotsky. In a brilliant pamphlet, "Our Political Problems," Trotsky defined his position regarding the dictatorship of the proletariat as well as Lenin's view of the party structure. He foresaw a situation, if the present course was pursued, in which the party would be replaced by the party organization, the organization by the Central Committee, and the Committee finally by the dictator. Provocatively enough the last chapter was entitled, "The Dictatorship over the Proletariat." With prophetic intuition he laid bare the anti-democratic germ-cell in Lenin's conception of socialism—even though he later turned away from this early insight.[7]

The First Attempt at Revolution

In the first years of the new century, several possibilities emerged for solving the burning social questions as well as matters of the relationship between Russian state and society.

One was along the lines of pro-reform liberalism, as advocated by friends of the Zemstvo self-government bodies. These circles had enlarged their program since the days of Alexander II. Opposition to the absolutist regime gathered momentum. When the government impeded the Zemstvo deputies in the discussion of their reform proposals and in gathering data, the liberal movement, too, had to resort to conspiratorial methods. In 1902 an illegal paper was founded abroad under the name *Osvobozhdeniye* ("Liberation"), with the ex-Marxist Peter Struve as editor. A League for Liberation followed the next year, which rejected class warfare and terrorism and worked for a democratic constitution, possibly in the form of a constitutional monarchy. Distinguished scholars, members of the nobility and the intelligentsia were among the leading figures of this liberal movement.

When a great Zemstvo Congress was banned on the eve of the revolution, the delegates nonetheless convened unofficially in November, 1904. The overwhelming majority of the delegates now went beyond the demand for a consultative assembly on the pattern of the old Moscow Zemskii Sobor. Instead they called for the abolition of absolutism and for democratized and enlarged self-government. The social problems of the peasants and the industrial proletariat were relegated to second place, and no steps were taken to interest the masses in the liberal program.

In complete contrast to this moderate opposition was the newly awakened terrorism of a group formed in 1902 under the name of Social Revolutionaries. Its leader was Victor Chernov. The Social Revolutionaries revived the traditions of the *People's Will* of the eighteen seventies. They instigated the assassination attempts of the pre-revolutionary years and spread revolutionary propaganda among the peasants.

When the imperialist policy of the Czarist government in the Far East led to war with Japan, the hour of the revolution had struck. The spark setting it off was a mass demonstration in front of the Winter Palace in January, 1905, which was received with rifle salvos. "Bloody Sunday" was the first of a number of revolutionary acts which reached their climax in the winter of 1905-1906.

Three basic trends soon became apparent. The revolution was, on the one hand, the struggle for a Russian constitution and for the fulfillment of the bourgeois democratic demands as advocated by the liberals of the Zemstvo movement. It was also a fight of the peasants for land, instigated primarily by the Social Revolutionaries. And finally it was a major milestone in the proletarian workers' movement; the revolution saw not only extensive street fighting in Moscow, but also the birth of workers' councils or Soviets.

Initially the Bolsheviks played a smaller part in these developments than the Mensheviks. Both wings of the Russian Social

Democratic movement convened at congresses abroad in the spring
of 1905; the Bolsheviks in London, the Mensheviks in Geneva.
They differed in their estimate of the revolutionary situation at
home. The Mensheviks believed that a democratic-bourgeois
revolution was in the making in Russia and that the working
classes should not yet demand to have the power, but support the
middle class in its struggle against autocracy. A socialist revolution was without prospects since Russia's economic development
was not yet ripe for it. It was impossible to skip any historical
stages. Here the West would have to lead Russia.

The Bolsheviks under Lenin took a diametrically opposed stand.
They were in favor of transforming the bourgeois into the socialist
revolution; they were for joint action by proletariat and peasantry.
The Third Party Congress in London issued a call to the peasants
to seize the landowners' estates and to prepare for armed insurrection. Party discipline was tightened, a special Central Committee was founded as well as a party organ, *Proletarii,* ("The
Proletarian"). In his pamphlet, "Two Tactics of Social Democracy
and Democratic Revolution," Lenin sharply attacked the Mensheviks, branding their attitude as treason to the working class. He
reiterated the theoretical basis for the views he had presented at
the Party Congress. In the peasant question Lenin looked upon the
alliance with the proletariat as the first phase of the revolutionary
struggle; only later, after dividing the peasants into wealthy and
landless elements, could one incite the latter, the semi-proletarian
classes among the peasants, against the richer classes, and thus
jointly—with the industrial proletariat—complete the revolution.
For Lenin the Russian revolution was significant within the framework of world politics. He believed that the proletarian-peasant
insurrection in Russia would enable Europe to make its own
revolution; that Russia would have to set the pace for the world
revolution in order to complete the socialist revolution with the
help of the European proletariat.

While these theoretical debates went on between the two Marxist
groups, the Czar maintained his refusal to consent to a democratic
assembly and reports from the front in the Japanese War sounded
increasingly gloomy. Tension rose and radicalism in Russia became
an ever greater threat. The peasants resorted to riots which developed into arson and murder. The industrial proletariat issued
strike calls which affected greater and greater numbers until a

climax was reached in October with an almost complete general strike throughout the country, paralyzing economic life.

The politically organized representation of the workers now came to assume greater importance. In May, 1905, the strikers in the textile works of Ivanovo-Voznesensk entrusted the leadership of the strike to an elected Workers' Council, basically only a kind of strikers' committee. In the fall of 1905, the printers' strike committee in St. Petersburg founded an overall "Soviet of Workers' Deputies," which soon made political demands as well. With its 550 delegates representing 250,000 workers, it was a political mass organization of the workers so far unheard of in Russia; it was to become the prototype of the Soldiers' and Workers' Councils of 1917, the Soviets of Bolshevik Russia.

The St. Petersburg Soviet was politically dominated by Mensheviks. It made the proclamation of a democratic republic part of its program. The first chairman of the Soviets was Khrustalev-Nosar, a lawyer. He was arrested in November, 1905, and Leon Trotsky, who had returned from exile abroad in February, took over the office for the remaining weeks of the Soviet.

With the emergence of Trotsky, a personality second only to Lenin entered the stage of the revolutionary struggle. The career of no other great Russian revolutionary can be as easily traced as that of Trotsky whose autobiography, in both content and style, must be classed among the great memoirs of world literature.[8]

Lev Davidovich Bronstein was born in 1879, the son of a Jewish farmer in the district of Nikolaev in Southern Russia. As a student in Nikolaev he became familiar with the ideas of the *narodniki,* and their influence made him at first oppose Marxism. He soon compelled attention by his keen argumentation and his skillful, aggressive technique in debating. Lenin was undoubtedly a man of far more profound learning, but Trotsky—he adopted this name in the course of his revolutionary activities—made up for many gaps in his knowledge by improvisation, by his quick-witted repartee, innate intelligence and boundless energy. In Nikolaev in 1897, he and his friends founded the South Russian Workers' Alliance based on Marxist principles. The reality of the revolutionary struggle was most important to Trotsky. Soon the authorities took action. The group was disbanded, Trotsky arrested and banished to Eastern Siberia.

At the *Iskra* in Geneva the gifted debater and writer was noticed and Trotsky was invited to contribute. He succeeded in escaping from Siberia. In Geneva he identified himself completely with the Menshevik course and vehemently opposed Lenin's centralism and bureaucracy. His pamphlet, published in 1904, "Our Political Problems," abounding in perceptive premonitions caustically settled accounts with the Bolsheviks. Nevertheless, he refused to let himself be fenced in on matters of party politics and often occupied a special position within the Menshevik group.

The revolution of 1905 provided a first test of his demagogic gifts. However, he presided over the St. Petersburg Soviet for only a short time. He was arrested early in December. His impressive bearing at the trial gained him wide notice. Again he was exiled to Siberia and ceased to exert direct influence on the revolutionary struggle.

At the time, it was chiefly the attitude of the army that prevented the workers from rising up in arms. Apart from occasional signs of disaffection among troops returning from the Japanese front, as well as among the reserves, and apart from the mutiny on the cruiser *Potemkin* in Odessa, the Russian soldier was not yet prepared to make common cause with the strikers.

The Czar's manifesto of October 17, 1905, almost halted the revolutionary momentum, split the opposition, and weakened the strike movement. The general strike gradually ebbed away; the crisis seemed overcome. The manifesto promised Russia a constitution, an Imperial Duma (parliament) based on universal suffrage, and civil liberties. For the first time Russia could create something like parliamentary parties. Now the right liberal "Octobrists" who were essentially a conservative party, and the left liberal "Constitutional Democrats" (Kadets) appeared.[9]

Unlike Trotsky, Lenin reached Russia, via Sweden and Finland, only on November 7, 1905. He commented on current events in a Bolshevik paper in St. Petersburg. On visiting the Soviet—which had come into being without his help and with some opposition from the Bolsheviks—he decided that such organs could very well serve as preparatory centers of armed insurrection. This concept differed considerably from that of the Mensheviks to whom the Soviets were mainly the instruments of the organization of the workers in their fight for freedom.

In Moscow, the Workers' Soviet was under the influence of the Bolsheviks. When the St. Petersburg Soviet was arrested on December 3, the Moscow Soviet had decided to answer this measure with

a renewed general strike which in turn would set off the hoped-for
armed uprising. The October manifesto had by no means completely pacified Russia. The government was dismayed when new
peasant revolts broke out; within a short period over two thousand
landed estates were burned down. The government did not dare to
use troops against the insurgent peasants. It feared that the "peasants in uniform" would refuse to fire on their non-uniformed brethren. In fact, here and there units of the army, and especially the
navy, staged mutinies. Unrest among the masses was increased by
anti-Jewish pogroms which, beginning in October, rolled like a wave
over western and southern Russia, undoubtedly encouraged and in
part inspired by ultra-reactionary circles such as the patriotic organization, "Union of the Russian People," called the "Black
Hundred."

This was the background for the events which took place in
Moscow in December. The Moscow Soviet had set up an armed
shock troop of about two thousand workers, and on December 9th
the rising broke out. Bitter fighting occurred on barricades and
streets, especially in the workers' district of Presnya. The revolutionaries did not succeed in winning the army over to their side.
Since this time the railroad workers did not join the strike, the
government was able to send loyal regiments from St. Petersburg
and Tver to Moscow. On December 20th the last desperate resistance in the workers' quarters died out. The government was again
in command of the situation. In the provinces, too, smaller risings
faded out. A rigorous clean-up was carried out by court martial
and punitive expeditions.

Lenin did not hasten to Moscow in order to direct the uprising.
He stayed in Finland and there convened a Party Conference, at
which the Bolsheviks decided to boycott the elections for the Duma.
Outwardly, however, the fiction of Social Democratic unity was
maintained. Subsequent party congresses were still held jointly. But
the difference became deeper.

The "Unity" Congress in Stockholm in April 1906, (called by
the Bolsheviks the "Fourth" Congress since they had held a separate
one, the "Third," in 1905) apart from debating what attitude to
take toward the Duma, mainly concerned itself with the agrarian
question. Lenin advocated nationalization of the land and its distribution among the peasants. Collective cultivation of the peasants'
land with state aid was already then being considered and, oddly
enough, it was Stalin, in contrast to Lenin, who proposed the estab-

lishment of individual peasant holdings. The party congress, however, adopted the Menshevik agrarian program providing for the transfer of the expropriated land to the Zemstvos which were to lease it to the peasants.

The last common Party Congress convened in London in May, 1907. Among the Bolsheviks attending, aside from Lenin, were Voroshilov, Zinoviev, Kamenev, Stalin and Maxim Gorky; among the Mensheviks besides Plekhanov, Axelrod, Martov, the Georgian Irakli Tsereteli achieved notice; and among the Polish delegates, Rosa Luxemburg. 105 Bolshevik delegates and 97 Mensheviks attended. The Polish, Latvian and Jewish Social Democrats were again represented; the first two cooperated with the Bolsheviks, the latter with the Mensheviks. Against the proposal of the Mensheviks to preserve the neutrality of the trade unions, the majority succeeded in subordinating them to the party. The Congress wound up with an undeniable victory for Lenin; the Bolsheviks were in control of the Central Committee. For tactical reasons vis-à-vis the Duma, it previously had become necessary for Lenin to revise the stand, taken in 1905, of not participating in parliamentary proceedings. The congress decided to take part in the elections and to use the sessions of the Duma as a propaganda sounding board.

When, in June 1907, the Government also dissolved the Second Duma, all 65 Social Democratic Deputies were arrested and exiled to Siberia. A decreed election law turned the Third Duma into a more pliable instrument of the government. The reactionary, nationalist Prime Minister, P. A. Stolypin, succeeded in having his agrarian reform bill passed; simultaneously national intolerance and reaction triumphed, putting their mark on the entire period until the outbreak of the First World War.

The Years of Reaction

The blow against the party also endangered Lenin in Finland. He fled to Switzerland, settling in Geneva, where he published the *Proletarii,* and later moved to Paris. In the ensuing years his main preoccupation was with the theoretical disputes within the party, and even within the ranks of the Bolsheviks, who underwent a crisis, due to a measure of disenchantment and disillusion following the failure of the plans for revolution. As a result, a number of intellectuals left the party. On the ideological plane, two highly educated Bolsheviks, Bogdanov and Lunacharsky, made the remarkable attempt, based on the philosophical school of Mach and Avenarius, of reconciling Marxist theory with elements of idealist philosophy and religion. They acted partly from frustration, partly from tactical propaganda considerations. Lenin made short shrift of this trend, advancing the thesis that evolution—both in nature and history—consists not only of continuous quantitative changes, but also of sudden qualitative changes. Applied to practical politics this meant that the advent of socialism was to be expected not as the result of gradual reforms, but of a sudden turn in events. Thus a socialist had to be a revolutionary, not a reformer.

With such a fundamental cleavage in attitudes little could be expected from a temporary rapprochement of the different wings. Hence a party conference in Paris in December 1908 rejected the idealists mentioned above who, for tactical reasons, proposed to recall the Social Democratic deputies from the Duma in order to infuse the party with new vigor. The spokesmen of this group[10] were expelled from the party.

As a result of these disputes a common line was reestablished among the Bolsheviks in 1910. They developed increasingly into a conspiratorial group with a common program of action, perfecting their cell organizations on Russian soil in underground illegality. Now their job was to consolidate strength for a new revolutionary situation and, in the meantime, to counteract the growing disappointment and apathy of the workers. It was also necessary to obtain money for the expensive propaganda at home and abroad, to operate the clandestine printing presses and, generally, to keep on the alert. A special type flourished in this atmosphere; men of ruthless energy, cunning, and skill who had to be sufficiently unscrupulous for the sake of the supreme goal; men in whom high intelligence was not a prerequisite.

Stalin was one of these men. Unlike Lenin and Trotsky, he ascended in the party in the penumbra of illegality; his name was mentioned very infrequently.

Joseph Vissarionovich Djugashvili was the son of a Georgian shoemaker who was in the habit of beating his wife and son when he was drunk. The mother, of Ossetian descent, adored her son who was born, the only surviving child, on December 21, 1879, in Gori near Tiflis. Her ambition for his future was boundless; the career of a priest seemed the logical choice. In 1894 he entered the Theological Seminary in Tiflis. She was probably unaware that the Seminary in Tiflis was the center of the radical student movement in the Caucasus. The young generation of Georgians was surprisingly united in its revolutionary fervor. The young Djugashvili was at first a model student. The priestly vocation offered, after all, the unique opportunity of gaining social status without very much mental—and especially without physical—exertion. Soon, however, he was caught up in the rebellious and heretic spirit which marked the Seminary. As a result he was expelled from the institution, presumably because of a violation of discipline. That he played a major role in the revolutionary activities from the time he entered the Seminary, and that he was expelled for Marxist agitation, is apocryphal.

Stalin—he, too, soon adopted a symbolic, revolutionary pseudonym—obtained a subordinate post at the Tiflis Observatory which enabled him to take part in underground revolutionary work. His interest in this phase of the revolutionary struggle apparently springs from that time. Soon he went underground as a professional revolutionary; occasionally he was active in Batum, the Black Sea port. In 1898 he joined the Social Democratic Party; in 1902 he was arrested for the first time and exiled to the province of Irkutsk in Siberia. However, he managed to escape in January 1904 and turned up again in Tiflis and Batum. But he could not compete with outstanding Georgian revolutionary leaders, such as Jordania, Chkheidze, and others who had greater learning and highly skilled dialectic. He had a boundless ambition, a wild determination to succeed. Principles and ideologies meant little to him. Gifted with all the arts of dissimulation and full of guile and patience, taciturn and suspicious, he set about to achieve his aim. In Baku he found the atmosphere more suited to his purpose. He soon played a leading part among a number of Armenian-Russian revolutionaries, the proletariat of the oil industry, and it mattered little to him that these Armenian workers had a traditional hatred for their Georgian neighbors.

Transcaucasia was far distant from the actual centers of revolutionary events and Stalin's importance in no way transcended provincial limits. It was an important milestone for him when he met Lenin for the first time in 1905 in Tammerfors; he was impressed —and this influenced his own later attitude toward all things ceremonial—by Lenin's matter-of-fact and easy-going behavior.

After the revolution it was important for the party leaders to have men in the country who would keep the revolutionary fire going and work for the financing of party activities. In the summer of

1907 a successful coup was brought off. A raid on a money transport of the Tiflis branch of the Imperial Bank netted 250,000 rubles. Stalin had directed this "expropriation"; in Paris Maxim Litvinov was arrested while trying to exchange the money. A donation of several thousand rubles to the party treasury by the Moscow merchant Morozov while exceptional, was not the only one of its kind.

The repressive course adopted after the dissolution of the Second Duma also resulted in more energetic police measures. In 1908 Stalin was again arrested and banished to the province of Vologda. He managed to flee, only to be re-arrested in 1910 and to escape again. In 1912 he reported for duty to the editorial offices of *Pravda* in St. Petersburg.

In January of the same year a Bolshevik Party Conference had met in Prague which was to become an important milestone of the revolutionary movement in Russia. What had begun in 1903 was now completed. The rift between the two Social Democratic factions became even wider. Lenin was now determined to make a clean sweep. The Prague Conference constituted itself as an independent Bolshevik Party. Lenin, Zinoviev, Ordjonikidze, and Spandarian were elected to the new Central Committee, and the candidates included Bubnov and Kalinin; Sverdlov and Stalin were co-opted *in absentia*. The Prague Conference, on the basis of the 1903 program, proclaimed the following important goals: creation of a democratic republic as a step toward the dictatorship of the proletariat, introduction of the eight-hour working day, and expropriation without compensation of the big landowners.

What caused Lenin to include a Georgian revolutionary, practically unknown even in party circles, in the top council of the party? Lenin's respect for Stalin in 1912 was caused by the leading role the latter had played, since the 1905 Revolution, in financing the party by violent "expropriations" in the Caucasus. As a tireless fighter on the home front, Stalin had become indispensable to the Bolshevik Central Committee at a time when the leading figures were still abroad. Lenin could use Stalin, not as an intellectual, but as a tough and skillful collaborator and unscrupulous conspirator. Party members active inside Russia were doubly important now that the controversy between Lenin and Trotsky added to the Menshevik-Bolshevik friction presented so great a threat to the unified leadership of the workers.

In the years before the outbreak of World War I, Trotsky attempted, from Vienna, to bring about his own Social Democratic fusion of the two extremes. His polemic against Lenin became progressively more hostile. Even if some of it was later misrepresented in Stalin's struggle with Trotskyism, there is no doubt that Lenin had to beware of his rival's sharp tongue. However, Trotsky failed in his efforts to find a third way acceptable to both Mensheviks and Bolsheviks.

Meanwhile the situation in Russia during the last years before the outbreak of the war was approaching its boiling point. The spring of 1912 saw a new big wave of strikes. It started with a strike of the gold workers on the river Lena; a battle with troops sent to the scene cost the lives of 250 persons. This massacre inflamed public opinion. In many cities of European Russia protest strikes were called in which almost half a million workers took part. "The shots on the Lena," wrote Lenin, "have broken the ice of silence, and the torrent of the people's movement has been unleashed." The strike movement became continuous from then on. In 1913 more than 850,000 men stopped work; early in 1914 the number had reached one and a half million.

Lenin seemed to scent that things were going his way. In order to be nearer to the home front, he moved to Cracow in Austrian Galicia. In St. Petersburg a new Bolshevik paper, *Pravda* ("Truth"), was founded; the first issue appeared on April 22, 1912, with articles by Kamenev and Stalin. The paper soon had a circulation of 40,000; the Menshevik *Luch* ("The Ray") had only 15,000. On the day Stalin's article appeared, he was arrested and exiled to Narym in Western Siberia. Soon he escaped and reappeared in St. Petersburg at the beginning of the election campaign for the Fourth Duma. After the elections in November, 1912, Lenin convened the Central Committee in Cracow for a survey of the situation. Stalin attended, and early in 1913, he repeated his visit to Cracow for a further meeting with the Bolshevik members of the Duma. This time he stayed abroad for six weeks. Here he was told by Lenin to write a survey of the nationality problem in Russia. His own views and experiences demonstrated his knowledge and interest in this field.

Stalin went to Vienna to gather impressions and material among the Babel of nationalities of the Habsburg empire. One of the ablest scientific thinkers among Lenin's followers happened to be in Vienna at the time—Nikolai Ivanovich Bukharin, who later became highly esteemed as the party's theoretician. Both Bukharin's parents were teachers. Born in Moscow in 1888, he had early shown exceptional interest in scientific problems and became a well-read student. The revolution of 1905 found him a convinced Marxist and follower of Lenin. Arrested on several occasions, he escaped abroad from his exile in Northern Russia. In Vienna he studied economics under Boehm-Bawerk, laying the foundation for his future eminence in economic questions. It is fair to assume that Bukharin helped Stalin in writing his pamphlet, particularly as the latter must have encountered linguistic difficulties in the use of Vienna's libraries. It is certain, however, that Lenin had drawn up the outline for the work.

Stalin's pamphlet, forty pages in length and entitled "Marxism and the Nationality Question," was a programmatic exposition of the Bolshevik stand as opposed to that of the Austrian Social Democrats. It was based on the right of self-determination, while rejecting a territorially independent "national cultural autonomy." The definition of the nation as a "historically evolved, permanent community of language, territory, economic life and psychological features finding expression in a common culture," became the basis of future Soviet nationality policy. One could not foresee that already during Lenin's lifetime but more strongly after Lenin's death this definition would become a façade behind which the government freely disregarded the will of the population when considerations of domestic or foreign policy superseded concern for national characteristics.

The Fourth Duma, elected in the fall of 1912, contained seven Mensheviks and six Bolsheviks. The Kadets were almost squeezed out of the political picture by the tremendous growth of the extreme Right.

The government of Nicholas II, a ship without helmsman after Stolypin's assassination, came increasingly under the influence of the nationalist Right, which looked to an aggressive foreign policy for welcome distraction from domestic troubles.

The Problem of the Russian Center

The question again rises: Where were the forces of the Center which, by way of evolution, could rescue the state from the confusion of domestic troubles and foreign temptation?

In the first half of the nineteenth century the liberal idea had lost contact with the national concept, then in the strait-jacket of an officially-standardized national dogma directed by reactionary forces. Later, after the Crimean War, when new impulses arose in the reform era, national tendencies coincided with liberal-democratic endeavors. Augmented by a now secularized messianic conviction, they soon assumed exaggerated forms. While Pan-slavic slogans helped launch the Turkish and Balkan wars and finally unleashed World War I, a chauvinistic nationalism grew rapidly inside the country. Its rotten fruits were the russification measures enforced on the non-Russian nationalities of the Empire, the fight against the denominations outside the established church, and the racialism directed particularly against Jews. For a second time in modern Russian history, liberal thinking parted company with national aspirations and was again restricted to radical and extremist solutions.

Herein lies the tragedy of the Russian political center. The reformist tendencies of Zemstvo liberalism carried lively hopes of attaining the first stages of democratic development in self-governing bodies operating within the framework of a constitutional monarchy. These trends found expression in the movement of the Liberation Union, which fathered the Constitutional Democratic Party (Kadets). But it was precisely these circles that were caught up in a nationalist wave after the 1905 Revolution. Under the flag of Neoslavism it appropriated the aggressive Panslavic demands—this time directed more against Austria-Hungary than Turkey.

Only a few Russian politicians were sufficiently realistic to see that the nationality problem deserved equal attention with the urgent social and economic problems, and that its solution was *not* a national statism which fundamentally represented a narrowing of the Russian imperial idea. The Kadets, under Professor P. Miliukov, paid as scanty attention to these questions as to the social wants of the peasants and workers. Russian liberalism was twice guilty here and we cannot hold the Russian national character responsible but, instead, the generation which happened to be at the helm.

As matters stood, the monarchy was ripe for its fall. With its frivolous entry into World War I it dug its own grave.

The Russian Socialists and the War

In the early days of the war Lenin was arrested by the Austrian authorities. He managed to get to Switzerland and in Berne he established, together with G. Zinoviev, the headquarters of the Bolshevik movement.

The Bolsheviks alone among the radical Russian parties consistently rejected the war. As early as September, 1914, Lenin wrote that Czarist Russia's military defeat was the indispensible condition for the victory of the revolution, the basis for any success. Lenin bitterly assailed the Socialists in all countries who remained loyal to their governments, labeling them social chauvinists. He challenged the Second International, and at the beginning of the war he already played with the idea of founding a new Third International. Among Lenin's opponents was Plekhanov. The Mensheviks were not quite united among themselves. Their right wing under Plekhanov considered the defense of their country a necessary preliminary of the revolution. The left wing, under Martov, demanded a peace based on the right of self-determination of all nations and the renunciation of annexations and reparations.

Two international conferences in Switzerland served to bring the standpoint of both parties into sharper focus. At Zimmerwald, in September 1915, the majority supported not Lenin, but the German Social Democrat Kautsky. He came out against a domestic truce, and while considering it the task of the Socialists to force their governments to conclude peace, rejected the use of active revolutionary tactics. The vote showed twenty-three for and seven against the moderate proposal. The leader of the left wing of the Russian Mensheviks, Martov, also had rejected Lenin's formula of "transforming the war into a civil war" and demanded a consistent pacifism. Henceforth Lenin's ire was directed against the "Social Patriots (Chauvinists)" as well as the "Social Pacifists." At Kienthal, in April 1916, the picture was the same. The majority remained loyal to the Second International; the workers of Western Europe were disavowing Lenin. Most of the Western Socialist leaders looked upon him, anyhow, as a fanatical, romantic, revolutionary sectarian. Nor was he at a loss for a suitable epithet for his opponents; to him the workers of Western Europe were hopelessly bourgeois.

In Russia the Bolshevik underground organization had in September, 1914, at a secret conference in Finland, passed and distributed a resolution against the government and the war. The government was not slow to act. In October, the Bolshevik Duma deputies and other party members were arrested and indicted for high treason. Early in 1915 they were bundled off to Siberia, where, in different localities, a sizable number of prominent party members were already assembled, among them Sverdlov, Ordjonikidze and Stalin. In 1913 Stalin had been arrested for the sixth time in his revolutionary career and exiled to the village of Kureika, in the

Turukhansk district on the Yenisei, not far from the Arctic Circle. The exceedingly harsh climate did not much bother him. However barren and isolated the region, Czarist exile compared favorably with what the Soviets had to offer later to its victims. Stalin, the political exile, could receive books, write and receive letters, move freely within a sizable radius, hunt and fish and sell what he caught. Here he sat out the war until 1916; during the last three weeks of the Czarist regime he was moved to the neighborhood of Krasnoyarsk.

In St. Petersburg quick action by the police had wrecked the Bolshevik organization. The Russian Bureau of the Central Committee, set up in 1912, ceased to exist for eighteen months. It was reopened only in the summer of 1916 by A. Shliapnikov, who had returned to Russia from Paris via Switzerland and Sweden. He enlisted the services of a young man who had done editorial work for *Pravda*. His name was Molotov.

Vyacheslav Mikhailovich Molotov came from the same part of the country as Lenin, the eastern part of European Russia, between the Volga and the Urals. There he was born in 1890, in a village in the province of Vyatka, of lower middle class parentage. His name was originally Scriabin. His school in Kazan brought him into contact with revolutionary groups. Abstract theory was not the forte of the slow mind of the young man; he craved action and soon he was organizing a task force which occupied itself with the manufacture of bombs. Quite early he developed a preference for the organizational and bureaucratic side of conspiratorial work; the statutes of a Pan-Russian revolutionary union of high schools and universities, drawn up in the years after the 1905 revolution, are his work. Exiled in 1909 to the Province of Vologda, he began to propagandize assiduously among the railroad workers and organize a Bolshevik cell. After his return from exile he entered the Institute of Technology in St. Petersburg. He began to contribute to *Pravda* and became its editorial secretary. With the police after him he moved to Moscow; there, however, he was denounced by an informer and imprisoned and in 1913 sent to Siberia, to the Province of Irkutsk. He managed to escape. During the war he reappeared in St. Petersburg and attempted to rally the scattered party members until Shliapnikov asked him to help reestablish the Bureau of the Central Committee. Publication of *Pravda* was out of the question for the time being.

At the same time Lenin was working in Zurich on his great

work, "Imperialism, the Highest Stage of Capitalism." He examined the close relations between capitalism of the day—with its financial monopolies and trusts—and imperialist foreign policy. He concluded that since capitalist states would continue to settle their differences by wars, only the end of the capitalist system would also put an end to imperialist wars. It is important to note that Lenin started from the assumption that political realities had undergone a fundamental change since the days of Karl Marx, and that to the exploitation of classes had been added that of entire peoples. Lenin was thus able to transfer the doctrine of the class struggle from the domestic to the international scene, furnishing the premises, deduced in the Stalinist era, for the future role of the Soviet Union as vanguard of the world revolution.

Although the basic theory of Lenin's book—that a Socialist state and imperialist policies are mutually exclusive—is refuted by the experiences of the Stalinist era, Marxist dialectics glibly rationalizes that truly imperialistic wars are only waged by capitalist nations, while a Socialist state conducts only just wars, particularly if it is encircled by capitalist powers.

In those days, before such arguments became necessary, the Russian Leninists considered Lenin's latest work as a kind of New Testament to the writings of Karl Marx, deserving of similar reverence.

In judging the actual political situation, Lenin was skeptical. As late as 1917 he said, in a speech before Swiss workers, that the old generation would not live to see the decisive battles of the coming revolution in Russia; the next generation, however, he hoped, would carry the revolution of the proletariat to victory.

Six weeks later the Czarist regime collapsed.

CHAPTER 1

THE REVOLUTION

Czarist Russia and the War

Russia's strategic plans collapsed quickly during the First World War. The invasion of Austrian Galicia, ideologically supported by the forces of Pan-Slavism, seemed to promise success. But the invasion of East Prussia, which France had demanded to ease the burden in the West, led to the catastrophic defeats of the Czar's armies in the battles of Tannenberg and the Masurian Lakes. In the course of the great German counter-offensive of 1915, not only Poland, but Lithuania, Courland, and West Russian territories up to a line extending from the Dvina to the Rumanian border were lost.

The collapse of the Russian Western front created a crisis among the Russian military leaders, resulting in a marked weakening of the entire political structure during the second war winter and in a loss of confidence in the Imperial Family. After the failure of the Allied campaign in the Dardanelles the burden of the war against Turkey was shouldered by Russia almost alone. The critical situation on the Western front also forced the Allies to ask Russia for renewed efforts against the German and Austrian armies. But the Brusilov offensive in the summer of 1916 proved to. be a Pyrrhic victory. It led to a German counter-thrust, under a new, firmer command, which was carried into Rumania and Serbia. The year 1916 ended in gloomy hopelessness. Hand-in-hand with the continued economic disintegration grew the opposition in the country against Nicholas II's reactionary court coterie and against the uncontrollable influence of Rasputin and other sinister figures. It began in liberal circles. An example of the asperity of the protests voiced at the time were the words of the leader of the Kadets, the historian P. Miliukov, who said, at the session of the Duma in

November, 1916, that the incompetence of the government bordered on high treason. Rather than relieving it, Rasputin's assassination by members of the Russian nobility in December, 1916, considerably increased the tension.

At the beginning of the new year, 1917, an Allied mission arrived in order to survey Russia's military potential (but actually also for a spot check on the political situation), but all its attempts to persuade the Czar to make concessions to the liberals proved futile. As a result the Western Powers, particularly England, dropped the Czar and pinned all their hopes on a political upheaval along liberal democratic lines. The memoirs of the British and French ambassadors to St. Petersburg, Buchanan and Paléologue give a vivid picture of the events leading to the revolution and reveal the threads that had been spun between their governments and the liberal opposition in Russia.

The February Revolution

During the month of February demonstrations became more frequent, caused at first only by the increasing scarcity of food. In addition there were strikes threatening the output of munitions. Rodzianko, the president of the Duma, and a representative of the Russian upper middle class, vainly appealed to the Czar to change the composition of the government in accordance with the desires of the liberal groups. Two factors became decisive for the collapse of the Czarist regime. The units of the St. Petersburg garrison that had been activated during the initial demonstrations and some units of the tradition-bound guard regiments proved to be unreliable. They made common cause with the demonstrators, refused orders and, in some instances, mutinied. The second important factor was the Duma. It seemed to contain the germ of a future democratic Russia; here the foes of reaction and corruption seemed to have their most promising forum.

When, on February 26 (March 11, Gregorian style which was introduced in Russia in February 14, 1918) the Czar dissolved the Duma, it ignored his order and remained in session. That night, with the city lit up by huge fires and the men of the Volhynian guard regiment murdering their officers, the Duma members met in the Tauride Palace. They felt themselves to be the true representatives of the people's sovereignty. On February 27 (March 12) the Duma constituted an Executive Committee which assumed dictatorial powers. Its members came from the so-called Progressive Bloc which had been formed earlier in the war, and which was now extended toward the left. Thus, the road to revolution had been entered upon even by the highest representative body of the people.

That day, the 27th of February (March 12), all the revolutionary instincts of the mob were unleashed. The prisons were opened, political and other prisoners mingled with the demonstrators; there were street fights with troops and police units still loyal to the Czar. The Cabinet, at this point still in office, urgently appealed to the Czar, who was at Headquarters, to return to St. Petersburg. It was too late, however. The government as such no longer possessed any authority. One after the other, its members were arrested by the insurgents.

It was of great importance that on February 27 (March 12), apart from the Executive Committee of the Duma, another body constituted itself which sprang from the Socialist opposition. An Executive Committee of the workers' and soldiers' councils was founded, modeled after the 1905 pattern. It was led by Chkheidze, a Georgian Menshevik. The Soviets at first limited themselves to occupying the Duma and to addressing appeals to the people. Both sides cooperated but also began to compete for popular favor. But the Duma Committee retained the political initiative. The left elements were represented, apart from Chkheidze, by Alexander Kerensky, a lawyer of outstanding rhetorical gifts. His popularity with workers and soldiers provided a certain amount of backing for the Duma Committee—as well as for the later Provisional Government.

On March 1 (March 14), the Czarist regime was overthrown in St. Petersburg. The uprising in Moscow had also succeeded. The Duma Committee sent a delegation to the Czar in Pskov and forced him to abdicate on the evening of March 2 (March 15). It was too late to issue a ukase for a new ministry. Consultation with the commanders of the Army showed Nicholas II that his renunciation of the throne was unavoidable. When his brother, the Grand Duke Michael Alexandrovich, refused the crown on March 3 (March 16) because he insisted on first hearing the will of the people in a constituent assembly, the fate of the House of Romanov was sealed after three centuries of rule.

Nicholas II was arrested on March 8 (March 21) at his Army

Headquarters, and for the time being was interned with his family in Czarskoe Selo. In Ekaterinburg in the Urals, today called Sverdlovsk, the Czar and his family were murdered by the Communists in July, 1918.

The Provisional Government and the Soviets

Since March 3 (March 16) Russia had become a *de facto* republic. Power lay in the hands of the Provisional Government, which had grown out of the Executive Committee of the Duma which from March 2 (March 15), wielded the actual powers of government in St. Petersburg. The government was initially based on a few liberal monarchists who did not have real contact with the people, or the necessary experience. They were honorable, educated and patriotic men but by no means equal to the tasks of such a turbulent, new situation. Prince Lvov became Prime Minister— a phlegmatic, passive personality guided by Tolstoy's philosophy of non-resistance against evil. Professor Miliukov took over the Ministry of Foreign Affairs. Kerensky, as Minister of Justice, represented the left wing; Chkheidze had refused the Ministry of Labor offered to him. Members of the Provisional government generally aimed at political, not at social revolution. But matters had come to such a pass in Russia that one of the most urgent requirements of the day was, if not social revolution, at least a thorough program of social reform. Such a program would have had to comprise a solution of the agrarian question, as well as labor legislation remedying the deplorable position of the industrial proletariat.

As one of its first measures the Provisional Government proclaimed civil liberties on March 2 (March 15) and promised to convoke a Constituent Assembly. All political prisoners were given amnesties and those exiled to Siberia were permitted to return. The police were replaced by a people's militia.

Postponement of elections for a Constituent Assembly until the fall was a tragic mistake for the government. It quickly became apparent that the authority of the government was severely limited by the workers' and soldiers' council, i.e., the Soviets. On March 1 (March 14) they issued their Order No. 1, calling for the formation of soldiers' councils in every military unit and the election of all officers by the troops. The consequence of this notorious order in the army, where discipline had already been shaken by recent events, was confusion of catastrophic proportions. It became doubtful, in these circumstances, that a continuation of the war could be considered at all.

The Social Revolutionaries were at first in the majority in the Soviets. Above all, they considered themselves to be the representatives of the peasantry. In addition there were the Menshevik and Bolshevik Socialists. The members of the Soviets had been elected in factories, workshops and barracks. The St. Petersburg Soviet consisted of 2,500 representatives, one worker for each thousand, one soldier for each company. Following the capital's pattern, similar Soviets were formed in other cities and, later, in the rural areas. They formed a broad representation of the people, from which however, the nobility, the upper middle class, and the educated classes were excluded. The deputies in the Soviets were not elected for any particular period. The moral authority of this popular representation stemmed from its close contact with the electors and from the reality of its power; as the line between legislative and executive functions was blurred its conduct gained in effectiveness. The revolutionary dynamic operating among the Soviets' deputies spelled both strength and weakness; strength vis-à-vis the Provisional Government which soon lost touch with public opinion, weakness when confronted with determined and disciplined small groups which would oppose their unorganized, elemental manner of functioning with a well-disciplined organization.

In St. Petersburg a Central Executive Committee of the Soviets was formed, chiefly consisting of the leaders of the Socialist parties and headed by a Presidium.

The Provisional Government and the Allies

The problem of the war was at this point the most important among the big political questions. There were two extreme and sharply opposed opinions. In the Provisional Government the dominant opinion of the moderate elements favored a continuation of the war on the side of the allies until victory was won. Among the Socialist parties, the Bolsheviks were the most uncompromising in their view that an immediate peace "without annexations and reparations" was to be concluded as quickly as possible. The majority of the Soviets was at first uncertain; its members realized that the people were tired of the war, but they did not want to risk admitting the military collapse.

The influence of the Allies made itself felt to a considerable degree at this point. Their representatives in St. Petersburg, who had not been entirely uninvolved in the fall of the monarchy, quickly assured the Provisional Government of their sympathies. On March 9 (March 22), the U.S.A. was the first of the powers to recognize the new Russian government; England, France and Italy soon followed. It seemed to them that in its present composition this government was the most likely to insure that Russia would not back out of the war. The support given to the Provisional Government in the spring of 1917 had a strategic advantage; it was necessary, at any cost, to tie down as many German divisions as possible in the east. The Western Powers were troubled to see Socialist trends on the increase. They suggested a broadening of the Government of Lvov. In the spring of 1917 representatives of English and French left wing circles tried to strengthen the bridge to the new Russia by visiting the country. Following Vandervelde, the chairman of the Second International, Albert Thomas, the French Minister of Armaments, and Henderson, as representative of the British Labor Party, came to St. Petersburg. Henderson had been cast as successor to Sir George Buchanan, whose position was considered undermined because of his connection with Czarist circles. However, after some observation, Henderson himself, realizing the Ambassador's familiarity with the situation, suggested that he be retained. It may be that he himself was not attracted by a task which was admittedly exceptionally difficult. The Allied representatives left Russia no less skeptical than their predecessors at the beginning of the year.

The controversy between the provisional government and the leftists soon came out into the open. On March 5 (March 18) Miliukov, in his speech addressed to the Allied representatives, had promised that Russia would fight on the side of the Allies until victory was won. On March 14 (March 27) the Soviets gave their answer. In a proclamation addressed to the peoples of the world they unequivocally demanded peace. Henceforth the Socialist parties hammered at Miliukov's "militaristic and imperialistic" foreign policy. On March 27 (April 9), in response to this pressure the Provisional Government, too, saw itself forced to advocate a peace without annexations and reparations.

This meant that Miliukov was discredited. When he nevertheless dared to repeat in a note to the Allies dated April 19 (May 1) what he had promised before, the storm broke. Demonstrations in the streets demanded the resignation of the Foreign Minister. On

May 5 (May 18) the government was reorganized; Miliukov and the War Minister, A. J. Guchkov, resigned. Lvov's second cabinet included Kerensky, this time as Minister of War and the Navy, as well as some other Socialists. Miliukov's note of April 19 was withdrawn. The Provisional Government, constituted as it was now, supported the demands for peace without annexations and reparations based on the principle of the nations' right of self-determination. It was small comfort to the Allies that the cancellations of the treaties of 1914 and 1915 also meant the withdrawal of Russian demands for the Turkish Straits. A further blow for the Western Powers was the news that Mensheviks, as well as the Social Revolutionaries, were ready to support the plan of the German Socialists to convoke an international Socialist conference in Stockholm. When Albert Thomas, the French Socialist, visited St. Petersburg, one of his most important tasks was to dissuade the Russians from following through on this. The plan itself was actually dropped soon afterwards.

The Western Powers also managed to interest the Provisional Government—despite its basic desire for peace—in a plan for a big summer offensive which was to be a follow-up of the Brusilov offensive of 1916.

The Kerensky Offensive

Kerensky thought it possible to combine two goals—an offensive against the Central Powers, and a democratic reorganization of the Russian military command. It appeared, however, that the second objective—in the middle of the war—greatly jeapordized the first.

On May 9 (May 22), Kerensky issued his "Declaration of Soldiers' Rights", which was based on the Order No. 1 of March 1 (March 14). It provided for the appointment of commissars in the army; it was hoped that with their help the somewhat problematic Soldiers' Councils could be handled more easily. In the meantime the disintegration of the army progressed rapidly. The Soldiers' Soviets issued orders contradicting those of the commanders, and systematically undermined the authority of the officers' corps. Defeatist literature smothered the last sparks of fighting spirit, and fraternization across the trenches, purposely promoted by the Germans and Austrians, made rapid progress.

Kerensky tried to boost sinking morale by making an inspection

tour of the front. He visited the most forward lines and attempted
in several rousing addresses to inspire the soldiers with new fighting
spirit. He thought the way was paved and the offensive was launched
in July, 1917. Its course reminds one, on a smaller scale, of the
events a year before. An initial breach was made in the Austrian
lines. However, the first German counter-attack spelled doom. During the first attack discipline had been maintained only with difficulty. Now whole regiments mutinied and left their posts. The
enthusiastic shock troops of the first days had been slaughtered
early in the advance. The offensive had hardly started when it
collapsed.

Under the pressure of the defeat, one of the commanding generals, General Kornilov demanded the immediate re-establishment of
military discipline, relentless punishment of all deserters and similar
measures. He was even supported by the regimental commissars.
On July 17 (July 30), Kornilov was made Commander-in-Chief in
place of General Brusilov. These measures, however, were no longer
supported by the popular will. The war weariness had spread, even
among those who until then had advocated the continuation of the
war. The war had long ceased to be the focus of the people's attention; the effective tactics of the Bolsheviks now held their interest.

Lenin's Return

Since the February Revolution confusion had reigned in the Bolshevik party. The party was directed by a temporary bureau of the
Central Committee, consisting of three comparatively young men:
V. M. Molotov, the *Pravda* contributor before the war, Shliapnikov
and Zalutsky, two energetic self-educated workers. None of the
three possessed sufficient political experience to enable him to
proclaim a definite policy in the face of the events taking place.
The outbreak of the revolution had surprised them. The party itself
was split into a right and a left wing. The Bureau belonged to the
left wing; there was no one who could have carried the whole party
along with him into unified activity.[1]

Pravda, edited by Molotov, strongly opposed the extension of the
war by the Provisional Government and also branded the Mensheviks as "traitors to the fatherland." The slogan was, "Resignation of
the Government and all power to the Soviets." The right wing of
the Bolsheviks, which included L. B. Kamenev after his return from

exile, was prepared to support Prince Lvov and to continue the war; it demanded that the split of 1905 be healed, i.e., a reunion with the Mensheviks in order to unify the Social Democratic Party.

J. V. Stalin, together with Kamenev, had returned to St. Petersburg from exile on March 12 (March 25). Since he was the senior member of the Central Committee which had been founded in 1912 he closed down the Bureau and, with Muranov and Kamenev, took over the editorship of *Pravda*. Stalin himself was as yet hardly known among the St. Petersburg party members. Chkheidze remembered his countryman from the revolutionary spadework in the Caucasus. Stalin had no authority in party circles where Kamenev's name carried greater weight. The first issues of *Pravda* were characterized by a more conciliatory tone toward the provisional government. In an editorial of March 15 (March 28) Kamenev came out for national defense. On the following day Stalin supported him.[2] When Lenin, annoyed by this behavior, protested in several of his "Letters from Afar," Stalin tried to justify the support of the government[3] at a Party Conference which was held on March 29 (April 10). It was only later that he submitted to Lenin's views.

The Party Conference started with the assumption that for the time being one should be satisfied with the democratic results of the revolution before realizing the Socialist demands. Everybody talked only of a democratic republic of workers and peasants, not of a dictatorship of the proletariat. The moderate Bolsheviks insisted that the party should support the Provisional Government; the radical Bolsheviks stressed that the revolution must not only be anti-feudal but also anti-capitalist.

The direction of the conference was in Stalin's hands. With great shrewdness he maneuvered between the two wings, trying to prevent the threatening split. At heart he was not even averse to approaching the Mensheviks, and negotiations to that end were started. The way to a moderate Socialist Russian democracy seemed open, the danger of a radicalization of the revolution seemed exorcized.[4]

Then on April 3 (April 16) Lenin returned. Socialist friends had obtained permission of the German Government and High Command for him to travel in a sealed train across Germany. In return he had to assume no other obligation than the promise to help a group of German civilians in Russia to return home. There was an identity of purpose between Imperial Germany and Bolshevism, aiming at the downfall of the Provisional Government.[5] Lenin received a triumphal welcome at the station in St. Petersburg. Thousands of workers, soldiers and sailors greeted him jubilantly. Chkheidze welcomed him in the name of the Soviets. But Lenin's reply was addressed not so much to him as to the people, and he cheered not the triumphant Russian revolution, but the coming world revolution. He was not interested in lengthy speeches of welcome. For him the revolution was only in the making.

First of all he had to enforce his will on the party. In great haste he committed his ten theses to paper as ammunition to bombard the joint meeting of Bolsheviks and Mensheviks, called for the following day at the Tauride Palace.[6] Lenin unequivocally demanded a breach with the Provisional Government; to trust it, he said, would spell the death of socialism. It was noteworthy that he rejected both the "Social Patriots" and the Pacifists and refused any collaboration with the moderate Socialists. Therefore he attacked *Pravda* without pity. True, the Bolshevik party could not immediately assume power. For this they needed a majority in the Soviets. But until that time they would have to win the masses for themselves. And now Lenin hammered his program of action into the ears of his audiences: liquidation of the standing army and the police, liquidation of the bureaucracy, socialization of the banks, control by the workers of production and distribution of goods, division of the land among the peasants. The effect of his first speech was tremendous. No one had expected such a degree of radicalism. "I shall never forget the speech," writes the Socialist N. Sukhanov, "which broke like lightning over the assembly and shook and confused not only me . . . it seemed as if all the elements had been let loose, as if the demon of destruction was rising from his depths. . ."[7]

The St. Petersburg Party Committee at first rejected the April Theses. But within a few days Lenin knew how to marshal all his arts of agitation. When old comrades reminded him of his former thesis that Russia was not yet ripe for Socialism, he scolded them as conservative and inflexible. One must not cling to old formulas but must always revise them critically. Russia's development could only be viewed in connection with that of Europe, it was Russia's mission to pave the way for the European revolution.

There was strong opposition, of course. Some said that these were views which formerly had been heard only from Trotsky. Others painted Lenin as an anarchist conspirator, a new Bakunin.

A special party conference in St. Petersburg, however, gave him

a majority of 20 votes out of 35. At the All-Russian Party Conference which had been convened at the end of April (beginning
of May), there were excited debates. Lenin's proposal to break
immediately with the international workers' movement and to found
a new International was turned down. So was his proposal to re-
name the Social Democratic Party and call it Communist. On the
other hand, the assembly supported his stand on the nationalities
question. Every nationality was to be given the right of self-
determination "including the right to secede." A compromise was
made regarding collaboration with other left wing groups and relations with the Soviets. Many of the older Bolsheviks, Kamenev,
Zinoviev, Bukharin and others opposed Lenin in these debates.
The final resolutions were passed 71 for, 39 against and 8 abstentions. The majority of the party was in Lenin's hands.

In these April days the party had gained a new orientation. The
next step was to win over the masses. Lenin mounted the rostrums
and each time cast a greater spell over his audience. His speech
sounded staccato and unmusical. And there were listeners who described it as repellent rather than fascinating.[8] But they, too, were
aware of its persuasive power. And nowhere was it more effective
than among the working class. He communicated the irresistible
feeling that here was a man of the people, although neither by birth
nor occupation could Lenin be called a proletarian. But even
beyond these circles grew the conviction that the millions of the
downtrodden and oppressed in the great country of Russia had at
last found a spokesman in this thick-set man with the intellectual
brow and the diabolic glitter in his eyes; a spokesman who really
wanted selflessly to serve their cause and not his own. His phrases,
such as "Take back the loot" (*Grab nagrablennoye*) were greedily
taken up. The contradictions in his speeches of his earlier ideology, the primitive, demogogical over-simplifications which sprang
from the tactics of the day-by-day struggle, were largely ignored.
People were swept away by the immense will power of this extraordinary man; the sparks of his rhetoric fell among the masses—
made into dry tinder by war and revolution—and started a fearful
blaze.

It was the anarchistic instincts of the masses which Lenin, whom
many considered to be an anarchist himself, knew how to arouse.
His great goal was the mobilization of the masses. They were to be
set free and go into action. Any stabilization of conditions, any

contentment with liberal-democratic freedoms was to be prevented.[9] The revolution, once started, must not stop; the Russian revolution was to set off the world revolution.

The freeing of the masses was, however, only one of Lenin's goals. The other was to direct the movement and to use it for putting the Bolshevik party into power. Lenin assumed that there was to be no conflict between the will of the masses and the will of the party, that developments would lead to the rule of one party. The heart of Lenin's teaching is that the masses need the guardianship of an elite party. The fanatical masses, however, who listened in fascination to his speeches and who avidly read his articles, were not aware of his real thoughts. And, since Lenin saw himself as the executor of a natural course of events, they became the tools of his tremendous drive for power.

Bolshevik Tactics in the Spring of 1917

A new Central Committee was elected at the first All-Russian Congress of the Bolsheviks held at the end of April. It consisted of nine members, among them Lenin, Zinoviev, Kamenev, Sverdlov and Stalin. The 133 delegates to the Congress represented about 76,000 party members. Their number had doubled since February. It was but a small band among the hundreds of thousands of Social Revolutionaries and Mensheviks, but they were well organized and disciplined and their aim was to take over all key positions gradually. This was Lenin's *avant garde* of the revolution, an elite, which soon became a willing tool in the hands of its leader. It grew in numbers day by day, but its influence on the masses grew even more quickly. While Lenin, supported by Zinoviev and Kamenev, fought by means of resolutions and speeches, Sverdlov and Stalin maintained contact with the party representatives in the provinces and with the delegates to the Soviets.

Stalin had quickly taken his cue from Lenin's ten theses. Now he hastened to defend them in *Pravda*. He took particular interest in the peasant question. When the Minister for Agriculture, Shingarev, forbade the peasants to till the land of the landlords before the land reform was legally settled, Stalin called on them in an article, *Land for the Peasants*, to form committees and to help themselves to the land. Besides that he made the nationality problem—in which he had already shown a theoretical interest before the war—his special domain. At the April Congress, in the matter of Finland, he had already advocated a nation's right to separate from Russia if it so desired.

A month after Lenin, Trotsky, too, had returned to Russia. After leaving the United States, he had at first been kept in a Canadian internment camp, and then was arrested in London, until the British Government, under pressure from the Provisional Government, allowed him to continue his journey. Now he plunged into the battles of rhetoric of St. Petersburg, employing his brilliant, passionate eloquence against the Provisional Government. He was interested in collaborating with Lenin. He no longer cared to re-unite the Mensheviks and Bolsheviks. On his return to St. Petersburg he found that the Mensheviks had moved to the right, while the Bolsheviks, on the other hand, had freed themselves of their narrow sectarianism which, in his opinion, had afflicted them during their underground period. (A *quid pro quo* position. Trotsky accepted Lenin's sectarian party—Lenin accepted Trotsky's sectarian view of a proletarian revolution.) The fact that Lenin had accepted Trotsky's view that the dictatorship of the proletariat was the real goal of the Russian revolution also made it easier for Trotsky to join the Bolsheviks.

Until July he was still head of a small splinter group of talented and influential Socialists, intellectuals, who called themselves "Mezhrayontsy," i.e., the inter-districtors. Among them were Lunacharsky, the future Commissar of Education; Pokrovsky, the well-known Marxist historian; Ryazanov, the biographer of Marx; the future diplomats Manuilsky, Joffe, Karakhan, and Yureniev; and others. In July they joined the Bolshevik party, and substantially raised the intellectual level of the party leadership. Party tactics, thanks to Trotsky, became more radical, a fact which many old Bolsheviks opposed for some time to come.[10] The Provisional Government continued with varying composition until Lenin overthrew it.

When in May the Provisional Government under pressure from the Soviets was replaced by a Provisional Government consisting of a coalition of Kadets, Mensheviks and Social Revolutionaries, the battle between government and Soviets ceased. Mensheviks and Social Revolutionaries were now also responsible for government policies. As a result the Soviets lost more and more ground among the urban masses, particularly in the capital. In the eyes of the peasants, on the other hand, the Social Revolutionary Party was all the more discredited as it delayed the promised division of the land.

Lenin agitated now more and more openly for "All Power to the Soviets." This formula was doubtless risky because the moderate Socialists still held the majority in the Soviets. When the first All-Russian Soviet Congress opened on June 3 (June 16), the Social Revolutionaries had 285 delegates, the Mensheviks 248, and the Bolsheviks only 105.[11] But when a demonstration of many hundreds of thousands of workers and soldiers marched through the streets of St. Petersburg shortly afterward, their posters and flags bore almost exclusively Bolshevik slogans. The effect was inevitable on the many Soviet delegates from the provinces. Lenin was firmly convinced that in time he would conquer the Soviets from within. The slogan "All Power to the Soviets" was his cloak for demanding the dictatorship of the Bolshevik party.[12]

The July Uprising

Actually the Bolsheviks were not yet ready to assume power—a fact proven by the failure of the uprising of July, 1917.

As a result of the revolutionary propaganda, which had steadily grown in volume since April, tension in the workers' quarters and in the barracks of the capital had reached a dangerous point by the end of June. Rumors that conservative and liberal circles were preparing a counter-revolution had brought the atmosphere to fever pitch when the July offensive began. On the afternoon of July 2 (July 15) a delegation of soldiers demanded that the Bolshevik Party leadership give the order starting the revolution. The party, however, renewed its prohibition of demonstrations, since it did not expect to benefit from a clash with elements loyal to the government at that time. "We had decided," one of the early official accounts states, "to await the offensive and in no case let ourselves be provoked, but rather give the Provisional Government time to reach the end of its rope."[13]

Toward evening thousands of armed demonstrators, soldiers of the garrison and sailors from Kronstadt gathered in front of the party offices. The Bolshevik leaders shrewdly re-directed the masses, which refused to disperse, to the Tauride Palace, the seat of the Soviets. The demonstration started amid the strains of the "Marseillaise." The Tauride Palace was beleaguered throughout the night, and the executive body of the Soviets was entreated to depose the Provisional Government and assume power. (Some accounts report that for a time the demonstration had disrupted the unanimity of the Bolshevik leadership. A sizeable section advocated immediate action but was overruled.)

Tension increased hour-by-hour. Several ministers were molested. Zinoviev spoke tirelessly to the crowds from a balcony of the palace and appealed to them to go home and save their energies for a later day. When these appeals proved futile, the party leadership decided to take part in the demonstration in order to "direct it into peaceful channels." [14] In fact, however, the party leaders were in large measure responsible for the excesses that took place. Lenin, who arrived in the city on July 4 (July 17) realized that the action taken had been imprudent. [15] In the following days the government managed to gather some reliable forces. Although the demonstrations continued and here and there resulted in bloody clashes, the movement gradually lost its momentum. Insurgents who had barricaded themselves in the Peter-Paul Fortress were persuaded by Stalin, Kamenev, and Lieber, a Bundist Menshevik, at the request of the Executive Committee of the Soviets, to surrender themselves not to the government but to the Soviets.

It is apparent that the Bolshevik party had played a double role in the July revolt. The official account of events, which Stalin gave the Sixth Party Congress [16] at its meeting a few weeks later, must be read with caution. [17] It appears that the rising of the workers and soldiers was actually prepared by Bolshevik propaganda, and that the Bolshevik leadership assumed that the unleashing of these forces would immediately be followed by a general popular rising against the government. However, the party leadership failed to push matters in this direction and could not keep control over the chaotic potentialities of the mob. The night in front of the Tauride Palace was the test. If the Executive of the Soviets had been swept away by the spirit of the revolt, there would have been nothing to stop the Bolshevization of the Soviets; the great coalition would have broken down and the path for a Bolshevik government would have been open. The opposition of the moderate Socialists in the Soviets turned out to be stronger than had been believed. They did not allow themselves to be railroaded by the mob unleashed by the Bolsheviks. When the Party Executive recognized this on July 4 (July 17), it called for a retreat.

In the meantime the government had ordered a cavalry division from the front to the capital. This division was decisive in putting down the rising. On July 7 (July 20) order was re-established. The Bolshevik party offices and the editorial offices of *Pravda* were occupied. Trotsky and Kamenev were arrested. Lenin at first went into hiding in a worker's home and then, on July 11 (July 24), fled across the border to Finland. He did not return to St. Petersburg until the eve of the October revolution. Zinoviev also vanished. Of the members of the Executive Committee, Stalin alone remained untouched; his name was too little known at that time. He temporarily assumed the leadership of the party and tried to steer it through the crisis. The Bolsheviks went underground once more. At this juncture they were joined by Trotsky's group which considerably improved the caliber of the party leadership. At the Congress which met at the end of July, he was elected to the new Central Committee. Apart from those already mentioned, the following Bolsheviks who were to become well-known were members: Rykov, Bukharin, Krestinsky, Dzierzynski, Joffe, Sokolnikov, Muranov and Madam Kollontay. During the debates, a controversy between Stalin and Rykov, Preobrazhensky and Bukharin attracted considerable attention. Opposing the thesis that the socialist reconstruction of the Russian social order could only be carried out if the revolution was also victorious in Western Europe, Stalin said that one should not lose sight of the possibility that it might be Russia itself that would be the pioneer of Socialism. "We must free ourselves of the out-dated prejudice," he said, "that only Europe can show us the way. There is a dogmatic and a creative Marxism. I have decided in favor of the latter."[18] This was a messianic Socialism reminiscent of Herzen and Lavrov, and the forerunner of the line adopted in the thirties.

At the August Congress, 240,000 party members were represented, three times as many as in April. The failure of the July revolt, while momentarily restricting the party leadership's freedom of political action, had not affected the party unfavorably.

The immediate conclusion which Lenin drew from the July events and which he discussed in his article, *"On Slogans"*, consisted in the demand that the existing slogan, "All Power to the Soviets," be changed, since their majority had joined the side of the counter-revolutionaries. The watchword now was to be, "The Dictatorship of the Masses," with the Bolshevik party to be the *avant garde* of the masses and to realize the demands of the peasants. Lenin freely admitted that now, after the government had openly proceeded against his party, he thought a peaceful transfer of power to the

Soviets was unlikely. He now advocated a combination of legal and illegal steps to play power into the hands of the party.[19]

For the Provisional Government the result of the July rising and the lost offensive was that Kerensky consolidated his position. After Prince Lvov resigned on July 8 (July 21) he took over the Prime Ministership, without, however, relinquishing the War and Navy Ministry. However, in the Ministry of War, the Social revolutionary Savinkov, one of the strangest figures of the Russian revolution, came more and more to the fore as its actual head.

Boris Victorovich Savinkov had for many years been head of the Social Revolutionary terror groups; he had held the strings directing the attempts on lives of ministers and grand dukes before and during the revolution of 1905. He mastered the technique of political murder to perfection. After the revolution of 1905 he began, under a pseudonym, to write novels[20] which strikingly portrayed the psychology of the terrorist. His contempt for men and death showed the influence of Constantine Leontiev, the reactionary writer of the 19th century. During the war, Savinkov had used his talents for writing nationalistic war reports. Now Kerensky made him Deputy Minister of War and Political Commissar of the High Command.

There was now a shift of the government to the right. The Kadets who had resigned in May, again assumed some ministerial positions. When Kerensky appointed General Kornilov as Commander-in-Chief, the left wing parties began to fear that events might take a course along Bonapartist lines.[21] Aside from the question of Kornilov's fitness for this job, a civil war between the two extreme wings seemed in the offing, as the Soviets were rapidly losing influence.

The Kornilov Revolt

The general situation in the country had deteriorated more and more. The crisis, gradually affecting all parts of the economy, became more pronounced. Production had come to a halt, transportation was disorganized. When the administration of the railroads had been handed over to committees of railroad men in July, the transport system collapsed completely. Government finances were in a hopeless state.

In the rural districts the peasants began to become impatient. The Provisional Government did not want to anticipate the decisions of the Constituent Assembly and postponed the distribution of land. The peasants, incited by the propaganda of the Social Revolutionaries and the Bolsheviks, struck out for themselves, using arson and violence against the landlords in many places. Inevitably this created a shortage of food in the cities and at the front. The quality of bread became progressively poorer, with potatoes and bran being added to it. On April 11 (April 24) the government had instituted a grain monopoly with fixed prices but the farmers refused to make deliveries and sabotaged the government's food program. The atmosphere became more and more mutinous. The failure to find an immediate way for satisfying the peasant's hunger for land proved one of the biggest mistakes of the Provisional Government. Only by a determined and speedy solution of this century-old problem could it have kept the support of the rural population.

In industry, too, a constructive program and determined action were lacking. The adoption of the eight-hour day had come about suddenly. Managers were dismissed. The consequences were inevitable. Work discipline grew lax, production dropped rapidly, and broke down completely in some very vital sectors. Altogether, production dropped to 30-40% of the pre-revolutionary level. Arthur Henderson, the British Labor M.P., had, on his visit, proposed government control of the factories. Actually, however, this control was passed on to the workers who were not capable of handling managerial tasks.

As a further result, prices rose rapidly and the currency became devaluated. Government expenses increased but were not being met by taxation. When the government began to print emergency currency, the so-called *Kerensky* bills[22] for 20 and 40 rubles, it embarked on the path of inflation.

After the failure of the Kerensky offensive, a continuation of the war could not be seriously considered. The prestige of the government had suffered greatly. Was it possible to hold the liberal ministers who had resigned responsible for all the failures at home and abroad? Kerensky, at least, lived in the hope that the suppression of the July coup and the reorganization of the Provisional Government into a primarily Socialist one (with places always kept open for non Socialists) would suffice to strengthen his authority. First of all he needed a broader democratic basis for his position. The "National Political Conference" which he had called for late September in Moscow, was to be a stepping stone to this. He hoped that in Moscow he would be better able to avoid the troublesome St. Petersburg Soviet, and rumors of an impending transfer of the government to Moscow were not without foundation. The clumsy propaganda of the Bolsheviks which interpreted this plan as an intention of abandoning St. Petersburg to the enemy was of course a malicious fabrication.

At the Moscow Conference, which Kerensky tried to use as a new forum for his rhetoric, the right wing noticeably applauded General Kornilov. His promotion to Commander-in-Chief had turned the Army Headquarters into a highly important political factor. The general immediately laid down two conditions: no interference by the government in military questions, and re-establishment of military discipline. These conditions were essential if the deterioration of the army was to be arrested. However, the question was whether their imposition would not lead to conflict. What was Kornilov's purpose?

The details of the Kornilov coup of August, 1917, are difficult to interpret. One thing is certain; after the July revolt, Kerensky had decided to settle accounts with the Bolsheviks. For this purpose he asked Kornilov to send reliable troops to the capital. Kornilov agreed because he believed that together with Kerensky, he would be able to establish order. However, each man had a completely different picture of what was required and what political solutions were within the realm of the possible. The chance for fruitful collaboration betwen the two men was highly doubtful. Kornilov cannot be accused of planning from the start to attack the Provisional Government at the same time as he proceeded against the Bolsheviks—an idea often suggested. He merely wanted to make the government more independent of the Soviets and more amenable to the influence of the military.[23]

The contrast between these two worlds, as expressed by their two exponents, almost inevitably led to misunderstandings even while attempts were being made at cooperation. It was an insignificant, unimportant person who created much of the confusion. The Duma Deputy Lvov (not to be confused with the Prime Minister of the same name) visited Kornilov in his headquarters shortly before the planned action against the Bolsheviks. From Lvov, Kornilov received the impression that Kerensky was ready to work hand in hand with him and was willing to give him dictatorial powers so long as Kerensky would be given a post in the new government. A request for such powers was then conveyed to Kerensky by Lvov in the form of an ultimatum, which Kornilov had by no means intended. On August 26 (September 8) Kerensky telephoned Kornilov to confirm what he had been told by Lvov. Kornilov gave this confirmation without being aware that he was confirming Kerensky's suspicion that he, Kornilov, intended to overthrow the government. On August 27 (September 9) Kerensky ordered Kornilov's dismissal and instructed him to come to St. Petersburg immediately. Kornilov now decided to take action. He refused the order and, on August 28 (September 10), issued a proclamation to the Russian people asking that they support him against the Provisional Government. General Krimov was ordered to advance on St. Petersburg with the Third Cavalry Corps.

Kerensky's reply was a kind of *levée en masse* in the capital. He tried to strengthen his position with the help of the Left. All Socialist organizations were called upon to make common cause in fighting the counter-revolution. Even the sailors of Kronstadt, the most radical element in St. Petersburg, took part in the united front after Trotsky had advised them from prison to liquidate Kornilov now, and Kerensky later, rather than both at the same time. The decisive factor was the fact that the railroad unions also put themselves at Kerensky's disposal. They gave the necessary instructions and, at the approach of Kornilov's troops, tracks were pulled up, trains re-directed and the attack forestalled.

Kornilov and his staff were arrested. He was not born to be a dictator. He lacked an arresting personality, keen political insight, and the gift of leading men. Essentially, he was only a good officer. Nor was this son of a Cossack a representative of reaction. He had no thought of a Czarist restoration. He only wanted to "put Russia in order." After his seizure of power there would have been many possible solutions, even that of a democratic republic.

After the suppression of Kornilov's revolt, Kerensky proudly felt that he had gained a victory over the left as well as the right. Lenin had fled, Kornilov was in jail. On September 1 (September 14) he officially proclaimed Russia a Republic. He himself assumed the office of Commander-in-Chief of the Army. Savinkov was made Governor General of St. Petersburg. However, Kerensky's supposed triumph was a serious self-deception. His quick defeat of the Right with the help of all radical forces led inexorably to his own defeat and to the burial of the February Revolution. Kerensky could not maintain control of the situation. The breakdown of his system, based on half measures, was imminent. The Bolsheviks alone had profited from the situation.

The Situation Abroad in the Fall of 1917

Surprisingly, the German counter-thrust after the unsuccessful Kerensky offensive did not occur at once. The Russians were granted a breathing spell but they could not use it; their strength was exhausted. On August 21 (September 3) the Germans occupied Riga, before whose gates—beyond the Dvina—they had stood since 1915. In October they took the Baltic Islands of Oesel and Dagoe in a surprise attack and were in control of the Northern Baltic. The effect on Finland was soon to be felt.

During the summer Russia's Western Allies had become more and more concerned about her. In a rather sharply worded note of October 9 (October 22) they demanded that Kerensky thoroughly reorganize Russia's military and economic forces, insure an increase in production, and re-establish discipline in the army. Kerensky was offended; he did not want any interference in the domestic affairs of his country and accepted the note only under protest. He was pleased that the United States had not signed the note. In June, when a special American mission had visited Russia, Kerensky had discussed with Senator Root the idea of relying more on American than on English and French aid. He hoped for American credits, particularly for reconstructing the railway system. After the German occupation of the Baltic Islands, however, he had no other course than to ask Buchanan on October 25 (November 7) for English naval units to be sent to the Baltic. But his efforts were in vain. In view of the German position in the Baltic, the British Admiralty did not want to risk its fleet in waters which could easily become a trap.

In November a big Allied conference was to meet in Paris. The Russian delegate was to be Kerensky's Foreign Minister, Tereschenko. Important decisions were expected which would also affect Russia's conduct of the war. But Kerensky's days were numbered.

The October Revolution

After the Kornilov coup, Kerensky's prestige in liberal circles had sunk considerably. In the light of this, government by the Soviets was generally favored, because it was thought—a grave misinterpretation of the actual situation—that a quick breakdown and complete disappearance of such a regime could be counted on.

In these circumstances Kerensky drew closer to the radical

parties. He made a number of concessions to them. In the middle of September a number of Bolshevik leaders who had been arrested in July were released. Kerensky hoped at least to be able to maintain himself until the Constituent Assembly met. Elections were scheduled for November 25 (December 8). What would happen then remained to be seen. Gradually, however, Kerensky lost control over the leftist circles which, at the beginning, he himself had represented. Both the Social Revolutionaries and the Mensheviks developed left wings which demanded the immediate division of the land and an immediate peace. They withdrew their representatives from the Cabinet, among them the Minister for Agriculture, Victor Chernov. Kerensky could not keep up with these radical developments. Against his will, the balance of his government had once again shifted to the right. (The Bolshevik theory that this was a conspiracy aiming at a Monarchist dictatorship is untrue.)

In the critical days of September the Bolsheviks had taken part in the suppression of the Kornilov revolt. The new situation gave them a great deal of leverage. Lenin asked the Mensheviks and Social Revolutionaries to sever the coalition with the Kadets and to form a government of their own, based on the Soviets. He promised that the Bolsheviks would then play the role of a loyal opposition in the Soviets. Significantly enough, at the time of this offer, the Bolsheviks had just obtained a majority in the St. Petersburg Soviet. During the September elections more than 50% of the seats in the city Soviets went to the Bolsheviks; in July they had mustered barely 10%. The Central Executive Committee of all Soviets in the country (VTsIK) was still in the hands of the Social Revolutionaries and the Mensheviks—but for how long? Within the Soldiers Councils of the Army, too, the Bolsheviks were gaining more and more ground. Among the Bolshevik leaders released by Kerensky was Trotsky. He was now elected President of the St. Petersburg Soviet by a bloc consisting mainly of Bolsheviks and Left Wing Social Revolutionaries. He urged it to demand from the VTsIK that a second All-Russian Soviet Congress be called and that all power be vested in it.

The slogan "All Power to the Soviets" now meant something quite different. An assumption of power by the Soviets could now easily lead to the assumption of power by the Bolsheviks; the slogan really meant power for the Bolsheviks as the representatives of the majority. Thus Trotsky's demands were already aimed at a new revolution.

Lenin, too, in his exile, was convinced that the time had come for the overthrow of the Provisional Government. For him it was a matter of course that the Soviets', that is the proletariat's, seizure of power would be followed by the seizure of power by the Bolshevik party. The seizure of power, he wrote in September, would fulfill the masses' wish for peace, the peasants' wish for land and the workers' wish for the socialization of the factories. The revolution in Russia would be accompanied by revolution in other countries, particularly in Germany. If this opportunity was missed, the forces of the counter-revolution would gain control. Having no immediate contact with the actual situation in St. Petersburg, he felt that he could trust only the city's Bolshevik organization. In the Central Committee of the Party, preparations for an armed insurrection were to be made. By his letters he sought to influence the long discussions which were being held.[24] When the question of an armed insurrection was first debated on September 15 (September 28), Zinoviev and Kamenev sharply opposed it. They felt the plan was impractical and too dangerous. Trotsky agreed with Lenin's basic idea but differed with him on its execution. Lenin mainly warned against an amateurish trust in a spontaneous popular uprising. Trotsky's concern was different. He felt that the base of the Bolshevik party was too narrow; that it was the rejection of the broader base that was amateurish and impractical. Lenin was in favor of starting as soon as possible; Trotsky planned to couple the insurrection with the meeting of the All-Russian Soviet at the end of October and use the greater authority of this supreme proletarian body to sweep it along.

Trotsky had a clearer picture than Lenin on how to base the tactical planning on the complicated alignments of power in the triangle of Provisional Government, Soviets and Bolshevik party. In masterly fashion he managed to camouflage all preparations for the revolution as security measures of the state against the danger of a right-wing counter-revolution. Under the lawful cloak of a broadly elected, popular-representative body, the Soviets, the conspiracy could be planned and prepared with a degree of carefulness which made Lenin's plan for a spontaneous coup by the Party appear to be an irresponsible adventure.

While the storm that was to destroy his regime was brewing, Kerensky moved unaware along old-established parliamentary paths. He assembled a preliminary Parliament, a representative body which he planned to play-off against the Soviets. The Parliament was to bridge the period until the meeting of the Constituent Assembly, but its weakness lay in the fact that it had only an advisory function, its members being delegated by parties and other non-governmental bodies. When the preliminary Parliament was opened by the Prime Minister on October 7 (October 20), after the Duma and the State Council had been officially dissolved on the previous day, the right wing demanded immediate stringent measures against the Bolsheviks.

The Bolsheviks had the choice of participating in this body. The question was discussed at an All-Russian Party Conference. Although Trotsky and Stalin favored a boycott, Kamenev and Rykov successfully advocated participation. Lenin castigated this acceptance as a "deviation from the proletarian and revolutionary path." However, Bolshevik participation was short-lived; they walked out after a statement by Trotsky.

Meanwhile the interplay of power had shifted to another level. The military strength available in the capital came to be a decisive factor. The rumor that the government intended to shift the capital to Moscow in order to surrender St. Petersburg to the enemy was enough to make the Soviets decide to take responsibility for the defense of the city. When the Soviet assumed the right to decide on all troop movements in St. Petersburg and the surrounding districts, the government had been outplayed in a vital matter. On October 13 (October 26) the Executive Committee of the Soviets established an extraordinary Military Revolutionary Committee, which, strangely enough, had been proposed by a Menshevik, who was quite unaware of the implications. Its chairman became *ex officio* president of the St. Petersburg Soviet. Thus Trotsky had created for himself a General Staff for the coming insurrection. As his immediate deputy, he appointed the Bolshevik Antonov-Ovseyenko.²⁵ All threads of the conspiracy were gathered in Trotsky's hands.

While the actual decision was here in the making, the Central Committee of the Party was still heatedly debating fundamental questions. From his hiding place in Finland, Lenin tried to eliminate the resistance of Kamenev and Zinoviev. "The crisis is here," he wrote early in October from Viborg, where he had moved from Helsingfors in order to be nearer to St. Petersburg. He warned against waiting for the Congress of Soviets, which, he felt, would mean missing the right moment for the revolution. He even threatened to resign from the Central Committee. He finally prevailed upon the Bolsheviks to walk out of Kerensky's preliminary parliament on October 7 (October 20). Echoing Trotsky's cry: "Petrograd[26] is in danger! The revolution is in danger! The People are in danger!" the Bolsheviks left the hall. On the next day Lenin appeared secretly in the city in order to participate in the historic session of the Central Committee of October 10 (October 23).

In vain Kamenev and Zinoviev entreated their party comrades to wait for the Constituent Assembly: "We don't have the right to stake the entire future on the single card of an armed uprising." They warned against immediate insurrection for two reasons; they believed that its advocates underestimated the government's powers of resistance and they counted on the imminent outbreak of a proletarian revolution in Western Europe. They were to be proved wrong on the first point; the second proved to be wishful thinking.

Lenin disregarded all objections and considered the pessimism of his two opponents unfounded. Twelve members of the Central Committee were present for the vote; ten voted for the revolution. Kamenev and Zinoviev were isolated. It was also decided to establish a Political Bureau of the Party which would be responsible for political direction. Lenin, Trotsky, Stalin, Sokolnikov and Bubnov—and Kamenev and Zinoviev, too—were elected as its members. This was the birth of the Politburo which later became so powerful. October 20 (November 2) was chosen as the day of the uprising.

But in the last two weeks before the October Revolution it became increasingly apparent that the Central Committee of the Party or the new Politburo was still reluctant to strike the decisive blow. Lenin returned to his hiding place and concentrated on trying to convert his two opponents by letter. St. Petersburg now appeared unsuitable to him as the starting point of the revolution. He suggested striking the first blow in Moscow. Then he even thought of letting the revolution begin in Helsingfors and letting it carry from there into Russia. Trotsky's idea of combined action with the Soviets obviously still pained him.

Then on October 16 (October 29) the Central Committee affirmed once again the previous decision regarding the rising.[27] Strangely enough Kamenev and Zinoviev did not hesitate to warn publicly against the rising in the magazine *Novaya Zhizn* (New Life), published by Maxim Gorky. Lenin was beside himself with fury and demanded the immediate expulsion of these "scabs" from the Party.[28] Stalin in his sly and cautious manner tried to mediate.

For the time being Kamenev's and Zinoviev's resignations from their posts in the Central Committee were accepted as sufficient.

The All-Russian Soviet Congress was to convene on October 20 (November 2). The Central Committee of the Bolshevik Party elected Lenin and Trotsky as its speakers at the Congress. When the executive body of the Congress, dominated by the Mensheviks, postponed the meeting by five days, i.e. to October 25 (November 7) they enormously helped the Bolshevik cause. More than a week was now available for the actual preparation of the insurrection. In accordance with Trotsky's proposal, to have the rising coincide with the assembly of the Congress, October 25 (November 7) was fixed as the date.

Actually, the rising was to take place on the evening before this date. The attitude of the troops in the garrison became a decisive factor. When the representatives of all St. Petersburg regiments gathered for a conference on October 21 (November 3), they recognized the Military Revolutionary Committee as sole authority of the garrison and resolved to obey no orders that were not counter-signed by Trotsky or one of his deputies. That was the first step toward mutiny against the Kerensky regime. Two days later the Military Revolutionary Committee appointed commissars for all military units in and around St. Petersburg. This was nothing less than Soviet assumption of control of the military. Henceforth, the commissars were to countersign all marching orders or the orders were not to be obeyed. Officers who resisted were arrested.

On October 24 (November 6) the government prepared its first counter-stroke. Loyal troops occupied the offices of the newspaper *Rabochi Put* (The Path of Labor), the Bolshevik organ edited by Stalin, which had replaced the prohibited *Pravda*. This gave Trotsky a welcome pretext for striking the first blow. The revolution began. Without firing a single shot, insurgent troops occupied all bridges, railroad stations, post offices and other strategic points. Serious resistance was encountered only at the Winter Palace, the seat of the government. Here Antonov-Ovseyenko, Trotsky's deputy, led the attack. The cruiser *Aurora* bombarded the Palace from the river. Only a few ensigns and a batallion of women soldiers defended the Cabinet assembled in the Palace, but in vain. During the night of October 25-26 (November 7-8) the government capitulated. Most of the ministers were arrested. Kerensky hurriedly left the capital to collect reliable troops, but his attempt—at this stage—was futile.

In the late evening of the day of the revolution, the Second All-Russian Soviet Congress met. Though the Bolsheviks did not have an absolute majority they could rely on the support of the left wing Social Revolutionaries. The sessions had hardly begun when the right wing Social Revolutionaries and Mensheviks declared that the Congress could not continue to meet under the threat of arms the bombardment of the Winter Palace had just signaled. As a protest against the insurrection they left the hall. In so doing they surrendered the field to the Bolsheviks. With triumphant scorn Trotsky could now reject all cooperation with the moderate Socialists: "Your role is played out," he shouted. "Go where you belong from now on—into the rubbish-can of history." [29]

At this point the left wing Mensheviks under Martov had no choice but to leave the Congress too. The Bolsheviks now had an absolute majority and could sanction what had happened.

The rising in St. Petersburg had succeeded. The Bolsheviks were in power.

The Establishment of the Bolshevik Regime

The All-Russian Soviet Congress could no longer be considered representative of the people as a whole. Nor did the Bolsheviks in any way attempt to make it appear as such. In their opinion it represented that part of the "working class" that was most important, the urban and rural proletariat. The slogan "All Power to the Soviets" had become a reality. The difference, as compared with the situation that had prevailed in the spring, was that within the Soviets the Bolsheviks had now outmaneuvered the other Socialist parties.

On closer inspection, it is obvious that the urban and rural proletariat were taken unawares by the rising of October 25 (November 7). The soldiers' councils, consisting mostly of representatives from the villages, favored the Social Revolutionaries rather than the Bolsheviks. The workers' councils in the city had indeed been dominated by the Bolsheviks since the summer, but it is pure fiction to maintain that it was the workers who took over the government the day of the October Revolution. It was the Bolshevik party which, in the name of the working class but in reality over its head had usurped power.

When Lenin received the news of the arrest of the Provisional Government, he went into the plenary hall of the Congress where he was greeted by stormy ovations. It was his first public appearance since the spring. In his speech to the truncated Congress he outlined a government without any participation by the bourgeoisie whatsoever, a proletarian, socialist state. He demanded an immediate end to the war and expressed his conviction that a "world wide Socialist revolution," a trend toward which had already started in Italy, Germany and England, would become a reality almost immediately.

On October 26 (November 8) the Congress constituted the first Soviet government. Its cabinet was called the "Council (i.e., Soviet) of the People's Commissars," soon to be generally known by the abbreviation which the Bolsheviks had given it—"Sovnarkom." Lenin became its chairman. A. I. Rykov took on the Commissariat of the Interior, A. V. Lunacharsky that of Education, Trotsky that of Foreign Affairs, Stalin the Commissariat for Nationality Affairs. Other People's Commissars were appointed for Agriculture, Labor, Commerce and Industry, Finance, Justice, Food and Postal Services. V. Antonov-Ovseyenko, N. V. Krylenko and Dybenko were entrusted with the Committee for War and Navy Affairs. A new Central Executive Committee of the Soviets was headed by Kamenev who, together with Zinoviev and Rykov, represented the Party's moderate wing which had not given up hope of achieving an understanding with the other Socialist parties.

The first decrees submitted to the Congress concerned the termination of the war, and the land question. The Congress decided to offer a "democratic peace" and an immediate truce to all nations engaged in the war. The Land Decree provided for liquidation of private ownership of the land and its immediate distribution to the peasants and workers. The execution of the decree was entrusted to the village councils, i.e., to the peasants, simply legalizing their taking matters into their own hands, which they had already been doing. It was further decided to set up revolutionary committees in all military units.

In these two vital decrees Lenin adopted, in part, the program of the Social Revolutionaries, possibly because the Bolsheviks were dependent on the support of the left Social Revolutionaries. Both decrees were intended primarily to meet the wishes of the peasants and were closely connected; without the return of the soldiers no division of the land would be possible. The demand for an immediate truce meant that Lenin had given up his original plan to obtain peace only through world revolution. He was aware of the tactical importance of immediately satisfying the Russian people's longing for peace.

Recalling the first evening after the Bolshevik victory Trotsky wrote, "Lenin's wide-awake eyes rested on my tired face. 'You know,' he said hesitatingly, 'to pass so suddenly from persecution and underground living to a position of power. . . .' he searched for words and then suddenly finished in German—'it makes one dizzy'—and moved his hand around his head. We looked at one another and smiled." [30]

So far, however, firm control had only been established in St. Petersburg. Kerensky had gone to Headquarters in Pskov. Most of the generals had turned him down. Only General Krasnov, although a monarchist and an opponent, was ready to support him. Krasnov ordered his Cossacks to march on St. Petersburg to overthrow the revolution. On November 9, Gatchina was occupied and on the next evening Krasnov's troops marched into Tsarskoye Selo. Now the position taken by the railroad workers' union became decisively important. Like most important unions it was controlled by the Mensheviks. It refused to recognize the new government and ordered all railroad workers to strike against transporting the troops of either side. Since this action paralyzed movement of Kerensky's troops, it served only to help the Bolshevik government. When the Prime Minister received warnings that Krasnov's Cossacks would turn against him he decided to flee. Disguised, he managed to escape from Gatchina across the Finnish border and to France.

However weak Kerensky's authority may have been, the opponents of the Bolsheviks were now completely without leadership, torn and split internally. Kerensky himself had robbed the army leaders of initiative; the troops were now either tired of war and politically indifferent or had already been bolshevized.

Could Kerensky have saved Russia from Bolshevism? Fedor Stepun,[31] an eye witness of the revolution, has attempted to rehabilitate this fateful man of the year 1917. He praises his "youthful" faith in the importance of the individual in history and, thereby, in himself; the honest enthusiasm which permeated his speeches; the uprightness of his idealism, which sprang from the ideas of the French Revolution and from Schiller. But Stepun, too, cannot deny that behind Kerensky's moving rhetoric lay weakness. His unforgivable fault was not that he led Russia down the wrong path after the February revolution, but that he failed to lead it with sufficient firmness. Russia in 1917, after the fall of the monarchy, needed a Russian Cromwell. Kerensky was not the type.

A last attempt at resistance was made in St. Petersburg when a small group of ensigns staged an uprising. After a brief street fight they were disarmed and executed. In Moscow, Bukharin was leading the Bolsheviks and, at first, had some difficulties. The Social Revolutionary Mayor Rudnev, and the Town Commandant, Colonel Ryabtsev, had suppressed the first attempted uprising, organized a "Committee of Public Security," and arrested the Bolshevik Revolutionary Committee and the Bolshevik commandant of the Kremlin. For almost a week it was possible to keep the Bolsheviks in check with the help of a few thousand ensigns and volunteers, mostly students. There was a brief truce but street fights broke out again after the Bolsheviks received reinforcements. On November 13 the Committee of Public Security had to capitulate. Thus Moscow, the heart of Russia, was in the hands of the Bolsheviks. Except in the South, particularly in the region of the Don Cossacks, there was no further organized opposition. Within a week Lenin and his party had gained victory.

The tasks which the new government now faced were tremendous. The fighting slogans of the agitators had to be translated into concrete administrative measures. The war had to be ended. The opposition had to be restrained and the economic crisis resolved. In conservative and liberal circles the men of the new government were considered insurgent terrorists, agents of the Central Powers, traitors to the Western Allies; these circles hoped that the ineptness of the Bolsheviks, after a few weeks of governing, would become apparent. The new government also had to reckon with serious opposition from the ranks of the population. The civil servants of the old regime refused to cooperate. The State Bank and some other institutions stopped operating; the financial system collapsed.

Indeed, in any of the Western European countries the Bolsheviks would have come to grief because of their amateurishness in political and administrative matters. In Russia, however, it was this very trait [32] that helped them maintain power. Within four to six weeks the governmental apparatus was fairly firmly controlled by the Council of People's Commissars. One of the chief methods to bring this about was the Terror.

On November 9, 1917 freedom of the press which had been a typical achievement of the revolution, was already curtailed. On December 1 all non-Bolshevik newspapers, with the exceptions of

Maxim Gorky's *Novaya Zhizn* and the Social Revolutionary paper *Dolya naroda*, were forbidden. A few papers appeared illegally for a few more months until they, too, disappeared from the scene.

Even more far-reaching was the creation of an "Extraordinary Commission for the Suppression of the Counter-Revolution" on December 7 (December 20). Soon this new state and secret police force of the revolution was known as Cheka.[33] It was headed by the Commandant of the Bolshevik headquarters in the former Smolny Institute, Felix Dzierzynski, the son of a wealthy Polish landowner from the Vilna region, who had joined the Polish Social Democratic Party at an early age and had spent a good part of his life in prisons and in Siberia. Dzierzynski was known as the great "Puritan" among the Russian revolutionaries. He was a man of fierce self-denial and incorruptible honesty coupled with an icy disregard of the opinion of others. He was blindly devoted to Lenin and sought to play the role of Grand Inquisitor of the Russian Revolution. While others sought the public eye, he preferred quiet but fanatic work in seclusion. His activities quickly became indispensable to the Bolshevik government.

Now the "Red Terror" against all enemies of the state was proclaimed. In the winter of 1917-1918 the number of victims rose considerably, but the climax was reached the following year. Lenin said that no dictatorship, including that of the proletariat, could be conceived without terror and force. In a conversation with Gorky he remarked, "The cruelty of our life, which is forced upon us by circumstances, will one day be understood and condoned." The Terror was an integral element of Bolshevik governmental practice from its very beginning. The Party saw it as an immutable necessity in order to gain victory for its ideals. In his first speech as chief of the new office, Dzierzynski said, "Do not believe that I am concerned with formal justice. We do not need any laws now. What we need is to fight to the end. I request, I demand the forging of the revolutionary sword that will annihilate all counter-revolutionaries!"[34] For Dzierzynski the class struggle meant the liquidation of "the enemies of the working class;" the term included all who opposed the Bolshevik dictatorship.

The course of Bolshevik despotism was firmly set. It was characteristic that not only the upper classes who had once ruled, the nobility, the bourgeoisie and the clergy, were affected. All strata of the population suffered, including peasants and workers, the middle class and the intelligentsia. The number of victims reached into the thousands. There were hostages murdered, there were official Cheka executions and semi-official courts-martial carried out by individual Bolshevik groups. Both those who were guilty in the eyes of the new regime, and those who were not, suffered arrest. By means of torture, threats, and force, confessions were extorted from the prisoners. Short work was made of interrogations and executions. Normal processes of law were suspended for some time to come. A state of emergency reigned, with all its terrible concomitants.

The rehabilitation of the economy proved to be much more difficult than control of the government apparatus. The crisis snowballed along the downward path which the economy had entered after the February Revolution. Prices reached fantastic heights, and the value of the ruble sank rapidly. Food rationing was introduced, and administered along political lines. Only members of the Bolshevik party, Soviet officials and workers were assured of supplies in the cities. The peasants, in spite of the Land Decree of October 26 (November 8), did not comply with their delivery obligations. Because the settlement of the land question had been delayed so long, they had begun to help themselves and had divided up the estates even prior to the October Revolution. Now they refused to make deliveries. Special requisition battalions of the Red Army and the Cheka poured into the countryside and began to confiscate food by force. Here and there peasants resisted and hid their stores. The more distant the area, the more violent their opposition. This was an extremely serious problem for the Bolshevik regime which had yet to devise solutions for it. For the time being the peasants still considered the Social Revolutionary Party to be the historic representative of their interests.

The Constituent Assembly

The relationship between the Bolsheviks and the other Socialist parties was now of great importance. Lenin's foremost aim was to prevent the formation of a unified non-Bolshevik opposition by the other Socialist groups. Kamenev disagreed and stubbornly fought for mutual understanding of all Socialists during the first week after the seizure of power. On the fifth day of endless discussion in the Central Committee of the party, Lenin ruthlessly threatened to split the party by using the terrorist sailors if his views were not accepted.[35] In answer to this, Kamenev submitted the problem to the Central Executive Committee of the Soviets, and thereby forced Lenin to give in. On November 2 (November 15) the Bolshevik Central Committee also decided in favor of a coalition government with the other Socialists.

In the new government then formed, the Bolsheviks held not more than half of the seats. Lenin, however, retained its leadership. After receiving news of the final victory of the revolution in Moscow, he had gained the upper hand again and exerted brutal pressure on his opponents in the party in order to deprive them of the initiative in negotiations with the other parties. Kamenev and Zinoviev, whom Lenin once again branded in the press as "scabs," temporarily left the Central Committee. Some People's Commissars also resigned their offices and the left Social Revolutionaries withdrew from the Soviet executive body.

Lenin, again firmly established, this time opened negotiations with the left Social Revolutionaries himself. A special conference of the Peasants' Soviets which met in St. Petersburg on November 10 (November 23) clearly showed the animosity of these circles for the Bolsheviks. When Lenin began to speak he was at first shouted down. However, he adroitly managed to play the various groups against each other and, finally, to persuade the Social Revolutionaries to participate again in the government, thus making a common front of all non-Bolshevik Socialists impossible. The executive bodies of the Workers and Soldiers' Soviets and of the Peasants' Soviets were combined. The final split of the Social Revolutionary party, on which the Bolsheviks had depended all along, soon occurred. Lenin's real intentions became apparent when the Constituent Assembly met.

The election date for the Constituent Assembly had been postponed several times by the Provisional Government. Finally it had been set for November 12 (November 25). Since April Lenin had urged that the elections be held sooner and, in his attacks on the Provisional Government, had criticized its delaying tactics in setting the date. One of the most disastrous mistakes of the Kerensky regime was its failure to realize the importance of a meeting of the Constituent Assembly at the earliest possible moment. Even if the Bolshevik leaders had early thought of taking the Assembly by surprise, they could hardly have done so before their seizure of power, unless they had been able to use the convening of the Constituent Assembly for their own purposes in the way they had used the Soviet Congress on October 25 (November 7).

After the October Revolution Lenin planned to postpone the elections. Trotsky, however, reminded him of the frequent promises that had been made to convene the Constituent Assembly as quickly as possible, once the Bolsheviks had gained power. The elections took place. The result was discouraging for the new Soviet Government. Of the thirty-six million who went to the polls, only nine million voted for the Bolsheviks, while nearly twenty-one million cast their ballots for the Social Revolutionaries. Of the 707 seats in the Constituent Assembly, the Social Revolutionaries won 370, which gave them a clear majority. The Bolsheviks received 175 seats; the left Social Revolutionaries, 40; the Mensheviks, 16; the Narodniki, 2; the Kadets, 17. In addition there were 86 representatives of national minorities, and one independent.[36]

The majority of the people had thus spoken against the Lenin government. Lenin drew conclusions from this, although not according to the rules of the parliamentary game. While the Social Revolutionaries and the Mensheviks used the time before the opening of the Assembly for practical preparations, working out proposals and programs, assigning various speakers to the debates, the Soviet Government tried to gain the support of the masses in St. Petersburg through relentless agitation. It appeared that at first the workers preferred to wait and remain passive. The agitation in the St. Petersburg garrison, led chiefly by the ensign Krylenko, did not achieve the desired success either. At this point Lenin ordered a division of completely reliable Latvian sharpshooters to be sent from Moscow in order to support the Red Guard and the Bolshevik sailors of the Baltic squadron. On December 11 (December 24) he forced the Central Committee of the party to approve his plan to break up the Constituent Assembly. The following day, in *Pravda,* he challenged the Assembly as not being truly representative of the people. Thus, even before it met, the Constituent Assembly had been condemned to death.

When the Constituent Assembly finally was opened on January 5 (January 18), 1918, in the Marinsky Opera House, it met under military guard supposedly stationed there as a measure of protection against counter-revolutionary provocations, but actually as the blind tool of the Bolsheviks. The seats on the right side of the hall were empty, for on November 28 (December 11), the Kadet Party had been prohibited, and its leaders arrested. Public galleries could be entered only with admission tickets issued by Uritsky, the chief of the Petrograd Cheka. Thus the government had made sure that it would get an appropriate response. When thousands of demonstrators with red flags and revolutionary posters gathered toward noon for a public expression of approval of the Constituent Assembly, they were greeted with machine gun salvos and dispersed. Altogether, nearly a hundred persons were killed or wounded in Petrograd that day.

The first session of the Constituent Assembly was opened by an old revolutionary veteran of the *Narodniki*, whose words were lost in the uproar of Bolshevik obstructionist tactics. Then in the name of the Central Executive Committee of the Soviets, Sverdlov read a Bolshevik declaration which demanded the immediate transfer of all governmental power to the Soviets. The Assembly, instead, elected Victor Chernov, the leader of the Social Revolutionaries, as President. Despite constant disturbances, Chernov managed to make his opening speech which centered around the demand for a solution of the land question and for a general peace. He appealed to the Soviets to work hand in hand with the Constituent Assembly as the highest freely elected authority of the people; if they were not ready for this, he said, there was the danger of civil war. Later Tseretelli, the leader of the Mensheviks, held the attention of the audience intermittently with his eloquent defense of civil liberties and his urgent warning against a civil war. The tumult in the hall grew louder; in the galleries the audience gave vent to its feelings without restraint.

Lenin induced Bukharin to demand that Sverdlov's declaration should be put at the head of the agenda. When this request was turned down after a lengthy debate by 237 against 138 votes, the Bolshevik delegates left the hall. With some hesitation the Left Social Revolutionaries followed them. The majority of the Assembly remained in its seats; there could be no question of a lack of a quorum or that the meeting had been broken up. Untiringly, Chernov conducted the subsequent deliberations, not allowing the guards' continued molestations to perturb him. When the dawn broke, he brought the decrees concerning the liquidation of the private ownership of land and the convening of an international Socialist peace conference to a vote. Both were accepted. In a formal ceremony, the majority of the Assembly proclaimed Russia a Democratic Federal Republic. The session finally closed in the morning. The Assembly members who remained believed that a new era had dawned for Russia. The Bolsheviks, however, knew that this was not a struggle for right, but of might.

When the delegates wanted to assemble again toward noon of January 6 (January 19) they found the entrance to the Marinsky Opera House occupied by armed troops. Even artillery had been drawn up. A decree of the Council of People's Commissars of the same day ordered the dissolution of the Constituent Assembly. "Everything has turned out for the best," Lenin said, "The dissolution of the Constituent Assembly means the complete and open repudiation of the democratic idea in favor of the dictatorship concept. This will be a valuable lesson." [37]

The same night two prominent Kadet leaders, Professor F. Kokoshkin and Dr. A. Shingarev, were murdered in a hospital by a group of Bolshevik sailors. When Lenin heard of the ensuing protest meetings held by the Social Revolutionaries and the Mensheviks, he said cynically: "Let them protest, let them bubble over with rage, let them rave some, sigh some, drink a lot of tea and talk until dawn; then they will surely soon fall asleep." [38] "Only knaves and idiots," he wrote later, "imagine that the proletariat must first gain a majority in elections held under the bourgeois yoke and that only then can it try to rule . . . We, on the contrary, maintain that the proletariat must first overthrow the bourgeoisie and take power into its own hands and then use this power, that is, the dictatorship of the proletariat, as the instrument of its class, in such a way that it gains the sympathy of the majority of workers." [39]

This coup of the Bolsheviks was followed by a reign of terror which declared all exponents of democracy to be enemies of the state and outlawed them. Does the success of the coup justify the argument that democracy could not be realized in Russia because it lacked a sufficiently solid basis? [40] The transition to democratic government would have been an extremely difficult one for Russia after the people had been corrupted by autocracy for centuries. But such transition was not impossible unless one is ready to deny the Russian people any need for liberty, however much their concept of it differs from Western ideas. Not only the liberal-democratic solution failed in Russia in 1917 because its representatives lacked the determination and ability to follow through. The moderate Socialists, too, such as Tseretelli, Chkheidze, Dan, Chernov, and others, lacked sufficient political aptitude and clear-cut planning. As Waldemar Gurian points out, they were paralyzed by the contradiction between their revolutionary promises on the one hand and their efforts to avoid anarchy on the other. [41] Theirs was a policy

of half-measures and withdrawal in critical moments which caused
them to lose the initiative on all the important questions of those
months. They had no sense of the vital meaning of power; Lenin
understood it thoroughly.

Did Lenin subordinate theory to his will to power? Consciously,
certainly not. The Marxist ideology was his basis of action. But he
knew how to learn from experience and he was very much aware
of changing power relations and changing opportunities.[42] And
these he knew how to use.

Could Lenin alone have led the Bolsheviks to victory? The
Bolshevik victory was decisively favored by the collaboration between Lenin and Trotsky. They formed a partnership of singular
effectiveness. What they shared between them in demagogic pas-
sion, cold cynicism, demonic will to power, fanatic intolerance and
unscrupulous ability, sufficed for their goal to be reached after
the three attempts in May, June and July. Each made up for the
other's failings. Trotsky's vanity, his tendency to be carried away
by his feelings, and his rude individualism, were balanced by
Lenin's intellectual sharpness, his greater understanding of collective psychic processes, and his quick eye for tactical advantages.
But Trotsky's fiery revolutionary *élan* and his natural military and
strategic gifts were of great importance in the Bolshevik rise to
power.

In the light of this, the subsequent official legend of Stalin's
leading role in the October rising collapses quickly.[43] It is not without irony that on November 7, 1918, the first anniversary of the
Revolution, he quite readily acknowledged Trotsky's part in the
successful *coup d'état* in a *Pravda* article.[44]

The Peace of Brest-Litovsk

As a result of the October Revolution the war had become of
secondary importance in the minds of the people.

Under the new regime, ending of the war seemed more a matter
of course than ever before. Only in a few scattered Rightist groups
was a continuation of the war on the side of the Allies tied up
with an overthrow of the Soviet government. The Bolshevik slogan
for immediate peace was very appealing. It was a very natural
demand, particularly when connected with the hope that the revolution, starting in the Central Powers, would spread throughout
the world.

On October 26 (November 8) the Soviet Congress addressed a radiogram to all nations and governments, calling for an immediate armistice based on the nations' right to self-determination and repudiated all annexations and indemnities.[45] On November 7 (November 20) the Council of Peoples' Commissars ordered Army Headquarters to propose cessation of hostilities to the Central Powers without delay. The Commander-in-Chief, General Dukhonin, refused to carry out this order, maintaining that the initiation of peace negotiations was a matter for the government. He was relieved of his command and, soon after, was murdered. His place was taken by Ensign Krylenko. The government decided to approach the Allies at this point. On November 8 (November 21) Trotsky, as Commissar for Foreign Affairs, addressed a note to all Allied ambassadors in St. Petersburg, in which he proposed an immediate armistice on all fronts.[46] Two days later this note was also forwarded to the neutral powers. Presumably, the Allied military attachés were not surprised; they must have been aware of the Bolsheviks' basic intentions. However they had doubts that those intentions would really be acted upon. On Nov. 18 (December 1) the American Military Attaché, General Judson, went to Trotsky in order to persuade him to change his mind.[47] He was unsuccessful.

The Western Powers were particularly shocked by the speedy publication of the secret agreements entered into by the Czar's government. Within six weeks, seven parts had been made public. Apart from the 1905 Treaty of Bjoerkoe between Nicholas II and Wilhelm II and other sensational, but important matters, the publication of the English-Russian agreement of 1907 concerning Persia and the so-called Sykes-Picot agreement of 1915 concerning the division of Turkey was most compromising to the Western Powers. The Soviets had every intention of discrediting them in the eyes of non-European and colored nations. The impact on foreign public opinion, particularly American, was tremendous.

The last shock of this kind suffered by the Allies was the Soviets' decree of January 28 (February 10) 1918, annulling the national debts of the Czarist regime. Loans worth millions of dollars were repudiated with a stroke of the pen, loans which had come primarily from the French and had made possible, since the end of the previous century, Russia's rearmament and war preparations.

Germany had informed the Soviet Government on November 14 (November 27) that she was ready to negotiate. Imperial Headquarters counted on the imminent fall of the Bolshevik regime with its peace policy and, therefore, was interested in hastening the conclusion of peace in the East. However, there was also a plan under consideration, particularly by General Hoffmann, of the staff of the Eastern headquarters, to push on to Petrograd, overthrow the Bolshevik Government, and establish contact with Rightist groups whose representative was considered to be the Grand Duke Paul Alexandrovich.[48] This possibility, however, did not offer enough assurance that a new right-wing government would be so ready to conclude a separate peace.

On the basis of the German answer, Lenin once more asked the Allies whether they were prepared to open peace negotiations together with Russia on November 18 (December 1). In adding that Russia would negotiate on her own if no answer was received, Petrograd showed that it did not seriously count on the Allies' readiness to make peace.

On November 20 (December 3) truce negotiations were opened with the Central Powers at Brest Litovsk. There had lately been no fighting to speak of, and the Russian Army was in complete dissolution. The soldiers were eager to return home as quickly as possible in order to share in the distribution of land. "They voted for peace with their feet," Lenin was fond of saying. On December 2 (December 15) a truce was agreed upon for four weeks, and on December 9 (December 22) peace negotiations began.

The Russian Delegation was headed by Joffe. The German-Austrian conditions were the cession of the non-Russian Western territories, i.e. Poland, Lithuania, and Courland. The future fate and boundaries of these countries were to be decided later.

When a Ukrainian delegation appeared at Brest-Litovsk, demanding self-determination for the Ukraine, this extremely difficult problem had to be faced. Germany and Austria, during the war, had already supported Ukrainian separatist attempts. The core of the Ukrainian movement was in Austrian Galicia. A Ukrainian legion had been used by the Central Powers. In the Russian Ukraine, too, attempts to win autonomy grew. In July, 1917, the Provisional Government granted the Ukraine autonomy within the Russian Empire. A Ukrainian Central Rada was established as the highest representative body of the Ukrainian people. The October Revolution strengthened in all non-Bolshevik Ukrainians the desire to move from autonomy to complete independence. It was inevitable that the Central Powers would further such a development in every way. They invited the Ukrainian delegation to Brest-Litovsk. When the Ukrainian Rada proclaimed its independence on January 9 (January 22), 1918, the action was, however, also recognized by England and France.

The Soviet delegation at Brest-Litovsk had to reckon not only with the loss of the Western territories and of Finland, but also with that of the Ukraine. At the end of December, having been acquainted with the German demands, the delegation left Brest-Litovsk. A suggestion of the Council of Peoples' Commissars of December 20, 1917 (January 2, 1918) to transfer the negotiations to a neutral country was turned down by the Central Powers. When the parleys were resumed at Brest-Litovsk in January, 1918, Trotsky himself took over as chief of the Soviet delegation. The Soviet Government used the tactic of dragging out the negotiations because it believed that in Germany, too, the prerequisites for the outbreak of a revolution were growing daily. And it also realized that Germany and Austria had differences of opinion about the Polish question.

Thus by formally protesting the German conditions on January 10 (January 23) Trotsky tried to gain better conditions, or at least time. He was unsuccessful, and on January 7 (January 20) he returned to Petrograd to report. Shortly after that, on February 9, 1918,[49] the demands of the Central Powers were submitted again in the form of an ultimatum. Trotsky reacted with a strange declaration. On February 10, in the name of the Council of People's Commissars, he refused to sign the German demands, but declared the war to be over.[50] The formula "Neither War nor Peace" was enticing. However, it was the slogan of an agitator, it ignored reality. Since their conditions were not accepted, the Germans resumed their offensive.

Setting out from Riga, on February 18, they conquered Livonia and then, from the Baltic Islands, Estonia. At the end of the month the Baltic countries were occupied. In the north, the advance halted at the historical border near Narva, and south of the Peipus the Germans advanced as far as Pskov. A continuation of the advance to Petrograd was not unlikely. In the south the Germans pushed into the Ukraine from Poland. On March 1 Kiev was occupied. Farther afield, the German troops penetrated into the Crimea and beyond Rostov into the Northern Caucasus.

In the Ukraine, a struggle between the nationalists and the Bolsheviks had broken out. Bolshevik troops occupied Kiev on

February 8 but, on the following day, the Germans had concluded an agreement with the Ukrainian delegation at Brest-Litovsk. The so-called "Bread-Peace" of February assured the German Command of raw materials and food, mainly grain. The German occupation of the Ukraine meant at this point that the country was secure from the Bolsheviks' grasp; together with the German troops, Simon Petlura, the leader of the Ukrainian Right Socialists, had moved into Kiev.

In the Council of People's Commissars and in the Central Committee an extraordinarily violent debate now took place; should one accept the conditions of peace or reject them and continue the war? Bukharin was an ardent advocate of rejection of the terms. The Russian Revolution, he asserted, would dishonor itself if, in order to save its own skin, it betrayed German and international socialism by resigning itself to the fact of annexations by the German Empire. By making peace with Russia, Emperor William II would have a free hand for fighting the revolution in Germany. Even if the continuation of the war was to lead to defeat and annihilation, it was still better than a life of dishonor and betrayal, he said. The Left Social Revolutionaries supported Bukharin's view.

Lenin thought less than nothing of this heroic gesture.[51] Cool realist that he was, he rejected theatrical gestures. He worked with facts only. "I speak for the Russian peasant," he said and knew that he had the backing of the people. The people no longer wanted the war. After the war had taken two and a half million men, a *levée en masse* could no longer be envisaged. Lenin tried to convince his colleagues of the complete hopelessness of the military situation and the senselessness of continued resistance. In order to save the young and not yet firmly established Soviet Republic one would have to give in to the demands of German militarism, he said. Should Russia finally collapse under the German onslaught, every hope for a revolutionary eruption in the West would be buried. The lands surrendered now would not be lost for all eternity; it was necessary to cede space in order to gain time.[52]

Considerations of foreign policy carried additional weight. Lenin was not interested in a victory of the Western powers over Germany. He expected that a peace in the East would lead to a continuation of the war in the West, thus serving the cause of world revolution.

At first Lenin's arguments fell on deaf ears. He was supported only by Sverdlov, Sokolnikov, Smilga, and later, Stalin. The majority was in favor of rejection and continuation of the "revolutionary war." A split in the party was to be feared as the Moscow Party Committee was dominated by Bukharin. However, under the impact of the rapid German advance to which hardly any resistance could be offered, Lenin, after many stormy debates, succeeded in gaining the agreement of the Central Committee seven votes to six to accept the German conditions. "Should the Germans demand the overthrow of the Bolshevik government we would, of course, have to fight,"[53] he said, but all other demands could and should be accepted. However, the German advance was carried forward by its own momentum. Despite a Russian telegram of February 19 signalling acceptance, the advance rolled on. The situation became critical, since no one knew the goals of the advance, and had to reckon with an attack on Petrograd. Lenin was willing to take these final consequences. At any rate, the decision was made to transfer the seat of the government to Moscow.

The final German conditions were presented on February 22-23. Russia had to renounce not only the southern, but also the northern Baltic provinces and conclude peace with the Ukrainian Rada and evacuate all Ukrainian and Finnish territory; to hand over to Turkey all occupied territory and a few Trans-Caucasian border regions; to demobilize the army and to renew the German-Russian trade agreement of 1904 in amended form. The Soviet government further had to pledge itself to cease all Bolshevik agitation in the territories occupied by the Germans.[54]

Only forty-eight hours were granted for signing the agreement. Now the passions of pro and con reached their climax. The Left Social Revolutionaries suggested asking the Allies for help and referred to an offer along these lines which the French Ambassador Noulens had made. Lenin roundly rejected such an idea. At most he would agree to negotiate for the purchase of arms. He moreover declared that "toying with revolutionary phrases" had to cease and threatened to withdraw from the government and the Central Committee if there were any more talk about continuing the war. The decisive vote (with four abstentions) showed seven for and four against acceptance of the German conditions.[55] On February 24 the German conditions were accepted by telegram.[56] On March 3, 1918, Sokolnikov, who had replaced Trotsky, signed the peace treaty in Brest-Litovsk.[57] It was ratified by the Soviet Congress on March 15.[58]

The Treaty of Brest-Litovsk is one of the most unfortunate peace treaties in history. For Germany it represented only a partial solution, because in view of the unstable political situation in Russia, considerable forces were tied up in the East which were needed in the West. For Russia, on the other hand, it was a national catastrophe of tremendous proportions. While national and historical arguments could validly be used for the secession from Russia of Western territories in Finland and Poland and of the Baltic countries, the situation was different in the south. The Ukraine was tied to Great Russia by innumerable bonds deeply anchored in historical consciousness. The common cultural heritage was stronger than linguistic differences. The loss of the Ukraine was economically unbearable; it meant the loss of Russia's richest granary and coal and iron deposits. It also meant that Russia had been pushed back from the Black Sea and was reduced to an area equivalent to that of the Muscovite Duchy of the Sixteenth Century. However one may sympathize with the justified Ukrainian demands for autonomy, the Ukrainian question demonstrated the need for a federal solution of Russia's nationalities problem.

In the Peace of Brest-Litovsk, Russia lost 26% of its population, 27% of its cultivated area, 26% of its railroads, 33% of its textile industry, 73% of its iron and steel industry, and 75% of its coal mines.

Lenin fought for the conclusion of the peace with iron logic. However, he did not try to justify the demands. He called the treaty "shameless," and compared it with the Peace of Tilsit, with which Napoleon had humiliated Prussia in 1807. He also pointed out that Prussia, through this humiliation had found the way to important reforms which enabled it later to perform great feats of arms.[59]

The differences of opinion concerning the Brest-Litovsk Peace had important consequences for conditions within the party. Bukharin's opposition lent substance to a group of Bolsheviks who were guided primarily by considerations of ideological loyalty, and who could not make concessions to political reality. To the members of this group the uncompromising purity of the revolutionary faith meant everything; they were the forerunners of the left wing opposition. The opposition of the Left Social Revolutionaries to the treaty meant that the coalition of the October Revolution broke asunder. In March 1918, the Social Revolutionary Peoples' Commissars left the government. Thus the Council of Peoples' Commissiars became a purely Bolshevik Cabinet.

The Seventh Party Congress, opened on March 6, also gave outward expression to the final break between Bolsheviks and Socialists. At Lenin's request the official name of the party, the Russian Social Democratic Party, was changed to the Russian Communist Party. The decision to transfer the seat of the government was also carried out then. Dzierzynski and his Cheka made themselves at home in the building of an insurance company at No. 22 Lubianka Street. Soon that name was to become a household word. Lenin arrived in Moscow on March 11 and living quarters were reserved for him in the Kremlin. And the Latvian sharpshooters were recalled from Petrograd and entrusted with guarding the Kremlin.

CHAPTER 2

THE CIVIL WAR

Background Factors. The Nationality Policy of the Soviets.

The outbreak of the great Russian civil war, which lasted almost three years, can be traced to national, social and party-political problems. Its course was considerably affected and complicated by the intervention of the Allies.

From the standpoint of party politics, the Bolshevik coup against the Constituent Assembly was sufficient reason to brand the regime as one of usurpers who had ignored the democratic representatives of the people. This view was shared by the conservative right and the liberal Kadets, as well as by the non-Bolshevik Socialists. There was at first no contact between the groups. The Bolshevik government organs treated the bourgeois elements so ruthlessly that they seemed completely devoid of influence on the course of events. However, left-wing parties could be expected to come to the defense of democratic rights against the dictatorship of the Soviets.

The main social issue of the civil war was the passive resistance of the peasants. After the Bolsheviks had introduced the slogan of class warfare into the villages, the resistance of the more well-to-do peasants turned into open opposition to the Soviet Government.

The nationality problem had arisen over the people's right to self-determination, which the Bolsheviks had demanded at the Party Congress of April, 1917. Stalin, in charge of nationality questions, insisted that all people oppressed by Czarism should have the right to remain within the Russian confederation, or to secede. In spite of strong opposition from Piatakov and Bukharin, this view, which happened to be Lenin's won the day. Lenin himself made it quite clear, that Poland and Finland had an undeniable right to secede. He felt that the other peoples—even should they decide in favor of secession—would be increasingly attracted to a proletarian Russian state.

At first it was a matter of the people's own initiative. They were soon in contact with each other. On May 29 (June 11) 1917, a Soviet of the national Socialist parties of the Ukrainians, White Russians, the Baltic and Caucasian peoples, the Jews and Mohammedans constituted itself in St. Petersburg; the Russian element was represented in this Council of Nationalities by a political group related to the Social Revolutionaries. The program of this Council envisaged at first only national autonomy, either on a territorial or individual level. Since secession from Russia was considered contrary to proletarian interests a federalist structure was advocated for the Pan-Russian Republic. Secession was to be sanctioned by the Constituent Assembly. An Executive Committee elected by this "Peoples' Soviet" addressed demands to the Provisional Government along these lines, and made preparations for the Congress of Nationalities convoked by the Ukrainian Rada for September in Kiev.

The Congress met from September 6-15 (September 19-28) in Kiev. The ninety-three delegates represented most of the peoples of Russia. Only the Poles[1] and the Finns considered themselves outside the planned confederation. By unanimous vote it was decided to transform Russia into a democratic federal republic; the desire was expressed that the Provisional Government adopt this decision and issue a proclamation to this effect even before the Constituent Assembly convened.

If the Kiev resolutions had been put into practice, the national groups, i. e. the people in the natural sense, would, for the first time in constitutional history, have been recognized as juridical entities. Russia would thereby have become a federation of nationalities, i. e. of peoples, in contrast to the later Bolshevik federation of nations in the sense of *national territories.*[2]

Thus Russia's transformation into a confederation seemed to have been initiated by the Kiev conference. After the failure of the July coup there was no apparent danger from the side of the Bolsheviks and, after the Kornilov coup had likewise been put down, the Centralist right-wing circles could no longer interfere with the nationality movement or the establishment of an all-Russian nationality state either. The Provisional Government, it was believed, would in the long run be unable to resist the powerful pressure for self-assertion of the peoples of Russia. From Kiev, as once before in the days of St. Vladimir, a new state was to be born.

The Provisional Government did not fulfill these hopes. When Kerensky proclaimed Russia a republic on September 1 (September 14) his statement did not contain any precise declaration regarding the structure of the republic—be it unitary or federative.

Once they had seized power, the Bolsheviks countered the vacillating half-measures of the Provisional Government by a firmly drawn program intended to win the sympathies of the nations on the fringes of the empire, especially the Ukrainians. Part of this program was the declaration of November 2 (November 15) to the peoples of Russia in which the Soviet Government defined its policy on the nationality question. Its author was Stalin, as People's Commissar for Nationality Affairs, and it bears his and Lenin's signature.[3] The four points of this declaration are: 1. Equality and sovereignty for all peoples of Russia; 2. The right of self-determination including that of secession and complete independence from Russia; 3. The abolition of all national and religious privileges and restrictions; 4. The free development of all national minorities and ethnic groups within Russian territory.

At first the Bolshevik propaganda voices reached only that part of the population in the border regions who were already sympathetic to the party. The anti-Bolshevik majority rejected both the "democratic centralism" of the Provisional Government, as well as of Bolshevism—which at that time did not yet use this formula—however much the latter promised the right of self-determination, including the right of secession from Russia.

Actually, after the Bolshevik advent to power, the Russian empire was torn asunder. The Ukrainian Rada started the process. At the end of September, the Ukrainians, having an acuter sense than Kerensky and his ministers of the threatening radicalization of political develpoments all over Russia, started to pursue a policy different from that of Petrograd; the representatives of the Kadet party had left the Rada. On the eve of the October revolution separatist tendencies had already gained the upper hand. After October 25 (November 7) the Rada refused any kind of recognition of the Soviet government and in a Third Universal of November 6 (November 19), 1917 proclaimed the establishment of a Ukrainian People's Republic which was to be part of the envisaged Pan-Russian federation.

Although not formally separating from Russia, the Ukraine, to all intents and purposes had established its factual independence.[4]

The Kiev Bolsheviks, in order to forestall this development, had attempted an armed insurrection on October 30 (November 12), but were overwhelmed in a brief counter-action. In December 1917, the Soviet government presented an ultimatum to the Rada and threatened to intervene by force of arms if it were not accepted. The Rada, however, rejected the Bolshevik demands. The Bolsheviks took action. At a Congress of Workers', Peasants' and Soldiers' Deputies convoked in Kharkov, they succeeded in gaining a majority. A Bolshevik government was formed which was supposedly Ukrainian, but in reality was strongly inspired by Petrograd. From Kharkov, the Bolsheviks advanced to Ekaterinoslav and Poltava, gradually gaining control of the whole region.

In this dangerous situation the Rada looked to foreign aid. In the summer of 1917 contacts had actually been established with the French and British. In December, Britain and France recognized Ukrainian independence. However, it soon became apparent that the Ukraine was in no position to pay the price that had actually been demanded for this recognition—i.e. to continue the war in the East against the Central Powers in the place of Russia. After considering its own position and the general political situation, the Rada decided to insure its own freedom by doing the opposite of what the Entente expected. It entered into immediate peace negotiations with the Central Powers. It was hoped that the country's new independence could best be protected by depriving the Russian Bolsheviks of the possibility of speaking for the Ukraine at the peace negotiations with the Central Powers which Russia had, in the meantime, also initiated.

Thus the question of the Ukrainian right to self-determination became one of the foremost and difficult problems of Bolshevik nationality policy. It became abundantly clear that the consequences of the line established on November 2 (November 15), 1917 could become a deadly danger to the Russian state. The possibility that the Ukraine, at first with German help, might become an independent bourgeois state, forced the Bolshevik rulers to restrict the freedom that had been proclaimed. At the Third All-Russian Soviet Congress which met in January, 1918, Stalin demanded that the self-determination right of the small nations be interpreted not as the right of the bourgeoisie, but of the "working masses of a nation." It was to be used as a means in the fight for Socialism and was to be subordinated to the principles of Socialism.

Speaking for the Mensheviks, Martov pointed out the incon-

sistency in the attitude adopted toward the Finns on the one hand
and the Ukrainians on the other. Why was freedom granted to the
former, and denied to the latter? Stalin replied that Soviets had
already been established in the Ukraine while in the other border
territories in question, including Poland, there were none; there was
no point in regressing to bourgeois parliamentarism where Soviets
were in existence.

The accounts of the Bolshevik nationality policy usually over-
look the fact that the border line between the two possibilities was
ill-defined. If the self-determination right was to be subordinated
to the principles of Socialism (in the Bolshevik sense) it meant that
in those territories, too, where there were no Soviets, the development of affairs could be guided in that direction. Lenin's hope that
even those nations which had separated themselves from Russia
would move along the revolutionary path toward a reunion was
not confined to theory. In keeping with the spirit of Bolshevik dynamics, it was vigorously implemented by the exercise of influence
on the domestic development of the nations in question. The Finnish civil war between the Whites and Reds in the winter of 1917-
1918 is the best known example of this. Another is the invasion of
the Baltic countries in November, 1918, by Bolshevik troops. In
both cases, Russian Bolshevik forces were supposed to speed-up
the movement toward reunion.

Centrifugal forces were felt in many parts of the empire. In the
Caucasus, regional efforts toward federation had been made since
the spring. In May, the North Caucasian mountain peoples formed
a Central Committee of the Union of North Caucasian Peoples and
the Daghestani, which functioned as a kind of local provisional
government. On September 7 (September 20), 1917 the Second
Congress of the Mountain Peoples accepted the constitution of the
"North Caucasian Federalist Republic." In Trans-Caucasia a committee of the three great South Caucasian peoples was founded on
November 2 (November 15); however, each nation also continued to pursue its own particular goals. The nation with the most
highly developed cultural and historical consciousness, the Georgians, formally declared their independence of Russia on November
9 (November 22).

In the Baltic provinces of Estonia, Livonia, and Courland, the
Baltic Germans still held the leading role in the country and, to
a lesser extent in the towns. However, since the 1880's aggressive
"Russification" and centralization had systematically encroached on

this form of self-government. As the indigenous population, the Letts and Estonians, became nationally conscious, they demanded an increasing share in the shaping of their cultural and social life and a voice in the administration of their country, these demands becoming more and more radical after 1905.

Here, too, the February Revolution rendered the question of the future relationship to Russia more urgent. Generally speaking, the Estonians and Letts adhered at first to the idea of an all-Russian federation within which they hoped to see their desire for autonomy realized. The October Revolution, however, accelerated the desire for complete separation from Russia. While the Letts still hesitated, an Estonian People's Assembly arrogated itself sovereign powers on Nov. 15 (28), 1917. This did not mean that all ties to Russia had been finally severed; the convening of the Constituent Assembly still seemed to promise the realization of the plans for an all-Russian Federation—a goal made more remote by the October Revolution.[5]

Finland alone arrived at a definite decision before the end of the year. As a first practical step after the declaration of November 2 (November 15), the Soviet Government issued a law on December 18 (December 31), 1917, granting independence to Finland. On December 22 (January 4, 1918) Stalin explained and defended this step in the VTsIK of the Soviets.[6] Party members such as Bukharin and Dzierzynski considered this policy a futile concession to the bourgeois nationalism of the small nations. But this was Lenin's line. He hoped that in the course of time, all the small nations who were now seceding from Russia would pass through proletarian revolutions following the Russian example and would sooner or later return to the fold.

The Finns, however, by a vast majority, rejected this path. Towards the end of November, 1917, they formed a right-wing bourgeois government headed by Per Svinhufvud, the "grand old man" of the struggle for autonomy, who had been able to return from his Siberian exile in the spring. On December 6 a declaration of independence was proclaimed. Outwardly the Council of the Peoples' Commissars recognized the new status unconditionally —a policy that differed from that adopted towards the Ukraine and was influenced by military and geopolitical considerations as well as the good will that Lenin had felt toward Finland during his last exile there. On December 31 he signed the document recognizing Finland's independence.[7]

Behind both the signature and the good will were still other reasons. The dubiousness of the Bolshevik concept of the right of self-determination was never more clearly demonstrated than in Stalin's speech to the Twelfth Party Congress in 1923. "There are instances," he said, "where the nations' right of self-determination conflicts with another, higher principle, namely the right of the working class to consolidate its rule once it has seized power. In such an event the right of self-determination cannot and must not become an obstacle to the working class in assuming its rightful dictatorship. The former principle must give way to the latter!" [8] This statement, which on this occasion referred to the invasion of Poland in 1920, can easily be applied to other situations as well. Why, since pro-Bolshevik military units remained stationed in Finland, should the declaration of independence not one day be changed by the "free resolve" of the Finnish people?

This was how the Bolshevik government speculated. On this speculation the civil war which broke out in Finland early in 1918 was based. General Mannerheim became the leader of the Finnish struggle for liberation. By the middle of February, North and Central Finland had been cleared of Bolsheviks, and in April the important industrial center of Tammerfors (Tampere) was liberated. A German auxiliary corps under General Count von der Goltz which landed at Hangö on April 1, played a significant role in the liberation. On April 20, Finnish troops moved into Viborg and the Battle of Lahti (April 30 to May 2) brought the final decision. The Russians suffered extensive losses. When Mannerheim victoriously entered Helsingfors (Helsinki) on May 16, Finland was free. The Finnish-Russian union of 1809 had come to an end, a fact to which Moscow had to reconcile itself.

After the Bolshevik coup against the Constituent Assembly of January 5-6 (January 18-19) the loyal representatives of the border territories knew that there could be no hope of achieving All-Russian Federation under bourgeois or socialist auspices. As early as January 9 (January 22) the Ukrainian Rada, in its Fourth Universal, proclaimed the Ukrainian People's Republic as the independent sovereign state of the Ukrainian people. This proclamation was made in the nick of time; on the night of January 15 (January 28) a Bolshevik insurrection took place in Kiev, and was supported by Bolshevik troops from the outside. On January 26 (February 8) the Ukrainian Government had to leave its capital and establish itself temporarily in Zhitomir. Nonetheless the Ukrainian peace treaty with the Central Powers was concluded on January 27 (February 9) at Brest-Litovsk. In the course of the German advance, beginning at the end of February, anti-Bolshevik Ukrainian troops succeeded in regaining Kiev on March 1.

Although the Ukraine had been recognized by the Central Powers as a sovereign state and as a partner for negotiations, the Germans did not recognize the White Russians when they realized that all plans for federation had collapsed and proclaimed their "independent and indivisible White Russian People's Republic." At the time, this proclamation was proof of their decision to cut loose from Bolshevik Russia, but it was the White Russian Republic which, after the retreat of the Germans, was first returned to the fold of the Moscow rulers. On January 1, 1919, it was transformed into an "independent Soviet Republic," which for the time being was to remain part of the Soviet Republic of Lithuania.

At the turn of the year 1917-1918, the effects of the Bolshevik terror began to make themselves felt in the Baltic countries. The expected continuation of the German advance, which had halted at Riga in 1917, was of more importance here than the collapse of the Constituent Assembly. On January 28, 1918, a representative of the Estonian and Livonian knighthood presented a declaration of independence to the Russian representative in Stockholm, an historically significant gesture which put an end to 200 years of membership in the Russian Empire.[9] However, it ignored entirely the political reality of the dynamic forces which were at work among the Baltic peoples themselves.

While the anti-Bolshevik forces among the Letts were still weak, only an insignificant section of the Estonian people was pro-Soviet. The greater part were friendly either to the Entente or to the Germans. As the German troops approached it became important to establish Estonian sovereignty in order to forestall German plans for annexation. On February 24, 1918, one day before the Germans occupied Reval and in the critical situation created by the flight of the Bolsheviks, Estonia's independence was proclaimed. K. Paets became Prime Minister of a government which was not recognized by the German occupation force.

In the treaty of Brest-Litovsk of March 3, 1918 Russia surrendered Courland, Riga and Oesel; Germany reserved the right to determine the fate of these regions in agrement with the local populations. In the complementary agreement to the Treaty of Brest-Litovsk of August 27, 1918, Russia also renounced her sovereignty over Estonia and Livonia.

Only after the collapse of the German Empire did the Latvians catch up with the Estonians. A Latvian People's Council, founded on November 17, 1918 in Riga, proclaimed Latvia a republic. Its first Prime Minister was K. Ulmanis.

In the Caucasus, finally, the liberation movement of the North Caucasian mountain peoples as well as the larger Trans-Caucasian nations was in full swing, accelerated by the events in St. Petersburg. Following the development sketched above, a North Caucasian Federal Republic constituted itself on May 11, 1918. The Don and Kuban Cossacks, too, began to stir toward independence, coincidentally with the first phase of the Civil War which began that winter.

In the Trans-Caucasus, the Trans-Caucasian Committee proclaimed the independence of the "Trans-Caucasian Federal Republic" on April 22, 1918. But the age-old historical rivalries of the three nations involved were too strong, their interests too different. The federation fell apart after only four weeks and, instead, the three national republics of Georgia (May 26, 1918), Armenia (May 28, 1918) and Azerbaijan (May 28, 1918), were established. All three entered into close contact with the German occupation forces in the summer of 1918. Subsequently, they were drawn into the whirlpool of the struggle between Whites and Reds and between British and Turkish interests.

What were the initial results of this development? The peoples of Russia, after the overthrow of the Czarist regime, had first pinned their hopes on their own progressive forces to fulfill their wishes, to help bring about Russia's transformation into a nationality state, a federal republic or a federation of republics. The first to be disappointed were the bourgeois-nationalist circles of the alien peoples. Even the Bolsheviks admitted that the Provisional Government would have found its most loyal allies among the nationalist bourgeoisie of these nations, if only it had shown some understanding of their demands.[10] The Bolshevik July insurrection in 1917 once more offered a chance for a common front, but the chance was lost. The Provisional Government remained, as before, a slave of the narrow, nationalist and centralist thinking of the overthrown Czarist regime, and recoiled from a constructive over-all solution of the Russian question which would take its peculiar ethnic structure into account. It was not prepared to renounce nationalist one-sidedness. It did not avail itself of the opportunity to gather all the diverse non-Bolshevik forces within the borders of the former empire. Thus, this empire had to break asunder into its national components.

Kerensky's proclamation of the Russian Republic, the October Revolution, and the forcible dissolution of the Constituent Assembly were further stages of this development. Due to their close co-operation in the summer of 1917, the Leftist elements among the alien peoples seemed to have a better chance than the Rightists of attaining their goal of a federal democratic republic. This goal was, in fact, reached, but it was of theoretical value only since the Bolshevik seizure of power led Russia into completely different paths. Under the impact of the new power politics even those groups of the border nations which so far could only have been called particularists became separatists. The solidarity of the so-called Russian International snapped, while in the border regions the National Front gained perceptibly from 1917 to 1918.

The result was that when the Civil War began, the Bolsheviks were not only faced with the opposition of the other socialist parties and the peasants, and with Allied intervention, but also with all the ethnic groups fighting for liberation from the central government. Territorially speaking, the Bolshevik government at the beginning of the civil war was, for all practical purposes, confined to the territory of the Grand Duchy of Moscow as it existed in the days of Ivan the Terrible, just as Lenin's opponents had prophesied in the Spring of 1917.

The Beginnings of the Civil War—Spring and Summer, 1918

Domestic resistance against Bolshevism centered amongst the Cossacks of the South. Here, far from the actual centers of revolutionary events, the propaganda of the Soviets had not taken hold. The Cossacks' pronounced love of freedom offered no encouragement for Bolshevist agitation. As early as the winter of 1917-18, General Alexeyev and General Kornilov, the former Commander-in-chief, organized the anti-Bolshevik resistance movement. They relied above all on the Don Cossacks and their hetman, Alexey Maximovich Kaledin. On January 10 a "Don Republic" was proclaimed. The German advance into the Ukraine produced a revulsion of sentiment. In the face of the collapse of the Russian defense, many persons doubted that it was right to oppose a government which, although Bolshevik, was still the political representation of the Russian state. When Kaledin could no longer completely rely on his Don Cossacks, he committed suicide on February 13.

In these circumstances Alexeyev and Kornilov had to confine themselves to non-Cossack volunteer contingents. After a brief advance they retreated with five to six thousand men into the Kuban region and the Northern Caucasus. In the fighting which broke out in Yekaterinodar (now Krasnodar), Kornilov was killed on April 13. General Anton Denikin took over as Commander-in-Chief. However, he could not maintain himself in the Kuban territory. After the Don Cossacks had elected a new hetman, Peter Nikolayevich Krasnov, on May 11, 1918, they were once again ready to fight the Bolsheviks. Denikin, descending from the Northern Caucasus to the Don, was able to replenish his ranks. Novocherkask was conquered after heavy fighting.

Krasnov and Denikin differed in their attitude toward the foreign powers. The former favored the Germans and attempted to establish contact with the German troops who had advanced in the vicinity of Rostov. Denikin wanted to cooperate with the Western Allies. Nonetheless, their collaboration in military matters was not affected. By a joint effort, the Don and Kuban regions were cleared of Bolsheviks in the early summer of 1918.

It was now Krasnov's aim to establish contact with anti-Bolshevik groups beyond the lower Volga, in the region between the Volga and the Urals. He managed to disrupt the railroad between Moscow and Tsaritsyn. Moscow was cut off from the food and oil supplies of the Northeastern and Southern Caucasus. An extremely serious situation arose for the Bolshevik government, particularly since conditions in the capital had become increasingly critical. The control of Tsaritsyn as a bulwark on the lower Volga came to be of decisive importance. The city had to be held at any price in order to prevent the merging of the South Russian and the East Russian anti-Bolshevik movements and in order to re-establish the railroad connection with Moscow. The fact that Stalin played a certain part in defending this position led Stalinist hagiographers to weave a particularly glowing but mythical halo around the story of these battles.

In the Ukraine some workers' battalions from the mining districts of the Don, under the leadership of the Party Secretary of

Lugansk, Kliment Yefremovich Voroshilov, had been fighting the advancing German troops since March, 1918. Voroshilov, born in 1881 in the Province of Ekaterinoslav, the son of a poor railroad guard, was himself a worker and since 1903 a member of the Bolshevik Party. In June, 1918, he and his unit managed to fight their way through the steppes controlled by the Don Cossacks. and reached Tsaritsyn. Here Voroshilov's unit received replacements, was formed into the Tenth Red Army, and he was put in command.

On June 7, Stalin arrived in Tsaritsyn. He had been ordered to ensure safe passage for the grain transports coming from the Northern Caucasus to Moscow. He immediately tightened economic controls; rationing of food and price control were among his first measures. Then he tried to organize the traffic on the lower Volga which had become quite chaotic. He was able to work successfully with Voroshilov who had been in the same Party Committee in Baku ten years before. The Political Commissar of the Tenth Red Army was an old Caucasian comrade-in-arms, the Georgian Serge Ordjonikidze. Finally Semyon Mikhailovich Budyenny, who was later to become one of the most popular figures in the Red Army, was also one of the Tsaritsyn group. Budyenny, a Cossack, was born in 1883, and had risen to the rank of cavalry sergeant in the Czar's Army. The small Cossack unit which he had set up in his village after the October Revolution had grown into a regiment, then into a brigade, finally into a division. He now tried to get Trotsky's permission to enlarge his division into a cavalry corps.

The Tsaritsyn group became more and more sharply opposed to the military policy of Trotsky who had just concluded his reorganization of the Red Army. There was opposition and instances of insubordination toward the Commander of the Southern front, General Sytin, a former Czarist officer, and conflicts with Trotsky, which seem like omens of the later break between Stalin and Trotsky.

In July, 1918, Krasnov's advance unit which had pushed beyond the railroad was beaten back, and the connection with Moscow was re-established. The food transports from the Caucasus reached Moscow once more; Tsaritsyn had passed its first test of strength.

In the Ukraine the significant element was the collaboration between the Germans and the Ukrainians. The so-called "broad peace" of Brest-Litovsk, which had ensured German supplies, had been followed on April 23, 1918 by a German-Ukrainian economic treaty which was very favorable to Germany but seemed unbearable to the Ukrainian Socialists. The Socialists were overthrown and replaced by a more conservative government led by the hetman Skoropadsky; he was in favor of close collaboration with the Germans, because he considered it the only means of realizing Ukrainian national aspirations. Despite the peace of Brest-Litovsk the German advance continued; on May 8 the Germans occupied Rostov and the Caucasus was thus within their reach.

In the course of time a second center of resistance against the Bolshevik government had come into being in Siberia. Here the Czechoslovak Legion was the paramount problem. At the initiative of the Western Powers a volunteer legion had been formed of deserters and prisoners of war from the Austro-Hungarian army which was to be put into action against the Central Powers. In the summer of 1917 its members had taken part in the Kerensky offensive. Now, after the Peace of Brest-Litovsk, the Czechs demanded to be transferred to the Western front. The only way open to them was through Siberia *via* Vladivostok. It was far from easy to transport approximately 40,000 men. In the spring of 1918, Trotsky in his capacity as Commissar for War, suddenly ordered them to be disarmed, a step toward making them prisoners-of-war. (The opinion has been expressed that he acted upon secret demands from the Germans.) This step proved to be fateful for the Bolshevik regime. On May 26 the Czechs refused to surrender their arms and rose against the Soviet government. Instead of going east toward Vladivostok they turned, and in June, 1918, marched west. The whole Siberian railroad was soon in their hands; they then pushed forward into the western foothills of the Urals and occupied one city after the other.

The result was a general anti-Bolshevik rising in the East. The opposition elements were composed of dissatisfied peasants, national minorities—the small Finnish and Tartar peoples between the Volga and the Urals—the Ural Cossacks, and representatives of the upper classes. The driving force was, at first, the Social Revolutionaries. In the summer an anti-Bolshevik Government was formed in Samara (later Kuibyshev) on the Volga, consisting of a group of thirty-four, mostly Social Revolutionary deputies of the dissolved Constituent Assembly, under their chairman V. Chernov. The "White" Government in Samara very soon decided to raise a "People's Army." It established close contacts with the Czechoslovak troops. When Kazan was taken on August 8, the gold reserves of the Russian Imperial Bank stored there fell into the hands of the Whites. In the west a front line was established along the Volga and Kama.

In September, protected by the military successes of the rising, an "All-Russian National Conference" convened in Ufa. Its goal was the amalgamation of all anti-Bolshevik forces. In Omsk, in Siberia, another "government" had also been formed. In contrast to the one in Samara, this was nationalist-conservative in character and had managed to establish somewhat tenuous control over the whole of Siberia. Its momentum was supplied by the right-wing circles; its most colorful personality was the former commander of the Black Sea Fleet, Admiral Alexander Vasilyevich Kolchak.

In Ufa, the two groups merged and formed a common Directory, consisting of five members. Here, too, the Social Revolutionaries were at first dominant. General Alexeyev, before his death, was selected to be the Directory's head. Admiral Kolchak took over the War and Navy Ministry. The murder of the Czar had weakened any thoughts of re-establishing the monarchy. (A Bolshevik terror group had executed Nicholas II and his entire family on July 16 in Ekaterinburg when the Czech troops drew near.) Even if Kolchak and other like-minded persons considered themselves trustees of the monarchy, the question of the future form of government was not an urgent one. It remained to be seen what political, psychological and military strength the Directory would be able to muster. One thing was certain: the spreading of the insurrection up to the Volga posed a serious threat to the Bolshevik government, a threat intensified by various other events.

The Beginning of Allied Intervention and the Revolt of the Social Revolutionaries

The attitude of the Western Allies was crucially important. Russia had concluded a separate peace and had withdrawn from the war. Superficially, it seemed that the Allies would now ignore the developments in the East in order to concentrate their forces in the West where heavy fighting was expected in the summer of 1918.

However, things were not that simple. In Russian ports, in Murmansk, Archangelsk and Vladivostok, supplies of ammunition and arms intended for the Russian front had been stored. After the Baltic countries had been occupied and German troops had landed in Finland, it was believed that a German offensive against St.

Petersburg, and an advance to Murmansk had to be reckoned with. The Allies feared that military supplies, both there and elsewhere, would fall into German hands. It was felt that appropriate measures should be taken in the South to prevent a German invasion of the Caucasus and a surprise attack on the Russian oil center of Baku which could easily be carried out, possibly by the Turks. The Allies were not sure, either, how far the Germans and the Bolsheviks would collaborate, and were most reluctant to let additional military supplies fall into Bolshevik hands.

The British, and later the French, government felt that intervention was essential. In March 1918 British troops landed in Murmansk. In April more units disembarked in Vladivostok, aided by the Japanese, who also sent contingents to the mainland. In June, the British troops in Northern Russia were reinforced and General Poole was put in command; in August a further shipment of British soldiers arrived in Archangelsk under General Ironside. By the end of the year there were about 10,000 to 15,000 Allied troops in Northern Russia; these were joined by 7,000 to 8,000 White Russians under General Miller.

With the backing of these military forces, an anti-Bolshevik government, consisting mostly of Social Revolutionaries under the leadership of N. V. Chaikovsky was set up in Archangelsk.

In a similar manner, after an anti-Bolshevik coup, a White Russian government was set up under Funtikov at Ashkabad in Turkestan. It, too, was backed by British forces who had advanced through Beluchistan and Persia and had occupied the Trans-Caspian area, including the city of Krasnavodsk, in August 1918.

In view of the Japanese activity in the Far East, in July 1918 the United States also decided to send troops to Russia. According to a State Department announcement of July 17, the United States continued to be against the idea of intervention in principle. It was said that the troops were simply intended as a support for the Czechs. After the landing of new British, French and Japanese units on August 3, 9, and 17, about 5,000 American troops from Manila and from the States arrived on August 16 and September 3. They were followed by Italian and more Japanese units. Japan finally had 17,000 men on Russian soil.

The decision of the Czechoslovak Legion to march west would probably not have occurred without encouragement from Allied representatives. The Entente also had a hand in the subsequent consolidation of White forces between the Volga and the Urals.

Now, the Bolsheviks received news of the latest Allied movements against them—the landings in Archangelsk. They were apprehensive and anxious; it was almost the last straw.

In the meantime, a serious domestic crisis had developed during July. It was caused by the increasing opposition of the Social Revolutionaries. Because the Left Social Revolutionaries had joined the Bolsheviks in the Constituent Assembly, some of their leaders were included in the cabinet of the People's Commissars. But the peace negotiations at Brest-Litovsk disturbed this new-formed unity. The Social Revolutionary Peoples' Commissars as well as Bukharin favored the rejection of the German demands. At the Fourteenth All-Russian Soviet Congress, the Left Social Revolutionaries voted against ratification; when ratification was nevertheless carried through, they resigned and the Cabinet became a one-party government.

The opposition of the Right Social Revolutionaries was even more outspoken. At their Party Conference which they were still able to hold in May 1918, in Moscow, their political goal was clearly defined—to overthrow the Bolshevik dictatorship and to continue the war on the side of the Allies. The Mensheviks, too, under Martov and Dan, did not hide their opposition to the regime. The Bolsheviks drew conclusions and saw to it that the All-Russian Central Executive Committee (VTsIK) passed a resolution on June 14, expelling the Right Social Revolutionary as well as the Menshevik delegates.

Even though the Left Social Revolutionaries were not affected, their relationship with the ruling party bcame more and more strained. In their attempts to carry the class struggle to the peasants, the Bolsheviks met with the opposition of the Social Revolutionaries who supported the land-owning peasants against them. In addition, attitudes differed concerning the question of capital punishment. The Cheka, in whose organizations the Social Revolutionaries cooperated, had carried out summary executions since February without due process of law. Now, for the first time, a death sentence against a counter-revolutionary admiral was made public. Referring to the decision of the Second All-Russian Soviet Congress to abolish capital punishment, the Social Revolutionaries protested to the VTsIK against the sentence. When they failed to make themselves heard, they withdrew their representatives from this organization as well.

When the Fifth All-Russian Soviet Congress met in Moscow

on July 4, 1918 the summer's heat was at its worst. The atmosphere was tense. On July 1st, martial law was declared in the city in order to guard against all eventualities.

Of the 1132 delegates to the Congress, 352 were Left Social Revolutionaries, the other 745 were Bolsheviks. Soon after the opening there was a heated debate on the agrarian question and the attitude to be adopted toward the German troops in the Ukraine. The Left Social Revolutionaries advocated active measures against the Germans, revocation of the Treaty of Brest-Litovsk, and breaking off of relations with the Imperial German Government. On July 6, the Congress was alarmed by the news that the German Ambassador, Count Mirbach, who had reached Moscow on April 24, had been murdered. The whole city was thrown into violent confusion. The assassins, Blumkin and Andreyev, who had entered the German Embassy on the *Denezhny pereulok,* had turned out to be members of the Left Social Revolutionaries and of the Cheka. Upon entering they had presented passes signed by Dzierzynski. It is obvious that this act was intended to provoke a breach between the Soviet Government and Germany. At the same time it was the signal for a number of Social Revolutionary uprisings aimed at the overthrow of the Bolshevik government.

The leader of the Social Revolutionary rebellion was Boris Savinkov, the experienced terrorist and Kerensky's associate in the War Ministry of the Provisional Government. At the trial of the Social Revolutionaries in 1922 he admitted that he had received 2,500,000 francs from the French Ambassador Noulens in order to finance the undertaking.

In Moscow the rebellion was directed by a woman—Maria Alexandrovna Spiridonova—a well-known terrorist who had joined the revolutionary movement when she was still almost a child.[10a] She was fanatically opposed to the Bolshevik government's Brest-Litovsk policy, and admired the Western powers. This led her to close contact with the French Military Mission in Moscow and involved her in the preparations for the murder of Count Mirbach. When the Cheka, aware of the threat she represented, put a price on her head, she requisitioned a Social Revolutionary bodyguard which was responsible for her safety.

With the rising in Moscow, simultaneous insurrections took place on July 6 in twenty-three Central Russian cities. In Yaroslavl the Social Revolutionaries succeeded in gaining complete control. The revolt posed a particular danger to the Bolsheviks for it was beginning to infect the troops along the Volga who were holding the front against the Whites and the Czechs. On July 10 General Muravyev, the Commander of the Eastern front, demanded immediate peace with the Czechs and the continuation of the war against the Germans.

In Moscow the Social Revolutionaries occupied the telephone exchange and stormed the Pokrovsky barracks under the personal command of Spiridonova. The position of the government became precarious. But at noon truck loads of Bolshevik reinforcements arrived. After an artillery bombardment lasting half an hour, the Social Revolutionary barracks were taken and the barricades cleared. In the Lubianka the number of arrested Social Revolutionaries rose by the hour. Among them were almost all the Social Revolutionary delegates to the Congress. Thirteen Social Revolutionary members of the Cheka were summarily executed; Spiridonova was exiled to Tashkent. Savinkov succeeded in escaping abroad.

On July 10 the interrupted sessions of the Congress were resumed. Now that the Bolsheviks were in sole control, the draft of the Constitution of the Russian Socialist Federal Soviet Republic was unanimously passed. It became effective on July 19.

The insurgents in Yaroslavl held out longest—until July 23. When Bolshevik control was reestablished there too, 350 persons were shot. Executions were carried out in a number of cities along the Middle Volga up to the Urals region. In Nizhni Novgorod, the principal victims were former officers; in Penza, Lenin personally ordered a merciless mass terror against all wealthy farmers (*kulaks*), clerics, and White Guardists; anyone offering resistance was put into a concentration camp outside the city; hostages were taken from the peasants who guaranteed with their lives the prompt delivery of grain." The shooting of the Czar and his family in Ekaterinburg was part of this resurgence of the Terror, although special factors were the immediate cause of the execution.

But the Social Revolutionaries did not yet give up. They returned to their old method of Czarist times, the political murder of representatives of the government. In June the Bolshevik orator Volodarsky was murdered in Petrograd. On August 30, Uritsky, chief of the Petrograd Cheka, was also assassinated. On the same day, the Social Revolutionary agent, Dora Kaplan, fired several shots at Lenin, seriously wounding him.

Surprisingly enough the Bolsheviks countered with an attack

on the British missions. Party circles had become very embittered that same month when news had come of the renewed landing of British troops in Archangelsk. The Soviet press published violent accusations against the British government. In Petrograd, Uritsky made inflammatory speeches, trying to incite the people against Britain.

The accusations, that the British were intervening in domestic Russian affairs, apparently were based on facts. When the British Consul General, Bruce Lockhart, was arrested in Moscow on August 31 he seemed heavily compromised. The interrogations showed fairly conclusively that he had had contacts with General Poole in Archangelsk, and with the White insurgents and the Czechs. While the former was understandable, the latter, however, was in the nature of a conspiracy against the government in power. From this and from the ties between the French representatives and the Social Revolutionaries, a picture emerged showing both Western powers scheming to overthrow the Bolshevik rulers. Even more compromising material was disclosed by the interrogation of the Odessa-born British agent, Sidney Reilly. Lockhart, who later described his experiences in a sensational book,[12] was held in Moscow for two months and then released in exchange for Litvinov who had been held in London.

A more serious situation was provoked by a spontaneous action of the Petrograd Cheka. A detachment had forced its way into the British Embassy; in the ensuing melee the Naval Attache Cromie was shot. The post of ambassador had remained vacant after the departure of Sir George Buchanan but the remaining members of the embassy staff were arrested. The British succeeded in transferring the staff of the Consulate General from Moscow to Vologda where, in the course of time, almost all the legations of the Allies and some of the neutral countries had assembled. The British soon retreated even further, to Archangelsk, under the protection of their troops. Diplomatic relations between the Soviet Government and England and France could be considered broken off. The neutral countries, too, followed the example of the great powers and asked for the recall of the Soviet representatives in their countries.

For a time Soviet representatives were only accredited in Washington and Berlin—after amends had been made for the murder of Mirbach—until in Berlin, too, five days before the outbreak of the German revolution, the Soviet representative Joffe was handed his passport. It had been established that he had been actively engaging in revolutionary propaganda.

The political isolation of the Bolshevik government had now reached its climax. In the light of the mounting tension in Soviet relations with the Western Allies during the summer, Soviet Foreign Commissar Chicherin, even before the actual break, had begun to consolidate the position adopted at Brest-Litovsk in order to find a way out of isolation.

Chicherin and Germany in the Summer of 1918

Georgi Vasilyevich Chicherin was a member of a distinguished aristocratic Russian family. As professor of Constitutional Law, his uncle, Boris Nikolayevich, had been a leading light at the University of Moscow as well as among Russian liberal intellectuals. He himself was the son of a diplomat, born on his father's estate in 1872, and after studying law, he chose his father's career. Nervous and of weak constitution, he was nonetheless distinguished by the breadth of his knowledge and his keen intellect. In 1904 he had established ties with revolutionary circles and soon he joined the Menshevik wing of the Russian Social Democratic Party. During the war he lived in London, was in contact with English radicals and headed a Russian Aid Committee for political emigrants. In August, 1917, he was arrested for defeatist propaganda. Only after the October Revolution did he join with the Bolsheviks. Lenin toyed with the idea of appointing him ambassador to England; Trotsky threatened reprisals against Englishmen living in Russia and thus forced his release. After his return, Chicherin first became Deputy Foreign Commissar and in May took over the direction of Russian foreign policy.

Chicherin's concept of foreign policy was strongly colored by anti-British resentment. London for him was the real center of world capitalism, and he considered the colored and colonial peoples, whose leadership was to be assumed by Russia, as natural allies in the struggle against Great Britain. Chicherin placed great hopes in China. Among the European states he considered Germany of great importance, especially since he had no illusions about Soviet Russia's precarious position in foreign affairs.

The murder of Count Mirbach seriously interfered with his efforts; he had received the German Ambassador with great courtesy and had facilitated the work of the prisoner-of-war commissions.

Lenin and Trotsky both visited the German Embassy soon after the assassination in order to express their regrets. Berlin merely issued a protest demanding a thorough investigation, but did not break off diplomatic relations. On July 28, the new ambassador Helfferich arrived in Moscow. The situation was tense. Every day threatening letters arrived at the Embassy. On July 30, Colonel-General Eichhorn, the German commander-in-chief in the Ukraine, was murdered. But the Bolshevik government did not allow itself to be diverted by these provocations which mostly emanated from the Social Revolutionary camp. The tension within the country, its precarious relations with the Western Allies, the dangerous situation on the Eastern front on the Volga, all called for exceedingly tactful treatment of the Germans.

This situation furnished the background for the sensational proposals which Chicherin, coming directly from a session of the Council of People's Commissars, submitted to the German Ambassador on August 1. The Foreign Commissar suggested that the German troops in the South should sever their contact with Krasnov and advance against General Alexeyev. In the North they were to join with the Finns and prevent an advance of the British from Murmansk towards the South. The Kremlin believed that the British were planning an attack on Petrograd; some of the material confiscated in the Embassy seemed to point in that direction. In the North, reliable Red troops were concentrated only in Vologda; Petrozavodsk on Lake Onega could not be held and was evacuated. The road to Petrograd seemed open to an aggressor from the North.

To all intents and purposes, Chicherin's proposals represented an appeal for help from the Soviets, an appeal which in view of popular opinion could not be expressed in the form of a regular alliance. Would Imperial Germany, which in April 1917 had allowed Lenin to pass without hindrance, now act to save the Bolshevik regime? The only consideration which would be decisive here was the fight against the British who were aiming at the re-establishment of a new front against the Germans in the East.

Helfferich forwarded Chicherin's offer to Berlin. In stating his own views, he urged its rejection and the adoption of a diametrically opposed course. He suggested that, without delay, the embassy be transferred to Petrograd, perhaps even to Pskov, which was occupied by the Germans. Contact was to be established immediately with the Whites. Helfferich thus adopted the view of his military attaché, Major Schubert, who believed that a few German battalions would suffice to restore "order" in Moscow. Even more important was the fact that the plan to break with the Bolsheviks was also discussed in military circles at German Head- quarters. Would it not be feasible to entrust General von der Goltz in Finland with an extension of operations directed against Petro- grad? The Germans had connections with Russian right-wing circles who wanted to proclaim the Grand Duke Paul Alexandro- vich Czar, and leaders of the Kadets also had recently advocated collaboration with Germany.

General Hoffmann, Chief of Staff of the Eastern headquarters was one of the most energetic advocates of this idea, without realizing its utopian character. A Russian government of the Right based on German bayonets could never have survived, once the revolutionary instincts of the masses had been aroused. (Such a government, incidentally, might have renounced its claim to the Baltic provinces, but never to the Ukraine.) The German Sec- retary of State for Foreign Affairs, Admiral von Hintze, had at one time been chief of the German military mission in St Peters- burg. His knowledge of Russia caused him to reject the plan to intervene in Russia in favor of the Whites. But he, too, could not be won over by Chicherin's wooing; the Military Command would never agree to such a step. Thus a compromise was adopted along the lines of the Brest-Litovsk policy. In a supplementary agreement to the treaty of August 27, the Russian territories east of the Berezina were evacuated by the Germans. Russia renounced claims to Estonia and Livonia and declared its willingness to supply greater quantities of oil and to pay indemnities totaling 6 billion gold marks. That was the price for which Germany agreed not to sup- port the Whites. Helfferich was recalled.

The Red Army and the Turning Point on the Volga

After the exciting days of the Social Revolutionary coup in July, the first August week was one of the most dangerous and tense periods for the Bolshevik regime. To the perilous situation on the Volga front was added the possibility of a change of German policy toward Russia.

This danger was eliminated by August 10 when the additional agreements were signed and, at the same time, a turning point ar- rived on the Volga front. On the same date, August 8, on which the untenability of the German positions in Western Europe became obvious after the failure of the last offensive in France,—the *dies ater* of the German High Command—Kazan on the Volga was taken by Czech and White Russian troops. This represented the climax of the anti-Bolshevik offensive of that year. Here too, it was Trotsky who, after reorganizing the Red Army, brought about the turn of events.

The Red Army had not been built in a day. Only later was its birthday fixed on February 23, 1918, the day when some resistance had been offered to the German advance near Pskov. This resistance was supposed to have halted the continuation of operations against Petrograd. In reality, as we have seen, such an advance had not seriously been planned by the German High Command.

The first military auxiliary forces used by the Bolsheviks after October consisted of irregular revolutionary workers' battalions, of units of the Petrograd and Moscow garrisons, and of Latvian sharpshooter battalions. The disordered and haphazardly assembled units soon became known as the Red Guard and their members as Red Guardists. Soon young workers as well as soldiers of the old army augmented its ranks. Good food and prompt pay were promised. The "Red Peasants' and Workers' Army" grew apace. Very soon, too, discipline was noticeably tightened. The next step toward solidifying the military power of the Soviets was taken by Trotsky in the summer of 1918 when he accepted Czarist officers, thus easing the critical shortage of military leaders. The worsening of the general conditions of the Soviet state in the midst of the Czech revolt in the East, the activities of White groups in the South, the German occupation of the Ukraine, and the British intervention in the North, contributed to a gradual change in the cool attitude of the officer circles toward the regime. Almost 40,000 so-called "military specialists" received their commissions in this manner and thus insured expert leadership of the Red Army. A former Czarist colonel, T. S. Vazetis, by birth a Lett, was appointed Commander-in-Chief. A further measure making for greater efficiency among the troops was the abolition of the revolutionary soldiers' soviets which were replaced by "war commissars." These now represented the proletarian-revolutionary principle side by side with actual military leadership, without subjecting each command to the paralyzing debate of a soldiers' soviet.

The reorganization of the Red Army was a major venture. Even Lenin hesitated to follow Trotsky's plans. He felt they were magni-

ficently conceived but too risky. Subsequent experience often justified Lenin's reservations. In the course of the civil war many
Czarist officers deserted to the Whites, often with their units. Serious differences of opinion frequently arose between Czarist officers
and commissars which had an adverse effect on military operations.
Nonetheless, Trotsky's experiment, to which Lenin had finally
consented, proved to have been unavoidable. Several of these
military specialists of 1918 later became important leaders in the
Red Army.

After the reorganization was accomplished, Trotsky, in his
capacity as Chief of the Revolutionary War Committee, took the
initiative on the Volga Front in the summer of 1918. In his famous
armored train he went to Sviyazhsk in the neighborhood of Kazan,
took over the command of the Red troops stationed there, and repelled the advancing anti-Bolshevik forces. For the time being, the
advance of the Whites on Moscow had been halted.

In September the fortunes of war seemed to change in the South,
too. Voroshilov managed to throw the Whites back across the Don.
Stalin reported to Moscow that Tsaritsyn seemed out of danger.
Soon, however, the city was again imperiled. By the middle of
October it was once more surrounded by White troops. They were
again thrown back, this time for good.

Soviet Russia and the Collapse of Germany

The November Revolution in Germany signaled a complete
change in Soviet Russia. The chances for a further spread of the
world revolution seemed immensely increased. The rulers in the
Kremlin must have thought that all that was necessary was to turn
the bourgeois revolution in Germany into a proletarian, Communist
one. For some time now the Bolsheviks had been active there. The
Independent Social Democrats had been provided with money and
propaganda literature as early as the spring of 1917. After the
collapse of the monarchy, the Spartacus League under Karl Lieb-
knecht and Rosa Luxemburg demanded closest collaboration with
Moscow and the creation of a Soviet Germany. Very soon Lenin
appointed Karl Radek head of Bolshevik propaganda in Germany.

Radek came from Galicia. He had met Lenin in Switzerland and
had returned with him to Russia. He was a well-read, able journalist
and he made himself indispensible to Lenin. Occasionally, he was
given small diplomatic assignments. Radek had a cynical contempt

for people and preferred to work behind the scenes. Now he was in his element. In an inflammatory address to the German Workers' and Soldiers' Councils on November he demanded a united front against the victorious capitalist powers. He was behind the Spartacist uprising which got under way early in December, resulted in some bloody clashes by Christmas, and came completely into the open on January 5, 1919. With Radek's help, the Communist Party of Germany (KPD) was constituted at the National Conference of the Spartacus League on December 30, 1918; its aim was the overthrow of the Ebert Government and the establishment of the dictatorship of the proletariat.

From then on Moscow counted on a quick success in Germany. The complete victory of Communism was expected by the middle of March at the latest. The Bolshevization of Germany was considered of the utmost importance, it was the prerequisite for successfully spreading the world revolution. "The circle of the nations," Radek wrote, "is almost completed. Only the most important link, Germany, is still missing."

Apart from these activities within Germany, the Bolsheviks also worked to bring outside pressure to bear. On November 13, the Soviet Government declared the Peace Treaty of Brest-Litovsk null and void. The Red Army was ordered to march into the regions occupied by the Germans. On November 25, the Germans evacuated Pskov and, on November 28, Narva. Soon the greater part of Estonia and Latvia was overrun by Red troops. Only Reval and Riga held out. On November 29, an Estonian Soviet Government was set up. On December 14, a Latvian Soviet Government was established and, three days later, released a highly significant manifesto. It said in part, "Behind us is the coming revolution which will lead within a very short time to a common union of the Socialist Soviet Republics, not only in Germany, but also in the rest of Europe, a union to which we, too, will belong . . ."[13] On January 3, the Bolsheviks took Riga. At the beginning of February the Red troops advanced west, via Vilna, as far as the border of East Prussia. It seemed to be only a question of time before the current of the Red revolution in Berlin and that in the Baltic countries would unite into one great flood.

In January and February, Soviet republics were established in innumerable North and Central German cities. There were bloody insurrections and street battles. The situation was most serious in Bavaria. In February 1919, a Soviet Republic was proclaimed there after the assassination of the Independent Socialist Prime Minister, Kurt Eisner. Like Radek in other places, a Russian, Eugen Leviné, played a part. A Red Guard was established. In the Ruhr, a Communist insurrection took place, and a Workers' and Soldiers' Republic was proclaimed.

In the meantime, however, Ebert's Government had begun to take countermeasures. The army was reorganized and strengthened, volunteer units were established. On February 12, Radek was arrested in Berlin. Government troops marched into the Ruhr. General von der Goltz took a division to Libau in order to protect East Prussia's flank and give support to the anti-Bolshevik volunteer corps in the Baltic. In May, Munich was taken by the Government troops and an end put to the Communist reign of terror.

The Russian Policy of the Allies in the Winter of 1918/19

Before events had taken this course, the Western powers had two alternatives in their policy toward Russia after their armistice with Germany. One alternative, now that it was no longer necessary to maintain an Eastern Front against Germany, was the withdrawal of all Allied troops from Russia. On the other hand, now that troops had been freed from action in the West, it became possible to use them in a "crusade" against Bolshevism in the East. As long as no peace had been concluded with Germany, the Allies were primarily worried by the specter of German-Russian collaboration under Red leadership. The events in Germany from November 1918 to February 1919 were disquieting enough. Radek's appeal had been heard in the West, too. From this viewpoint it seemed necessary to strengthen the Allied troops in Russia and to establish contact with anti-Bolshevik forces. A certain delimitation of spheres of interest was considered advisable in order to prevent friction in the collaboration between the British and the French. Two days after the Armistice in the West, on November 13, 1918, operational areas were established based on an agreement of December 23, 1917, which had been signed by Milner and Cecil for England and Clemenceau, Pichon and Foch for France. The British were to be in control of the Caucasus and the Trans-Caspian region, while the French sphere comprised the Ukraine with Bessarabia and the Crimea. The Don was the approximate line of division. British interests in the North Russian forest region were tacitly acknowledged. On the next day, the British Cabinet decided to support

General Denikin with arms, and to give *de facto* recognition to Kolchak's Government in Omsk. On November 15-16, a British and French squadron entered the Black Sea. After that British troops landed in Batum and Baku, and on December 18 French troops landed in Odessa.

While the British, however, avoided direct contact with the Bolshevik troops and were satisfied with shipping arms and ammunition to the Whites, France was more active in the Ukraine. After the departure of the Germans, Skoropadsky's Government had been overthrown on November 15 and been succeeded by the Socialist government of General Simon Petlura, who hoped to fend off the Bolsheviks with the help of the Allies. He made an agreement with the French High Command which supported him in raising Ukrainian troops. The troops under French command increased to nearly 45,000 men; they consisted of two French and two Greek divisions, as well as Rumanian, Polish and Serbian units, plus a White Russian brigade. In March 1919, joint operations were started against the Red Army.

At this point it is necessary to look behind the scenes of Allied policy. Apart from the German question, the Russian problem, too, was by no means a secondary item at the Paris Peace Conference. Not only were there differences of opinion between the Allies, but also bitter political controversies in the individual countries.

In England, a letter to the London "Times" calling for energetic measures against the Bolsheviks, written by the Secretary of War, Lord Milner, on December 19, 1918, had aroused lively comment. Chicherin replied to it with a sharp, official protest. There were two opinions in the British Cabinet. While Lloyd George was in favor of a very cautious treatment of the Russian question, Winston Churchill was outspoken in his opposition to Bolshevism. Lord Milner's demand was in keeping with Churchill's attitude. At the Inter-Allied conferences of January 22, 1919, a mediation proposal by the American President, Woodrow Wilson, was to be debated. It envisaged a conference on Russia on the Principo Islands in the Sea of Marmara to which all parties, Bolshevik and anti-Bolshevik, were to be invited. On February 4, the Soviet Government declared that it was ready to take part in the Conference but when, on February 16, the White governments indignantly refused to sit at the same table with the Bolsheviks, the plan came to naught. The Allies then met in February in Paris for decisive consultations. The questions at issue were—should intervention in

Russia be continued, should a military conflict with the Bolsheviks over and above the indirect support of the Whites be envisaged, seeing that diplomatic relations had been broken off since the summer of 1918? The meeting was impressed by the statements of the British Prime Minister, Lloyd George, who pointed to dangerous symptoms in the British Army. Strikes and Bolshevik agitation among the population were disquietening. The British soldier, too, was tired of the long war. Even Churchill could not ignore these facts.

The active forces thirsting for intervention were now concentrated in Marshal Foch. On February 19 he said to Wilson that the Allies would lose the war if they did not find a satisfactory solution to the Russian question. While the members of the *entente* had so far been satisfied with the concept of a *cordon sanitaire* which the border states, Poland and Rumania, were to put around Bolshevik Russia for the protection of Europe, Foch now drew up a detailed plan of active steps to be taken against Russia in a "crusade" against Bolshevism. The news from Germany no doubt played an important role in the conception of this plan. The Communists were still in power in Bavaria. News received in March 1919, of the outbreak of a Communist rising in Hungary under Bela Kun was grist for Foch's mill. Added to this was the fact that Germany had not yet decided whether it would accept or reject the Peace of Versailles. If Germany were to go Communist and refuse to sign the Versailles Treaty, Foch argued, the West would be in serious danger. It was important to forestall this.

Under a French High Command Foch wanted to unite all anti-Bolshevik troops in the border states, in Poland and in Rumania, as well as German prisoners-of-war, volunteers, and Allied detachments, for a general march on Russia. He felt that he could be certain of the support of the French cabinet. But, apart from outside criticism, he met dissent in his own camp, where there were misgivings about the Napoleonic visions of the ambitious Marshal. The opposition was headed by Clemenceau. On March 27, 1919, Foch's plan was rejected by the Supreme Council of the Allies. The opposition of the Americans was the decisive factor. In the begining of the year, William C. Bullitt had been to Russia on a secret mission and returned convinced that a further weakening of Russia would not be to the advantage of the United States in view of Japan's position in the Pacific and East Asia. This had decided Wilson to oppose the plan.

With the collapse of plans for direct, aggressive intervention, a new phase of Allied policy toward Russia began in April 1919. It was characterized by the decision to withdraw Allied troops from Russia. French units were the first to be recalled. Mutinies which had taken place in the French Fleet stationed in the Black Sea—on one cruiser a Red flag had been hoisted—seemed to make this recall advisable. At the beginning of April, Odessa was evacuated, and then Sebastopol. The Red Army, advancing through the Ukraine where it had occupied Kiev on February 3, pushed on to the Black Sea. On April 8, 1919 the Ukrainian Soviet Republic was proclaimed. The Anglo-French front, which had extended from the Rumanian to the Turkish border, had been broken.

Great Britain was not in so great a hurry. As late as May, 1919, Churchill, on his own responsibility, succeeded in having the British detachment in Archangelsk reinforced. Subsequently, the troops were put under the command of the White Russian General Miller who had taken over the High Command of the anti-Bolshevik forces in the area. In the Caucasus, however, British troops were recalled in the course of the summer. In July they left Baku; in August, Tiflis. Only in Batum did some British units remain until the summer of 1920.

It was calamitous for the Russian economy and, particularly, for the continued struggle of the Whites that in the course of their withdrawal the *entente* troops ravaged the considerable grain and tobacco stocks of the Ukraine. An even greater loss was the requisitioning of nine-tenths of the Russian Black Sea fleet; during the evacuation of Odessa alone, 112 merchant vessels were commandeered.

The Summer Offensive of the White Armies in 1919

The fact that the Allies had abandoned active military intervention did not mean cessation of indirect aid, i.e. the supply of arms and ammunition and moral support. Part of this was the Allied recognition of the Kolchak government.

Backed by the British Cabinet, Kolchak had, on November 18, 1918, overthrown the predominantly Socialist government in Omsk and assumed power. With the title of Regent, he headed a government which considered itself the provisional executive of an all-Russian centralist monarchy. Whether the crown was going to be offered to the Grand Duke Nikolai Nikolayevich or Kyril Vladimirovich, did not matter at this point. Much more important was the fact that this anti-Bolshevik movement assumed a reactionary form aiming at the restoration of the monarchy; it had no plans whatever for the constructive social transformation of Russia. Kolchak was a man of unquestioned honor, but he lacked political ability and experience in land warfare. Nor was he familiar with the special political and social conditions in Siberia, and his government, with few exceptions, had no outstanding men. An added danger for him was the opposition of the Social Revolutionaries who continued their agitation among the Siberian peasants and the Czech troops. In the East, Kolchak's power extended, at best, as far as Lake Baikal. In the Far Eastern province the Japanese were the *de facto* rulers. They supported the Cossack Ataman Semenov, undoubtedly with plans for annexation in mind.

In March 1919, when a French-Ukrainian offensive was expected in the Ukraine, Kolchak also attacked. He had about 125,000 men at his disposal.

He conquered Perm (Molotov) and Ufa (Chkalov) and advanced toward Vyatka and Kazan. In April he was only 20 miles from the Volga. The front ran from Glazov-Buzuluk-Orenburg to Uralsk. On May 26, the Supreme Allied Council in Paris decided to recognize the Kolchak government and to support it on the following conditions: Kolchak had to promise to convoke a new Constituent Assembly, to guarantee free elections and the abolition of class privileges, to grant independence to Poland and Finland, and autonomy to the Baltic and Caucasian states. On the whole, Kolchak's reply was positive; he pointed out that the Constituent Assembly would be the supreme authority for the settlement of all Russian domestic questions. The Allies declared themselves satisfied and, on June 12, confirmed their promise to support the White army with supplies and ammunition.

It was undoubtedly tragic for the White army leaders that the withdrawal of the Allied troops took place precisely at the moment when they started their offensive. Nonetheless, the anti-Bolshevik forces approaching Moscow from all four sides during 1919 seemed to have considerable chance of success. Apart from the distribution of purely military strength, it was now a question of which side, the White or the Red, would be able to exert the greater moral, political and propagandistic pressure.

After Kolchak's, Denikin's armies were the most important. During the winter of 1918-19 Denikin had held his positions in the Eastern Ukraine. In the spring he began to extend them. Any cooperation with the Ukrainians under Petlura was impeded by mutual distrust; they knew that Denikin was an adherent of the "one and indivisible Russian Empire" and that he rejected Ukrainian autonomy, let alone independence. However, at this point these questions were postponed for future settlement. The Bolsheviks' breakthrough in the Western Ukraine in the spring of 1919 and their advance to Odessa, had little effect on Denikin. In the middle of May, he began his advance in the direction of Moscow with an army which had grown to 160,000 men, among them the Don Cossacks under Krasnov. Like Kolchak, he, too, was assigned a few British officers as advisers and technical experts, in addition to receiving British arms and ammunition. The guns, motor vehicles, tanks and about one hundred airplanes were of special importance. All told, Britain is supposed to have invested about fifteen million pounds in aid to Denikin.

Partly because of the Bolshevik invasion of the Western Ukraine, Denikin had originally planned to march up east of the Volga in order to establish contact with Kolchak. When the latter was finally recognized by the Allies in June, 1919, he placed himself under the Admiral's command. Tsaritsyn had been assigned the role of a Bolshevik stronghold on the Lower Volga during the summer and fall of 1918; this fact made it doubtful whether an advance in that direction would succeed. On the other hand, the weakness of the Bolshevik positions in the Ukraine was a temptation to transfer the weight of the offensive further west. Here Denikin could also hope to establish contact with Rumania and Poland.

That summer, the Bolsheviks had to withdraw again from the Ukraine. In June, Ekaterinoslav (Dnepropetrovsk), Kharkov, and Tsaritsyn (Stalingrad) fell into Denikin's hands. Red counterattacks failed because the Bolsheviks were unable to agree on a uniform plan although, on July 3, the Revolutionary War Committee had been reorganized, and S. S. Kamenev, a former Czarist officer, had succeeded Vazetis as Commander-in-Chief of the Red Army. When Trotsky's proposals were rejected by the Politburo, he submitted his resignation as Commissar for War and Chairman of the War Committee. It was not accepted, and Trotsky yielded. An offensive begun against Denikin in the middle of August, at the suggestion of Kamenev, was a complete failure. On September

21, Kursk had to be surrendered; on October 13, Orel. The approach to Tula, center of the armaments industry, was open. And beyond Tula lay the road to Moscow.

Denikin's movements were facilitated by peasant revolts behind the Bolshevik lines. In mid-October he had reached the line of Voronezh-Orel-Chernigov-Kiev-Odessa. The line of the White positions showed a considerable bulge, with the consequent danger of an open flank in the North West. Nonetheless, Denikin hoped to reach Moscow by winter and overthrow the Bolshevik government. General Yudenich's simultaneous successes before Petrograd also served to make him optimistic.

The Baltic Front—Yudenich before Petrograd

In the fall of 1917 Britain had refused to accede to Kerensky's appeal to send her fleet into Baltic waters. Now, after Germany's collapse, she no longer feared a trap. As early as December 1918, British naval units entered Libau and Reval. The purpose was to support the national independence aspirations of the Estonians and Letts, who placed great hopes in the Western powers, especially Britain. But the hopes were futile; when the Bolshevik troops approached Riga in January 1919 and the city had to be evacuated, the British warships sailed away without intervening in the battle. This was even stranger than the demand of the British Admiral Sinclair that the remnants of the German troops in the Baltic area were to remain there as long as was deemed necessary by the Allies—as the only protection against the Bolsheviks available at the time.

Local forces, too, had begun a resistance movement. In Estonia, the young Estonian army in joint action with the German-Baltic Regiment and Finnish volunteers had forced the Bolsheviks back across the Narva. In February, General Von der Goltz assumed leadership of the German defense in Courland. The *Baltische Landeswehr,* consisting of German-Baltic volunteers, a Lettish battalion and a White Russian unit fought side by side with remnants of the German occupation army which had been reinforced. The Bolsheviks were pushed back step by step. On May 22, 1919, the bold sortie of the *Baltische Landeswher* liberated Riga.

By the summer of 1919, Bolshevik rule in the Baltic region had collapsed. The native population wanted nothing more than to shape the future of their countries according to their own wishes, completely independent of Russia. But the anti-Bolshevik Russian units which had been assembled in the Baltic countries looked upon the fighting merely as an overture to extensive operations aimed at the overthrow of Bolshevism in Russia.

In May, a Russian volunteer army under General Yudenich and General Rodzianko advanced East across the Estonian border. Yamburg and Pskov were conquered and the advance was continued toward Petrograd. On June 12, 1919, Krasnaya Gorka was occupied and contact was established with dissatisfied elements of the Seventh Red Army. These advance positions, however, had to be evacuated again when the guns of Kronstadt battered Krasnaya Gorka. The first operation had failed.

In the summer, the White Russian troops were reorganized and put on a broader basis as the Russian Northwest Army. In July 1919 General Nikolai Nikolayevich Yudenich took over as sole Commander-in-Chief. The political reasons for this step were not clear at first. When differences of opinion arose between Yudenich and the representatives of the various Russian groups, the British military representative in Reval, General March, forcefully intervened and insisted that the opposing factions meet. This led to the establishment of a Northwest Russian government under the industrialist Lianosov. He was prepared to recognize British interests in the Baltic region and in Persia. In return, the British promised financial support and arms. The inclusion of the Persian question shows the surprising continuity in British aims in that part of the world as exemplified by British-Russian agreements on the eve of the First World War; it also indicated clearly how important the British deemed this Russian counter-government to be for the future.

With this political backing General Yudenich proceeded to prepare his conquest of Petrograd. The offensive began in October 1919. Yudenich believed that, simultaneous with the advance of the troops in Ingermanland, the British fleet would attack Kronstadt as the decisive factor in the final struggle for Petrograd. It was not entirely clear how this military cooperation could be reconciled with the decisions of the Supreme Allied Council in Paris in March of the same year, nor with the general attitude of the British Cabinet. But since the background of the Allied intervention policy could not possibly be known at the time, Yudenich's staff hoped that the British fleet would intervene.

The advance continued. On October 20, Tsarskoye Selo and Gatchina were occupied. The Whites were now at the gates of Petrograd. The mood of the city was desperate. The population was prepared for the possibility of street fighting. Trotsky hastened to the beleagured city. In the event that Estonian and Finnish troops should join the battle, he worked out a plan of withdrawal in order to "preserve the elite of the Petrograd working class from extermination." [14] Should Denikin's advance near Orel continue, Lenin was even prepared to evacuate Petrograd in order to move reinforcements to Moscow. But for the time being Trotsky attempted to mobilize all available forces for the defense of the city and he did, indeed, succeed in arousing a fanatic determination to resist.

October 21 was the decisive turning point. The following day the Red Army assumed the offensive. Conflicting counsel and lack of discipline became noticeable in the conduct of the White troops. Contrary to an explicit order, railroad traffic from Petrograd to Moscow had not been disrupted. Thus the Fifteenth Red Army could be brought up from the south to threaten Yudenich's right flank. The British naval guns remained silent. The fleet had meanwhile left the waters of the Gulf of Finland and withdrawn to Riga.

The spirit which had gripped the Red defenders of Petrograd also marked the subsequent battles. They were fought hard and bitterly, and atrocities and excesses were committed on both sides. Yudenich's offensive collapsed and his forces ebbed back to the borders of Estonia. When the Estonian government initiated armistice negotiations at the end of the year—negotiations which led to the peace of Dorpat on February 2, 1920—Yudenich's army was demobilized.

In Latvia, too, a White Russian army had been formed under the Caucasian adventurer Bermondt-Avalov. He harbored a grandiose plan of advancing jointly with the German units directly eastward to Moscow, in order to enter it victoriously and, possibly, even in advance of Kolchak or Denikin. When he met with opposition from the Letts, he decided to improve his position by a surprise attack on Riga. However, British naval units had arrived from the Gulf of Finland; the intervention of their guns, for which Yudenich had waited in vain, and the arrival of an Estonian armored train, put a quick end to Avalov's coup. His other plans, too, came to nothing by the end of the year.

Kolchak's and Denikin's Defeat

At the end of 1919 Denikin could no longer hope to establish contact with Kolchak on the middle Volga. While the road to Moscow seemed to open up for him during October, Kolchak had been pushed back considerably to the east.

A union of the southern and eastern White Armies was only conceivable if Kolchak's left wing had advanced by way of Samara and Uralsk, and Denikin had joined him by way of Tsaritsyn. This shows the tremendous importance which Tsaritsyn once again assumed for the Bolsheviks. This position on the lower Volga had to be maintained at all costs. Actually, since October, 1918, traffic on the Volga, right down to the Caspian Sea, had never been seriously disrupted. Mainly due to the determination of the Commander-in-Chief of the Eastern Front, Michael Vassilevich Frunze, the Bolsheviks, by making a counter-attack from the Samara region in the direction of Ufa, were also able to prevent Kolchak from extending his operations southwestward.

Kolchak probably made a fundamental mistake in concentrating his strongest troops not here, but on his right wing, which was to advance from Perm via Vyatka toward Vologda, in order to establish contact with General Miller's troops which were advancing south from Archangelsk. Czech troops, under General Gayda, were there. They were subordinate to Kolchak, but collaboration was made extremely difficult by mutual distrust, jurisdictional squabbles and arbitrary acts on the part of the Czech leaders. The densely wooded areas west of the Kama also presented a considerable obstacle.

It was the weakening of the center, which Kolchak had permitted to strengthen the right wing, that proved to be most disastrous. Here the Red Armies under Frunze and V. V. Kuibyshev pressed forward, broke through, and threw Kolchak back behind the Urals in the fall. Kolchak was able to set up a new front line only when he reached the Tobol in Siberia. Lenin's order of the day of May 25th— "If we do not reconquer the Urals by the winter, the collapse of the revolution is inevitable"—had been justified. On November 19, Omsk, the seat of the White Government, was taken by the Bolsheviks. Everywhere in the hinterland, north and south of the Trans-Siberian railroad, the peasants rose, incited chiefly by Social Revolutionary agitation, dissatisfied with the

absence of an agricultural program which would have met their
hunger for land, and repelled by the essentially reactionary attitude of Kolchak's cabinet. In many localities newly-formed partisan groups began to make trouble for the White troops behind
the lines. They were given more and more supplies, encouragement
and leadership by the Bolsheviks. The Siberian railroad was entirely in the hands of the unreliable Czechs, with whom the Whites
were continually at odds. There were disagreements among Kolchak's staff, and it became obvious that the "Regent's" authority
was very limited. It also appeared that the support of the Allies,
on which Kolchak had based considerable hopes after the an-
nouncements of May and June, 1919, was insufficient. In the relationship with the representative of the Supreme Allied Council,
the head of the French Military Mission, General Janin, real trust
was lacking. In the winter of 1919-20, the position of the Kolchak
Army daily became more hopeless.

For Denikin, too, the turning-point had come in October 1919.
The Red leaders had regrouped their forces in the South. After
Yudenich's defeat before Petrograd, the situation was most dangerous. There were two plans for the counter-attack. The Commander-in-Chief, Kamenev, supported by several party chiefs,
including Stalin, envisaged an attack from the northeast *via* the Don
region. Trotsky energetically advocated an offensive directed from
the Donets coal basin in the north, where the population was
sympathetic to the Bolsheviks. He saw, more clearly than others,
the special connection between the military and social factors of
the Civil War.[15] When Denikin arrived at the gates of Orel, Lenin
backed Trotsky.[16]

One army group was assembled northeast of Orel for an advance against the railroad line Orel-Kursk. Another group, headed
by Budyenny's Cavalry Corps, was stationed east of Voronezh.
When the Bolshevik armies began their counter-attack, Denikin
was forced to withdraw his advance detachments from Orel. However, the pressure did not diminish. The enthusiasm which had inspired the defenders of Petrograd as they had fought off Yudenich,
was now infecting the armies in the south. The Red Cavalry Corps
gained legendary fame in these battles, after Denikin's defeat it
was enlarged into the First Cavalry Army.

In the southern fighting region too, popular opinion turned
against the Whites, for reasons similar to those in Siberia. The

Ukraine posed an additional problem. In the region behind the lines, a daring Ukrainian peasant leader, Makhno, organized his "green" bands, who wanted to have nothing to do with either the Whites or the Reds. As Bolshevik propaganda, ably conducted, also made its influence felt, only far-reaching concessions in agricultural and social affairs, and in regard to the Ukrainian desire for autonomy, could have led to any significant change. Denikin wrongly considered these matters something to be settled after the fighting was over. Peasant risings flared up in various places, contact was made with the advancing Bolsheviks, and Denikin's retreat could no longer be halted. Before the end of the year he had to surrender Kiev and Kharkov. At the beginning of 1920, his troops fell back to their initial positions in the Kuban region after evacuating Rostov on January 8. The rest of his volunteer army and some of the Don and Kuban Cossacks, in March retreated in panicky haste to a last redoubt in the Crimea.

The winter of 1919-20 also brought Kolchak's campaign to a bitter end. The retreat along the Siberian railroad became an unspeakable martyrdom; an increase in partisan activities and the depressing knowledge that the army was trapped were added to hunger and cold. The troops were not fated to reach a refuge on the coast. When Kolchak, with his staff and government, reached Irkutsk, a rising of a "Revolutionary People's Army" took place which was outwardly non-Bolshevik, but was really in secret agreement with Moscow. The Czechs, long considered a suspect and unreliable element, adopted a most equivocal attitude. The actual decision, surprisingly enough, was made by the French General Janin. He delivered Kolchak, who had sought his protection, to the "People's Army." He was given a court martial, and together with some of his colleagues, was shot on February 7, 1920. "Admiral Kolchak," the British Military Representative A. Knox, wrote in his memoirs, "appeared to be too weak to merit support." With this formula the *entente* washed its hands of the affair. Two weeks later the Red Army marched into Irkutsk. It found the region suitably prepared. Trotsky had long hesitated to pursue Kolchak's troops any distance beyond the Urals. Now he gave in to the urging of various party leaders, among them Stalin.[17] The Soviet Government was thus able to expand its control as far as Lake Baikal. The Far Eastern region between Lake Baikal and the Pacific remained under Japanese control for the time being.

Wrangel's Insurrection and the War with Poland

At the beginning of 1920 the Soviet Government was granted
a short breathing spell. The liquidation of Kolchak and Denikin
took its course. On the Baltic front, peace negotiations with Estonia had been started and, after the conclusion of the Peace of
Dorpat on February 2, 1920, similar negotiations were begun with
Latvia, Lithuania and Finland. The Supreme Council of the Allies
decided in January, mainly at the instigation of British circles
interested in trade with Russia, to lift the economic blockade which
had held Soviet Russia in an iron vise since the fall of 1918. This
was a measure which, it was maintained, did not represent a change
in the basic attitude toward the Bolshevik regime. But it did result
in a perceptible easing of the economic situation. In Copenhagen,
Litvinov initiated economic talks with representatives of the British
Government which led to a provisional agreement in February,
1920. In May, 1920, a Soviet Trade Delegation went to London.

The fact that Soviet Russia now had access to the centers of
agricultural and oil production in Siberia, the Donets Basin and
the Northern Caucasus was of great economic importance. In the
Ukraine a "Military Revolutionary Committee" consisting of five
members—three of them Bolsheviks—was established and paved
the way for a Soviet Ukrainian regime under Rakovsky, a Bolshevik of Rumanian descent, who had previously been temporarily
in power during the spring of 1919. The constitution of the Ukrainian Soviet Republic of March, 1919, was thus put into effect.

The Kremlin hoped that sooner or later even the last resistance
of anti-Bolshevik forces on the Crimea and in the adjacent area of
Kherson, would be eliminated. But in fact, a new operation against
the Bolsheviks was being prepared there in the fall of 1920. In
conjunction with Polish activities, this was to grow into the last
formidable threat to the Soviet Government. The Whites were
given one last chance.

In April 1920 Denikin transferred the command of the remnants
of his troops which had fled to the Crimea to General Baron Peter
Nikolaevich Wrangel. Wrangel, scion of a Russified branch of the
well-known Baltic-Swedish family, possessed greater military and
personal qualities than his predecessor, and he also had an appreciation of political necessities. He was at first intent on a consolidation and reorganization of his troops. Severe measures re-

established discipline and raised morale. Draconic punishments were meted out for arbitrary requisitioning and similar offenses.

Wrangel's agricultural law of June 7, 1920, which was drafted by the former Czarist Minister of Agriculture, Krivoshein, was of particular importance. It promised the peasants a generous allocation of land. But it was two years late. If Denikin and Kolchak had adopted it at the beginning of the Civil War it could have been most effective; now its impact was negligible. Confidence in the cause of the Whites had been destroyed. The war between Whites and Reds had unleashed all the cruelty and brutality of a fratricidal struggle uncontrolled by any conventions of international law. Prisoners were given no pardon; they were usually shot for security reasons. In the battles between the small, often irregular, units the fighting reached an unparalleled degree of bitterness and bestiality. Brutal excesses, tortures and abuses were not unusual. They were by no means confined to the Bolshevik side. The intensity of the Red Terror was matched by the White Terror. The peasants of the Ukraine were tired of the struggle. As far as they were able to think politically, Wrangel's Great Russian-Centralist schemes proved that he would not fulfill the desire for autonomy. Far more than the Czarist general, their peasant-anarchist leader Nestor Makhno, still with considerable forces at his command and playing his own game between the fronts, seemed to many peasants to be a representative of their political aspirations. In him, it was believed, the old Cossack tradition lived on.[18] Wrangel did not manage to gain Makhno's lasting cooperation although Makhno did cooperate at decisive moments. A Cossack rising in the Don and Kuban regions failed. The great mass of the population remained passive when Wrangel's army advanced north during the summer. The British government informed Wrangel that it was no longer prepared to support the Whites.

A continuation of the struggle was senseless. Lloyd George had already declared on November 8, 1919, that the Bolsheviks could not be vanquished by force of arms. Britain was about to establish direct contact with the Soviets. At the most she was prepared to cover the defense of the Crimea with her fleet; and she also offered to act as mediator in Moscow. But Chicherin refused; Wrangel was to deal directly with the Soviet government.

Despite British warnings, Wrangel decided to start an offensive with his 70,000 men, as the Poles had just invaded the Ukraine.

Unwilling to renounce their eastern territories, the Poles were not prepared to accept as final the Curzon Line which the Supreme Allied Council had designated on December 8, 1919, as the permanent Polish frontier in the east.[18a] As early as the fall of 1919, Polish troops had invaded White Russia, after occupying the Lithuanian region of Vilna; in the south they had crossed the borders of Volhynia and Podolia. In view of Denikin's successes, the Poles decided to hold back, since Warsaw did not expect much from territorial negotiations with a victorious White General. They resumed their operations only in January 1920. While General Haller occupied Duenaburg, Mozyr and Gomel, General Pilsudski penetrated deeply into the Russian Ukraine and on May 7, 1920, occupied Kiev. Thus to the many political possibilities and forces which had been facing the Ukrainian workers and peasants since 1918 a new one was added. The rural population especially confronted the Poles with undisguised hostility. Remembering the experiences of the 17th century which were kept alive in Gogol's tales, they were fearful of again coming under the rule of Polish landowners. Their opposition was motivated by national, religious and social considerations. The question was how, in these circumstances, Petlura, who had appeared in Kiev in the wake of the Polish troops, could hope again to succeed in winning the population over. This time he had sided with the Poles and was even prepared to abandon the old Ukrainian claims to Galicia. But the Polish occupation of the Ukraine remained merely an episode. By June 11, Pilsudski had to evacuate Kiev.

Far beyond the Ukraine, the Polish attack aroused a wave of patriotic sentiment which communicated itself to the entire country. The German advance in 1918 and the Allied landings took place at a time when the population was still exhausted and its emotions dulled by war and upheaval. But now the people were alive to the fact that hostile foreign armies had occupied the soil of Mother Russia. The appeal of General Brusilov, the last Czarist Commander-in-Chief, to all officers of the Czarist army to support the Red Army in its fight against Poland to the best of their ability, fell on fertile soil. Many an enemy of Bolshevism made his peace with the Soviet state at that time.

Soon the Red Army began its counter-attack. In the north, Tukhachevsky, advancing through White Russia, penetrated far into Poland. In the south, Yegorov and Budyenny threw Pilsudski back across the Bug. The question now arose whether a halt should be made at a line which represented approximately the ethnic border between the Poles and Ukrainians and an offer of peace made to the Poles, or whether the offensive should be continued. Trotsky advocated the first alternative. He warned against a march on Warsaw because he feared the resistance of the Polish population. Lenin, on the other hand, supported by Zinoviev and Kamenev, demanded the invasion of Poland. He hoped the Red Army would arouse revolutionary sentiments in the Polish working class. Beyond Poland he wanted to establish direct contact with German Communism and lend it support. Then "Europe was to be tested by the bayonets of the Red Army." [19] There were violent discussions in the Politburo; Trotsky, Dzierzynski and Radek were out-voted. Stalin, who had at first shared Trotsky's misgivings, changed his mind and joined the majority. In the meantime, Tukhachevsky had reached the suburbs of Warsaw but his troops were exhausted and his reserves depleted. The lines of communication had been stretched dangerously far. On July 10, 1920, Pilsudski appealed to the Allies. A little later a French military mission, headed by General Maxime Weygand, appeared in Warsaw. Allied war material was sent through Germany and by sea to Poland. The Soviet High Command now ordered the Southern army to turn north in order to ease the pressure on Tukhachevsky and to cut short Pilsudski's counter-offensive. But Yegorov and Budyenny, supported by their Army Commissar, Stalin, were not satisfied to play a subsidiary role and leave the triumphal entry into Warsaw to Tukhachevsky. Ignoring orders, they continued their march west in order to conquer Lvov. Thus, on August 15-16, the "miracle on the Vistula" occurred which brought the great turning point.

The Poles, under Pilsudski and guided by their French advisers, threw the Russians back. The retreat of Tukhachevsky's army soon degenerated into a wild rout and came to a halt only outside Minsk. When Yegorov and Budyenny hastened to the scene, it was already too late. The conquest of Poland had failed.

In the meantime, Wrangel had made use of the war with Poland and broken out of his redoubt. He gained some territory north of the Sea of Azov and threatened the Don basin. But before he could establish contact with the Poles, they had already been repulsed. The *de facto* recognition of his "Government of Southern Russia" by France on August 12, 1920, undoubtedly provided moral support, particularly since England had held back. However, France never actually gave any material help. After an armistice was concluded between Poland and Russia on October 12, the Red Army was free to concentrate on the one opponent left in the south. In bitter fighting, Wrangel was pushed back into the Crimea by the troops of M. V. Frunze, the Commander of the Southern Front. The Isthmus of Perekop was the scene of a desperate final battle in November, 1920. The Red troops advancing in the night of November 7-8 were supported in a surprise action by units led across the ice of the Sivash lagoon, who attacked the defenders from the rear. On November 16, the Red troops entered Kerch.

Wrangel realized that further resistance was hopeless. Retreating to the interior of the Crimea, he managed, in the middle of November, to evacuate almost 130,000 soldiers and civilians by sea from Crimean ports to Constantinople. Most of the members of Wrangel's army later found a haven in Yugoslavia.

The End of the Civil War

The Civil War in Russia had come to a close. The Whites had failed. They lost because they had no constructive program for the future, no plan reflecting the political and social aspirations of the masses. They lost because they could not come forward with any idea which, beyond the slogans of the negation of Bolshevism and Czarist restoration, could have aroused the enthusiasm of the people. Their opponents, the Bolsheviks, had managed to find a balance between the rationalist doctrine of their leadership and the chaotic subconscious of the masses. The terse and simple points of their program, supported by the unbridled use of violence and terror, played a large part in their success.

Added to this was the dual nature of the intimate bond between civil and Allied intervention. After the idea of a crusade, proclaimed in the winter 1918-1919, had been abandoned, the support given to the Whites was too feeble to bring about decisive success. "An intervention with hopelessly meager means was one of those wretched half-measures which are criminal in politics. . . . Our intervention in Russian chaos would have had to be successful from the first day, if it was to achieve its purpose," Bruce Lockhart wrote in his memoirs.[20] Sir George Buchanan[21] and Winston Churchill held similar views.[22] These "wretched half-measures" were perhaps most drastically demonstrated by the behavior of the British Fleet before Petrograd in October 1919.

Examining Britain's attitude without prejudice, it is not suffi-

cient to point to the fact that Lloyd George's Liberal Cabinet had
begun to realize the importance of Soviet Russian trade for the
British economy. It was the traditional British approach—even in
the case of political and military conflict—not to disturb the free
play of forces in a foreign country by decisive interference in its
domestic affairs. Instead it was British policy to let these forces
find their own balance. The Allied shipments of arms were meant
to give the anti-Bolshevik forces a chance to carry out their plans;
when the spiritual and moral strength of their ideas and aims
proved to be too weak, the chance was lost, and the Nemesis of
history took over.

To this must be added one other unfortunate fact. The Allies
did not intend to prolong the bloodshed in Russia by their moral
support and armaments. However, as things turned out, this was
the result of their intervention. Without the help of the Allies, the
Civil War might have been ended as early as the spring of 1919.
Without intervention, the Soviet leadership would have been robbed
of its excuse to intensify the Terror in the years 1918 and 1919.
It would have been more to the purpose not to seek a compromise
in this case, but to choose one of the alternatives. This would have
meant either pursuing the policy adopted at the end of 1918, and
following it through to its final conclusion, i.e. an open declaration
of war against Soviet Russia; or else a recognition of the Bolshevik
regime and the withdrawal of support of the Whites. But no one
could foresee in the winter of 1918-19 that the Bolshevik "ama-
teurs," who were generally expected to achieve only speedy bank-
ruptcy in their political and social experiments, would prove to be
stronger than their adversaries.

The war with Poland was finally ended on March 18, 1921,
when peace negotiations were concluded at Riga. One of the conditions was that Soviet Russia renounced its territories west of the
Curzon line, which were claimed by Poland. Thus Poland came
into possession of a region that was actually within the old historical
borders of the former Polish kingdom, but which had only a small
Polish population; the majority of the inhabitants were White
Russians in the northern part, and Ukrainians in the south. This
was a settlement which remained in force until the collapse of
Poland during the Second World War.

The situation had also been stabilized in the whole of the Baltic
region. With his dialectic dexterity, Lenin described the Peace of
Dorpat with the Estonians, which meant an abandonment of the

Bolshevik plans of November 1918, as a "remarkable victory over international imperialism . . . a window on Western Europe for the Russian worker." [23] Now, when these Baltic lands were being surrendered, it was paradoxical to use this simile about the Western Window which Peter the Great had coined after reaching the Baltic during the Northern War. The surrender of these non-Russian regions was in full accord with the nations' right to self-determination which had been repeatedly proclaimed by the Bolsheviks. The most important link in the chain of Peter the Great's acquisitions, Ingermanland with Petrograd, remained within Soviet Russia.

On July 12, 1920, the peace treaty with Lithuania was signed in Moscow, and that country's independence was recognized; the treaty with Latvia was signed in Riga on August 11. On October 14, another Peace of Dorpat was signed between Finland and Soviet Russia, establishing Finland as an independent state and granting it the port of Petsamo to give it access to the Arctic Sea.

The Reconquest of the Caucasus and the Far East

The Transcaucasian peoples' aspirations for independence were not crowned with the success attained by the Baltic nations. Until November 1918, actual power was wielded by the German and Turkish troops that had occupied Transcaucasia. After the collapse of the Central Powers, England occupied the political vacuum; British troops, advancing from Persia, took Baku. Although the White generals refused to concern themselves with the independence of the Transcaucasion republics, the Supreme Council of the Allies granted them *de facto* recognition in January 1920. Meanwhile, the British troops had been withdrawn again; only a small garrison remained in Batum until July, 1920.

It thus became possible for the Bolsheviks to engineer a rising in Baku in January of 1920. A local administration, independent of the Azerbaidjan Republic, had been formed in May, 1918, by Shaumian, an old comrade of Lenin's. This led to the establishment of an Azerbaidjan Soviet Republic. On May 7, 1920, Moscow recognized Georgia's independence. At the end of the year, Turkish troops invaded Armenia from the south; Bolshevik units, in turn, entered from the northeast and made possible the establishment of an Armenian Soviet Republic. In an agreement with Turkey on December 20, 1920, the border was fixed; Armenia was divided, the southern parts becoming Turkish. The Bolshevik regime in Armenia, after sporadic uprisings, became firmly established in April, 1921.

For a time Georgia presented a refuge for non-Bolshevik elements. A Menshevik Cabinet which greatly valued close contact with Western Europe was in power there; as late as September 1920, leading members of the Second International, among them Kautsky, Vandervelde, and Ramsay MacDonald visited Tiflis. In January, 1921, Georgia's independence was recognized *de jure* by the Allied Supreme Council. It was a short-lived triumph. Stalin feared that Georgia might become a bridgehead for further Allied intervention and, after things had been settled in the Ukraine, he brought about Soviet intervention. On February 21, 1921, Bolshevik troops, consisting at first only of Georgians, crossed the Armenian-Georgian frontier; Tiflis fell four days later. A Georgian Soviet Republic was proclaimed. Soviet Russia was once more in possession of the whole Caucasus.

The reconquest of the Far Eastern territories also took place. In the Trans-Baikal region an independent democratic Far Eastern Republic had been set up on April 6, 1920, after the collapse of Kolchak's army. Its leaders were two Russian emigrants from America, Krasnoshchekov and Zhatov. Assuming an attitude similar to the one adopted toward the Georgian Republic, the Soviet Government temporarily recognized this buffer state on May 14, 1920.

During the same period, the Japanese—who had shortly before withdrawn their forces from Siberia—landed troops anew in Vladivostok in response to an incident in Nikolaevsk. A special local administration was able to maintain itself in this coastal area, backed by the Japanese occupation forces. But in April 1921, when it seemed to show a tendency to join the Far Eastern Republic, it was overthrown by a right wing group under Merkulov. Two states continued side by side from then on. The coastal republic soon became a meeting place of White military elements who had either been members of Kolchak's army, or had belonged to the fighting force of the Ataman Semenov.

The Far Eastern Republic also held elections for a Constituent Assembly which was opened in January, 1921. On April 27, 1921, it adopted a constitution with bourgeois democratic forms. However, the influence of the Bolshevik delegates could not be overlooked. Further, the Republic's armed forces were headed first by

Bluecher, then by Uborevich—both later well-known representatives of Soviet military leadership.

Negotiations were opened in August 1921 between the Republic and Japanese representatives but remained fruitless. As time went on, England and the United States exerted increasing pressure on Japan to withdraw her troops permanently from the continent. In direct negotiations with a representative of Soviet Russia, Japan finally declared itself ready to evacuate its armed forces. This decision was made on September 14, 1922, and in October the last Japanese left the coastal region. The departure meant the collapse of the White government in Vladivostok. The coastal region joined the Far Eastern Republic, which was then in control of the whole region between Lake Baikal and the Pacific.

The Republic's life was short. After the withdrawal of the Japanese troops, the Soviet Government had no more reason to respect the buffer state. Soviet influence in the Assembly of the Far Eastern Republic brought about a proclamation dissolving the state on November 10, 1922, and incorporating it into the Russian Soviet Republic.

With the exception of the Western border regions and cessions of territory to Rumania and Turkey, the entire territory of the former Russian Empire had once more been gathered into a political entity. It was not by chance that in the same year when the Far East again joined Russia, the somewhat loosely joined federation of states was more firmly integrated into a Soviet Union.

CHAPTER 3

THE ERA OF THE NEW ECONOMIC POLICY (NEP)

The Economic Position after the Civil War

Civil war and intervention had hit Russia hard. As long as fighting was the order of the day, there could be no thought of domestic reconstruction. Make-shift measures had to suffice and the requirements of defense against internal and external foes had absolute priority. Bolshevik historians call the period from 1917 to 1921 the era of Military Communism.

By the end of 1920 mile after mile of arable ground had lain fallow for many years. The Ukraine in particular had been a battle field with constantly shifting front lines. Many times the harvest had been destroyed while still in the fields. The constant fluctuation of the fortunes of war between the Whites and the Reds often had made work in the fields completely senseless. Resigned, the peasants sank into dull passivity or took to their primitive arms to participate in the fighting. In Central Russia especially the mood of the peasants became more and more hostile. Forced requisitions killed any remaining initiative. Everyone began to produce only enough for his own needs. A steady stream of refugees from the cities to the countryside increased the difficulties. During the Civil War several rural areas had suffered near-famines when the harvest had been poor. The failure of the harvest in the summer of 1920 had been particularly disastrous.

Industry, too, was completely disrupted. Production had sunk to one seventh of the pre-war figure. Most factories lay idle, many mines had been destroyed. Catastrophe had hit the iron industry. In 1921 pig iron production was only 3% of pre-war. The stocks of metal and industrial products had been exhausted. The most essential things, food, consumer goods, and fuel, were lacking.

Not only the war had paralyzed the economy. Overly rapid socialization, which was to make the Party program a reality, was also a factor. Lenin, quoting Marx, had demanded the "expropriation of the expropriators." In December, 1917, the banks had been expropriated; in January, 1918, the merchant marine; in February, the grain dealers; in May, the mines; in June, the oil industry. This was followed by the expropriation of all large enterprises whose capital was between one-half million and one million rubles. Only businesses with less than ten workers were left in the hands of their owners. Socialization was often carried out amateurishly. There was a lack of men with the necessary knowledge to manage the nationalized plants. From 1919 on, Lenin was very concerned with the rehabilitation of industry. In contrast to many party comrades, e.g. Rykov, he believed that the management of the nationalized industrial plants was to be entrusted to individual directors appointed by the state. His colleagues thought in terms of collective administrations in keeping with the concept of the workers' councils.

Dissatisfaction spread among the workers. Factories were shut down from lack of raw materials and fuel and there was a consequent loss of wages. Many persons were forced to seek other work, often in rural areas. The government intervened with coercive measures. It became clear that the place of the private employer had not been taken by the worker, but by the state. It was the state that now collected the profits from factory production and felt itself bound to supervise production in the factories. It could demand that the employee work in a particular place even against his will, or else could transfer him without consulting him. Thus the "socialization of the means of production" became a nationalization strictly centralized and backed by extensive power. The state, of course, was bound to pass the fruits of production on to the consumer, that is, to everybody. For this, it used a cumbersome bureaucratic apparatus; its slow, or a times faulty, functioning led the worker to feel that he was, in the end, short-changed.

Trade was at a standstill. Not only the big firms, but eventually the small enterprises, too, were closed down. Starting in 1920, private trading was prohibited. After the private ownership of land and houses had been abolished, an order was issued to hand over all precious metals and to deposit all cash, except a small amount for current use, in the state bank. The vacuum created by the collapse of legitimate trading was filled by illegal black marketeering. Mostly this involved food and thus favored the peasants. Prices reached dizzy heights. Between 1920 and 1921 the price of bread increased eleven and a half times.

The Soviet government had retained the war-time food rationing system. Before it had been an emergency measure necessitated by problems of a wartime economy; now it was a means of controlling the people. A uniform food allocation was fixed for the urban population, the so-called *payok;* it was determined not according to the individual, but according to his place of work. This led to considerable abuse, as many people tried to show that they were working in several places, with a resulting decrease in output.

The Kronstadt Rising

In February 1921 the rations of the workers in the Petrograd factories had to be cut because of the general situation. The response was a wave of strikes which far exceeded in importance the occasional strikes of earlier days.

The basic reason for them was the general dissatisfaction and disappointment of the workers with the very questionable achievements of the Revolution. The hoped-for relaxation of the war-time regime had not come about. Nor was there greater individual freedom as expected. The practice of directing labor particularly embittered the workers. It became a political issue which could become dangerous to the Bolsheviks. Mensheviks and Social Revolutionary ideas were expressed in pamphlets that were circulated among the workers: "Down with the Communists! Down with the Soviet Government! Long live the Constituent Assembly!"

At the end of February, the strike wave in Petrograd reached its climax. In addition there were many demonstrations, particularly in the industrial district of Vasilievsky Ostrov, the big island in the Neva delta, from which one could see Kronstadt across the gulf. Zinoviev, as Party Secretary of Petrograd, ordered the Red Army to scatter the demonstrators and proclaimed martial law. Troops were called from the provinces to reinforce the garrison. Those who were arrested were deprived of their *payok.*

However, the spirit of revolt now infected the Navy. At a revolutionary meeting of the sailors in Kronstadt on March 1, 1921, the civilian demonstrators were assured of the Navy's sympathy. Since the October Revolution, the rank and file of the fleet had been replenished by new peasant recruits. Village attitudes were thus carried over. A meeting on March 2 demanded free elections in the Kronstadt Soviet, and ended with bitter accusations against the Bolshevik dictatorship. The Commissar of the Baltic Fleet, Kuzmin, and the Chairman of the Kronstadt Executive Committee, Vasiliev, were arrested. A "Provisional Revolutionary Committee" took over. The battlecry of a "third revolution"—in addition to the two of 1917—seemed about to be realized.

In the "Newsletter of the Revolutionary Committee" a forthright tone was adopted. Mention was made of "the Communists' three years of bloody destruction," of the "cruelties which the Bolsheviks had committed throughout Russia," etc. Demands were made for new secret elections with full freedom for agitation, freedom of speech, freedom of the press and freedom of assembly. No party functionaries were to fill government or military positions, there was to be equality in rationing, abolition of trade restrictions, freedom for artisans and small industries, no restrictions on the peasants' livestock holdings.[1] The fact that the freedoms only applied to workers and peasants shows that they were not intended as democratic freedoms, but as a new form of Socialist radicalism which was obviously closely tied to the Social Revolutionary program. The slogan "Soviets without Bolsheviks!" did not fail to be effective; its echo retains importance even for the Russian emigrees of today.

As the Kronstadt Committee began to consider itself the spokesman for the entire country, particularly the peasantry, the danger of a third revolution was obvious, Lenin was resolved to act. At first he sent Mikhail Ivanovich Kalinin, the Chairman of the VTsIK, who was popular among the peasants, as a government emissary to Kronstadt. Kalinin called a meeting and tried to pacify the insurgents. His attempts were in vain. His words were drowned in a storm of protest and he barely escaped arrest. Now the government adopted military measures. The reinforcements led by Tukhachevsky, which Zinoviev had requested, arrived. Trotsky arrived in Petrograd on March 5 and his order of the day demanded that the rebels be shot one after the other, "like ducks on a lake," if they did not surrender.

At first the atmosphere in Kronstadt was optimistic and aggressive. The officers demanded offensive operations against Petrograd. The majority of the sailors rejected this in order to avoid unnecessary bloodshed. They hoped that the workers and soldiers of Petrograd would rise and join them. The government realized that it would have to act quickly. In a few weeks the ice would melt and then it would be too late to attack the rebellious fortress with land troops. On March 7 at 6 p.m., Tukhachevsky gave the order to open heavy artillery fire on Kronstadt. Amid a raging snow storm his troops, camouflaged with snow shirts, began their attack across the ice. Trotsky's ultimatum had run out. The Kronstadt Committee called upon the people for the last and decisive battle. Radio messages enabled the whole world to listen in on their heroic resistance. On March 11 this announcement went out: "Fellow workers, Kronstadt is fighting for you, for those who are hungry, cold and unprotected . . . Kronstadt has raised the banner of rebellion and is certain that millions of workers and peasants will answer this call. It is unthinkable that the dawn which rose in Kronstadt will not become the light of day for the whole of Russia . . ."[2]

The Kronstadt garrison consisted of 14,000 men, of whom 10,000 were sailors. A broad front had to be defended. For ten long days and nights the outnumbered insurgents under their commander, General Kozlovsky, fought off the attackers. Their courage also infected the regiments stationed on the opposite shore in Oranienbaum. They made common cause with the people of Kronstadt. Their mutiny was immediately and bloodily suppressed by Cheka troops who hurried to the scene. In the night of March 16, Tukhachevsky made preparations for storming the city. The fire of the coastal batteries was supported by aerial bombardments. The final battle was undescribably bitter. The sailors fought fanatically. In the morning of March 18 the last machine guns were silenced. The resistance had been broken. The last living rebels were shot, or banished to prison camps.

Lenin Changes His Course—March, 1921

The conclusions which Lenin drew from the Kronstadt rising mainly concerned the security measures to be taken against opposition movements. The insurrection also clearly pointed to the dangers which the Bolshevik regime would face unless it found a way to solve the economic emergency.

By February 22, 1921, a "National Planning Commission" (*Gosplan*)[3] had been set up in the Council for Labor and National Defense. The events of the spring strengthened Lenin's determination to steer a radically different course in his economic policy and to find a way out of the chaotic confusion which "militant communism" had brought about in the country. The peasants' interests in production had to be aroused, the food supply had to be ensured. Domestic trade had to be resumed and industrial production strengthened. This was not possible without modifying the Marxist economic program. Without making basic changes a compromise between theory and reality had to be found. This compromise was expressed in the "New Economic Policy" (NEP).[4]

It was not easy to win acceptance of these changes at the Tenth Party Congress which met on March 8, 1921, but Lenin managed to gain his point. He admitted frankly that the Party had gone too far, that the immediate transition to a purely socialist division of property exceeded the strength of the country. It would first be necessary to introduce a mixed economic system in which the socialized concerns would compete with private enterprise. It was hoped that the socialized part of the economy would gradually expand while private enterprise would gradually die out. Of socialism's final victory there could be no doubt, but it could not be hurriedly precipitated.

This meant that the large industrial plants, transportation, the big banks, and foreign trade remained, as a matter of course, in the hands of the state. In the rest of the industrial field and in domestic trade, private enterprise was once more permitted. The food levy at fixed prices in the rural areas was abandoned and a "grain tax" was substituted. The peasants could once more sell part of their produce on the open market. The right to private ownership was re-established within certain limits and private mutual benefit societies were again permitted.

Foreign capital was again welcome, to restore the economy. Foreign firms were asked to resume their activities in Russia—even in the field of heavy industry. Restrictions on trade agreements with other nations were lowered. It was no coincidence that in the same March of 1921, the Riga peace treaty with Poland, a friendship pact with Turkey, and a trade agreement with Britain were concluded.

Industrial production soon quickened. The relaxation of strict controls over the workers, together with a graduation of wages according to ability and output—the so-called specialists received higher *payoks*— were inducements for higher output. The execution of one of Lenin's favorite plans could now be undertaken. He felt that an increase in electric power in the rural areas would result in an increase in production and raise the living standards of the peasantry as well. Lenin was fond of speaking of the proletarian era of electricity as opposed to the bourgeois era of steam.

The new policy was successful, but not instantaneously. The winter of 1921-22 was very hard, the harvests of both years insufficient. Reserves had long ago been used up or destroyed. The NEP came too late to prevent the first great famine of the Soviet era. According to official estimates, no less than five million people died of starvation in Russia at the time. In July, 1921, a special Aid Committee for dealing with the famine was established including non-Bolsheviks and even some former Kadets. The following August a great international aid organization directed by Herbert Hoover, later President of the United States, was set up in answer to an appeal by Maxim Gorky, and the Soviet Government had no choice but to accept it.[4a]

At first Lenin had considered the famine a welcome means of decimating the bourgeoisie, while the governing classes, Party functionaries and workers were protected by the rationing system. However, the famine spread to the people as a whole and became a national emergency, particularly affecting the peasants. It was characteristic that the Aid Committee was soon outlawed and that its bourgeois members were arrested on different pretexts. However, the aid program was continued with collections made by Quakers and with other measures initiated by the great Norwegian Arctic explorer Fridtjof Nansen. About 700,000 tons of food from the United States were distributed in Russia during that time.

The famine was accompanied by epidemics and disease; there was still a danger of typhoid fever which the Civil War had brought; and typhus epidemics were added. The misery of extensive sections of society increased rapidly; rations were still very low.

Nevertheless, some signs of slow economic improvement were evident. Agricultural and industrial production were starting again, and trade became more active. The transportation system slowly began to function. Mechanization made progress. In the beginning of 1923, the worst seemed to be over.

As a result of the NEP, a money economy, supposed to have been abolished in accordance with Marxist theory, had been reestablished. (Credit and money were considered to be the pillars of the capitalist order.) Money transactions again became common in every sphere; even the *payok* was paid out in money again. On December 1, 1922, the currency was stabilized. In 1924, the paper ruble, which had fallen to a fantastic low, was abolished. The State Bank issued new bank notes, 25% of which were backed by precious metals and foreign currencies. A new monetary unit was introduced, the chervonets, valued at 10 rubles.

New laws concerning labor and agriculture, passed in 1922, supplemented previous measures for the rehabilitation of the economy. Nevertheless some of the basic elements of the Bolshevik doctrine were retained; the private ownership of the soil, of forests and streams remained prohibited, and they could not be bought, sold or mortgaged. At the Third Congress of the Comintern in 1921, Lenin described the new economy quite openly as State Capitalism, although it was capitalism in a proletarian state which was to be developed against the interests of the bourgeoisie, and for the benefit of the workers.

The atmosphere in Russia grew calmer. The widespread dissatisfaction which had been expressed quite openly at the beginning of 1921—it had not been confined to those against whom the new regime had discriminated—gradually died down. The one-party rule of the Bolsheviks appeared to be better accepted. For the first time in seven long years, the economy showed symptoms of recovery. Now there were possibilities for accumulating capital, which benefited merchants and peasants. It remained to be seen whether this was the beginning of an evolutionary development of the Soviet State, whether or not the New Russia, under State Capitalism, would be less dependent on the coming of a world revolution than it had been in the years of militant communism.

The End of the Anti-Bolshevik Opposition Parties

The Kronstadt rising was the pretext for getting rid of the last remainders of the anti-Bolshevik opposition.

After the unrest of the summer of 1918 and the civil war, the Mensheviks and Social Revolutionaries had been shown enough consideration to give the impression of tolerance toward differently oriented political movements. As late as August 1920, a Menshevik Party Congress could still be held in Moscow. Allowances had to be made for the fact that sympathy for the Mensheviks was still strong in the trade unions. The Eighth Congress of Soviets, in December, 1920, for the last time brought together Bolshevik, Menshevik, and Social Revolutionary. By the beginning of 1921, the situation had become dangerous for the leaders of the opposition groups. The Menshevik leaders, F. I. Dan and J. O. Martov, and the leader of the Social Revolutionaries, V. M. Chernov[5] went abroad. From then on, the headquarters of the Mensheviks was in Berlin, that of the Social Revolutionaries in Paris.

Soon there were reprisals against the Mensheviks, followed by reprisals against the Social Revolutionaries. In February 1922 arrests began to be made. The Cheka had to cope with an adversary with a particularly rich experience in conspirational activities. At that time the Cheka was transformed into a department of the Commissariat of Internal Affairs and received the inoccuous name of "State Political Administration." The Russian abbreviation[6] GPU soon carried the same ominous connotation as Cheka. Dzierzynski continued to head the office until his death in 1926. Very soon it was to become an independent organ within the Soviet apparatus.

In the summer of 1922, Bolshevik Russia's first political trial, the prosecution of the Social Revolutionaries, took place. The events of the summer of 1918 were now examined at great length. The tense atmosphere of the proceeedings was heightened by the fact that Boris Savinkov, who even during the war against the Poles had been organizing anti-Bolshevik forces and had soon afterward fallen into Russian hands, was one of the defendants. The trial ended with fourteen death sentences, only two of the defendants being pardoned. Appeals for mercy made by prominent revolutionaries, including the novelist, Maxim Gorky, and the German Communist, Clara Zetkin, were turned down by Lenin. The condemned were kept in prison as hostages of a sort. When capital punishment was re-introduced two years later, it was Stalin who finally ordered their execution.

This was the end of a revolutionary movement whose agrarian communist and anarchist tendencies were typical phenomena of Russian radicalism.

The Problem of the Trade Unions and the Dictatorship of the Party

It was significant that at the same time as the economic dictatorship of the Bolshevik party was relaxed, the reins of political dictatorship were tightened. After the anti-Bolshevik opposition parties had been brought to trial, steps were taken against the opposition elements within the Party. These measures were provoked by debates about the position of the trade unions in the Soviet state, which took place at the same Tenth Party Congress in the spring of 1921 at which Lenin defended his New Economic Policy.

This debate started on the eve of the Kronstadt insurrection. Four different opinions were voiced. The so-called "Workers' Opposition" led by Mme. Alexandra M. Kollontai and the former People's Commissar for Labor, A. G. Shliapnikov, a friend of Molotov's from the early days of the Party, advocated that all decisions about economic matters be made by the trade unions. This proposal was an expression of labor's dissatisfaction with the economic dictatorship of the Party bureaucracy. The ruthless manner with which the rights and interests of the workers had been ignored were sharply criticized. Mme. Kollontai demanded that the trade unions, as the immediate representatives of the working class, be given the responsibility for planning and directing the national economy. They were to balance the weight of the Politburo and of the Government, i.e. of the Party bureaucracy. Significantly, the union leaders, Tomsky and Rudzutak, did not support this proposal; they considered themselves representatives of the state.

Mikhail Pavlovich Tomsky, born in 1880 in St. Petersburg, the son of a laborer, had been an old fighter in the Russian labor movement, spending long years in prison and exile. From 1917 on he played a leading role in the consolidation of the labor unions. At the end of that year he became chairman of the Moscow Trade Union Council and, in 1918, Chairman of the All-Russian Association of Trade Unions, Tomsky succeeded in establishing contacts with the British Trade Union movement. (In 1925 he took part in the Anglo-Russian Trade Union Congress at Scarborough, England.) Since 1919, he had been a member of the Central Committee of the Party. Later he was also appointed to the Politburo.

Janis Rudzutak was born in 1887, the son of a Latvian day laborer in Courland. As a worker in Riga he had come in contact with the Latvian and Russian revolutionary movements and had become one of its earliest Bolshevik exponents. He took an active part in the Latvian revolution of 1905. After the October Revolution, he played a leading role in the Moscow trade union organization, and in 1920 was elected a member of the Party's Central Committee. In 1922, he attended the Genoa Conference as the Soviet delegate. After Lenin's death he rose still higher, became People's Commissar for Transport and, in 1926, Deputy Chairman of the Council of People's Commissars and member of the Politburo.

Another group taking part in the debates, the so-called "Democratic Centralists," demanded the relaxation of the bureaucratic centralism within the Party. They were led by V. V. Osinsky (Prince Obolensky), T. V. Sapronov, and V. M. Smirnov.

Of even greater importance was the radical wing of the Bolsheviks under Trotsky and his followers. In contrast to the "Workers' Opposition," they wanted to incorporate the unions entirely into the governmental apparatus. Trotsky believed that the trade unions had outlived their function. The state was now a state of the workers. The Government was the legal representative of the total proletariat, i.e., also of the workers. The demands of individual workers' associations could not be allowed to run counter to general needs. Instead of representing individual occupational interests, the unions were to submit unconditionally to state and Party. Bukharin supported Trotsky's views.

Lenin used all his dialectic gifts in order to find a middle way. He was particularly sharp in his attack on the "Workers' Opposition" and the "Democratic Centralists" whom he described as anarcho-syndicalists. In their very words he saw a "direct danger to the future of the proletarian dictatorship." In this respect he agreed with Trotsky. At the same time, he defended the continued existence of the unions as a means for the workers to protect themselves against trespasses by the state. Simultaneously the workers had to protect the state as the dictatorship of the proletariat, and to protect themselves against the state. They were not to be forced to join a union. He also reminded his listeners that the proletarian state was not only a state of the workers, but a state of the peasants as well.

In the Kollontai-Shliapnikov opposition, Lenin considered most dangerous, not its concept of the role of the unions in the state, but the motive behind it—the curbing of the dictatorship of the Party. For this reason, all opposition groups within the Party were prohibited. Three Party secretaries, Krestinsky, Serebriakov and Preobrazhensky were relieved of their offices and replaced by more reliable Party members, among them Molotov and Yaroslavsky.

Little did Trotsky, who voted for the suppression of the opposition, suspect the consequences this would have for him, nor the trend he had helped inaugurate. Only later he wrote that the outlawing of all other parties was in flagrant opposition to the "spirit of Soviet democracy," and that these events were to be understood as a "temporary act of self defense."[7] But had not Trotsky himself,

in 1904, prophesied the dictatorship of the proletariat would lead
to the dictatorship of the Party apparatus if the centralist bureaucratic path upon which Lenin had entered were pursued?[8] Perhaps
the formulation of "the necessary self defense of the state apparatus" is an indication of how weak the government still felt itself
to be in the spring of 1921.

Starting with the Tenth Party Congress, the transformation of
the Party into a bureaucratic apparatus progressed rapidly. It
ceased being a "free association of independent, critically thinking,
and courageous revolutionaries." The administrative officers began
to replace the ideologists; in the committees, the bureaucrats and
party functionaries replaced the idealists.[9] Trotsky's and Bukharin's
stars began to wane; Bolsheviks of a new type slowly emerged into
the limelight; among them were men like Stalin and Molotov.

Bolshevik Federalism and the Founding of the Soviet Union

The concept of federalism has always had a twofold meaning
in multi-national states.[10] It permits the continual existence of
differences and peculiarities in a racially heterogenous political
structure. It may also serve to promote the expansionist tendencies
of a state; it softens the impact of an annexation; indeed, it may
make the idea of joining a larger political unit appear attractive
to a smaller state.

We have already shown how the nations' right to self determination, proclaimed by the Soviet Government, had been modi-
fied by the accompanying hope of a reintegration with Russia. The
Bolsheviks used the federal idea shrewdly, and it became a very
important tool for them.

An outline for a constitution of the Soviet state, providing for
a federal structure, had already been submitted to the Third Congress of Soviets in January, 1918. Events had forced even Stalin to
give up his original centralist position which he had advocated in
1913. The methods for implementing the federalism were important. The new federalist enticements were ineffective in impeding
the development of the Western border states. However, as noted,
the Civil War led to the return of the Ukraine, White Russia, the
Caucasus, and the Far Eastern Provinces.

With the exception of the last, all these provinces formed separate Soviet Republics, which at first were only loosely connected
with the Russian core of the Bolshevik state. The Russian Socialist

Federal Soviet Republic (RSFSR) encompassed the entire area of Great Russian settlement, including the whole Northern and Eastern part of European Russia, as well as Siberia and Central Asia to the borders of Persia and China, and to the Pacific coast. At least 60% of the total population lived in this area. The RSFSR had received a constitution on July 10, 1918, based on the concept of Soviets and the dictatorship of the proletariat. The head of the state was the Chairman of the VTsIK of the All-Russian Soviets, the government was in the hands of the Council of the People's Commissars of the RSFSR.

The RSFSR was decidedly a nationality state. Almost 50% of its population, 64 million of the 140 million, belonged to various non-Russian nationality groups. They represented extreme ranges of cultural and social development, from the Western European character of the large Russian cities to the primitive, semi-nomadic tribal life of the Central Asiatic peoples. Beside the Finnish-Ugrian tribes of the Chuvash, Mordvinians and Mari (Cheremiss) between the Volga and Urals, there were the Mongol Kalmucks in the Northeastern Caucasus, the Mohammedan tribes of the Northern Caucasus, the Tatars in the Crimea and along the Volga, the Arctic and Siberian Samoyeds, Yakuts, and Voguls, the Turkestan Kazakh, Kirghiz, Turkmenians and Tadzhiks. Few of these people had a conscious feeling of nationality; many had not yet found the way out of the primitive tribal family to a distinctive social development.

This conglomeration of nationalities provided a great opportunity for Bolshevik welfare policy. If the Soviets brought them political and social organization, economic aid and elements of civilization, the Bolsheviks would soon appear as liberators from the Czarist yoke, as the ones who encouraged tribal and national characteristics. The People's Commissar for Nationality Affairs was quite aware of these possibilities. In keeping with his own maxim, "national in form, socialist in content," illiteracy was fought, popular education and local literature were fostered, and into the forms thus developed, regardless of their differences, the same content of Bolshevik ideology was inevitably poured.

At the end of 1922 the top Party authorities decided to tighten the bond which connected the RSFSR with the Ukrainian, White Russian and the three Caucasian republics. This followed the transition from militant communism to peaceful collaboration with the other states, making a closer union of the Soviet Republics desirable. The connection between the RSFSR and the other Soviet Republics had so far been extremely loose, actually consisting only of the Bolshevik party, which ruled them all. In June 1919, a Federation of the Russian, Ukrainian, White Russian and, wishful thinking, of the Latvian and Lithuanian states, had been envisaged for the first time in a decree of the VTsIK. The first concrete steps were taken in treaties with White Russia and the Ukraine on January 16 and December 28, 1920, when the first joint People's Commissariats were created. The next step was the standardization of constitutions.[11]

Now nothing stood in the way of a final union. At the end of 1922, the Tenth All-Russian Soviet Congress was presented with a report from Stalin which planned the establishment of a Soviet Union. On December 27, 1922, the proposal was accepted by the Congress. Thus the Union of Soviet Socialist Republics (USSR) was created. The Congress itself was immediately extended to become the First All-Union Congress of Soviets by the addition of members of the congresses of the other republics. On December 30, the decision was ratified.

On July 6, 1923, the Union received its constitution. In October, 1924, two further Soviet Republics were born within the RSFSR: the Uzbek and Turkmen in Central Asia;[12] they were joined in 1929 by the Tadzhik Republic as the ninth Soviet Republic.[13]

Within the Soviet Republics, especially within the RSFSR as the largest among them, settlement areas of individual tribes and communities were consolidated into autonomous republics or autonomous territories, according to the stage of their development. There was, e.g., a Volga German, a Bashkir, a Buryat autonomous republic, and autonomous territories of the Kalmucks, Votyaks and others.

The constitution of the Soviet Union of 1923 differentiated between the governmental bodies of the Union and those of the individual republics. Foreign policy, foreign trade, economic planning, defense, the administration of justice, education and public health were solely the concern of the Union. The supreme governmental power of the Union was represented by the All-Union Soviet Congress which was convoked every year by the Central Executive Committee (TsIK) of the Soviets. It consists of delegates from the Soviets. But only the lowest in the hierarchical pyramid of the Soviets, the village and city Soviet, was elected by the people themselves. The franchise was confined to adults over eighteen who derive their "own productive work," to officials and soldiers, but not to priests and members of the bourgeosie. All higher Soviets, the county, province and state Soviets, were composed of representatives of the Soviets immediately below; the voice of the voters was expressed only indirectly at these levels. The Executive Committee, elected from among members of the Congress, was the permanent governing body. It was authorized to issue decrees and exercised full governmental authority between congresses. The actual functions of the Committee were carried out by its Presidium. Its chairman, in turn, was considered the actual personal representative of the Union and its President. He was, however, nothing more than a figurehead.

The first president of the Presidium of the TsIK, Mikhail Ivanovitch Kalinin, was elected in 1923. Kalinin was born in 1875 in the Province of Tver (Kalinin), the son of poor peasants. At the age of 14 he went to St. Petersburg as a house servant. He tried to complete his primary education by tireless reading. At the age of 18 he became a worker in a munitions factory. In 1898, he joined the Social Democratic Party. Soon he was arrested and exiled to Tiflis in the Caucasus. Here, too, he plunged into revolutionary work as he did later in Reval. Most of the time he was either in prison or exile. In the Revolution of 1905, Kalinin agitated among the workers in St. Petersburg and, by 1906, he had become a delegate to the Party Congress in Stockholm. During World War I, he made anti-war speeches and contributed to *Pravda*. When in 1916 he was exiled to Eastern Siberia, he obtained permission to pay his own fare there and, in the course of the trip, succeeded in escaping. After the February Revolution, he was elected to the Petrograd City Duma; after the October Revolution he became Mayor of the city; after Sverdlov's death, he became chairman of the VTsIK. Now the Party called on him to become head of the Union.

Kalinin's personality was complicated and he tended to subordinate himself. He was almost universally liked because of his friendly, modest manner. He was extremely loyal to Lenin, and later transferred this loyalty to Stalin. During periods of unpopular agricultural policies he was of great use in pacifying delegations of angry peasants. He never wielded great influence and actual government functions were carried out by the Council of People's Commissars.

In the highest echelons of the Party, the Central Committee, the

Politburo, the Bureau of Organization (Orgburo) and the General Secretariat, the actual threads of policy met, and all directives were prepared. Personal ties with the Council of People's Commissars, gave the latter the character of one of the executive organs of the Party. The principle of decentralization had thus become illusory, both in the top supreme governing bodies of the Union as well as in the relationship between the Union and individual Soviet Republics. Here, too, the governmental bodies were confronted with the rigidly organized Party apparatus which had its leadership in the Kremlin.

Family and School

While these great external and internal political decisions were being made, and the country's economic life and social structure were undergoing a transformation, Bolshevism was also having far-reaching effects on the private, intellectual and religious life of the nation.

In keeping with the social radicalism of the first years, the family was denied its importance as a social institution. It was degraded to a relic of the bourgeois epoch and considered a bourgeois prejudice. When in December, 1917, civil marriage was introduced as the only recognized legal form, this change could still be considered as part of the emancipation of public life from the Church. However, the marriage laws of 1918 indicated that a relaxation of marital and family ties was also intended. According to these, an entry into the public marriage register was sufficient for concluding a marriage. Divorce became a matter of form; the notice of one marriage partner to the other stating the intention of dissolving the marriage was sufficient. Only the fate of the children was subject to legal control. Illegitimate and legitimate children were both treated on the same basis. From 1920 on, abortions were permitted without restriction.

Tension in the relationship between the generations was also exploited for the systematic undermining of family life. Particularly among members of the more conservative groups, whether the former upper classes or the peasantry, differences of opinion between parents and children frequently carried a disquieting political coloration. The systematic indoctrination of the children in Bolshevik ideology and propaganda often created a deep rift between younger and older generation. The youth organization "Komsomol" was largely responsible for this. Denunciations by children of their parents were provoked, encouraged and rewarded.

In the confusion of the Civil War and the years of the famine, many families had been torn asunder; hordes of children without parents tramped through the country. They formed gangs led by adolescent boys or girls, terrorized the population and committed thefts, murders and other crimes.

The moral deterioration of the "Bezprizornye," these homeless youths, was unequalled. In the twenties they became a disquieting element which seriously endangered public safety, health and order. The state was finally forced to proceed against them with extreme measures. Wherever the local militia was insufficient, the military was called in. There were cases where gangs of children and adolescents who put up resistance were mowed down with machine guns.

The unbridled sexuality within these particular groups only reflected an attitude that was generally in vogue. Free love was propagated everywhere. The great prophetess of free love was Mme. Alexandra M. Kollontai. Born in 1872, the daughter of a Czarist general, she was one of the early revolutionaries and in 1915 joined the Bolsheviks. It was hard to match her cultural and moral radicalism; her books and articles on these subjects repelled Lenin.

The Soviet school system, too, was at first run under the slogan: liberation from bourgeois shackles and prejudices. Not only was the influence of the Church eliminated; the authority of the teacher was restricted to such an extent that the new order made an organized teaching program impossible. The program itself was to be freed of superfluous ballast. This included ancient as well as modern foreign languages. History was abandoned in favor of a sociologically oriented social science which used historical material to fortify Bolshevik ideology. There was a special need for the teaching of the natural sciences. Here, however, the dearth of qualified teachers made itself felt. In the twenties, the main emphasis was placed on the development of manual skills and the loss of factual knowledge soon assumed catastrophic proportions.

In 1923 there were signs of an awakening even among those close to the Commissar for Popular Education, the Bolshevik *bel esprit,* A. V. Lunacharsky. It was realized that the discussion of political and social questions would remain useless unless a basic elementary education was provided. The necessity for concrete factual knowledge and organized teaching was re-discovered. From 1925 on, the teaching of political doctrine was more subordinated to a basic elementary education. Compulsory school attendance was reintroduced and discipline reestablished. The Russian alphabet was simplified and sports, which had always been neglected in the schools of Czarist Russia, were promoted. These were trends which introduced the new era of the thirties.

The Persecution of the Church

The Bolshevik's attitude toward church and religion was logically derived from dialectical materialism and Marxist ideology. According to Marx, religion is "the opium of the people." Lenin gladly adopted this formula. Religion, it was said, diverts the attention of the worker from the miseries of this earth to the world beyond, and thus promotes the interests of the exploiters. All forms of religious life were sharply opposed, particularly the Greek Orthodox Church and the other religious communities.

The Greek Orthodox Church had used the fall of the Czar as an opportunity to appoint a clerical leader as its head, a practice followed before Peter the Great. A Church Council which met on October 15, 1917, elected the Metropolitan Tikhon as Patriarch. Under his leadership the Church energetically opposed the atheism of the Bolsheviks. All Bolshevik members of the parishes were excommunicated and the policies of the Soviet Government were sharply attacked. This forthright stand against the new regime, while undeniably heroic, was unable to stem the course of events. The Church had lost its power over the people's souls; the people more or less silently accepted the anti-clerical measures of the state.

The complete separation of State and Church marked the beginning of a number of other measures which thoroughly isolated the life of the Church and excluded it from public affairs. The clergy were deprived of its civil rights. Religious instruction of the young was prohibited in 1921; the Criminal Code of 1926 decreed forced labor as the punishment for any violation of this prohibition. The state's hostile attitude toward religion was clearly expressed in the new school text books. All religious literature was banned and parochial schools, seminaries and monasteries were closed.

The resistance of the clergy, and particularly the open enmity of the Patriarch Tikhon, made the religious battle increasingly bitter. The persecution of monks and priests began. Countless numbers of them were among the first victims of the Cheka and died as martyrs; there are some statistics that indicate that altogether 28 archbishops and bishops and 6,775 priests were killed. Church lands were expropriated; church treasures and sacerdotal objects were confiscated. Finally almost all of the surviving ecclesiastical dignitaries, including the Patriarch, were arrested.

But this was not enough. Party and state now initiated an active propaganda campaign in order to win the younger generation. In 1925 the "Association of Militant Atheists" was founded. Its mission was to ridicule religion and to undermine the authority of the church. The Association pursued its aims through speeches and articles and by means of exhibitions and anti-clerical museums, which were usually located in requisitioned churches. A greater knowledge of the natural sciences was to serve as a constructive counterbalance to "religious superstition and obscurantism," and promote the materialistic ideology. The chief newspaper of the "Association of Militant Atheists," called *Bezbozhnik,* was, however, a poor journal which combined importunate stridency with inferior content.

There were some among the clergy who could not bear the burden imposed by a conflict with the state. They demanded a compromise with Bolshevism and the severance of all connections with counter-revolutionary forces. A special group was formed which called itself "The Living Church." It considered Lenin's persecution of the Church to be a just retribution for the Church's attitude during Czarist times, when it was indifferent to social injustice, and served as a tool of the Government. A reconstruction of the Church along Communist lines was demanded. The state welcomed these trends as the first signs of the disintegration of the Church. When Tikhon died in 1925, the successor whom he had designated was prevented from carrying out his office.

Here, too, the New Economic Policy made certain concessions necessary. The resumption of relations with other countries made necessary some consideration for public opinion abroad, a public opinion which had been shocked by the religious persecutions during the period of War Communism. To some extent, religious services were permitted again, but only in halls especially hired for this purpose. The "Living Church" managed to regain a few minor liberties. In his encyclical letter of July 16, 1927, the Patriarchical Vicar, Sergius, asked the faithful to adopt a loyal attitude toward the state. At the end of the year he ordered a prayer for the state and government. This was as far as the Church was willing to go in its conciliatory attitude. However, the basically anti-religious attitude of the state did not change, and the activities of the "Association of Militant Atheists," led by E. Yaroslavsky, steadily increased.

"Proletarian Culture"

The revolution and the Civil War had led to the complete collapse of Russia's intellectual life. Many of the intellectuals, who had chiefly belonged to the upper classes, had come to violent ends, had died in prisons, or had succumbed to hunger and cold. Internationally known scholars had left their country as emigrants; among them were the philosophers and theologians S. Bulgakov, N. Berdyaev, L. Karsavin, V. Zenkovsky and F. Stepun, and the historians M. I. Rostovtzeff and G. Vernadsky.

Only after the Civil War was there a revival of the universities and of academic life. Then Lenin himself stressed that in the Soviet state, too, research and teaching must not be allowed to wither. In line with a readiness to compromise, characteristic of the NEP period, the revival of public education was achieved mainly with the help of the bourgeois experts who still survived. This situation continued until 1928. Bolsheviks by conviction, such as the Marxist historian, Prof. M. Pokrovsky, were aware that this could only be an interlude. The liberal-democratic or nationalist-conservative political philosophy of these circles contrasted sharply with the official Party opinions concerning the role of the arts and sciences in the state.

In the eyes of the Party only dialectical materialism, Marxism's philosophical core, was to have validity and form the essence of a new, over-all scientific system encompassing the natural and social sciences, philosophy and law, history and languages. In the dialectic process of history this scientific system has no independent function in the search for truth and knowledge, but plays the role of a servant of the Socialist state and the Party. The former is the executor, the latter the trustee of this process. What this would mean in practice was expressed by Andrei Vishinski, when he stated that it was the function of the law to serve "the preservation, strengthening and development of those social conditions which are in the interest of the ruling class." If jurisprudence was to submit to the needs of the Party, the ideological bond of philosophy and history with dialectical and historical materialism would inevitably also lead to a total transvaluation of values in these fields.

Apart from changing the basic orientation of scientific thought, it was also the task of Bolshevik educational policy to attract the proletarian and peasant classes to the institutions of learning. Not only the secondary schools but the universities had to serve the ends of proletarian society. In 1919, special Workers' Faculties (rabfak)—the favorite scheme of the Deputy Commissar for Education, Prof. Pokrovsky—were instituted, providing accelerated matriculation courses. The children of workers and peasants were given preference in admission to the universities, while members of the bourgeoisie were excluded from higher education. The result of this proletarization of the universities was a rapid decline of the general intellectual level, attributable to the lack of a systematic curriculum and shallowness of thinking.

In art and literature, the first years after the October revolution were dominated by elation at having been freed from all the old inhibitions and bonds. The expressionistic and symbolist tendencies of the pre-war period now came into their own; what had until then been called decadent, was now considered the discovery of new continents. Evolving from futurism, several of the poets sought a new naturalism. Among these, S. Yessenin and V. Mayakovsky are typical. Both committed suicide, in 1925 and in 1930, respectively. Painters and architects showed a tendency toward the ultra-modern during the twenties when a certain creative individualism was apparent. In music, the development led from Scriabin and Rimsky-Korsakov to Igor Stravinsky and Serge Prokofiev; Dmitri Shostakovich, too, was at first among those who sought for new ways of expression. The theater and the ballet, after having temporarily closed down completely, continued along conventional lines. In the art of the film, S. M. Eisenstein's pioneering genius was revolutionary; he discovered much that was new and worthwhile and his *Potemkin* (1926) offered the film world completely new artistic effects and techniques.

In the course of time the Party recognized the tremendous propaganda possibilities in art and literature, the theatre and films. Radio was another excellent means for influencing public opinion for political and ideological purposes. At first the state had been satisfied with encouraging and fostering the artistic creativity of the workers, for example, through the organization "Proletkult" in the labor unions. Now it proceeded to exercise an increasing influence in all areas of artistic creation and activity. Censorship and directives began to set limits to independent expression and to stifle individual artistic initiative. Actors, dancers and musicians were able to enjoy greater economic security, but the theatres, concert halls, and the like were more and more controlled by educational and political directives which the Party issued in order to propagate its doctrines.

In poetry a new "Socialist Realism" became dominant. The great Russian writer Maxim Gorky described its task as "not only to present critically the past in the present, but also to contribute to the strengthening of the present of what the revolution had achieved, and to shed light on the goals of the Socialist future." Gorky, the intimate friend of Lenin and the spokesman of proletarian literature, had left Russia in 1921 because he did not approve of Bolshevism's hostile attitude toward bourgeois culture. When he returned in 1928, his international fame had faded; his literary activity was on the decline. In spite of this, his influence on the new generation of Soviet writers can hardly be exaggerated; A. Fadeyev, M. Sholokhov, K. Simonov, and many others learned from him.

The historical novel celebrated its return with Alexei Tolstoy's *Peter I* (1930). Tolstoy, a relative of the great Leo Tolstoy, returned to Russia in 1923 from voluntary exile abroad; eventually he received all the honors at the disposal of the Bolshevik state. His work, together with the whole shift of cultural orientation to the Russian past, is part of the new Soviet patriotism of the thirties.

Outlines of Soviet Foreign Policy: Focus on Asia

The Soviet Government's very first steps in foreign policy were an affront to its former Western Allies. The annulment of the Czarist debts and the publication of the secret treaties had created a tense atmosphere. This finally led to the *de facto* breaking off of diplomatic relations in the summer of 1918, when the first signs of Allied support for the anti-Bolshevist forces became noticeable. That the intervention did not become a regular state of war was only due to the obvious war weariness of the West.

With Germany, too, diplomatic relations were subjected to varying degrees of stress and strain. The annulment of the Peace of

Brest-Litovsk and the intervention in Germany's domestic revolutionary troubles in the winter of 1918-1919 had prevented the establishment of official contacts with the Weimar Republic.

Lenin's appeal for an international revolution was the equivalent of a declaration of war on the bourgeois world. The Bolsheviks of that time felt that the core of world capitalism was in the British Empire. The democratic socialists of the West were looked upon as fellow travelers of the capitalist system; the Bolsheviks reserved a special hatred for them as renegade brothers. From this point of view, the Social Democratic countries of the defeated Central Powers were counted as a matter of course among the hostile totality of the capitalist world.

Turning away from Europe, Soviet Russia began to become more demonstratively friendly toward the Asiatic nations. The transfer of the capital from Petrograd to Moscow in the spring of 1918 symbolized, to some extent, the close of the European period of Russian history which had begun with Peter the Great. (But the immediate reasons for the transfer were based on considerations of foreign policy and military strategy. The concentration of all forces in the center of the country proved to be essential during the civil war.) A characteristic aspect of the Asiatic orientation was that Bolshevik proclamations of the "nations' right of self-determination" were accompanied by scathing attacks on the imperialist colonial policies of the West. This formulation was primarily intended for consumption by the Asiatic peoples. The Bolsheviks could count on a vigorous echo to these slogans, from Turkey in a wide semicircle to China.

It was significant that the particular Bolshevik leader entrusted with the nationality question considered this focus on Asia of special importance. Stalin, who grew up in a half-European, half-Asiatic world where there had been much contact with Turks, Tatars, and Persians,—in a country which, although inhabited by an ancient Christian people, belongs geographically to Asia, or at least bridges the continents—showed particular understanding for the Eastern aims of Bolshevism. During the days when the attention of the heads of the Party was monopolized by the events of the German November revolution, he published two very significant articles. One was entitled "Don't Forget the East!" the other "Ex Oriente Lux."[14] Stalin by no means underestimated the importance of European events for the cause of the World Proletariat. But his attacks on capitalism contained an anti-European note which did not appear, for example, in Trotsky's publications. Pointing to a conference of Communist Mohammedans, which was to pave the way for Communism in Persia, India and China, he drew attention to the tremedous possibilities open to Bolshevik propaganda and influence.

Russia itself was inhabitated by millions of Mohammedan citizens. During the Civil War, the Bolshevik regime was sometimes in danger of losing the territories of Central Asia. Fostered by the Turkish politician, Enver Pasha, a Pan-Turanian movement had gained momentum there. It finally collapsed in 1922. The former protectorates, Bukhara and Khiva, were conquered and subordinated to the RSFSR, as were the Russian Turkestan provinces. Gradually they were transformed into separate Soviet republics. All national aspirations had to give way to Bolshevik centralism.

Beyond the Russian borders, it was to the advantage of Bolshevik propaganda to add more and more fuel to the nationalism of the semi-colonial world. In Moscow a special "League for the Liberation of Islam" was founded. At a Congress of Peoples of the Orient, in September 1920, the Hungarian Communist Bela Kun, deviating from usual Marxist dogma, said that a Communist regime could also be established in the economically backward Asiatic countries which lacked an industrial proletariat.

In February 1921, the RSFR concluded its first agreements with Persia and Afghanistan. The treaty concluded with Persia on February 26, was of particular importance. In it, Lenin made a definite break with "the imperialist policy of the former Russian government." As a token of good will Russia renounced all claims to the railroads and military highways which she had built in Northern Persia, as well as to all lands owned by the Persian Bank. In return Soviet Russia obtained control of fishing rights in the Caspian Sea and a voice in determining Persian tariffs. Article VI of the treaty gave Soviet Russia the right to march into Persia if the Persian government was unable to prevent attempts of a third power to use the country as a base of operations against Soviet Russia. Russian trade with Persia, now in sharp competition with British trade, advanced to second place.

On March 16, 1921, a treaty of peace and friendship was concluded with Turkey. The Soviet government gave up Kars and a few other border regions along the Caucasian frontier. Both nations, Soviet Russia as well as Turkey, which had been weakened by the war, could expect much from this cooperation. In the Far

East, after the collapse of the last anti-Bolshevik forces, Outer
Mongolia, which had been under Russian influence since 1912,
also came under Soviet sway; only a little while before this area
had served as the base of one of the last of the daring leaders of
the White Army, the Cavalry General Baron Ungern-Sternberg;
then his venture, too, was liquidated. In the treaty, which was
concluded on November 5, 1921, with the "Mongolian People's
Republic," China was not mentioned at all. After the return of the
Far Eastern Republic in 1922 a direct agreement was made with
Japan. China followed Japan's example. A trade agreement which
the Soviet Union concluded with Eastern Turkestan (the Chinese
province of Sinkiang) represented another milestone on the road
which Bolshevik policy had mapped out for itself.

Nevertheless, Bolshevik Russia alleged to the outside world that
it was the natural protector of all suppressed colonial peoples and
of the exploited semi-colonial world. Bolshevik propaganda violently attacked the imperialism of the Western nations, and Russian historiography did not hesitate to condemn Czarist imperialism,
but in reality expansionist ambitions were by no means foreign to
the newly founded Soviet Union.

The Founding of the Communist International: Hopes for World Revolution

The fact that the Soviet government was directed by a party
which had universal goals, extending far beyond the territorial
borders of the state, presented it with unique possibilities. In March
1919 Moscow had become the seat of the Communist International
(Comintern) which broadcast its slogans and orders all over the
world. Since that time, the policies of the Kremlin have been characterized by a strange two-facedness.

On November 1, 1914, at a time of conflict with the patriotism of
the Social Democrats of several of the belligerent nations, Lenin
for the first time spoke of the necessity of creating a Third International beside the right-wing Socialist Second International.[15]
In his April Theses of 1917, he urgently demanded the founding of
this Third International. In January 1919 he addressed an open
letter to the workers of Europe and America, calling for its creation. On January 24, official invitations to a Congress which was

to meet in Moscow in March were sent out by Soviet Foreign Commissar Chicherin. A manifesto by Trotsky ended with the stirring words: "In the name of the Soviets, the workers, the revolutionary battle for power and the dictatorship of the proletariat, under the banner of the Third International, workers of all nations, unite!"

The Congress was opened in the Kremlin on March 2, 1919. The delegates represented only some of the countries which had been invited, and their choice had frequently been quite accidental. All the speeches vibrated with tremendous emotion. It was said that the Third International would continue the work of the Second by ridding it of its opportunistic, social-chauvinistic and petty bourgeois deviations, and realize the dictatorship of the proletariat on a world wide scale. How all-embracing a goal was envisaged is shown in the New Year's proclamation to the Soviet People in 1920, which said: "We shall establish workers' and soldiers' councils in Berlin and Warsaw, in Paris and London, and the might of the Soviets will one day extend throughout the whole world." [16]

Grigori Zinoviev, one of Lenin's earliest collaborators, was elected President of the new International. Behind him stood Lenin himself, as undisputed master and intellectual mentor. Henceforward Comintern and Soviet Union were closely interlocked by an unwritten personal union.

The Second Congress of the Comintern was opened in Petrograd in June 1920, and later transferred to Moscow. This time, delegations from 37 countries were present. The discussions centered around the methods to be adopted for the world-wide dissemination of Communist propaganda. The Congress worked out a plan to set up secret Communist centers in every country. These were to work for the proletarian revolution while the various official Communist parties were to further the same cause legally through their parliamentary representatives. The Second Comintern Congress adopted Lenin's twenty-one points, [17] and they became directives binding on all Communist parties desirous of belonging to the Third International. Principally, they demanded a rigid subordination and strict discipline, a vigorous fight against social democratic ideas, and active propaganda in the labor unions and armies. Subsequent congresses went even farther. As time went by, party activities in the various countries were more tightly coordinated and more stress was put on the need for subordination to the orders of the Central Offices.

As at the end of 1918, the chief hopes of the Comintern centered on Germany. In the spring of 1920, Germany seemed ripe for Bolshevization. Set off by the reactionary Kapp coup, a Red insurrection broke out in March in the Ruhr, where a "Red Army" of nearly 50,000 men was organized.[18] At the same time a Communist rising took place in Thuringia and Saxony, and in the Vogtland, Max Hoelz proclaimed a Soviet Republic. Order was not reestablished until May.

That the German question continued to occupy the Bolshevik leaders is illustrated by an exchange of opinions between Lenin and Stalin in June 1920. For the Second World Congress of the Comintern, Lenin had worked out some commentaries on the national and colonial question which he had shown to, among others, Stalin.[19] In a letter of June 12, 1920, Stalin opposed Lenin on some points. The matter at issue was the future constitution of the Soviet State. In surprising contrast to his former skepticism regarding the federal idea, Stalin now urged the creation of a loosely organized confederation instead of a highly centralized federal state. The various peoples of the old Russia, he believed, were accustomed to a strong central power and would continue to accept it. But the nationalities had never belonged to Russia and had developed their own forms of government. In certain circumstances they "might see themselves forced by a superior power or by events to enter into some form of political union with Soviet Russia." "Let us assume," Stalin said, "the future existence of a Soviet Germany, Soviet Poland, Soviet Hungary or Soviet Finland; these nations which had their own state and their own army . . . will, even as Soviet states, hardly agree to enter into an immediate federation with Soviet Russia after the manner of the Bashkirs or Ukrainians." For such countries, he believed, only a loose confederacy with Soviet Russia would be feasible.[20]

While this document discloses how extensive were the plans for Bolshevisation of the Peoples' Commissar for Nationality Questions, the events of October 1920, reveal something of the methods by which this goal was to be reached. It was then that the Independent Social Democratic Party of Germany (USPD) obtained almost five million votes in the elections and became the second strongest party, next to the Social Democrats (SPD). The Party Congress of the USPD, held in October 1920 in Halle, included among its guests no less a personage than the President of the Comintern, Zinoviev. The leader of the Mensheviks, Martov, was also invited. Zinoviev harangued the assembly in a German speech lasting four hours; the result was that 224 delegates voted for affiliation with the Comintern and only 158 against it. This was the culmination of a development which the left wing had been urging for a long time. The USPD joined the Communist Party of Germany (KPD), while the right wing joined the SPD. The USPD thus ceased to exist.[21]

These events took place against the background of the Polish-Russian war. At the Congress in Halle, Martov revealed Soviet intentions of drawing Germany into this war by making shrewd use of the nation's opposition to the Treaty of Versailles. Radek had tried to establish contact with the German High Command and to advocate military cooperation against Poland. A revision of the German Eastern boundary was allegedly the reward on which Germany could count. These fantastic plans came to nothing, and probably not only because the "miracle on the Vistula" had created an entirely new situation.[22] For some time, Germany continued to be a field of active operations for the Comintern, a field which offered numerous possibilities for establishing closer relations, even though the enticing suggestions of German-Russian solidarity against the West did not draw any significant response.

At the beginning of 1921, it became clear that the World Revolution which had been expected since 1917 was no longer imminent. At the Tenth Congress of the Russian Communist Party, Lenin admitted, on March 8, that an early victory of the Revolution could not be counted upon, and for this reason he felt justified making concessions to the bourgeois world at home and abroad.

Soviet Russia and the Western Powers
The Treaty of Rapallo

The Russian problem had been discussed at Versailles in the absence of Russian representatives; a new order had also been established in Eastern Europe without Russian participation. So, too, at the beginning of the twenties, the great decisions in world affairs were made without consulting Soviet Russia.

When the League of Nations was established, neither Germany nor the United States had become members. But when Soviet Russia was not invited to the great international disarmament conference in Washington in 1921, Moscow considered this a great blow, because the Kremlin was now once again anxious to participate in the deliberations of the great powers. Trade negotiations with Great Britain had been initiated in the spring of 1920. Maxim Litvinov, as Soviet delegate, went to Copenhagen in order to establish contact with British representatives. At first there were difficulties and the talks were broken off but they were resumed in November. On March 16, 1921,[23] they led to the signing of a British-Russian trade agreement. As matters stood, this signified the *de facto* recognition of Soviet Russia by the British government.

The first breach had been made in the hostile front which had surrounded the Bolshevik state since 1918. Undoubtedly British businessmen were interested in making investments in Russia. But great obstacles still had to be surmounted before regular relations could be established. When Leslie Urquhart, a director of the Anglo-Russian Consolidated Ltd., arrived in Russia in 1921 for negotiations about mines and other property owned by his company in Central Asia, he realized that the Soviet government showed no willingness to return the property. When the British Cabinet raised the question of Czarist debts, the Soviet government countered with a demand for 20 billion rubles as indemnity for the damage Russia had suffered as the result of intervention. In these circumstances, a formal *de jure* recognition of the Bolshevik regime could not yet be considered. If Chicherin's foreign policy was based on out-and-out anti-British sentiments, he was matched in London by the Foreign Secretary, Lord Curzon. The former Viceroy of India was well-known to be a strong opponent of Bolshevism.

At this time Russia therefore registered most of her gains in the economic field. The trade agreement with Great Britain was followed by similar agreements with Norway (September 2, 1921), Austria (December 7, 1921), Italy (December 26, 1921) and with Germany. The first German-Russian agreement was the treaty of April 19, 1920, which concerned the return of prisoners of war and civil internees. Skilfully prepared by the Soviet expert for foreign trade, L. Krassin, it was extended on May 6 1921, into a trade agreement. For the first time since August, 1918, a German plenipotentiary went to Moscow again. At the same time, strictly secret military talks, of great significance to the German Reichswehr, were begun. The intention was to circumvent the restrictive clauses of the Versailles Treaty and to train German pilots and tank officers on Soviet territory. Russia, in turn, was interested in the help German experts could give in expanding the Russian armament industry.[24]

Against this background the Treaty of Rapallo can be better understood.

Both Germany and Soviet Russia were invited to the Economic Conference which opened in Genoa on April 10, 1922. For the first time, Soviet diplomats—having been awaited with keen curiosity—appeared at an important international affair. Chicherin let the Western powers know that in certain circumstances the Soviet government was prepared to recognize the debts of the Czarist regime and to pay compensation for foreign losses in Russia—if it were granted a loan and *de jure* recognition. The British Prime Minister, Lloyd George, who had always been ready to come to terms with the Bolsheviks, did not seem averse to starting negotiations on this basis. British oil concerns showed a strong interest in Russian oil exports. Beyond this, Lenin's NEP seemed to promise commercial advantages. France, Belgium, and the United States were considerably more reluctant. The negotiations were stalled, and threatened to halt completely. Into this deadened atmosphere burst the amazing news, on Easter Sunday, April 16, that Chicherin had met with the German Foreign Minister, Rathenau, at Rapallo. The Russians hoped to gain in an agreement with Germany what they had been unable to gain from the Western powers. The rapprochement between the two powers, both suspect to the West, had taken place quite unnoticed. Chicherin had had informal talks with the German Chancellor, Wirth, on his way through Berlin. Now he managed to overcome Rathenau's hesitations. The result was the Treaty of Rapallo, a German-Russian friendship pact in which both parties renounced indemnities (Article 1), reestablished diplomatic relations (Article 3) and granted preferential treatment to each other in their mutual trade relations (Article 4). The Germans renounced the six billions in reparations demanded at Brest-Litovsk and compensation for expropriated private property in Russia (Article 2). The Russians, on the other hand, gave up all financial demands on Germany. The treaty also provided for mutual consultation prior to all important International agreements.

The Treaty of Rapallo was a heavy blow to the policies of the former Allies in Europe. It brought about the fall of Lloyd George's Cabinet in England. But the West's assumption that Germany had completely thrown in her lot with the East and that secret military clauses would have other, even more far-reaching consequences, was wrong. There were no secret clauses and a man like Rathenau was incapable of choosing an Eastern solution against the West. For Germany, Rapallo meant the preservation of its independence between West and East at a time when Russian weakness meant that there would be no danger.[25] For Soviet Russia, the treaty provided the door through which it could once more enter international politics.

It was important that these successes in foreign affairs were achieved on the eve of decisive domestic changes. A few weeks before the conclusion of the treaty of Rapallo, Stalin had been nominated Secretary General of the Communist Party; at the end of the year Lenin suffered his second stroke which was to exclude him more and more from political life.

CHAPTER 4

STALIN'S RISE AND STRUGGLE WITH THE OPPOSITION

Lenin's Death and His Successors

After the change of course decided on at the Tenth Party Congress and the launching of the New Economic Policy, it became obvious that Lenin was gravely ill; although only fifty-one years old he showed symptoms of cerebral sclerosis. Toward the end of 1921, his health deteriorated still further. Nevertheless, at the Eleventh Party Congress in March, 1922, he delivered, as usual, the principal address, in which he presented the results of the NEP. But on May 26 he suffered a stroke, and for two months he was unable to move, speak or write. Only in October did he return to the Kremlin to resume his work.

At the Fourth Congress of the Comintern in Moscow, in November 1922, Lenin appeared to have regained his former buoyant energy. In a great speech to the Congress, and later before the Moscow Soviet, he explained how the NEP would in due course lead to a fully Socialist state. However, in the middle of December his health again took a turn for the worse. He was no longer able to participate in conferences, though he remained in contact with the leading officials by telephone and letter. His wife, Nadezhda Krupskaya, who had shared his life and struggles since 1898, and who had accompanied him into exile in Siberia, helped him with his work. His sister, Maria, nursed him. Around the turn of the year Lenin dictated his so-called testament—his final recommendations regarding the men who were to lead the Party after his death. In March 1923, he had a third stroke and for the first time the Party Congress—the Twelfth —in April, had to meet without him. His physical decline could no longer be arrested. In October he dragged himself again to his office in the Kremlin, then returned

155

to his country house in Gorki near Moscow, where he died in January 21, 1924.

Lenin's body was embalmed and buried with tremendous pomp and circumstance in a mausoleum on the Red Square in the Kremlin. His tomb became the nation's holy shrine and his memory was surrounded by the halo of a quasi-religious idolatry. The name of his birthplace was changed to Ulyanovsk, and St. Petersburg (Petrograd) was henceforth known as Leningrad. A Lenin Institute, founded for the purpose, was given to the task of publishing his works, including his letters and notes. Since then four editions of Lenin's Collected Works have appeared.[1]

At first a triumvirate, a *troika*, as the Russians called it, consisting of Zinoviev, Kamenev and Stalin took over the reins. Very soon Stalin succeeded in gaining the dominant position in this body and in pushing aside his two colleagues as well as Trotsky, his most dangerous antagonist.

Stalin had never been very close to Lenin. He had never belonged to Vladimir Ilyich's intimate circle of friends. Zinoviev, Kamenev, Bukharin, even Trotsky, had been closer to him. The story of Lenin's last illness is the story of a constantly growing, but already helpless distrust of Stalin. We do not have to rely alone on Trotsky's doubtlessly very subjective report of the events of the years 1922-23 [2] for this; other sources, too, furnish confirmation.[3]

Stalin had managed to enlarge and fortify his position constantly. To the post of Commissar of Nationalities which he occupied until the office was abolished in 1923, he added in 1919 that of Commisar of Workers' and Peasants' Inspectorate (Rabkrin), charged with supervising the entire state apparatus in order to eradicate two chief evils, incompetence and corruption. The nature of the agency eventually enabled its head to pry into every office of the various administrative divisions. But it had a second purpose as well—the training of a reliable and competent civil service. The new Commissariat came to be the incubator of the later all-powerful "apparatus" of the Party. Besides these government offices, Stalin had gradually succeeded in occupying key positions in the Party. Since 1912, he had been a member of the Central Committee and, since 1917, a member of the Politburo.

During the civil war, the Politburo consisted of only five men: Lenin, Trotsky, Stalin, Kamenev and Bukharin. While Lenin and Kamenev, as his deputy, were running the government, while Trotsky was responsible for the conduct of the war, and Bukharin for press and propaganda, Stalin had even then assumed the actual organizational leadership of the Party. Next to the Politburo, the Organization Bureau (Orgburo) grew in importance; it dispatched Party functionaries into all the civilian and military offices. Early in 1919 Stalin was the only liaison man between Politburo and Orgburo. In this capacity he strove for co-ordination between Party policy and organization, and directed the forces of the Party, gaining prestige and increasing his knowledge of personnel and routine.

At the Eleventh Party Congress in 1922, a new, enlarged Central Committee was elected and new statutes drawn up; at the same time it was decided to create the office of General Secretary of the Party. On April 3, 1922, Stalin was appointed to this post. Trotsky relates that Lenin accepted Stalin's candidacy, which was supported by Zinoviev, with skepticism. "This cook will serve us nothing but peppered dishes," he is said to have commented privately. But he did not oppose it. V. M. Molotov and V. V. Kuibyshev were appointed as Stalin's assistants.

Henceforward the Politburo, to which Tomsky and Zinoviev had now been elected as well, represented, as it were, the brain trust of Bolshevism. The Bureau of the General Secretary, although subordinate to the Politburo, developed into the real center of governmental power. Eventually, the General Secretariat became the actual executive organ of the Politburo; it could, however, not only influence execution, but by planning the agenda and furnishing data for Politburo sessions, also influence its decisions.

A further point must be considered. At the Tenth Party Congress in 1921 a supreme control commission had been created for the supervision of Party morale, representing on the government level a counterpart to the Workers' and Peasants' Inspectorate. The main task of the commission consisted in carrying out the periodically necessary purges of the Party, which were as yet completely harmless. They meant a reproach, or at worst, expulsion from the Party. The Central Commission in Moscow became the highest court of appeal for all purges throughout the country. These were to be carried out completely independently of the upper Party echelons. The General Secretariat gradually became the co-ordinating link between the Central Commission and both the Central Committee and the Politburo. Thus Stalin was in a position to influence the purges. A carefully kept card index furnished him with the necessary data.

No one among the Party leaders envied him his jobs. They were all of a character that had no attraction at all for the highly gifted intellectuals among the Politburo members. The daily grind of Party service required a thorough, persevering and at the same time prosaic routine, a "patient and sustained interest in every detail of organization."⁴ Nobody had any inkling that through persistence, intrigue and brutality, Stalin, the subordinate Party functionary, was about to become Lenin's successor.

Lenin's displeasure at the growing power of the inner Party apparatus was aroused in October, 1922, between the first and second phases of his illness. When Lenin resumed his official duties, he was, according to Trotsky, dismayed by the alarming growth of "bureaucratism" in the government apparatus; he wanted to establish a special commission to abolish these abuses. Trotsky suggested that this anti-bureaucratic campaign be extended to the Party sector as well. In a letter to the First All-Union Congress of Soviets of December 23, 1922, therefore, Lenin proposed to raise the membership of the Central Committee from fifty to one hundred.⁴ᵃ Lenin's relapse did not permit the execution of the plan.

On December 25, Lenin dictated his testament.⁵ It was based on his fear of a split in the Bolshevik party. Two classes, he wrote, provided the foundation of the Party—workers and peasants; if there was no harmony between them the Party would inevitably fall apart. This danger was far distant. At the moment he was concerned with the threat of a rift arising from more immediate causes, viz., possible differences of opinion in the Politburo. He then turned to a review of his possible successors. Trotsky was, without a doubt, the ablest man in the Central Committee, but he had far too much self-confidence. Lenin pointed out that Trotsky was too strong an individualist and too little inclined to subordinate himself to party discipline. About the second of the two party members mentioned in detail, he stated: "Since Comrade Stalin has become General Secretary, he holds immense power in his hands, and I am not convinced that he will always know how to use this power with the necessary moderation."

He also mentioned in passing the fact that Zinoviev and Kamenev had shown lack of resolution during the October Revolution; of the other party leaders, N. I. Bukharin was characterized as the "favorite of the entire Party" and the highly respected theoretician G. L. Piatakov as very able but not wholly reliable. These were apparently thoughts dictated at random which were later to be defined more precisely. No concrete statement regarding the succession was contained in the testament.

Lenin, in his concern about rifts arising from personal differences, must have thought of the antagonism between Trotsky and Stalin above all. Particularly, Trotsky's antipathy toward the Georgian was well known. It went back to the very early days, even though Trotsky's memoirs may have dramatized these first impressions. The contrast became fully apparent during the civil war when Trotsky's fame was at its height. It outlasted the Polish war and was nourished by Stalin in the party apparatus. Lenin was bound to fear that once his authority was gone, the contrast between two such strong personalities might destroy the Party.

Lenin was further bound to doubt whether Trotsky's impulsive energy, his vain ambitiousness, could be restrained in the future. Moreover, Trotsky, by reason of his authority in military circles, might make himself sole dictator of Party and country. The thought that such Napoleonic ambitions might also be slumbering in Stalin's breast, seemed far-fetched at the time. Interpreting Lenin's reflections, the most feasible solution must have seemed a collective Party council of old Bolsheviks, including Stalin, which would not only keep him in check, but would also restrain Trotsky and neutralize their mutual antagonism.

On January 4, 1923, Lenin added a codicil to his testament. "Stalin," it stated, "is too rude and this failing . . . is intolerable in the office of the General Secretary. Therefore I propose to the comrades to find a way to remove Stalin from this post and to appoint a successor for him . . . who is more patient, loyal, courteous and considerate toward the comrades and less temperamental, etc." These details may seem insignificant, but if a split was to be avoided, and if concern existed about the relations between Trotsky and Stalin, even such trifles could assume decisive importance.[6]

The immediate cause for this increasingly skeptical attitude toward Stalin was Stalin's uncompromising attitude on the Georgian question about which Lenin had received new data at the turn of the year.

The Georgian Republic, which on May 7, 1920, had been recognized by the RSFSR, was confronted with a *fait accompli* when Red Army units invaded it in February 1921, and transformed it into a Soviet Republic. The Georgian people, consisting mainly of peasants and petit bourgeois, resisted the sovietization of their country. Not only the Mensheviks among the population wanted independence; the Georgian Bolsheviks, too, envisaged a Georgian soviet republic independent of Russia, tied to Moscow only by common political aspirations.[7] Precisely for this reason Lenin advocated a flexible and cautious policy in Georgia. Stalin, who had visited his native country in 1921, carried out a ruthless program of bolshevization which took no account of Georgian national pride. He did this through his countryman, S. Ordzhonikidze. When signs of resistance appeared, he played off one group of Georgian Bolsheviks against another without the knowledge of either Lenin or the Central Committee. He also saw to it that Lenin was left in the dark about the true state of affairs. When Lenin, despite his illness, succeeded in informing himself accurately with the aid of authentic reports, he became so incensed that he decided to break with Stalin.[7a] On December 30, the very same day on which the first Soviet Congress of the USSR was opened, he set down his intention of holding Stalin responsible for the latter's "Great-Russian-nationalist" action in Georgia. Soon after he had dictated the codicil to his testament, he began an open and total attack on Stalin. In a *Pravda* article dated January 25, 1923, he criticized—still mildly—Stalin's activities as Commissar of the Workers' and Peasants' Inspectorate. He followed this up with a second article which was considerably sharper in tone. This did not appear in print until March 4, four weeks after it had been written. The following day he had a heated personal discussion with Stalin and, in a brief letter which he dictated immediately afterward, he informed him that he was breaking off all personal relations with him.[8] This campaign was completed by a telegram sent on March 6 to the Georgian opposition group in which Lenin assured it of his agreement and his support; at the same time he entrusted Trotsky with the protection of Georgian interests.

Lenin's third stroke on March 9, 1923, presumably brought on by the intense aggravation of the preceding days, interrupted a development which would no doubt have undermined Stalin's position seriously; the renewed and fatal deterioration of Lenin's health came just in time for Stalin.

An episode reported by Trotsky helps complete the picture. Trotsky alleged that Stalin, at a Politburo meeting at the end of February, stated that Lenin had recently called him in order to ask him for some poison for he felt that his condition was hopeless. The others present protested violently. Trotsky thought it possible that Lenin had actually expressed this tragic wish, since

Stalin alone was interested in fulfilling it, and that Stalin had indeed considered taking a hand in preventing Lenin's recovery. Whatever the facts, even if planned, Stalin did not need to resort to violence. The agitated discussion of March 5 set the stage for the final elimination of Lenin from political life on the 9th.

The Triumvirate of 1923-1925
The First Stage in the Fight against Trotsky

During Lenin's illness, Kamenev had already taken over the chairmanship of the Politburo. He was, without a doubt, closest to Lenin among the older comrades. Before his death Lenin had entrusted him with the publication of his works. He was probably the most intelligent of the old Bolsheviks, the real expert in the strategy of inter-party struggle, well versed in all questions of doctrine. As Party Secretary in Moscow he was backed by the Party organization of the capital.

There were close ties between him and Zinoviev. Through all the shifting fortunes of the subsequent party struggles, the Party's Castor and Pollux could not be separated. Zinoviev was an able speaker and a demagogue who knew how to appeal to the masses. As Party Secretary of Leningrad, he too could count on substantial local support. Abroad, in the circles of international Communism, he was the most popular figure among the Russian party leaders; his position as Chairman of the Comintern enhanced his authority in the Soviet Union as well.

At first, Stalin shrewdly stayed in the background. During Lenin's illness, he had exhibited the most exemplary devotion. An article in *Pravda,* entitled "Communist Strategy and Tactics," which he had written in March 1923, abounds in respectful references to the sick master. Carefully veiling his differences with Lenin, he steadily strengthened his position. At the Twelfth Party Congress which opened on April 17, 1923, he had a definite headstart over the two other triumvirs. He diplomatically proposed that Trotsky deliver the main report in Lenin's place. Trotsky declined, proposing Stalin, who also refused. Zinoviev then gave the report but was listened to in "oppressive silence"; both Trotsky and Stalin carefully noted this fact. The Georgian question, raised by Zinoviev and Bukharin, he pushed aside by calling it "provincial chauvinism," pointing to similar equally reprehensible occurrences in Turkestan and in the Ukraine. Also important was the fact that the

Central Control Commission was now merged with the Workers' and Peasants' Inspectorate, with Stalin's faithful follower, V. V. Kuibyshev, as its director. The membership of this body was raised from seven to fifty, and in addition there were to be ten candidates. Thus began a course which brought the Commission in dangerous proximity to the GPU, until it finally became a kind of special division of the State Security organs.

After the congress, Zinoviev began to realize that the real threat to a collective leadership of state and Party came not so much from Trotsky as from Stalin. His own position had deteriorated as a result of the failure of the Communist *coup d'état* in Germany. At the end of the year ominous symptoms of the disintegration of government authority appeared throughout the country. Strikes in industry broke out sporadically. They were illegal, as every strike in the Soviet Union always has been. The consequences of the NEP were long and painful. Undernourishment and low wages goaded the workers to desperation. When the trade unions refused to mediate, discontent exploded spontaneously. The opposition groups of the Tenth Party Congress became active again, demanding greater freedom of opinion in the Party.

At this point Trotsky took action for the first time. Openly he attacked the triumvirate and criticized the growing bureaucratization of the Party apparatus. Why were most Party secretaries no longer elected but appointed from above? The discipline necessary during the civil war must now make way for greater, freely assumed responsibility within the Party, he said. Trotsky's attack called forth an important declaration by forty-six prominent Communists, among them Piatakov, Preobrazhensky, Antonov-Ovseyenko, Muralov and others. Its content, by and large, paralleled Trotsky's statement. The policy of the Central Committee was considered mistaken and dangerous for the country.

The triumvirate saw that it had to give in. It proposed a democratic party reform which was unanimously accepted by the Politburo. The questions which had been raised were now to be discussed publicly. Stalin delivered a very astute speech to the workers of Krasnaya Presnya, an industrial district in Moscow, in December 1923. He seemed to agree to Trotsky's demands but in reality, his speech was intended to provoke Trotsky to make further demands. Trotsky actually did this in an open letter to the workers of the same district. He wrote that some comrades seemed to overestimate the importance of the Party apparatus and to think too little of the vital force of the Party itself. Central direction could certainly not be dispensed with, but the Party should control its machinery. Addressing the younger generation, Trotsky pointed out that not infrequently old fighters of the Revolution became bureaucrats. This had happened in the Social Democratic movement of the West and might happen to the Bolsheviks too.

This meant open warfare. Zinoviev, Kamenev and others attacked Trotsky. Stalin knew Trotsky's still undeniable popularity had to be taken into account. He proposed a Party conference for January 16 to 18, to discuss the questions. Here at last Stalin openly opposed Trotsky. He read out a list of "six mistakes" by Trotsky. The most serious were that he incited the Party against the Party organization as well as the youth against the Party; that, although a member of the Politburo, he spoke for the Opposition, for the "petit bourgeois intelligentsia." The Party had to be homogeneous, monolithic! The conference ended with a condemnation of the attacks as a "petit bourgeois deviation from Leninism" and with the resolution that the Central Committee could expel its own members from the Party if they acted contrary to its interests. These were significant portents of serious future disagreements.

In the meantime the *troika* began a two-pronged drive to weaken Trotsky and the Opposition. In February 1924, a number of Trotsky's supporters were sent abroad in the course of a reshuffle of diplomats. Christian Rakovsky was sent to England, N. N. Krestinsky to Germany, A. Joffe to China. Rakovsky's removal from the Ukraine, where he had been chairman of the Council of the People's Commissars, was of particular significance. Strong measures were mapped out for the Ukraine, one of the chief strongholds of the Opposition. One of Stalin's closest associates, Lazar Moisseyevich Kaganovich, was entrusted with carrying out a purge there. Stalin submitted another proposal of great importance to the Party Conference: 200,000 workers were to be admitted to the Party "directly from the workshops in order to instill a healthy proletarian atmosphere." In truth Stalin hoped by thus enlarging the Party, to strengthen also the influence of his party machinery.

Trotsky had not taken part in the January conference. He had contracted influenza while duck hunting, and suffered from an alarmingly high fever which caused him to go to the south on January 18. The explanation of this astonishing fact—Lenin's death was expected any day—is probably that Trotsky wished to avoid the impression that he wanted to assume power after Lenin's death. His pride and vanity led him to believe that the Party, tired of the struggles for power within the Politburo, would ask him to lead the Party anyway, and that it was appropriate to keep in the background. If this explanation is correct,[9] Trotsky's attitude toward Stalin shows the same low estimate of the man that runs like a bright thread through all his works; an undervaluation by the scintillating, intellectual and fiery politician of the diametrically opposed type of a different species, which was to cost him so dearly.

Trotsky did not attend Lenin's funeral, as he himself reports, because Stalin misinformed him of the time for the ceremony and he was unable to reach Moscow from the Caucasus in time.[10] Thus Stalin became the dominant figure at the cermonies.

The Loyalty Oath, the "great pledge," which Stalin read on January 26 at the Second Soviet Congress is a ceremonious oath in which "the style of the Communist Manifesto is strangely mingled with that of the Greek Orthodox prayer book."[11] This oath initiated the subsequent Lenin cult. Two days later Stalin delivered his great speech at the official memorial ceremony in which he very shrewdly managed to represent himself as the legal executor and official interpreter of Lenin's spiritual heritage.

After Lenin's death neither Zinoviev nor Kamenev, but Rykov, one of the most colorless of the Bolshevik leaders, became chairman of the Council of People's Commissars of the USSR and, at the same time, of the RSFSR.

Alexei Ivanovich Rykov, born in 1881 in Saratov, the son of a former peasant in the Province of Vyatka, grew up in the greatest poverty. As a law student in Kazan he was drawn into radical circles; in 1902 he took an active part in the revolutionary demonstrations in Saratov, then went underground, frequently changing his residence. After a brief meeting with Lenin in Geneva he plunged into the revolution of 1905. As delegate of the Moscow group he took part in the Third Party Congress in London at which he was elected to the Central Committee. In the usual fashion he, too, lived through periodic arrests and exile. In the intervals he went abroad for consultations with Lenin. After February 1917, he played a role in the Moscow Soviet; after the October Revolution he became People's Commissar of the Interior. During the Civil War, as chairman of the Supreme Soviet for Economic Affairs, he organized the nationalization of the economy and devoted a good deal of energy to organizing the food supply of the Army. The price control law of 1923 was his work.

Kamenev became Rykov's deputy. For the time being, various Commissariats remained under their former heads.

In May 1924, the reading of Lenin's testament led to a difficult scene at a meeting of the Central Committee. It was to be decided whether or not this document should be made public at the coming Party Congress. According to an eye witness,[12] an embarrassed silence settled on the meeting when the passage about Stalin was read. Stalin himself showed perfect self-control and remained calm. The situation was saved for him by Zinoviev. He said that Lenin's every word was law and that the vow to fulfill everything that he had ordered would be kept. Fortunately, it was apparent that in one respect Lenin's fears had been groundless. Everyone could testify that collaboration with Stalin was completely harmonious. Kamenev appealed to the Central Committee to leave Stalin in office. This meant, however, that the testament could not be published.

Trotsky, who was back in Moscow, remained silent. Lenin's widow protested in vain against the suppression. The proposal to communicate the testament confidentially to the district delegates was accepted by 40 to 10. It became generally known abroad two years later when Max Eastman, formerly an American Communist and supporter of Trotsky, published it in *The New York Times*.[13] Not until the Twentieth Party Congress in February 1956 was the so-called Testament, and other relevant documents, released in the Soviet Union.

At the Thirteenth Party Congress in May 1924, Trotsky seemed ready to resign and to renounce his opposition. However, Zinoviev overplayed his hand; he asked that Trotsky should not only cease future criticism but also admit that his past criticism had been mistaken. The ugly cloud of "crimes of conscience" of the later show trials cast its first shadows. Trotsky's statement proved not entirely satisfactory. He said that in the last resort the Party was always right. But he could not admit that his criticism had been erroneous. It is evident, from his statements, that Trotsky looked upon his opinions as the correct interpretation of the Party line and, therefore, refused to renounce them.[14]

Trotsky was by no means ready to capitulate. In the fall of 1924 he opened a second campaign against the triumvirate. His pamphlet *The Lessons of October*, published in October, discussed

anew the loss of Party democracy. In contrast to the Workers'
Opposition and other opposition groups, he did not demand a
multi-party system; he consistently advocated the one-party concept. He also maintained that it was nonsensical to consider the
Party as a closed, forever static, entity. In 1917 it had been a
small elite group but now it had become a mass party, and this
called for a fresh, non-dogmatic reappraisal of its role in the state,
he said. These thoughts were colored by some personal considerations. Comparing the situation of the German Communists in
1923 with that of the Russian comrades in 1917, he represented
Zinoviev and Kamenev, by innuendo, as the frightened waverers
who had been willing to miss the hour of decision!

The details of the polemic which followed are uninteresting. But
an important result was that both the men attacked by Trotsky,
as well as Trotsky himself, lost stature in the eyes of the masses.
The winner in the controversy undoubtedly was Stalin. While he
backed his two partners and attempted to minimize Trotsky's role
in the October Revolution, the quarrel helped him to establish
himself above Zinoviev and Kamenev. It was in 1924 that he
elaborated the idea of "Socialism in one country." The same year
was characterized by a succession of further failures of Comintern
politics. Apart from the conflict with England arising from the
so-called Zinoviev letter, there were abortive *coups d'état* in Estonia
and Bulgaria. Zinoviev's reputation was in decline. The Fifth
Comintern Congress, which met in Moscow in June 1924, revolved
around the fight against "Trotskyism." However, the disappointment over the lack of accomplishments by the Comintern affected
all participants.[15] Stalin was the one to benefit by dissatisfaction.
The German delegate, Ruth Fischer, gives an impressive account
of how Stalin quietly, almost furtively, made contact with the
younger foreign delegates to whom revolutionary oratory meant
less than expert organization.

Trotsky, however, was still a power in the country, particularly
in his capacity as Commissar for War, thanks to the halo surrounding him from the Civil War days and the authority he commanded among the younger generation. Would he know how to
use this moral capital. Would he, backed by the Army, join battle
with the Party machinery?

In January 1925, a Party decision by the Politburo forced
Trotsky to resign as Commissar for War. Trotsky did not demur
nor did he call on the Army to resist. Obediently he devoted

his energy to insignificant economic tasks which the Politburo assigned to him. He continued as a member of the Politburo but avoided any public controversy. Was it resignation or party discipline that caused him to forego a Bonapartist solution? Trotsky never had a high opinion of Stalin. In his autobiography he cites a conversation with a Party comrade in 1925, in which he called Stalin the "most eminent mediocrity in the Party." [16] But how, asked his interlocutor, was it possible for a mediocre man to become a leader? "That is the reaction following on the great social and sociological adjustments of the first years of the revolution. The victorious counter-revolution may have its great men; but its first stage, the Thermidor, needs mediocrities." When writing this he was as yet unaware that Stalin embodied both the Thermidor and the Counter-revolution. However, later, in his Stalin biography,[17] he recorded his forebodings. According to this, he had told a friend in 1924 that Stalin would become dictator of the Soviet Union. "So mediocre a person, such a colorless nonentity?" "Mediocrity yes, nonentity no," had been Trotsky's reply. "The dialectic of history has already grasped him and will raise him higher. Everyone needs him . . . all the worms which are crawling out of the soil ploughed up by the revolution . . . he speaks their language and knows how to lead them. Of course, great events . . . may intervene and upset all speculations. But if everything continues to develop as automatically as now, Stalin will just as automatically become dictator."

Trotsky's refusal to put up a fight cannot be explained as quiet submission resulting from physical debility. The gifted ideologist and analyst was born to be a revolutionary, not a dictator. Such a man dared not reach beyond the Thermidor.

Hardly had Trotsky withdrawn into the background than the ties which had so far kept the *troika* together snapped. Curiously enough, while Zinoviev demanded still harsher measures against the all but vanquished adversary, Stalin firmly refused to have him excluded from the party leadership. Soon Stalin began to dissociate himself from his two partners. He ceased to consult them and obtain their agreement on measures which he planned to submit to the Politburo. But he still adhered to the principle of collective leadership by the Politburo. The Big Seven of the Party still belonged to it: Zinoviev, Kamenev, Stalin, Trotsky, Bukharin, Rykov and Tomsky. The *troika,* however, fell apart in the course of 1925.

The "Permanent Revolution" and "Socialism in One Country"

Stalin's theory of "socialism in one country" was developed quite accidentally. Its future importance was not foreseen. In his pamphlet *The Foundations of Leninism*, published early in 1924, Stalin maintained that the proletariat, while able to seize power in a particular country, could not create a socialist economy in that country. The strength of one country might suffice to overthrow its bourgeoisie, but for the final victory of socialism the efforts of one country were insufficient. For this the proletarians of several countries had to join forces.[18]

However, in the course of the same year, Stalin changed this thesis. In an article entitled "The October Revolution and the Tactics of the Russian Communists" which appeared in December 1924, he maintained that he had employed that formula only for tactical purposes in the controversy with the Trotskyites.[19] Socialism could very well be established in one country. Late in April 1925, Stalin submitted his theory to the Fourteenth Party Conference[20] and defended it successfully against all attacks.

Stalin's thesis was, in effect, his answer to the theory of the "Permanent Revolution" which Trotsky had taken over from Marx and applied to the Russian Revolution. According to it, the revolution would of necessity develop from an anti-feudal (bourgeois) revolution into an anti-capitalist (socialist) one. Although it had broken out first in Russia—contrary to the Marxist view, in a backward country—socialism could not be realized here alone. The revolution could not stop at national borders and it had to pass into its international phase. Only when the West revolted as well could socialism be realized on a broad, international foundation. Thus Trotsky conceived the revolution as first being intensive and then extensive; this constituted its double permanence.

Originally, Lenin had a different concept of the Russian Revolution. He believed the Russian peasant was the chief stumbling block in transforming the anti-feudal goals of the revolution into anti-capitalist goals. Hence for the time being Russia would have to be content with the first phase. In 1917, however, Lenin changed his mind and demanded an immediate transition from the bourgeois to the socialist revolution, thereby acknowledging its permanence. The prerequisite for the success of the socialist revolution in Russia continued to be for him its international expansion.[21] In the final analysis a socialist society could only be realized on a world scale.

Disappointment at the failure of the world revolution in the years 1918-1921 prompted Lenin to slow down the speed of socialization. He certainly continued to focus his expectations on the victory of the world revolution and the coming expansion of the socialist experiment. But just as during the long drawn-out transition period he forged the state, which according to Marxism was doomed, into a more solid instrument of the dictatorship of the proletariat, i.e. the Party, the experiences of the Comintern also forced him right up to his last tragic years increasingly to restrict the socialist development to the Soviet Union itself. One searches in vain for any sharp contrast between Lenin's and Stalin's views as announced immediately after Lenin's death. When Stalin announced himself as Lenin's willing disciple and endeavored to furnish in his *Problems of Leninism* a comprehensive exposition of Lenin's views, he could do so without directly misrepresenting him: the difference is apparent solely in an increased simplification and a shifting of emphasis.[22]

Stalin realized that a theory such as Trotsky's of the permanent revolution would in the long run provoke the masses to skepticism as the prospect of world revolution receded ever farther into the future. The Party, too, might become tired of waiting forever. Was the fate of the Russian revolution to depend on the position of Communism abroad? Should one not for the time being be satisfied with building a Russian socialist society?[23]

Here he implied realistic aims which appealed to the young communists of the 'twenties and 'thirties more than the dialectical rhetoric, brimming with ideology, of the great theoreticians.

But even though Stalin entered upon the path of nationalist Communism with his new theory, which quickly was to become dogma, his Marxist schooling as well as his common sense prevented him from abandoning his intellectual fundamentals. All his polemic arguments notwithstanding he knew full well that the Russian peasant, with his stubborn love of private property and the soil, represented an obstacle in the path of the socialist society which could only be realized under conditions of greater productivity of labor and a highly developed industry, not in an economically backward country.

The simplest way out was to solve these two difficulties by means of state intervention. The peasants had to be persuaded, by force if necessary, to carry out collectivization; and Russia's industrialization had to be speeded up. This would silence the two most important arguments against the realization of socialism in Russia. However, the means to be employed were not in harmony with official theory. They consisted above all in perfecting the state's machinery to the highest degree, developing a strong totalitarian political system using terror. This was to be the inevitable result of the trite-sounding theory of "socialism in one country."

Stalin between Right and Left Opposition (1925-1927)

Trotsky's Banishment

In the course of the controversy with Trotskyism and the battle of minds over Stalin's new theory, a re-grouping within the Party leadership took place, beginning in 1925. Gradually a right wing led by Rykov, Bukharin and Tomsky faced a left wing headed by Zinoviev and Kamenev.

This differentiation had little in common with the usual distinction between radical and moderate and nothing at all with the party groupings of the year 1917-18 for example, when Zinoviev and Kamenev represented the moderate point of view and Bukharin the "left" wing. This time the left was characterized by a marked internationalism and a tendency to consider politics from an ideological point of view, while the Right advocated the theory of Socialism in one country and approached the situation from a practical viewpoint, though it wished to limit the use of force out of consideration for the workers and peasants. Remarkably enough even Bukharin, "the greatest theoretician of the Party," now advocated a more realistic policy. It even seems that he had furnished Stalin with the theoretical arguments for the development of his position and that it was only his collaboration that fashioned the primitive rudiments into a scientific structure to support his manoeuvers.

Stalin had a great deal of everyday administrative contact with Rykov, the head of the government, and Tomsky, the trade union chief. This meant a certain identity of viewpoint. Nevertheless, here, too, Stalin sought continually to strengthen his position, by appointing devoted party comrades, on whom he could rely, to important posts. In December 1925, Molotov, Voroshilov and Kalinin were elected to the Politburo to give it ten members. Thus a Stalinist "center" was created within the top body. "Molotov, slow-minded, dull, but endowed with enormous patience and capacity for work, had followed Stalin like a faithful shadow from the days when, in 1913, he had helped Stalin to issue the first number of *Pravda*. Stalin exercised upon him the fascination which an astute and ruthless man often exercises upon people lacking such qualities." [24]

The peasant question became the main issue of controversy. A peasant rising in Georgia in the summer of 1924 was due, in part, to nationalist resistance against the ruthless Bolshevization of the country which Lenin had tried in vain to stop. It also stemmed from the peasants' deep discontent which was by no means confined to Georgia. NEP was in the final analysis a hybrid, encouraging on the one hand private initiative while again and again bringing it into conflict with the socialist sector of the national economy. The peasants, while calling for a larger supply of cheap consumer goods, demanded the highest prices possible for their own products. Industry picked up only slowly, produced little and that at high prices, yet demanded cheap food and raw materials. Bukharin wanted to eliminate this clash of interests by making concessions to the peasants as an incentive to produce and market more food. The development, for example, of efficient farms could be encouraged to supply the cities. Viewed thus the big farmer, the *kulak*—who by Western standards was still a small producer— need not be a threat to the socialist state, as long as the latter controlled industry, banking and transportation. Already demands were being voiced to reduce agricultural taxation, to abolish the restrictions on the hiring of farm laborers, and to permit the long-term leasing of land.

Bukharin was not at all pleased that this neo-NEP was enthusiastically acclaimed in bourgeois circles, as far as they could still express their opinion. Professor Ustrialov, for example, the representative of the bourgeois specialists, who since 1923 were again being used in the nation's economy, greeted Bukharin's peasant policy as a return to normal capitalist methods of production.

The Left hoped to find a way out of the blind alley of NEP by making changes at the opposite end: it demanded a more rapid industrialization, with the idea that an increase in industrial production would also revitalize agriculture. As things stood, the rural areas were threatened by a chronic food crisis. Taxation should be lowered but only for the "middle" and poorer peasants, not for the *kulaks*. In the place of the large farms, collectives should be created, though not overnight and by force, but gradually with the peasants' consent, stimulated by government aid in the form of seeds, machinery, etc.

The debates and controversies over this paramount economic problem, which from 1925 to 1926 generated increasing heat, were not Stalin's first concern. He considered them merely as accompanying phenomena of the real problem, the problem of power. He supported the Right but without entirely following Bukharin's bold agricultural policy; in his eyes the *kulaks* found as little favor as before. His own agricultural and industrial policy, embodied in the First Five Year Plan, was soon to go far beyond what the Left demanded at this point, although with reversed markers. He supported the Right for reasons of power politics, rather than economics. In January 1926 he answered Zinoviev's pamphlet *The Philosophy of an Epoch* with his work *Problems of Leninism*, a collection of essays in which the whole weight of the argumentation was marshalled against Zinoviev and Kamenev. While Zinoviev and Kamenev had obtained the support of Krupskaya, who was closer to them than to any other group, for a memorandum, Stalin in his new book tried to give the impression that he was offering nothing more than an interpretation of Lenin's opinions.

This was also the time when "red corners" *(krasnyi ugol)* were instituted both in private homes and public buildings, where portraits of Lenin and soon also of Stalin were to take the place of the formerly traditional icons with their little oil lamps. Within a few years their number rose in the factories from 7,000 to 42,000.

For a time it seemed as if a reconciliation between Stalin and Trotsky could be achieved, especially as the former had lately refrained from polemic attacks on Trotsky. Radek, in particular, tried to bring the two together. When, in October 1925, M. V. Frunze, Trotsky's successor as Commissar of War, submitted on Politburo orders to a fatal operation, it would have been possible to recall Trotsky. But it was Trotsky himself who accused Frunze's doctors of being willing tools of the Kremlin, which was interested in removing the popular military leader because he was a supporter of Zinoviev. Trotsky was not interested in a reconciliation with Stalin. He felt more and more drawn to the Left by its increasing use of his arguments. Frunze's place was taken by K. E. Voroshilov who followed Stalin's line.

The Fourteenth Party Congress in December 1925 [26] brought the decisive clash with the Zinoviev faction. The Congress had been postponed several times and was now awaited with impatience. From the very start the atmosphere was more highly charged than it had been in years. [27] In his report for the Central Committee, Stalin submitted an economic plan which for the first time clearly pronounced as a goal "the transformation of the Soviet Union from an agricultural into an industrial country." This was based on Stalin's concept of socialism in one country, and unhesitatingly he equated the establishment of a state industry with socialization. Zinoviev's and Kamenev's protests against this blending of concepts, and their fearless opposition to the highhandedness of the General Secretary, provoked Stalin to a stinging counterattack in which he sought to discredit them as "strike breakers of the October revolution." Both sides endeavored to fortify their arguments with quotations from Lenin. The Leningrad party members backed their Party Secretary. Kamenev, too, had his following. But for all that, they were still in a minority. When Kamenev called for a vote of no confidence in Stalin, the majority of the assembly rose and burst into an ovation for the Party, intermingled with quite a few shouts of "Long live Stalin." Did Tomsky imply a warning for Stalin when, replying to Kamenev's attack on the former, he observed that the Politburo had a collective leadership and would never permit the unlimited rule of one individual? Perhaps Stalin remembered these words when ten years later Tomsky was driven to commit suicide.

With a majority of 459 to 65 (with 41 abstentions), the Party Congress accepted Stalin's and Bukharin's political platform. Zinoviev and Kamenev had been defeated. Many of their Leningrad and Moscow comrades had not dared to vote for the opposition.

Drawing his conclusions from the Congress, Stalin's first step was to undermine Zinoviev's position as Party Secretary of Leningrad. To this end he dispatched one of his followers, Sergei Mironovich Kirov, to Leningrad. Kirov had been Party Secretary of Baku, had occasionally been used for special projects of the Central Committee and had proven himself as an energetic organizer and able orator. He managed to make a breach in the citadel of the opposition, Leningrad, and in 1926 he was elected Party Secretary there in Zinoviev's place. Now Zinoviev and Kamenev had no choice but to join Trotsky. Stalin easily discredited them in the public eye by re-publishing their mutual attacks during the past years. Zinoviev and Kamenev had no illusions about Stalin's ruthless drive for power. But they were mistaken if they looked upon their new *troika* with Trotsky as being on a par with the "Stalinist Center." Kamenev believed that if Trotsky and Zinoviev appeared together on the rostrum the whole Party would be won over.[28] Trotsky himself was considerably more skeptical. Stalin's power had already reached such heights that Krupskaya observed that if Lenin were still alive Stalin would probably have him arrested. Nevertheless, after convalescing in Germany, Trotsky seemed to have regained some of his former fighting spirit.

The leaders of the opposition held their conferences in a forest near Moscow. Trotsky still clung to the hope that he had the sympathy of the Red Army circles. Lashevich was still Voroshilov's deputy, even after Frunze's death, and he was a supporter of Zinoviev. Trotsky probably did not plan a direct *coup d'état* against Stalin. But, in the event the new *troika* should succeed in obtaining a majority in the Party, he wanted to create a powerful basis for it. The army was to be for them what the party machine was for Stalin. However, the old revolutionaries shrank from the last decisive step because they believed that a new, fratricidal revolutionary civil war might result in victory for the counter-revolutionary forces. Trotsky did not dare to take the Bonapartist leap and Zinoviev was hardly cut out for such a role.

At a plenary meeting of the Central Committee in July 1926, the opposition, or as it called itself, "the bloc," appeared for the first time before the party membership as a separate group. They made a statement which Stalin sarcastically dubbed the "mutual amnesty." Their criticism accused the leadership of weakening the position of the working class and the poor peasants as against the *kulaks,* the NEP officials and the bureaucrats, and favoring the forces which sought to steer the country back into capitalist tracks. As regards foreign affairs, they observed a decline in the international position of the Soviet Union. A member of the opposition, Y. A. Ossovsky, even went so far as to demand the admission of a new proletarian party. In the place of the current neo-NEP, the "bloc" demanded increased industrialization and a participation of the workers in management through the trade unions. This was an unmistakable declaration of war against the monopolistic control of Soviet industry by the government and the Party, against the perversion of the workers' party into a government party.

The arguments of the opposition were not entirely lost on the meeting. All the more reason for Stalin to isolate it by several changes in personnel, which followed the July meeting in rapid succession. Zinoviev was removed from the Politburo, Kamenev had to give up his post as Commissar for Foreign Trade to A. I. Mikoyan, an Armenian comrade of Stalin's. Lashevich was relieved of his military post and expelled from the Central Committee. Dzierzynski suddenly died from a heart attack at a party meeting on July 20, 1926. Menzhinsky took his place as chief of the GPU and V. V. Kuibyshev succeeded him as chairman of the Supreme Economic Council. If Dzierzynski himself had followed Stalin's and Bukharin's line, the two new functionaries supported Stalin even more willingly. Kamenev had declined the ambassadorship to Japan because he was not yet willing to give up the fight in Moscow. On the other hand, Mme. Kollontai, who was Minister to Norway did not protest when she was transferred further afield to Mexico. The possibility of expulsion from the Party began to hang threateningly over the heads of the opposition. In order to forestall this danger, Trotsky, Zinoviev, Kamenev, Piatakov and Sokolnikov retreated a little and on October 4, 1926, signed a statement admitting that they had offended against the statutes of the Party and pledging themselves to disband their "party within the Party." They also disavowed some of the extremists in their ranks.

This admission of guilt notwithstanding, Trotsky and his associates continued their criticism of the Stalin-Bukharin course with remarkable firmness. Their agitation became dangerous when they began to attend some cell meetings in order to exercise direct influence on the factory workers. The party apparatus took countermeasures; in turn it sent representatives to the meetings, arranged protest demonstrations against opposition members, had their speeches interrupted and sent spies to all cell meetings. A few arrests and deportations began to be made.

A plenary session of the Central Committee and the Central Control Commission, meeting from October 22 to 26, instituted further measures against the bloc. Trotsky was expelled from the Politburo, Kamenev lost his position as candidate of the Politburo, Zinoviev his chairmanship of the Comintern. The fact that Zinoviev was given a seat in the presidium of the governmental planning commission was cold comfort, but it was of some importance that all opposition leaders were still members of the supreme party body, the Central Committee.

The winter of 1926-27 brought a kind of truce. The struggle flared up again following a number of reverses suffered by Soviet foreign policy. In May diplomatic relations between Great Britain and the Soviet Union were broken off, following an incident in the Soviet trade delegation in London. In June, Voikov, the Soviet envoy in Warsaw, was murdered by a Russian émigré. At the same time Stalin's China policy suffered a heavy blow when Chiang Kai-shek turned against the Chinese Communists. In September the Anglo-Russian Trade Union Committee was dissolved.

Encouraged by this accumulation of mishaps, eighty-three leaders of the opposition issued a declaration in the summer of 1927 in which they held Stalin and his associates responsible for these failures. In the midst of the resulting debates in the Central Committee Trotsky's so-called "Clemenceau statement" assumes special importance. It must first be noted that at the time the Kremlin was in the grip of a psychotic fear of an imminent general war against the Soviet Union. In this connection Trotsky stated that in the event of such a war he would take a position similar to that of Clemenceau during the 1917 crisis in France, when accusing the French government of showing insufficient determination, he asked for and obtained dictatorial powers. Here it was again—the spectre of the Bolshevik Bonaparte! It was considered outrageous for Trotsky to accuse the Soviet government of lack of foresight and to declare that if necessary he would work for the overthrow of the government in order to unify the country against a foreign attack. What was customary during a crisis in a bourgeois country sounded like treason in the Bolshevik state.

The result was the expulsion of Trotsky and Zinoviev from the Central Committee. The opposition once more tried to appeal to the masses. For the tenth anniversary of the October revolution they arranged separate demonstrations in Moscow and Leningrad. While not directly aggressive in character, they gave Stalin the opportunity to take decisive measures against his opponents. On November 14, 1927, Trotsky and Zinoviev were expelled from the Party at a joint meeting of the Central Committee and the Central Control Commission. Two days later Trotsky's close friend, the former diplomat Joffe, committed suicide.[29a] A daily mounting terror was now unleashed against the members of the opposition.

The Fifteenth Party Congress which met in December 1927 became a scene of turmoil. In vain did Kamenev and Rakovsky try in a dignified manner to defend the principle of opposition. In vain did the members of the future right wing opposition demand the right of open criticism as part of true party democracy, even though they recognized the need for party discipline. The words of both sides were drowned in a storm of interruptions, whistling and general uproar, until Stalin finally took over with the words: "Enough, Comrades, an end must be put to this game. . . ." The Congress demanded that the leaders of the opposition immediately renounce their opinions and show contrition. This was the price asked for their continued membership in the Party. Kamenev pointed out that such a process was unheard of in the history of Bolshevism, that if they yielded they would dishonor themselves without gaining the respect of the other party members. It was all in vain.

On December 18 the Congress expelled seventy-five leading members of the opposition from the Party. Trotsky refused to meet the demands of the Congress. He was deported to Alma-Ata in Kazakhstan. Zinoviev and Kamenev recanted. The Congress, however, did not accept their surrender, leaving the decision to the General Secretariat.

Collectivization and Industrialization
The First Five Year Plan (1928-1932)

The tenth anniversary of the October Revolution, celebrated with great pomp on November 7, 1927, provided a festive occasion for Stalin to outline his new program.

While peace and international collaboration were stressed as foreign policy goals, the General Secretary proclaimed two paramount aims in the domestic field: radical collectivization of the peasants and creation of a powerful Russian industry. At the same time he promised lower taxes, and old age insurance for workers, peasants and soldiers. Women were to obtain equal status, the fight against illiteracy would continue and the cultural aspirations of the people would be given intensified support.

A month later the Fifteenth Party Congress of December 1927

sanctioned the draft program, thus initiating Russia's great agrarian revolution and forced industrialization, linked to Stalin's name. It was decided to launch the collectivization program and "to pursue the offensive against the *kulaks.*" At the same time the State Planning Commission was entrusted with working out the first Five Year Plan for the entire economy of the Soviet Union.[30]

The pro-peasant era of the years 1925-1927 had primarily been the work of Bukharin. Stalin had let matters take their course, without completely identifying himself with Bukharin's line. He approached this delicate problem with the greatest caution in order to avoid all disturbances in the country during his fight with the left-wing opposition. Even after the Fifteenth Party Congress there was as yet no sign of the subsequent thorough-going collectivization. It developed gradually during the following years, simultaneously with the struggle against the right-wing opposition. But it may be assumed that Stalin was already in 1927 committed to total implementation of his program of socialism in one country. For tactical reasons he may have judged it wiser to progress by stages.

Officially it was admitted[31] that in 1928 it became evident that government grain purchases were short by two million tons of the minimum necessary for feeding the urban population. In other words, a new famine was in the offing because the peasants did not fulfill their quotas. What had happened? Was the reason that the smaller peasants had been unable to produce enough grain to feed the cities and that thus in the final analysis the effects of the agrarian revolution of 1917 over ten years had to be held responsible? Could the feeding of the cities only be assured by larger agricultural units? Or was it that the consequences of sabotage on the part of the *kulaks,* and perhaps of the medium farmers as well, had now become obvious?

Two things must be noted here. On the one hand, in spite of the many defects of the NEP, an improvement in the living standard during the years 1924 to 1927 was indisputable. According to reports from Leningrad, for example, the free market in food showed a sufficient supply as late as 1927; only at the beginning of 1928 did an abrupt shortage of necessities set in. If the improvement in the food supply coincided with the pro-peasant course of the Bukharin era, it may be assumed that sabotage must be ruled out for that period. But what could have caused the peasants to have kept back two million tons when delivering the harvest in

1927, thus suddenly initiating a course of sabotage which cannot be explained by any coercive measures before the year 1928? For nothing is known of a failure of the harvest in 1927.

What is known is that the purchase of foreign grain had always been rejected because is was said that no foreign exchange was available and the Soviet Union had been refused credits. But during all these years, even those of the famine, the export of Russian grain at dumping prices had not been abandoned—a measure which is explicable not in terms of the Soviet Union's economic policy, but the strategy of the Comintern. In the case of a drastic failure of supply, how easily could demand have been satisfied by renouncing this type of export. Thus we are amply justified in doubting the authenticity of the alarming reports of January 1928. They were necessary as a plausible overture for speeding up the collectivization program.

From the viewpoint of the Bolshevik program, the closed season granted to the peasants from 1924 to 1927 had admittedly been an unsatisfactory kind of temporizing. The necessity for thorough collectivization was often discussed even outside Stalin's circle But even Zinoviev and Kamenev, whose economic program wa decidedly based on urban and industrial considerations and who did not possess any real knowledge of rural conditions, advocated a partial and gradual collectivization, in order not to shake the state to its foundations. They favored greater reliance on unions for furthering industrial production and the agrarian economy, too, could undoubtedly be given new life by a system of peasant co-operatives. Such ideas, however, were anathema to Stalin. In them he scented Menshevik or Social Revolutionary deviations. He would rather tolerate the apparent return to capitalist forms— perhaps so that later he could make Bukharin and his assistants responsible for the ideological and, possibly, the economic consequences.

And thus the Politburo, taking its stand on the above-mentioned report, decreed "emergency measures" early in 1928, which were further intensified in the summer. Thus began the campaign against the *kulaks;* its tactical steps consisted in sudden raids on *kulak* farms, requisitions and arrests. Stalin still denied in July 1928— that he wanted to expropriate the *kulaks*: in the existing circumstances that would be folly,[32] and he still shrank from drastic, final solutions. The Five Year Plan, accepted late in 1928, provided for the collectivization of a maximum of 20% of the farms by 1933. As late as the spring of 1929, Stalin still asserted that private agriculture would continue to play a dominant role.[33]

A few months later collectivization was in full swing. Private agriculture had been sentenced to death. And in the last days of 1929 Stalin issued his threatening order for "the counteroffensive against the *kulaks*," in which he spoke of liquidating them as a class. Now he advocated their unqualified expropriation.[34] Now he did exactly what Yuri Larin, a Menshevik economist, had demanded in 1925—directed a second revolution in agriculture. Then Stalin had sternly rejected it as "fanning the class struggle on the land."

What took place in those two years of 1929 and 1930 in Russia was a gigantic agricultural revolution which mercilessly sent the *kulaks* to their doom. An attempt has been made to arrive at a numerical social classification of the total of 25 million Russian peasants—not counting their families. According to it, there were 15 to 18 million middle income peasants between the two extremes of 5 to 8 million poor peasants and 1½ to 2 million *kulaks*.[35] The middle income peasants could be regarded as the actual mass of the Russian peasantry which had to be won over for the reform. It has been correctly pointed out[36] that increasing the supply of tools and machines, credits and technical experts to the collectives *(kolkhozes)*, would have made them attractive to the middle income peasants, whose existence was as precarious as that of the poor. By encouraging economic competition between the *kolkhozes*, with their expected higher living standard, and the private farms, a mixed system of agriculture could have evolved, which might have once again assured a satisfactory food supply for the entire country. A reform of this kind, however, would probably have taken decades, if not generations, to complete in view of the primitive Russian conditions and the lack of adaptability of the Russian peasant. Stalin, on the other hand, was in a hurry. He was in a hurry to prove his theory of socialism in one country in order to solidify his power. And he was a man of such unparalleled brutality and unscrupulousness as to attempt the attainment of this end even at the price of the economic and physical annihilation of millions of human beings.

He decided to try to incite the "village poor" against the *kulaks* by promising them a secure existence as workers in a *kolkhoz*, furnished by the state with machinery and by the expropriated *kulaks* with livestock. In the event, it became clear, the alleged will of the small peasants was too feeble to carry through collectivization. The police were the real galvanizers of the change. The mass of the "middle" and the rich peasants met it with bitter resistance. Food, in huge quantities, was gathered in hidden stores, cattle slaughtered in nihilistic despair, crops were burned, implements broken. It was one of these great elemental peasant revolts against state power which had periodically shaken Russia since ancient times; now it was a Red Czar against whose measures bitterness raged in impotent despair, and the place of a Pugachev or Bolotnikov was taken by the nameless *mouzhik* of the twentieth century as the exponent of Russia's betrayed liberty.

The government was unable to make headway by administrative means. As resistance increased it took to military measures. Rebellious villages were surrounded by Red Army or GPU units and forced to surrender at the point of machine guns. The recalcitrant *kulaks,* even peasants who were suddenly termed *kulaks,* were arrested and deported *en masse* to arctic regions. It was no longer sufficient, said Stalin in a speech of December 1929, to expropriate the *kulaks.* Now it was too late to permit them to join the *kolkhozes.* The result was that millions of peasants, *kulaks* and others, were driven into misery from which there was hardly ever any return.

After the second winter since the start of forced collectivization Stalin himself recoiled from the results of his methods. In a proclamation of March 2, 1930, he tried to put a brake on the drive. The officials entrusted with carrying out collectivization had become "dizzy with their success": this is the headline which Pravda gave to the proclamation.[37] Stalin pretended that his orders had been misunderstood. The officials were made responsible for their excess of zeal. *Kolkhozes* could not be set up by force; whoever tried that was a reactionary fool. A stop had to be put to all excesses.

Thus Stalin suddenly and shrewdly slowed down the process which he had originally speeded up and again established himself as the "spokesman" of the peasants. He probably feared that the agrarian revolution would turn into a peasant revolt against the proletarian state. Protests were made which Stalin answered on April 3, 1930, by having the order to stop all forcible measures represented, not as his personal view, but as that of the Central Commitee.[38]

While on January 6 of that year it had been decided to conclude collectivization along the middle and lower Volga and in the Northern Caucasus by the fall, or by the spring of 1931, this process was now slowed. From 1930 to 1933 only 10% of the remaining peasant holdings were collectivized. At the end of the first Five Year Plan 60% of all holding had been collectivized.

What was a *Kolkhoz?* Each *kolkhoz* was a co-operative forming an independent economic unit which consisted of smaller and larger holdings with joint cultivation of the land. On the average, about 75 peasant families belonged to a *kolkhoz* and they were required to work 100-150 days for the co-operative. All produce in excess of needs was handed over by the *kolkhoz* to the state, primarily grain and potatoes, cattle for slaughter, occasionally sugar beets, vegetable produce, etc. Each *kolkhoz* was administered by a chairman and his assistants, responsible for labor discipline, deliveries, and the increase of production through competition.

At first the "agrarian revolution from above" which was carried out from 1928 to 1930 had catastrophic consequences. A few years later the economic results were disclosed. In January 1934, Stalin himself announced a few figures.[39] In 1929 Russia possessed 34 million horses, in 1933 only 16.6 million were left; 30 million head of cattle and almost 100 million sheep and goats had been slaughtered. Large tracts of land had gone untilled, as during the civil war ten years before. The result was a new famine which was not confined to the cities but invaded also the richest agricultural areas of the Ukraine.

The decimation of the supply of horses had another consequence. An accelerated mechanization of agriculture now became a matter of life and death. The use of oxen or even cows as draught animals had never been customary in Russia; but even now it would not have been feasible as here, too, the losses had been catastrophic. Besides, the *kolkhozes* covered extensive areas and could not be cultivated without tractors. This had been realized even before the mass slaughter of horses. Now speed was imperative. In addition to the 7,000 tractors available in the whole country, 30,000 more were manfuactured in the course of 1929 alone. This, however, was only a beginning. More tractors and machinery of all kinds were urgently needed. New factories had to be set up, iron and coal production had to be increased. More fuel was needed. The country had to be electrified, new power plants had to be erected overnight.

Added to this was the problem of training the peasants and acquainting them with mechanical agriculture. Instructors and agronomists were needed, a new generation of *kolkhoz* farmers had to be raised. Political enlightenment had to keep pace with occupational training. The chairmen and functionaries of the *kolkhozes* had their hands full. Beside the *kolkhozes,* motor and tractor stations (MTS), which were to serve as technical and political centers, were formed into a network which was gradually to extend over the whole country. With the help of the MTS the government could retain a firm hold on the *kolkhozes;* the technical set-up of the MTS could easily be combined with a political apparatus for purposes of surveillance.

This was a task which would have needed decades or generations to evolve organically and without excessive hardships. Here it was compressed into a short span of a few years and tied in, beyond the actual agricultural and industrial requirements, with the victory of a system which, while claiming to be a socialist society, merely represented the consolidation of Stalinist autocracy.

The mechanization of agriculture was obviously connected with Stalin's program of industrialization. When in 1927 the People's Commissar of Finance did not want to allocate more than 650 million rubles for capital investment in industry, Stalin had the Supreme Economic Council raise this sum to 825 million. In fact, during the first year of the Five Year Plan 1,300 million were invested. In the middle of 1929 the capital investments were increased to 3,400 million rubles. In June 1930 the Sixteenth Party Congress was astounded to hear from Stalin that agrarian Russia was about to be transformed into an industrial country; in many branches of industry the Five Year Plan would be fulfilled in 2½ to 3 years. The slogan was to be—the Five Year Plan in four years! In the current year industry would increase production by no less than 50%. Stalin stressed that the Soviet Union was far behind the capitalist countries in the important sectors of basic industries. According to the Plan, the production of pig iron was to be only 5.5 million tons at the end of 1929 as compared with 13.4 million in Germany, and 10.5 million in France. Hence the pace was not to be slackened and whoever advocated that was to be considered a class enemy.

In this way Stalin forced production up. However, the target figures were not always reached. From 1930 to 1931 coal and steel production did not increase by 50% but by 6 to 10%. The development of mining was much too slow and hindered the production and processing of iron. Therefore Stalin constantly pressed for the opening up of new coal and iron mines in the Urals, Siberia and Central Asia. John Scott, an American who worked in Soviet plants during the thirties, tells of the speed with which blast furnaces were erected in the Urals wherever new industries were located, in Magnitogorsk and in other places; he did not ignore the great loss of life in this "battle of the iron producing industry," but he was impressed by the enthusiams of the workers who were imbued with an increasing pride in their achievements.[40] In many instances it was no doubt genuine. This represents the other side of these brutal slave driving methods of Russian industrialization, a side which must not be overlooked.

Its origin must be sought in the patriotic pride which Stalin managed to kindle in the workers during the 'thirties. Characteristic is the famous speech which he made to the industrial executives on February 4, 1931, about "the tasks on the industrialists." [41]

Stalin openly admitted the "bitter experiences" in trying to meet the Plan quotas. The increase had been less than had been expected. It was important to prevent a further slowdown of industry. After a sober and factual discussion of the economic and ideological bases of the problem, he suddenly addressed the meeting with great emotion. Occasionally the question had been raised whether the pace of production could not be slackened. "No, comrades, the pace must not be slackened! On the contrary, we must quicken it as much as is within our powers and possibilities. This is dictated to us by our obligations to our own workers and peasants, to the working class of the whole world. To slacken the pace would mean to lag behind; and those who lag behind will be beaten. But we do not want to be beaten. No, that we do not want!" He went on to say that the history of old Russia had always been that she was primarily beaten because of her backwardness. Beaten by the Tatar Khans, by the Turks, by the Swedes, the Poles and the Japanese, and by the Anglo-French capitalists. "She was beaten because of her backwardness, because of her military, cultural, political and industrial backwardness. She was beaten because to beat her was profitable and went unpunished. Remember the words of the pre-revolutionary poet—'Thou art poor, Mother Russia, but thou art plentiful. Thou art mighty, but thou art helpless, Mother Russia!' " And he continued: "In the past we had no fatherland and could have none. Now, however, that we have overthrown capitalism and the workers wield power in our country, we have a fatherland and shall defend its independence. Do you want our Socialist fatherland to be beaten and to lose its independence? If you do not want that, then you must abolish its backwardness and develop a really Bolshevik pace in the establishment of its Socialist economy. There are no other ways. That is why Lenin said in the time of October—'Either die or overtake and surpass the advanced capitalist countries' *(dognat i peregnat)*. We are fifty or a hundred years behind the advanced countries. We must make good this lag in ten years. Either we accomplish this or we will be crushed." [42]

With this, one of his most important speeches, Stalin shrewdly appealed beyond all reason and ideology to the emotions of his listeners. He re-awakened the dormant patriotism of the Russians, he legitimized it in its new socialist guise and thereby made it palatable also to non-Russian Soviet citizens. The famous old thesis of the admirers of the Europeanization of Russia, of the friends of the West, and of the liberals, that Russia was many generations behind Western European development, that Russia had to make good the headstart of the West—all this was cleverly combined with a quotation from Lenin and coined into a political and economic slogan to spur the already wild pace of industrialization.

Stalin's appeal was meant to fire the imagination and energy of the working masses. Where there was not enough of them, the necessary pressure was applied. He thus drove the people with every means at his disposal into the first Five Year Plan which combined vast achievements with terrible sacrifices. At the end of 1933 pig iron production was already at 10 million tons, at the start of the war with Germany, it stood at 17 million tons. Within a few years Germany and France seemed to have been overtaken —at least in this respect—and the demands voiced on February 4, 1931, had been fulfilled at least in one sector. Within a few years Russia had become an industrial nation.

Did this mean that the goal of the left-wing opposition—which from 1925 to 1927 had opposed the pro-peasant course of the government—had been attained after being appropriated by the government? Had not Stalin made "super-industrialization," which he had then ridiculed, into his own program and carried it to its extreme? The industrialization plan of the opposition and Stalin's

Five Year Plans are not the same. They have different points of departure and most likely lead to different forms of society.[43] One must not forget the role which the opposition had assigned to the unions: participation in management. Though not to the extent demanded by the Workers' Opposition of Shliapnikov in 1921, the Zinoviev group had arrived at an increasingly conscious rejection of state socialism which was bound to turn the employee into a helpless tool of management and its government functionaries, and had indeed already done so in many respects. Stalin's industrialization of the thirties would have been impossible without the prior destruction of all intra-party political labor groups. As it was, not the slightest objection was to be feared from the unions; they had long since ceased to represent the workers. Stalin's industrialization bore the same terrorist character as his collectivization.

Stalin Settles Accounts with the Right-wing Opposition (1928-1931)

Stalin's partnership with Rykov, Tomsky and Bukharin had lasted for the duration of the struggle with Trotsky and the left-wing opposition. Now after the defeat of the common enemy, it soon broke down—just as the *troika* had fallen apart after the first fight against Trotsky.

Rykov, Tomsky and Bukharin themselves thought, after the Fifteenth Party Congress which had pronounced sentence on Trotsky, Zinoviev and Kamenev, that their policy had prevailed. In the Comintern, Bukharin had replaced Zinoviev as chairman. In the Politburo, which now consisted of nine members, the three believed that they could also count on the votes of Kalinin and Voroshilov, so that Stalin with his three supporters—Molotov, and the newly elected members Kuibyshev and Rudzutak—would have remained in the minority. Actually, however, Kalinin, under pressure, and Voroshilov, were loyal followers of Stalin, their moderate pro-peasant views notwithstanding. Among the candidates for the Politburo, Kirov, Kaganovich, Andreyev and Mikoyan also were supporters of Stalin. Because he was able to rely on a majority, Stalin used his old tactics and began to oust Bukharin's supporters from influential administrative positions in the government and in the Party, refraining from an open fight for the time being.

The battle began early in 1928 when Stalin intensified the coercive measures against the *kulaks*. The more stringent the forms of collectivization became, the more obvious became the rift between Stalin's machine and the right-wing opposition.

From March to June 1928 purges took place within the Party involving all functionaries who had not shown the necessary severity in applying the "emergency measures" against the recalcitrant peasants. A further indication that the NEP period had come to an end and that neither bourgeois specialists nor the *kulaks* could any longer expect consideration, was the *Shakhty* trial. In the *Shakhty* district in the Donets basin, acts of sabotage instigated by Russians and foreign capitalists were allegedly discovered. The show trial of the "saboteurs of *Shakhty*" took place in May 1928 and a little-known lawyer, Andrei Y. Vishinski, represented the Party so ably that he was soon launched on his successful career as Public Prosecutor. Stalin suggested that the conclusions to be drawn from this trial were that the Bolshevik industrial executives must acquire the necessary knowledge in order to be independent of the bourgeois experts. This represented, apart from anything else, a rejection of the more conciliatory trend which Bukharin had recently set in motion toward representatives of bourgeois economic concepts.

Outwardly the fiction was still maintained that the Politburo was completely united on the new measures. This was kept up until the end of the year. Only in the spring of 1929 did Stalin drop his mask and openly name Bukharin as the leader of the right-wing opposition. Bukharin himself had become aware of the coming storm. At an early stage of the controversy, in July 1928, he had attempted to establish contact with Kamenev who, like Zinoviev, had been exiled to Northern Russia. According to the report of the former Comintern functionary, Boris Souvarine, Bukharin freely opened his heart to the fallen Party comrade, devoid of any illusions regarding Stalin. He spoke of him as a ruthless intriguer who lived only to satisfy his uninhibited appetite for power; when it suited him he changed his convictions in order to get rid of an opponent. Stalin's policy was bound to have a disastrous effect on the revolution, it was leading the country to the abyss.[44]

Bukharin's plan of joining the former left-wing opposition in a new front against Stalin was no longer feasible. Both Party and people were tired of the eternal squabbles among the elite which had now gone on for five years. Kamenev's and Zinoviev's popularity had waned just as Trotsky's star was on the decline. In addition, Stalin exercised an increasing pressure on the whole political life of the country. Who was still willing to speak his mind openly when the party machine and its security organs had been perfected to such an extent that a thorough control of public and private life was possible? Stalin had brought more and more of his supporters into the machine; each one of them exerted some influence on public opinion, not only of the masses but also of former oppositionists. The number of recanters and opportunists among them grew daily and quite a few of the prominent Trotsky-ists and Zinovievists returned from exile. Among them were Radek, Piatakov, Sokolnikov, Smilga, and finally Zinoviev. Many of them imagined that Stalin's rejection of the right-wing opposition and of the pro-*mouzhik* course might mean a renewed rapprochement with the viewpoint of the former left-wing opposition. They failed to see the gulf which Stalin's industrialization and the persecution of the *kulaks* had created between his and their ideas on these problems.

The exponents of a moderate peasant policy believed that with his tirades against the *kulaks,* Stalin would soon create such confusion in the country that one day his resignation would be inevitable. They thought it would simply be a matter of letting time do its work and being prepared to seize the reins at the right moment.

The right opposition gained supporters from the most varied camps. While Bukharin gathered around him remnants of the bourgeoisie and Tomsky had adherents among the labor functionaries, Rykov stood high in the eyes of leading officials in the Soviets. He found particular support in the Moscow party organization, Kamenev's former domain. Here opposition was voiced not only against the liquidation of the *kulaks,* but also well-founded misgivings were expressed regarding the speed-up in heavy industry. N. A. Uglanov, the Moscow Party secretary, opposed the erection of the Dnieper power plant and demanded that instead of developing heavy industry, more attention should be paid to light industry, as for instance, the Moscow textile factories.

Early in 1929 the right opposition submitted a statement of its views to the Central Committee. It was rejected and and its authors were reprimanded. When Rykov, Tomsky and Bukharin thereupon handed in their resignations, the step was denounced as sabotage.

Stalin continued to consider Trotsky his most dangerous opponent who, from his exile in far-away Alma Ata, persisted in his attempts to influence public opinion. From April to October 1928, he sent 800 political letters, among them a number of quite extensive discourses, and about 550 telegrams, receiving at the same time about 1000 letters and 700 telegrams.[45] In December 1928 a GPU representative handed him an ultimatum to relinquish the "direction of the opposition" against Stalin. Reprisals were taken against his relatives. On January 18, 1929, Stalin requested the Politburo to deport Trotsky from the Soviet Union, an unprecedented step. Over Bukharin's protests, the proposal was passed. Trotsky went to Constantinople, but the arm of his opponent reached him wherever he went—be it legally, through diplomatic pressure on the country of his refuge, or through terrorist measures by GPU agents against him or his family. He was forced from country to country, from Turkey to Norway, from there to Mexico. In the latter he seemed to have found peace.

Next to Trotsky, Stalin directed his hatred against the members of the right opposition. The three leading party members were relieved of their offices in the course of 1929; in November Bukharin was ousted from the Politburo by a plenary meeting of the Central Committee, Rykov and Tomsky were reprimanded. In 1930 V. M. Molotov was appointed Rykov's successor as chairman of the Council of People's Commissars. The post of chairman of the Comintern which Bukharin had last held, remained vacant. D. Z. Manuilsky became one of the most influential figures.

Before the year 1929 was out, Bukharin, Rykov and Tomsky recanted. For the time being they were spared public indictment and trial, actually gaining a delay of nine years, but as they spent most of the time in exile in the provinces, they no longer exerted political influence. The right-wing opposition had been smashed just as the left-wing opposition had been smashed two years before.

But even then the party apparatus could not completely forego the pleasure of making public its victory. In 1930 an "Industrialists' Party," allegedly headed by an engineer, Professor Leonid Ramzin, was portrayed as a branch of the right opposition, suspected of Menshevik sympathies, and accused of sabotaging industrial expansion and conspiring with foreign powers. In a great trumped-up show trial in 1931 almost all defendants were sentenced to prison or exile.

Stalin's victory carried everything before it. A new generation of émigrés — Trotskyists and other oppositionists—gradually made its way abroad. The struggle for power within the Soviet Union was to gain importance for world communism in the thirties; for a time there was talk of founding a Fourth International. The

Soviet Union itself, however, had entered on the path of an autocratic dictatorship by a small oligarchy of party functionaries.

The man who headed this group let himself be glorified by Party
and masses. Already in 1925, only one year after the city on the
Neva had been given Lenin's name, another city, Tsaritsyn, symbol
of the victorious civil war and the dawn of industrialization, had
in his honor become Stalingrad. He was at the height of his power.
Before the close of the fateful year of 1929, Stalin celebrated his
50th birthday on December 21. In Lenin's case, the same anniversary had been celebrated in 1920 in a very modest manner.
Now all the houses and walls of Moscow were covered with huge
portraits of Stalin. Every shop window displayed his bust. In each
district every party secretary praised him in flowery phrases. Stalin
was presented not only as a trustee of Lenin's heritage, but as his
lineal heir who was to complete his work.

CHAPTER 5

SOVIET FOREIGN POLICY 1922-1932

Russian-German Relations after Rapallo

The treaty of Rapallo initiated an era of manifold co-operation between the Soviet Union and the German Republic.[1] The first German ambassador to go to Moscow was Count Ulrich von Brockdorff-Rantzau. As in the summer of 1918, and in accordance with the express wish of the Soviet government, a representative of the "Junker" class rather than a spokesman for the German leftist parties had been sent. Very soon a peculiar kind of confidential relationship developed between the German ambassador and the Foreign Commissar, Chicherin. They were at one in their anti-British views and both favored the medium of informal confidential talks in small groups with a minimum of ceremony.

The treaty of Rapallo gave the Soviet Union a chance to develop its economic relations with foreign countries. Very soon negotiations were started with a view to stepping up German-Russian trade. Brockdorff-Rantzau's efforts were primarily directed toward a strengthening of existing mutual economic ties. In his opinion an exclusively east-oriented German policy was dangerous and he, therefore, rejected the idea of forming a political front against the West. One should try, he believed, to restrain Russia from military experiments; therefore he warned against military collaboration and opposed the trend in that direction, followed by German and Russian military circles.[2]

The primary concern of the Kremlin, however was at first neither the economic nor the military aspect of its relations with Germany, but rather the development of the revolutionary movement in that country. Here it was not so much Chicherin, the exponent of the official foreign policy, as Zinoviev, chairman of the Comintern, who had first say.

In this respect the French occupation of the Ruhr in January 1923, presented an excellent opportunity to steer the agitation of the working masses into proper channels. Officially the Soviet government opposed the French sanctions and pointed out that they might conjure up the danger of a new war. At the same time it assured the German proletariat of its sympathy. Events seemed to be moving toward a Communist rising in Germany; the question was what attitude the Comintern was to adopt in such an event. On March 25, 1923, a district party congress convened in Essen to map out a program for the seizure of local power by the Communists. A workers' Republic in the Rhineland and in the Ruhr was to be the base from which a Red Army was to advance on Central Germany and seize power in Berlin.[3]

The Executive Committee of the Comintern, however, rejected the plan of the German Communists and threatened to disavow any insurrection in the Rhineland that might take place. In the meantime the great Bolshevik expert on Germany, Karl Radek, set the stage for a dangerous game in Berlin. Since the occupation of the Ruhr, German-Russian relations had grown so friendly that he could officially establish himself at the Soviet Embassy. From there he put the finishing touches on publications of the *Rote Fahne;* from there he also entered into discussions with representatives of the government and the military as to what stand the Soviet Union would take should war break out between France and Germany. Backed by authority, Radek was in a position to promise a friendly neutrality. At the same time, Moscow put its seal of approval on the passive resistance movement which the German government had proclaimed against the occupation of the Ruhr. This became apparent in Radek's famous "Schlageter speech" in Moscow. Leo Schlageter, as representative of nationalist resistance groups had organized acts of sabotage in the Ruhr area, had been convicted by a French court martial and shot on May 26, 1923. Radek honored his memory as a "brave soldier of the counter-revolution" who also deserved the sincere admiration of the soldiers of the revolution.

It was obvious that Radek could not have thus paid tribute to nationalist groups in Germany on his own initiative. He had been authorized by the Politburo to do this. The Soviet Union extended a hand to Berlin because it feared nothing so much as a German-French settlement and because Anglo-Russian tensions had again intensified during this period. Radek's suggestions were based on a concept about which Zinoviev himself, it is true, was not very enthusiastic, but which was of considerable importance to the Bolshevik economist, Bukharin as well as the Hungarian Communist, Eugene Varga. It was the idea that through the policy of reparations, Germany would sink to the status of an industrial colony of England and France—a threat affecting equally the German worker and the bourgeoisie. This would lead to the necessity of a German "National Bolshevism," or a common front with the bourgeoisie as demanded by Bukharin at the Fourth Comintern Congress.

In the summer of 1923 the Ruhr crisis moved towards its climax. While separatist currents grew stronger in the Rhineland, the Communists organized military formations and called upon the factory workers and agricultural laborers to go on strike. In August the German government resigned. In several cities risings took place, in Bavaria right-wing radical groups became active, Germany seemed to fall apart. Then suddenly the picture changed when Stresemann was entrusted with the task of forming a government. Strict orders outlawing the general strike were issued and an end to the passive resistance in the Ruhr was agreed upon with England. Fearing Bolshevization, the moderate parties gave up the continuation of the pro-Soviet plans of the spring. In Moscow, on the other hand, this turnabout was considered so serious that the leaders of the Comintern interrupted their vacation in the Caucasus. The Politburo decided to drop the National-Bolshevik line and to organize a Communist rising in Germany,[4] Everywhere illegal military units of the KPD were organized. At the same time an apparatus for the spread of terrorism was set up. All these organizations were promised unlimited financial assistance. In the year 1923 alone more than one million dollars were poured into Germany, some *via* the Berlin embassy, some directly to the "apparatuses."[5]

Definite dates had been set for the outbreak of the Communist rising in Germany. The details of the plan were arranged during a special session of the Executive Committee of the Comintern which Zinoviev had convoked in Moscow at the end of September. Streamers could already be seen in Moscow carrying the slogans: "How Can We Help The German Revolution?" or "The German October Is Near!" In fact the Kremlin planned to let a Communist revolution break out in Bulgaria at the end of September and one in Germany at the beginning of October.[6] Trotsky even urged the preparation of an exact timetable with the date of climax set for November 7 or 9, the two symbolic dates.

Although the rising in Bulgaria miscarried, the following program was contemplated for Germany. After a brief period of preparing the ground by intensive propaganda, Communist representatives were to take over the governments of Thuringia and Saxony, and workers were to be armed as battalions of the "Red Hundreds." As soon as the rising had been proclaimed, one Red Army was to march from Saxony to Berlin and another from Thuringia to Munich and gather all the revolutionary forces on the way. Special significance must be attributed to the decision to send several hundred Red Army officers to Germany as military experts to command the military formations of the KPD.[7] Among them were many non-Russian Communists who were believed to have a better knowledge of conditions in Central Europe. They were under the jurisdiction of the special international liaison division of the Comintern (OMS),[8] which had its representatives at the Soviet Embassy in Berlin. The direction of this military-political organization in Germany (MP), which was intended to form the nucleus of the future German Red Army, was in the hands of a Soviet Division Commander, Skoblevsky.[9] A number of leading Comintern delegates went to Germany, headed once again by Radek. With feverish energy, preparations for the great insurrection were made in all sectors. A Commission of Seven in Berlin directed operations. Excitement was mounting daily. The outbreak of a nationalist *coup d'état* was to be feared at any moment. Meanwhile inflation soared to an all time high.

On October 10 the Communists, as planned, formed a new government in Saxony; four days later President Ebert ordered the occupation of Saxony and Thuringia by German troops. Now everything depended on the directives issued by the Comintern. The Comintern had an altogether wrong conception of the striking power of the German Communists. A telegram from Zinoviev ordered the immediate arming of fifty to sixty thousand men;[10] everything else was to be decided by a conference of workers' organizations in Chemnitz. They did not know in Moscow that the bulk of the military equipment existed only on paper and that preparation for the rising had been organized extremely poorly. The great Communist insurrection in Saxony and Thuringia turned out to be a bubble which burst at the first breath of reality. In Chemnitz the leaders could not make up their minds about calling a general strike. Incidents occurred when the German Army marched in, but measures against the Communists were carried out nevertheless. The insurrection had failed.

A handful of activists rose on October 22 in Hamburg. Led by E. Thaelmann, the Communists attacked the police precinct stations. They thought that all Germany had risen and that Russia would soon come to the assistance of the KPD. Rumors spread to the effect that the Soviet fleet was ready to enter the port of Hamburg, that the Red Army had marched into Poland, etc. It was only at the end of the second day of the fighting that the leaders of the "Red Hundreds" received the order to retreat. On the third day the Hamburg rising, too, collapsed.

November 9, 1923, thus did not mark the climax of a Communist revolution as Trotsky had hoped, but on the contrary, it was the National Socialists under the leadership of Adolf Hitler who sought to rouse the masses with their "Munich Putsch" and failed just as the Communists had in Saxony, Thuringia and Hamburg. The KPD was temporarily prohibited in Germany and went underground.

For the Comintern the failure of its greatest and most representative revolutionary attempt in the heart of Europe meant a severe set-back. It went hand in hand with a considerable loss of prestige for Zinoviev and contributed not a little to his downfall in his struggle for power with Stalin.

After the events of 1923, relations between Berlin and Moscow became considerably cooler. In May 1924 a serious conflict arose. The German Communist Bozenhardt sought asylum in the building of the Soviet Trade Delegation in Berlin. Although the extraterritoriality of the Trade Delegation had been guaranteed in the trade agreement, since the monopolization by the Soviet government of Soviet foreign trade conferred governmental status on Soviet foreign trade agencies, the German police forcibly entered the building and searched it. The Soviet government thereupon broke off economic relations with Germany; the Trade Delegation was closed down. At the end of July 1924 however, the conflict was settled and Germany recognized once more the extraterritoriality of the Trade Delegation. The same year saw the show trial of two German students in Moscow who were accused of having planned attempts on the life of Soviet dignitaries. They were sentenced to death but were exchanged, together with twelve other Germans, for Russian Communists who had been arrested in

Germany in 1923. German engineers, too, who had been hired in Russia as foreign experts during the NEP period, were suspected of sabotage, tried and sentenced.[11a]

In spite of these strains, trade between the two countries increased. An important stage was reached by the trade agreement which was concluded on October 12, 1925.[11] The most-favored nation clause applying to both countries was of great importance. On this basis trade between the two countries expanded considerably. Germany granted long-term credits to the Soviet Union and started delivering installations for mines and coking plants, machines for the metal, paper and sugar industries, electro-technical goods, etc.

Stresemann, the German Foreign Minister, was watched somewhat suspiciously by the Kremlin because of his efforts to reach a settlement with the West. It is true that he warned more than once against "flirting" with the Bolsheviks; in a strangely prophetic vein he wrote in a letter dated September 7, 1925:[12] "When the Russians will have reached Berlin and the Red Flag will wave from the Palace, they will be satisfied to bolshevize Europe as far as the Elbe and will throw the rest of Germany to the French to devour." Otherwise, however, he was "quite ready to reach an understanding on a different basis with the Russian state in whose evolutionary development" he believed.[13] For example, he was all in favor of strengthening trade ties. In this respect, however, he was somewhat influenced by the latest NEP phase in the Soviet Union and the tendencies in relation to the capitalist forces which Bukharin represented. He imagined that an increasingly closer inter-relationship between the Soviet Union and the capitalist West would pave the way for an evolutionary development in Russia.[14]

After the signing of the Locarno Treaty on October 16, 1925,* Stresemann emphasized that Germany wanted to maintain cordial relations on both sides. In the Kremlin the news of the conclusion of the Locarno treaty at first caused some alarm. Stalin maintained at the Fourteenth Party Congress in December 1925, that Locarno was pregnant with a new war in Europe, that it was nothing but a continuation of Versailles.[15] In reality, Germany proved by the trade agreement of October 12, that the conclusion of the treaty with the West did not affect its relations with the Soviet Union. It was of particular significance that Germany expressly reserved the right to refuse, on the basis of Article 16 of

* The actual signing took place in London, on December 1, 1925.

the League of Nations Covenant, to participate in possible sanctions against the Soviet Union. A discussion during December 1925 between Stresemann and Chicherin, who had stopped over in Berlin after a visit in Paris, brought mutual satisfaction.

In the Berlin Treaty of April 26, 1926, it was thus possible to continue along the lines adopted at Rapallo. Both states agreed to remain in friendly contact as before and to consult with each other on all political and economic questions. In case one of the two partners was attacked by a third power, the other was to maintain neutrality; the same was to apply in case of an economic boycott. It was agreed to submit any disputes between the parties to arbitration. The Treaty of Berlin was to be in force for five years; in 1931 it was extended for another three years.

While Soviet Russia remained somewhat distrustful of the "Spirit of Locarno," the news of Germany's entry into the League of Nations in September 1926 was received with equanimity. It was only later that Germany's efforts to maintain the middle ground between West and East, were depicted as a deceitful game in which Germany used its relations with the Soviet Union as a bargaining object in its dealings with the Western powers.[10] In reality the Treaty of Berlin at the time gave the Kremlin the asurance that Germany would not join any anti-Soviet interventionist bloc, a fact which was to be of no mean importance in the tense world situation of the coming years.

German-Russian trade took another upward swing in 1927. The government in Berlin set aside the sum of 330 million Reichsmark for so-called "Russian credits" as security to German exporters. Soviet payments were actually made punctually. When Count Brockdorff-Rantzau was succeeded as ambassador in Moscow by Herbert von Dirksen, trade activities between the two countries were nearing their peak—during the period between 1928 and 1933 tens of thousands of German engineers and skilled workers were in Soviet employ. A trade agreement of December 21, 1928 and the creation of a "Russian Trade Committee of German Commerce and Industry" contributed to a further increase of German exports to Russia. A "German Industry Week" which was organized in January 1929 in Moscow by the German-Russian Society for Culture and Industry under the sponsorship of Einstein, bore witness to this. The fact that even during the world-wide economic crisis of 1929-1932 the Russian market could still be expanded, showed how important business with Russia was for the German industrial export trade. During the period from 1929 to 1932 alone, Russia's share of the total German exports of machine tools, for instance, rose from 10% to 75%! At the height of the crisis, in February 1931, representatives of leading German industrial plants went to Moscow at the invitation of the Soviet Government in order to study Russian market conditions. As a result, a new agreement was signed in August 1931, guaranteeing further deliveries valued at a total of 300 million Reichsmark.

During these years military collaboration between the Red Army and the Reichswehr continued undisturbed. Apart from the training of German pilots and tank crews in Russia, visits were exchanged by members of the General Staffs and there was an exchange of experiences gained at maneuvers.[17] At the Soviet maneuvers near Kiev, in 1931, the Chief of the German Army Command, General von Hammerstein, for the first time watched the performance of paratroops.

Occasionally, news of this collaboration reached the general public, particularly through German Social Democratic or pacifist media. It even became the subject of parliamentary debate in the Reichstag in Berlin; in Soviet Russia the public paid little attention to it. German Communists were in a quandary. In 1927, when the dock workers in Stettin, unaware that the German armaments industry also supplied the "Fatherland of the Workers," refused to load munitions for the "imperialist powers," their strike was quickly called off by Moscow. The possibility which existed at that time even for a meeting of intellects, was demonstrated by the Russian Historians' Conference which was held in Berlin in 1928, on the initiative of the Russian expert, Professor Otto Hoetzsch. This was the last occasion when exponents of official Marxist thinking were re-united at one table with Russian émigré bourgeois scholars. This experiment, however, remained an isolated event and it may not have been by mere chance that immediately following the Berlin Congress, steps were taken to purge Russian historical science of bourgeois elements.

The political relations between Moscow and Berlin during these years lacked the closeness which they had had during the spring of 1923. Simultaneously with Brockdorff, his actual counter-part on the Soviet side also withdrew from the political scene. As a result of Chicherin's illness, the conduct of the current affairs at the Foreign Commissariat devolved increasingly on M. Litvinov. When the latter finally took over the direction of the Commissariat on July 21, 1930, Soviet foreign policy entered a new phase. It was to lead to a growing understanding with the Western powers and the Little Entente.

Conflicts with Great Britain

After the surprise of the treaty of Rapallo, Soviet-British relations were again overshadowed by distrust.[18] The course of those years is marked by a whole chain of incidents. English fishing vessels were confiscated near Murmansk, a British steamer before Odessa was fired on; English experts in Russia were under constant suspicion and the arrest and shooting of several engineers was a characteristic example of the harshness of Soviet methods. Again and again anti-British demonstrations took place in Moscow. Hostile propaganda accusations were exchanged. Chicherin accused England of anti-Soviet agitation in the Baltic states; Lord Curzon, understandably, was upset by the support the Sinn Feiners in Ireland received from the Comintern, until things were settled late in 1921. During the single month of April 1922, the Comintern, in fact, spent 5 million gold rubles exclusively on the financing of revolutionary incitement in England and in France.

The center of these agitations was not, however, in Europe but in Asia. When in the spring of 1923 the incident of the fishing vessels occurred in the Far North, the British admiralty dispatched a cruiser to the White Sea. The ultimatum of the British government of May 8, threatened to break off trade relations, but the chief demand of the note was the cessation of anti-British propaganda in India, Persia and Afghanistan. In view of the immediate danger of an armed conflict, the Soviet government, by a note dated May 23, gave in to the British demands and paid compensation for the confiscated vessels as well as damages to the next of kin of the British subjects who had been killed. Regarding the question of anti-British agitation in Asia, the note contained a long and ambiguous statement.

In contrast to the British conservatives, the Labor Party advocated a more conciliatory Russian policy. While it had already exerted pressure in this direction, Ramsay MacDonald's first Labor Cabinet granted *de jure* recognition to the Soviet Union on February 2, 1924. It set off an entire chain of recognitions by other nations. A few days later, on February 8, Fascist Italy followed the British example; then Norway followed on February 13; Austria on February 25; Greece on March 8; Sweden on March 15; Denmark on June 18; France on October 28; several non-European states followed too.

Recognition by Britain, however, did not stop the Comintern from continuing to stage mass demonstrations for the independence of Ireland, Egypt and India. The revolutionary ferment in England was to be aided, precisely at this stage, with all possible means. "We shall support MacDonald as the rope supports the hanged," Zinoviev exclaimed with tasteless cynicism. And Lenin seconded him with "MacDonald remains a bourgeois pacifist through and through, a petit bourgeois reformer who knows the class struggle only as a rhetorical cliché, like all those imposters, sophists and schoolmasters of the bourgeiosie." In this work the Comintern had at its disposal a number of information bureaus, special missions and other agencies as operational bases. Besides the official diplomatic offices, the trade missions particularly were first and foremost used as espionage and agitation centers. Protests regarding Communist propaganda were usually countered in Moscow with the observation that the Soviet government was not responsible for the activities of the Comintern organs.

Christian Rakovsky became the first Soviet ambassador to London. He had formerly been the president of the Supreme Soviet of the Ukraine, and in 1922 had been a member of the Soviet Delegation at the Genoa Conference. However, King George V ignored the representative of a regime which had killed his cousin, the Czar,[19] at all social functions. No agreement was reached regarding the Russian debts or compensation for British private property lost in Russia.

The Anglo-Soviet negotiations dealing with these questions and also with the Soviet request for a loan, were opened in London on April 14, 1924. They dragged on and finally on August 8 they led to the conclusion of a general agreement which postponed the settlement of the debt problem until a later date. The trade agreement signed at the same time was to replace the Anglo-Soviet agreement of March 16, 1921; it granted to both parties the most-favored-nation treatment. The Soviet trade delegations in England were granted the privilege of extraterritoriality.

However, the agreements of August 1924 were not to become effective. The incident of the Zinoviev letter became the stumbling block.

On October 10, 1924 the British Foreign Office came into possession of a document allegedly representing a letter from Zinoviev to the British Communist Party. In it the party was ordered to go beyond ordinary agitation and to form special cells in the British Army as well as in armament factories and munition supply depots. "In the event of an imminent war," it said, "one can, with the help of the latter and in co-operation with the transport workers paralyze all war preparations of the bourgeoisie, thus transforming the imperialist war right from the start into a class war." Finally, steps were to be taken to train military specialists as future leaders of the British Red Army.[20] The letter was signed by Zinoviev and the Finnish Communist, Kuusinen, as chairman and secretary of the Comintern, respectively. MacDonald asked the Foreign Office to test the authenticity of the letter and to address a protest to the Soviet Embassy. Meanwhile the Zinoviev letter became one of the most important weapons in the British election campaign. The editor of the British Communist paper "The Workers' Weekly," had issued an appeal to the British soldiers not to shoot at the workers during illegal strikes. He had been arrested but had soon been released at the Attorney General's request. A vote of no confidence in connection with this episode led to new elections. Scared by the Communist threat, the electorate repudiated the Labor party and the MacDonald government resigned. On November 21 the Conservative Cabinet, led by Stanley Baldwin, denounced the treaties with Russia.

The genuineness of the Zinoviev letter has never been proved. Zinoviev himself in an interview with foreign correspondents branded it a forgery. An investigation commission appointed by the Labor party reached the same conclusion. Strangely enough, the affair seems to have played a decisive role in the power struggle within the Russian Communist party. It may have suited Stalin to see Zinoviev branded as the marplot of an Anglo-Soviet rapprochement in his position as chairman of the Comintern.

The new Conservative Cabinet resumed complaints about anti-British agitation. The Secretary of State for India, Lord Birkenhead, pointed out in Parliament that unrest was being stirred up in Asia by a foreign power which aimed at the destruction of the British Empire; Bolshevism, he said, was "a strange and serious epidemic." The new Foreign Secretary, Sir Austen Chamberlain, also assumed a firm attitude in December 1924 when he came to an agreement with Herriot in Paris regarding counter-measures against Communist propaganda in the colonies. The plan of a joint démarche in Moscow, however, was dropped.

When the great coal strike broke out in England in 1926 the press saw, not entirely without reason, the hand of the Comintern. On June 12 the Cabinet protested the funds reaching England from Russian trade unions for the support of the strike, and published a "Blue Book" containing documents found during a search of the offices of the British Communist Party. The British oil industry demanded an economic boycott of the Soviet Union and the severing of diplomatic relations.

The Soviet press, too, was unsparing in its attacks during this period, singling out Churchill and Chamberlain as chief villians. The latter was a particularly popular target of Soviet cartoonists; unrestrained by considerations of taste, a straw effigy of Chamberlain was burned at a big demonstration in Moscow amidst the derisive howling of the mob.

The situation became even more tense when on May 21, 1927, the British police, on orders of the Home Secretary, forced its way into the London offices of the British-Soviet concern "Arcos," [22] confiscated the diplomatic mail of the trade mission, and even searched the persons of the Russian employees. The surprise raid brought substantial material to light. It became apparent that "Arcos" and its staff of almost one thousand people had become a regular center of Bolshevik espionage and subversive propaganda in England. Among the confiscated documents taken to Scotland Yard in three trucks, there were photocopies of secret documents regarding the most recent discussions between the General Staffs of England and France. A White Book assembled a number of documents for a massive indictment of the Soviet Union. Subsequent Soviet protests did not convince British public opinion.

Decisive debates concerning this situation were held at the end of May. Although Lloyd George spoke at length about the harmful economic consequences of a diplomatic break with the Soviet Union, a majority in Parliament agreed with the Cabinet. Severance of diplomatic relations and termination of the trade agreement were voted by 346 to 98. On May 27, 1927, Chamberlain informed the Soviet chargé d'affaires, Rosengoltz, of the decision. Canada likewise broke off relations with Russia.

In Moscow there was considerable excitement. The Fourth Congress of Soviets, meeting in Moscow in April 1927, had already been told that the foreign situation was perturbing, even dangerous. Several speakers, attacking the League of Nations, described it as a mouthpiece of French and British imperialism. The endeavors of the Geneva disarmament commission. in whose deliberations a Soviet representative had participated, were denounced with biting sarcasm. Now, as diplomatic relations with Great Britain had been broken off, Rykov, as chairman of the Council of People's Commissars, described the British decision as a first step toward war. The Moscow press accused Great Britain of aggressive intentions. In all seriousness England was thought to be preparing for a "crusade" against the Soviet Union, at least for a blockade similar to that of the civil war years. That this was not intended is, for example, proved by the discussion between Chamberlain and Stresemann in Geneva in June 1927. There, in view of the friendly relationship between Germany and the Soviet Union, the British Foreign Secretary asked his German colleague to intervene with the Moscow government.[23]

The estrangement continued through 1928. The Labor Party changed its pro-Russian attitude. The tension was finally lessened for economic reasons. Up to this point the Soviet Union had occupied a high place in England's foreign trade. Now British-Russian trade had shrunk uncomfortably and Germany was about to gain a big economic advantage. Decisive, however, were the efforts of a group of American oil companies, headed by John D. Rockefeller, to obtain favorable delivery agreements from the Soviet Union. In view of this competition, Sir Henry Deterding, the president of the British Royal Dutch Oil Company abandoned his antagonism toward the Soviet Union in the spring of 1929. In the summer, a delegation of British industrialists went to Russia. The British textile industry was also in need of markets for its products. An Anglo-Russian committee was created to study the possibilities of economic co-operation.

MacDonald's second Labor government (1929-1931) also favored the resumption of diplomatic relations. The first gesture in this direction was the refusal to grant Trotsky a British entry permit. On July 17, 1929, the Norwegian Minister in Moscow handed Litvinov, the Deputy Foreign Commissar, a note bringing the "cold war" of the years 1927-1929 to an end. Litvinov's very presence at the foreign office ensured a more cordial relationship between the two countries. Married to an Englishwoman, the niece of the newspaper publisher Sir Sidney Low, he had found in England a second home during his years of exile. He spoke English fluently and enjoyed the role of a great admirer of English life and culture. In December 1929 the new Soviet ambassador, G. Y. Sokolnikov, presented his credentials in London. The Soviet Union assured the British government that it would not interfere in the country's domestic affairs.

Soviet Russia and the Border States

Since the Revolution a broad zone of buffer states separated Soviet Russia from central and western Europe. The so-called border states from Finland down to Rumania had either completely seceded from Russia or had wrested territories from the former Russian domain, substantial as in the case of Poland, less substantial as in the case of Rumania. Russia's former western allies had tried during the civil war to transform this intermediate zone into a kind of *cordon sanitaire* which would prevent the further westward spread of Bolshevism. They had sought to give moral support to these nations in their fight for freedom even if actual military help had been supplied solely by Germany; after the peace treaties they continued to promote the independence of these states. British efforts were concentrated mainly on the Baltic states,[23a] the French were concerned with Poland and with the countries of the Little Entente to which Rumania belonged. Finland, supported by the strong sympathies of the Nordic and Anglo-Saxon countries, particularly the United States, was the first country able to stabilize its domestic and foreign status.

In the peace treaties of 1920 and 1921 the Soviet Union had recognized the independence of the border states; only with Rumania no treaty was concluded and Russia had not committed herself to relinquishing Bessarabia. It was, therefore, understandable that as early as March 3, 1921, Rumania concluded a military agreement with Poland.

Poland, whose ambitions to become a great power had been encouraged by the grant of a council seat in the League of Nations, attempted to extend her influence northward. In March 1922 the Polish government invited Estonian, Latvian and Finnish representatives to a conference in Warsaw. Lithuania had not been invited in view of the tension with Poland over the Vilna question. The result of the talks was the Warsaw agreement of March 17—

a non-aggression pact to run for five years, providing for mutual consultation in the event of an unprovoked attack by a third party. Undoubtedly it represented an attempt to form a bloc under Polish leadership which was to protect the participating countries from Soviet aggression. In a sense France sponsored this Warsaw creation as she was eager to provide a counterweight to possible British ties with Germany as well as with Russia. In no case, however, did this represent a general anti-Soviet trend; the bloc resulted from the Baltic states' natural need for security which had its origin in the experiences of the years 1918-1920. This was also the motive for the alliance concluded by Estonia and Latvia in1923. Russia, however, tended to denounce any such attempts at forming regional groups along her immediate borders as hostile acts.

Immediately after the Warsaw agreement, the Soviet government suggested a conference with the Baltic states with a view to expanding trade relations. However, the true reason for this meeting, which took place at Riga during March 1922, was the desire to undermine the united front of the Baltic states.[24] Neither Finland nor Lithuania took part in the conference. The results were a few unimportant agreements concerning rail traffic and barter trade and some academic statements about a reduction of armaments. A disarmament conference, convened in Moscow in June of the same year, at which the states not represented at Riga were also present, remained barren of results as the Soviet government rejected the proposal of the border states to conclude a non-aggression pact first and then to reduce armaments.

Relations between Soviet Russia and the border states remained correct but very formal; trade revival, too, was negligible. The policy of the Comintern made sure that the small nations' distrust of Soviet Russia was not diminished. Its chairman, Zinoviev, was particularly interested in Estonia which he regarded as being located at the very doorstep of his Leningrad office. The Soviet envoy in Reval, Mikhail Kobetsky, was his special confidant and at the same time the Comintern agent. When, in November 1924, the Estonian government, in the light of the events in London, conducted a search of the Estonian Communist Party's offices and made some arrests, Zinoviev decided on an audacious surprise operation which he also hoped would boost his sinking reputation. A group of sixty Red Army officers was smuggled across the border and charged with the organization of a *coup d'état* in Reval.[25] On

December 1, 1924, the Communists went into action. However, the Estonian army countered promptly and vigorously. After a few hours the attempted *coup* was crushed.

Stalin's adherents in the Communist party of the Soviet Union saw in Zinoviev's Reval fiasco a new defeat for their opponent and a welcome aid in bringing about his removal from the leadership of the Comintern.[26]

Events such as those experienced by Estonia made constant watchfulness advisable. In all the border states the Soviet embassies served at the same time as agitation centers for the indigenous Communist parties. In January 1925 Poland once again initiated new negotiations, this time including Finland. At a conference in Helsingfors the question of an arbitration agreement was discussed; beyond that Poland was desirous of concluding a military agreement. Of the three Baltic states, Lithuania maintained its hostile attitude to Poland over the Vilna question; however, Latvia and Estonia, too, showed little inclination to be dragged into bigger conflicts under Poland's leadership.[27] Finland was more concerned with her Scandinavian relations. Poland's plan thus came to nothing and in other respects, too, the close ties between the border states were loosened during the late twenties, the Latvian-Estonian alliance alone remaining.

This development was welcomed in Moscow. For a long time a weak point in the front of Baltic solidarity had been sought and this was found in Lithuania where leftist circles were inclined to heed Soviet proposals. Early in 1926 the Soviet Union proposed non-aggression pacts with the border states, including Poland and Finland. It would undoubtedly have been safer to meet the Soviet Union collectively rather than individually; however, when Poland made this the excuse for rejecting an agreement with Moscow, she was also motivated by the desire to play a leading role among the border states. The Soviet proposals found an all-the-more-willing listener in Lithuania when a leftist government was formed in May. On September 28 Lithuania struck out on her own and signed a friendship and neutrality pact with the Soviet Union. At this point Latvia, where a left-wing government was also at the helm,[28] agreed to negotiate too. But a Latvian-Soviet neutrality agreement, drawn up in the spring of 1927, was never signed as the Latvian government had to resign on account of it; for the time being the only result of the negotiations was a trade agreement. Only Estonia still refused to conclude a treaty with the Soviet Union.

No diplomatic relations had so far been established with the countries of the Little Entente. In Czechoslovakia and, especially, in Yugoslavia numerous Russian émigré organizations had been formed and the remnant of Wrangel's army had found refuge there. Rumania tried to obtain guarantees regarding her claim to Bessarabia. In 1926 she renewed her military pact with Poland and concluded agreements with France and Italy in which Bessarabia was recognized as part of Rumania. Moscow's protests in Paris and Rome were ineffective. Franco-Soviet relations, which had always been very cool, became even colder. In 1927 the Soviet Union's foreign relations were subjected to severe strains in Eastern Europe too. On June 7 the Soviet ambassador, P. L. Voikov, was shot in Warsaw by a Russian émigré, an incident reminiscent of the attempted assassination of V. V. Vorovsky, the Soviet representative in Lausanne in 1923. The Soviet government took reprisals against alleged Polish spies in Russia. Only after the signing of the Kellogg-Briand pact outlawing war, was Soviet foreign policy once more able to resume its plan for a treaty system in Eastern Europe.

In the absence of diplomatic relations with the United States, the Soviet Union had not been invited to the negotiations preceding the pact. After it had been signed on August 27, 1928, by the representatives of the Western powers as well as by Germany, Italy, Poland, Czechoslovakia and Japan, the Commissariat for Foreign Affairs sharply criticized the pact, characterizing it as aggressively aimed at the encirclement of the Soviet Union. These accusations were invalidated when the Soviet Union was subsequently invited to sign the pact. On September 6 Russia agreed to do so.

Now the Kellogg-Briand pact was to be used as a basis for the creation of a series of Eastern European treaties. In December 1928, the Kremlin proposed to Poland and Lithuania that the pact be regarded as effective even if other states should not ratify it. Lithuania agreed to this in principle and, after some hesitation, Poland also agreed on the condition that similar simultaneous agreements were to be signed by Estonia, Latvia and Rumania. Litvinov agreed to this. On February 9, 1929, the East Pact was signed in Moscow by representatives of the Soviet Union, Poland, Rumania, Estonia and Latvia. The Soviet government hoped thus to prevent the Kellogg-Briand Pact being used for the creation of an anti-Soviet front. For the first time an agreement had been reached with Rumania in spite of the Bessarabian question, without the Soviet Union, however, recognizing the existing border. Subsequently Lithuania, Turkey and Persia also joined the East Pact. On May 17, 1929 a trade agreement was concluded with Latvia, similar to the one that existed with Estonia. It is obvious that the Baltic states now had fewer misgivings about the situation than two years before, because the agreements with their powerful Eastern neighbor were now backed by the more far-reaching Kellogg-Briand system. However, in order to establish some counter-balance to these agreements with the Soviet Union, Estonia stressed even more strongly its spiritual ties with Finland (which significantly enough had not taken part in the Moscow meeting) and with Sweden.

The East Pact of 1929, the so-called Litvinov Protocol, was a significant success for Soviet foreign policy. It was due mainly to Litvinov's astute tactics as a negotiator. For the first time since the revolution, the nations of the Eastern and Central European "intermediate" zone had joined a treaty system which, although originally conceived in the West, was put into effect and signed in Moscow. Soon the fear would arise that this system would also find its pivot in Moscow.

Apart from the desire to assume a dominant position in Eastern Europe, Moscow's East Pact policy had another motive. In view of the tensions in East Asia, characterized by the conflict with China between 1927 and 1929, and Japan's threatened intervention on the Asiatic continent, the Bolsheviks thought it advisable first of all to protect their European rear.

Soviet East Asian Policy

Since the October revolution cordial relations had existed between the Bolshevik and Chinese revolutionaries. Lenin did not forget the telegram in which Sun Yat-sen had congratulated him after his seizure of power. In a manifesto to the Chinese people in July, the Soviet government solemnly renounced all Czarist claims to Chinese territories and property.

After the Civil War, closer contacts could be established. In Moscow a Communist Far Eastern Institute and the Sun Yat-sen University were founded, the latter attended by nearly one thousand Chinese students. One of the pupils of the Moscow Military Academy was Chiang Kai-shek, Sun Yat-sen's military adviser. Sun Yat-sen himself requested the Comintern to send him political and military advisers.[29] Naturally they were chosen from among Russian functionaries. The group left for China headed by Adolph Joffe. His first talk with the Chinese President in the summer of 1923 was to be epoch-making for the subsequent collaboration between the two countries and the two systems. Next to him stood Mikhail Borodin (Grusenberg), who had long lived as an émigré in the United States, and who was soon to become an influential figure in the government of Sun-Yat-sen. In 1924 a military academy was founded in Canton headed by Chiang Kai-shek. He was assisted by a Soviet military mission led by a man who for the time being called himself General Galen and whose origins remained obscure. The organization of the Chinese army was patterned after that of the Red Army, and political commissars, who very often were Communists, wielded strong influence.

The premise for this collaboration between nationalist Chinese forces and Communism was a concept which at this time gained recognition in the Central Committee of the CPSU. In an effort to make up in the Far East for the failures of world Communism in Europe during the past years, Stalin and Bukharin in 1924 convinced the Politburo to give full support to the Chinese nationalist Kuomintang party. This was a kind of preview of the future "popular front" tactics, because official support went to the nationalist forces rather than to the Communist party of China which had been founded in 1921. The latter was ordered by the Comintern to collaborate with the Kuomintang. Two Chinese Communists joined the nationalist government. A "united front" between nationalist bourgeoisie, peasants and workers was demanded.

Trotsky, Radek and Zinoviev sharply attacked this new China policy. The opposition demanded a quicker Bolshevization of China according to the Russian pattern and the introduction of the system of soviets. It rejected collaboration with the Kuomintang. It is, however, noteworthy that Adolph Joffe, Trotsky's close friend and sympathizer, also believed that a remodeling of China entirely along Russian lines was not advisable. In a joint statement with Sun Yat-sen he advocated the independent development of China and rejected the introduction of the Soviet system.[30]

After Sun Yat-sen's death in March 1925 it at once became apparent how important the mediating role of the great Chinese statesman had been. In Canton the Communists broke the truce and in the summer of that year assumed leadership of the Kuomintang.

Chiang Kai-shek took action immediately. After the death of Sun Yat-sen he had become head of the Kuomintang. In March 1926 he arrested several Communist leaders in Canton, accused them of conspiracy and had them executed. Stalin nevertheless continued his policy of supporting Chiang Kai-shek even when the latter ruthlessly proceeded against the Chinese Communists in April 1927. But when these incidents were repeated in May, the breakdown of Moscow's China policy could no longer be kept secret.

Just when diplomatic relations were severed by England, the Soviet government had to recognize that Chiang Kai-shek, too, was determined to end his collaboration with Communism.

Soon after the events of May 1927, Chinese police entered the Soviet embassy in Peking and made a search which brought incriminating documents to light. The Soviet missions in Shanghai and in Canton were also forcibly entered. As Chiang Kai-shek rejected the sharply worded protest of the Soviet ambassador, Karakhan, the Soviet government broke off diplomatic relations with China on December 14, 1927. At first the Soviet position in Manchuria remained unaffected but here, too, incidents were to occur. On May 28, 1929 Chinese police violated the extraterritoriality of the Soviet Consulate General in Harbin, conducted a search and arrested the Consul General, as well as the Consul General of Mukden who happened to be present. A little later the Russian officials of the Chinese Eastern Railroad were arrested and the road taken over by the Chinese. Russian influence in Manchuria had now been practically eliminated. An attempt at mediation by the Great Powers was unsuccessful.

The Soviet Union had gathered considerable forces in the Far East under the legendary General Vassily Konstantinovich Blücher, who was none other than the former General Galen. In October 1929 some units advanced into Manchuria, occupied Hailar and proceeded to Harbin. However, there were no military engagements of any importance. The Chinese accepted the Soviet demands and reinstated the Russian employees of the Manchurian railroad. These negotiations were concluded by an agreement signed in Khabarovsk in December 1929 along the lines of former agreements.

In view of her domestic difficulties, China decided to make advances to the Soviet Union. However, an international Communist Trade Union Congress which met in Vladivostok while negotiations were in progress, and whose special task was the subversion of East Asia, clearly revealed to the Chinese government the dangers threatening the country. In December 1931, a Chinese soviet government was set up in the Province of Kiangsi with its seat in Juichin. Mao Tse-tung was elected its chairman. Within a short time a Chinese Red Army was created which, by the end of 1933, included 350,000 regular troops and 600,000 men organized in irregular units.[31] This was the beginning of the Chinese civil war. Henceforward the Chinese Communists could count on Moscow's wholehearted support.

During the thirties Japan became increasingly active on the mainland. The Japanese had not recognized the Soviet government until 1925. Two points were at issue between the two countries, going back to Czarist times. One was that of the fishing rights of Japanese fishermen in Russian waters, a vital matter to the island empire. Another was that of the Japanese concessions on the island of Sakhalin, the southern part of which had been awarded to Japan in 1905 by the Treaty of Portsmouth. Agreements regarding these problems which were made in 1925 and 1928, led to a considerable increase in trade between the two countries, particularly in Russian exports to Japan. As these agreements, however, concerned Russian rights of sovereignty, they carried the germs of further complications.[32] At the beginning of 1931 the bitter feelings over the fishing rights found vent in an attempt on the life of the director of the Soviet trade mission in Tokyo.

An added source of friction was Japan's interest in Manchuria. As in Czarist times, political and economic forces collided here. The expanding network of the Manchurian railroad had been of considerable value to the country. Colonists streaming in from over-populated China found work in the course of the rapid industrialization. Japan was quick to give moral support to the autonomous spirit which these groups showed vis à vis Russia. At the end of 1931 the Japanese felt it necessary to protect their interests by military means as well. Troops were sent to the railroad between Taonan and Tsitsihar in northern Manchuria and at the same time a separatist Manchurian government was set up. When, in 1932, quarrels arose between Chinese and Japanese in Shanghai, the Japanese government intervened with land and naval forces and bombed the city. This was the overture to the Chinese-Japanese war which was to break out a few years later.

The Soviet government was faced with the possibility of losing control in Manchuria. Litvinov succeeded neither in persuading the League of Nations to intervene in the Manchurian situation, nor in interesting Japan in a non-aggression pact. Renewed, although considerably exaggerated, activity on the part of anti-Bolshevik Russian emigrants in Manchuria contributed to a further increase of Moscow's nervousness. There seemed no way of putting a halt to Japan's advance.

On February 5, 1932, Japanese troops occupied Harbin and two weeks later the independence of Manchuria was proclaimed. On March 9 the new state was named Manchukuo. Now the Bolsheviks had no alternative but to resume their relations with the Chinese government in Nanking which had been broken off in 1927. On June 29, 1932, a Soviet-Chinese non-aggression pact was signed in Moscow. As regards Japan, too, there was no other course but to accept matters as they stood. Conceivably, a friendly gesture from the United States could, in view of the undoubtedly conflicting American-Japanese interests in the Pacific, have led to a stiffening of the Russian attitude in the Manchurian situation, and even to a common anti-Japanese front of the United States and the Soviet Union. But as the United States had not recognized the Soviet government, the Kremlin decided to approach Japan directly.

In August 1932 a new agreement concerning the oil concessions on Sakhalin, and Japanese fishing rights, had been concluded. In March 1933 Litvinov once more proposed a non-aggression pact to Japan and in May Japan offered to buy from the Soviet Union the northern lines of the Manchurian railroad, which were still in Russian hands, for thirty million rubles. Moscow at first asked ten times that amount but yielded since, in the event of a breakdown of negotiations, a further Japanese advance in the direction of Outer Mongolia was likely. The negotiations opened in June 1933 in Tokyo, were interrupted several times and seriously reopened in September, 1934, and led to a preliminary agreement on March 23, 1935. For 170 million yen the railroad lines which had so far been controlled by the Soviet Union were transferred to the government of Manchukuo. The result was a slight lessening of tension between Russia and Japan.

The conciliatory attitude toward Japan, however, did not mean that the Soviet Union renounced its interests in the Far East, nor had it permanently capitulated to the Japanese plans of pan-

Asiatic domination. Settlement of the disputed issues was simply postponed until a more propitious time. Exactly ten years later Moscow was to make demands on Japan. In the meantime the Soviet government took steps further to strengthen its strategic position in the Far Eastern provinces.

Russia and the United States

Prior to 1933, no official diplomatic relations existed between the Soviet Union and the United States. Although recognition of the Bolshevik regime was advocated in the Senate and in the House of Representatives as early as 1920, as for example by Senator Borah, the government and broad sections of the people were filled with a deep dislike of Soviet tyranny. As in the case of the pogroms against the Jews in Czarist times, now the persecution of the Church, atheist propaganda and, to no less a degree, the terror methods of the GPU, strongly prejudiced American public opinion against the Bolsheviks. The fear that Bolshevik ideas could infect America if diplomatic relations were established, also played a role even though the living standards of the American workers made them by and large immune to the propaganda slogans of the Comintern.

When Moscow appealed to President Harding in 1921 to avail himself of the mutual advantages of a resumption of trade relations, the United States government pointed out that there was no purpose in doing this until Soviet production was based on private property, the inviolability of contracts, and the freedom of labor.

This criticism of the basic principles of Communism did not, however, prevent the United States from consistently adhering to the concept of the inviolability of Russian territory. This explains why the American government did not establish diplomatic relations with the Baltic border states until 1922; and for the same reason it was very interested in not permitting the Japanese to establish themselves permanently on Siberian soil in the Far East. Soviet Russia was not represented at the Washington Naval Disarmament Conference of 1921; nevertheless, the American Secretary of State, Charles E. Hughes, insisted on the protection of Russian interests in the Far East. As a result of general diplomatic pressure the Japanese were obliged during the following years to withdraw their support from the anti-Bolshevik forces in the coastal province. While in this instance America's own interests, which did not include a powerful Japan in the Pacific, played a role, Hoover's relief mission during the first famine of 1922-1923 was based on purely humanitarian motives.

When President Coolidge assumed office in 1923 possibilities of an economic rapprochement seemed to open up, particularly as the Soviet Union's NEP promised a return to former economic principles. Nevertheless, Secretary of State Hughes, pointing to the continued existence of Communist propaganda, rather brusquely rejected Chicherin's approaches.

However, American business, nourished on the concept of free enterprise, did not let this state of affairs interfere with the establishment of trade contacts with the Soviet Union. In 1926 American firms acquired concessions for gold prospecting on the Amur, in 1927 satisfactory contracts were signed between the Standard Oil Company and Soviet government agencies. That same year American firms granted sizeable trade credits to the Soviet Union. The International General Electric Company, for example, signed a contract with the Soviet government for the sale of electrical goods for more than $20,000,000. A great number of engineers, technicians and experts went to Russia to be employed in connection with the industrialization program of the First Five Year Plan. While American-Russian trade had reached a total value of $37,000,000 during the period 1921-1925, i.e., three fifths of the annual figure of the pre-war period, it rose to $95,000,000 in the following years, i.e., almost double the pre-war figure. Already, American exports to the Soviet Union by far exceeded imports.

The Kellogg-Briand Pact of 1928 outlawing war was a new source of conflict as the American Secretary of State, F. B. Kellogg, originally had not wanted to include the Soviet Union. The latter thereupon used its subsequent invitation for its own purposes.

What was more important for American-Soviet relations was the beginning of the Great Depression which opened up quite unexpected opportunities for Soviet foreign trade. Wheat and cotton, coal, manganese and oil were dumped on the American market in order to increase the difficulties of the capitalist economy. This "Red trade threat" caused serious concern and was countered by the United States with an embargo on a number of Soviet goods such as wood and cellulose. By pointing out that these were being produced by prisoners, it was intended to attach a moral blemish to trade with the Soviet Union. The result was a rapid shrinking of trade on both sides. While the total value of Russian exports to the United States in April 1931 had still been $7,000,000, this figure dropped to $2,400,000 in the course of the year, while the American export figures were $6,800,000 and $1,300,000 respectively. In these circumstances Moscow's animosity toward the United States during 1931-1932 is understandable. During the conflict with Japan in Manchuria it was reflected in further irritability with the United States which, Moscow assumed, favored Japanese expansionist tendencies on the Asiatic continent.

In time, however, it became apparent that it was extremely difficult to exclude permanently so tremendous an economic area as the Soviet Union from world trade without exposing the capitalist economic system itself to certain hardships. Thus in the early thirties a resumption of normal trade relations and the diplomatic recognition of the Soviet Union was increasingly demanded in the United States. This was particularly true of the Democratic party which assumed power in 1933 with the election of F. D. Roosevelt.

The Non-Aggression Pacts of 1931-1932

The Soviet Union's rapid integration in a network of treaties with Western and Eastern European states after 1930 was the work of Maxim Maximovich Litvinov, who had succeeded Chicherin as Commissar for Foreign Affairs. This subtle diplomat with his air of comfortable respectability, had for some time been equally well known to the accredited diplomats in Moscow and in the lobbies of the League of Nations in Geneva, where with great eloquence he used the Disarmament Commission as a forum for Soviet disarmament propaganda, without making himself personally disliked. Now he successfully and tirelessly set to work to expand the Soviet Union's relations with the capitalistic states, following up the NEP, as it were, with a new diplomatic era, to last from 1930 to 1938.

M. M. Litvinov was an old Bolshevik. Born in 1876 in Bialystok in the then Russian part of Poland, he became acquainted at an early age with Marxist ideas and even before the turn of the century began to play a role in Social Democratic circles. In 1903 he joined the radical wing of the Party. During the years following the first Russian revolution he successfully participated in the illegal procurement of arms for the Bolshevik movement.[34] He was arrested abroad while attempting to exchange Russians bills obtained from the Tiflis bank robbery in 1906. In 1918 he was in an English prison; he was released in exchange for the British Consul, Bruce Lockhart who had been arrested in Moscow, and returned to Russia. There he soon became Chicherin's indispensable collaborator.

At the end of 1931 the Soviet government decided to establish even closer relations with the border states on the basis of the Moscow East Pact of 1929. As a first step Litvinov, in November, proposed a non-aggression pact to Poland. In 1926 similar negotiations had been unsuccessful because Poland had rejected a unilateral treaty and demanded a collective treaty covering all the border states. This time the Soviet Union yielded and approached the border states as well. The first state to agree to enter into negotiations was Finland and on January 21, 1932, a Finnish-Soviet non-aggression pact was concluded. It guaranteed the frontiers established in the peace of Dorpat on October 14, 1920, and provided for arbitration procedures. It was to run for three years with a two year extension in case of non-termination. This agreement was followed on July 25, 1932 by a Polish-Soviet non-aggression pact laying down similar conditions but without guaranteeing the frontiers. Nevertheless, Poland believed that Article 3 of the agreement gave her assurances against German revisionist claims concerning the Polish western frontier. It was thought in Warsaw that the agreement had exorcised the spectre of a possible Russo-German deal regarding Poland.

On February 5 and May 4, 1932, similar agreements were signed with Latvia and Estonia respectively; here, too, there were no frontier guarantees. Both non-aggression pacts were quickly ratified. On November 27, 1932, Poland ratified her treaty, the Finns took their time, not acting until July 22, 1933.

The relations between Rumania and Soviet Russia were particularly tense. After negotiations had been started, with Poland acting as intermediary, they were wrecked by the intervention of the Rumanian envoy in London, Titulescu, who immediately thereafter became Foreign Minister in a new Cabinet. For him Rumanian foreign policy centered on the Bessarabian question which was not open to discussion. The Soviet press adopted an increasingly aggressive tone toward Rumania and the Rumanian Communists received systematic support from Russia.

Only when on July 3, 1933, the so-called "definition agreement" which was to define more clearly the aggressor in a case of war, was signed in London by the signatories of the Kellogg-Briand Pact Rumanian and Soviet signatures appeared once again, as in 1929, on the same document. The London agreement was also signed by the East European signatories of the East Pact of 1929, among them the Soviet Union and Rumania. The concrete result of this settlement of the problems at issue, was the resumption of traffic between the two countries. Railroad traffic was resumed across the new Dniester bridge near Tiraspol in October 1935.

As stated above, the treaty policy of the Soviet Union in Eastern Europe had a double motivation: to protect the Soviet rear in view of the increasing tension in East Asia, and to create, under Moscow's control, an interlocking treaty system among the border states. If any of the Great Powers had an interest in these efforts, it was France. France had ties with the countries of the Little Entente as well as with Poland, some of them contractual, some historical and cultural, some dating far back, but most of them arising out of the Versailles treaties. The stabilization of conditions in Germany induced France to renew her search for security and gradually the relationship with the Soviet Union appeared in a different light. France's advocacy of an anti-Soviet *cordon sanitaire*, strong during the 1920's, was tempered by a growing readiness to resume relations with Moscow, a shift of emphasis made easier by the innocuous and accommodating look of Litvinov's foreign policy.

The understanding achieved between Poland and the Soviet Union in 1932 was a great help in clearing the way. Added to this was the anxiety in Paris caused by the dynamic developments in Germany on the eve of Hitler's seizure of power. Accordingly, the discussions concerning a French-Soviet non-aggression pact which had begun in 1931 and which were accompanied by trade negotiations, were now speeded up. On November 29, 1932, a conciliation agreement and a non-agression pact were signed between the Soviet Union and France.

The non-aggression pact pledged one country to assist the other with arms in the event of an attack by a third power. Interference in domestic affairs, economic boycott, as well as military organizations directed against the treaty partner were to be banned. In conformity with the Kellogg-Briand Pact all controversial questions were to be solved peacefully by arbitration.

Although on the face of it not incompatible with the treaties of Rapallo and Berlin, the Franco-Soviet agreement resulted of necessity in a cooling off of German-Russian relations. For other reasons, too, these were soon to enter a critical stage. The world political situation was changing from the post-war situation of World War I to the preliminaries of World War II.

CHAPTER 6

DOMESTIC DEVELOPMENTS BETWEEN THE SECOND FIVE YEAR PLAN AND THE OUTBREAK OF THE WAR

The Economic and Social Situation after 1932

The Five Year Plan terminating in 1932 had undeniably been successful in its Bolshevik aims—at least in terms of controls if not of production. In the course of collectivization approximately three-quarters of the arable land had been divided into *kolkhozes;* in the Ukraine, in the Northern Caucasus and in the lower Volga region the change had been particularly speedy. The often incredibly primitive cultivation of the soil had given way to modern methods; mechanization had made great progress and, according to the official reports of the day, agricultural production had reached its pre-war volume by 1930. (More recent reports indicate that *per capita* production has never yet reached the 1916 level in cattle, grain, butter, etc.)

In industry the production of coal and iron had been given priority. The most important coal center, the mines in the Donets region had been mechanized and expanded. Production of iron and steel had reached an unprecedented level; new smelting works had been built, for example in Krivoy Rog and in Zaporozhye. The tractor plant at Stalingrad, the combine for pig iron and rolling mill products in Magnitogorsk in the Urals, were examples of gigantic new plants. Oil was being prospected for in the Caucasus and in Siberia. At Dnieprostroi on the Dnieper, Europe's greatest power station with an output of 650,000 kilowatts was erected in 1932. The road network had been enlarged and an important new railroad, the "Turksib" which connected Siberia with Turkestan, was completed in 1930.

In spite of these remarkable achievements there could, of course, be no question of a final "Victory of Socialism" as Stalin had

bombastically called it in January, 1933, in his speech to the
Central Committee. In the following year at the Seventeenth Party
Congress [1] he himself admitted the gaps in the fulfilment of the
plan. Defects had become noticeable in the industrialization program as well as in agricultural collectivization. These, it was hoped,
would be eliminated by a new Five Year Plan which had already
been launched.

The most important tasks of the second Five Year Plan (1932-
1937) were ostensibly to increase the production of consumer
goods, raise the living standard, complete the modernization of
industry and agriculture, and improve the quality of production
in every field. But in actuality, the emphasis fell, not on human
welfare, but on those measures which strengthened the economic,
political, and military potential of the state.

The task was to render the Soviet Union as independent as
possible of foreign countries by speeding up industrialization. Within the framework of total planning, the regional modernization of
the economy was assigned a special role. Between the various
economic sectors of a region planned collaboration was to be
established—a typical form of this being the industrial complex
which combined the various industrial branches of a region, e.g.
coal mines, foundries and chemical plants, in order to enhance
their productivity. The Ural-Kuznets combine in Siberia became
the biggest project of this kind—a striking example of the growing
importance of the Asiatic regions in the industrial development of
the country. The intensification of the exploitation of the Central
Siberian and Turkestan mineral deposits led to a steady eastward
shift of the center of industrial production, even beyond the Volga-
Ural region. Generally speaking, the gigantic combines of the
various branches of industry were characteristic of the trend toward
the colossal, the dangers of this "gigantomania" not yet having
been realized.

The expansion of communication and the electrification of the
country accompanied this development. In the north-eastern part
of European Russia the Kotlas railroad was to open up the coal
mining region on the Pechora river, and in Central Asia the
Turksib was extended. In addition to the electrification of the railroads special attention was to be paid to the expansion of inland
waterways and shipping. After the completion, in August 1933,
of the White Sea Canal, which was named after Stalin, the construction of the eighty mile long Moscow-Volga Canal became the

major project, opening up a highly important inland waterway. From 1935 on, the Ministry of Transport was headed by L. M. Kaganovich, one of Stalin's closest collaborators.

Military considerations were the driving force behind the expansion of the transport system, the encouragement of heavy industry, and the development of power plants. This motive was clearly marked in a speech by Stalin on January 7, 1933; it was equally manifest in all the speeches made at the Seventeenth Party Congress, particularly in an address by Voroshilov.

Industrialization was accompanied by the collectivization of agriculture. Behind the goal of changing the peasant into an agricultural worker completely dependent on the state—a rural proletarian—was the intention of the Party to erase eventually the difference between him and the urban proletarian, to replace the two classes of peasant and worker by the single one of the "toilers." However, the other side of the accompanying modernization and mechanization was black indeed. In essence, the collectivization of the Russian peasant was the beginning of a new serfdom. The loss of individual initiative was accompanied by an unexampled and hopeless pauperization. The self-confident and energetic members of the peasantry had already been broken or destroyed in the turbulent years of the agrarian revolution. The millions of *kolkhoz* peasants became the patient work animals of the nationalized economy, able to claim only a small segment of their existence as their own.

The change-over from the first to the second Five Year Plan coincided with the climax of the great agrarian crisis and the second famine of the Soviet era. The brutality with which collectivization had been carried out resulted in the *kolkhoz* peasants' conviction that there was no point in working, as—regardless of their industry and output—the outcome of their labor remained always the same. The general dissatisfaction and indolence led to a considerable drop in production. When delivering the harvest the peasants tried to help themselves by secretly holding back a part of it, although since August 1932, they risked the death penalty for such action. Frequently, in their desperation, the *kolkhoz* farmers took a step which resulted not only in reprisals but also in great hardship for themselves; they went on strike and left the fields untilled. The results soon became apparent when the great famine of 1931-1933 ravaged the land—a famine which was, in part, government-planned.

This time the famine struck hardest in those regions where collectivization had been enforced most rigorously, although in part this included the most fertile black earth lands of the Ukraine and the Northern Caucasus. The situation was disastrous along the Volga, where there was always the danger of drought. Relapses into barbarism occurred, hardly imaginable in their horror; starving peasants attacked whatever persons they met in isolated areas, butchered them and ate the meat themselves or took it to market. Cases were reported of brutalized parents killing their own children in order to still their ravenous hunger. The number of victims of the catastrophic famine is estimated at between ten and eleven million.[2] The disaster was carefully concealed from foreign eyes; this time no relief committees were organized abroad.

In 1932 the final year of the first Five Year Plan, the crisis through which the country was passing became noticeable. Dissatisfaction did not remain confined to economic matters but found political outlets too. Restlessness infected the villages and provincial towns and did not stop before the walls of the Kremlin. The rumblings of the tense struggle with the Right Opposition and of the settling of accounts with Rykov, Tomsky and Bukharin had not yet died down. The shocks of the first show trials of the 1920's and 1931 were still felt. On the other hand, the courage to make a stand had not yet been wholly extinguished. Among Stalin's close associates pamphlets were circulated urging that it was high time to oust the General Secretary. They were signed by men who, only a short while ago had served Stalin well in the fight against Trotsky and Bukharin. They were soon arrested, accused of high treason and sentenced to imprisonment. And yet they had not planned a revolt, but merely Stalin's replacement in his party office.[3]

From afar Trotsky exercised a certain amount of influence. It's importance should be neither exaggerated nor underestimated. At the end of 1932 his *Bulletin* published a survey of the economic situation in the Soviet Union, containing many facts which could only have been obtained from informed government circles.[4] The article concluded with these words: "As the present leadership evidently is no longer able to find a way out of the hopelessly confused economic and political situation, the Party is becoming more and more convinced that a fundamental change must take place in the leadership."

The Ukraine, in particular, was seething with discontent. Here economic misery was combined with nationalist-autonomist trends which in the past years had been allowed to develop without hindrance. On January 24, 1933, Stalin sent P. Postyshev, an old Bolshevik of half Russian, half Tunguz descent, to the Ukraine as his special confidant and plenipotentiary with orders to stifle Ukrainian nationalist tendencies. The GPU was at his disposal. In Kiev Postyshev carried out a thorough purge of the Ukrainian government and the local party. This earned him the title of "Hangman of the Ukraine," a name once assigned to Count Muraviev in Lithuania. The Chairman of the Council of People's Commissars, Chubar, was removed from office; the People's Commissar for Education, M. Skrypnik, one of Lenin's oldest comrades, committed suicide. 28,000 members were expelled from the Party, 237 Party secretaries were dismissed. The Ukrainian intellectuals, in particular, were persecuted. Several writers were exiled, the Ukrainian Academy of Sciences was placed under the control of the Moscow Academy. The well-known Ukrainian historian, Professor Hrushevsky was exiled to Moscow.[5]

Outside the Ukraine, too, discontent was rife, even in Party circles and in the Komsomol. Stalin took action. Hundreds of thousands of Party members were expelled, Zinoviev and Kamenev exiled to Siberia.

At the same time a tragedy occurred in Stalin's own family. The all-pervading atmosphere of crisis had not passed his house by. His second wife, Nadezhda Alliluyeva, the daughter of a Petrograd worker and Bolshevik partisan, had so far blindly followed her husband's line. She led a quiet, retired life. Every day she went to work in a chemical laboratory, showing little interest in political questions. Now, in the face of the peasant's misery, the ruthless battle of collectivization, the doubts which began to pervade even the highest party circles, she, too, began to lose confidence in the policy pursued. Alexander Barmine[6] relates how one evening in November 1932, Stalin and his wife were Voroshilov's guests. Other members of the Politburo were present and the conversation turned to political questions. Mme. Stalin, too, expressed her opinion. She did not hide her concern over the general discontent and the Terror. This was more than Stalin could stand. He made a scene and in the presence of the other guests overwhelmed his wife with abuse. Nadezhda Alliluyeva left the house and that same night ended her life.

Another Bolshevik émigré, Victor Serge, reports the consequences of this suicide, which came as a great shock to Stalin.[7]

At a meeting of the Politburo he offered to resign. The members, unsure of themselves, received this announcement with obvious discomfort. No one dared to say a word, no one moved. Then Molotov broke the embarrassing silence. Jumping up he shouted, "Stop it, stop it! You have the Party's confidence!" Thus the only offer of resignation which Stalin made during all the years between 1922 and his death, was turned down.

However, this incident did not remain without consequences. In January 1933, the month Hitler seized power in Germany, Stalin issued a directive at a session of the Central Committee which signified the reversal of the agrarian policy. He opened the granaries of the Red Army and distributed the stores. Great quantities of grain were bought on the Baltimore grain exchange.[8] The Party machinery was mobilized in order to combat the famine. In the villages the directors of the political divisions of the Machine and Tractor Stations (MTS) were given dictatorial powers and all Party organizations were subordinated to them. A propaganda campaign directed at the peasants soon began to bear fruit. Work was resumed everywhere and the excellent harvest of 1933 played its part in allaying popular unrest.

The Government, without changing its basic attitude, began to make some concessions to the *kolkhoz* peasants. Originally almost everything the peasant owned had been declared communal property; he was paid for his work in the *kolkhoz* like a day-laborer. From now on the *kolkhoz* peasant was allowed to cultivate a small piece of land for himself, to keep some poultry, one or two goats or sheep, and even a cow. He was to share in the net profit of the *kolkhoz* from the sale of surplus produce on the free market.

In a speech before the "shock troop workers" of the *kolkhozes* on February 19, 1933, Stalin once again attempted to explain the necessity of collectivization looking at it from every angle. There could be no doubt that he wanted to sound encouraging, and the theme "Our next task is to make all *kolkhoz* peasants wealthy!" had an almost sensational effect. "Yes, comrades," Stalin exclaimed once more before his incredulous audience, "they shall be wealthy!" He was rewarded with wild applause and the record of the speech notes at the end: "Cheers and ovations . . . calls of 'Long live Comrade Stalin' . . . 'hurrah, long live our leader!'"[9]

In addition, the *kolkhozes* were clearly favored over the large government farms, the Soviet estates or *sovkhozes*. Initially the *sovkhozes* with their vastly better equipment were held up as model enterprises to the *kolkhoz* peasant. This idea was now dropped. Most *sovkhozes* were dissolved and the land, almost forty million acres, distributed among the *kolkhozes*. Thus the air was cleared and gradually the bitter resistance against collectivization, if not the discontent, died down so that shortly thereafter almost all peasant holdings could be collectivized.

In January 1933, Stalin made a speech at the Central Committee session in which he said, "We had to spur the country on . . . it was a hundred years behind in its development and was confronted with a deadly danger." [10] This time he admitted that the first Five Year Plan had not been fulfilled, and in explanation he cited the supposed danger of a war in the Far East. However, in his speech of February 19, 1933, he viewed collectivization from yet another angle. He said that if the Party did not remain alert, the *kolkhozes* could, in certain circumstances, become a far greater danger to the Government than even the private peasant holdings. The peasants were now well organized and could be centrally directed better than ever before. Should they at any time take action against the Government, they would be far more effective than before. He insisted that it was necessary that organs of the Party keep effective control of the situation. With this in mind, special "Political Detachments" were created which became active throughout the country. The pressure which had just been relaxed economically became more intense politically.

At the Seventeenth Party Congress in January 1934, Stalin boasted that two million peasants who had never before handled an engine had been trained as tractor drivers, that about the same number of men and women had been schooled for administrative work, and that about 110,000 agronomists and engineers had been distributed all over the country. Two years later, in 1936, the number of Machine Tractor Stations had increased from 4376 to 4951.

During these years the rise in prices and the need for price controls continued to be a difficult problem. The free market had ceased to exist in 1928. The state had fixed maximum prices and regulated distribution by a system of food rationing; once again, as in the days of the Civil War, the ration card played a decisive role. The inflation came to a halt toward the end of 1931; but the supply of food and other goods decreased due to the agricultural underproduction caused by collectivization. What few consumer goods were available were absorbed almost entirely by the bureaucracy; the workers saw hardly any of them. At this point the abolition of rationing and a revision of the price regulation system would have been in order. However, the Government retained both, because only by means of the double price system and the *Torgsin* preference stores,[12] designed to lure foreign currency and gold reserves from the population and bring them into circulation, was there hope of concealing the misery of the broad masses, the shortages of food and other goods, not to mention the famine in the south. The rationing system served as a screen for preferential treatment of those classes of the population which were important to the existence of the regime.

Rationing was abandoned in December 1934 and the result was a general rise in prices. At the same time, the value of the money was again being appreciated and people realized that the road to money led *via* increased production. In the light of this, the Government believed that the people were once again ready for wages graded according to skill and output.

To mechanization of production, one of the fundamental tenets of the second Five Year Plan, was added the need for a rise in the quality of output. The means adopted for this were a sliding wage scale, piece work pay, and special bonuses for skilled workers. In a speech on June 23, 1931, Stalin had given his blessing to these methods, portraying the differentiation between skilled and unskilled labor as an essential characteristic of the social transition stage preceding the achievement of communism. The stepping up of productive efficiency required specialized training and this, in turn was closely linked to the general level of education, to the fight against illiteracy. Thus educational and economic policy were interlocked.

In a speech on May 4, 1935, Stalin demanded an increase in industrial output. It sounded very well when he contrasted the hitherto current slogan "technology is all-decisive," with the man who had mastered this technology; when he asked for skilled workers and specialists and called the "human cadre" the most valuable and decisive element in the work process. But despite the high value placed on expert knowledge and the preferential treatment it enjoyed, the demand for an increase in output also had its negative aspects. Admittedly, the Russians had always worked at a very leisurely pace and the desire to speed up the work rate in the course of industialization was understandable. But when on August 31, 1935 a miner in the Donets Basin, Alexei Stakhanov, mined 102 tons of coal in one shift, thus exceeding the normal quota by 1300%, he originated a movement which was to lead to the merciless exploitation of human labor.

In other fields of production imitators of Stakhanov established outstanding records. Among the *kolkhoz* workers, the peasant Maria Demchenko gained fame. Similarly, during 1935 an order for speeding up harvesting work involved piece work wages for tractor drivers, i.e., payment according to the acreage worked, not according to the hours spent on the job. 1936 was named "Stakhanov Year." Shock troops of Stakhanovites pushed the output of work crews up, raising the levels of so-called socialist competition, seeking to achieve a well-nigh perfect mechanization of labor. If Soviet man had mastered technology better than ever before, he now faced a system of mechanized work direction, with government and Party organs in the role of overseer.

With the reestablished grading of wages according to skill and output, the old battle cry of the proletariat—piece work is murder —died down. The State which, in the course of implementing full socialization, had taken the place of the private entrepreneur, had no trouble in suspending the customary prerogatives of labor, such as strikes and the right to arbitration. Leaving one's place of work or moving from one locality to another was becoming more and more difficult and sometimes impossible.

This raises the problem of the Soviet labor unions and their ability to protect the workers.[18] From the inception of the planned economy the unions were subjected to a process which progressively led to their becoming an instrument of the state, a "labor front," as they were called in Hitler's Germany. Ever since then the main function of the unions has been the raising of the level of productivity and the transmission of the orders of State and Party. They have become part of the machinery of the Bolshevik dictatorship. Their task is to extract the last ounce of productivity from the workers by means of collective agreements regarding wages and work norms. In close co-operation with the state, pressure is exerted on the worker when, for instance, he wants to change his place of work—he then loses his right to social welfare benefits.

Hence the Soviet worker cannot expect any protection from his union if his employer, the state, infringes his rights. In practice the right to strike cannot be exercised because, in a nationalized economy, it can easily be represented as sabotage. The heaviest blow to the Soviet worker was the change-over between 1938 and

1940 to a system of obligatory work, buttressed by severe penalties. A decree of June 1940 provided penalties for loss of more than twenty minutes working time or for being slack three times within one month, or for being slack more often within two months. The penalty could be a cut of 25% in wages or imprisonment up to six months. For repeated or more serious violations of work discipline, the punishment could be exile to forced labor of varying degrees, or sentencing to forced labor camps.

Very characteristic of Stalin's new social policy of the thirties was his fight against "egalitarianism." When the principle of equal pay was abandoned in 1931, it was a clear renunciation the almost ascetic ideal of the old Bolsheviks who, like every elite in its initial stage, knew that success could only be attained by self-discipline. In Lenin's time no member of the Party, including the highest functionaries, could earn more than a skilled laborer. Now it was found impossible to obtain the qualified workers required for the needs of industrialization unless they were attracted by better salaries. Stalin pointed out that his new wage policy was supported by a sentence in Karl Marx which stated that in a classless society, too, workers were to be paid primarily according to output and not according to need. He waged a bitter battle against rigid egalitarianism. As time went on, difference in wages and salaries became so vast that they could no longer be reconciled with Marxist principles. Between the masses of unskilled and underpaid workers on the one side and the privileged worker aristocracy, the bureaucracy and the higher functionaries on the other, a continually widening rift opened up.

This was the moment when the so-called "technical intelligentsia," the class most characteristic of present-day Russia, began to receive economic recognition as well. With the party functionaries, the representatives of the Soviets, and the new Soviet intelligentsia, they formed a new privileged class in the Bolshevik state. As the number of Soviet intelligentsia grew, it became correspondingly easier to dispense with the services of the remaining bourgeois intellectuals. The trial of Professor Ramzin was typical of this change. Here and there members of the old intelligentsia were still used to train the new generation, but gradually they became superfluous and could be replaced by Bolshevik experts.

Stalin's barbed rebuttals of his Trotskyist critics, who attacked his new social policies, and his venomous criticism of the "egalitarians," merely stressed the dependence of his system on this

new privileged class of the Soviet intelligentsia—it had become
one of the main props of his regime.

Ideological Changes During the Nineteen Thirties.

The years of the second Five Year Plan were also years of
profound ideological changes in the Soviet Union. This was manifest in the relationship between the Soviet citizen and the state and
in undisguised "restoration" tendencies in cultural affairs.[14]

Stalin's oft-quoted speech before leaders of industry in February
1931, in which he passionately pleaded for bridging the technological gap between Russia and the West, was in a sense an appeal
to the patriotic instincts of the people of Soviet Russia. It was the
first harbinger of an ideological change which traced directly
back to the thesis of "socialism in one country."

Three years later, in the spring of 1934, the icebreaker *Chel-
yuskin* was caught in an ice floe during a polar expedition and
had to be abandoned. The crew of 104 men drifted for weeks
on an ice pack until finally, without loss of life, they were rescued
by air through the heroic efforts of the pilot Papanin and his men.
It was a stirring exploit and received due recognition when the
rescuers and the rescued were officially welcomed in Moscow.
In calling the recipients of this honor "sons of our great fatherland,"
Stalin struck a surprising note and re-introduced the use of a
terminology which had been condemned since the October revolution. The press took up the new line. Henceforward not only *rodina*
(birthland) but occasionally the word *Rossiya* (Russia), too, could
again be heard in public. In May 1936, the year of the new
constitution, *Izvestia* wrote that it was the duty of every Soviet
citizen to love his native land and to know its history. At the same
time the border skirmishes with the Japanese in the Far East served
to arouse patriotic emotions. In December 1936 *Pravda* wrote:
"The Soviet land is great and mighty, without boundaries, joyous
and happy. Truly, we workers of the Soviet Union love our fatherland. We are patriots. . . . even the air of the Soviets is holy to us."

Soviet patriotism, hitherto a strangely crepuscular phenomenon,
had finally come into the open. At first it lacked the Great Russian-
nationalist note and appealed to the common national consciousness of all Soviet peoples. The film "Circus" is an eloquent example
of this. But gradually the return to historical tradition, including
the stress on specifically Russian elements, became characteristic.

The previously-held concept of history, was no longer satisfactory. This led to the attack on one of the fathers of Marxist historical research, Pokrovsky, and the liquidation of his school.

Until his death, M. N. Pokrovsky (1868-1932) had been the almost unchallenged dean of Bolshevik historians. Some critical voices had been raised in 1931. At the end of that year Stalin sent an open letter to the editors of the magazine *Proletarskaya Revolutsiya* (Proletarian Revolution) in which he discussed "some questions concerning the history of the revolution" and violently criticized another article dealing with the attitude of the Bolsheviks toward German Social Democracy before 1914. Present-day Soviet historiography considers this letter the beginning of the battle against Pokrovsky.

The reform of the teaching of history was discussed in the Central Committee of the Party during 1932-33 and was further debated at the Seventeenth Party Congress in 1934. A resolution of the Council of People's Commissars and the Central Committee adopted on May 16 of that year, demanded that the history text-books for secondary schools be re-written and that history once again take the place of the courses in Marxist social studies which Pokrovsky had introduced. At the universities, too, faculties or chairs of history were re-instituted and frequently filled with bourgeois historians who had been dismissed only a few years earlier.[15]

A statement issued in August 1934 and signed by Stalin, Kirov and Zhdanov, examined most critically the various outlines for a new textbook which had so far been submitted, and gave directions for the approach to all principal problems in the teaching of history and in the establishment of historical concepts. Despite this, according to a statement issued by the Central Committee and the Council of People's Commissars on January 26, 1936, the textbooks which were finally published still did not pay sufficient homage to the "greatness and dignity of the national past of the peoples of the Soviet Union." Subsequently a contest was announced on which Stalin and Molotov expressed themselves publicly in April 1936; in 1937 the results were published. The new textbook had been decided upon.

In all these statements, in the accompanying discussions in the press, in the extensive collection of scientific monographs published in the years 1939-1940, Pokrovsky's conception of history is taken to task. He was accused of deviating from dialectic materialism in favor of a narrowly economic or even mechanistic materialism, thereby degrading history into a colorless sociological schematism. Concrete facts and events had been submerged in a sea of abstractions. He was charged with neglecting to appraise the meaning of spiritual factors as well as the role played by the men of genius; with completely ignoring the history of the more distant past or using it only as a quarry for his sociological abstractions; with denying history its scientific character by describing it as "politics projected into the past."

The new Stalinist concept of history was, more than ever, "politics projected into the past." But it attempted to restore the link with the Russian past. It endeavored to bring about a synthesis between national and Marxist ideas. It differed from Czarist history by including all the peoples of the Soviet Union whose history in some instances was now explored and described for the first time. Nevertheless, the focus was Russia and Russian national traditions. Hero worship was revived and homage paid to the Grand Dukes and Czars, the saints and military leaders of old Russia. Films and the theater, literature and the arts also rediscovered and glorified the Russian past. In November 1936 the Soviet poet, Demyan Bedny, who, until then, had enjoyed great public acclaim and whose doggerel persiflage about the Gospels had been very popular, was officially branded as an "infamous blasphemer of the patriotic emotions of the Russian people," because he had ridiculed the old Russian medieval heroes, the *Bogatyri*, in the libretto of a comic opera. After some official corrections, in which Stalin took a personal interest, Ivan the Terrible appeared in an Eisenstein film as an imposing and inspired personality. The Alexander Nevsky film became a chauvinistic diatribe against the Order of Teutonic Knights, its primitive black and white scenario effectively supported by Prokofiev's rubato music.

In literature, the writer Count Alexei Tolstoy, who had returned from abroad in 1923, erected a grandiose monument to Peter the Great in his magnificently colorful novel. In it the Czar, despite a well-drawn profile, appears almost like a fore-runner of Bolshevism. In 1937, Glinka's opera "A Life for the Czar" was produced again under the title "Ivan Susanin" at the Great Theater in Moscow. The hymn to the Czar, which the text contains, was no longer suppressed. The painter Repin, who had been branded a counter-revolutionary, was reinstated, particularly for the sake of his historical pictures. Among the writers of the past, Dostoevsky continued to be treated with reserve, but appreciation of Tolstoy was encouraged. On June 6, 1937, the hundredth anniversary of Pushkin's death was observed as a great national holiday. A special committee headed by Gorky made the arrangements.

The military past of the Czarist empire, also, seems to have been rehabilitated. Suvorov and Kutuzov have been resurrected in films and on the stage. The battle of Borodino was commemorated in September 1937, 125 years after its occurrence, although a few years previously the Church of Our Saviour in Moscow, built in memory of the Wars of Liberation, had been pulled down, supposedly because it hampered traffic.

In the schools, too, restoration trends could be noted. After history had been re-introduced, Latin became a school subject again. A new education law of September 3, 1935, re-established the authority of the teacher and the need for discipline among the pupils. Report cards and marks, which had been discarded as a bourgeois malpractice, were again used as a means of evaluating achievement. The teaching of arts and crafts, until then considered reactionary, was once more permitted.

Many laws were passed to protect the family. On April 7, 1935, measures were taken to cope with delinquent children; some were committed to correctional colonies. The death sentence became applicable to children of twelve or more years old. The *bezprizorny* ceased to be a public problem.

Was it a coincidence that Stalin permitted the newspapers to treat his visit to his mother in Georgia almost as a political event, or should this gesture be considered as his symbolic "descent to the mothers," symbolizing the return to Russian tradition? A law of June 27, 1936, re-instituted the family once again as the basis of the state. Divorce was made more difficult and there were to be tax exemptions and subsidies for families with many children. Abortion was declared a criminal offense except when medically authorized. In the spring of that year, the Party had submitted this part of the law to the people in all the factories, offices, kolkhozes, etc., for discussion. This was an unusual step. Opinions were expressed only reluctantly but gradually a definitely critical attitude emerged, particularly among the women. This was due partly to the housing shortage, partly to the general hardship of living. Despite the results of this "plebiscite," the government implemented the law most vigorously, apparently in the hope of replacing the victims of collectivization and the famine by increasing the birth rate. (The opinion has been expressed that this unusual public discussion was really initiated in order to explore the general public attitude and that the negative response assured Stalin that the masses of the people had not yet been sufficiently educated to appreciate his wishes and plans for them.[16] It is said that this experience strengthened his determination to fight the old revolutionaries to the bitter end.)

Apart from motives of population policy, the desire to foster a certain law-abiding spirit also played a part in the formulation of the 1936 family law. Considerations of national security also entered into it. By strengthening marital and family ties the principle of collective responsibility of the family for its members could be applied more easily. Every Party member is in duty bound to exercise "revolutionary watchfulness," even in his family circle. Such watchfulness which in some cases implies denunciations, is more difficult when family ties are loose. In case of persons traveling abroad, it is useful to keep back the marital partner as a hostage only if the marriage is a meaningful one. Legally the concept of regarding kinsfolk as hostages had been established in the high treason decree of June 8, 1934, and within the Party these ideas had been applied to some extent even before that. In 1938 they were also spelled out in a decree in which the relatives of a person who had fled the country (thus committing high treason and forfeiting his life), were held co-responsible and could be sentenced to up to fifteen years of forced labor.[17]

In the armed forces, too, there was a return to tradition and discipline.[18] In 1934 the Revolutionary War Council, dating back to the first years of Bolshevism, was dissolved. The People's Commissariat of Defense and its head was given greater powers. The decree of June 8, 1934, re-introduced the concept of high treason. Stalin's well-known speech to the graduates of the military academies on May 4, 1935, in which he stressed the importance of the "human cadre," i.e. of qualified leadership, became the signal for a number of reforms. They are inseparably connected with the name of Tukhachevsky. A new active service manual, issued in 1936, set down the regulations for training. The new constitution eliminated the last restrictions on non-workers and members of the former ruling classes, the so-called *lishentsi*. Universal military service was enacted in paragraph 132 of the constitution and military service was described as the honorable duty of every Soviet citizen. The principal staff of the Red Army was again called the General Staff. A decree of September 22, 1935, re-established service ranks in the army, thus creating a special military caste. Henceforward the highest rank was that of marshal. The development concluded with the issuance of special regulations concerning Soviet orders and awards and the introduction of the title, "Hero of the Soviet Union" (1936).

What caused most surprise, perhaps, particularly abroad, was the change of attitude on church matters. In the history textbook controversy of 1936, the official attitude had been to stress the "progressive character" of Christianity. Pokrovsky was accused of having overlooked the important role played by the Greek-Orthodox Church in education in Kievan-Rus for example, or the activities of the monasteries in the colonization of the Russian interior, particularly in the northeast. On April 3, 1937, Pravda sharply criticized intolerance towards the Church and frowned upon the disciplinary punishment of a school teacher in whose home an icon had been found. At a joint meeting at the end of 1938, the Academy of Sciences of the Soviet Union and the League of the Godless held a debate on the relationship between Christianity and Communism and it was concluded that Christianity had done more to promote the general progress of mankind than any other religion, and had contributed to the founding of a new social order.

Certain restraints were then placed on the League of the Godless, restraints which were not relaxed until after World War II. This period of tolerance during the years 1936-1938, which coincided with the big purges, was apparently designed to placate foreign observers of the Soviet Union and to prevent Russia's declining moral prestige from taking a fatal plunge. This development was also the logical outcome of the reestablishment of ties with the Russian past, although at first no decisive changes in the status of the Church resulted from it.

The Stalin Constitution of 1936. State and Party during the 1930's

The Stalin Constitution of 1936 symbolized the change which the Marxist concept of the state underwent in the Soviet Union during the Stalinist era.

The withering away of the state which Marx had envisaged, continued to be the stated ultimate goal of Communist hopes. It could not be realized until an end had been put to capitalist encirclement. Until then, the Soviet state had to lead the fight against capitalism. It is the state which plays a leading part in the Soviet superstructure; the civil service, literature, art, philosophy, morality and law are subservient to it. The state represents the Soviet social order, protecting, strengthening and developing it. The Soviet citizen had to adjust himself to this concept of the state; it was the backbone of his patriotism. The constitution which had united the Soviet republics in 1924, was no longer adequate for this strong, authoritarian one-party state which the Party, going far beyond the state's nominally federal structure, had tightly centralized. In 1935, the Seventh Congress of Soviets decided to draw up a new constitution and a commission headed by Stalin worked for almost six months on the draft, which was unanimously adopted by the Eighth Congress of Soviets in November 1936.

According to the Soviet (Stalin) Constitution of 1936, the USSR is a federal state consisting of eleven Soviet republics (RSFSR, the Ukrainian, White Russian, Georgian, Armenian, Azerbaidjan, Kazakh, Kirghis, Uzbek, Turkmenian and Tadzhik Soviet republics). The Union is the arbiter in questions of peace and war, national defense, foreign trade, economic planning, banking, postal services, communications and transport. Theoretically a secession from the Union is possible for the individual republics. In practice, however, the local Party organizations could never disregard central Party headquarters so that in actual fact secession could be carried out only by way of revolution; this obviously, could always be suppressed by the military and police forces of the Union.

All citizens have equal rights no matter what their nationality, race or sex. The various nationalities enjoy the protection of the Constitution which enables them to pursue their own cultural development.Here, however, the old principle, "national in form, socialist in content," applies, and the Bolshevik ideology common to all citizens is merely served up in varying styles. However, the unifying pressure which had been directed at the republics, particularly the Ukraine, since about 1929, undoubtedly diminished after 1936.

The Supreme Soviet of the USSR is the highest organ of the state. It consists of two chambers, the Soviet of the Union and the Soviet of Nationalities. Elections (held every four years) for the two chambers are universal, equal and direct. Franchise and eligibility for office are not subject to any restrictions, provided the candidate or voter has reached the age of eighteen. Even clergymen and former Czarist officials and officers are not excluded— after almost twenty years they were no longer considered a danger to the state! The only exceptions are the mentally ill and persons who have been deprived of their right to vote by a court of law. It is significant that this last category increased considerably after the great purge of 1936-1938.

The Supreme Soviet elects in a joint session of both chambers a Presidium and the Council of the People's Commissars of the USSR. The Chairman of the Presidium corresponds approximately to the head of the state in a Western democracy, the Council of the People's Commissars to the Cabinet of Ministers. A separation of powers is not provided for in the Soviet Union; neither Executive and Legislative nor Executive and Judiciary are sharply separated.

All citizens are guaranteed the right to work, recreation and education, as well as to public assistance in their old age and during sickness and disability. All citizens are granted freedom of conscience and, significantly, freedom of anti-religious propaganda. However, freedom of "religious propaganda," i.e. propagation of the gospel and religious observances, is not explicitly guaranteed and depends in the last resort on the interpretation of the freedom of conscience. The Stalin Constitution also guaranteed freedom of speech, press, assembly and association, the inviolability of person and domicile, secrecy of the mails, etc. However, the operative clause in this context is: "in the interest of strengthening the Socialist society." The means for abrogating the above mentioned freedoms are always at hand. An enumeration of the duties of the citizen—to obey the laws, to observe work discipline—was likewise an expedient for depriving alleged enemies of the state of their civil rights.

The exceptional position accorded the Communist party of the USSR in the constitution is also important. "The most active and purposeful citizens among the working classes and other classes of the toilers unite in the Communist Party of the Soviet Union which is the vanguard of the toilers in the struggle for the strengthening and development of the Soviet system and forms the core of all organizations—political and governmental—of the toilers." According to this formulation the admission of other parties was bound to appear absurd. The natural consequences are one-party elections.

An overall picture of the development of the Communist party since the late twenties is revealing.[19] While the Party had only 500,000 members in 1923, preserving in a way the character of an elite party, within ten years of Lenin's death it had become a mass party of 3½ million. During 1925 and 1926 alone, a contingent of 200,000 new members was admitted; Stalin sought to strengthen his position against the opposition with their help. Through the purges of 1936-1938, membership dropped below 2 million. On January 1, 1939, it stood at 2,306,933 and from that time on—apart from the enormous blood-letting of the war—it has been on the increase.

The Communist party of the Soviet Union exercises no direct governmental functions. Nevertheless, it is the decisive power in the state. Its influence on domestic and foreign policy is absolutely final and by and large it can be identified with the state. The top organ of the party is the Central Committee, consisting of about 150 members and candidates, but actual power is not exercised by it but rather by its executive organs: the Politburo, the Orgburo, the Secretariat and the various central agencies. The Politburo, above all, constitutes the actual leadership council of the party, consisting of about twelve members and candidates. Together with the Secretariat it is the *de facto* government of the Soviet Union. In addition, the Politburo exerts great influence on the administration of justice and the appointment of judges. Organizational questions are dealt with by the Orgburo, many of whose members are also members of the Politburo. The Secretariat of the Party— Stalin held the post of General Secretary from 1922—was in the ascendency during the thirties; together with Stalin's special private secretariat it exceeded in importance, especially during the great purge, even the Politburo.

The outstanding development in the party and its organs in the thirties was the progressive loss of its proletarian character. Whereas the new Soviet intelligentsia, the class of the party functionaries and the new academic upper strata, the high industrial executives, etc., constituted about half the membership, the number of proletarian members dropped to about 30%, or half the former figure. Since the thirties, incidentally, data concerning the social origin of party members have remained confidential, a fact which speaks for itself. In March 1939, the Eighteenth Party Congress raised the social status of the intelligentsia to that of the workers and peasants, amending the Party statutes accordingly. The privileged position of the proletariat was thus finally abolished and the social dominance of the top functionaries recognized within the party.[20]

The Great Purge (1935-1938)

The period of the Second Five Year Plan, of the birth of Soviet patriotism and of the Stalin Constitution, witnessed also the most severe domestic upheavals, which resulted in an extensive realignment of the social structure of the entire population as well as of the Party.

These upheavals were set off by the murder of a prominent Party member, the Leningrad Party Secretary, Sergei Mironovich Kirov. The murder, which occurred on December 1, 1934, started a chain reaction of arrests, interrogations and executions which found its climax in the great purge, the *Chistka* of 1937-1938.[21] According to conservative estimates about 7 to 8 million people— according to others, 23 million—became victims of this purge.

The background of the Kirov murder is now quite clear. According to the original official version the murder was committed by the Trotskyite student Nikolayev on orders of a conspiratorial organization, the "United Center," which was directed from abroad. The same organization, according to official accounts, also planned the murder of other leading party members—Stalin, Voroshilov, Kaganovich, Zhdanov and Ordjonikidze. In 1934 several attempts had allegedly already been made on the life of Stalin and other Bolshevik leaders, but had failed. Kirov's murder was to have set off a series of assassinations.

This version soon met disbelief and there was some talk about such completely unpolitical motives as jealousy. Even the trade union leader Tomsky was suspected, most unjustly.[22] Much more likely was the idea that Yagoda acted as provocateur, either after hints or instructions from higher up.

Kirov was known as the advocate of a more moderate policy. In view of the achievements of the First Five Year Plan, the 1933 policy shift on the peasant question and the elimination of the Trotskyites, he considered it time to stop the terror and to dissolve its executive organs. In the summer of 1934—shortly after the phrase of "the sons of the great fatherland" had been coined and the new patriotic concept of history had been decreed—the GPU was dissolved. This was the end of an institution which the people had felt to be the symbol of government terrorism. Its functions were taken over by the newly created People's Commissariat for Internal Affairs, an organization which at first was in no way tainted by governmental caprice or arbitrary justice. One was tempted to think that after the liquidation of the regime's enemies the ship of state was going to enter calmer waters.

It soon became apparent that the new agency, which combined the regular, criminal and political police in one state police organization and maintained close ties with the government, was even more powerful and had more extensive functions than its predecessor. Its importance was particularly enhanced by the fact that it was, in some instances, responsible for the execution of sentences. In the light of this, Yagoda, who had been put at the head of the new Commissariat, had reason to fear that Kirov would endanger his new position, all the more so as Kirov's more moderate line was supported by some members of the military, particularly Voroshilov and Bluecher. Both were apprehensive about the effects which the discontent of the peasants might have on the morale of the Army. In the Far East Bluecher was able to prevent the peasants from being compelled to enter the *kolkhozes*. Kalinin, too, sympathized with Kirov's more moderate course. On the other hand, Molotov and Kaganovich particularly, advocated rigid and uncompromising severity.

The trial of Kirov's assassins was held *in camera,* in accordance with an *ad hoc* law which denied the accused all legal assistance. It is very suspicious that a man from Kirov's personal guard was the victim of a traffic accident on December 2 while on his way to a hearing, although no others in the automobile were in the least harmed. This odd fact was brought out by Khrushchev in his secret speech of February 25, 1956. Obviously this man was designedly silenced, perhaps because he knew that Stalin himself was interested in the liquidation of Kirov. Nikolayev and his associates were executed. Zinoviev and Kamenev were charged with a multitude of involvements but denied having been directly connected with the murder. For the time being it was sufficient that they were ready to admit some indirect guilt. Zinoviev was sentenced to ten years and Kamenev to five years of forced labor. That same spring some other men who had been close to Stalin were also condemned without much of a stir being created.[23] In Leningrad, Andrei Zhdanov, as Kirov's successor, was entrusted with mopping up suspect elements in the city. Tens of thousands were deported from Leningrad to Siberia.

On the surface peace and quiet seemed to have been restored. Secretly the purge continued. An ever widening circle of investigations prepared the great show trials of 1936-37. With the appointment on May 13, 1935, of a special Security Commission of Stalin, Yezhov, Zhdanov, Shkiryatov and Vishinski, it became obvious that very thoroughgoing measures were to be expected. Going over the heads of the existing agencies, this Commission was to "liquidate the enemies of the people." It was also decided to investigate all Party members, both publicly and in secret. All Party officials were asked to redouble their vigilance and to be unsparing in criticism of others and of themselves. The result was a torrent of denunciations throughout the whole country.

When the first of the big trials, the "Trial of the Sixteen," began in August 1936, it was noted with some surprise that it was being held publicly and that the examinations were not only conducted by the NKVD but also by the Public Prosecutor. Perhaps Stalin even then had a certain distrust of Yagoda; perhaps the latter had really had too much to do with the events leading up to the Leningrad murder. The government agencies concerned with the trial maintained all the appearances of due process of law. As these were cases of high treason, the conduct of the trial, which was held from August 19 to August 24, was assigned to the military court of the Supreme Court of the USSR.

The defendants were accused of preparing a conspiracy to overthrow the government and to remove Stalin and other leading members of the Politburo. Among these, it was revealed on August 22, were also to have been Kossior and Postyshev, the latter a future victim of the *Chistka*.

A. Y. Vishinski, as Chief Public Prosecutor, skillfully played off one defendant against another and managed, in a variety of ways, to extract the desired confessions.[24] Vishinski, who was born in Kiev in 1883, was professor of criminal law in Moscow who had managed to gain Stalin's favor after Lenin's death even though he had formerly been a Menshevik. Under his presidency, the University of Moscow was transformed into a Bolshevik educational institution in response to the government's request. He became a Public Prosecutor in 1924 and, in 1933, he was appointed Chief Public Prosecutor.

In the trial of the so-called "Terrorist Center" he rested the case for the prosecution with the words: "I demand that all these mad dogs be shot."[25] The Court endorsed the Public Prosecutor's plea. On August 24, 1936, all the defendants, among them Zinoviev and Kamenev, were sentenced to death and the sentences were carried out the following day.

During the trial Zinoviev could only be prevailed upon to make self-accusations; Kamenev's statements, however, seriously implicated a number of old Bolsheviks. Thus this first trial immediately had further consequences. When Tomsky, the very popular Trade Union Secretary, committed suicide shortly afterward, many an old Bolshevik became jittery. At a meeting of the Central Committee in September 1936, open resistance to Stalin's proceedings against the opposition was expressed. Stalin did not react to this as expected. He did not change his course but, under the democratic mantle of the new Constitution, he decided to proceed with even greater severity and to spare not even his old party comrades if they resisted his measures in any way. Yagoda fell into disgrace. On September 26, 1936, he was relieved of his office and appointed People's Commissar for Postal Services, a post of no consequence. In his place Nikolai Ivanovich Yezhov was appointed. With him the purge neared its climax, the *"Yezhovshchina,"* as it was popularly called.

The NKVD maintained that it was able to prove that, at Trotsky's behest, a second purely Trotskyite Center had been formed in Moscow as another illegal conspiratorial organization paralleling the already existing "United Center" of Trotskyites and Zinoviev followers. This group was supposedly engaged in treasonable negotiations with Germany and Japan, and as soon as a Trotskyite government seized power in Russia, the Ukraine was to be ceded to Germany and the Amur territory to Japan. Its more immediate aims allegedly were an extensive network of espionage, subversion and treason within the borders of the USSR.

Even party members could not help being surprised when they learned that besides N. I. Muralov, G. Y. Sokolnikov and G. L. Piatakov (the deputy People's Commissar for Heavy Industry), the shining light of Bolshevik publicity, K. B. Radek, Lenin's old comrade in arms, had also been arrested as the leading spirit of this conspiracy. When once before he had been arrested by Yagoda, he had soon been released. At this point, however, when underground ties with foreign countries were to be proven, it was obviously advantageous to implicate a person whose name would have meaning in this connection.

The trial of the "Seventeen" was conducted in Moscow from January 23 to January 30, 1937 by the same tribunal that had sat six months before. While Muralov put up a great deal of resistance during the examination and a confession could be wrested from him only with difficulty,[26] Radek broke down soon after the start and, somewhat like Kamenev in 1936, incriminated a number of members of the so-called right wing opposition who had been sentenced to imprisonment or exile in 1931. The result of the trial was that Piatakov, Muralov and others were sentenced to death, while Radek and Sokolnikov received prison sentences of ten years each.

That same month, N. I. Bukharin, once the brilliant theoretician of the Party, successor of Zinoviev as Chairman of the Communist International and now also chief editor of *Izvestia,* was arrested after Radek and Piatakov had incriminated him. He had just returned from abroad where he had been convalescing. He was put on trial together with members of the former right wing opposition who had been incriminated by Kamenev. This, the largest of the Bolshevik show trials, the so-called third Trotskyite trial, required intensive preparations. It seemed necessary to assemble a great deal of evidence. All NKVD offices worked at high pressure for a whole year. In March 1938 everything was ready so that this trial too, the trial of the "Twenty-one," could be enacted. It was a time of greatest international tension—the first Czech crisis was then underway.

Among the other accused were A. I. Rykov, the former Chairman of the Council of People's Commissars (Lenin's direct successor in that office), N. N. Krestinsky, the deputy Commissar of Foreign Affairs, the diplomats C. G. Rakovsky[26a] and A. P. Rosengoltz, and Yagoda, the former People's Commissar of the NKVD. Differing from the second Trotskyite trial, the indictment this time explicitly stressed that the initiative came from abroad. It was stated that foreign espionage services had set up a new conspiratorial group, called the "bloc of Rightists and Trotskyites," whose goal was the overthrow of the Bolshevik regime in order to create a bourgeois-capitalist system (no longer a Trotskyite state). It also sought to detach not only the Ukraine and the Far Eastern territory, but also White Russia, Turkestan and Transcaucasia from the Soviet Union. It was maintained that Trotsky and his agents had been in contact with the German Secret Service since 1921, with the British Intelligence Service since 1926, and with the Gestapo since 1933; that they had engaged in negotiations with German military and Fascist groups—with Hess, Rosenberg, Niedermeyer and Haushofer—and had accepted orders from them. Supposedly, their aim had been to use all means to undermine the

Soviet regime, particularly to sabotage the armament industry and to organize resistance groups.

In the proceedings against Bukharin, his political past as far back as the Peace of Brest in 1918 was unearthed. Even then, it was alleged, he had plotted to undermine the Peace Treaty, to overthrow the Soviet government jointly with Trotsky and the left-wing Social Revolutionaries, to murder Lenin and Stalin, and to put a Bukharin government into power. Yagoda, surprisingly enough, was not accused of having been connected with the assassins of Kirov, but of having committed another heinous crime. On orders of the "United Center," he was said to have killed the novelist Maxim Gorky with an overdose of strophanthinine injections, assisted by Dr. D. D. Pletnev and his former house physician Dr. L. G. Levin. V. R. Menzhinsky and V. V. Kuibyshev, who had died in 1935, were said to have been done away with by the conspirators in a similar manner.

A gigantic wave of arrests flooded the country and the whole population grew tense. Suspect were all former oppositionists, followers of Trotsky, Zinoviev, Bukharin, former Mensheviks and Social Revolutionaries, anarchists, members of the Jewish Socialist Bund and others; also all sympathizers of pre-revolutionary left-wing parties; returned emigrants, Party members whose duties had taken them abroad, all citizens who corresponded with persons abroad, foreign Communists, members of religious sects, all those who at one time or another had been excluded from the Party, all Party members who had resisted the purging process. "Not infrequently," B. D. Wolfe writes,[26b] "it happened that a former examining magistrate met in his prison cell or in a concentration camp the same persons whom a few months ago he had tortured, forced to make confessions and sentenced to imprisonment. Among these unfortunates were millions of ordinary workers and peasants, members of national minorities, nomads who did not want to settle down and nomads who had settled down." According to calculations made by some of those involved, about five or six per cent of the total population of the Soviet Union passed through the pre-trial prisons of the NKVD during the period 1936 to 1938, i.e. eight or nine million, of whom only about two million were considered criminals. Among those apprehended were workers, peasants, clergymen, intellectuals and civil servants; all occupations were represented, none was spared. Of the 140 members of the Central Committee who had been elected at the seventeenth Party

Congress in 1934, only fifteen still enjoyed their freedom in the fall of 1937; of the twelve members of the Politburo eight were at liberty.

The purpose of the examinations was to extend the investigations progressively in order to involve the whole population. In continuous interrogations the prisoners were subjected to unspeakable psychological and physical tortures until their resistance was broken and they were ready to sign the statements put before them. While in tne prisons themselves no actual mistreatment took place, the examining magistrates increasingly began to use physical means to exert pressure. The so-called "great conveyor belt," the continuous interrogation which often stretched over several days and nights, took up much time. For this reason corporal punishment for the purpose of obtaining confessions was instituted in August 1938 in order to cope with the work pressure that the increasing number of arrests brought.[27] The prisoners reacted in different ways. While a highstrung person like Radek broke down at the outset, the old Bolshevik Muralov resisted the conveyor system for nine months. Weissberg-Cybulski tells of a Jewish tailor who submitted to an uninterrupted examination for thirty-one days and nights with a strength reminiscent of that of a fakir, without making a confession. It is not certain whether in addition to these measures drugs were also used in order to break down psychological resistance, drugs which are supposed to have a disintegrating effect on the central nervous system.

The desired results were obtained. The third Trotsky trial ended on March 13, 1938 with the pronouncement of the death sentence for the above-mentioned principal defendants and several others, with the exception of Rakovsky and S. A. Bessonov who were sentenced to twenty and fifteen years imprisonment respectively. The sentences were put into effect on March 15.

After investigations and examinations varying in length, all the defendants had, in the course of the trial, made their confessions. Some simply made short statements, others preferred to go into elaborate details in their self-accusations.[28] Only Krestinsky withdrew his confession at the public hearing and by this unexpected change in the program created a disagreeable sensation. Vishinski adjourned the session and handed Krestinsky over to the NKVD for a night of special treatment. At the next session Krestinsky stated that his revocation had been a counter-revolutionary maneuver in order to discredit the Court. After this there were no more interruptions.

It is important to note that among the prominent victims of the 1937-38 trials were not only the persons officially mentioned in Vishinski's speeches during the trial. A number of well-known Communists met their deaths in a variety of ways, sometimes quite mysteriously, during this period. It is not at all certain that the assassins of Menzhinsky, Kuibyshev and Gorky actually belonged to the opposition; according to some informants the fact that they simply had certain differences of opinion with the occupants of the Kremlin played a role in their sudden deaths. In Gorky's case, too, it is not certain whether his relationship with Stalin was as harmonious toward the end as the official historians would have us believe. Also, in the Central Committee Stalin's old comrade-in-arms from the Caucasus, S. Ordjonikidze, and P. Postyshev, Party Secretary of Ukraine, seem to have protested vehemently during the trials against the severity shown toward the old Bolsheviks. Indeed, more than any other member of the Politburo Ordjonikidze could afford to differ openly with Stalin. Soon afterward he suffered a heart attack to which he succumbed (1937). His death probably suited the NKVD. Postyshev disappeared in 1938.

A number of publications by former Bolsheviks indicate that Stalin's fellow-countryman and party comrade, Yenukidze, also fell victim to the great purge. The same was true of the former People's Commissars Borodin, Rudzutak, Karakhan, and of Mezhlauk, the Secretary of the Kharkov region; of the Politburo members Kossior, Chubar, Eiche and Petrovsky.[29]

Of special interest is the fate of the considerable number of prominent foreign Communists, among them top functionaries of the Comintern, who were sucked into the maelstrom of the *Chistka*. For example, it is not clear in what circumstances the German Communists Max Hoelz, Remmele and Heinz Neumann lost their lives in the Soviet Union during those years. The same is true of the Hungarian Communist leader Bela Kun[29a] who, in 1936, had participated in the Spanish Civil War, and of nearly all the members of the Central Committee of the Polish Communist party.

Among many others, the Austrian physicist, Alexander Weissberg-Cybulski, born in Galicia, who was with the Ukrainian Institute of Physics in Kharkov, was involved in the Bukharin

trial. After three years in the detention prisons of the NKVD where
he showed exemplary resistance to all attempts to extort confessions from him, he was handed over to the Gestapo in 1940.
Escaping after five further years of imprisonment, he was able to
draw a terrible and vivid picture of the horror of those times in
his book *The Accused* (New York, 1951).

Many of the pre-trial prisoners were never properly tried, many
were sentenced by an administrative commission of the NKVD
(the OSSO—*Osoboye soveshchaniye*) to forced labor camps. While
the OSSO could not impose the death sentence, it was empowered
in the fall of 1937 to go beyond the existing limit of five years of
forced labor.

The Soviet penal system had been reformed soon after the revolution, supposedly along humanitarian lines. Imprisonment was
to serve not so much as a punishment as a means of re-education;
the prisoners were to be employed in useful work. In the thirties,
when the struggle with the peasants who were resisting collectivization began, the number of prisoners grew into the hundreds of
thousands. For the construction of the White Sea canal alone,
Yagoda supplied 250,000 prisoners. Now all considerations of
"re-education" were discarded; punishment once again became
forced labor and Stalin's new watchword *"Tyurma tyurmoi"* (give
the prisoners what is their due),[30] applied to all prisoners. Over the
unhappy victims of Stalin's social policy rolled the insensitive and
cruel machinery of a slavery unknown since the days of antiquity
—differing from it only in the techniques employed by a modern
totalitarian and industrial state.

To these unfortunates were now added the victims of the great
purge. The opinion has been expressed that the need for large
numbers of laborers for the great technical projects in the Arctic
region and in Siberia, was one of the chief reasons for the mass
arrests. However, this would not satisfactorily explain the arrest
of innumerable scientists, engineers, military men and higher state
and party officials. While labor requirements played a secondary
role, they did, however, provide the arrests with an economically
"sound" rationalization. (It has indeed become the custom in the
Soviet Union to watch one's political p's and q's particularly in
the spring, the beginning of a new work season, when winter has
claimed the usual heavy toll in the work force of the labor camps.)

By the end of the thirties a large network of forced labor camps
covered Northern Russia and Siberia, with particular concentra-

tions in Karelia and on the Kola Peninsula, on the Pechora and the Northern Dvina, and in Central and Eastern Siberia. Between 1926 and 1939, the urban population of the Soviet Union increased by one hundred percent, the greatest increase taking place in the regions of Karelia and Murmansk. Here the increase was 558%, in Eastern Siberia 384% and in the Far East 329%. It was in these areas that most of the prison camps were located. For the years 1935-1937 the number of their inmates is given as five to six million, in the years 1940 to 1942 it rose to about ten million.[31]

After the completion of the White Sea Canal, the construction of the Moscow-Volga canal became the major project and was completed on July 4, 1937. The victims of the great *Chistka* could now be utilized in the main to double-track the Trans-Siberian railroad, and for the construction of the Baikal-Amur railroad. The gold-mining camp of Dalstroy on the Kolyma river in Northeastern Siberia, with its capital of Magadan, also grew into a giant complex during this time.

With rigid logic, the persecutions of 1937-1938 not only involved old Bolsheviks but also the leadership of the Red Army.

It can be assumed that Tukhachevsky and the other top officers of the Red army were horrified by the liquidation of the Party's old guard and did not hesitate to express their feelings. They were in control of the armed forces of the country and in command of the Moscow garrison. They could occupy the Kremlin at any time, perhaps under the face saving pretext of protecting the Politburo and Stalin. Subsequently it would be easy to arrest Stalin, Yezhov and some of the others. It is possible that Stalin was informed of these and similar ideas which were being toyed with privately. There is, however, no definite proof that the Red generals had planned a *coup d'état* and that Tukhachevsky had been the driving force behind this conspiracy in order to assume—in the event that the plot was successful— the role of the First Consul of the Russian Republic.[32] It is more likely that in their growing disapproval of the show trials the military leaders expressed so much criticism that Stalin was prompted to action. As regards Tukhachevsky in particular, Stalin may also have been influenced by Voroshilov who had for quite some time disliked the ascendancy of his rival.

Tukhachevsky had been implicated in passing by Radek at the Piatakov trial. Then, when Radek himself was on trial in January 1937, the Marshal's name was once again mentioned, but Vishin-

ski seemingly passed it over. Soon after that Tukhachevsky
vanished from Moscow and there were rumors that he had been
arrested. However, at the end of March he returned in order to
attend, among other events, a dinner honoring the Red Army at the
American Embassy, where, Ambassador Davies reports, he looked
"fresh and boyish." [33] Perhaps Tukhachevsky's permission to visit
Moscow, and the announcement in April that he was to be
the official representative of the Soviet Union at the Coronation
festivities of George VI of England, were designated to cover up
the fact that he was being investigated. By the end of the month a
decision was reached[34] and Tukhachevsky must have become
aware of it when he learned that Admiral Orlov was to go to
London in his place. At the big parade on May 1, it was noticed
that the Marshal looked disturbed and that everyone avoided him.[35]
On May 11 came the official announcement that Tukhachevsky
had been relieved of his position as Deputy People's Commissar
for Defense and had been consigned to a second rate post in Saratov
in the Volga region.

It was a sign that the Red Army was becoming suspect when
soon after this, on May 17 1937, the office of Political Commissar
for the military units (the *Politruks*), which had been abolished in
1925, was re-established. The execution of the decree was put into
the hands of L. Z. Mekhlis, the new director of the Political Administration of the Red Army. He had become prominent as Stalin's
secretary and now became Gamarnik's successor. On June 11,
1937 Tukhachevsky was arrested. It is said that he had resisted
and was wounded. He was brought on a stretcher before Stalin
and the latter had an argument with him.[36] Almost at the same
time a number of the most prominent leaders of the Red Army
were also arrested: General Putna, the military attaché at the
Soviet embassy in London, who like Bukharin and Krestinsky,
obeyed the order to return to the Soviet Union; General Kork, the
former Commandant of Moscow, currently director of the Military
Academy; General Yakir, the Commander of the Military District
Ukraine; General Uborevich, Commander of the Military District
White Russia; General Eidemann, Chief of Aerial Ground Defense
(Ossoaviakhim); General Primakov, Budyenny's deputy in the Cavalry Inspection; General Feldman, chief of the Red Army's Personnel Administration; the generals Dybenko, Yegorov, Bluecher
and many others.

Unlike the accused members of the Party elite, the military men were not tried in public. In their case a show trial did not seem appropriate. A military tribunal, held *in camera* and presided over by Voroshilov investigated the cases and imposed the sentences. Gamarnik also was to have been a member of this tribunal. He had been Chief of the Political Administration of the Red Army and of the Red Fleet and a member of the Party's Central Committee. He was a tall bearded man who, like Tukhachevsky, enjoyed universal popularity. Realizing that the accusations against Tukhachevsky were unfounded, he had a personal discussion with Stalin. This brought no results and at the end of May 1937 he committed suicide.

Budyenny also seems to have been under suspicion and possibly was arrested and detained for a time. However, he was soon released and, like Voroshilov, joined in the trial of his comrades. The arrested generals were accused of espionage for Germany and Japan, of having passed on strategic plans of the Red Army, and of having plotted an armed uprising. During the proceedings, the Anti-Comintern pact which Germany and Japan had concluded in 1936, was used to highlight the background of the conspiracy. The trial was short and on June 12, 1937 Tukhachevsky and the other generals were executed.

Meanwhile the preparations for the Bukharin trial continued, the whole country was seized by tremendous excitement. Was it possible that practically the whole General Staff had consisted of agents of foreign powers? Had Lenin really—with the exception of a single colleague—surrounded himself with traitors? Did not this carelessness and inability to judge people diminish his stature? Members of the innermost circles of the Party were shocked and a feeling of insecurity pervaded the ruling group.

There can be no doubt that the extension of the purges to the Red Army resulted in a catastrophic weakening of Soviet military power. At the time the Red Army probably had about eighty thousand regular, as well as eighty thousand reserve officers, of whom twenty thousand and thirty thousand respectively had participated in the civil war. According to well-informed sources, 75% of the members of the Supreme War Council, three out of five marshals, thirteen out of fifteen army generals, 62 out of 85 corps commanders, 110 out of 195 divisional commanders and 220 out of 406 brigade commanders were liquidated during 1937 and 1938. Perhaps 65% of the upper echelons (from colonel up) and ten percent of the lower echelons (altogether twenty thousand officers) were arrested. Of the six thousand high ranking officers alone, 1500 were executed. The others disappeared, at least temporarily, into prisons and labor camps.

In 1938 Voroshilov was forced to enroll ten thousand officer candidates six months before they completed their training as second lieutenants, in an effort to make good the loss in part. A rehabilitation Commission appointed by Beria after Yezhov's downfall, investigated, cleared and reinstated about three thousand officers. Among these were such military leaders of the Second World War as Rokossovsky, Tolbukhin and Yakovlev.

It is noteworthy that the military specialists taken over from the Czarist Army were less affected by the purges than the "Red Commanders," who were mainly members of the working and peasant class, mostly old Bolsheviks and veteran soldiers of the Civil War. The result of the purges was that primarily the proletarian element in the officer corps was decimated. The gaps were filled by military specialists of a younger generation who already belonged to the new Soviet intelligentsia. Thus, for example, in December 1938 the Politburo decided to introduce a special two-year General Staff course at the Military Academy and about one thousand high-ranking officers, most of them members of the new intelligentsia, were trained there. A similar change-over took place during the following years among the rank and file.

The strength of the Red Army was for the time being paralyzed, and this led to a weakening of the Soviet Union's political position in international affairs. This situation did not change until August 1939 when an alliance was concluded with the very power with which Tukhachevsky was supposed to have conspired. Perhaps he had been accused just because he had *opposed* the resumption of a collaboration between the Red Army and the Reichswehr, something which Stalin had considered even in 1937.

The question remains: what could have decided Stalin to subject the Soviet Union to this dangerous blood-letting by extending the purge to the Red Army? Tukhachevsky's great popularity among the people as a whole was undoubtedly of decisive importance. It exceeded that of any other Soviet leader. It was known that he had mechanized the army, had been the first to develop the use of paratroops, and had reformed the training methods for the recruits. As long as Tukhachevsky was at the head of the General Staff one could be assured that the country which, according to the official propaganda, was in constant danger from abroad, was in good hands. The great military reforms of 1934-1936 were also credited to Tukhachevsky. They had transformed the Red Army into a highly competent military force and enhanced its standing. To the people at large the Red Army had for some time now been a much more meaningful symbol of the new times and of revolutionary dynamics than the Party itself.

Even if Tukhachevsky did not prepare an uprising, it is not unlikely that he would have been ready to take such an action if he felt that Stalin's measures endangered the revolutionary achievements. This possibility was enough for Stalin to rid himself of a potential rival. The sacrifice of the one man of necessity led to that of the others.[37]

In the spring of 1938 the trials had reached their peak. Among those condemned to death in the Bukharin trial was Yagoda, the former head of the NKVD. The paroxysm of persecutions continued for a few more months. At the end of the year, however— it was the year of the first Czech crisis and of the Munich Conference—it petered out. A severe disciplinary action against the local NKVD organization in the Moldavian SSR made the people prick up their ears. It was a symptom of a coming change. In December 1938 Yezhov was relieved of his office as People's Commissar for Internal Affairs. Like Yagoda, who at one time had also been appointed to an unimportant post, Yezhov, too, was for the time being allowed to retain his office of People's Commissar for Rivers and Canals. He was succeeded by Lavrenti P. Beria, a Georgian compatriot of Stalin's who until then had been Chief of the State Police in Trans-Caucasia.

Beria was born in 1899 in Merkheuli in Georgia, probably the son of a poor peasant. As a student of the Technological Institute in Baku he joined the Bolsheviks, and as a young engineer he volunteered for work with the Cheka. He served during the Georgian rising of 1924 and in other revolts in the Caucasus, eventually becoming Chief of the Georgian GPU and Party Secretary of Georgia. For fifteen years he ruled the most restless of all Soviet republics, until in 1938 Stalin called him to Moscow where he was in charge of state security until a few months after the death of his powerful patron.[38]

When Beria appeared in Moscow, the slogan was: "Purge the Purgers!" and Yezhov was made the scapegoat of the allegedly overly severe measures of the *Chistka*. Within the NKVD a thorough house-cleaning took place. However, there was no change in the principle governing the state supervision of the Party's official pronouncements and opinions, the practice of administrative banishments and the use of forced labor camps. As heretofore, appropriate administrative measures provided the prison camps with the necessary labor force. Beria's handling of deportations differed from that of Yagoda and Yezhov in that they now took place noiselessly. The prominent persons among the persecuted had already been liquidated and shrill, propagandistic exposure was no longer opportune or necessary.

For an evaluation of the total process it is important to realize that the initiative for the purges did not come from subordinate organizations, nor from the NKVD and its chiefs. It lay entirely in the hands of Stalin and his intimates: L. M. Kaganovich, A. A. Andreyev, V. M. Molotov, A. A. Zhdanov. He also made use of his private secretariat (A. N. Poskrebyshev,[39] G. M. Malenkov), as well as of the NKVD apparatus and the office of the Public Prosecutor. The great *Chistka* was, therefore, a stage in Stalin's personal struggle for power. After the suppression of Trotsky's opposition, after the conclusion of collectivization, and after the passing of the great famine, this power was not actually endangered. It must once again be stressed that there is no proof that new terrorist cells were created in the Soviet Union at Trotsky's behest. Not until the first Trotskyite trial in 1936 did an oppositional trend appear which, however, remained as unorganized as the opposition of the peasants during the years of collectivization.

Stalin's position was, however, only safe as long as the "old guard" of the Party and of the Red Army would put up with the accumulation of dictatorial power in his hands. He had achieved the transition from the dictatorship of the proletariat to the dictatorship of the Politburo, *via* the dictatorship of the Party. From there he had gone on to the dictatorship of a small group within the Politburo. If the transition was to become permanent, it was necessary for the Party to wipe out the memory of the years of struggle for freedom, the Revolution and the Civil War. He was not concerned with the enemies of the Socialist revolution, nor with one or another opposition group within the Party. His concern were all those potential protagonists of real liberty who might arise from the innermost circles of the Party and of the Red Army. It was for this reason that foreign Communists who were staying in the Soviet Union, were sucked into the maelstrom of the persecutions.

Thus Stalin's *Chistka* also contained elements of the social realignment which, expressed in the popular saying "the revolution devours its own children," has been apparent in all similar events since 1789. However, the manner and the extent to which these events occurred cannot be understood without considering the personal motive of Stalin's struggle for power. In addition, the element of mass psychology must also be considered. As in witchhunting, and in the time of the Inquisition, collective insanity is palpably present in the "Witches Sabbath" of 1935-1938.

The fate of Stalin's most feared adversary must be accounted for. The final act of the great drama of the purges was not played in Moscow, but in Mexico.

In 1936 Trotsky was living in Norway. When the Soviet government demanded of the Norwegian government that it deprive Trotsky of the right of asylum and simultaneously threatened an economic boycott, the Norwegian Minister of Justice, Trygve Lie, was prepared to intern him but not to expel him, or hand him over to the Soviet Union.[40] Trotsky left Norway and went to Mexico where he continued his polemics against Stalin. The trials of 1937-1938 provided him with ample material. Several attempts were made on his life and all his children died in mysterious circumstances. On August 20, 1940, he too met his death. An obscure individual who had gained admittance by posing as a party comrade, splintered Trotsky's skull with an ice-ax while he sat at his desk at work on his biography of Stalin. "Thus," writes Deutscher, "the verdict of the Moscow tribunal which sentenced Trotsky to death, was carried out. Having mercilessly uprooted Trotskyism in Russia, Stalin now achieved his last dark triumph over the man himself, whose name like Lenin's had stood for the great hopes and the great illusions of the October Revolution. The banishment of those hopes and illusions was as if sealed by Trotsky's death. There was a tragic symbolism that the blood of Trotsky's head spattered the sheets of paper on which he had written down his account of Stalin's career. But in the whirlwind of that year—the summer of 1940—this epilogue to the Moscow trials passed almost unnoticed." [41]

From Purge to World War II

Unshaken by the horror of the Great *Chistka,* Stalin proceeded along the road he had mapped out for himself. The last year of the purges (1938) saw the appearance of a concise textbook of the history of the Communist Party of the Soviet Union, edited by a commission appointed by the Central Committee. Since the tenth anniversary of its publication, it has often been stated that the book was written by Stalin. While the compilation of the work had been personally ordered by Stalin, it was written by a group of historians under Zhdanov's supervision. The manuscript was reviewed by Stalin and annotated and corrected by him. He himself wrote only the section "On Dialectical and Historical Materialism" in Chapter IV, a section consisting of thirty-two printed pages (out of a total of 440 pages).

The work had to prove that Stalin was Lenin's only true disciple, and his closest friend, and the October Revolution had to be credited solely to those two, as all the other Bolshevik leaders of the years of struggle were deserters and traitors. The book, moreover, had to justify the legality of Stalin's personal dictatorship on historic grounds, and establish proof of his genius.

A direct road leads from the Stalin Constitution of 1936 to Stalin's history book of 1938. It was necessary to prove ideologically that the millions of victims who had fallen by the wayside had been necessary sacrifices.

The conclusion of the purges coincided with the beginning of the third Five Year Plan. At the Party Congress of 1939 defects and gaps in the second Five Year Plan were revealed. They consisted of a tremendous waste of manpower and equipment, and an alarming decline in the quality of the goods produced, as a result of the overemphasis on spectacular individual achievements in the Stakhanov manner. Frequently goods were unusable. Another matter of serious concern was the discontent of the workers due to the constant pressure and speed-up to which everyone was subjected as a result of the stellar performances of selected individuals.

The first two factors led to a new emphasis on quality rather than on speed and quantity alone, and to the issuance of official warnings against the so-called "gigantomania." Workers' discontent, however, was met with a tightening of work discipline. If output was not satisfactory, if a worker took time off or was merely late, he faced drastic reprisals, ranging from deductions from wages or social insurance to the withholding of vacations or eviction from housing provided by the plant, even to compulsory re-settlement or arrest.

The new serfdom of the *kolkhoz* peasants was now matched by the enslavement of the industrial worker. While official sources spoke of the six-fold increase in national income and the seven-fold increase in industrial production, the worth of these statistics in the face of the pauperization of the working masses is dubious. Certainly, as compared to Czarist times, social insurance, paid vacations, the possibility of recreational and convalescent trips and plant-provided housing, had resulted in a show of improvement in living conditions. However, just as the civil rights guaranteed in the new Constitution had remained paper freedoms—such as the right to associate, the right to strike, the freedom to change one's place of work, etc.—no true rise in the living standard of the workers had been brought about. The problem of a sufficient supply of consumer goods remained unsolved.

One of the main reasons for this failure is to be found in the tremendous increase in armament production from 1938 on. The military budget had been raised from five billion rubles in 1934 to 14.8 billion in 1936, and to 34 billion in 1939.[42] The standing force of the Red Army was constantly increasing:

1934 — 940,000 men
1935 — 1,300,000 "
1938 — 2,000,000 "
1939 more than 3,000,000 "
1940 — 4,000,000 " (5,000,000 men if the NKVD troops and the militia before the outbreak of war are included)

This growth of the military power, which devoured one fourth of the national income, was naturally attributed to developments abroad. Hitler's policy, which at first aimed at a re-establishment of German sovereignty and a revision of the borders drawn at Versailles, was seen as a threat by the Soviet Union; particularly as it was accompanied by an intensification of the ideological battle, and by the anti-Comintern pact which conjured up the spectre of an encirclement of the Soviet Union. After the purge of the Red Army, the High Command of the Soviet armed forces was reorganized. The Army and Navy were separated, a special People's Commissariat for the Navy was created. In place of the unwieldy eighty-member War Council of the Commissariat for Defense, a new Supreme War Council consisting of eleven members and a similar body for the Commissariat of the Navy were established. In order to co-ordinate all military matters and to underline their importance, a special Defense Committee headed by Marshal Voroshilov was set up within the Council of People's Commissars. A decree of September 1, 1939, ordering universal compulsory military service, abolished the territorial militia system of revolutionary times. Active military service was to last from two to five years, depending on the branch of the service.

When Marshal Timoshenko took over the People's Commissariat for Defense in May 1940, he took a number of steps further to strengthen discipline. The discussion of orders issued, which had until then been usual in the Red Army, was now condemned as "pseudo-democratic." A decree of August 12, 1940, re-affirmed the exclusive authority of officers which had been introduced in 1924 but temporarily suspended during the Tukhachevsky crisis in 1937. Desertion and absence without leave were punished with far greater severity.

The close connection between the military reforms introduced by Voroshilov and Timoshenko with the ideological line of Soviet patriotism is most clearly apparent in the announcement of a new oath on January 3, 1939. On February 23 all members of the Soviet armed forces were sworn in according to the new oath. While the old formula stressed the class consciousness of the workers, the world revolution and the brotherhood of peoples, nation, fatherland and state were now the focal points.[43]

There were many causes for the ideological changes in Stalinism in the thirties. The delay in the coming of the world revolution and the appearance of totalitarian regimes in several European countries had created a new situation which pointed to the necessity of strengthening the nation—of realizing "socialism in one country." This negative concept had to be provided, primarily for propaganda reasons stemming from the internal fight against the international line of the Trotskyites, with a positive angle. This was believed to have been found in the idea of the Socialist fatherland, in Soviet patriotism. By building bridges to the Russian past, by highlighting certain personalities and patterns of Russian history, it became possible during the thirties to counterbalance the pronounced upsurge of nationalist aspirations in the Ukraine with the Great Russian concept firmly centered in the multi-national empire of the Soviet Union.

Soviet patriotism, reinforced by Party mass indoctrination, fell on fertile ground, despite the considerable shocks to which public opinion had been subjected by the show trials and the forced labor camps on the one hand, and by the evident divergence from the ideology of the Marxist class struggle and Marxist internationalism on the other. It was the new generation which was most inclined to heed the appeal to hero worship. Side by side with the heroes of Russian history towered the great pioneers of "socialist reconstruction," closer at hand and more tangible. This generation soon revered the powerful dynamics of Leninism as applied also to the technological and organizational modernization of the country. Spellbound, one saw the Russian, together with the other inhabitants of the Soviet Union, seized by the spirit of technological and economic advance and saw unbelievable energies being released from the inert masses of the people. The opening up of new mineral deposits, the building of new roads, canals and railroads, the construction of giant industrial plants, pioneering achievements in Arctic exploration and in aviation—all these created, adroitly interpreted by propagandists, an enthusiastic pride of belonging to the world's most progressive nation, a nation which ruled one-sixth of the earth. Every map showing in global terms the tremendous expanse of the Soviet Union, triumphantly hammered this fact into the consciousness of every school child. Every single Soviet citizen could believe that he had had a part in this rise of his country. Proper standards of comparison with other countries were lacking—purposely. The terrorist methods of the regime, met by most of the older generation with resigned Eastern fatalism, were considered by the younger generation, which accepted Stalin's History of the Party as gospel truth, a necessary evil from which one turned to the business of the day.

Thus Soviet patriotism in the younger generation was not fictitious; it was not a phantom, but genuine. A kind of intoxication with technology and with Russia's limitless space was combined with the eschatological fascination of the Marxist messianic expectations. Evolving beyond Leninism, Stalinism seemed to some to lead the Soviet man toward "a happier future," even if the world revolution was tardy in coming.

It was the Komsomol, the Bolshevik youth organization, growing from one million to nine million members between 1925 and 1939, which nurtured this faith in a generation whose memory reached back neither to the Czar's nor to Lenin's days. Nevertheless, many of the defectors of the future were also of the generation brought up in the thirties.

The Soviet Intelligentsia

How did the Soviet intelligentsia arise?

After the state had become the sole owner of the means of production, the economic sector had as great a need for leadership personnel as Party and government. Cultural affairs and the sciences, press and radio, all centrally controlled, as well as public health and education, required a group of experts and government executives without whom public life would come to a standstill. Among the people this group soon became known as *apparatchiki;* they were the Bolshevik managers of the Soviet state socialism. According to official statistics they numbered about two million in 1926, nine and a half million in 1937, and had grown to eleven and a half million in 1940. In 1949 their number was estimated between fifteen and sixteen millions.[44]

The earnings of the *apparatchiki* far exceed those of the average Soviet citizen. Their share in the available national income has been put at 35%, although they represent only 14% of the working population. The corresponding figures for workers is 33% (22% of the population), for peasants 29% (53% of the population), while those engaged in forced labor (11% of the population), receive only two to three percent.[45] Thus the largest part of the national income is in the hands of the smallest class of the population. Usually they are also the winners of awards and Stalin prizes which frequently result in further privileges in the form of tax exemptions and free railroad travel.

As time went on the special position of the Soviet intelligentsia was consolidated. Higher education became their privilege. Until 1932, 65% of all students had to be members of the working class. After this requirement was removed, the proportion of working class students dropped to 33.9% by 1938, while that of children of civil servants rose to 42.2%. Since then no further figures have been published. On October 2, 1940 free tuition in secondary schools and universities was abolished. According to eye witnesses, this measure came as a stunning blow to the younger people,[46] who felt that a basic socialist achievement of which they had been justly proud, was being abandoned. Apart from recipients of scholarships, admittance to the universities was thus restricted to the well-to-do Soviet upper strata, which endeavored to fill vacancies from among its own ranks. This statement is not invalidated by the scholarships given to the children of proletarian parents, for such a grant necessitated a very definite mental subservience to the regime and its pillars—the new class of functionaries.

By a significant coincidence, on the same day (October 2, 1940) on which the abolition of free schools made higher education the privilege of the new intelligentsia, a Central Labor Reserve Office was established with the right to conscript children of both sexes between the ages of fourteen and fifteen for the trade, industrial and railroad schools which it maintained. Receiving free training and maintenance, the students of these institutions are considered "mobilized" and are obliged to work for four years after the completion of their training wherever the state chooses to place them. Freedom of vocational choice was sacrificed to the arbitrary power of the state and the Party.

The connection between the two measures is that the growing generation in both instances is placed at the disposal of the Bolshevik state and its agencies; in the former instance is is controlled mentally, in the latter physically.

Both the Party and its counterpart among the young people, the Komosol, reflect in their membership this structural change in Soviet society. The Party lost its predominantly proletarian character; the number of functionaries increased steadily and in 1949 they represented 64% of the membership, while the workers represented 21%, and the peasants 16%.[47] The Komsomol leadership has always been predominantly a preserve of the *apparatchiki.*

What, then, does Soviet patriotism represent? It is the credo of just those strata tied to the regime for better or for worse: the Soviet intelligentsia, the *apparatchiki,* the party leadership, the security service, the Red Army officer corps. Quite naturally it has a more emotional connotation to the younger age groups; among the older people, hardened by the years of intra-party strife and the *Chistka,* it is probably based on more rational and calculating considerations. Soviet patriotism withstood the great purge which in part reflected the struggle of the new intelligentsia against the old party leadership.

The possibilities of a further rise in patriotic sentiment are only thinly divided from the dangers of a crisis. The former could be promoted by a defensive war, the latter might appear if tensions arose between the new political and social classes, resulting in a real rift between the technological intelligentsia and the Party leadership proper.[48] It can easily be imagined how bitterly this newly arrived group, the *beati possidentes,* would oppose any attempts to turn back the clock for the sake of the original ideal of a classless society.

CHAPTER 7

THE SEE-SAW PERIOD OF SOVIET FOREIGN POLICY

Popular Front and League of Nations

As a result of the Soviet Union's entry into the League of Nations and the decision of the Seventh Comintern Congress to adopt the Popular Front policy, the year 1934-35 marked a decisive turning point in Soviet foreign policy.

The National Socialists' seizure of power in Germany played a preparatory rather than a decisive role, and we may question whether the Soviet public was really shocked by the news of January 30, 1933. After Bruening's fall, Moscow had become very suspicious of Papen's "Western Orientation," as the new German Chancellor was believed to be an advocate of an anti-Soviet French-German alliance. On the other hand, his successor, General Schleicher, who at the end of December 1932 received Litvinov on his way through Berlin, was considered a Russophile of the old Reichswehr school.

The prospect of the assumption of power by the National Socialists was viewed with equanimity, for Hitler was considered a pacemaker for Communism. Another fact pointed in this direction: as late as November 1932 the German Communist Party (KPD) and the National Socialists (NSDAP) had made common cause during a strike in Berlin. Contact between the Russian Embassy in Berlin and influential politicians of the German Social Democratic Party (SPD) was abruptly discontinued on Moscow's orders in January 1933. Moscow was convinced that Hitler represented but a stage on the road to a Soviet Germany.

Notwithstanding the anti-Marxist propaganda during the Reichstag Fire trial and the impassioned attacks on Goering with which Georgi Dimitrov had spiced his defense, Goering himself in an interview with a Dutch newspaper on March 21, 1933, and Hitler in a Reichstag speech on March 23, spoke in quite conciliatory tones of the Soviet Union. On May 5 the Berlin Pact of 1926 was readily extended. The replacement of von Dirksen, the German ambassador in Moscow, by Rudolf Nadolny and the appointment of Surits, one of the ablest Russian diplomats, as Soviet Ambassador in Berlin, seemed to ensure continued normal diplomatic relations: the men knew each other from their tours of duty in Ankara. These personal factors could be considered as conceivably pointing to a new diplomatic alignment.

The cause of the actual turn in German-Soviet relations was not ideological, but a political incident of which Moscow took a most serious view. This was the ten-year non-aggression pact which Hitler and Pilsudski concluded on January 26, 1934. Thus after National Socialist Party circles had long vacillated between a Polish and a Russian course, a decision, favored by Rosenberg's office, which had become the most important instrument of anti-Bolshevik propaganda, was finally made. It was Radek's opinion that in addition to this Polish policy, which held out hopes of regaining the Corridor by supporting Poland's desire for territory in the Ukraine, two other courses were open to Hitler. One was an alliance with France, which—in keeping with Papen's ideas, it was thought—would be directed against the Soviet Union; the other was Rosenberg's dream of an alliance with England and Italy which would be directed against both France and the Soviet Union.[1] Both courses, actually, could be combined with a settlement of German-Polish problems.

Polish Foreign Minister Beck was enough of a diplomat to leave for an official visit to Moscow shortly after the pact with Germany had been signed.[2] He was among the first Western statesmen to be received in the Kremlin and to some extent the event could be considered a success by the Soviet Union. The non-aggression pact of 1932 was extended, the legations of both countries were raised to embassies.[3]

The Soviet reaction to the German-Polish rapprochement is also proof of diplomatic skill. The Russians recognized that the dangers inherent in the pact could only be neutralized on a broad geographic basis by drawing both states into an Eastern pact system to which in addition, the Soviet Union, the Baltic states and Czechoslovakia would belong. Thus the German-Polish pact could, so to speak, be drowned in a larger treaty system. This system of an Eastern Locarno, which was strongly supported by the French Foreign Minister, Barthou, as a mutual military aid treaty, was submitted to Germany on March 28, but limited at this point to the Baltic states. The proposal was designed to counter the possibility that the Baltic nations intended joining the German-Polish pact. The Germans however turned it down when they saw that neither Reval nor Riga nor Kovno (Kaunas) evinced any desire to make use of a joint Russian-German guarantee.[4] Poland, too, rejected the Eastern pact. A joint protocol covering these questions was signed in Genoa only by the Soviet Union and France.[5]

It is entirely possible that the offer of a guarantee to the Baltic states concealed far more ambitious goals of Soviet foreign policy. The Russians may have envisaged a great territorial reapportionment which would assign the Baltic states to the Soviet Union and the Polish Corridor to Germany. Although the German Foreign Minister, Neurath, did not hesitate to tell Litvinov, when the latter called on him on his way back from Geneva, that Germany was not interested in the Russian proposals, Ambassador Nadolny once more tried to demonstrate the advantages of a continuation of the Rapallo course by appealing directly to Hitler. He pointed out that the Soviet Union could be considered the strongest military power in Europe and asked for an immediate friendly gesture toward Moscow.

Hitler, however, recalled Nadolny and the military collaboration between the Reichswehr and the Red Army, which had begun under Seeckt, was terminated. No restrictions were placed on trade but a transitory falling-off in German exports to Russia meant a temporary increase in British and American imports. On April 9, 1934, however, a new German-Russian trade agreement credited 200 million Reichsmarks to the Soviet Union so that German imports during 1936 amounted to almost thirty percent (British imports to about sixty percent).

Perhaps it was because of these economic factors that a journalist of Radek's caliber could still write in *Izvestia* on July 15, 1934 that he saw no reason why National Socialist Germany and the Soviet Union should not get along with each other, particularly as friendly relations had also been established with Fascist Italy. It is, however, also possible that this surprising statement, which Radek had undoubtedly been authorized to make, was a result of the strong impression which the quelling of the Roehm Putsch had made on Stalin that same summer. The murder of

Chancellor Dollfuss of Austria, and Hitler's growing dictatorial power after Hindenburg's death, were further evidence that, contrary to initial expectations, National Socialism was a reality to be reckoned with.

The German-Polish rapprochement and the failure of plans for an Eastern pact system brought about a shift in Soviet foreign policy toward an effort to draw closer to the Western powers. United States recognition of the Soviet Union was significant as a first success in this direction. It was granted in November 1933 after Roosevelt had been elected President and the Democratic party had come into power.[6] The Soviet government assured the United States that the lives and property of American citizens in the Soviet Union would be protected, and undertook not to engage in any Communist propaganda in the United States. The first American Ambassador to be appointed to Moscow was William C. Bullitt, a man who had travelled in Russia in 1919 and who had pleaded for American understanding of the upheaval then taking place. American public opinion, however, was divided or reserved. People were particularly shocked by the religious persecutions and atheist propaganda in the Soviet Union—as they had been shocked by the Jewish pogroms in Czarist Russia—and later the purges of the thirties were viewed with even more distaste. Bullitt himself met with the Kremlin's disfavor because of a pro-Japanese interview which he gave on December 1, 1935 in Berlin, and was accused of "anti-Soviet activities."

The example set by the United States was followed by the states of the Little Entente which, until then, had also not maintained any diplomatic relations with the Soviet Union. Particularly close ties were established with Czechoslovakia under Beneš, and with Rumania, too, relations became more friendly after Titulescu became foreign minister.

After Germany had left the League of Nations in October 1933, the possibility of the Soviet Union entering it was frequently discussed. In 1927 and 1932 Litvinov had participated in disarmament conferences of the League and had presented some quite bold proposals, undoubtedly made, in part, for their propaganda value. It is understandable that in view of the National Socialist racist policies he felt personally repelled by the Germans. In the Geneva cloakrooms, where he was a generally popular figure with the diplomatic crowd, he intensified his activities. He felt it was necessary to prevent the isolation of the Soviet Union, as had occurred in 1922 at Genoa and Rapallo, by taking part in the Western system of collective security. He had Stalin's support when the latter stated, "Comrade Litvinov is quite right. We want to join the League of Nations because otherwise we have to choose between the hammer and the anvil. We certainly do not want to be the hammer of the small and weak nations but we also do not want to become the anvil of the big powers."[7] On September 18, 1934, the Soviet Union was admitted to the League of Nations and was granted a permanent seat on the Council.[8]

At the Seventh Congress of Soviets of the Soviet Union which met in January 1935, Molotov, in his speech on the 28th, endeavored to justify this decisive step and interpreted it as increasing Soviet prestige in international affairs. At the same time he made it clear that a change in attitude towards Germany had taken place. When he referred to Hitler's *Mein Kampf* and the famous passage justifying an aggressive German policy in the East his audience could not help being affected. That same month, Goering, on the occasion of an official visit to Poland, had drawn Pilsudski's attention to the Ukraine and advocated a German-Polish alliance; in May (1935) Hitler in a conversation with Lipski, the Polish envoy, had spoken of Asia as the proper field for the Soviet Union's political activities; and in July of that year Beck was given a magnificent reception when he visited Berlin. It was, therefore, inevitable that Moscow would be alarmed by the intensification of German-Polish talks and these worries were further increased by the rise in German armament production. In January 1936 Tukhachevsky, in a speech to the Central Committee, expressed concern about the growth of the German army and—pointing to Hitler's successful rearmament—demanded an increase in Soviet armaments.[9] In a *Pravda* article of March 1937 he again drew attention to German re-armament and wrote that Hitler's army would reach 850,000 by the summer, when it would be forty per cent larger than the French army and as large as the Soviet army, although the population of the Soviet Union was 2½ times that of Germany and the Union's area ten times as large.[10]

In the meantime the Seventh Comintern Congress met in Moscow in the summer of 1935 (July 25). It had actually been planned for the end of 1934 but had been repeatedly postponed because of the international situation. It now issued directives for the Soviet Union's new foreign policy. For the first time in the history of the Comintern Congresses the Soviet state as such became the focus of the discussion. Joseph Stalin, the General Secretary of the Communist Party of the Soviet Union, was received with a burst of applause as a demonstration of the Soviet Union's leading position in world Communism. This was, however, also a significant symptom of the growing authority of the Soviet leader and of the new Kremlin etiquette. While, quite in accordance with Soviet propaganda tactics, naive observers from abroad, such as Joseph Davies, subsequently United States ambassador to the Soviet Union, felt that the results of this Congress represented the end of Bolshevik aims for world revolution; they were in reality simply a transition to more flexible methods.[11]

The thesis that Fascism and social democracy were twins was now filed away; instead, the defense of democracy against Fascism was declared to be the most important task of the workers' movement. Social Democrats and Communists were asked to stand together and form so-called popular fronts—a catch-all for every party, including conservatives and liberals, which was ready to fight against Fascism. This new order of the day meant the renunciation of one of the most important tactical principles of the Comintern, the prohibition of a Communist coalition with bourgeois parties. The support of all Communist parties in their fight against bourgeois governments was replaced by the order to maintain the domestic peace.

Manuilsky, the virulent opponent of social democracy in the Comintern, was replaced by the Bulgarian Communist, Georgi Dimitrov, the hero of the Reichstag Fire trial. His name became the symbol of militant anti-Fascism across party boundaries.

The resulting rapprochement between the Soviet Union and the Western democracies was most effectively confirmed by the visits of the West European foreign ministers in Moscow. Eden's stay in March 1935[12] was followed by Laval's visit in May.[13] For some time negotiations for a mutual assistance treaty between France and the Soviet Union had been in progress. Russia's failure to bring about an Eastern Locarno seemed to indicate that multilateral treaties would not be feasible and bilateral agreements would have to take their place. On May 2, a five-year treaty was signed in Paris guaranteeing mutual military assistance.[14] Immediately after this, Laval arrived in Moscow and, like Eden, was received by Stalin. That same month a similar treaty was concluded between the Soviet Union and Czechoslovakia, and was also given emphasis by Beneš's visit to Moscow in June of that year.[15] In this treaty a clause added to the second article was of great importance. According to it, the obligation to provide mutual aid was only to come into effect if France also went to the assistane of the injured partner. This passage which played such an important part in Czechoslovakia's collapse in 1939 actually turned the bilateral treaties with Czechoslovakia and with France into tripartite agreements.

Moscow was, however, disturbed by the fact that Paris delayed the ratification of the Soviet-French treaty for so long (until February 27, 1936), while Czechoslovakia ratified its agreement without hesitation even before Beneš left for Moscow. The treaty with France had no practical results, not even when Laval was replaced by the popular front government of Daladier and Blum, and Soviet politicians frequently complained about the lack of confidence which continued to exist between the two countries. While the domestic events of this year were certainly not such as to increase the reputation of the Soviet regime in French eyes, every diplomatic contact between the Western powers and National Socialist Germany, on the other hand, filled Soviet statesmen with the deepest misgivings.

The Spanish Civil War and the Anti-Comintern Pact

The new system of East-West military and diplomatic agreements was to be put to the test by the Italian attack on Abyssinia (October 1935) and the resultant international tensions. In June 1936 the Soviet Union was invited to the Conference of Montreux at which Turkey was given the right to fortify the Straits and naval negotiations were initiated with Great Britain.

It is noteworthy that in the spring of 1936, before German air force units actually went into action in Spain, Hitler seems to have played with the idea of changing his Polish card for the Russian.[16] Reports from the German embassy in Moscow, indicating that things had settled down again in the Ukraine, had a dampening effect on National Socialist plans for that area. Hitler's big Reichstag speech of March 7, 1936 in which he used the conclusion of the French-Russian pact as an excuse to denounce the Locarno agreement, was surprisingly free of attacks on the Soviet Union which had become so usual since 1934-35. It almost looked as if, after Locarno had been renounced, Rapallo was to become important again. However, this was apparently only a fleeting thought.

The summer of 1936 brought full-scale German and Italian support to Franco Spain, causing tension between Berlin and Moscow.

The Spanish Civil War of 1936-1938 had become an extremely serious international problem. The Kremlin found itself in a most difficult dilemma. While on the one hand Stalin had to prevent Franco's victory for ideological reasons, he realized on the other that with Fascist Spain as a neighbor France would feel encircled by Fascism and be virtually driven into Russia's arms as its only saviour. Conversely, a victory of the Left in Spain, following a whole-hearted Communist program, would diminish the possibility of a fruitful collaboration with the Western powers and drive France into Hitler's arms.

In the light of this dilemma the strange reserve which Stalin evinced toward the revolutionary intentions of the Spanish Republicans can be better understood. The Comintern gave instructions to the Spanish party to confine itself to the defense of the Republic against Franco and to abstain for the time being from all radical demands for the socialization of industry and the expropriation of the landowners. In a letter to the Spanish Socialist leader, Largo Caballero, who as a last resort had accepted Russian aid, Stalin recommended that the interests of the peasants be considered, that private property be respected and the investment of foreign capital not be discouraged.[17]

The aid which Hitler and Mussolini gave to the Franco regime made it impossible for Stalin to continue to stand aside. Soviet Russia's prestige as the stronghold and support of all revolutionary uprisings was at stake. Thus what had until then amounted to rather intangible propaganda aid, turned into actual financial and military help. It was characteristic that the Soviet Union supported the right wing of the Spanish Republicans and demanded the suppression of all anarchist, syndicalist and Trotskyite groups which were particularly prevalent in Catalonia. In the train of military specialists, agents of the GPU also came to Spain, experienced in the hunting down of political heretics and the organization of purges. Strangely enough the directions of purges among the Catalonian Communists was put into the hands of an old adherent of Trotsky, Antonov-Oveyenko, possibly in order to trip him up in this difficult task. Soon afterward he fell victim to the great *Chistka* in the Soviet Union.

Outwardly, the pretense of non-interventions was maintained. In August 1936 Litvinov, in response to a French request, signed a statement to this effect[18] and in December the Tass news agency denied reports of the presence of Soviet troops in Spain.[19] However not until February 20, 1937, were Soviet citizens forbidden to volunteer for the fighting and although in July the Soviet Union supported the British suggestion that all volunteers be re-called,[20] Bolshevik forces continued to participate semi-officially.

Thus Soviet intervention in the Spanish Civil War was governed by an endeavor to maintain at all costs the impression of a judicious solidarity with the Western powers and to avoid from the beginning anything that might lead to differences of opinion with the British and French governments. German-Russian relations, however, became considerably more strained as the ideological propaganda war between the two camps grew more intense and as both sides continued their participation in the Spanish fighting, albeit under camouflage.

These events in Europe coincided with a rise of Russo-Japanese tension in the Far East. Japanese intervention in Chinese affairs led to several incidents on the Manchurian border and the Bolshevik press used these to stir up patriotic sentiments. The Soviet government reinforced its troops in the Far Eastern Province and strengthened its friendly relations with the Mongolian Republic (Outer Mongolia) by concluding a new assistance pact. This was followed by a non-aggression pact with China the next year (August 21, 1937).

The Soviet Union and the Czech Crises

The Berlin-Rome axis was established in October 1936. It was followed by the conclusion of the German-Japanese Anti-Comintern Pact on November 25th. The Kremlin now felt that a direct connection between the European and Asiatic fronts of the "Fascist" powers had been established. While the Soviet Union probably did not seriously fear encirclement, the threat of it could be used successfully as a propaganda slogan in support of the new foreign policy. Salvation seemed to lie exclusively in Litvinov's new course of collective security and close collaboration with the Western powers. When in November, 1937 a new German-Polish agreement concerning national minority problems was published and Italy officially joined the Anti-Comintern Pact the same month, Litvinov's course and the popular front policy received renewed justification.

It must not be overlooked, however, that Soviet policies during these years, by no means prompted by one aim, were conducted along two distinct lines. Moscow was of the opinion that the new economic crisis which broke out about 1937 would seriously shake the capitalist world. The increasing number of unemployed in England and in the United States, coupled with the aggressive policy of the Anti-Comintern powers, led to the most pessimistic prognosis for the democratic West. The hour of Communism seemed once more to have struck. Contrary to promises made and despite the popular front truce, the opportunity for more vigorous Communist propaganda could not be passed by. A left wing victory in Spain, it was hoped, would set off similar developments in the other Western countries.

The increase in Bolshevik ideological propaganda was the chief reason for the West's distrust of the Soviet Union, and it interfered with the harmony of collective security. When this was followed by ever more sensational reports of the show trials in Moscow and the purging of the Red Army, the Soviet Union's prestige and importance in the eyes of the Western powers began to sink.

It was the Czech crises, however, which led to the final breakdown of the system of collective security between West and East.

As a result of the Nazi's surprise move into Austria in March 1938, the Sudeten German question soon became a vital problem for the Czechoslovak state. It became apparent how impossible it was, for geographic reasons alone, to deal with border problems in central Europe according to national principles and by means of plebiscites. After a first-hand examination of the situation in the Sudetenland and a series of personal discussions between British Prime Minister Chamberlain and Hitler, England and France urged Czechoslovakia to agree to relinquish the border territories. Responding to outspoken threats of violence, the Western powers decided to follow Mussolini's suggestion and give their advice more impact by arranging a Great Power conference in Munich. They believed that in this way they could save the peace. The Soviet Union, however, was not consulted.

In answer to a French inquiry at the beginning of September 1938, the Soviet Union had suggested that a joint statement be issued by the British, French and Soviet governments, an appeal made to the League of Nations, and a joint military plan with the Czech General Staff worked out. The Kremlin informed the Czech government that it was ready to carry out the assistance pact of

1935 if France honored her part in it. A protest was made against
the concentration of Polish troops on the Czech border. When the
United States offered to act as mediator, looking to a peaceful
settlement of the conflict, the Soviet government expressed its
interest in an international conference. It seemed a matter of course
that Russia would be invited.

However, the Western powers made no use of the Russian offers.
After the great domestic upheavals of the past few years, the West
felt justified in assuming that the strength of the Red Army had
been weakened to such a degree that the Soviet Union could not,
for the time being, be considered an effective partner in international affairs. Further, extensive Soviet interference in the central
European situation was in any event unwelcome. At the Munich
Conference, which took place from September 29 to September 30,
1938, Hitler's demands were accepted.[21] As French aid to Czechoslovakia was thus made impossible, the Soviet Union, too, was
relieved of its obligations.[22]

After German troops had invaded Czechoslovakia, the Soviet
Deputy Foreign Minister, Potemkin, could not restrain himself
from exclaiming to Coulondre, the French Ambassador in Berlin:
"Now we have no other way out but a fourth division of Poland!"[23]
This clearly shows that for the Soviet Union the Munich settlement
had a profound influence on Soviet-Polish relations. For some years
now the situation had grown tenser. In March 1938 the Polish
government, encouraged by Germany's annexation of Austria,
had sent an ultimatum to Lithuania, demanding that the rights of
Polish minority groups be respected and that Vilna no longer be
considered the capital of Lithuania. The Soviet government intervened at this point, exerted pressure on the Polish government,
and forced it to reduce its demands.

When, in September 1938, Polish maneuvers were held near
the Czechoslovak border, the Soviet government interpreted them
as troop concentrations and theatened to abrogate the Non-
Aggression Pact of 1932. After the Munich Conference and the
occupation of part of Czechoslovakia by German troops, Polish
troops also crossed the border and occupied the district of Teschen.
However, the Kremlin did not react to this immediately, nor to the
proclamation of a government for the Carpathian Ukraine in November 1938, at the same time as the final cession of the Teschen
district to Poland. An independent Carpathian Ukraine could
easily be seen as part of Hitler's Ukrainian plans, forming, in a

way, a Ukrainian Piedmont, as the germ of an independent Ukraine. That Moscow was aware of this is obvious from Stalin's speech to the Eighteenth Party Congress in March 1939, in which he spoke of the imbecility of planning to "join the Soviet Ukraine, an elephant in size, to the midget Carpathian Ukraine."[24] The fact that in December 1938 Hitler responded to Hungarian pressure and left the area in question to Hungary, is interpreted by some observers as the first conciliatory gesture toward Soviet Russia, forecasting the closer relations which the year 1939 was to bring.

During the second Czech crisis the Soviet Union again remained quite aloof. When Slovakia's declaration of independence, proclaimed in March 1939 on orders from Berlin,[24a] signaled the invasion of the remaining Czechoslovak territory by German troops and Hitler announced the creation of the protectorate Bohemia-Moravia on March 17, the Soviet Union did nothing more than send a quietly worded response on March 18. It disputed the constitutional right of the Czech President Hacha to agree to the German measures, and refused to recognize the incorporation of Czechoslovakia into the German empire.

Two Irons in the Fire

It was obvious that the policy of collective security had collapsed. Ribbentrop's visit to Paris had struck a serious blow at Litvinov's foreign policy. New ways had to be found if Soviet Russia was not to be excluded from all participation in the settlement of European problems or, worse, completely isolated. The snowball growth of German strength in the course of the past years and the conciliatory attitude of the Western powers gave rise to the opinion in leading Soviet circles that these powers planned to direct German expansionist efforts eastward. On October 4, 1938, the Tass Agency strongly repudiated the assertion that the decisions made at Munich had first been agreed upon with the Soviet government, which thus refused all responsibility for the fruits of Munich. However, in order to escape isolation, which was bound to become dangerous if Poland were to share the fate of Czechoslovakia, two roads were open. Either try to come to an agreement with the Western powers in order to strengthen the resistance to Hitler, or ally oneself with National Socialist Germany in order to participate in the division of Eastern Europe.[25]

In his speech of March 10, 1939 to the Eighteenth Congress of the Communist Party of the Soviet Union in Moscow (the first Party Congress in more than five years), Stalin left both possibilities open. He stressed the basic necessity of maintaining a certain degree of political flexibility within the limits of Marxist theory. While he mentioned the German expansion in the Danube region and Hitler's Ukrainian plans almost parenthetically and with derisive superiority, he spoke with biting acidity of the warmongers who, if what he said was to make sense, could only be sought in the camp of the Western powers. "We must take care that warmongers who are fond of letting others pull their chestnuts out of the fire, do not involve our land in a conflict." In his warning to the "aggressor nations" that they leave Russia in peace, he indicated that if they would do this he would be ready to make his own suggestions for arriving at an understanding; his own Munich, which would not be worse than Chamberlain's. The tenor of his remarks was sharply anti-Nazi and the trial balloon for Soviet-German understanding was carefully concealed. Nonetheless it was there. He was obviously first of all interested in leaving wide open the door to an agreement with Great Britain and France, but the back door, through which Ribbentrop one day was to slip, was slightly ajar.[26]

Mekhlis, the head of the Political Administration of the Red Army, who was not so much in the spotlight of international affairs, could after this speech afford to add that it was the task of the Soviet Union to meet its international obligations and to increase the number of Soviet republics. It became apparent that the Soviet Union proposed to match German expansion with similar expansion in its own sphere and the events of March 15-17, perhaps foreseen even then, were proof of this.

Later it became clear that Hitler was a better interpreter of the indirect and veiled offer which this speech contained than the governments of the Western powers of the more open hints which were addressed to them. Hitler's speeches on April 1 and April 28 of that year took a quite conciliatory attitude towards the Soviet Union. Since the beginning of the year the German Chancellor had been trying to manœuver Poland into a position that would result in a situation similar to that in Bohemia. When Beck visited him on January 4, Hitler's fanatic hatred of the Russians which had been so much in evidence during Beck's visit of the previous year,[27] had evaporated. Hitler stated that in his opinion the Ukrainian question was not of paramount interest and it was noticeable that his tone toward Poland had cooled considerably. The Ribbentrop plan, which had been discussed throughout the winter, provided for the return of Danzig and an extra-territorial railroad through the Corridor. However, in the spring Poland's attitude also stiffened. Lithuania's return of the Memel region to Germany on March 22, 1939 and an economically advantageous agreement with Rumania on March 23, did not, as Hitler had expected, make the Polish government more ready for concesssions but rather made it seek closer ties with the Western powers. Although on March 21 Beck, fearful of granting the right of passage to Russian troops, had turned down the British proposal to join France and the Soviet Union in a common defensive front, he told the German Ambassador categorically on March 28 that Poland would not accept Hitler's proposals. In this connection a good deal of importance has been accorded to the British guarantee of the Polish borders, which the Chamberlain government made on March 31, together with a promise of aid to Poland in case of a German attack. It has been said that this stiffened Poland's attitude toward Germany without being able to prevent the disaster in September 1939. For this reason English critics also have described it as an "unwise" move.[28] The facts, however, are that Beck was surprised[29] by this move, of which he was informed on the eve of the day on which it was officially announced. He had taken his stand against Germany two days before; all the British guarantee did was to strengthen the conviction of the Polish government that its attitude toward Germany was right. Neither Warsaw nor London foresaw Hitler's decision radically to change his course with regard to Russia, and on the basis of the new course, to risk a world war by carrying through his plan regarding Poland.

The British guarantee led to Hitler's putting his stake on the Russian card. On April 28 he unilaterally terminated the German-Polish pact of 1934. For the Kremlin the path to an agreement with Germany was now open. It had not yet become known that the British guarantee had only been given with a German attack in mind. (The fact that the Russians supported Roosevelt's suggestion of April 15 to convene an international conference for the clarification of the questions at issue, had little meaning.)

On May 2, 1939 Litvinov was replaced as Commissar for Foreign Affairs by Vyacheslav Mikhailovich Molotov, who assumed this post in addition to his office as Chairman of the Council of

People's Commissars which he had held since 1930. This initiated the new course of Soviet foreign policy. The person of the Commissar for Foreign Affairs should not be an impediment to a possible agreement with Germany and in this respect Molotov appeared a suitable figure.

On May 20 Molotov and the German Ambassador, Count von der Schulenburg, who had succeeded Nadolny, discussed for the first time political means of strengthening German-Russian trade relations. From then on the gradual development of closer German-Soviet diplomatic relations began to unroll before the eyes of international observers, starting with cautious explorations by subordinate officials, confidential conversations and hints, followed by official talks between the responsible policy makers up to the final decision in August 1939. The Soviet government managed to camouflage the German-Russian talks as skillfully as did Hitler's Foreign Ministry. The safeguard was even taken of temporarily recalling the Soviet ambassador in Berlin, Merekalov, and not having him return to his post for the whole summer. In the meantime Astakhov, the Soviet *chargé*, participated in highly important discussions which could, however, be disavowed if necessary. Sometime between May 27 and May 30 Hitler seems to have decided definitely to enter into negotiations with the Soviet Union. In a small Berlin restaurant on July 26 the outlines of a division of Eastern Europe were drawn for the first time, Poland being apportioned to Germany and the Baltic states, together with Finland and Rumania, to the Soviet Union.

The Baltic states had for a considerable time been subjected to strong Soviet pressure. Their efforts to overcome the limitations of their size by regular conferences between their foreign ministers and by expanding political and cultural exchanges in order to create a loose Baltic Entente, had aroused the wrath of the Bolsheviks as early as 1936. At that time Zhdanov, the Party Secretary of Leningrad, had turned the words of Peter the Great—that the window to Europe should be widened—into a timely threat. The official visit of Marshal Yegorov, Chief of the Red General Staff, to Reval and Riga in 1937 was proof of the Kremlin's growing concern about the Baltic countries. Nor did the very astute Latvian Foreign Minister, Munters, who visited Moscow that same year, succeed in dispelling the distrust with which the Kremlin viewed the formation of the Baltic bloc. And in June 1939 when Halder, the Chief of the German General Staff, visited Estonia on his way to

Finland, the Soviet Union again pricked up its ears. Even if rumors that the Germans intended to establish a footing on the Baltic islands were not true, the message which the Germans wanted to convey to the Soviet Union by this visit was well understood in Moscow and particularly in Leningrad. The best proof of this was Zhdanov's article in *Pravda* of June 29, 1939, which, with its sharp attacks on the Western powers, had been written for German eyes also.[30]

When Schulenburg hinted in a conversation with Molotov on August 3 that Germany was ready to respect Soviet interests in the Baltic countries, Molotov, according to Schulenburg, became communicative for the first time. He accepted the fact that this included for the moment only the two northern Baltic states and that the problem of Lithuania remained unsettled. However, he turned down the German proposal to include a political friendship clause in the preamble of the trade agreement which was now ready for signature. The Germans were not to get their way as easily as that and the Kremlin also showed reluctance and hesitation when Ribbentrop urged a personal meeting with Stalin. Molotov waited until August before informing the German government through the *chargé* Astakhov that the Soviet government was basically agreeable to negotiations taking place in Moscow.[31] The date, however, was left open.

In the meantime two things had happened. The Germans had sent a representative to London in the hope of using their trade agreements to further their political ends, but by July this plan had failed. The Soviet negotiations with the Western powers from April to August 1939 were of greater importance. They were based on the anger which Paris and London felt about the events of March 1939. In London, conservative politicians such as Duff Cooper and Churchill had repeatedly expressed the opinion as early as 1938 that so "gigantic a factor" as the Soviet Union should not be left out of account when it was a question of maintaining the peace. In the spring of 1939 the Labor Party also began strongly to urge that an assistance treaty be concluded with the Soviet Union. On March 17 Chamberlain announced in a speech that the British government would not only consult with Germany's immediate neighbors, but also with the powers beyond the European frontiers, about defense against German imperialist aims. At this point, however, the British government turned down as premature a proposal by the Soviet Ambassador Maisky that a major international conference be convened, and suggested only a joint declaration with Poland, condemning aggression, and an agreement to hold mutual consultations. This British counter-proposal, however, led nowhere as Poland refused to collaborate with the Soviet Union.

In April the Western powers, influenced by the growing tension, made further proposals. These primarily concerned the question of whether the Soviet Union was prepared to guarantee the borders of Poland and Rumania. Moscow, however, turned down a unilateral guarantee. The Soviet counter-demands, presented on April 17, envisaged an assistance treaty between the Western powers and the Soviet Union, a joint guarantee for all East-Central European states, and a military alliance. These proposals revived the Franco-Soviet East pact plan of 1934, extended into a military alliance, but under considerably less favorable conditions for the small states.

During the negotiations it became apparent that, apart from the right of passage through Poland, the Baltic question was now of paramount importance to the Soviet Union.[32] Here the Kremlin demanded a free hand. Although it was known that the Baltic states unequivocally rejected the automatic guarantee to be forced on them, France was nevertheless ready to accept the Soviet proposals. Great Britain remained considerably more hesitant at first and only on May 14 Chamberlain, under pressure from the Opposition, agreed in principle to the conclusion of an assistance treaty with the Soviet Union. As before, however, he felt that the consent of the states to be guaranteed was important. After Germany had concluded a non-aggression pact with Estonia and Latvia on June 7, Mr. Strang, the head of the middle-European division of the Foreign Office, was sent to Moscow to conduct the negotiations. The fact that no member of the Cabinet had been sent, did not exactly have an encouraging effect. The talks dragged on until Zhdanov's article of June 29, sharply attacking the Western powers and once more conjuring up the picture of the chestnuts which the Soviet Union was to pull out of the fire, had the effect of speeding matters up. The attitude of the British government grew more accommodating. At French urging, an agreement concerning the political treaty was achieved by July 24.[33] In line with the Soviet proposals, the Baltic states, Poland, Rumania, Turkey and Greece, and at the request of the French and British, Belgium also, were included in the list of states whose frontiers were to be guaranteed.

Despite certain British reservations, the Kremlin interpreted this treaty as Western consent to a free hand for the Soviet Union in the Baltic region. A week later—on August 3—Hitler was to give the Bolsheviks the same *carte blanche*.

In the final analysis, Molotov was not disturbed that the negotiations with the Western powers had taken so long, for this made it possible to test the second iron which the Kremlin had in the fire. On May 31 new proposals were submitted to the Western powers after Molotov had learned that not only Ribbentrop, but also Hitler, was interested in German-Soviet talks. It was necessary to play for time to come to an arrangement with the Germans. Because of this the negotiations were dragged out by constantly raising new points. The proposal to the Allies that they send a military mission to Moscow was made in order to increase the pressure on Germany, although the die was almost cast. The fact that Great Britain and France continued to send only subordinate personages and these *via* the slow sea route cast doubt on their good will in Moscow.

The military negotiations, which began on August 12, were to serve the Soviet Union as a means of extending the assurances obtained in connection with the Baltic states, to Poland as well.

Three days after Moscow had invited German negotiators to Moscow, Voroshilov, in his military discussions with the French and British, raised the extremely ticklish question of Soviet footholds in Finland and the right of passage through Poland and Rumania for the Red Army. The Polish government could not be persuaded to grant the Red Army this right. "With the Germans, we are in danger of losing our freedom, with the Russians our soul," the Polish Commander-in-Chief, Marshal Rydz-Smigly, is said to have declared in justification of this refusal. As the Western representatives did not want to agree to the right of passage against the wishes of the countries concerned, the negotiations were once again deadlocked. They were interrupted from August 17 to August 21 and it was one of history's minor ironies that during those days the German embassy in Moscow arranged a very successful garden party at which Strang, the head of the British mission, won first prize in a tennis tournament. On August 22, General Doumenc, the head of the French military mission, told Voroshilov that France would agree to the right of passage. Voroshilov replied that this was not sufficient, that formal approval by Poland and Rumania would be necessary. Only then could the treaty be signed, provided "that in the meantime the Polish situation had not changed."

It had already changed. On that very day it was announced in Moscow that Ribbentrop was on his way to the Soviet Union.

Stalin's Pact with Hitler

During the second half of August the German-Russian talks assumed concrete form. The political division of Eastern Europe was determined in outline and on August 19 a trade agreement was signed which granted the Soviet Union a two year credit of 180 million Reichsmark for the purchase of German goods. Hitler suddenly seemed to be in a great hurry to settle matters. German-Polish relations grew worse day by day; there was a chain of German-provoked border incidents countered by Polish excesses toward members of the German minority. Hitler was determined to force a military decision. On August 19 Schulenburg once again asked Molotov whether a date for a visit by Ribbentrop to Moscow could be set. This time, as before, the answer at first was no, but at 3:30 p.m. the German Ambassador was suddenly called back to Molotov. The Soviet Government, he said, would be ready to receive Ribbentrop in a week. It was Stalin himself who, in the intervening hours, had come to this decision. In a personal letter to Stalin, Hitler asked that Ribbentrop be received a few days earlier,[34] and Stalin agreed.

Ribbentrop arrived in Moscow on August 23. The negotiations took place in Stalin's presence in part, and made extraordinarily rapid progress. The result was a 10 year non-aggression pact, effective from the moment of signature, a very unusual diplomatic procedure. Both partners guaranteed each other absolute neutrality if one of them was attacked by a third party; and provisions were made for regular consultations on questions of mutual interest, and friendly discussions in cases of disagreement. Of particular importance was a secret codicil of which the world was not to know until much later.[35] It laid down, firstly, the division of Poland with the rivers Narev, Vistula and San as the demarcation line. The question of the existence of a Polish state remained open. Secondly, it dealt with the Baltic states. Here the division took place according to spheres of interest. Estonia and Latvia were allotted to the Soviet Union, Lithuania to Germany. In the negotiations over this point Ribbentrop had at first set his sights for the

Duena line which would have brought the southern part of Latvia, the province of Courland, under German control as well. However, Stalin wanted the Baltic ports of Libau and Windau on the coast of Courland. Ribbentrop telephoned Hitler directly from the conference room and obtained his agreement to this concession. Stalin was very much taken aback by this surprising readiness to yield, and according to his later statement, he suspected even then that Hitler considered these concessions only temporary and intended to take them back at the first opportune moment. The third clause of the secret codicil concerned Bessarabia. Here Ribbentrop declared readily that it was of no interest to Germany.

The news of the Hitler-Stalin Pact of August 23, 1939 hit the world like a bombshell. It had tremendous impact, particularly since the preliminary talks had been kept completely secret. The control of public opinion which both totalitarian states had mastered to an almost equal degree, enabled them at a moment's notice to put a complete stop to the hostile propaganda with which they had been bombarding each other. The press of both countries now reveled in mutual declarations of friendship and the editorials provided the necessary historical background by reminiscing about the Prussian wars of liberation in the early 19th century, Bismarck, and Rapallo.

After the rest of the world had recovered from the shock, it became clear that a most critical stage had been reached regarding Poland's fate. On August 25, England extended its guarantee to a treaty of assistance. At the same time intensive negotiations took place between London and Berlin, but they were rendered extremely difficult by Hitler's ever-increasing demands and the high-handed disregard of the usual diplomatic forms to which the British and Polish representatives were treated. The German government demanded that a special Polish plenipotentiary be sent to Berlin. Hacha's fate, however, warned Beck against coming to Berlin personally. The British assistance pact had encouraged the Polish government to adopt a firmer attitude so that even now it did not realize just how serious the situation was and what the consequences for Poland might be. A last mediation proposal by Mussolini gave Poland a short breathing spell. He suggested an international conference to which France readily agreed; Britain, however, refused to participate. On September 1 German troops invaded Poland. Two days later England and France broke off diplomatic relations with Germany. The second World War had started. While the capitalist states massacred each other, the Soviet Union hoped to harvest the fruits of the summer's diplomatic achievements.

Here it is relevant to ask what path Stalin's foreign policy followed during the summer of 1939. With his speech of March 10 he had put two irons into the fire, but it is difficult to say which he thought the more important. Undoubtedly he thought it best to keep the Soviet Union out of international conflicts for the time being, to remain an observer on the sidelines and, ultimately, to profit from the strife of others. Could he succeed in this? In the face of the dynamics of National Socialism he more and more doubted that the Western powers would oppose Hitler. Later he told Churchill that at that time he reckoned with the possibility that the Western powers might let Poland down as they had Czechoslovakia,[36] leaving Russia and Germany face to face alone. The tardiness with which Great Britain and France tackled diplomatic and military negotiations in the summer of 1939, strengthened Stalin's conviction that a real gain could only be made through an alliance with Hitler. Hitler's pressure since the beginning of August, and his readiness to concede to the Soviet Union an extension of its sphere of influence in Eastern Europe, seemed to confirm that he meant business. Thus, on August 19, the die was cast in the Kremlin.

In his notable speech, after the German attack on Russia, on July 3, 1941, Stalin attempted to justify his conduct. "It will be asked," he said, "how was it possible that the Soviet government signed a non-aggression pact with so deceitful a nation, with such criminals as Hitler and Ribbentrop?" And he supplied the answer: "We secured peace for our country for eighteen months which enabled us to make military preparations." Stalin did not, however, mention the territorial gains which the agreement with Germany had also brought, a strategic outfield which was important for defense and as an avenue for political infiltration of the West.

The Division of Poland

When Hitler's attack on Poland inaugurated the Second World War, the Soviet Union had been for some time engaged in tedious frontier battles with the Japanese. In the summer of 1938 there had been an incident on the Soviet-Manchurian border near Lake Khassan. Soviet reports spoke of skirmishes in which the Japanese had been thrown back. The newspapers made much of this, and during a time when Russia was living under the shadow of the recent purges, it stimulated patriotic sentiment. In May 1939 there were further incidents on the Manchurian-Mongolian border as the Japanese advanced into Western Manchuria. In accordance with the 1936 treaty, the Red Army was committed to aiding the Mongolian People's Republic and Soviet troops participated in the fighting which took place throughout the summer along the Chalchin Gol river. They inflicted some losses on the Japanese. The latter withdrew and negotiations were opened which coincided with the climax of the European crisis. On September 15, 1939, an agreement was signed in Moscow. Hostilities were terminated and a border commission formed. The Soviet Union was thus free to act in the West; the Anti-Comintern pact notwithstanding, Japan had not yet joined the military alliance between Germany and Italy which had been concluded on May 22, 1939, as an extension of the existing Axis pact.

German troops had broken Polish resistance by the time Soviet troops crossed the border on September 17, two days after the armistice with Japan. There is little indication that a joint military plan had been worked out between the Germans and the Soviet Union. However, the idea of military collaboration must have been considered. When on August 27 rumors circulated in Berlin that Soviet troops had already crossed the Polish border, Schulenburg was instructed to request Moscow to withdraw its troops, if the rumors should indeed be true, as the diplomatic preparations for the war had not yet been completed.[37] However, on September 3, the day of the British and French declaration of war on Germany, Ribbentrop asked the Soviet government "to mobilize its forces against Poland and to occupy the territory which it had been allotted in the secret agreement." Subsequently the German government repeatedly urged the Soviet Union to intervene.[38] However, on September 10 Molotov stated that the time had not yet come; preparations would still take another two or three weeks, but three million men had already been mobilized. Apart from the desire to reach settlement with the Japanese first, it seemed advisable for Russia's reputation both abroad and at home to start intervention only when it would no longer have an actual military character. Not until the Germans reported—prematurely as it turned out—

the imminent fall of Warsaw on September 15 (the city actually resisted until September 27), did the Soviet government begin to speed up its own invasion.

At first the Polish government had been as misled about Soviet intentions as the rest of the world. After the departure of the British and French military missions from Moscow, Marshal Voroshilov had stated in an interview that the Soviet Union was prepared to supply Poland with raw materials and arms. As late as September 2 the Soviet Ambassador in Warsaw proposed that negotiations be opened on this subject. When, however, the Polish Ambassador in Moscow reminded Molotov of this on September 8, the latter replied that the situation had now changed and that the Soviet Union had to concern itself first and foremost with its own interests. Soon after this the Soviet press began to report incidents along the Polish border. Informed Polish circles may have sensed what was up, but it was too late to prevent the catastrophe from running its course, particularly as the Western powers responded neither with military aid nor by declaring war on the Soviet Union[39] when the attack from the east took place.

The Soviet troops met hardly any resistance; the fate of the Polish army had already been sealed. The simultaneous movements of the German and Soviet armies led to a quick encirclement of the Polish troops. On the Polish side these operations led to the loss of 300,000 men dead, wounded and taken prisoner, while the Soviet losses were only 757 dead and 1,862 wounded.

In a public statement on September 17, Soviet intervention, despite several discussions of the wording with the German government,[40] was justified on the grounds that the population of Eastern Poland had to be protected from the Germans. Both the press and the propaganda agencies used the argument—most zealously abroad but with more caution at home—of the "liberation of Russia's Ukrainian and White Russian brethren in the territories in question." In later Soviet historical works the version of the "helpful brother's hand" which was extended to the Ukrainians and White Russians, has been given a good deal of space. The fact that the Polish-Soviet Non-Aggression Pact had been violated was coolly explained away by pointing out that like all other contracts it had expired when the Polish state had ceased to exist.

In the course of military operations German troops had at

some points crossed the demarcation line, and had to be withdrawn. To the surprise of the rest of the world, these movements took place without friction. The demarcation line now assumed the character of a military frontier. In Galicia the oil territory of Borislav-Drohobich on the upper San had been occupied by the Germans and they would have liked to keep this area. Molotov refused, but conceded the triangle of Suwalki between East Prussia and Lithuania (with the exception of Augustovo) on October 8, 1939.

Nothing had so far been settled regarding Poland's ultimate fate. The creation of a small Polish state under German protection was a strong possibility. On September 19, however, Molotov informed the German Ambassador that the Soviet government, and Stalin personally had changed their original intention to create a rump Polish state and were now in favor of a final division of Poland along the demarcation line. One week later Stalin asked Schulenburg to see him and informed him of his decision. The creation of any kind of Polish state, he thought, might lead to friction between the two powers. If Germany would give up Lithuania, he would gladly be ready to let her have the county of Lublin and part of the county of Warsaw as far as the River Bug on the eastern side of the demarcation line. The Soviet Union by thus ridding itself of areas where the Polish population might become a center for nationalist Polish and anti-Soviet tendencies, planned to secure for itself the possession of the whole of the Baltic territory up to the border of East Prussia. These proposals were to be the subject of negotiations with Ribbentrop.

During Ribbentrop's second visit to Moscow, a German-Russian border and friendship agreement was signed in September 28, with a codicil of the same date, and another one dated October 4. Stalin's proposals served as the basis for discussion and were accepted by Germany. They formed the content of the secret codicil.[41] Ribbentrop did not succeed in obtaining a change in the frontier on the Upper San and thus a part of the oil deposits; Stalin agreed only to supply Germany with one year's oil production—about 300,000 metric tons. It was a direct result of Stalin's policy and proposals when ten days later Hitler decreed the creation of the so-called *Government General* of Poland. Among the Polish inhabitants of the territory which Russia surrendered in September, were a great number of Jews, abandoned to Hitler's racial policy, i.e., to extermination. It is significant that the new border coincided with the so-called Curzon line which in 1919 the Allies had submitted to the Peace Conference. Even then Stalin was probably thinking ahead to the time when the Western powers would be asked to sanction this border. The Russo-German agreement provided for an extensive economic program under which Soviet raw materials were to be paid for by German deliveries over a long period.

The fourth partition of Poland, as Potemkin had prophesied, had taken place. The Soviet Union gained 20,000 square kilometers and almost thirteen million inhabitants. Of these, seven million were Ukrainians, three million White Russians, more than one million Poles, and more than one million Jews. The Polish "Eastern territories" which in the Middle Ages had been part of the Russian Kiev Empire, had been regained by Catherine II in the course of the first Polish partition in 1772, had been a bone of contention during the reign of Alexander I, and had now become a part of Soviet Russia. The Soviet Union presented itself to the people as a new "gatherer of Russian soil," exponent of ancient Russian national claims.

The Kremlin also lost no time in consolidating the diplomatic gains it had made in the Baltic area. As early as September 24, the Estonian Foreign Minister, Selter, had been requested to come to Moscow because of a supposed incident in Reval. On September 28, the same day Ribbentrop was in Moscow, Selter had to sign an assistance treaty in which Estonia made naval and air bases available to the Soviet Union. Soviet troops, at this point still modest in number, which were to occupy these points were granted admission. On October 5 it was Latvia's turn. She too had to make naval bases available at Windau and Libau. On October 10 similar conditions were imposed on Lithuania. The Vilna territory, which Lithuania had long coveted, was pulled out of the bankrupt Polish estate and presented to the Lithuanians as a morning-gift in acknowledgement of the new collaboration. All three assistance pacts were supplemented by trade agreements which changed the modest volume of the years following 1917 into mass deliveries which soon led to the impoverishment of the Baltic countries. Those among the Baltic politicians who had some insight knew exactly what lay in store for their countries. The road to final annexation by the Soviet Union had already been mapped out and the hopes which at one time had been placed in the Western powers, particularly England, had been shattered.

In the face of the political alignment which had crystallized since August 23, there seemed no other possibility of meeting the threatening developments than as intensive a collaboration as possible between the Baltic states.

In the secret codicil of September 28, a large-scale population exchange between Germany and the Soviet Union had been agreed upon. In collaboration with the local authorities, all persons of German nationality or of German origin were to be allowed, if they so desired, to re-settle in Germany or in the German spheres of interest, with full protection of their property rights. The same applied to Ukrainians and White Russians in those parts of Poland that had been allocated to Germany.

To the Baltic Germans re-settlement appeared a safety measure against the dangers of a bolshevization of the country. The transfer was carried out smoothly by joint commissions set up by the German and Soviet authorities. The subsequent re-settlement of the so-called ethnic German peasants from Eastern Poland (and later from Bessarabia and Bukovina) was handled in a similar manner.[42]

German-Soviet Cooperation and the Comintern.

An evaluation of German-Soviet cooperation reveals that both partners viewed the situation with stark realism and their relationship had the character of a marriage of convenience. They exploited the advantages of their alliance quite unscrupulously with regard to the outside world and with the greatest distrust toward each other. However, both Hitler and Stalin were not completely free from illusions.[43] Hitler believed he was witnessing a great change in Russia, a shift of Bolshevism from its international basis to an anchorage in Slavic-Muscovite nationalism.[44] Stalin's illusion was his belief that the agreements concluded with Germany would last for a long period. He envisaged a drawn-out, stubborn and bloody war in the West and thought that harmony with Hitler would last as long as that war, or at least until its last and decisive phase. Then the time would come when, as in the Polish campaign, he would appear on the side of the victor and pocket a share of the spoils.

The first political project on which Germany and the Soviet Union collaborated was a joint campaign for an immediate peace, set in motion after the Polish war. A joint declaration issued on September 29, held Great Britain and France responsible for the continuation of the war, if they refused to take part in another Munich. The Soviet Union would have been an important participant in such a new Munich conference. It was interesting that Stalin mobilized the whole Comintern apparatus for this peace campaign. In Italy, Belgium and the United States, Communists used sloganized protests against being "dragged into the war." In Great Britain, a so-called People's Congress in January 1940 opposed the "imperialist war" and the nationalist attitude of the Labor Party. The French Communists were particularly confused: at first they had voted for war loans, but at the beginning of November 1939 they were ordered to join the anti-war front. The leaders of the German Communists, who had fled to Russia, were especially vehement in their attacks on Great Britain and France. Walter Ulbricht, one of the Comintern secretaries, advocated Hitler's peace proposals and stated that the Soviet people and the German workers had a common interest in thwarting the British war plans. Things went so far that thousands of copies of Molotov's great "peace speech" (addressed to the Supreme Soviet on August 31), were dropped over France by German planes, and Czech Communist leaders were given permission by the German authorities to make tours of inspection in the protectorate of Bohemia-Moravia.

In all his official speeches between August 1939 and July 1940 Molotov stressed the theme that ideological differences need not stand in the way of a closer collaboration with Hitler. Europe needed a strong Germany, the responsibility for the war lay chiefly with Great Britain and France, who alone favored its continuation and expansion. The war which these two states perpetuated was an imperialist war, the sole purpose of which was to enable Great Britain and France to retain their colonies. This became the official foreign policy line of the Communist party of the Soviet Union and was echoed by the entire press and propaganda apparatus.

There was also collaboration in military matters. Recalling perhaps their relations during the twenties, military men on both sides now proceeded to develop a plan for working closely together. The primary area of concern was naval strategy. The Soviet Union supplied Germany with a naval base near Murmansk, which which was in use until the beginning of September 1940. In return Russia hoped to obtain blueprints of the latest German battle ships, construction plans for anti-aircraft batteries, armored turrets for naval vessels, etc. Negotiations started in September 1939.

Germany actually put the cruiser *Luetzow* at the disposal of the Soviet Union; German technicians went to build or remodel Soviet warships in the Leningrad docks; the German passenger steamer *Bremen* found refuge in Murmansk on its return from the United States, and all foreign ships were kept back until three days after its departure. But collaboration remained limited. Hitler could not overcome his distrust of the Soviet Union. For example, he turned down the proposal that German submarines be built in Russian docks or be purchased by the Russians, he refused to sell the heavy cruiser *Seydlitz,* and did not give permission for the blueprints of the battleship *Bismarck* to be passed to the Russians.

Economic programs functioned better. Stalin himself stressed the need for the proper observance of the conditions, and for consideration of additional German wishes. In a conversation with a German representative he stressed that if cooperation continued for another four to five years, the Soviet Union would be in a position to keep "two Germanies" supplied.[45] According to the major economic agreement concluded on February 10, 1940, Germany was to receive goods to the value of 800 million Marks in the course of the first twelve months, including 900,000 metric tons of petroleum, 100,000 metric tons of cotton, 500,000 m. t. of iron ore, 300,000 m. t. of scrap and pig iron, 2,400 kg. platinum and also manganese, lumber, feed grain, vegetables, etc. From the notes (dated September 28, 1940) of one of the German negotiators, it is apparent that the Soviet Union had supplied in one year almost one million metric tons of grain alone. Both sides stressed the political significance of their trade relations and *Pravda* celebrated the agreement most enthusiastically on February 19, 1940.

While Soviet deliveries were made in good order and punctually, German deliveries of manufactured goods were frequently delayed. In March 1940, the Soviet government found it necessary to send a reminder regarding the proper fulfillment of the terms of the contract. On its own part, it was so concerned with carrying out the agreement conscientiously that even goods obtained through other trade agreements were often made available to Germany. British rubber and tin which, under an agreement of October 11, 1939, had been supplied in exchange for Russian lumber, was in part passed on to Germany and when Britain asked for guarantees to prevent this, the Soviet Union refused to grant them. Other raw materials which Germany needed were also obtained abroad through the Russians or reached Germany via Soviet ports and Soviet railroads. Germany could thus obtain deliveries from the Far East and from overseas and, in part at least, evade the British blockade.

For the Soviet Union, the advantages of cooperation at first lay exclusively in the political sphere and efforts were made to increase them gradually.

The Winter Campaign against Finland

Aside from the Baltic states, Soviet foreign policy had a goal of which little mention had been made in the discussions during the summer of 1939. This was Finland, a country which enjoyed the friendship both of Germany and of the Western powers, particularly the United States. Although this fact had to be taken into account, the Kremlin thought that it could risk putting the recent successful collaboration with Germany to the test. The Western powers did not have to be considered at this point. Therefore following the settlement with the Baltic states, negotiations were opened with Finland on October 5. However things went by no means as smoothly as with the Balts. The Finns put up a stubborn resistance.

Soviet demands were mainly concerned with an adjustment of the border on the Karelian Isthmus. In an hour of weakness during the war against Gustav III of Sweden, Catherine II had already criticized her predecessor, Peter the Great, for having built the capital of the Empire so near the border. In 1919 the Soviets had gone through the experience of a threat to Leningrad by the White armies of Finland while Yudenich's troops were approaching from the southwest and the British fleet was menacing Kronstadt. Now the fortifications which the Finns had erected on the Karelian Isthmus seemed like a gun pointed at Leningrad. It was said that from there, only 32 kilometers away, the city could be attacked by long-distance guns; Kronstadt was open to attack from Viborg; and Finnish planes could reach Leningrad in two to four minutes. From the way in which the border ran across Karelia, the Murmansk Railroad was also thought to be exposed to Finnish attack. However, apart from the fact that Leningrad was no longer of the same importance as in the 18th and 19th centuries, the Russians ignored the fact that the so-called Mannerheim Line was not a belt of fortifications like the Maginot Line. Of the

96 concrete dug-outs along the 125 km. long line of fortifications, only 29 were up to modern standards.

The Soviet Union also wanted to lease the Hangoe Peninsula at the entrance of the Gulf of Finland, and the Finnish part of the Rybachii peninsula with Petsamo, Finland's only ice-free port at the Arctic Sea, in order to construct Soviet naval and air bases. In return the Soviet government offered Finland an area which was twice as big, but economically far less valuable, in Northern Karelia. Premier Paasikivi, who had signed the peace treaty with the Soviet Union in 1921, was ready to agree to all points except the lease of Hangoe, the key to the Gulf of Finland. He felt that this would mean risking the security of his country, and he knew that he had the support of his whole people. The negotiations were broken off on November 13.[46] Finland began to mobilize and to reinforce its troops on the Karelian front. The Soviet Union responded on November 28 with the abrogation of the non-aggression pact. Two days later thirty Russian divisions attacked at eight points along the extensive border and that same morning Helsinki was bombed by the Red Air Force. The Finnish Winter Campaign of 1939-40 had begun.

The Soviet plan envisaged that the attack and bombardment of the Finnish cities would in themselves suffice to provoke the Finnish nation to rise against its government. For this reason only a limited number of troops from the Leningrad military district were used. It had been expected that the campaign would be but a Sunday outing, that it would be easy to rout the Finnish troops. However, the Red Army's first break-through on the Mannerheim Line was met with unexpectedly violent resistance which was buttressed by the impassibility of the terrain with its forests, lakes and swamps, and by bad weather. Camouflaged Finnish ski patrols constantly swarmed around the enemy. They suddenly emerged from the forests, attacked Soviet columns, and cut them off from reinforcements. Hundreds of Russian tanks were immoblized in the snow and in the swamps, others were attacked with great courage and destroyed. The Red air attacks only served to strengthen the Finnish will to resist. The Soviet losses were tremendous. An attempt to break through to the Bothnian Bay via Kajaani at Finland's narrowest point failed. Only the surprise attack on Petsamo was successful. When the Soviet leadership realized that it could not expect to succeed in forest warfare in the North, it decided to concentrate its efforts on the Mannerheim Line in the hopes of forcing the issue there.

On February 2, 1940, Marshal Timoshenko attacked the Line with 27 divisions and a tremendous number of guns. After ten days he managed to break through. The Finnish resistance collapsed and starting February 15 the troops fell back. In the open terrain it was not possible to stem the Soviet tide. Finland was forced to ask for a truce.

In the meantime the rest of the world had been greatly angered by the Soviet attack on Finland. First and foremost public opinion in the Scandinavian countries was aroused. On December 7, 1939 the three Scandinavian Foreign Ministers had actually signed a declaration of neutrality, but the Swedish government attempted several times to intervene in Berlin on Finland's behalf. It received the only partially reassuring answer that Germany was not interested in an extension of the Finnish-Russian conflict. German-Russian consultations in February 1940 once more confirmed that Swedish neutrality would be respected; this was reported by Tass on March 3. Thus an intervention by the German government in Finland's favor did not come about. Supplies of arms which had been promised Finland out of the Polish loot were stopped in December 1939. This policy, in line with a decision made in August of that year, was obviously an unpopular one. In England, France and the United States "all the resentment felt against the Soviet government for the Ribbentrop-Molotov Pact was fanned into flame by this latest exhibition of brutal bullying and aggression. With this was also mingled scorn for the inefficiency displayed by the Soviet troops and enthusiasm for the gallant Finns." [47] There was a movement to help the Finns by sending them arms, ammunition and volunteers. Throughout the winter discussions were held between the governments and General Staffs of Britain and France regarding the dispatch of an Expeditionary Force to Finland. As for the delivery of supplies, there was only one route that could be used. This was via Narvik, through neutral Norwegian and Swedish territory. An important consideration in this was that such an expedition would at the same time also prevent the Germans from acquiring ore from the Swedish mines situated along this route.

However, the Western powers could not follow through with their plans. Norway and Sweden were not prepared to prejudice their neutrality. It is possible that Britain and France might have decided to overcome this obstacle, but the plan as a whole was viewed quite sceptically and made only slow progress. In Finland it was feared that a British and French landing in Norway would extend the battlefield to the whole Scandinavian north in such a way that there would be little hope for effective military assistance to Finland herself. It would have been too little and too late. The only positive action the western powers took was to exclude Soviet Russia from the League of Nations on December 14, 1939.

With its traditionally sober realism, the Finnish government decided to yield to the inevitable. A final Allied request made to the Scandinavian governments on March 11 and 12, 1940, to permit the passage of troops for the support of Finland, had been turned down. Britain's and France's decision to send an Expeditionary Force even without this permission and in that event to break off diplomatic relations with the Soviet Union, came too late. The peace negotiations had been started and on March 12 the treaty was signed in Moscow.[48]

Finland ceded the Karelian Isthmus and the region on the northern bay of Lake Ladoga with the cities of Viborg, Kexholm and Sortavala, in addition to parts of the Rybachii peninsula and several smaller islands in the Gulf of Finland, to the Soviet Union. On the Finnish western border, in the district of Kandalaksha, the border was pulled somewhat further back. The peninsula of Hangoe with the adjoining islands was leased to the Soviet Union for thirty years for the purpose of erecting a naval base at a yearly rent of eight million Finnish marks. Finland had to pledge herself to stay out of any hostile coalition against the Soviet Union. The port of Petsamo was returned.

The friendly relations between the Soviet Union and Germany had met the test of the Finnish war. In his reply to a congratulatory telegram from Hitler on the occasion of his sixtieth birthday, Stalin stressed that German-Soviet friendship was now "sealed with blood." On February 11, the German-Russian trade agreement was extended to meet German grain requirements more adequately. Although Stalin did not accept an invitation to Berlin which was extended to him in March 1940, the excuse given was that he hesitated to appear in a setting with which he was not familiar.

The Allied Plans in the Near East

In the spring of 1940 the Soviet Union not only faced the danger of hostilities with the Western powers in Northern Europe, but also the possibility of a military embroilment in the Near East.

General Weygand, Chief of the French military mission in Beirut, had been very active since August 1939. When in September 1939, the Soviet Union began negotiations with Turkey for the conclusion of a non-aggression pact, Britain and France consulted with each other about the means of strengthening their Near Eastern position. It was due to their close contact with the Turkish government that Turkey finally rejected the Soviet advances, especially as Soviet commitments were not to be applicable in case of a German attack on Turkey. On October 19 Turkey concluded an assistance treaty with Britain and France.

The Turkish government realized that its national integrity could only be endangered by the German-Russian alliance. Only by joining the Western powers could it hope for protection. Such a decision had, however, to be carried out most cautiously in order to give the Soviet Union no cause for reprisals. For this reason a clause in the assistance pact specified that it was in no case to lead to a conflict with Soviet Russia.

On January 20, 1940, an Anglo-French conference took place in Beirut which was followed by discussions in Ankara and Cairo. In addition to the plan to send an Expeditionary Force to Salonika in order to assist Greece against the Axis powers, the Allies also entertained the idea of cutting off Germany from the oil supplies of the Caucasus. This could only be successful if an operation were undertaken against the Russian oil industry; from February to April 1940 the French General Staff occupied itself with this scheme. Records of this are to be found in the notes of Premier Daladier and General Gamelin, in the reports of the French Ambassador, Massigli, from Ankara and in Weygand's letters to the General Staff.[49] It was hoped that an air attack on Baku and Batum by nine groups of modern French and British bombers from Persia and Iraq would paralyze 75% of the Russian oil production and would also bring the political advantage of arousing the Mohammedan population of the Caucasus. This operation was to be supported with a naval attack in the Black Sea. Unofficial enquiries in Turkey indicated that while the Government would hesitate to become involved in a war with Soviet Russia, it would not protest against Allied planes flying over Turkish territory. After the end of the Finnish war this plan assumed more definite forms because now the possibility of intervention in the North no longer existed. A shift of Allied activities to the Eastern Mediterranean also seemed to promise to create a deterring impression on Italy. The change-over in the French government on March 23, resulting in Reynaud's replacing Daladier, did not mean an abandonment of these plans. However, as some time was needed for preparations—planes from North Africa and France as well as supplies had to be dispatched, and Turkey required time to prepare herself against possible Soviet reprisals—Weygand proposed on April 17 to set the deadline for the end of June.

Moscow began to grow uneasy. The Turkish *chargé d'affaires* reported that the Russians had asked American experts what was the best fire-fighting method in case of a bombardment of Baku. They were said to have received a rather discouraging answer and had been told that the evacuation of the population to a distance of at least 50 km. would be necessary. The Soviet press began to adopt a threatening tone toward Turkey and accused the Turkish government of having deviated from its neutral position. On April 25 *Pravda* warned the Turks against the "machinations of the British and French imperialists."

The Annexation of the Baltic States and Bessarabia

The German attack in the West in May 1940 relieved the Soviets of this worry. On the date for which Weygand had planned the attack on Baku, France had already succumbed. In this sense, therefore, Moscow must have received the news of the outbreak of fighting in the West with satisfaction. It was also realized that only the August agreement gave Hitler the necessary protection in the rear to enable him to withdraw almost all troops from the Russian front and employ them in the West. However, it had not been expected that France would collapse so quickly and when the Kremlin sent its formal congratulations to Hitler they perhaps were somewhat forced. Germany's power was increasing so rapidly that Hitler from now on would not be as dependent on Soviet Russia as before. It was therefore necessary for Russia to strengthen her own position against all possible eventualities and in the face of the tremendous shift in the European balance of power, Stalin began to harvest the last fruits of the Ribbentrop pact.

In the meantime the Baltic states, under the impact of the Finnish war, far away from the Western Allies, and cut off from Germany, tried to establish closer contacts among each other.[50] The Soviet government thereupon accused the governments of Estonia, Latvia and Lithuania of having concluded, "behind the back of the people," a secret pact among themselves directed against Moscow. Supposed anti-Soviet provocations, particularly in Lithuania, gave the Soviets an excuse to intervene. Molotov, in a note handed to the Lithuanian envoy and also published in Riga and Reval, demanded a re-shuffle of the Lithuanian government, the punishment of the top officials who were guilty of the alleged provocations, and the right of passage for Soviet troops to the most important centers in the country. Lithuania collapsed under this tremendous pressure. The Red Army crossed the border and President Smetona fled the country. A special envoy of the Kremlin, the former ambassador to Berlin, Dekanozov, arranged for the creation of a communist government and made preparations for Lithuania's incorporation into the Soviet Union. Parallel developments took place in the other Baltic states. Vishinski was sent to Riga and Zhdanov to Reval—the latter eventually became responsible for the whole operation. In these countries, too, a small Communist group, strengthened by infiltrations from the Soviet Union, brought about a change in government.[51] President Paets of Estonia and President Ulmanis of Latvia were deported to Russia. The decisive element in this upheaval was not the popular will but Russia's armed might. The Red Army now fulfilled a function which according to the ideas of the old Bolsheviks should have been that of the working masses of the people. The events in the Baltic countries were indicative of the change which the Soviet Union had undergone from a revolutionary state to an imperialist power of the first order. It now claimed the heritage of the Czarist Empire quite openly.

In order to save face, mass demonstrations and parliamentary elections were held supporting incorporation into the Soviet Union. The election of new popular representatives had the desired results. In July they "unanimously" voted for the introduction of a Soviet government and requested to be received into the Union.

At the same time Moscow also advanced in the Southwest. In a note addressed to Rumania on June 26, 1940 Molotov demanded that "in the interest of justice," Bessarabia, which Russia had handed over to Rumania in 1918, be returned. However, as Northern Bukovina was linguistically, politically, and historically inseparable from Bessarabia, this province, too, was to be ceded, particularly as it was supposed to have expressed a desire in 1918 to join Russia (presumably the desire only of isolated Communist groups). While Bessarabia had been mentioned in the secret codicil of the August agreement with Germany, the Soviet demand for Bukovina was new. Hitler had already been annoyed by the precipitate sovietization of the Baltic lands and when Lithuania was occupied by Soviet troops, he informed the Lithuanian Soviet government on August 9, 1940 that he was cancelling the free port privileges which had been granted after the return of the Memel territory in 1939. Now, according to Ribbentrop's statement in Nuremberg, he gave vent to his displeasure about the Soviet break-through in the Balkans with the words: "I am no longer going to let the Russians push me against the wall." However, for the time being he decided to swallow this pill too.

After some hesitation and discussion with Berlin, the Rumanian government accepted the Soviet proposal and the Red Army occupied the two provinces. In contrast to Bessarabia, Northern Bukovina and its capital city, Chernovits, were ancient Austrian territory and had never belonged to Russia. (Bessarabia had been Russian from 1812 to 1918.) At the Seventh Session of the Supreme Soviet of the USSR on August 1, 1940, the representatives of the Baltic states and the Rumanian provinces were present. The Congress decided to admit the Lithuanian, Latvian and Estonian SSR into the Soviet Union; to constitute a special Moldavian SSR to take care of Bessarabia, and to admit Northern Bukovina into the Ukrainian SSR. Thus the "indissoluble ties" between the two Rumanian provinces were not even respected by administratively uniting them into one Soviet Republic. Since the Seventh Session of the Supreme Soviet, the Soviet Union consisted of sixteen union republics.[52]

German-Russian Rivalry in the Balkans

Soviet interests in Balkan questions extended far beyond Bessarabia.

Soon after France's capitulation, Molotov observed to the Italian Ambassador in Moscow that the Soviet government considered the war practically over, the Soviet Union's interests being now mainly centered in the Balkans. Its goal was to extend its sphere of influence to Bulgaria so that the Turks would not be the sole usufructuaries of the Straits. It must be left undecided whether Molotov, in not even mentioning Great Britain at that time, believed that there would be a British peace move, just as Hitler expected one before opening his air attack on the island and making plans for invasion. The fact is that Hitler ignored Russia's interests in the Balkans inasmuch as he drew no conclusions from his ambassador's report from Moscow in July 1940 that while Stalin had received Sir Stafford Cripps, the new British Ambassador, he had strictly rejected the possibility of a shift in the Soviet's German policy.[53] When on August 30 he arbitrated in Vienna a territorial exchange between Hungary, Rumania and Bulgaria, and subsequently Germany and Italy guaranteed the Rumanian border, Moscow could well have asked against whom this guarantee was thought necessary and why the Soviet Union had not been consulted. The German theory that, according to the secret codicil of August 23, 1939, the acquisition of Bessarabia was to satisfy all Russian interests in the Balkans, was mistaken;[54] on September 21, Molotov clearly indicated in a memorandum that the Soviet Union continued to be interested in the Balkans and objected to Germany's making decisions about countries which bordered on the Soviet Union without consulting his government. There could be no doubt that German-Russian collaboration was seriously endangered by Balkan questions. As early as September, Ciano, an attentive observer, thought the dream of harmonious relations between Germany and the Soviet Union had been forever disrupted by the Vienna arbitration.

In the meantime the Soviet Ambassador to Sofia, Lavrentiev, had become very active. A Soviet offer to Bulgaria to conclude a mutual assistance pact had been turned down in October 1939. In January 1940, however, a trade and air service agreement was signed and in the spring a direct air route between Moscow and Sofia was opened. After June 1940 it was evident that these ties were to be extended. In fostering the relationship with Bulgaria and in strengthening the Russian influence in the immediate neighborhood of the Straits, the Soviet government continued the pan-Slavic policy of the Czars of the nineteenth century. Relations with Turkey had deteriorated since the spring of 1940, but while at that time the goal had been to fend off British and French influence, the Russian Turkish policy became definitely anti-German in the fall of 1940.

Tensions with Germany also became apparent in regard to the Danube Commission. When Germany invited the states bordering on that river, as well as Italy, to a Danube Conference at which the existing International Commission was dissolved and a new Danube Statute was prepared, the Soviet Union was not repre-

sented. In the face of Molotov's protest, a Soviet representative
was finally invited in October 1940 and, on October 28, negotiations concerning the new Statute were started in Bucharest in his
presence. British objections, which looked upon this as a violation
of Soviet neutrality, were ignored by the Soviet Union.

Any likelihood of arriving at joint decisions on Balkan questions and of co-ordinating mutual interests, was soon thwarted by
Hitler's high-handed procedure in Rumania. Soon after the Vienna
pronouncement, a German military mission went there and, on
October 11, some German training battalions arrived in order to
protect German oil interests. After the occupation of Bessarabia,
Moscow had made it quite clear in a note that while Russia had no
objections to German economic interests in Rumania, the appearance of German troops could only be interpreted as a glaring provocation.

Did Hitler realize that the competition in the Balkans could no
longer be continued as he planned it? Two days after the arrival
of German troops in Rumania, on October 13, Ribbentrop wrote
his famous letter to Stalin in which Molotov was invited to a
conference in Berlin. Nothing less was planned than the inclusion
of the Soviet Union in the tripartite pact which had been concluded
on September 27 between Germany, Italy and Japan and which had
taken the place of the Anti-Comintern pact.

Here the connection between international politics and the military and political situation in the West becomes apparent.

Molotov's Visit to Berlin

After the disaster of Dunkirk, Hitler for some time lived in
hopes of a British peace offer. By the beginning of July this had
turned out to be nothing but wishful thinking and Hitler laid plans
for England's defeat by a multiple invasion, preceded by intensified
air warfare. This enterprise, dubbed "Operation Sea Lion," was,
after some vacillation, scheduled for September 21. But it was not
to take place. The ferocity of British resistance to the German air
attacks caused Hitler, on September 18, to halt the deployment
of the naval units, and in the middle of October the entire operation was, temporarily at least, called off. In the light of this the
Russian problem began to assume greater importance. At a military conference on September 26, Grand Admiral Raeder suggested that a conflict with the Soviet Union could be avoided by a

sweeping operation for the control of the Eastern Mediterranean and of the Near East. Hitler agreed, saying that Soviet Russia should be encouraged to move South, toward Persia and India, because access to the Indian Ocean was much more important to Russia than positions in Eastern Europe. By diverting the Soviet Union's attention to South Asia, he thought conflicts with Germany could be avoided; he was also attracted by the prospect of having Russia involved with Britain in that region.

These were the main points of German policy during the discussion with Molotov which took place in Berlin on November 12 and 13, 1940. Stalin had personally replied to Ribbentrop's letter and had expressed his confidence that a "long-term definition of the interests of both partners would further improve relations between the two countries." He was also prepared to continue personally the discussion begun with Ribbentrop in Berlin; however he postponed this on Ribbentrop's suggestion that Italian and Japanese representatives should also participate.

The interpreter, P. Schmidt, is the author of a fascinating eye-witness report of Molotov's visit to Berlin. Ribbentrop attempted at first to excite the Soviet Foreign Minister with a tempting picture of the carving up of the British Empire. The Soviet Union's sphere of interest was to be southwestern Asia in the direction of the Persian Gulf and the Arabian Sea, with free access to the Mediterranean. Molotov heartily agreed with this basic concept. He welcomed a new distribution of the spheres of interest based on the changes that had occurred in the world situation since 1939. But he was not in the least fascinated by the gigantic dimensions of Hitler's dreams of the future. Perhaps he was reminded, as far as his cut and dried mind was able to form historical associations, of Napoleon's refusal to surrender Constantinople to the Russians and instead suggesting to the irrational and romantic mind of Paul I, a Russian campaign against India. (This actually began in 1800 and petered out in the sands of the Kalmuck desert the following year thanks only to a sudden change in Russian sovereigns).

Molotov "met Hitler like an equal" (Schmidt), he remained cool and dispassionate; Hitler's demonic magic rebounded from his matter of factness. Persistently he pulled the conversation away from German fantasies by returning to the question: what areas in Europe was Hitler willing to cede to the Soviets? He also said that the Soviet Union was willing to participate in the Three Power Pact, but as a partner not as a subject for discussion.

During a second meeting two very large and complex questions
—of primary interest to the Bolsheviks—were put in sharper
focus. Regarding the Balkans, Molotov wished to know whether
the German guarantee of the Rumanian frontiers was also directed
against the Soviet Union. He let Hitler know that the Soviet government was planning a mutual assistance pact with Bulgaria,
guaranteeing the present regime and the monarchy, and also solving the problem of Russian security in the Black Sea by constructing military bases in the Dardanelles. In the Baltic region,
he demanded that Germany grant the Soviet Union complete
freedom of action in Finland and withdrawal of the troops sent
there. While he had observed the strictest neutrality in the winter
campaign against Finland, after the defeat of France Hitler had
concluded an agreement with Finland according to which German
troops and German material could be transported across Finnish
territory to Kirkenes in Norway. At the end of September 1940,
the first German ships had been unloaded in Finland. The fact
that Germany had concluded a similar agreement with Sweden and
that a kind of race had started between Germany and Russia for
the Finnish nickel mines in Petsamo, had considerably increased
Soviet distrust.

It was evident that Russia not only considered Finland exclusively within her sphere of influence, but also looked increasingly upon the Baltic Sea as a kind of Russian *mare clausum*. It
became clear from Molotov's words in the concluding discussion,
that for Russia the Turkish barrier at the Dardanelles corresponded
to the Danish Sound in the north. Inevitably one recalls on hearing
the Russian expansionist aims thus expressed, the words of the
French statesman and historian, Adolphe Thiers, who exclaimed
with regard to the pressure which the Czarist Empire had exerted
on Europe in the era of Nicholas I: "If the Russian colossus plants
one foot on the Dardanelles and the other on the Danish Sound,
the Old World will become enslaved and Liberty will flee to
America." Hitler, unlike the Western powers during the Crimean
War which, while not permitting the conquest of Turkey and the
control of the Straits, left Russia's position in the Baltic undisputed,
was reluctant to make concessions at either point. He maintained
that he was willing to abide by the August 1939 agreement regarding Finland and would, under no condition, tolerate a new war
in the Baltic area. He could on the other hand have yielded in
the Balkans in a manner that would not have conflicted with

"vital German interests." However, instead of assuring the Russians that he would promote their interests in the Balkans with Italy, he let it be understood that he first had to learn how Bulgaria viewed Russia's offer to lease bases and to know what Mussolini thought of this. He had no objections to a revision of the Montreux Treaty which would mean barring foreign naval vessels from the Black Sea and giving the Russians access to the Mediterranean. But he could not agree to the construction of Soviet bases at the Dardanelles.

Thus Molotov saw himself in the uncomfortable position of having to return to Moscow with empty hands. He knew that Stalin, the great realist, would not be satisfied with vague prospects regarding Persia and India. Many hours of discussion had not brought the two viewpoints any closer. On the evening of the second day of conferences, Ribbentrop tried once again to make definite proposals for an agreement that was to be complemented by two secret codicils. On November 14 Molotov left Berlin in order to report to Stalin. Twelve days later, on November 25, Molotov handed the German Ambassador the Soviet reply to the German proposals. The Soviet government, it said, was prepared to agree to the German project—but only under certain conditions, based on the two secret codicils of November 13. According to the first, the area south of Batum and Baku, i.e., Eastern Turkey, Northern Persia and Iraq would be recognized as a Soviet sphere of interest. According to the second, the Soviet Union would be granted the right to erect a military and naval base at the Dardanelles. Turkey was to be invited to join the proposed Four Power Pact; if she agreed to do so, her territory was to be guaranteed by Germany, Italy and the Soviet Union, but if she declined, the three powers were "to take the necessary diplomatic and military steps to safeguard their interests."

Beyond this the Soviet government made three further demands: that Germany immediately withdraw its troops from Finland, in exchange for which the Soviet Union would guarantee to maintain peaceful relations with Finland and to respect German economic interests there; that Japan renounce its coal and petroleum concessions in Northern Sakhalin; and that Bulgaria be considered as part of the Soviet security zone, whereupon a mutual assistance pact was to be concluded between the Soviet Union and Bulgaria.[55]

Although the Kremlin repeatedly requested a reply, the Soviet counter-proposals of November 25 remained unanswered. Hitler never mentioned them. Molotov's visit had not led to closer Soviet-German cooperation as Ribbentrop had envisaged in his letter of October 13. On the contrary, disagreement between Berlin and Moscow became increasingly greater. The visit initiated the *dénouement* of the Russo-German relationship which from now on drifted toward an open breach.

One might ask whether the Soviet government seriously believed that Hitler would be willing to discuss its additional demands or whether it intended to wreck the negotiations by excessive stipulations. We are inclined to doubt it. By concretizing its demands it could gauge Hitler's readiness to enter into serious discussions. Perhaps, if Hitler had given Russia a free hand in the Balkans and in the Turkish area, she in turn would have been willing to limit her demands in Finland and the Baltic. The problem of Sakhalin was in this context only of peripheral importance. If Hitler evaded a continuation of the discussions, this was indisputable evidence of the fact that he rejected one of the most fundamental means of diplomatic negotiations, the compromise.

A few years later Bulgaria and the rest of the Balkan states were included in the Russian sphere of influence. But the failure of the talks of November 1940, meant that Turkey maintained her territorial integrity. She not only managed to keep out of the war, but also avoided being pulled behind the Iron Curtain after 1945.

The Barbarossa Plan

That Hitler was already considering alternative solutions to the Russo-German deadlock as well as the entire military situation, when Molotov arrived in Berlin, was apparent from the preparations that were taking place under the code name "Barbarossa."

As early as June 1940 German troops had been transferred to the Eastern border. At a conference which Hitler held on July 21 military and political aims against Russia were mentioned for the first time in connection with the war against England and the possibility of an attack on Russia in the coming fall was envisaged.[56] The General Staff was instructed to draw up a plan of operations. On July 31 Hitler decided to postpone the attack on Russia until the spring of 1941 as more extensive preparations were necessary and greater clarity regarding Russian aims was to be achieved in the meantime. It was significant that both in Finland and in Rumania the Germans adopted a more unequivocal position against the Soviet Union. In Finland negotiations were in progress regarding the supply of arms and the passage of German troops on their way to Norway, and in Rumania the German guarantees were followed immediately by the arrival of German troops.

On November 12, 1940—presumably a few hours before Molotov's arrival in Berlin—Hitler issued Directive No. 18 concerning the military situation. It was based on the preparatory work of the German General Staff and apart from ordering continued operations against England, it contained the information that German troops would continue to be transferred to the East at the same time that the German government was attempting to obtain a clear picture of the attitude of the Soviet government through the discussions with Molotov. If in this directive Hitler once more mentioned Operation "Sea Lion" and hinted at the possibility that in the spring of 1941 it might be taken up again, this was done primarily in order to camouflage the troop concentrations in the East. Hitler believed that Great Britain could be more decisively defeated by the destruction of her position in the Mediterranean than by so risky an undertaking as an invasion. The intensification of military operations in the South was, however, to go hand in hand, if necessary, with a lightning assault on the Soviet Union, which would deprive England of its last potential ally on the Continent. Already on November 13, Hitler in a talk with Goering said that the Soviet demands in the Balkans were unacceptable. He believed that together with Soviet demands for an absolutely free hand in Finland they represented an ambitious attempt to encircle Germany and he was determined to prevent this. In making this decision, as Papen, then German Ambassador in Turkey, correctly put it, he had already lost the war.

At a conference in Berlin on December 3, 1940, the impending "big operation" was mentioned as such for the first time. In vain did Grand Admiral Raeder warn against a splitting up of the German forces and asked for a postponement of Operation Barbarossa until England was defeated. Hitler was intoxicated with the idea of a new gigantic "blitz" in the East which was to provide him with the economic means for concluding the war in the West. On December 18 the military were instructed to make preparations for a quick campaign for the destruction of Russia even before the end of the war against England and these preparations were to be concluded by May 10, 1941.

The Yugoslav Question. Matsuoka's Visit to Moscow.

The situation in Yugoslavia threatened a further increase in the tension.

Of all the European states, Yugoslavia had hesitated the longest before establishing diplomatic relations with the Soviet Union. The influence of Russian emigrés was even more pronounced there than it had been in Czechoslovakia or Bulgaria. Countless members of the Russian clergy and the Czarist officer corps had, after the collapse of the Wrangel army, settled in Yugoslavia, finding a last refuge in Belgrade. Now even here Hitler's successes in the West led to a lessening of misgivings regarding Russia. It is certainly no coincidence that a trade and air agreement between Belgrade and Moscow was concluded one day after the start of the German advance in the West and diplomatic relations were established two days after the conclusion of the Franco-German armistice. At the beginning of 1941 Russia was bound to have the impression that Germany was intent on pushing her out of the Balkans altogether. In January and March protests were issued against the appearance of German army units in Bulgaria. In view of Germany's refusal in November to support Soviet ambitions in the Balkans, these troop movements were provocative. On March 24 the Soviet government gave Turkey a pledge of neutrality.

Gafencu reports that Gavrilovich, the Yugoslav Minister in Moscow, was received in the Kremlin "like a brother" and was able to hatch conspiratorial plans with Stalin against his own pro-German cabinet under Stoyadinovich. In the night of March 26 to March 27 a *coup d'état* was carried out in Belgrade and Stoyadinovich was overthrown. On April 4 the new cabinet concluded a friendship pact with the Soviet Union, which gave evidence of the course it was going to follow.[57] Molotov told the German Ambassador that the Soviet government expected Germany to keep peace with the Yugoslavs. Two days later, however, German troops crossed the Yugoslav frontier and the German Balkan campaign began. While previously the rapidity of the German victories in Poland, Norway and France had disconcerted the Soviet government, here, in a terrain that was considered most unfavorable to military operations, the German speed had a downright frightening effect. Russian distrust grew into a feeling of being seriously menaced. Would the German troops, victorious in the Balkans, march through Turkey towards Suez, or were they now free to be used against Russia?

Stalin became aware of the seriousness of the situation. The Moscow military parade on the 1st of May was turned into an unusual display of strength. On May 6 the world was surprised by the news that Stalin himself had taken over the office of Chairman of the Council of People's Commissars which until then had been occupied by Molotov. He thereby for the first time assumed a government office, without however, giving up his seat in the General Secretariat of the Party. By becoming the head of the Government and remaining leader of the Party, Stalin assumed a twofold responsibility. What had caused him to step from the traditional semi-obscurity of his Party office into the limelight? Undoubtedly he was impelled by the premonition that the Soviet Union was on the eve of great decisions. It would either be necessary to make considerable further concessions to Germany and accept commitments under the Three Power Pact—perhaps even the extreme step of openly joining the war against the Western powers;[58] or, in the case of a German surprise attack, to concentrate in one man's hands all the powers needed to safeguard Russia. That man could only be Stalin.

The two visits to Moscow of the Japanese Foreign Minister, Matsuoka, in March and April of that year, throw an interesting light on the situation. Stalin received him both times with unusual courtesies. In lengthy discussions he hinted at the Asiatic characteristics common to both him and his guest, while the shrewd Japanese attempted to paint the war in China as a struggle against Anglo-Saxon liberalism by Japanese "moral Communism." The concrete object of the discussions,—the Japanese concessions on the island of Sakhalin—was thus pushed into the background. When Matsuoka returned in April from Berlin, where the changed atmosphere toward Russia had not escaped his attention, the Japanese-Soviet non-aggression pact was, to Germany's great surprise, concluded.

This neutrality agreement, dated April 13,[59] freed the Soviet Union of the risk of war on two fronts, in the case of a clash with Germany. (Later it also gave Japan the chance to take the offensive in the Pacific.) But even in regard to Soviet relations with Germany, this extra-curricular undertaking by the Japanese partner was bound to restore the prestige of the Soviet Union and cause Hitler to revise his brusque disregard of Soviet desires. That this latter thought was connected with Matsuoka's visit is apparent from the curious gesture which Stalin made at the departure of his guest: unexpected by the press and the diplomatic corps, he appeared at the railroad station and after embracing Matsuoka, he turned to the German Ambassador, Count Schulenburg, and the deputy military attaché, Colonel Krebs, and said "We must remain friends, come what may." While this remark undoubtedly stemmed from a desire to remove from the agreement with Japan some of its provocation to Germany, the hint that the door for new negotiations with Germany was still open, was also unmistakable.

With the same thought in mind, the Soviet government established diplomatic relations with the pro-German Persian government it had hitherto refused to recognize; and the Belgian, Norwegian, and Yugoslav ambassadors were handed their passports because their governments had ceased to exist.

The Eve of the War: Preventive War or Surprise Attack?

Germany did not respond to these gestures and Moscow's resulting uneasiness became more pronounced when the news of Rudolf Hess' flight to England became known. It was believed that as Hitler's personal emissary he had been ordered to arrange an alliance between Germany and Great Britain against the Soviet Union. In consequence, several things occurred which could be taken as harbingers of a coming war. Air raid drills were intensified, foreign diplomats were restricted in their movements, foreigners were refused travel permits. *Pravda* repeatedly reminded the people of their patriotic duties. There were troop reinforcements, noticeably on the Western frontier, especially in the neighborhood of Lvov. In the last days of April, Count Schulenburg returned to Berlin taking with him a Russian offer to deliver five million metric tons of grain in 1942. He strongly advocated the maintenance of peace between Germany and Russia and attempted to convince Hitler that the Russian troop concentrations along the border were prompted by the Russian desire for security and that Stalin was prepared for further co-operation with Germany and for further economic concessions.

It was in vain. Hitler had already made his decision. Throughout April there had been an increasing number of protest notes because of border violations, mainly by airplanes. Both sides were trying to explore the strength of the foe. One hundred and fifty

German divisions stood on Russia's western border; they faced a slightly larger number of Russian divisions. On April 4 Stalin received a warning from Churchill in London that a German attack was planned for June 22. Stalin did not quite believe it but he decided to make one last attempt at clearing the air. On June 14 the Soviet Telegraph Agency, Tass, issued a statement in which Sir Stafford Cripps, British Ambassador in Moscow, was violently attacked for circulating rumors regarding "an imminent war between Russia and Germany." All rumors according to which Germany had made territorial and economic demands on the Soviet Union which had been rejected by the Soviet government, were denied.[59a] That German and Russian troops were about to commence hostilities was a "false and preposterous provocation." Actually no demands had been made by Berlin. But it seems that Stalin was waiting for them and wanted to see whether the Tass statement would break the spell of silence between Berlin and Moscow.

When Schulenburg was at Molotov's office at 9:30 p.m. on June 21, the latter mentioned the war rumors and pointed out with some regret that Germany had not taken any notice of the Tass statement. Why was Germany dissatisfied, what had caused this tension? The German Ambassador was unable to reply to this and said he would ask Berlin. A few hours later he handed the Soviet Commissar for Foreign Affairs Hitler's declaration of war.

The question has been raised whether Hitler's attack on the Soviet Union forestalled a Soviet attack, i.e. whether or not his was a preventive war. As proof of the Russian desire for war, statements by Soviet Russian officers and functionaries have been quoted, as well as affidavits of German generals, from which it has been inferred that the Soviet government planned, or at least contemplated, an offensive use of its troops stationed along the Western frontier.[60]

The massing of very mobile troop units, including cavalry, on the borders gives one pause.[61] However, their location in the Northwest and Southwest of Russia conspicuously points to the probability that they were to serve as military support for Russia's political demands of November and December 1940. If Germany were to show herself ready to renew negotiations and were to grant the Soviet Union the freedom of action it desired against Finland and in the Balkans, these units could have been used for an advance in those directions—not for an attack against Germany![62]

As a matter of fact the massing of Russian forces on the Western border was intended in a sense as a means of pressure. The Soviet Union wished to discourage Hitler from his aggressive intentions, and to increase its own political weight. That Hitler was not to be frightened by these measures but went over to the attack, irresponsibly and boundlessly underestimating the Soviet potential, on the basis of the Finnish war, came as a complete surprise to the Soviet government.

A Soviet assault on Germany in the summer of 1941, at a time the United States had not yet entered the war, and Hitler seemed invincible, would have been lunacy. If to Stalin the Ribbentrop-Molotov pact meant time gained—and it did indeed mean that—it was not with a view to an early entry into the war, but to strengthen the Soviet potential under the protection of the war between the capitalist powers. Both the pact with Germany as well as the alliance with the Western powers from 1941 on must not blind us to the fact that for the Bolsheviks the war which began in 1939 represented the long hoped-for conflict among the capitalist states which could become the springboard for world revolution. By patiently biding his time, Stalin could expect to achieve more than by a premature participation in the war. The war worked for the Soviet Union. Only after the Axis powers and the Western allies had torn each other to shreds and Germany was finally vanquished, perhaps with the help of the United States, only then, perhaps at the eleventh hour, Stalin must have thought, would the moment for Russian intervention have arrived, and then only in order to share in the loot. This was Stalin's tactic in 1939 in the Polish campaign and again in 1945 in the war against Japan. He presumably also planned to act that way in the West's struggle with Hitler.

CHAPTER 8

THE "GREAT PATRIOTIC WAR" OF THE SOVIET UNION

Hitler's Surprise Attack on Russia

On June 22, 1941, at 4 o'clock in the morning, German troops suddenly invaded Russia without warning.[1]

On February 3 Hitler had approved the plan of campaign against the Soviet Union. At first the date was left open. On April 1 it was planned for some time during the second half of June; on June 6 Hitler fixed the date at June 22. According to some reports June 12 had been originally set, but as a result of Hungary's refusal to march, a ten day postponement became necessary.

World public opinion had been skilfully deceived as to Hitler's war plans. Many signs seemed to indicate that the summer of 1941 would be employed mainly in stepping up the Mediterranean offensive. The German victory in Yugoslavia, the landing on Crete and Rommel's successes in Libya all combined to support such an assumption. Among the German leaders Goering was well known as a vigorous exponent of these plans. The Reich Marshal had warned against an attack on Russia and recommended concentrating military action in the Mediterranean theater of war. When a German-Turkish Mutual Defense Pact was signed in Ankara on June 18, rumors arose about German troop movements from the Balkans in the direction of the Near East. There were also reports of a march of German troops through the Ukraine, also with the Near East as their destination. The rumors hid the real meaning of the troop concentrations on the Russian frontier.

Hitler's plan of campaign had been outlined, in a general way, as early as December 18, 1940.[2] It called for the destruction of the bulk of the Russian Army in Western Russia by deep thrusts of wedge-shaped tank units. The retreat of Russian combat troops into the vast Russian hinterland was to be prevented. A line was quickly to be reached stretching roughly from Archangelsk to Astrakhan making attacks by the Russian Air Force impossible. For the Germans the line would form a base for aerial bombardment of the industrial region in the Urals. Hitler was quite convinced that his plan would be successful and a "Fuehrer Directive" No. 32 of June 11[3] dealt with military measures to be taken against England after the conquest of Russia had been completed.

The Soviet troops stationed on Russia's Western border were overwhelmed by the surprise German attack. In the wake of heavy bombing raids, aimed at the airfields close to the border, and which had thrown the Russian air defense into confusion, Hitler's armies stormed into Russia in three great columns in the dawn of June 22. A central army group advanced in a pincer movement from East Prussia and from Poland in the direction of Minsk. Simultaneously a southern group crossed the Prut and invaded the Ukraine, while a northern group entered and occupied the Baltic states and threatened north west Russia. The German air force attacked targets far behind the front; at the same time German planes appeared over the ports of the Baltic, the Arctic and the Black Sea.

Simultaneously, Italy, Rumania and Slovakia declared war against Russia. On June 25 Finland followed the German example. Hungary followed suit on June 27.

Stalin, in spite of the tense international situation, had left Moscow on June 11, perhaps as a gesture to help lessen tension. He was accompanied by Malenkov and Voznesensky. In Moscow, Molotov was in charge. He silently listened to the German Ambassador who handed him Hitler's declaration of war on June 22 at 4 a.m.[5] Then he remarked abruptly: "It is war. Your aircraft have just bombarded some ten open villages. Do you believe that we deserved that?"[6] Schulenburg had instructions not to engage in any discussions.

A few hours later Molotov broadcast an announcement of the German attack to the Russian people.[7] Stalin at first remained silent. For the purpose of coordinating all defense measures, a State Committee for Defense *(Gosudarstvenny komitet oborony)* was organized on June 30, which was in the nature of a war cabinet and constituted the supreme executive organ. In addition to Stalin, Molotov and Voroshilov, Beria and Malenkov were its members.[8] Malenkov had recently become one of Stalin's closest collaborators in the General Secretariat of the Party. All members of the State Committee were also members of the Politburo.

At the front, operations were in the hands of three proven military leaders of long standing. Timoshenko was in command in the central sector, Voroshilov in the North and Budyenny in the South. However, they failed to slow the rapid advance of the Germans and their allies. After a tremendous tank battle near Smolensk, the forward thrust of the German attack in the central sector seemed somewhat weakened, but in the Ukraine the fiercest of the great encircling battles of the opening campaign developed before Kiev in September. After catastrophic losses, Budyenny was forced to retreat. The Soviet leadership had committed the fatal error of deploying too many troops too close to the front, giving the Germans a chance of annihilating them in gigantic battles by closing in on them in double pincer movements. The number of prisoners rose to hundreds of thousands; at Kiev it exceeded half a million. By the end of October the Germans had reached the line formed by the towns of Kursk-Kharkov-Stalino-Taganrog. In the middle of November the Isthmus of Perekop was stormed and Rostov, the gate to the Caucasus, was conquered.

The advance in the central sector had again reached full speed. The battle of Briansk was followed by the occupation of Orel, Tula, Viazma and Rzhev. On October 15 the German armored divisions stormed Mozhaisk, west of Moscow. Then, immediately outside the Russian capital, the advance came to a halt. In the north the Germans had advanced as far as Leningrad. They occupied Schluesselburg east of the old capital. The siege of Leningrad had begun. Would it be followed by the siege or conquest of Moscow?

On July 3 Stalin made a momentous radio appeal to the people.[9] He frankly admitted that the Soviet Union was in mortal danger. The situation was too serious for comforting words. However, he felt the need to justify his policy. He raised the question of whether the Soviet Union had made a mistake in concluding a non-aggression pact with Germany. He answered in the negative and pointed out the advantages which had at first resulted from that move. For a year and a half the country had been assured of peace and had thus been in a position to continue its military preparations. (He could also have mentioned the territorial gains achieved by the Soviet Union between 1938 and 1940.) He made the point that Hitler's troops had been fully mobilized on the outbreak of war with the Soviet Union, while his, on the other hand, had not. By stressing the fact that the Soviet Union had been surprised by Hitler's attack, he sought to awaken in the people a feeling of moral superiority. In his appeal to the people's will to resist he adroitly combined national with social arguments. The cruel and implacable enemy had set out, he said, to conquer the soil which Soviet peasants had tilled in the sweat of their brow, and to Germanize the peoples of the Soviet Union. He was out to turn the people of the Soviet Union "into the slaves of German princes and barons" and to restore the rule of the landlords and the Czars in Russia. Stalin urged the people to leave nothing but a desert in the wake of their retreat. The speech ended with a reference to Napoleon's fate in his Russian campaign of 1812 and to that of Kaiser Wilhelm II in the first World War. Both had enjoyed a reputation of invincibility, and both had been defeated in the end.

On July 19 Stalin personally took over the direction of the Commissariat of Defense; and thereby became Commander-in-Chief of the Army. The actual leadership of the armed forces was in the hands of "Headquarters" *(Stavka verkhovnago glavno-kommandovaniya)*, which was directed by the Chief of the General Staff. This post had for some time been occupied by General Shaposhnikov, a holdover from the Czarist General Staff. He was an able military theoretician and a tireless worker. He became indispensable to Stalin, by his almost servile eagerness to serve, not by his wealth of ideas.[10] Thus from the beginning military leadership was in essence entirely concentrated in Stalin's person even though this may not at first have been true for the administrative details of military planning. The actual direction of the high command of the army was entrusted to General Zhukov. In August 1942 the importance of his position was stressed by his appointment as Deputy Commissar for Defense.

Russia did not have a system of defense similar to that of the French in the West. The often-mentioned "Stalin Line" actually consisted merely of the swamps near Pinsk, near the old Polish-Russian border. The only defense plans which held any promise of success were based on the nature of the Russian terrain. As in the days of Napoleon, the Russians relied on the size of the country and on the hard winters. Space must be yielded so that time might be gained. Where resistance was in vain, where retreat had become inevitable, "scorched earth" must be left behind to greet the enemy. Not one locomotive, not one railway carriage, not one pound of flour, not one can of gasoline must fall into his hands. Thus Stalin expressed the idea on July 3. The farmers were told to lead away the cattle and to get the grain ready for removal. Whatever could not be moved was to be destroyed.

This was the atmosphere in which the Russian retreat from June to December took place, a retreat which led to the gates of Moscow. However, it differed in character from that of the Polish and French armies. The Germans had met an adversary whose leaders were determined to resist to the very end. Would the people put up the total resistance expected of them? This was the decisive question of the war.

Stalin called upon the people to wage guerrilla warfare. He demanded that in the areas occupied by the enemy, guerrilla units be formed, mounted and on foot. They were to harass the enemy unceasingly, to cripple him by sabotage, to blow up bridges and to set fire to warehouses and trucks, rolling stock, etc. For years the population had been trained in guerrilla fighting, now it had a chance to prove its mettle in the wide area between the Baltic and the Black Seas.

The German Policy in the Occupied Territories

The population was at first paralyzed by the lightning successes of the Germans. Then, suddenly anti-Bolshevik sentiment burst into the open, particularly in the non-Russian Western territories; it was especially striking in the Baltic countries, but also in Eastern Poland and Bessarabia, among the White Ruthenians and Ukrainians. In many places the German troops were greeted as liberators. Tremendous possibilities opened up for a German Eastern policy, provided the principles of psychological warfare were properly applied. Several alternatives existed: to play the trump of the liberation of the border states; to endow the fighting with the character of a crusade against Bolshevism as Marshal Foch had envisaged in 1919; to establish an anti-Bolshevik Russian Fascist regime; or to attempt an unscrupulous *divide-et-impera* policy and divide Russia into nation states.

Hitler did not follow any of these policies consistently. His real goal was to colonize the country and exploit its manpower. A German edition of Alsdorf's book about British methods of subjugating India had become a text book for the Nazis. Russia was probably scheduled to become a "German India." At first the Ukrainian desire for secession was encouraged in line with the German plans for the Ukraine during the first World War and the thirties. This was done to bait its population with the concept of a powerful autonomous Ukrainian state from the Carpathians to the Caucasus. But these pretenses were soon abandoned and, by 1942, German colonization plans were launched openly.

A number of decrees were characteristic of the spirit of National Socialism as it manifested itself in its eastern policy. As early as May 13, 1941, a decree provided that captured commissars be liquidated without trial. The so-called "Communist Decree" of September 16 provided that for every German soldier killed in occupied territory fifty to one hundred Communists were to be shot. The "Hostages Decree" of October 1 authorized the taking of hostages among non-Communists as well. The Under-Cover-of-Night Decree *(Nacht-und-Nebel-Erlass)* of December 7 provided that in case of acts of terror or sabotage, the civilian population was to be deported as unobtrusively as possible by the so-called Security Service for use in the German armament industry. A decree of December 1942 authorized reprisals against the relatives of saboteurs; and the Gang Decree of December 16, 1942 enabled the Chief for Gang Suppression to adopt drastic measures against the guerrillas.

Reichsleiter Alfred Rosenberg, himself born in Russia, had in anticipation been appointed Commissar for the Occupied Eastern Territories on April 21, 1941; on April 23 a Russia Committee of the German Foreign Office had been established. In the first flush of the advance a special Ministry of the Eastern Territories, headed by Rosenberg, was created on July 7; the political war aims in the East were worked out by this Ministry. The product was confused; there were overlapping and mutually contradictory plans and ideas, poorly thought out, immature in concept. Rosenberg started with the basic idea of a "national disintegration of the Soviet Union," according to which the state as a whole was to be dissolved into several areas—the Ukraine, a Caucasus federation, etc.—in order to prevent Russia from ever again becoming a threat to Western Europe. Whether the Baltic States and the Ukraine were to become independent or protectorates of Germany, what was to become of Poland and the Eastern Polish territories was never spelled out. Gradually it became accepted that Germany was to be the chief beneficiary of the conquests. It became customary to speak of *Reich* territories *(Reichslaender)*, in which military colonies and fortified farms were to be set up.

Chiefly because of Rosenberg's fanatically anti-Christian attitude

the promotion of a religious revival among the Russian population
was rejected. Thus a trump card, which could have had its political
impact, too, was left unused, a circumstance upon which Stalin
soon seized. German military efforts to counteract, modify or even
sabotage these political ineptitudes, as well as the immoral and in-
human terror, were no longer possible when the occupied territories passed into the hands of the civil administration of the
National Socialist Party.

In the course of this development the will to resist increased
among the disillusioned population of the occupied territories. This
became more and more evident as the German troops, after marching
through the White Russian and Ukrainian regions, entered the Great
Russian provinces beyond Smolensk. Soon partisan warfare flared
behind the front, creating ever-increasing difficulties for the Germans.

Cooperation with the Allies

The problem of political and military cooperation with the Western Allies was of greatest importance to the Soviet command.

Although Churchill had predicted to the day the beginning of
the German attack on the Soviet Union, the shock felt by the leading politicians and the population was still great. After a discussion
with Sir Stafford Cripps, the British Ambassador to Moscow, recently returned to London for consultations, Churchill drafted, as
he relates in his memoirs,[11] a major speech in which he promised
extensive aid to Russia. "No one," he said, "has been a more consistent opponent of Communism than I have for the last twenty five
years. I unsay no word that I have spoken about it. But all this
fades away before the spectacle which is now unfolding." On July
12 a Mutual Assistance Pact was concluded between the two countries, in which both parties undertook not to enter into any separate negotiations with the enemy.

In the United States a similar mood prevailed. Here, too, it was
believed that all doubts had to be cast aside in favor of common
action against Hitler.

British as well as American military experts took a most pessimistic view of the prospects of Russian resistance. In view of the
devastating crisis the Red Army had undergone in the purges of
1937 and its performance in the Finnish winter campaign, and the
known power of the German "blitz" campaigns, it seemed impossible that German troops should be tied down in the East more than
three months.[12] More perceptive was a memorandum by Joseph E.

Davies, the former United States Ambassador to Moscow. As early as July 8, he foresaw the difficulties with which Hitler would have to deal in the occupied territories as guerrilla warfare and sabotage commenced. Even after the loss of the Ukraine and White Russia, Stalin could, in his opinion, hold on for quite some time in the Urals; however, one had to bear in mind also that in such a situation Stalin's well known "realism" might lead to a separate German-Russian peace. Stalin was in any case informed that the Western powers, determined to defeat Hitler, were prepared to collaborate with the Soviet Union on a friendly basis.[13] In order to obtain a true picture of the Soviet Union's actual resistance potential and of Stalin's intentions, Roosevelt sent Harry Hopkins, his long-time associate and confidant, to Moscow in July 1941.

With instructions from the British as well, Hopkins flew from Scotland via Archangelsk to Moscow, and there managed to gain Stalin's confidence to a considerable degree. He explained to Stalin that the American government was fully determined to give the Soviet Union all possible aid as quickly as possible.

Stalin himself described the situation and needs of the Red Army with a frankness "unexampled in recent Soviet history."[14] He deeply impressed Hopkins by the lucid precision of his statements. He asked for anti-aircraft guns, machine guns, rifles, fuel and aluminum. He said that the safest transport route was via the Arctic route. On July 30 he told Hopkins that he had not believed that Hitler would attack, but nevertheless had taken all precautions. The Germans had underestimated the strength of the Russian Army which, at several points, was moving to counter-attack. Hopkins could not help but notice how desperately serious the situation was. Stalin had to admit that 75% of the armament plants were located in the areas around Leningrad, Moscow and Kiev. These areas were already directly threatened by the enemy. Stalin said that the war would certainly be hard, perhaps long and that one thing alone could assure the defeat of Hitler—the entry of the United States into the war. Hopkins left Moscow with the conviction that the Soviet government was ready to put up a determined fight and that American help was therefore called for. His report considerably fortified Roosevelt in his intention to support the Soviet Union's resistance.

American aid based on a Lend-Lease Agreement was to become decisive in Russian defense against the German attack.[15] It was given promptly and effectively. Just a week after the German attack, a committee had been created to organize aid to the Soviet

Union. In July, Roosevelt ordered that shipments for Russia be immediately prepared. Under the direction of Col. P. A. Faymonville, the American army's foremost expert on Russian conditions, 145 million dollars worth of goods were made ready for Russia in the first three months alone.

In September 1941 W. Averell Harriman headed a mission to Moscow to investigate the Soviet Union's needs. Lord Beaverbrook accompanied Harriman as British representative. Negotiations were difficult. Even then Stalin hinted at the demand which later was to wind its way like a bright thread through the history of collaboration against Hitler—he asked for the opening of a second front in the West in order to relieve the Russian front. During those critical days when the front was hourly moving closer to Moscow, the visitors could notice unmistakable signs of nervousness in Stalin. Just as he had previously told Hopkins that American troops—even under exclusively American command—would be welcome in every sector of the Russian front, he now asked Beaverbrook whether Great Britain could not send some of her troops to Ukraine. When Beaverbrook proposed a transfer of British troops from Persia via the Caucasus, Stalin, eternally distrustful and perhaps remembering the British advance along the same line during the civil war in 1918-19, rejected the offer.

The principal items on the agenda concerned the deliveries of war supplies and raw material. They were summed up in the so-called Moscow Protocol. The United States undertook to supply Russia with $1,015,000,000 worth of goods in the course of 1942. On November 7 Roosevelt described the Soviet Union as a "suitable partner" for a Lend-Lease agreement and established an interest-free credit of one billion dollars, repayment to begin five years after the cessation of hostilities. After the United States entered the war, it was of course vitally interested in the Soviet Union's successful prosecution of the war. The provisional agreements of 1941 were supplemented so that a final Lend-Lease Agreement defined the American aid program of which the Soviet High Command could make use until 1945. In order to expedite shipments a special order issued by Roosevelt on March 7, 1942, released all the material promised in the Moscow Protocol; it was to be shipped without delay and ahead of any other commitments. The Soviet Union was thus given priority in the allocation of war materials over all the other Allies, even over the United States own armed forces.[16] A special "Presidential Protocol Committee," headed by Hopkins, administered the Aid to Russia program. A supply mission, under

General Faymonville, was sent to Moscow to work directly with the Soviet authorities. For the Soviets Mikoyan, the People's Commissar for Foreign Trade, was responsible for the receipt of the shipments. Later the duties of the Supply Mission were transferred to the newly created American military mission in Moscow.

As a result of the American aid program 2,660 ships, carrying a total of 16½ million tons were sent to the Soviet Union between October 1, 1941, and May 31, 1945. More than 15 million tons actually reached their destination; 52 ships were rerouted to England; 77 ships were lost through enemy action. Trucks and tanks were the most important items sent: 427,284 trucks, 13,303 tanks, 35,170 motor cycles and 2,328 other vehicles were delivered. Next came oil products: more than 2½ million tons of aviation gasoline and gasoline additives, as well as fuel for all types of vehicles. Also important was the rolling stock delivered to Soviet railroads: 1,900 steam locomotives, 66 diesel engines, more than 10,000 railroad cars of all kinds. All these had to be built to fit the wide Russian tracks. In addition there were tools and factory equipment, spare parts, arms, medical supplies, textiles and shoes. A final important item consisted of food shipments, used mainly for the army, totaling nearly four and a half million tons of canned meats, sugar, flour, salt and fats. It has been calculated that with the average strength of the Red Army at about twelve million men, these deliveries assured each individual of more than half a pound of highly nutritive food per day. The total value of all American deliveries was approximately eleven billion dollars.

Among the military agreements between the Soviet Union and other Allies, the Military Agreement with Great Britain, concluded on July 12, was the most important. Soon Stalin took Sir Stafford Cripps, the British Ambassador, into his confidence, though in the summer of 1940 when Cripps had presented his credentials he had treated him very cooly, refusing to believe his warnings of a German attack. When the Germans approached Moscow, Stalin did not hide his concern from Cripps. He said that Moscow would be defended to the last but he admitted the possibility of the fall of the city. In that case, he said, the Red Army would have to surrender the whole of Russia west of the Volga. Even then, however, the Soviets would not end the war. But it would probably take many years before they would once more be able to advance across the Volga.

The Battle of Moscow

At the end of 1941 the question to be faced was whether, after the surrender of all the Western provinces, the Soviet Union was still in a position to continue resistance.

The area which the Germans had occupied by the end of 1941 contained about 40% of the total population of the Soviet Union; 65% of the pre-war coal production came from this area, 68% of its pig iron, 58% of its steel, 60% of its aluminum, 38% of its grain, and 84% of its sugar. About 40% of the railroad network had been lost. Between June and November, industrial production fell by more than half, steel production by more than two-thirds. The production of ball bearings was no more than five per cent of the peace-time output.[17]

In these circumstances the prompt relocation of the Western and South Russian industrial plants in the East and the resumption of production became, perhaps, the most important prerequisite for the continuation of the war. The plants were usually evacuated to places where similar enterprises existed. Merged with these they increased their productive capacity. Frequently, new plants had to be built from the ground up, particularly in Siberia and Central Asia. Soon after the relocation work was resumed here at stepped-up speed. Altogether 1,360 factories and workshops were shifted from the West to the East. Millions of workers with their families accompanied the machines and equipment. Henceforward the armament industry was concentrated in the cities on the middle and lower Volga, the Ural region, the Kuznetsk Combine and the area around Karaganda.

By October 1941 the German advance had reached its climax and the German *Reichspressechef* (Press Chief) declared that the war in the East was as good as over. The Red Army was said to have only sixty divisions still intact; all the others had been wiped out. In German military circles, however, the situation was regarded far more soberly and skeptically. It was realized that the Soviet Union could still divert some troops in order to invade Persia, in accordance with the plan made with England on August 25, 1941. Leningrad, encircled since the end of September, was putting up a heroic resistance and the Finns, true to their tradition of remaining neutral unless attacked, refused to march against the city. On October 29 the German General Staff asked that the offensive be halted and Field-Marshal von Rundstedt also demanded that the front be shifted back. On December 7 Hitler turned down these proposals, dismissed Field-Marshal von Brauchitsch as Commander-in-Chief of the Army and assumed the immediate command of the army in addition to his post of Supreme Commander of the *Wehrmacht* (German Armed Forces).

According to the order for the conquest of Moscow, issued on October 2, a gigantic ring of fifty-one divisions, of which thirteen were armored and five motorized, was to surround the Russian capital. The fighting grew desperate. The German outposts stood thirty miles from Moscow and one section of the front had moved to only six miles of the city's perimeter.

On October 13 the top Party leaders were called together in Moscow. The dangers threatening the city and the measures which had to be taken were discussed. Volunteers were formed into workers' battalions and sent to the front after only one week of training. The rest of the population was called up for the construction of tank traps, artillery positions and machine gun nests. The city was surrounded by a ring of defense lines. On October 19 a state of siege was declared. The central offices and the most important industrial plants were evacuated. The People's Commissariats and the government departments were moved to Kuibyshev (Samara) on the Volga. Records which could not be moved were burned.

On November 6 the Moscow Soviet met for the anniversary celebration of the Revolution in a station of the Moscow subway in order to be safe from air raids. The next day, Stalin, standing on the roof of the Lenin Mausoleum, reviewed the troops and the people's defense units. He sought to encourage the soldiers by recalling the difficult times of the civil war and by saying that in a few months, at most in a year, Germany would collapse. Then followed his unexpected invocation of the Russian people's national past. "Let the manly images of our great ancestors—Alexander Nevsky, Dimitry Donskoy, Kuzma Minin, Dimitry Pozharsky, Alexander Suvorov, and Mikhail Kutuzov—inspire you in this war." By pressing into service ghosts of Imperial Russia for the defense of the country, he seemed to put an end to the specifically Soviet patriotism which had been kindled during the thirties. After the parade, the troops marched straight from the Red Square to the front.

However, when the news spread that the most vital government bureaus were leaving the city, the population of Moscow was gripped by fear and dismay. Psychologically, this was the moment of greatest danger. The people thought that the city was to be surrendered. Looting and disorders took place, food stores were stormed, party members burned their membership cards and destroyed their badges. Everywhere there were symptoms of approaching anarchy. Gradually, however, the fact that Stalin himself did not leave Moscow began to have its effect; the atmosphere grew calmer when it became known that he continued to reside in the Kremlin. While Hitler, in his order of the day to the German troops, was promising that "the Kremlin was to be blown up in order to seal the fall of the Bolshevik system," Stalin refused to leave its walls. This strengthened the people's morale. The Kremlin became the symbol of the country and its fight for survival. (It may be that Hitler, in his stubborn refusal to leave Berlin 3½ years later, hoped to effect a similar miraculous result. However, in May 1945, German reserves were exhausted, while at the end of 1941 the Soviet strength was not.) The Soviet Union had been spared the mortal dangers of a war on two fronts. All of Germany's attempts to persuade Japan to enter the war were in vain. When, on December 7, the Japanese made their surprise attack on Pearl Harbor, Moscow knew that Japan would, in the future, be kept busy in another theater of war.

Towards the end of November the German advance on Moscow slowed down. The German units advanced only a few miles a day. Twice they had tried to storm the city, twice they were repelled. It also became evident that it was impossible to close the circle around the city. Then came the winter. As in 1812, it started early; and the Germans had been sent into battle without their winter equipment. On December 6 the temperature in the Moscow area dropped to 40° below zero. That day Stalin gave the order for a counter-offensive. Fresh Siberian units had arrived from the Far East and were immediately thrown into battle. The first climax of war had passed.

On December 8 Hitler announced that he had suspended operations because of the winter. The first campaign had been a failure. The Russian armies had been decimated but not wiped out. Neither Moscow nor Leningrad had been taken and the Caucasian oil fields continued to be beyond reach. Via Archangelsk, Persia and Vladivostok the Soviet Union was able to maintain its contact with the Allies. The relocated armament factories were producing at full speed and American shipments had started to arrive.

Apart from the bitter resistance of the Russian troops and Hitler's irresponsibility in setting grandiose and unattainable military goals, a very important contributing factor to the deliverance of Moscow was the difficulties the Germans faced in provisioning and replacing their troops. Neither the conversion of the Russian railroad network to continental track width, nor the transportation of reinforcements along the Russian roads kept up with the speed of the advance. The roads were inferior and, in the fall and winter, deep in mud or snow. The Russian winter also disabled the *Luftwaffe* (German Air Force). The effectiveness of German military units which, in some instances, had advanced beyond Moscow, was dissipated because they could not be reinforced.

The Russian counter-offensive was not a pursuit but rather an unceasing infiltration westward bypassing the centers of German resistance. As in 1812, the Russian troops advanced, not along the roads, but through the fields. They consisted in the main of Cossack divisions, supported by artillery on sleds, and ski troops. These regular units were joined by guerrilla groups which grew in number as the mood in the occupied territories changed. As time went on the battles were fought with increasing brutality.

The Germans retreated along the whole front. It was thrust farthest back in the middle sector, as far as Kalinin and Tula. After Kalinin the Russians retook Kaluga, they then reached Velikie Luki and occupied Mozhaisk. In the Leningrad area the Germans had to give up Tikhvin as early as December 9. The Russians continued to press forward and, by constructing a road across the ice of Lake Ladoga, reestablished contact with Leningrad. At Staraya Russa the bulk of the German 16th Army was cut off from its lines of communication and, after great suffering, the population of Leningrad found itself freed from the enemy's clutches. In Moscow, too, the first and second winter had brought great hardship. The people had suffered hunger and other privations. Fuel, light and gas supplies frequently broke down. But Leningrad, in the winter of 1941-42 probably suffered the most. The number of deaths from starvation is estimated at 600,000. The corpses, which could only be buried with difficulty, were often kept in the houses so that the occasional rations allotted to the household would not be cut.

In the South the Isthmus of Kerch was retaken with the help of the Black Sea fleet and Feodosia in the Crimea was occupied.

The German High Command withdrew its troops behind lines of defense; again and again "hedgehogs" were formed in which the isolated units tried to maintain themselves. They suffered incessantly from the cold as winter equipment had not been provided and voluntary gifts from home were not to make up for it. On both sides the losses during this winter were unexpectedly great and Hitler found himself compelled to shift reservists and troops from the West to the Eastern front, something which he had not planned to do until summer.

About February 23 inactivity set in on the whole front. The momentum of the Russian armies seemed to be spent. Compared with the tremendous expanse of territory which the Germans still held, the reconquered areas appeared insignificant. But they provided a kind of bulwark for the capital so recently endangered and removed it further from the German grasp. The aggressor had lost the initiative, but the danger was still great.

According to Hitler's secret instructions on April 5, the front was to remain stationary in the middle sector. In the north, however, he still hoped for the conquest of Leningrad; in the south, for a break-through to the Caucasus. After defeating the Soviet troops on the middle course of the Don River, the Caucasian oil fields were to be taken and the armament and communication center of Stalingrad was to be paralyzed.

As a preliminary to the main operations, General Manstein prepared for an advance on the Crimea. He liquidated the Soviet bridgehead on the Kerch Peninsula, besieged the city of Sevastopol and on July 13, took it by storm. The whole Crimea was in German hands. The main offensive was to be led by Bock's Army Group consisting of more than one hundred divisions and supported by 1,500 planes. Due to a costly but skillful attack by Timoshenko on Kharkov on May 12, the offensive was delayed for four weeks—a loss of time which it later appeared could not be retrieved.[18] Thus the German operation did not start until the end of June. East of Kursk and in the Eastern Ukraine the Russian front was pierced at various places. The enemy advanced to the gates of Voronezh where heavy fighting flared up and the Don river was crossed. But then a Russian army, concentrated north of the city, joined in the fighting and resistance grew stiffer. Voronezh itself could only be partly occupied and a break-through further east—in the direction of Saratov—proved impossible. Since the German advance progressed in the South to the middle course of the Don river, and Rostov had been occupied at the end of July, it could be assumed that Hitler had decided to change the direction of his thrust from the middle Volga, as his April instructions called for, to a direct attack on the lower Volga near Stalingrad. Indeed, part of the German units, crossing the middle Don, advanced toward Stalingrad while other armies further south crossed the lower part of the Don near Rostov and invaded the North Caucasian plains.

The German decision not to advance further north was actually of great service to the Soviets. The Soviet troops north of Voronezh regained their full freedom of movement; they could be re-grouped and subsequently used in Stalingrad. However, if the advance was to be made in the direction of the lower rather than the middle Volga, the question arose as to what extent Hitler's plan to gain two strategic goals was compatible with military reality. Was it conceivable to reach for both the Caucasian oil fields and Stalingrad? Nowhere were the grave difficulties of such a splintering of the advance more clearly realized than in the German General Staff. Halder, Chief of the General Staff, knew that the Red Army, despite great losses, had not been decisively beaten, let alone destroyed; and he also knew the dangers inherent in stretching the lines of communication which a further advance would inevitably involve. At the beginning of September 1942 he proposed to Hitler that the front be taken back to the line Kiev-Riga. Hitler turned down this suggestion and replaced Halder with a more tractable successor. At the same time a number of German Field Marshals were also removed from their positions. However, if, in opposition to Halder, an offensive war was to be continued in the East, it would have been wise to confine it to the attainment of one of the two goals. Despite the great importance which rapid and direct access to the Caucasian oil fields had for the German war economy, an advance immediately eastward to the lower Volga was of incomparably greater urgency and might even have proved decisive for the whole war. Continued upward along the Volga to the region around Saratov it could have cut off Moscow from the industrial areas in the Urals and in Siberia, as well as from Marshal Timoshenko's forces in the south, leaving the city exposed to an annihilating German attack, this time also from the east. This would have been a plan of unexampled audacity; it would certainly have required special sources of fuel and would have been based on the assumption that in the fall and winter of 1941-42 the strength of the

Red Army had been sapped, not just temporarily but permanently. As matters stood, such a plan, even if restricted to Stalingrad, was most likely to fail, and utterly utopian was the idea of combining the Stalingrad enterprise with a continuation of the advance into the Caucasus.

In an important speech at the beginning of October 1942 Hitler revealed his strategic goals and these did, in fact, envisage the fatal double offensive.

The German advance into the Northern Caucasus was at first accompanied by considerable success. After the occupation of the Kuban region, the Maikop oil fields, at the foot of the Northern Caucasus, were gained. Within a short time the Terek river was reached and Novorossisk, the important naval base on the Black Sea was taken. Then, however, the Germans ran out of fuel. Russian resistance stiffened in the difficult mountainous terrain. Before Grozny the German Caucasus campaign came to a halt. Hoisting a Swastika flag on Mt. Elbrus did not make up for the fact that the Trans-Caucasian oil fields remained out of reach.

All forces were now concentrated on Stalingrad. The city, formerly called Tsaritsyn, was a sprawling industrial center with half a million inhabitants, situated on the right bank of the Volga, not far from the bend of the river. The river here was of imposing width and difficult to bridge. The German troops would have needed to occupy a sufficiently broad operational base on the bank in order to get across. Only after the river had been crossed would the circle around the city have been closed. Instead the German army made the attempt to take Stalingrad by storm. Incessant attacks took place for a whole month. They were met with the stubborn resistance of the garrison under General Chuikov. Stalin had recognized Stalingrad's critical position some time in August. The new Chief of the Russian General Staff, Vassilevsky, had been sent to the scene, together with General Zhukov, and Malenkov, member of the Politburo. An order of the day, "Not a Step Back," charged Chuikov and his 62nd Army to defend the city to the last man. The workers from the Stalingrad factories joined the troops of the garrison. In October the position of the defenders grew critical. On the site of the Tractor Plant and two other factories every foot of soil, every building, every street was bitterly fought over. By the middle of November the Russians were maintaining themselves only in isolated positions on the river bank. The city was a heap of ruins. Section by section, artillery and air attacks had systematically levelled it. The Red Army dug itself into the earth, into the cellars, ruins, and dugouts. It might have been sufficient if the Germans had awaited the effects of the stoppage of all shipping on the Volga, especially as the vital oil supply line, Baku-Moscow, had also been paralyzed. However, Hitler insisted on attaining his goal, to win the city which bore the name of his hated adversary. After the conquest of Leningrad and Moscow had failed, he had to have Stalingrad.

In the meantime, Stalin was able to assemble troops north of the Don without interference. The importance of the connection between Moscow and sources of supply to the east beyond Saratov became more and more apparent. From the Urals and Siberia, where the factories that had been evacuated and assembled there had in the meantime reached their top output, supplies of all kinds reached Moscow via Saratov or were shipped directly to the southern theater of war. A direct railroad line from Astrakhan to Saratov made possible the transportation of American and Persian supplies across the Caspian Sea and in Chkalov (Orenburg) the oil wells of the so-called "second Baku," between the Caspian Sea and the Urals, could be used. From the long range point of view the possession of the lower part of the Volga could only be of use to the Germans if they also held Astrakhan. For Astrakhan and Saratov were, in the final analysis, equally as important as Stalingrad.

In the beginning of November 1942 General Paulus was appointed Commander in Chief of the German Sixth Army, which was to bear the burden of the battle for Stalingrad. Its twenty-two divisions, consisting of about 300,000 men, were concentrated in a small area west of the city. The adjacent defense positions in the northwest on the Don were held by Rumanian and Italian units; in the south other Rumanian troops linked up with them.

The Russian plan of attack was made up of two operations. The first consisted of distracting skirmishes on the central front between Velikie Luki and Rzhev in order to prevent possible German reinforcements; the other envisaged the relief of Stalingrad. On November 19 the Russian counter-offensive which, in an order of the day on October 14, Hitler had described as unlikely, began. The whole operational reserve was put under Zhukov's orders. He divided them into three armies which were to press from the north, northwest and south on the flanks of Stalingrad. They were led by Generals Rokossovsky, Vatutin and Yeremenko. The artillery was under the command of General Voronov. Concentric blows were to be struck at the rear of the German besiegers in order to prevent their breaking through to the west, which it was thought they might attempt.

When the offensive began on November 19 it was initially directed at the weakest links of the German front. First of all, the Rumanian and Italian positions in the north were broken up and Russian tanks forced a crossing of the Don. Further west the Russian troops cut deep into the German rear on the middle Don and joined with forces advancing westward from the south. The circle around the Sixth Army had been closed. Paulus was ordered to maintain the siege of Stalingrad; it was thought that supplies could be assured by air. In the meantime relief troops were dispatched under General Manstein. With about 150,000 men he broke through the Russian lines on December 12 and in bitter fighting some territory on the middle Don was regained. Now, however, Stalin ordered that the Sixth Army be ignored and everything be concentrated on the German relief troops. The powerful Russian thrusts prevented the relief operation from being successful and the situation of the Sixth Army grew desperate. The aerial supply line proved to be inadequate and a great number of planes were lost. Manstein's suggestion to risk the loss of half his troops and break through the Russian lines, was rejected by Hitler. At the beginning of January Rokossovsky asked the Germans to surrender but Paulus refused. The destruction of the Sixth Army continued. On February 2, 1943 its remnant capitulated, shortly after Paulus and twenty-three generals had been taken prisoner.

Even during the fighting for Stalingrad the German position in the Caucasus had become untenable. As a bridgehead opposite Kerch, only the Taman Peninsula remained in German hands. After the catastrophe of February 2, the Eastern Ukraine also could no longer be held. During February the Russians also reconquered Bielgorod and Kharkov. Repercussions were felt everywhere. In the central sector the Germans were forced to give up their advance position near Viazma. When the Russians retook Schluesselburg on Lake Ladoga their contact with the beleaguered city of Leningrad had been reestablishd.

When the thrust of the Russian advance began to slow down, in the middle of February, Manstein carried out some completely unexpected attacks. At Dniepropetrovsk he had gathered a new army of twenty-four divisions, of which twelve were armored, and with these he attacked on February 21. South of Kharkov he pushed the Russians back across the Donets river, avoided exposing himself by further pursuit, and was content with the reconquest of Kharkov on March 12. Then the thaw began and stopped operations on both sides. The winter campaign of 1942-43 had ended. The initiative had passed to Russian hands. The German drive had been exhausted in the battles for Stalingrad and Grozny. The psychological effects of the battle of Stalingrad were immense on both sides. In the Soviet Union its outcome bolstered morale tremendously.

The Return to Tradition

The mortal danger which had threatened the Bolshevik regime during the victorious advance of the German troops in the first two years of the war had induced Stalin to use any and every means to strengthen the national will to resist. This was the great hour of Soviet patriotism.

As the number of Russians in German prisoner-of-war camps increased, it became a matter of course to appeal to the national consciousness, to awaken the forces of the nation's tradition and history and to employ these energies in the defense of the fatherland. This approach was successful. Where reports of German excesses and coercion in the Occupied Territories did not suffice, where the instinct to resist was not as spontaneous as, for example, among the members of the Komsomol, results were achieved through pressure and unceasing propaganda.

Particularly in the Red Army, the nationalist and traditionalist slogans fell on fertile ground. Highly treasured customs and institutions which still carried the halo of the Revolution and the Civil War were thrown overboard. In October 1942 when the outcome of the battle of Stalingrad had become clear, a special decree was issued abolishing the office of political commissar in the armed forces, re-established only fifteen months 'before. The place of the commissars was taken by Deputy Commanders for Political Affairs who held officer's rank. In the small units the function of the *Politruks* was handed over directly to the Commanding Officers. This was done chiefly for military reasons. Unity of command was a prerequisite for effective discipline and the greater efficiency of the troops. A *Pravda* article of November 1942 stressed that the soldier had no socialist obligations, that his task was simply to serve his fatherland as his forebears had done.

"Socialist competition" within the army was therefore out of place. That same year the first new guard regiments were formed. Their members received special insignia. The shock regiments were renamed guard regiments. The time when the guard regiments, the most effective symbol of Czarist power, had cut down the revolutionaries of 1917 seemed centuries away from the present battle. The flags, however, remained red, including the special Red Guard flag created in 1943; they were protected by new decrees enhancing their importance.

Of considerable significance was a decree of July 1943 which reorganized the ranks of privates, non-commissioned officers, officers and generals. That meant a change in the leadership of the Red Army in that a two-fold officers' corps was established. In October of the same year new ranks for the senior generals were introduced. Specialists attached to the quartermaster and engineer corps were given officer's rank. At the beginning of 1943 new insignia of rank had been introduced; the golden epaulettes, which the October Revolution had abolished as symbols of the counter-revolution and of the reactionary caste system, had been reintroduced. New awards, such as the Kutuzov and Suvorov Orders, were links with the tradition of Czarist times. Cossack formations, once notorious as tools of Czarist oppression and important centers of counter-revolutionary resistance in the Civil War, were revived. Saluting was reintroduced and strictly enforced. Exclusive Officers' Clubs and even separate messes for field and staff officers were set up. Among officers great value was attached to good breeding and correct behavior.

On March 6, 1943, Stalin himself assumed the rank of Marshal and was formally appointed Supreme Commander in Chief of the Soviet Armed Forces. He awarded marshal batons to his ablest commanders. In December 1943 alone 360 officers were promoted to the rank of General; the newspapers were filled with lists of appointments and promotions. Stalin took advantage of every opportunity to stress his personal solidarity with his commanders and the officers' corps.

Russian patriotism was set to work also outside the military sector. After the loss of the White Ruthenian and Ukrainian provinces in the west and in the south, it was more important than ever that the fighting spirit of the actual Russian core of the Soviet Union be maintained. Already during the first winter of the war all slogans had been couched in language that would appeal to

Russian national feeling. The slogan "Proletarians of All the Countries Unite" which several newspapers carried as bannerheads, was replaced by "Down with the Fascist Invader." As in 1812, when Napoleon's troops had advanced as far as Moscow, the holy soil of Russia had to be defended. And when Leo Tolstoy's country house in Yasnaya Polyana, near Moscow, was devoured by fire in the course of the fighting, his immortal story, *War and Peace,* gained a new, uncanny reality. The work of the historian, E. Tarle, on Napoleon's invasion of Russia, which had appeared first in 1937, sold rapidly in its second edition in 1943. Experience showed that the Russian soldiers' fighting spirit was not in the main aroused by the somewhat vapid Soviet patriotism, but by their attachment to "Mother Russia." Stalin himself admitted this in talking with Harry Hopkins.

The Russian state and the Russian people became the focus of patriotism. The press stressed that the Russian people had been the actual instrument of Russian history. The new National Anthem read: "Unbreakable Union of free-born Republics, Great Russia has welded forever to stand." Stalin's theory of socialism in one country had become so nationalist in tenor that in the crucible of war the Bolshevik regime assumed more and more a national-Bolshevik character.

In this connection, Stalin's comment concerning National Socialism is of importance. While the battle for Moscow was still raging he said "Can the followers of Hitler be regarded as Nationalists? No, they cannot. The Hitlerites are not Nationalists, but imperialists." He said that at one time Hitler could have been considered a German patriot, but he had lost the right to this appelation when he began to annex non-German countries. This positive interpretation of nationalism was joined to the positive conception of patriotism which had been promoted in the Soviet Union since 1934. With full awareness, Stalin thus legitimized Russian nationalism, using it as a weapon against the "imperialist aggressor."

The bridge which had thus been built to the pre-revolutionary past also made it possible to re-establish contact with the world of the Greek-Orthodox Church. Stalin's new policy toward the Church was dictated by the need to utilize all the sources of the nation's resistance. It was initiated in 1942 by the loyalty declarations of the ecclesiastical dignitaries and by church collections for armaments. On November 7, 1942, the Metropolitan Sergius and Stalin exchanged telegrams for the first time to celebrate the twenty-fifth

Anniversary of the October Revolution. After Stalingrad, representatives of the Church were permitted to enter the Kremlin. On September 4, 1943, Stalin received the Metropolitan Sergius, the head of the Russian Church and of the other Russian metropolitans. In a long and friendly discussion they planned the election of a new Patriarch. The reasons given for the conclusion of peace between the Party and the Church were that the Church had, in the course of the war, worked wholeheartedly for victory and had thus proven its loyalty to the Fatherland. On September 8 a clerical Synod, consisting of metropolitans and bishops from the lands under Soviet dominion, elected the Metropolitan Sergius Patriarch. The State on its part set up a Department for the Affairs of the Greek-Orthodox Church in the Office of the Chairman of the Council of People's Commissars, to which similar departments for the other religious denominations were soon added.

Religious and pro-church sentiments had never completely died out in the Soviet Union, especially among the older generations of peasants. In the midst of the deprivations and trials of the war these sentiments were strengthened. By its new church policy the government hoped to draw these sections of the population to its side.

Outside Russia, Stalin's reconciliation with the Church was of particular importance in the Balkan countries on which Soviet policy and war aims were increasingly focussed during the second part of the war. With open eyes, Stalin followed the policy of the Czars who also had used the Church as a political instrument, while the Church itself, on the other hand, had been the source of certain political ideas. It did not, however, play that role now. The present task was to stress everything that the Russian and the Orthodox churches of the Balkan countries had in common, preparatory to the construction of a political bridge. It is possible that the revival of Panslavism was planned when Soviet foreign policy first showed an interest in Rumania and Bulgaria and friendly relations were established with Yugoslavia. The outbreak of the war made a more intensive pursuit of this line advisable. In the summer of 1941 a All-Slavic Committee was formed in Moscow among whose most sedulous members were the historian Grekov and the poet Alexei Tolstoy. The "slogans" of the Communist party for the anniversary of the Revolution in November 1942 avoided any reference to the world revolution and instead appealed to the common interests of the "fraternal Slavs."

The new emphasis on national tradition was perhaps most strongly

demonstrated in the dissolution of the Comintern in 1943, a measure
which was rightly expected to make a strong impression abroad. The
fact that it coincided with the re-establishment of the Greek Orthodox Church in the Soviet Union was bound to lead to the assumption
that world revolutionary aims had finally been discarded. This impression was underlined when the "Internationale," the hymn of the
labor movement of the world, was replaced by a specially written
and composed Soviet national anthem with a pronounced nationalist
and patriotic flavor.

It was obvious that for the duration of the war, at least until the
acute danger was over, Stalin had to eliminate all domestic quarrels
and tensions. A domestic truce and patriotic solidarity cloaked all
the controversies and ideological deviations of the thirties; actual
or alleged adherents of existing or fictitious opposition groups were
brought back from exile or concentration camps whenever there was
a need for their services. Among the generals reaching the highest
ranks and honors in the Red Army were Rokossovsky, Tolbukhin
and Yakovlev, all of whom had been punished during the Tukhachevsky trials, but had been pardoned by a rehabilitation commission even before the outbreak of the war. Rokossovsky, who with
Zhukov was chiefly responsible for the victory of Stalingrad, had
been Tukhachevsky's contact man with the Comintern. Professor
Ramzin who had been sentenced in the early thirties for high
treason and industrial espionage was also released, greatly honored,
and reinstated in the Civil Service.

Ostarbeiters, Partisans and Prisoners of War

In the occupied territories the Germans were in the meantime
doing their best to lose the initial sympathies of the population. On
March 21, 1942, Hitler had appointed Sauckel, the Gaulciter of
Thuringia, as "Plenipotentiary for the Recruitment of Labor." He
immediately began to put into practice Hitler's idea of exploiting
the "inexhaustible reservoir of labor" in the occupied Eastern territories for the German war economy. Without any consideration for
the wishes of individuals or for human ties, and without any psychological understanding of the mentality of the population of the
Western Soviet Union, a mass recruitment of labor was started in
the early summer of 1942 and people were forcibly transported to
Germany. Several millions of so-called "Eastern workers" were
in this manner made available to the German war economy. In

order to guard against the danger of political sabotage they were housed in separate camps, had to wear a degrading East Badge, and were exposed to many other humiliations. There were of course German protests against the inhumanity of the method of recruiting, which frequently degenerated into man hunts, and against the degrading treatment meted out to the laborers also. On the whole the Germans had no reason to be dissatisfied with the output of these workers.

The psychological effect of the slave labor operation was, however, soon to be noticed in the occupied territories. Favorable conditions for anti-Bolshevik propaganda quickly vanished. When the labor recruiting officers approached a settlement, the population fled to the woods. It frequently preferred a hazardous free life, full of deprivations, to assured income in a foreign country. When the German military police organized search parties, they met with resistance. In the forests, the Partisan groups increased. Skillful Bolshevik propaganda gave them moral and patriotic support and a steady stream of agents and contact men, smuggled through the front lines, provided them with propaganda literature, leadership, arms and ammunition. The partisans severed the German lines of communication, destroyed supply columns, attacked reserve units and isolated posts, dynamited roads, bridges and munition depots. With heroic zeal, young people fought their way through the front lines in order to execute their missions. One of them was Zoya Kosmodemyanskaya, a high school senior and member of the Komsomol. During a winter night she cut German telegraph lines and set fire to a munition dump in a village in the central sector of the front. Apprehended and executed as a partisan, her picture, assiduously spread among the Soviet public, became the symbol of heroic self-sacrifice and patriotic resistance. Month by month the unrest grew in the territory behind the front, particularly in the forests and swamps of White Russia. Routes which in the fall of 1941 could be used by German vehicles without danger, a year later could only be travelled by guarded convoys. In the Ukraine too there were signs of unrest. Here the members of the nationalist Ukrainian movement, at first supported by the German authorities, were disillusioned. While the transfer of the Carpathian Ukraine to Hungary in March 1939 had caused resentment, the incorporation of Galicia into the Polish Gouvernement-General met with vigorous criticism. Even worse was the transfer to Rumania of a broad piece of Ukrainian border territory, re-named the Province of Transnistria, and including the city of Odessa. When to this was finally added the particularly ruthless and brutal administration of the *Reichskommissar* for the Ukraine, Erich Koch, the nationalist Ukrainian organization OUN went underground and engaged in active resistance. In the course of time an extremely ingenious resistance army, the UPA, developed in the Ukraine, fighting on two fronts, as it also considered Bolshevism its enemy.

The German authorities were helpless in the face of this development. Having no experience with illegal organizations, a complex net of camouflage, and the methods of partisan fighting, they met this ingenious system either naively with blind confidence, or else with ruthless force. Constructive ideas and suggestions submitted by some informed officials were strangled by red tape, or were, when they reached him, branded by Hitler as illusionary or sentimental. To him the Slavs, particularly the Eastern Slavs of Russia, were inferior "swamp dwellers," sub-humans who did not deserve humane treatment and whose sole *raison d'être* was to serve as labor in the attainment of the German goals he envisaged. Nevertheless he did not hesitate in 1942 to establish his headquarters at Vinnitsa in the Ukraine from June to November. Here Goering, Himmler and the Supreme Command of the Army also set up their staff quarters, quite oblivious of the fact that they were surrounded by a skilfully camouflaged net of Soviet agents.

On both sides the partisan fighting became more and more cruel. Not infrequently hostages were shot, there were mass operations against the male population, whole villages were burned, and so on.

Persecution of the Jews was pursued independently. SS commandos saw to it not only that the Nuremberg Laws were applied to their fullest extent in the occupied territorties, but also that all Jews who could be caught were deported to Auschwitz and other extermination camps. It appeared that the Jews of West Russia were completely unaware of the German policy on the Jews, as they, possibly quite deliberately, had not been warned of the dire consequences of staying on when the Soviet authorities retreated.

Added to the slave labor and partisan problem was that of the prisoners of war. The numbers taken prisoner were so tremendous from the beginning of the advance that even the best organization could not have coped with them. The mass deaths in the big collection camps behind the front, caused by insufficient medical aid and care,[21] replaced the initial joyful surprise that not every prisoner of war was immediately shot (as Bolshevik propaganda had tried to tell the Red Army, particularly the officers), with deep disappointment and discouragement. This had an effect on the whole emotional climate in the occupied territories. When conditions gradually became more normal and the situation became tolerable in the large permanent camps, a good deal of good will had been lost.

For the rural population the question of the continuation or dissolution of the collective farms was a very important test. In general, the Bolshevik methods of forced collectivization during the 'thirties, the deportation of the so-called *kulaks,* the exactions of the state, were well remembered. There were sound psychological prerequisites for a constructive German agrarian reform along lines of private enterprise. In White Russia an attempt was actually made. From one day to the next the collective farms were dissolved and divided into individual peasant holdings. In the Ukraine where the solution of this question was even more urgent for psychological and economic reasons, Erich Koch opposed it most energetically, arguing for the retention of the collective economy on economic grounds. He sabotaged and, by appealing to Hitler, completely blocked a new agrarian system (February 15, 1942),[22] and an "ownership declaration" (March 6,1943),[23] which the Ministry for Eastern Affairs had worked out along the lines of Stolypin's reform ideas, envisaging the creation of a class of peasant proprietors.

The Western Powers and the Problem of the Second Front.

The Japanese attack on Pearl Harbor on December 7, 1941, brought the United States actively into the war.

American support of Soviet military operations in the form of loans and shipments intensified. Shipments were sent mainly via the Pacific and, alternatively, by the northern route via Murmansk and Archangelsk. Along the latter route the convoys had to face the constant danger of German submarine attacks. Here the situation became increasingly difficult so that England began to urge the curtailment of shipments. Churchill cabled Roosevelt that the convoys required were exceeding Britain's strength. Since 1942 the Soviet Union urgently required planes, particularly fighters. For a long time, the Soviet government objected to American suggestions for ferrying them to Russia via Alaska and Siberia. A good deal of distrust still existed between the Eastern and Western Allies. Each side did not exclude the possibility of the other concluding a separate peace with Hitler. To Stalin the gulf between the liberal capitalism

of the Western powers and the totalitarian system of the Axis
countries seemed much smaller than it really was. On the other
hand, the Western allies could not discount possible surprise moves
on Stalin's part. The pact of August 1939 was not forgotten.

As Stalin urgently needed Western aid, he studiously avoided
waging the war under the flag of the world revolution. All previous
orders to the Communist parties in the various countries to sabotage
the war effort were cancelled. The new line demanded that the
Communists follow a policy for which in 1914 they had bitterly
upbraided the Socialists. They were to subordinate themselves to
whichever government was in power and devote all their energies
to the war effort. Thus they would help the Soviet Union, the fatherland of all workers. Also within the resistance movements in the
German occupied countries, the Communists were to follow the
nationalist-bourgeois leadership. The word "democracy" became the
common symbol in the fight against "Fascism." The nationalist,
patriotic course adopted in Russia would prove to the Western
powers that Bolshevism was being domesticated. The dissolution of
the Comintern sealed this development; it did not fail to have its
effect abroad: the Communist parties reacted with shock, governments with relief.

But his deep-rooted distrust of the West led Stalin to express
disappointment at Allied hesitation in making an all-out effort and
greater sacrifices. When a British Cabinet member, Lord Brabazon,
stated in the days of the German invasion of the Soviet Union, that
it would be best for the Western powers to wait until the Germans
and Russians had exhausted each other, Stalin was particularly
offended, perhaps because from 1939 to 1941 he had entertained
a similar idea regarding the war between the West and Hitler. Hence
his continued demand for the Second Front in the West. This became one of the main issues of Allied-Russian military collaboration
between 1941 and 1944. In a letter to Churchill on September 4,
1941, Stalin had already demanded the opening of a second front
"in the Balkans or in France" during that year, in order to divert
thirty to forty German divisions from the East. Ten days later,
Stalin requested that twenty-five to thirty British divisions be sent
to Archangelsk, or via Persia to Southern Russia, a plan which
could not be realized, chiefly because of the scarcity of transportation.

In order to protect himself against a separate peace by the West
and to speed the opening of the Second Front, Stalin sent Molotov

to London and Washington in the spring of 1942. The signing of a Soviet-British alliance for twenty years on May 26, 1942, was a great political success for the Soviet Union.[24] Molotov was unable to obtain definite promises for a Second Front, but both Churchill and later Roosevelt in Washington, told him privately that a landing in France could be counted on that year. However, things were not that simple. When, on his return from the United States, Molotov stopped over in London, a joint communiqué was drafted on June 11. This stated "that in the course of negotiations concerning the urgent tasks of opening a Second Front in Europe during 1942 a complete understanding was reached." But this communiqué was in the first place intended to mislead the enemy. In reality the Western allies had in the meantime realized that insurmountable obstacles lay in the way of carrying out such a project.

In a note drafted at the same time as the official communique, Churchill told Molotov the plain truth. "I made it clear," he writes in his Memoirs, "while we were trying our best to make plans we were not committed to action and that we could give no promise."[25] Also as regards the question of a new lend-lease program, which was to be inaugurated on July 1, Molotov, contrary to original expectations, had to accept a curtailment of the shipments planned from four million metric tons to two and a half million because of the critical shipping situation.

In addition to the problems which concerned the immediate conduct of the war, there was the extremely thorny question of the Soviet Union's future Western frontier, the most complex aspect of which was the Polish situation.

The Baltic and Polish Questions

When Eden visited Moscow in December 1941, Stalin had demanded the re-establishment of the pre-war frontiers and thus British recognition of all Soviet territorial acquisitions since the fall of 1939.[26] At that time Eden had successfully evaded the question but had nevertheless managed to persuade the Soviet Union to enter the alliance of the United Nations. The declaration concerning this was signed by Ambassador Litvinov on January 1, 1942, in Washington. This, however, in no way meant that the Soviet government had renounced its territorial claims. That same month Churchill declared with a good deal of feeling that the surrender of the Baltic nations to the Soviet Union was incompatible with Britain's honor. However, the Kremlin maintained its stand and in March of that year Churchill, under the pressure of events, retreated from his original position. Although the American Secretary of State, Cordell Hull, had until then strictly refused any concession in this area, Roosevelt supported Churchill after stipulating the desirability of free emigration for all inhabitants of the Baltic countries who did not want to accept annexation.

When the British and American governments promised an increase in lend-lease shipments, Molotov, after consulting with Stalin, declared himself ready to agree to the British draft of an Anglo-Soviet alliance. Article 5 of this provided that the partners agreed "neither to aim at territorial expansion for themselves nor to intervene in the domestic affairs of other states," but the Kremlin took the point of view that this passage did not refer to Soviet territorial acquisitions between 1939 and the conclusion of this alliance.[27]

The opposition of the Western Allies to the Kremlin's Polish plans was stiffer than on the Baltic question. The war with Hitler had been started because of Poland and the prestige of the Western powers demanded that Polish rights be safeguarded against the Soviet Union.

In London a Polish government in exile had been set up. When in the first days of the war the Soviet government declared that the Ribbentrop Pact of August 1939 was null and void, the head of the Polish government-in-exile, General Sikorski, interpreted this as Soviet readines to give back the eastern Polish territories. However, the Kremlin had no such intention, and when Stalin offered to enter into negotiations with Sikorski, the latter refused all discussion of frontier questions. Nevertheless, on July 30, 1941, the Soviet government concluded an agreement with the Polish government-in-exile, similar to that concluded with Czechoslovakia on July 18, providing mutual aid during the war and the creation of national military units on Soviet soil. However, a really harmonious collaboration between Soviet Russia and the Poles became more and more difficult and the tension between Moscow and the London Poles grew. The British government had its hands full trying to keep Sikorski from making provoking gestures, such as baptizing the British cruiser which had been assigned to him "Lwow." At the same time, however, London was of the opinion that Stalin desired a strong post-war Poland, including German territories, and that in the East he would be satisfied with the Curzon line.[28]

When Molotov raised the Polish question in London, the British government refused to agree to the annexation of Eastern Poland as incompatible with the British-Polish agreement of August 1939. It similarly opposed Russian claims to Rumanian territory.[29]

One of the weightiest problems in Polish-Soviet relations was the fate of 14,500 Polish internees who in September 1939 had fallen into Soviet hands. Among them were about 8,000 officers. They had been housed in three internment camps in the district of Smolensk. Until the spring of 1940 news of them had been received occasionally but then complete silence enveloped the three camps and their inhabitants. After June 22, 1941, the Polish government repeatedly asked the Soviet government for details regarding the fate of the internees, and asked for their release so that they could join the new Polish army. No concrete answer was given. During a conversation between Polish Ambassador Kot and Stalin on November 14, 1941, the latter, after calling the NKVD on the telephone, dropped the subject abruptly; on December 3 he assured General Sikorski that the internees had escaped via Manchuria.

Local investigations were impossible as the Germans were occupying the area in which the three camps were situated. In the spring of 1943 the sensational news made the rounds that the Germans had discovered a mass grave of Polish officers at Katyn, near Smolensk. The German radio accused the Soviet government of having murdered the Poles. An investigation by international and neutral experts established that the executions had taken place in the spring of 1940 when the area was still under Soviet control. Although Churchill told General Sikorski that he was skeptical about the usefulness of a Polish statement on this matter, the Polish government published a *communiqué* on April 17 in which the International Red Cross was asked to undertake an investigation of the incident.

As a result of this *démarche*, the Soviet government cancelled the Polish-Soviet agreement of 1941. Stalin informed the British government of this step in a special note to Churchill and despite British mediation, relations with the Polish government-in-exile were severed.[30]

As regards the Katyn incident, in January 1944, after the Smolensk area had been reconquered, the Soviet government published a report of a Russian investigation commission which attempted to saddle the Germans with the responsibility for the murder of the Polish officers. At the War Crimes Trials in Nuremberg the Katyn affair was passed over in silence and the Soviet representatives did not take the opportunity to refute the German accusation of 1943.[31] However, the latest Polish reports and also the results of an American investigation commission set up in 1952, leave no doubt that the murders took place prior to the German occupation of the territory in question.[32]

Churchill in Moscow

In the middle of the summer of 1942 the Allies' conduct of the war had reached perhaps its most critical phase.

While Rommel's advance in North Africa was making rapid progress and a landing at Dieppe had failed, German troops in Southern Russia advanced in a double move both on Stalingrad and into the Caucasus. People with vivid imaginations already saw the outlines of a gigantic pincer movement which in the north reached across the Caucasus and in the south across the Suez Canal in order to meet at the oil wells of Iraq and Iran.

The time for a Japanese mediation attempt, made in the late summer of 1942, was thus not badly chosen. Perhaps these calamitous weeks before the clash at Stalingrad were the only time since the battle of Moscow when Stalin would have been seriously available for a *pourparler*. Halder may have felt this when—consciously limiting himself to the military sector—he warned against splitting the strategic goals of the German advance and recommended pulling back the front and conducting a defensive war. Churchill also sensed that this was a fateful hour. Now was the time to act, to prevent a weakening of the coalition, or the loss of the Soviet Union to the alliance.

In August the British Prime Minister, accompanied by W. Averell Harriman whom Roosevelt had assigned to him for this mission, went by air via Cairo to Moscow. The task in hand was to coordinate the military operations of the two partners. For the first time Churchill met Stalin, "the great revolutionary chief and profound Russian stateman and warrior," with whom he was for the next three years "to be in intimate, rigorous, but always exciting, and at times even genial, association."[33]The initial negotiations took place in a "somber, depressed atmosphere." Churchill brought the news that the British and American governments had decided to schedule the invasion, not for France, but North Africa and Sicily. For 1943, a more extensive operation in France was planned for which even now American troops were being assembled in Britain; for the time being, however, only Operation Torch could be carried out in the Mediterranean.

Even during the first discussion Stalin had "begun to look very glum." [34] He felt that in a war risks had to be taken, he could not understand why the Anglo-Americans were so afraid of the Germans. He maintained that this represented a mortal blow for Soviet public opinion. Churchill managed to infect Stalin with a temporary enthusiasm for the new plan but the "atmosphere of cordiality" of which the official communiqué spoke was not real and the discussions of the military experts—Voroshilov and Shaposhnikov, Brooke, Wavell and Tedder—also left much to be desired and ended somewhat abruptly. In the last meeting between Churchill and Stalin the latter assured his guest that Soviet troops would in any event block the Germans from access to the Caspian Sea and the oil of Baku and prevent a break-through to Persia and Turkey. After the conclusion of the discussions Churchill accepted Stalin's invitation to a nocturnal visit to his private apartment in the Kremlin which lasted for more than seven hours. In his memoirs Churchill himself describes this visit with unsurpassed vividness. The Prime Minister managed to get his host to make some interesting comments about collectivization, [35] the communiqué was once more discussed, a pig and a good deal of liquor was consumed. However, when the possibility of a meeting between Stalin and Roosevelt in Iceland and a visit by Stalin to Britain was mentioned, the latter became evasive.

It was two full years before the Soviet Union could consider the promise of a Second Front fulfilled with the invasion of Northern France. Until then the real difficulties of the British and Americans in conducting the war met with little understanding. With the intensification of the battles around Stalingrad the whole burden of fighting the Germans seemed to rest on the Red Army.

While the Western allies discussed the question of Germany's unconditional surrender, the battle for Stalingrad was nearing its end. The Russian victory made a tremendous impression in the West as well. According to Sherwood it "changed the whole picture of the war and the future in as far as this could be predicted. As the result of one battle Russia assumed the position of a great international power . . . " [36] Stalin's repeated demands for a second front now carried more weight. The demands became more energetic and insistent and reflected both the growing irritation of the

ruler of the Kremlin and the regained self-confidence of the Red
Army.

The Battles of the Summer of 1943:
The Russian Volunteer Units

The winter fighting following the battle of Stalingrad had resulted in a front line which west of Kursk showed the Russian
positions considerably advanced, but they were flanked by the cities
of Orel and Bielgorod, still in German hands.

The German military leaders felt that, chiefly for psychological
reasons, they could not afford to withdraw the front farther, as previously suggested by Halder. In order to fortify German morale
and to delay the expected Russian offensive, Hitler decided to risk
a tactical advance. The bend in the front near Kursk was to be
straightened out in Germany's favor. Commanded by Field Marshal Kluge, thirty-six divisions advanced in pincer formation into
the country beyond Kursk on July 5.

The attack miscarried. The Russians under General Vatutin not
only maintained their positions but also recaptured the two bases
of the German offensive and flooded westward in a broad wave.
Kharkov, Stalino, Taganrog to the south, and Smolensk north of the
break-through point, were reconquered by the Russians in the course
of August and September. The Germans in the Ukraine, attempting
to hold at least the Dnieper line, were surprised when the summer
battle for Kursk grew into winter fighting. At the beginning of October the army groups of General Rokossovsky, General Vatutin and
General Konev crossed the river at three points. The Germans
yielded Dniepropetrovsk and Melitopol. Their position in the Crimea became critical. By a vigorous counter-attack General Manstein tried to hold Krivoy Rog in the Dnieper bend in order to avoid
geting into a similar position as in the previous winter in the Don
bend. But in vain. In November Krivoy Rog and Kiev fell into
Russian hands. They then advanced to the railroad line Mohylev-
Odessa and occupied Zhytomir. Here Manstein once more intervened with twelve divisions, reconquered the city and forced the
Russians back almost to Kiev. In the meantime the winter had
come—the third winter in Russia.

This is the place to consider one of the most important elements
in the German conduct of the war which at times promised to

become a real threat to the Soviet Union—the use of anti-Bolshevik Russian forces against the Red Army.

In spite of the disappointing experiences with the German authorities in the occupied territories, despite the initial bad treatment of the prisoners of war, despite the labor levies, a countermovement to the partisans came into being. From among the prisoners of war, thousands were recruited by the German army as auxiliary units, partly as the result of anti-Bolshevik propaganda, partly by virtue of the wish of the volunteers to escape the camps. In each regiment and in each battalion so-called "Hiwis" (German abbreviation for "volunteers") gathered as drivers, stable-boys, cooks, medical orderlies, and interpreters. They were constantly augmented by an unending stream of deserters who flooded across the lines, all the efforts of Bolshevik propaganda and the Soviet military successes since Stalingrad notwithstanding. At the end of 1942 nearly one million "Hiwis" were serving in the German armed forces. In the course of time some of them were absorbed into volunteer units which had been formed on a national basis; and these were consolidated in 1943 under a *General der Osttruppen* (General of Eastern Units). At the end of the war General Koestring, formerly German military attaché in Moscow, occupied this position.

In the front sector of Orel a singular attempt at constructive co-operation with the Russian population was made in 1942. The district of Lokot was taken out of the hands of the German civil administration and set up as a self-governing, autonomous territory. Its head was a Russian of Polish background, an engineer by the name of Kaminski, who worked out a plan to organize supplies and security, ensure deliveries to the German authorities, and set up a Russian school system. He also created a fighting unit and gained the confidence of the Germans to such an extent that they gave him a completely free hand and even put other districts under his control. The German retreat in the late summer of 1943 wiped out this particular set-up. But Kaminski, who had been evacuated with 30,000 people, repeated his experiment in the district of Lepel. The collapse of the German front in 1944 sucked him into the whirlpool of the Warsaw uprising, during which he came into conflict with the German authorities, was court martialled, and shot.

In White Russia a different kind of venture was tried during the winter of 1943-44. In the middle of the partisan territory an official of the German Ministry for Eastern Affairs created a kind of Youth

Aid program and obtained practical training in Germany for young people between the ages of fourteen and eighteen. There they were not treated as slave workers but as on a level with their German fellow workers. Some ten thousand young White Russians, and later Russians and Ukrainians also, came in the course of this program into contact with West European working and living conditions and had an opportunity to test the validity of Bolshevik propaganda concerning the capitalist West.

The earliest instance of collaboration was that with volunteers from the Caucasus and the Turkic peoples. In October 1941 the basis was laid for establishing a Turkic division within the German armed forces. Turkestanian and Caucasian prisoners of war received preferential treatment. As time went on, Georgian, Armenian, Azerbaidjanian, North Caucasian, Turkestanian and Tatar legions were formed. In the occupied Northern Caucasus an autonomous state was proclaimed in the territory of the Karachay and Kabardinians which at first benefited the population, but which was doomed by the German retreat. Of the approximately 650,000 men who in 1944 were under the command of the General of Eastern Units in prisoner of war or construction battalions, more than 100,000 were Turkestanians, more than 100,000 Caucasians, 35,000 were Tatars, and there were even twenty-nine squadrons of Kalmucks.

The Cossacks were in a special position. In the summer of 1942 when the war reached their territory, 70,000 of them went over to the Germans in order to join the fight against the Soviet regime. A Cossack Corps, commanded by the German General Pannwitz, consisting of two divisions, and a Cossack Militia under Ataman Domanov were set up. Although the Cossacks considered themselves either Russians or Ukrainians, the German authorities attempted to stamp them as a special tribe in order to stress the heterogeneity of the population of Russia. However contrived such attempts may have been, the Cossacks themselves in part accepted them for the sake of expediency in their fight against Bolshevism.

It was all the more significant that as time went by these non-Russian or not uniformly Russian, formations were joined by purely Russian anti-Bolshevik groups. Outstanding among them was the Vlasov movement. While the Kaminski experiment could not be considered a national Russian undertaking, having come into being accidentally, due to local conditions, and with a Russian as its leader, it was different with Vlasov.[37]

Andrey Andreyevich Vlasov was the son of a peasant from the Nizhni Novgorod region. At seventeen he had taken part in the October Revolution and had swiftly risen in the Red Army. After 1930 he belonged to the Communist party. During the great purge he was military adviser to Chiang Kai-shek in China. At that time, according to his own account, he experienced the first doubts regarding his Bolshevik views. Nevertheless, at the outbreak of war, he followed his duty as a soldier, distinguished himself in the great battle of Moscow and was decorated with the Order of the Red Flag. As Commander of the Second Army he was unable to prevent his troops from being encircled at the Volkhov river after heavy fighting. For weeks Vlasov and the rest of his men wandered around in a no-man's land; and here it was that he arrived at the decision to arouse the Russian people to the fight against Bolshevism. His plan assumed more definite shape as he became acquainted with the Germans during his captivity. In the summer of 1942 he attracted the attention of the Eastern Division of the German General Staff. The idea took shape of placing this intelligent and determined man at the head of a grandly conceived political project which was to unite all anti-Bolshevik forces to further a positive Russian program. That same fall, attempts were made to use Vlasov propagandistically. However, he did not appeal to the Russian people until the spring of 1943 when in an "Open Letter," dated March 3, he described in detail the "reasons why he had entered the battle against Bolshevism."[38] In the letter all Russian prisoners of war, the civilian population of the occupied territories, and beyond them the total population of the Soviet Union, were exhorted to participate in the fight "against Stalin, for peace and a new Russian." A few days later the appeal appeared in the prisoners' of war newspaper *Dobrovolets* (The Volunteer) and was then broadcast in millions of leaflets. In Smolensk a Russian liberation committee was formed under Vlasov's leadership which on April 12 addressed an appeal to the whole Russian people.[39]

Among the prisoners of war and the "Eastern Workers" Vlasov had for a time had an audience. The first result of the project was an increase in the number of desertions at the front. A propaganda trip to Smolensk and the territory behind the central sector of the German-Russian front, and later through occupied Northwestern

Russia as far as Pskov and Novgorod, was a great success. Soon even old-time Russian emigrants began to take an interest. In newspapers and leaflets continual appeals were now made to join the Russian liberation army. The German authorities responsible for the project wanted to put Vlasov in charge of the army which, as an allied force, was to fight shoulder to shoulder with the German *Wehrmacht* against Stalin. The Germans even thought that the time had come to set up a Russian counter-government, possibly in Smolensk.

However, behind the scenes of the successfully developing Vlasov movement a stubborn battle was being fought between the various German authorities. Rosenberg's Ministry of Eastern Affairs from the beginning concentrated its propaganda on the non-Russian peoples in order "to liberate them from Russian hegemony" and thus to break up the Soviet Union. While Hitler had long ago, in line with this policy, agreed to the use of volunteers from among the non-Russian peoples, he rejected the military use of Russian prisoners of war. Only as time passed did those concerned with Eastern policy realize that the Russian question could not possibly be solved without the Russian people. The Russian people, it was rightly stressed, had always been the central political element in Eastern Europe. Therefore, only a large, comprehensive East European movement, not a motley organization of countless small ethnic groups whose national sentiment was often but a German invention, could be an effective force in fighting Bolshevism.

Although this concept was backed by a number of far-sighted Russian experts and was put forward in many constructive outlines and proposals, it did not gain the acceptance of the top German authorities. The various reports submitted lost their effectiveness on their way through the maze of red tape, or were simply filed away. If Hitler was approached directly, he could not be convinced; he clung stubbornly to the illusion that all problems could be solved by purely military means—by force— and he opposed any political program which recognized Russian national aspirations.

At the end of 1943 the Vlasov project was suspended on Hitler's orders. The General himself for the time being was again swallowed up in the mass of prisoners of war, until the OKW (*Oberkommando der Wehrmacht*, the Supreme Command of the German Armed Forces) managed to house him in a villa in Dahlen in a state of honorable internement. From there he exercised a certain influence on the training of Russian volunteers in Camp Dabendorf near Berlin.

At the end of 1944 the progressively deteriorating situation at the Russian front recalled the Red General to mind once more in German government circles. Soviet victories, however, had meanwhile resulted in fewer and fewer deserters. The Soviet authorities gradually succeeded in stamping out the symptoms of demoralization marking the first years of the war, desertions at the front and self-mutilation behind the lines. A special division within the NKVD, called *Smersh*, watched over the entire military apparatus with ruthless severity.[40] Discipline and fighting morale were restored to their normal level.

German-Russian Peace Feelers during 1943.

The year 1943 which had begun with the Soviet victory at Stalingrad and the Casablanca formula of unconditional surrender, brought a whole series of tests of the alliance between the Soviet Union and the Western allies.

Having gained in self-confidence after Stalingrad, the Russians took note of the fact that the Second Front in the West, which had been promised for 1942, had still not been started, and the burden of the land war was still almost exclusively shouldered by them. In the course of the year Hitler threw eighty to ninety per cent of his total land forces into the war on Russia. Was it not possible that the Vlasov movement might lead to a breakdown of the partisan warfare and to a progressive undermining of the morale of the Red Army itself? Were the responsible men in the Kremlin not bound to consider a separate peace with Hitler quite seriously as a means of escaping further dangers by accepting a territorial gain along the lines of the Molotov conversation of November 1940?

Such speculations occupied the minds of members of German military circles in November and December 1941 and again in September 1942.[41] Several times Japanese offers of mediation along these lines were made to the German government, the last in September 1942, before the defeat at Stalingrad. At that time Ribbentrop had brusquely rejected any further efforts in that direction. Hitler's Axis partner Mussolini also pressed his ally to go over to a defensive war in the East, even to conclude a separate peace with the Soviet Union and then proceed to fall full force on Great Britain.

When in March 1943 and again in July he broached the subject, the propitious moment to convince Hitler—when he was gripped by that mood of depression following on Stalingrad—had really passed. That same July Mussolini was overthrown. The efforts of Papen, German Ambassador to Turkey, to get Turkey to act as mediator were also unsuccessful. Kempner, the former American Chief Prosecutor at Nuremberg mentions four German attempts to enter into a peace discussion with Moscow: first after the landing of the allies in Africa at the end of 1942; then in the spring of 1943; and finally in the summer and fall of 1943.[42]

Unless Kempner was thinking of other, less well-known incidents,[43] he could only refer to the peace feelers with which in 1942 and 1943 Peter Kleist was concerned. Kleist was an official of the German Foreign Office who, as early as the summer of 1939, had engaged in talks with the Soviet attaché Astakhov in Berlin, for the purpose of bringing about German-Russian negotiations. Later he worked temporarily in the Ministry for Eastern Affairs. In December 1943 he succeeded in establishing contact with a Soviet go-between in Stockholm. This agent, by the name of Clauss, assured him that if Germany agreed to the 1939 frontiers, she could have peace within a week. At a second meeting in June 1943, Clauss said that the Soviets were not willing to fight for the interests of Great Britain and the United States one day more than was necessary. Hess was being held in honorable confinement by the British and no steps were being taken for a Second Front. Instead there was a plan to invade the Balkans to which the Kremlin was definitely opposed. Clauss managed to make a German-Russian agreement sound quite plausible to Kleist and he suggested a meeting with Alexandrov, the Head of the Central European Division of the People's Commissariat for Foreign Affairs. For nine days Alexandrov waited in vain in Stockholm for an answer from Berlin. Kleist, temporarily arrested by the Gestapo, received Ribbentrop's authorization to resume contact with the Russians in the fall. When on September 4 he, once more met with Clauss in Stockholm, he sensed a stiffening in the Soviet attitude. As a preliminary to negotiations, the Kremlin demanded a gesture which would indicate Germany's readiness for a change of line, such as the dismissal of both Rosenberg and Ribbentrop. The Russian war aims were now the frontiers of 1914, a free hand in both Straits (Dardanelles and Cattegat), and in the whole of Asia. This information supposedly came from the Russian Embassy Counsellor, Semyonov, who had been authorized to pass it on by Ambassador, Mme. Kollontai. The Deputy Commissar for Foreign Affairs, Dekanozov, formerly Ambassador in Berlin, was supposed to have been instructed to meet with Kleist. His appointment as envoy to Sofia was an invitation to the Germans to demonstrate readiness to negotiate by a similar gesture—Kleist suggested the sending of Schulenburg to Bulgaria.

Germany did not respond to these peace feelers with any seriousness as Hitler's thinking was too fanatical and Ribbentrop's diplomacy too rigid. Among other things, Hitler objected to the fact that the Soviet negotiator was not one hundred per cent Aryan. Actually, it is doubtful whether Stalin seriously thought of a separate peace with Germany once the Red Army had broken through the Dnieper front. However, these contacts could at any rate serve as a weapon for pressuring the Western Powers to open the Second Front in France. In anticipation of the Foreign Ministers Conference which was to meet in Moscow, he was bound to welcome some trumps in his hand. If nothing else, the Stockholm peace feelers created anxiety.[43a]

The Crisis in the Relations of the Allies

In the course of the summer, Russia's relations with her Western Allies seriously deteriorated. At the beginning of March Moscow had been pained and angered when it became known that the American Ambassador, Admiral William H. Standley, had told American newspaper reporters that Russia was getting American supplies in quantity but was keeping this fact from the people and was leading them to believe that Russia was fighting unaided.[44] On March 15, 1943, Stalin drew Churchill's attention to the fact that Germany had moved thirty-six divisions from the West to the Eastern front. He reminded him of the Allied promise to open the Second Front in France in the spring of 1943 without fail. He pointed out that it was of the utmost importance for the Red Army that this blow from the West take place in the early summer. From the view-point of the common cause a further delay would be "very dangerous" and the vagueness of the Anglo-American statements were arousing grave anxiety in him.[45]

That same month an American offer to act as intermediary between Finland and the USSR to bring about Finland's withdrawal from the war, was turned down by the Soviet Union.[46]

A further blow for Stalin was a letter from Churchill on March

30 saying that until September Great Britain and America would be forced to discontinue sending convoys to the Soviet Union because of preparations for the campaign in Sicily.[47] This aroused considerable ill-feeling in Moscow.

Moreover, relations between the Allies were strained by the Polish question which that same spring entered the critical phase already discussed. When Soviet Ambassador Maisky went to see Churchill in great agitation, bearing a message from Stalin which contained the news that the Polish-Russian agreement was to be cancelled, Churchill refrained from entering into a discussion of the embarrassing Katyn affair, but he failed to prevent a breach between the Russians and the Poles. The fact that in the meantime three Polish divisions under General Anders had been formed in Persia on British orders, increased Soviet distrust.

The announcement of the disbanding of the Comintern in May 1943 did not fail to have its effects on the Western Powers as it seemed that the Soviet Union was giving up all plans for world revolution. However, with the approach of the summer offensive, Moscow grew increasingly irritable because the Second Front once more failed to materialize. Roosevelt tried to improve Stalin's mood by sending him a message in May through Joseph E. Davies, the former ambassador, suggesting a personal meeting. Roosevelt had recalled Ambassador Standley after the latter's indiscretions in March and would have liked to entrust Davies with the job again if his health would have permitted. Hopkins, who in turn was suggested by Davies, was indispensable in Washington. After a lengthy discussion with Stalin, Davies managed to break the ice and got him to agree to a meeting with Roosevelt on July 15. But at the end of June Allied relations once again grew tense as a result of a cable which Stalin sent to Churchill in which "he reviewed at length all the assurances that had been given during the past thirteen months relative to the opening of a Second Front, and concluded with words which could be interpreted only as charges of deliberate bad faith by the Western Allies."[48] The British Prime Minister answered with equal sharpness. When on top of this Stalin recalled Maisky from London and Litvinov from Washington, the atmosphere became "alarmingly reminiscent of that which had preceded the Molotov-Ribbentrop Pact of August 1939."[49] The meeting between Stalin and Roosevelt was indefinitely postponed. If reports are correct that at that time Stalin was not only backing the Yugoslav Communist Leader Tito against the nationalist partisan leader

Mikhailovich, whom the British supported, but was also encouraging him to establish contacts with the German authorities,[50] it is not surprising that fears of a separate Russian-German peace haunted the Western capitals.

Against this background Kleist's Stockholm talks assume a greater importance than he himself could have guessed. The Western Powers may have known of these Soviet peace feelers. In the First World War Stockholm had been a meeting place for all the secret services; it was no different now. But Hitler had no idea that the coalition of his enemies was so brittle and that he had such surprising diplomatic chances at this moment! Even if it was premature to speak of the possibility of a final break between the Allies, as Sherwood[51] does for example, it cannot be denied that the anti-Hitler coalition was showing signs of a serious crisis. It is true, however, that at that time Hitler would have had to buy peace from Stalin with incomparably greater sacrifices than in the fall of 1942.

Stalin certainly did not count on a change in Hitler's attitude and a collapse of the coalition. For him the exploratory contacts with Germany, as well as the sharpness of his complaints to the Allies, simply served the purpose of getting the latter to take a more active part in land warfare and to force them to promise bigger concessions in the post-war period.

In these circumstances it was important to get together with the Russians to insure that the dangerous rift did not widen. After conferring with Harriman, Churchill managed to dissuade Roosevelt from his planned *tête-à-tête*. Instead he proposed to convene a preliminary conference of the three Foreign Ministers in Moscow. Roosevelt accepted this.

Hopkins submitted a document dated August 10, 1943, to the Anglo-American Conference in Quebec, which had been written by American military experts and concerned the Russian situation. The basic idea in this appreciation was that Russia's post-war position in Europe would be a dominant one, which no other power, including Great Britain, would be able to oppose. For this reason, it was concluded by the American government that everything possible had to be done to obtain Russia's friendship. To this end, Russia had to become an active ally in the war in the Pacific against Japan. This more or less outlined the policy which was to guide the decisions made at Teheran and Yalta.[52]

During the Quebec Conference Stalin's consent to the meeting of the Foreign Ministers arrived at last and was enthusiastically greeted

by the Western representatives. Eden and Hull went to Moscow
where the talks took place from October 15 to 30, 1943. For the
first time the question of the division of Europe into spheres of
influence was raised.[53] The military representatives participating in
the meeting informed the Russians of the plans to cross the Chan-
nel, operation "Overlord,"[54] but the Russians for their part did not
show their cards.

After extended talks with Cordell Hull at the Moscow Conference Stalin finally agreed to a meeting of the "Big Three" in Teheran. It was he who suggested this place and he stubbornly stuck to
it. He maintained that it was impossible for him to go farther away
from Moscow. He turned down a proposal to meet in Cairo with
Chiang Kai-shek. When Roosevelt suggested several other localities,
he threatened to postpone the conference until the spring of 1944
when he would be agreeable to a meeting in Alaska. Finally Roosevelt and Churchill yielded and on November 28, 1943, the Teheran
Conference convened.

The Teheran Conference

In Teheran, which was occupied by Soviet and British troops,
Stalin could feel at home. What was most important was that he
could make unhampered use of the whole security machinery of the
NKVD. He invited Roosevelt to be his guest in a villa in the Russian Embassy compound. He thought this would be the best means
of preventing too close a contact between the President and
Churchill. Despite this no really close relationship between Roosevelt and Stalin came about. Even during Molotov's visit to the
United States Roosevelt had had the feeling of being helpless in the
face of the Russian phenomenon. This feeling now increased. Later
he once said about Stalin "there was nothing human about him to
which one could become related." Nevertheless, he did not tire in
his efforts to gain Stalin's trust. Little attacks on Churchill as well
as an almost naive readiness to make concessions to the Soviet
Union, particularly in Eastern Europe, were used to keep Stalin in
a good mood.

When Churchill submitted to the Conference his plan of a triple
Allied invasion in Northern France, in Italy and in the Balkans,
Stalin's animosity broke through with renewed sharpness. He suspected that the operation in the Balkans was to forestall a Russian
occupation, depriving the Soviet Union of a sphere of influence

which Hitler had also refused to grant in 1940. Stalin rejected Churchill's combination plan on the grounds of the supposed danger of frittering away Allied strength and insisted that the landing be concentrated on Northern France. He also did not want to hear anything of subsidiary operations in Northern Italy and on the Adriatic to support Tito because they would not be decisive in ending the war. He argued that in Northern France the Allies had the advantage of short and safe supply lines and the nearest and shortest path to the Ruhr area and to the Rhine.

Churchill himself defended his combination plan with military and political arguments. He stressed that from a military view point the invasion of the Balkans required no forces or shipping space beyond that already available in the Eastern part of the Mediterranean. Politically speaking he speculated on Turkey's entry into the war which he thought was inevitable once the Aegean Sea was won. It may be that especially the proposed participation of Turkey annoyed Stalin as he had no desire to face in the post-war period a victorious Turkey which might even have expanded territorially. Although in the final protocol he agreed to a formulation which mentioned aid to Yugoslav partisans and efforts to bring Turkey into the war, the fact that no special military operations were to be undertaken in the Eastern Mediterranean robbed these plans of practical importance.

Decisive for the abandonment of the Balkan project were the arguments of Roosevelt's military experts who, in keeping with the general American reluctance to concentrate troops in a limited space and fight in difficult terrain, managed to convince the President. It was decided to concentrate everything on operation "Overlord" which was to be started in May or June 1944, at the latest in July. This could be interpreted as a big success for Stalin. Europe had thus been divided into two operational zones. After the German collapse there would now be nothing to hinder the expansion of Soviet influence in Eastern Europe. One of the first fruits of this successs was the private meeting of the "Big Three" about the future Polish frontiers. The Foreign Ministers had not been able to agree on this when they had met in Moscow shortly before. A decision had to be made as the Red Army was approaching the former Polish border; it was impossible to wait until the final Peace Conference. Churchill, therefore, consciously deviating from the British attitude during Molotov's visit in London, proposed to recognize the Curzon Line of 1920 as the Polish eastern frontier, the same frontier which Stalin had envisaged during Russo-German negotiations in 1939-40. An attempt by Eden[55] to save a part of Galicia with the city of Lvov for Poland, was unsuccessful. Stalin pointed out that the line ran west of the city. He accepted the Curzon Line and suggested that Poland be compensated at Germany's expense for loss of her eastern territories. This had the advantage for the Soviet Union that the future Poland would, in view of the certainty of German demands for revision, be completely dependent on the protection and good will of the Kremlin.

Did Churchill think he would be able to halt Bolshevism at this new Polish border? Did he think that Stalin would be content with a bourgeois, western-oriented government for the Polish state-to-be, and that he would resume the disrupted relations with the London Poles? Immediately after the break with Sikorski in the spring of 1943, Stalin had made arrangements for the creation of another, pro-Soviet Polish government. Shortly before Teheran he told a group of Polish Communists in the Soviet Union that he would welcome the creation of a political association of Poles which would dispute the claim of the Polish government in London to be the sole representative of Poland. One month after the Teheran Conference such an association under the name of "Polish National Council" was actually formed. In the course of time it assumed the character of a second government in exile. A Soviet-Czechoslovak agreement,[56] concluded on December 12, 1943, was a second step along the road to the sovietization of Eastern Europe which had been entered upon in Teheran. Unaware of the coming difficulties of the post-war era, the London *Times* greeted the agreement on Dcember 13 with the words: "This agreement means a further step for the Russians towards achieving their full share in European affairs and once again gives rise to the idea that Russia has a great mission to fulfill on the continent."

The Polish question was closely connected with the fate of Germany.[57] Quite early, in his discussions with Eden in December 1941, Stalin had proposed the dismemberment of Germany, suggesting that East Prussia be handed over to Poland. While the British government had a moderate view on this matter, Roosevelt, in opposition to his advisers, among them Secretary of State Cordell Hull, very soon agreed to Stalin's plan. In May 1943 Stalin adopted Roosevelt's terms of unconditional surrender for Germany which in January had become the basis of Allied policy in Casablanca.

This did not, however, mean that he would have opposed an interim draft of territorial and economic peace conditions. It is also possible that he hoped this would prevent a stiffening of German resistance as some knowledge of conditions under which the war might be ended were better material for sober reflection than none at all. In September 1943 the leading economic adviser in the Kremlin, the Hungarian Communist, Professor E. Varga, advocated heavy German reparations to all the Allies in the form of commodities. In Teheran it was Stalin again who was the first to bring up for debate another important demand regarding Germany. He declared that Poland should extend as far as the Oder. In addition he proposed transferring Upper Silesia completely to Poland. The details of the frontier were for the time being left undefined. Only in the case of East Prussia, which he had promised to Poland as early as December 1941,[58] he expressed the wish that the ice-free port of Koenigsberg be assigned to the Soviet Union. When at this point Roosevelt pleaded that the Baltic Sea be freed to all merchant shipping, Stalin thought the President was about to raise the question of the Baltic states. He declared categorically that the Baltic states "had expressed in plebiscites their desire to join the Soviet Union and the question was therefore not open to discussion." After the misunderstanding had been explained, he agreed to guarantee the safety of Baltic shipping.

When Stalin demanded Koenigsberg, neither Roosevelt nor Churchill thought of mentioning Windau and Libau or the Memel territory which he tacitly also claimed and which were all ice-free ports.[59]

The proposed Oder border for Poland had been turned down by the Polish government in London as late as November 7, 1943; only after Teheran did the Poles adopt Stalin's proposal.[60]

Apart from the foregoing, Stalin was not particularly interested in plans for dismembering Germany. Of Roosevelt's proposal to divide Germany into five autonomous states, he said that he could see little differenc between the population of one part of Germany and that of another. Very firmly he opposed Churchill's plan for a Danube Federation with or without parts of Southern Germany. If they were to participate there was the danger that the Germans would try to become dominant. He felt that both Austria and Hungary should remain independent. However, no final decision regarding Germany's territorial fate was made at Teheran.

Stalin was also in favor of rendering the German officer corps

and the German General Staff harmless. He thought that the liquidation of about fifty thousand German military experts would be a
guarantee that Germany's military might could not be revived. He
considered the measures proposed by the United States and Great
Britain for the subjugation and control of Germany as insufficient.
Churchill protested violently against these brutal and primitive
views.[61]

After operation "Overlord" had been agreed upon in principle,
Stalin took a lively part in the discussion of the details of putting it
into effect. According to Deutscher he assumed an attitude of bene-
volent superiority, the attitude of a veteran victor towards allies
who were only now about to embark on their first really big venture.
"He offered helpful advice and drew readily on his fund of experience." [62] It was he who urged the Western Allies to create a uniform
Command immediately. In response to this, General Eisenhower
was appointed Supreme Commander in Chief.[63] Stalin gave advice
for the camouflage of the operation through maneuvers of diversion
and *ruses de guerre*, and promised to launch strong supporting
offensives the moment the Allies landed in France.

Two important sets of problems which were discussed concerned
the post-war period. Over and above the European plans, the
Americans were particularly interested in having the Soviet Union
participate in the Pacific War and in the new international organization planned for after the war, the United Nations Organization.
At the beginning of the Conference Stalin had already promised to
intervene in the war against Japan as soon as he could withdraw the
necessary forces from Europe.[64] At the final session Stalin also
agreed to Roosevelt's favorite plan for the organization of the
United Nations—apparently willingly, but basically with the greatest caution and mistrust. He was reassured when Roosevelt told him
that the Executive Committee of the Organization would not have
the power to make binding decisions, but only recommendations.
Roosevelt's proposal to entrust the real power to the four World
Powers, the United States, the Soviet Union, Great Britain and
China, the so-called "four policemen," was met sceptically by Stalin
both in principle and in particular as regards the inclusion of China.
On the other hand he advocated the control by the United Nations
of bases both within and outside of Germany, among them Dakar
and the Japanese Islands, apparently in order to avoid unilateral
American control.

Stalin's successes at Teheran were considerable. Concerning both the Baltic and the Polish question he had managed to push through the Soviet demands. The failure of Churchill's Balkan plans made room for the possibility of incorporating the Balkan area, and perhaps also the Danube area, into the Soviet sphere of influence along with Poland. Stalin gained prestige personally. Placed side by side with the two Anglo-Saxons he had not cut a bad figure in his bearing and argumentation and had shown consistency, self-assurance and diplomatic skill during the sessions. Without himself assuming any major obligations, he had obtained important concessions from the Allies. He had seized the diplomatic initiative which he was to retain at Yalta and Potsdam.[65] The Crusader's Sword which Churchill handed him in the name of King George VI, he accepted with well acted emotion; when at Churchill's birthday celebration in Teheran Churchill toasted him as "Stalin the Great," he pointed with dignity to the Russian people to whom really belonged the honors shown to him; it was easy to be a great leader if one had to do with a people such as the Russian![66]

When the "Big Three" bade farewell to each other on December 1, 1943, full harmony seemed to have been re-established between them. In reality, however, from a political view point, the terms of unconditional surrender which the Allies had in January of that year stipulated for the Axis powers, they had now, in the face of Soviet demands,[67] accepted for themselves.

The Soviet Advance in the Winter of 1943-44 and Spring 1944

When the fall fighting ceased, three German Army groups stood on Russian soil between the Baltic and the Black Sea. The front of Army Group North stretched south of Leningrad to west of Nevel; that of Army Group Center from there to west of Ovruch; while Army Group South held the line up to the Black Sea, including the Crimea. The three Army groups were no longer connected by rail since the Leningrad-Odessa line had been crossed by the Red Army at Nevel and Ovruch.

The two northern Army groups were more difficult to attack than the one in the south, both for topographical reasons and because of their strongly built defense constructions. Army Group South moreover formed a salient projecting far eastward. It began southeast of Kronsten, continued in the direction of the Dnieper south of Kiev and eventually ended in the Dnieper bend at Kherson. The mere existence of this bulge was an invitation for Soviet strategy either to encircle the German troops by attacking their flanks or to push them back as far as the River Bug or farther, thus tearing a wide gap into the German front between the Pripet Marshes and the Carpathians.

There was also the political temptation of reconquering the Ukraine, including the western territories inhabited by Ukrainians, and thus gain a spring board for an advance into the Danube basin and the Balkans. The assumption that Vienna is a more important strategic key for the conquest of Eastern Europe than Berlin may be correct.[68]

With these considerations in mind, the Soviet High Command ordered the Army groups of Vatutin, Konev and Malinovsky to encircle the German troops under Manstein in the Dnieper bend. This big offensive was preceded by four more limited operations, perhaps necessitated by supply difficulties and the extreme winter cold. On Christmas eve Vatutin went into action, conquered Korosten and Berdichev on each side of Zhytomir, then Zhytomir itself. He poured motorized units into the resulting gap and reached Sarny on the railroad line Vilna-Lvov, south of the Pripet Marshes, early in the new year. At the same time Rokossovsky advanced north of the Marshes and took Mozyr and Kalinkovichi on the railroad line Leningrad-Odessa, thus protecting Vatutin's strategic flank in the rear.

On January 18, 1944 Manstein opened a powerful counter-attack in the area of Vinnitsa and threw the Red Army back nearly sixty miles northeast and east of the city. Thus ended for the time being the forerunner of the first Soviet offensive. In the meantime a second offensive had been started south of Leningrad. Here General Govorov, breaking out of Leningrad, was to encircle the German troops under Lindemann. He was to be supported by General Meretskov from the east. When on January 15, 1944, the ice of the Volkhov river and Lake Ilmen seemed solid enough to permit an advance, the attack was opened. Krasnoye Selo, Novgorod and Novo-Sokolniki were retaken. The Germans began a general retreat. In February Luga was occupied, the German "hedgehog" near Staraya Russa was wiped out, and finally the important railroad junction, Dno, was taken. Lindemann fell back as far as the defense line Pskov-Ostrov-Opochka which in the south was joined by the line running east of Vitebsk. Thanks to these Russian successes, the German threat to Leningrad was thus removed after more than two years.

In February 1944 General Konev succeeded in encircling eight German divisions in the area of Cherkasy on the Dnieper, south of Kiev. At the same time Vatutin advancing south from Sarny gained Rovno and Lutsk and approached Kovel and Dubno. Manstein saw himself forced to rush troops west in order to prevent the Russians from entering Galicia.

The last of the four partial offensives was the advance of General Malinovsky in the big Dnieper bend. In February, he retook Sofiyevka and Apostolovo south of Dniepropetrovsk, cut the German forces into two, pushing one group back toward Nikopol and the other toward Krivoy Rog, until at the end of the month that much fought over city was finally occupied.

On this basis the great Soviet offensive of the spring of 1944 was developed. Before it started Vatutin was replaced in the High Command of the first Ukrainian Army Group by Marshal Zhukov, Stalin's deputy in the Supreme Command, while Marshal Vassilevsky, Stalin's Chief of Staff, was given the job of co-ordinating the operations of the third and fourth Ukrainian Army Group under Malinovsky and Tolbukhin. Between these two groups Konev, who had just been promoted to the rank of Marshal, continued to be in charge of the second Ukrainian Army Group. Zhukov's and Konev's goal was to reach the Odessa-Lvov railroad line which ran more or less parallel to the front.

On March 4 Zhukov advanced along a line almost sixty miles wide. The German positions were shattered, the railroad line was reached as planned and the Soviet troops stood close to Tarnopol. At the same time Konev managed a successful blow at a German base near Uman where five hundred tanks and twelve thousand trucks were taken. The Germans retreated. Their position between the rivers Dnieper and Bug became untenable. In complete confusion they surrendered Zhmerinka, Vinnitsa and Kamenets-Podolsk. Konev's advance continued west and approached the Rumanian border. At the end of March he had reached the river Prut.

Taking advantage of Konev's initial successes, Zhukov turned south early in March and advanced on Chernovits, the last rail connection between the German armies in Eastern Poland and Southern Russia. At the end of March his troops crossed the River Dniester and occupied Chernovits.

During the period when the first and second Ukrainian Army Group reached the Dniester and the Prut, Malinovsky reconquered Kherson and Nikolayev in the Southern sector. On April 10 Odessa was taken without a fight. Soon Malinovsky reached the Dniester and at Dubosari established contact with Konev's left flank. In the meantime Tolbukhin turned toward the Crimea. He conceived the plan of crossing the Sivash lagoons, the shallow sea adjoining the Perekop Isthmus, as soon as they had frozen over and simultaneously to attack the German fortifications on the Isthmus. When it became clear in March that a freezing of the Sivash could no longer be expected, Tolbukhin decided to have some of his troops wade across it at shallow points as had been done in the civil war in the fighting against Wrangel, and to transport the major part of his men on pontoons and rafts.

In the early morning of April 8 he opened his attack with concentrated artillery fire on the Perekop positions. The first defense line was breached on the next day. While the second still resisted the Russian troops, a surprise attack via the Sivash took place. The Rumanian troops could hold their positions in the Northern Crimea with as little success as the Germans near Kerch. A general retreat began toward Simferopol and from there to Sevastopol. In May the last German troops surrendered at Cape Kherson on the southern point of the peninsula, after Sevastopol had been evacuated on May 9. The Crimea was again in Russian hands.

The Russian winter offensive of 1944 ended with "one of the most brilliantly conceived and executed campaigns of this remarkable year." [69]

The Summer Campaign of 1944

In its winter and spring campaign the Red Army had almost everywhere in the north and in the south reached the pre-war Russian borders and in some places crossed them. Only in the central sector an important German salient still extended into old Russian territory, enclosing the Pinsk Marshes and the towns of Vitebsk, Mohylev and Bobruisk.

With their poor flank communications and the lack of reserves it was only a matter of time before the Germans would have to give up this salient. But in the north and south, too, a continuation of the Russian advance into the Baltic countries, Galicia and Poland proper and particularly into Rumania, where the oil fields of Ploesti were the prize, had to be expected in the summer of 1944.

The Soviet spring attacks had already been remarkable for their carefully co-ordinated operations. They took place with clockwork precision, one taking over from the other, so that German combat reserves in the neighboring sector were always unexpectedly needed just where they stood and new break-throughs made a systematic defense impossible. In the summer and fall of 1944 this strategy was to bear further fruits. The Soviet Command did not let itself be goaded into far-flung offensive thrusts in order to flatten out the enemy and destroy him in big pincer movements. It remained steadfastly cautious and contented itself with an unending number of limited local actions. Throughout the year the Soviet High Command shifted the focus of the fighting from north to south and then again to the center "with astonishing regularity, power and circumspection, like a boxer who systematically covers his opponent with telling blows without expecting that one single blow will knock him down." [70]

Soviet war historians speak of "Stalin's ten blows" in 1944, [71] with which he finally repelled Hitler's attack on the Soviet Union. In contrast to the Western conduct of the war, the tactical goal of the Soviet armies was not necesssarily the annihilation of the enemy but rather his exhaustion, if annihilation meant too great a sacrifice. Whenever the resistance of the Germans stiffened so that a continuation of the attack was no longer profitable, it was diminished and re-opened at another sector of the front. The vast expanses of the East seemed to make this tactic the only appropriate one.

When on June 6, 1944 the invasion of Northern France, which had for so many years been demanded and hoped for by the Soviet Union, was started and developed favorably for the Allies, it also served as a signal for the opening of the Russian offensive. It was politically wise to begin the attack at a point where a waning of the war effort had become noticeable by the end of 1943—the Finnish front. On June 10 General Govorov opened the attack on the Karelian Isthmus, broke through the Finnish fortifications and took Viborg. The whole of East Karelia had to be evacuated by the Finns. Although Hitler had tried to prevent Finland's quitting the war by sending Ribbentrop there in June and Keitel in August, events could no longer be prevented from taking their course. When on August 1 Marshal Mannerheim became President in place of Rytl, who had concluded and was identified with the pact with Germany, contact was established with Moscow via Sweden. Negotiations which were opened on August 25 ended in the Truce of Moscow on September 19.

In addition to the peace conditions of 1940, the headland of Porkkala, which was to be leased to the Soviet Union for fifty years, and the port of Petsamo, Finland's only access to the Arctic Sea, were substituted for the peninsula of Hangoe. Reparations amounting to three hundred million dollars were to be paid in the course of six years in the form of commodities.[72]

At the end of June the main offensive in the central sector was opened. Four army groups, the First Baltic Army Group and three White Russian Army Groups, altogether one hundred divisions, went over to the attack. The Russian plan envisaged the encirclement of the German army groups in the triangle Minsk-Vitebsk-Zhlobin and the destruction of all "hedgehogs." General Bagramyan advanced north of Vitebsk, General Chernyakhovsky north of Orsha, General Zakharov north of Mohylev, while General Rokossovsky stormed Zhlobin. In the last days of June the other "hedgehogs" were also taken. Then the crossing of the River Berezina was forced, after bitter fighting, Borisov fell on July 1, two days later Minsk was occupied as well as Polotsk. On July 4 the Soviet troops crossed the Polish frontier of 1939. The conquest of Vilna and Grodno and the establishment of a bridgehead on the River Nieman then opened up the road to East Prussia.

In the north the army groups of General Yeremenko and General Maslennikov broke through the German defense lines near Opochka, took Ostrov and Pskov and continued into the Baltic states. While in Estonia at first only Narva was taken, the Soviet troops marched deep into Latvia as far as Courland, conquered Mitau and temporarily severed the only railroad connection with Germany. The Germans were forced to withdraw their troops from Estonia and Livonia.

A third battle area developed in Galicia and Central Poland. During July Konev's troops took Brody and Rava Ruska, crossed the River San and established a bridgehead on the Vistula near Baranov. Advancing on a wide front, Rokossovsky in the meantime reached the River Bug, crossed it and took Chelm and Lublin. On July 25 Lvov surrendered to the Russians. At the beginning of August the Galician oil territory of Drohobich and Borislav was occupied.

Late in July, Bialystok and Brest-Litovsk, both just east of Warsaw, were captured. Rokossovsky's troops advanced straight on Warsaw, were temporarily delayed by German counter-attacks, but on August 15 entered Praga, the eastern suburb of the Polish capital. In Warsaw a Polish insurrection had broken out on August 1.

To the consternation of the Polish resistance fighters, the Russians suddenly stopped their advance.[72a] Until January 1945 the front in Poland ran from the East Prussian-Latvian border east of Warsaw in an almost straight line to the Czechoslovak border.

The Soviet High Command was more interested in the conquest of Rumania. From the two bridgeheads on the western bank of the Dniester, Tolbukhin advanced into Rumania on August 20. Rumanian resistance collapsed. When Jassy was occupied on August 23, King Michael dissolved Antonescu's government and began negotiations with the Allies with whom he had already established contact in the spring. As Molotov had clearly stated in a radio address on April 2, 1944 that the Soviet government was making no claims to Rumanian territory except Bessarabia and had no intention of tampering with the social structure of the country, those close to the King believed that a Russian occupation of the country would not affect its political sovereignty. The sixth German Army was encircled and destroyed by Tolbukhin and Malinovsky near Kishinev. Immediately afterward Ismail and Galatz on the Danube were taken and in the last days of August Ploesti and Bucharest also.

Italy and Finland had ceased to be Germany's allies. Rumania, too, was now lost to the Germans and with it its oil and wheat. It was inevitable that this had repercussions on Bulgaria. On August 26 it withdrew from the war, on September 16 the Russians occupied its capital, Sofia. Rumania and Bulgaria were now under Soviet control.

Political Problems of the Year 1944

How the Western Allies reacted to this Russian advance into the Danube and into the Balkans on the one side and into Poland on the other, leads directly to a consideration of the political problems of 1944, the time between Teheran and Yalta.

Every time the victorious Soviet troops crossed the old borders of Soviet territory, political problems of far-reaching import arose. It was necessary to clarify to what extent the *carte blanche* given to Stalin at Teheran held good.

When the Red Army entered Polish territory in the Rovno and Lutsk areas in January 1944, the London Polish government declared that it alone was entitled to administer those areas. This claim was rejected. An offer to mediate by the American Secretary of State, Cordell Hull, was badly received in Moscow, brusquely turned down. Stalin would brook no interference with his Polish policy. In a *Pravda* article of January 17, 1944, the British government was accused of secret negotiations with Hitler regarding a separate peace. Did the Kremlin know that a few weeks earlier such "peace feelers" made by the Germans had been rejected by Great Britain? [73] Was the article meant to hint that if necessary Moscow herself was ready to negotiate with the Germans? [74]

While Stalin's attitude regarding the Polish question made it clear that he considered Eastern Europe exclusively a Soviet sphere of interest, he did not, on the other hand, fail to demonstrate that he was uninterested in the domestic affairs of the Western countries. There the Communist parties were still required to subordinate themselves to bourgeois resistance movements and to collaborate in national fronts. In March 1944 it had caused surprise that Moscow was willing to recognize the government of Marshal Badoglio in Italy although the Italian left wing parties had opposed him. When shortly thereafter they demanded the King's abdication, *Izvestia* advised the Italian Communists to play down the conflict with the crown for the time being. In France the Communist party had to subordinate itself to General de Gaulle's movement. [75] In both countries the Communists, although numerically the strongest parties, were content to hold second-rank posts in the coalition with the bourgeois center, leaving the army and the police in the hands of anti-Communists. When in December 1944 civil war broke out in Greece, the Communist-dominated partisans of the ELAS movement received no assistance from the Soviet Union; there was not even moral support from the Soviet press and radio; they were left entirely to themselves.

However, as time went on the Kremlin's growing interest in all questions concerning Italy, the Balkans and the Eastern Mediterranean was bound to worry Great Britain. The place of a Comintern policy operating with fifth columns had been taken by purely nationalist ambitions of a great power which aimed at having a finger in every pie. Was this a fruit of Roosevelt's idea of World Policemen safeguarding order which he had suggested to Stalin at Teheran? [76]

Faced with this attitude the British government felt it necessary clearly to delimit the various spheres of influence, particularly where hitherto this had not been done with any precision, specifically the Balkans.

Churchill himself admits that when at Teheran he proposed a landing in the Balkans he had not been motivated by the threatening expansion of Soviet dominion. This thought did not occur to him until May 1944 when the Rumanian troops were driven from the Crimea and the Red Army advanced to the borders of their country.[77] To deny Rumania, Bulgaria and Yugoslavia to the Russians, as Hitler had tried in November 1940, was perhaps unthinkable. But one had to try to keep Greece out of the Soviet sphere to prevent Russia gaining a foothold on the Mediterranean.

In June 1944 the British government proposed to the Soviet Union that Rumania and Bulgaria be considered part of the Russian zone but that Britain exercise unrestricted control over Greece.[78] Stalin agreed immediately. When Churchill and Eden came to Moscow in October this division of the Balkans was confirmed. Indeed they did not hesitate, with a cynical pedantry of which perhaps not all parties were conscious, to lay down in percentages the extent of the respective spheres of influence in each country! According to the American Ambassador's report to Washington, the Soviet Union was to have a 75% to 80% priority in Bulgaria, Rumania and Hungary, while in Yugoslavia the ratio was to be 50:50.[79] The Soviet Union promised not to interfere in Greece if the British government should find it necessary to take military action there. In return the British agreed not to intervene in Rumania.[80]

The solution of the problem of spheres of influence in Poland turned out not to be so simple. It soon became clear that the British hope with regard the Curzon Line was not to be fulfilled. In the summer of 1944 when Soviet troops marched into the central regions of Poland, Stalin entertained the Polish Committee of Liberation, which had been organized in Russia, at an official reception in the Kremlin. After the capture of Lublin, the city became the headquarters of the Committee. The only thing that the Western Powers felt they could do at this point was to persuade Stalin to enter into negotiations with the new head of the London Polish government. After the death of General Sikorski, the conservative peasant leader Stanislaw Mikolajczyk had taken his place. He was one of the few Polish emigré leaders who were prepared to consider the Curzon Line and if necessary accept it. But when Mikolajczyk went to Moscow in July he found to his consternation that the Soviet government had shortly before *officially* recognized the Lublin Committee. Stalin could easily allege that he had no intention of meddling in domestic Polish affairs, for his crowd was in charge. Mikolajczyk was benevolently counselled to come to terms with the Lublin communist government.

The hopelessness of a western-oriented development was dramatically demonstrated by the Warsaw rising. The insurrection broke out on August 1, 1944, led by officers with many years of experience in the Polish underground movement, who followed the orders of Mikolajczyk's government. At the time, the Red Army was approaching the suburbs of Warsaw under Rokossovsky, himself of Polish origin; it was believed that the Germans were about to evacuate the city. To the insurgents no sacrifice seemed too great if they could free the Polish capital through their own efforts before the Russian troops arrived. The Polish position toward the Russians would be quite different if Warsaw was in Polish hands. But the leaders of the insurrection failed to co-ordinate their actions with those of the advancing Russian troops; they struck too soon. Rokossovsky had been stopped outside the city by the Germans and was even temporarily thrown back. The German garrison had no thought of evacuating Warsaw but threw its whole weight against the insurgents. "A somber and desperate battle developed, in which the Poles fought with unique romantic heroism, and the Germans revenged themselves by burning and pulling down street after street and house after house, until the city of Warsaw virtually ceased to exist."[81]

In those anxious weeks Mikolajczyk appealed to Stalin personally. The latter at first tried to deny that there was an insurrection. Then he promised help. But it never came. Was Rokossovsky not strong enough to storm Warsaw and relieve the insurgents? With the great offensive against Rumania in full swing, was it impossible to alter plans and send reinforcements? All this is possible. However, one thing is certain: the Warsaw rising in no way fitted into Stalin's plans. As he could have no part in directing the revolt, it was all right with him if the insurgents bled to death and Warsaw was not liberated by its own people. This interpretation is confirmed by the Soviet attitude to British planes which were to drop arms and food for the insurgents. The Soviet command refused them permission to land on Soviet airfields behind the Russian lines in order to refuel and return to their bases. Only when it was too late did Russian planes appear over the burning city which was now beyond help.

When Churchill was in Moscow in October 1944 he tried once

more to make out a case for his protegé, the Polish government in London and for Poland as a whole, but in vain. Stalin would not withdraw his territorial demands for Galicia nor modify his insistence on counting the whole of Poland as being within the Russian sphere of influence.

Vlasov between Hitler and Stalin

The tremendous successes achieved by the Soviet troops since the great turning point early in 1943, naturally vastly strengthened popular morale and resistance. And conversely, all further successes were accompanied by an aura of patriotic fervor which at first was consciously promoted and directed but gradually entered into the deeper consciousness of each individual Red Army soldier and Soviet citizen.

However, the Soviet leadership had to keep a careful eye on public opinion in order not to lose control of the spirit which it had conjured up. An immediate problem was that of the non-Russian peoples of the Soviet Union who, having been lost to the Germans in 1941-42, had now been freed from German occupation. It was questionable how wholeheartedly they would consider themselves "liberated." As long as the war was still on the time had not come to retaliate against those who had collaborated with the Germans. On the contrary, while in 1941-42 "Little Mother Russia" and the sacred Russian soil were fervently revered, it now became important to put greater emphasis on the multi-national character of the Soviet empire. Such considerations would eventually spread from the field of propaganda to the military sector.

During the debate concerning the Constitutional Amendment law of February 1, 1944, national military units within the Red Army were discussed in the Supreme Soviet of the USSR. Among them were Estonian, Latvian, Lithuanian, Georgian, Azerbaijan, Armenian and Kazak formations. The law itself was to give the individual republics of the union the right to raise autonomous national military units. In defending this measure, Molotov attempted to show that heretofore such units could not be set up because of the lack of military leadership, but that now the necessary officer corps was available. This explanation was not particularly convincing.

The true reasons for this measure were probably the determined resistance to sovietization by the Baltic peoples and the success with which the Germans had recruited volunteers for their side.[82] These volunteers were in the main members of the various ethnic groups within the Soviet Union but later there were also some Great Russian volunteer units. Moreover, the representative, though not the organizational head of the movement was a former commanding officer of the Red Army, General Vlasov, an extraordinarily able and popular man.

The law of February 1, 1944, is evidence that the Kremlin did not consider the anti-Bolshevik volunteer army under German auspices a mere scarecrow, but a reality. The possible dangers arising from it for the maintenance of Soviet patriotism had to be met by greater concessions to the national consciousness of the various ethnic groups.

The fact that in the fall of 1944, when the first Russian offensive on the soil of old German national territory was opened, Hitler remembered Vlasov and the possibilities latent in his movement, was a warning to Moscow, flushed with the year's victories, to be on guard even now. It was however uncertain how far Hitler was prepared to recognize the autonomous character of the Vlasov movement.

In the summer of 1944 German circles favoring it succeeded in interesting Himmler in the use of Russian forces against Stalin. Himmler did not, of course, change his mind regarding the inferiority of the Slavic race. Vlasov's theory that Russia could only be conquered by Russians was to him as inconceivable and far-fetched as it was to Hitler. However, he decided to suggest to Hitler the use of these Russian forces.[82a] One of the difficulties was that Vlasov's point of view differed from the official views of the Ministry for Eastern Affairs which were also those of Hitler. Vlasov was a Russian patriot and opposed to the division of Russia into its national components, i.e. the independence aspirations of the Ukraine, the White Ruthenians, the Caucasians and the Turkic peoples. However, his program of a "single and indivisible Russia" *(Yedinaya nedelimaya Rossiya)* differed considerably from the rigid centralism and the unitary concept of the Czarist empire and the White Guard Russians of the civil war of 1919. He made no claims to Poland and Finland and it seemed as if the indepedence of the Baltic nations was something that could be discussed with him. Moreover his program for an "indivisible Russia" left room for certain autonomous and federalist aspirations of the non-Russian groups.

As a first step he was interested in unifying all anti-Bolshevik forces in his hands. All "Hiwis" and all Eastern volunteers had to be transferred from the German formations, and all Eastern battalions had to be organized into special divisions of the Russian Army of Liberation (*Russkaya Osvoboditelnaya Armiya*—ROA). The German military authorities raised difficulties about whether the ROA divisions were to fight under their own leaders and only be tactically subordinated to the Germans, or whether the leadership was to be German. It was a victory for Vlasov that in the meantime the use of "Eastern Badge" which the Eastern workers had been obliged to wear, which they looked upon as a discriminatory measure and whose abolition he had repeatedly demanded, was discontinued. The same applied to corporal punishment which the Germans had introduced for Eastern workers in the occupied territories as "a measure in keeping with the Slavic mentality" without being aware that in the Soviet Union, in contrast to Czarist times, such measures were reserved to the NKVD, and had otherwise been discarded.

It was important that in the fall of 1944 the German Foreign Office, also, began to think of the effect that a systematic promotion of Vlasov would have abroad. Vlasov was received by Ribbentrop who assured him that it was entirely up to the Russians how they arranged their relations with the other Eastern peoples. But the absence of a uniform, purposeful Russian policy was demonstrated only two days later when Rosenberg assured the President of the White Ruthenian Central Council, Professor Ostrovsky, that the German government was in favor of the creation of an independent White Ruthenian state. During his first discussion with Himmler, Vlasov proposed that all the various national committees which had been formed be subordinated to a "Supreme Committee for the Liberation of the Peoples of Russia" which he was ready to head. The minutes of this meeting are conspicuous, however, for their lack of clarity. The SS was from the start to play a double game with Vlasov. By replacing his former intelligent German advisers with members of Himmler's staff, Vlasov was to be systematically prevented from making independent decisions.

Perhaps in the end it was due to the interest shown by the German Foreign Office that despite all obstacles a conference, staged as an official act of state for the founding of the Committee for the Liberation of the Peoples of Russia, took place in the Hradčan Castle in Prague on November 14, 1944. Prague had been suggested by Vlasov because of the city's Slavic background. In the presence of representatives of the Orthodox Church, of Eastern workers, numerous Czarist emigrants, and official representatives of the German government, Vlasov was elected President of the Committee; his manifesto was then read and accepted.[83] Its climax was a demand for the overthrow of "Stalin's tyranny, to liberate the peoples of our homeland from the Bolshevik system and to give them back the rights which they had successfully fought for in the popular revolution of 1917." It also demanded that after the war, steps be taken to create "a new political structure of the people without Bolsheviks and exploiters."

An official agreement was concluded between the Committee of Liberation and the German Foreign Office, and Vlasov's financial support was not to come from propaganda funds, as heretofore, but to be considered a state credit.[84]

Three divisions under the direct command of Vlasov were at once to be set up and sent into action. This was a small number in view of the fact that in 1943 almost one million Russians were serving in the German army. However, even this minimum program came too late and never got beyond the preparatory stage. The first Division was organized and stationed in Prague, a second was on the way to being organized. Some Russian battalions were used in Denmark and in France. Only at the beginning of 1945 was a battalion of the ROA sent into battle against the Red Army in Silesia, with the result that two Soviet regiments came over to it.[85]

The First ROA Division in Prague became involved in a risky game with high stakes when the Soviet troops approached. When the collapse of Germany became evident, Vlasov wanted to assemble all ROA formations stationed in Czechoslovakia and Austria in order to establish contact with anti-Bolshevik resistance groups in the Balkans where—in his opinion—a conflict between Soviet and Western interests was most likely. When at the beginning of May 1945 the Czechs rose against the Germans in Prague, one of Vlasov's generals decided on his own to intervene with his troops, making common cause with the insurgents. Following the Warsaw example, the city was to be liberated before the arrival of the Red Army in order to hand it over to national Czech groups. The fact was overlooked that the Czech insurgents were by no means anti-Bolshevik; nor was it known that the Americans would halt their advance on Prague at Pilsen, and withdraw to the Czech-German border, in agreement with the Soviets.

The ROA troops, including Vlasov, were interned by the Americans and handed over to the Soviets. After being kept in prison for fifteen months Vlasov was executed in Moscow in August 1946.[86]

The Fall Campaign of 1944

As early as August the troops of the First Baltic Army Group had approached the East Prussian border from Vilna and Schaulen. In their first break-through, Soviet units advanced as far as Goldap in the eastern part of East Prussia. For the first time German civilians had a taste of land warfare on their own soil.

Hitler still refused to transfer his HQ from Rastenburg in western East Prussia. It was here that he was struck by the bomb of the conspirators of the 20th of July without, however, being seriously wounded. In this book we confine ourselves to examining what contacts the conspirators had with the Soviet Union. In 1942 a Soviet espionage headquarters had been set up in Berlin under the name of "Rote Kapelle," run chiefly by two romantic idealists of Communist leanings. Both had for a considerable time supplied the Russians with information. When a Soviet agent was arrested by the Gestapo this loose organization was destroyed and the two leaders executed. Here, too, certain socialist ideas were strangely mixed up with the Prussian tradition of alliances with Russia. The same was true of the young diplomat, Trott zu Solz, who early in July 1944 sought to find out from Mme. Kollontai in Stockholm how the Soviet Union would react to a *coup d'état* against Hitler. In the person of Count Schulenburg, these circles thought to have found not only an outstanding expert on Russia, but also a man who had a good chance of being looked upon as *persona grata* by Stalin. If the attempt on Hitler was successful it was planned to establish direct contact with the Kremlin via Schulenburg.[87]

How the Soviet government would actually have reacted to such a turn of events is difficult to say. The fact that a "Free German Committee" had been established in Moscow with the cooperation of the German generals Paulus and von Seydlitz, making extensive use of German nationalist slogans and symbols, seems to indicate that if the 20th of July had taken a different turn, the attempt might have been made to suggest to the Western Allies a compromise peace with this new, non-Nazi Germany, in the hope that it would follow a pro-Soviet course.

After the failure of the *coup* there was no let-up in the Soviet military advance. In September the Leningrad Army Group under

General Govorov began the conquest of the Baltic countries. Reval was captured on September 21, by October the Baltic islands had also been taken. Simultaneously the third Baltic Army Group under General Maslennikov advanced into southern Estonia, captured Valga and threw the Germans back in the direction of Riga, while General Bagramyan's First Baltic Army Group approached Riga from the south. The German troops—about twenty divisions—on the west coast of Courland were encircled after Bagramyan's vanguards had reached Polangen and Tauroggen. Fighting was still in progress here when the news of Germany's surrender became known in May 1945. Riga was stormed on October 13, 1944, thus completing the conquest of the Baltic countries. A considerable number of upper class Estonians, Latvians and Lithuanians tried to leave their native countries with the German troops, in flight from the Bolshevik terror; many succeeded, after hair-raising adventures, in escaping across the sea to Sweden. A time of unspeakable suffering began for the rest of the population.

The last phase of the northern offensive was the conquest of East Prussia. General Chernyakhovsky had orders to break through to Koenigsberg by way of Gumbinnen and Insterburg. On October 16 Soviet artillery began to bombard the first German defense line. Eydtkuhnen was taken, the fighting spread to the forest of Augustovo and the second defense line near Stallupoenen and Goldap was stormed. At the third line near the small river of Angerap the Russians were stopped by five German tank divisions. Violent fighting caused Chernyakhovsky to halt the attack and for the time being confine himself to defensive actions.

The largest territorial conquests were made, before the year was out, in the south, in the Danube area. At first Malinovsky's Second Ukrainian Army Group advanced from northern Bukovina into Transylvania, where in September he occupied Karlsburg, Temesvar and Arad. In the meantime Tolbukhin, who had been made a Marshal, wheeled north from Bulgaria in the direction of Belgrade. He crossed the Danube south of the Iron Gates and on October 1 established contact with Tito, the Yugoslav partisan leader, near Negotin. At Turnu-Severin he linked up with Malinovsky's left flank. On October 19 the Germans were ejected from Belgrade. Malinovsky now crossed the Hungarian border and at Szeged forced a crossing of the river Tisza. The Germans and Hungarians withdrew toward Budapest. From the north, from the Carpathians, General Petrov's Fourth Ukrainian Army Group meanwhile slowly made its way through difficult country. There was heavy fighting with well equipped fresh German divisions and the important junction of Chop changed hands several times. At the end of October Malinovsky occupied Novi-Sad on the Danube, Kecskemet and Cegled, and on November 11 he already stood in the outskirts of the southern and eastern suburbs of Budapest. The Tisza was crossed at several places and early in December Malinovsky and Petrov linked forces.

The entire plain between the Tisza and Danube was occupied by the Russians with the exception of a small area east and north of Budapest. Since two Hungarian armies and twenty-five German divisions were still facing Malinovsky, he was ordered to wait for support from Tolbukhin. There was a short breathing spell, which, however, could not conceal the fact that Hungary was lost.

Responsible Hungarian leaders had realized this for some time, especially after the country had been occupied by German troops in March 1944. In September Horthy approached Moscow and asked for a truce. It was granted on October 16. On the same day, however, Hitler arrested Horthy and appointed a new Hungarian government which was to continue the fight.[88] Hungary was thus, for better and worse, tied to the fate of National Socialism.

The Russian Breakthrough in January 1945

From August 1944 to January 1945 the central sector of the Russian-German front in Poland was surprisingly quiet. It may be that during this time all efforts were aimed at conquering the Baltic states and Hungary and that reserves were sent there. These same five months were used by the Soviet High Command to regroup its armies.

In the north, two army groups under Chernyakhovsky and Rokossovsky were made ready for the invasion of East Prussia. In the center Zhukov was to attack Warsaw and to march straight on to Berlin, while Konev was to make Upper Silesia his goal. In the south Malinovsky and Tolbukhin, supported by Petrov, were to clear the Carpathians and Slovakia of Germans, to occupy Budapest and to advance on Vienna.

Altogether about three hundred divisions and twenty-five tank armies, besides numerous Cossack formations, had been assembled for this final phase. They were opposed by scarcely one hundred German divisions, already partially depleted.

On November 29 the Russians started northward for Budapest from the Plain of Mohacs, where in 1526 Sultan Suleiman the Magnificent had assembled his forces.At the same time other formations pressed east. At the end of the year the Hungarian capital had been encircled. German counter-attacks from Komarno were temporarily successful, but in the end it could not stem the Russian advance. On January 18, 1945, Pest was taken and on February 13, Buda. The road to Vienna was open.

At the same time the path to Berlin was freed. On January 12 the Russians attacked the bridgehead of Baranov, south of Warsaw, after intensive artillery bombardment. While Konev advanced rapidly towards Kielce, Zhukov proceeded west across the River Pilicia, then turned north and threatened Warsaw from the west. Germans were forced to evacuate the Polish capital. On January 17 it was occupied by the Russians. On January 19 Cracow, Kutno and Lodz fell.

In the meantime the two northern Army Groups had invaded East Prussia. Chernyakhovsky advanced across the River Memel on Tilsit and Insterburg and then broke through the Masurian defense lines. Rokossovsky crossed the Vistula near Pultusk, took Neidenburg, crossed the battlefield of Tannenberg and at Plock his left flank linked up with Zhukov's right flank. On January 22 Osterode, Deutsch-Eylau and Allenstein were taken, on January 26 the Baltic was reached near Elbing. This meant that the land route between Germany and East Prussia was cut.

The only real obstacle on the way to Berlin was now the River Oder which was defended by a number of fortifications both old and modern. Konev had no particular difficulty in invading Silesia and reaching the river there. He encircled Breslau and passed it by, then crossed the Oder and came to a stop on the border between Silesia and Saxony near Bunzlau. Meanwhile Zhukov surrounded the city of Posen, crossed the German-Polish border and reached the Oder just behind Kunersdorf, one of the battle fields of the Seven Years war. On February 10 his advance, too, slowed down.

Before crossing the Oder, Zhukov decided to occupy East Pomerania as his rear communications could be attacked from there. On March 9 his troops reached the Baltic coast in the neighborhood of Kolberg. After Rokossovsky had taken Danzig, his troops became available for the support of Zhukov. At the begining of March the latter threw two bridges across the Oder, north and south of Kuestrin. Chernyakhovsky in the meantime annihilated the remaining German resistance in East Prussia where about twenty divisions were still fighting stubbornly. On April 9 Marshal Vassilevsky, after having been mortally wounded, forced the surrender of the city of Koenigsberg. Thus East Prussia was completely in Russian hands.

In the south the Danube campaign was entering its final phase. A vigorous German counter-attack on Lake Balaton had at first been highly successful; but then they ran short of fuel, just as in the battle of the Ardennes. This gave Tolbukhin and Malinovsky the opportunity to catch up. The whole area between the Danube and the river Drava was reconquered and on March 29 the Austrian frontier was crossed. The Russians now concentrated all their forces on Vienna. On April 3 Bratislava was taken and on April 13 the ancient imperial city was in Soviet hands.

The Yalta Conference

In the fall of 1944 Roosevelt had expressed the wish for another conference with Churchill and Stalin in order to discuss the problems which had been left unsolved at Teheran, as well as those that had risen since. As Stalin did not want to leave his country during the great Russian offensive, the two Western statesmen and their staffs embarked once more on a long journey.

The conference was held from February 4 to 10, 1945, in the old Czarist palace of Livadia near Yalta in the Crimea.[89] Now the Soviet Union was no longer the only ally that had achieved major victories. The invasion of Northern France had been successful, the Allied troops stood on the Rhine. However, the Russians were about to cross the Oder and attack Berlin. The heightened Russian self-confidence, the fact that they were on home ground, and Stalin's indestructible vitality, contributed as much to an extensive adoption of the Soviet point of view on a whole range of questions as Churchill's nervousness about the imminent election and Roosevelt's illness and fatigue.

Apparently all parties thought that it would be possible to carry the unity achieved during the war into the post-war period. As of old, the regulation of international affairs was envisaged as a task of a condominium of the "Big Three," i.e. a division of the world into gigantic spheres of influence. But differences of opinion arose as to whether a fourth great power was to be included. As Roosevelt at Teheran had pleaded that China be included, Churchill and Eden now pleaded vigorously for a share of the fruits of victory for France. Stalin, who had not taken very much to de Gaulle when the latter visited Moscow at the end of 1944, showed little inclination to accord so important a place to a country which in his opinion had not made enough sacrifices. He consented only reluctantly to the establishment of a special French occupation zone in Germany and to France's subsequent admission to the Allied Control Commission.

During the debates on the organization of the United Nations the outlines of future dissensions were apparent. Agreement had been reached concerning the veto power which the great powers were to have in the Security Council, and Stalin wished to have it particularly effectively worded so that there could be no possibility of it being evaded or weakened. However, when in this context Churchill said that the United Nations should also be able to proceed against one of the great powers, which might perhaps aim at world dominion, Stalin asked him maliciously to name the power he thought capable of this. Presumably Great Britain and the United States had no such plans in mind. Churchill adroitly met this discovery of his mistrust of the Soviet Union by pointing out that as long as they, the three men who had jointly conducted this war, were alive, there was no danger of conflict. However, one had to think of the future.

It was characteristic of Stalin's concept of international affairs that he stubbornly opposed every proposal which might give the small nations a chance to make their weight felt in the United Nations. He feared that the big powers might one day mobilize the small nations against the Soviet Union. When his proposal that the United Nations have its own armed forces, particularly its own international air force with bases in the different countries, was turned down, he realized that an oligarchy of the great powers could not be achieved. Thereupon, in order then to secure more votes for the Soviet Union in the Plenary Assembly, he insisted that the Ukrainian and Byelorussian (White Russian) republics be separately admitted to the United Nations, a step made possible by a revision of the Soviet constitution in February 1944. Roosevelt tried to oppose this move; he is supposed to have said earlier that in such an event he would ask for 48 votes for the United States! [90] However, as Churchill supported the Soviet proposal, he gave in, and even waived the three votes which Stalin had offered the United States in return.

The most important subjects for discussion were the Polish and the German problems,[91] and the participation of the Soviet Union in the Pacific war. At Yalta—aided by haphazard procedure— Stalin dealt skilfully with Roosevelt's main concerns at critical moments in negotiations, first by pretending hesitancy, then by showing sudden enthusiasm, and thus gained the points in which he himself was most interested. When Roosevelt and Churchill asked that Galicia with its oil wells and the city of Lvov be given to Poland, he demanded with passionate emphasis that the original Curzon Line must be made the basis of the border settlements in the east, which meant that the aforementioned region would be allotted to the Soviet Union. In the west, Stalin proposed that the Polish borders be pushed forward to the Oder and Neisse rivers at Germany's expense. Churchill's warning that the Polish goose should not be so stuffed with German fodder that it would die of indigestion, was ignored. After many discussions the Soviet representatives were able to persuade the Western Powers to agree on a general recognition to Poland's right to compensation in the west, on the condition, however, that Polish independence be re-established. The Russian attempts to have the Neisse line accepted as the future German eastern frontier were firmly rejected by the Western Powers.[91a] On the issue of Galicia, however, Roosevelt was ready to withdraw his objections once he though that his wishes regarding Russia's participation in the UN and in the Pacific war were going to be fulfilled. The British representatives then contiued to fight a solitary battle for some days more to have the Polish exiled statesmen included in the reconstruction of the new Polish government. The final solution, to expand the Lublin Committee by a number of "democratic leaders," proved to be so elastic a formula that the Soviet Union found enough loopholes to disregard Polish sovereignty.

As regards German affairs, Stalin unequivocally advocated the dismemberment of the country. Churchill was against any commitment on this matter for the present and without France's opinion having been heard. As on this issue too, Stalin was supported by Roosevelt, Churchill finally agreed to dismemberment being spelled out in the capitulation conditions. A joint occupation policy was agreed upon. In vain the British representatives, remembering the experiences of the first World War, warned against excessive reparation payments. "If you want your horse to pull the cart," Churchill said to Maisky in his familiar picturesque manner, "you must give it some oats, or at least some hay." But here, too, he did not succeed in convincing his partner. The Russians demanded that of a total of twenty billion dollars they receive ten billion. After Harry Hopkins had spoken in favor of the Soviet demands, Roosevelt declared himself ready to recognize them as a basis of later discussions by a Reparations Commission. This compromise was recorded in the final protocol.

The problem of Soviet participation in the war against Japan was discussed on February 8, not in the joint meeting, but between Roosevelt and Stalin in a secret session. So far Stalin had managed to keep his country out of the Pacific war; he could be glad that the Japanese had not invaded Siberia, as Hitler wanted them to do. The Soviet government had no enthusiasm for adding to the exertions of the war with Germany the burdens of an expedition in the Far East. However, Roosevelt had been pressing for this for quite some time. In 1943 Stalin had promised participation in the Japanese war without, however, committing himself to the extent and place of attack. Roosevelt was now eager to have these promises realized, particularly since his sources estimated that anywhere up to a million Americans might be lost in the attempt to defeat Japan without Russian help. Roosevelt undoubtedly overrated the hazards of the Pacific theater of war and the strength of Japan,[92] but the effectiveness of the atom bomb, which was actually to make Russian intervention totally unnecessary, could not have been foreseen.

Intervention held no great risks for Stalin; and it promised to be very profitable. The secret agreement opened not only Manchuria but also Korea to Soviet influence. In exchange for promising to intervene two or three months after the German capitulation, Stalin obtained guarantees that the status quo would be maintained in Outer Mongolia, that Russia would retain its predominant influence in Northern Manchuria, and that the Chinese Eastern railroad which had been sold to Japan in 1935 would be returned to Russia, as well as the harbor zone of Port Arthur and Dairen which had been ceded to Japan in 1905. From the territory of Japan proper, the Kurile Islands which had belonged to it since 1875, and the southern part of the Island of Sakhalin, which had been surrendered in 1905, were demanded.[93]

Apparently, Roosevelt did not realize that by agreeing to this arrangement he sacrificed to some extent the principles which had been so emphatically announced in the Atlantic Charter, and reiterated in a special Yalta communique concerning the liberated areas.[94] In logical continuation of the line adopted at Teheran, the Soviet Union was granted concessions at Yalta the full implications of which could at the time not be completely appreciated. In order to gain Russia's participation in the Pacific war and in the UN, she was granted a dominant position in the Far East which the American occupation of Japan could only partially balance, and the whole of Eastern Europe, with the sole exception of Greece, was surrendered to her. Not until later was it realized in the West that Hitler's tyranny had been replaced by another.

The Occupation of Berlin and the End of the War in Europe

In the final phase of the battle for Germany, political questions became as significant as strategic. While the Western Allies wanted to overthrow Hitler's regime and for this purpose force the German armies to capitulate, the Russians, apart from their military goals, endeavored to expand their own *"Lebensraum"* as far into Central Europe as possible. This made it desirable to advance as far as possible into Germany and, if possible, occupy Berlin and the central German industrial area before the Western Allies got there.

On April 17, four days after the fall of Vienna, Zhukov assembled his troops for the assault on Berlin, hoping to advance beyond the Reich capital as far as the Elbe. In the early morning of that day his troops advanced from the bridge heads near Kuestrin, broke through the German fortifications and on April 22 reached the Autobahn encircling Berlin, along which they advanced westward to Spandau. At the same time Konev advanced with his troops from the bridgeheads on the western part of the Neisse, ordered his left flank to march on Dresden and Torgau, and his right flank and center to turn north and proceed toward Berlin. On April 25 Berlin was completely surrounded; on the same day the advance guards of the Russians and the Americans met each other at Torgau. In Berlin street fighting broke out which continued until May 2. On April 30 Hitler shot himself in the bunker of the Reich Chancellery. When General Krebs went to the Russians in order to negotiate a capitulation, he was informed that the surrender was to be unconditional. On May 2 the fighting ceased and the Red Army was in possession of the German capital.

While Konev meanwhile overcame the remaining German resistance in Prague, some of Zhukov's troops reached the Elbe in the first days of May. Germany was thus almost completely occupied by the Allied armies.

In view of the political implications of a Russian occupation of Berlin and of a Soviet zone extending far into the West, not only up to the Elbe and in some places a little beyond, but soon to include Thuringia, the question has been raised as to why the Western Allies did not hasten to occupy Berlin and Prague, even Vienna, before the Russians. Even if the political situation in 1945 did not yet carry the tensions which were to arise later, the alliance with the Soviet Union, necessary for the overthrow of Hitler, need not have led to such a surrender of eastern Central Europe, particularly as the efforts of the Allies since the invasion of France fully justified a central role in deciding the future of the continent.

For some time there had been warnings and forebodings caused by the fear of being left behind in the common race for victory. In May 1944 Churchill clearly recognized the consequences of an excessive permissiveness toward the Russians, at least as regards the Balkans and the Danube region. However, he too was not in a position to remain uninfluenced by the dynamics of the Russian military successes and Stalin's very logical political arguments. That Rumania, Bulgaria, Hungary and in part Yugoslavia were left to the Soviets in the partition agreement of June 1944 and finally, although reluctantly, Poland also, indicates how much Great Britain had to think of her spheres of interest outside the European theater. Britain, particularly the Conservatives, considered a Russian expansion in the Eastern Mediterranean and Asia Minor as being almost more dangerous than the surrender of Eastern Europe. Nevertheless, Field Marshal Montgomery had advocated a plan of marching on Berlin by making a second landing on the German North Sea coast, in the hope that the war could be ended in the fall of 1944. After the landing in Normandy, the British had also suggested that instead of advancing along a broad front, a pointed wedge should rapidly be driven to the Rhine and into the Ruhr, carrying the troops of the Western Allies to Berlin before the Russians got there.

For the Western Supreme Command, especially for Eisenhower, the problem was not a political one at all, but strategic. Just as the Americans had mistrusted an operation in the Balkans because they had no experience with fighting in a limited space and in mountainous country, they now preferred to advance in France along a broad front rather than in a wedge formation as Montgomery proposed, bringing about inevitably the thorough but slow conquest of Germany. The importance of Berlin as a stategic goal was overshadowed for them by Hitler's "Alpine Stronghold" in Southern Germany, the conquest of which was thought to require considerable forces; it was not then known that the stronghold was chiefly a figment of the imagination. Added to this were the fears of Omar Bradley and other Americans, that an advance on the capital would mean excessive losses—he thought about 10,000 men. Thus the occupation of Southern Germany was carried out energetically and thoroughly, but the advance was halted in front of Prague and slowed down in the direction of Berlin.

The belief that in the train of military successes the political problems would solve themselves, proved disastrous.[95] In the spring of 1945 strategic considerations were given precedence over extremely important political problems; it was not realized that a war could be lost on the political front even if it had been won strategically.[96]

The Potsdam Conference

Germany was conquered. Hitler was dead. The war in Europe was ended. When on May 24, 1945, Stalin received the commanders of the Red Army in the Kremlin, he toasted not the citizens of the Soviet Union, but significantly enough the health of the Russian people "the most outstanding nation among the peoples of the Soviet Union." The Russian people, above all, had in this war shown intelligence, perseverance and patience, and proved itself to be the "driving force" of the Soviet Union.[97] While these words were certainly an acknowledgment of the patriotic fervor which had motivated resistance, an astute observer could not help noticing that in the speech Stalin also praised the Party as the "inspirer and organizer of the people's struggle."

The Soviet losses had been great. But the Kremlin could be satisfied that the fight had not been in vain. It had led not only to the repulse of the enemy and the liberation of the homeland, not only to the maintenance of the possessions of 1939 or 1940, but also to the extension of the Soviet territory by about 193,000 square miles with a population of almost sixty million.

In addition to the Baltic countries, Eastern Poland and Bessarabia, North Bukovina, East Karelia with Petsamo and Porkkala, and the northern part of East Prussia now belonged to the Soviet Union. The Soviet sphere of influence reached even beyond, farther than Manchuria in the Far East, in Europe covering the whole of eastern Central Europe from Finland to the Aegean Sea and to the Adriatic.

One of the chief political aims of the Soviet Union at the Potsdam

Conference was to gain recognition by the Western powers of these possessions. Apart from being in control of Central and Eastern Europe, the Soviet Union also showed a special interest in the Mediterranean and the Near East. It demanded a revision of the Montreux Agreement and expressed the desire to participate in the trusteeship of the Italian colonies.

The Potsdam Conference lasted from July 17 to August 2. Stalin and Molotov repeatedly tried to conjure up the spirit of Teheran and Yalta in order to collect the dividends of the many promises and assurances which Roosevelt had given. The American President had died in April 1945. His successor, Harry Truman, was faced with the great difficulty of becoming familiar with his new office and could not afford to lose prestige at the outset of his term by having the Conference fail. In the middle of the Conference Churchill was replaced by Attlee as a result of the election victory of the British Labor Party. The British and American foreign ministers, Bevin and Byrnes, were also new to their jobs. Thus the Soviet statesmen remained the only interpreters of the decisions of Teheran and Yalta.[98] This explains why compromises so favorable to the Soviet Union were made at Potsdam.

On the question of the German eastern borders, Stalin presented the Western Allies with a *fait accompli*. The whole area east of the Oder and the Neisse, including the former Free City of Danzig, was already under Polish administration. The Soviet government had not found it necessary to consult its allies before it so generously handed this territory over to the Polish Communist government. At Teheran it had not been completely clear as to which of the Neisse rivers was meant,[99] the Eastern or the Western Neisse, but this too had been settled: the Polish control extended as far as the Western Neisse.[100] There were extensive debates regarding this difficult question. After listening to the Polish representatives, and after compromise proposals made by the Allies had been turned down, the United States and Great Britain saw themselves forced to agree to the temporary administration of these territories by Poland. However, Byrnes and Bevin repeatedly stressed then and later that this decision was provisional. The Soviet claims to the northern part of East Prussia were on the other hand recognized without question. Here, too, however, it was to be a trusteeship until the final decision at the Peace Conference.

It was also of importance for Soviet policy in Germany that after Yalta the Kremlin had changed its original views quite definitely. As

Stalin had already stated in his speech of May 9, and at the end of the month had told Hopkins,[101] he no longer intended to "dismember or annihilate" Germany. The more tensions grew between the Allies, the more a new orientation of Soviet policy in Germany seemed necessary. After the Polish desires had been satisfied, a Germany that was only divided into occupation zones rather than into several independent states, would be better suited to meet Soviet demands for reparations. The details of a peace treaty with Germany were to be worked out by the newly founded permanent Council of Foreign Ministers in which France was also included after Soviet hesitations had been overcome.[102] It was to be seen how far this body would be able to meet the problems of the peace and maintain international order.

The Soviet Share in the War with Japan

The fact that the Soviet Union and Japan did not attack each other during the Second World War but maintained their neutrality, was to their mutual advantage.

When the Siberian reinforcements arrived in Moscow in December 1941 to ward off the German assault, a Japanese attack could have been disastrous.

The Japanese, however, preferred at that time to advance toward the West rather than the East. The news of Pearl Harbor was heard in Moscow with a sigh of relief. However much the Germans urged the Japanese to take action in Siberia, they did not let themselves be deflected from their own program. The war would have taken a different course if at the time of Stalingrad the Russians had had to fight on two fronts.

In 1945 it was no longer a risk for Stalin to enter the Pacific war, as he had repeatedly promised Roosevelt. As in 1939 in Poland, he intervened at the twelfth hour in order to secure his share of the spoils.

On August 8, 1945, two days after the first American atom bomb had been dropped on Hiroshima, the Soviet government declared war on Japan because it had refused to capitulate unconditionally to the Allies of the Soviet Union.

Marshal Vassilevsky was the Commander in Chief of the military operations. The plan called first of all for the occupation of Manchuria. This was carried out from two sides: by the troops of the Transbaikal Army Group under Malinovsky which advanced through the Mongolian People's Republic in the direction of Mukden and Port Arthur, and by the troops of the First Far Eastern Group under Meretskov from the Vladivostok region. The enemy troops which had been encircled in this manner were then split into two parts by the troops of the second Far Eastern Army Group which advanced from Khabarovsk. In the meantime the fleet and air force cut communications with Japan.

The day on which the Russians started their intervention in the war, the second American atom bomb was dropped on Nagasaki. On August 10 the Japanese government was ready to capitulate. It is quite characteristic of Soviet historiography that the part played by the United States is not mentioned in the account of the end of the Japanese war,[103] nor are the Pacific operations which preceded the use of the atom bombs mentioned, although the Japanese capitulation would surely have come about even if Soviet troops had not intervened.

The way in which Stalin told his people of the Soviet Union's participation in the subjugation of Japan was also quite remarkable. In his proclamation he depicted the war as Russia's revenge for the Japanese victory over the Czarist Empire in 1904-05. "The defeat of the Russian troops in 1904," he said, "left bitter memories in the hearts of the Russian people. It was a blemish on the tradition of our country. Our people hoped and believed that the day would come on which Japan would be defeated and this blemish be erased. For forty years we, the men of the older generation, have waited for this day. Now it has finally come."[104]

Actually the defeat of the Czarist government had at that time been hailed by all radical parties, even by the liberals, as a step on the way to freedom. Lenin himself had celebrated the victory of the Japanese as a prologue to the rising of the European proletariat.[105] Now, however, the interpretation was in keeping with the return to a nationalist view of history and to Russian tradition.

The year 1945 saw the Soviet Union emerging from the Second World War in a position of power which was far removed from the nadir of the year 1938 and exceeded the wildest expectations of the Kremlin. A Bolshevik Empire had been born which was closely linked with the name of Stalin. Only the United States of America could compete with this world empire. Would the post-war world see the colossi living peacefully side by side? This was a question which millions asked themselves with fear.

CHAPTER 9

THE END OF THE STALIN ERA

Economic Recovery:
The Fourth Five Year Plan

The war made unheard of demands on the Soviet economy. The extent to which production was put into the service of the war effort was astounding even by Soviet standards. The rhythm of the five year plans had been interrupted. The fulfillment of the Third Five Year Plan (1938-42) was delayed by seven to eight years.[1] However, after the battle of Stalingrad, the big turning point of the war, the production of the plants that had been shifted to the East became highly significant. The destruction of industry in the fighting zones and in the enemy occupied areas was in part balanced by the erection of new works. American Lend-Lease aid and technological advice, the introduction of new processes, and a sweeping standardization proved to be very advantageous. The evacuation of industrial plants to the East accentuated a general eastward shift of Soviet industry, which had been in process for some years, but which now had to be speeded up, and was therefore accompanied by many improvisations. Hence, the subsequent return westward was only partial, and, of about 2,500 plants that were moved to the East during the war, 1,360, or more than half, remained there permanently, in spite of the fact that 6,000 plants were re-opened in the course of economic reconstruction in the Western provinces.[2]

Despite these facts, one cannot ignore the tremendous misery that the four years of war had meant for the country and the people. Vast regions of western and southern Russia had been laid waste during the fighting, In the course of the German retreat, or as a result of guerrilla warfare. Innumerable townships had been destroyed, and the housing shortage was appalling. The number of homeless was estimated at about 25 million. The total loss of life was about 20 million. Many of these had died of hunger or during air attacks, many met death in Hitler's camps, others were so weakened by malnutrition or over-exertion that they succumbed prematurely.

The Soviet Union was hardly able to cope with this situation on its own. The aid of the Allies was of paramount importance, even after hostilities had ceased. In its own economic planning, the Soviet Union returned to the Third Five Year Plan. With the help of UNRRA and British and Swedish credits for the purchase of machinery and of raw materials—particularly rubber and tin—the basis for reconstruction could be laid. In addition, there were reparation payments and the transfer of machinery from the enemy countries. The satellite states had to supply minerals, oil, optical and electrical instruments, and sugar and fats in amounts that meant ruthless exploitation. By its control of the German Soviet zone, the Soviet Union commanded 36% of Germany's 1936 industrial capacity, or 41% of the 1943 capacity. Reparations were arranged in such a way that as much as 80 to 90% of the production of certain highly specialized finishing industries went to the Soviet Union. In Hungary and Rumania the situation was similar. Although dismantling was often carried out in so impractical and slipshod a manner that the machines were useless when they reached the Soviet Union, assets of inestimable value nevertheless streamed into the country. The Jena Zeisswerke, including personnel, was shipped complete to Russia. Numerous highly skilled German workers and engineers, among them atomic scientists, were forced to go to Russia, representing an intellectual potential that can hardly be overestimated.

A very important factor in reconstruction was the speed-up. The forty-hour week, which had been introduced in 1937, had been raised to forty-eight hours in June 1940 by governmental decree,[3] and it continued in force, accompanied by strict discipline.

On August 19, 1945, the top party and government authorities ordered the preparation of a new Five Year Plan. The program was worked out by the spring of the following year, and was approved by the Supreme Soviet in the middle of March 1946. The Fourth Five Year Plan (1946-50) was marked by faulty planning attributable to the difficulties of the post-war situation.[4] De-control of grain had been scheduled for the fall of 1946, but this date could not be met, allegedly because of the bad harvest. Only on December 16, 1947, shortly after a currency reform had also been carried out, was grain derationed.

One of the main features of the Fourth Five Year Plan was its extensive housing program. Even before the war, the crowding of Soviet cities had created living conditions that would have been

unthinkable in Western Europe.[5] Building restrictions and destruction during the war had rendered the situation utterly catastrophic.
In the cities alone, 60 million square meters of living space were
to be built in the course of reconstruction. In 1950, statistics showed
that the goals of the plan had been exceeded in the cities, but only
80% achieved in the rural areas.[6] The rise in population within the
old borders of the Soviet Union must also be taken into account.[7]

Apart from the goals envisaged for the basic industries, five large-
scale construction projects for the improvement of the electricity
supply, the irrigation system, and the communication network were
a special feature of the Fourth Five Year Plan. These were the
power works on the Volga near Kuibyshev[8] and Stalingrad, the
power works at Kakhovka on the River Dnieper, the Turkemenian
canal in Central Asia, and the Volga-Don canal. It was expected
that the new hydroelectric power plants would increase the production of electricity in the Soviet Union by about 22.5 billion kilowatt
hours per year, or by more than one-fifth. With an excess of bom-
bast, the works were described as "Stalin edifices of Communism,"
their task being to "change nature" and to convince the world of
the purely peaceful aims of Soviet reconstruction while the United
States and the other capitalist powers were "feverishly" arming for
a new war. But alleged Western plans for aggression served as an
excuse for Soviet armament. The law decreeing the Fourth Five
Year Plan called for "the further extension of the defensive strength
of the USSR and the equipment of its armed forces with the most
modern weapons."

Heavy industry continued in the forefront of Soviet planning. The
1950 reports about the results of the Fourth Five Year Plan indicated, despite the questionable reliability of Soviet statistics, that
pre-war production had not only been reached but considerably
exceeded. The industrial production of the Soviet Union now held
second place in the world.[9] It is of particular importance that the
quota for steel production was exceeded; 27.3 million metric tons
of raw steel and 20.8 million metric tons of rolled steel were in the
main used for the construction of heavy machinery, factories, railroad equipment, and armament. In a speech on February 9, 1946,
Stalin—thinking far ahead of the current plan—set the Soviet economy the goal of producing 60 million metric tons of steel annually
by 1960, 500 million metric tons of coal, and 60 million metric
tons of oil. These figures were devised before the outbreak of the
Cold War, and they sound rather utopian. It was not very likely that
the Soviet economy would find it easy to catch up with the United
States.

As was to be expected, the production of consumer goods, particularly textiles, shoes, and household appliances, had to take second place, although, on the eve of the initiation of the Five Year Plan, Stalin had particularly stressed the necessity for expansion in this sector. According to the sparse details regarding the fulfillment of the quotas laid down by the Plan, a target was exceeded only in the production of woolen textiles, while other items did not reach the expected quotas. Household appliances were not even mentioned in the reports.[10] In his report of November 6, 1951, Beria simply spoke of an increase in the production of consumer goods, quoting isolated percentages, in keeping with Soviet usage.

The revival of agricultural production was of special importance for sound and balanced economic development. Particularly great difficulties had to be coped with. Not only had the stock of cattle been decimated, but there was a catastrophic lack of tractors and horses. In the spring of 1947, one could still see peasant women tilling the fields with spades. During the previous summer there had been a drought that was assessed as the worst since 1891. Rationing, which was supposed to end in 1946, had to be continued. In the winter of 1946-47, there were hunger revolts in Kharkov, accompanied by violent incidents that had to be suppressed by the NKVD.

The lack of workers and transportation frequently meant that the harvest could not be gathered in time. The production of tractors, reaping and threshing machines, and other agricultural machinery was therefore considerably speeded up. The motorization of agriculture made further progress, and, in his report of 1951, Beria said that power-driven plows were being used almost exclusively on the collective farms. Machines were also handling 60% of the harvest.[11]

By the end of the Fourth Five Year Plan, it appeared that the stipulated production quotas in agricultural yields had been achieved. Among them were programs for the extension of artificial field irrigation, the planting of wooded shelter belts,[12] soil conservation, and soil improvement. In 1948, a Fifteen Year Plan for the forestation of the steppes was initiated. There were also new political plans for agriculture, among them a program for the creation of giant collective farms and agricultural cities.

The collective farm system had been somewhat less rigidly controlled during the war. In the areas that had been spared German occupation, the burden of work was borne chiefly by women. In order to increase production, certain rules had been relaxed so as to spur private initiative. Thus, there had been an increase in individual ownership as private vegetable fields grew because of un-

official "annexations" by their owners. Now, however, the reins
were tightened again, and a special decree for the protection of the
collective farm system was passed. In September 1946, A. A.
Andreyev, a member of the Politburo, became the head of the newly
formed Council for Collective Farm Affairs, within the Council of
People's Commissars of the USSR. As a first step, a thorough purge
of the directors of the collective farms was undertaken, and the
privileges that the war had brought were abolished. It was remarkable, however, that considerable clemency was exercised, and
kolkhoz directors who were dismissed in the course of investigations
were not punished further. Concomitantly, Andreyev advocated the
extension of the system of individual work groups, which had
proved useful in raising output as early as 1940. In the course of
time, these groups achieved a certain independence within the collective farms; this was particularly pronounced in the case of the
so-called isolated groups. The formation of these groups, in which
family ties were accorded a good deal of consideration, was promoted in every way during the period 1947-49.

During these years, it was noteworthy that the local Party and
Soviet organizations were granted a somewhat greater degree of
autonomy, and centralization was no longer enforced quite so rigidly. This more "liberal" phase of domestic policy also coincided
with the period during which capital punishment was abolished in
the Soviet Union (May 1947 to January 1950). In addition to this,
a law was passed on August 26, 1948, granting each Soviet citizen
the right to build, buy, or inherit his own home. Although in practice only the well-to-do of the *apparatchiki* were able to make use
of this provision, the combination of all these factors created a contrasting background for the growing isolation in foreign policy and
cultural affairs that occurred during these very same years.

When delays in grain deliveries occurred in the fall of 1949, those
who rejected Andreyev's policy attributed the slowdown to discontent among the peasants, particularly those working in groups. The
opposition centered on Nikita Sergeyevich Khrushchev, the chairman of the Council of Ministers of the Ukraine. At the end of the
year, when he was transferred to Moscow as Secretary of the Party's
Central Committee and as Party Secretary of the Province Committee, he began to attack Andreyev. Khrushchev had a different concept of agrarian policy. He advocated the combination of three to
five collective farms into one giant collective farm, within which
the work was to be carried out, not by small groups but by work
brigades 100 to 150 strong. Near Cherkassy, in the Ukraine, the
first giant farm had already been founded at the end of 1949. Now

further mergers were made, although the resulting farms did not always run smoothly. At the end of 1950, 250,000 collective farms had been combined into 125,000 giant farms. Beyond that, Khrushchev planned the erection of special "agro-cities," in which the peasants from the collective farms were to live in mass housing projects where, incidentally, they would be easily available for propaganda purposes. At issue was nothing less than the abolition of the existing type of peasants, who were to be replaced by skilled workers employed in fully mechanized agricultural plants.[13]

Early in 1951, the opposition against this ruthless new agrarian revolution began to make itself felt. It appeared that even in the Politburo, where Khrushchev, Beria, and Malenkov had joined forces to oppose Zhdanov, strong differences of opinion existed. Khrushchev's plan to take the private vegetable fields away from the collective farm peasants and move them to the periphery of the new giant farms was most sharply criticized. At first, Stalin apparently watched the clash of opinions calmly. Then he intervened as a mediator. Andreyev remained at his job. The collective farm mergers were to take place more gradually and the erection of agro-cities was to be postponed. The complete uprooting of the Soviet peasant had been averted.

Ideology: The Zhdanovshchina

While the war was still in progress, a violent attack by the leading Party organ *Bolshevik* on the third volume of *A History of Philosophy,* which appeared in 1943, created a stir. The authors were taken to task for having described the classic period of German philosophy as the acme of pre-Marxist philosophical thinking, without sufficiently stressing the Russian philosophers of the 19th century. This criticism subsequently became the credo of a vigorous ideological school.[14]

This school demanded that everything Russian come first, a line it had been thought necessary to follow during the war in order to promote fighting morale. After the war, it needed to be continued, it seems, in order to safeguard not only ideological principles but also national pride, both of which were threatened by the close contact with the Western world that hundreds of thousands of Red Army men, slave laborers, prisoners-of-war, and Vlasov's soldiers had had, creating a situation not unlike that after the wars of liberation against Napoleon. Stalin's toast to the Russian people on May 24, 1945 (the end of the war in the West), officially introduced this new course and signaled the beginning of a continuous intervention by the state in Soviet intellectual life, which took place during the subsequent years. During the first period—until 1948— A. A. Zhdanov was chiefly responsible for what was done, and the term *Zhdanovshchina*[15] was soon coined to identify his program.

A. A. Zhdanov was born in 1896, in Mariupol, on the Sea of Azov. At the age of 19, he entered the Bolshevik party, and at the end of the First World War was serving as an ensign. During the Civil War, he rendered a valuable service to the Bolsheviks in winning over the Ural region, one of the strongholds of the Social Revolutionaries. From 1924 to 1934, he directed the Party in Nizhni Novgorod. It was decisive for his further career that he vigorously supported Stalin's fight against Zinoviev, Tomsky, and others. During the Seventeenth Party Congress of 1934, he moved into the top ranks of the Party hierarchy. In 1939, he became a member of the Politburo. As Party Secretary of Leningrad (from 1934 until his death), his name is inseparable from the defense of the city during the Second World War.

One of the best educated of the Communist Party leadership, Zhdanov had exercised considerable influence on Soviet cultural policies as early as 1934-38. He had played a considerable part in the cultural revolution of Soviet patriotism and, as a Great Russian, the stress on Russian nationalism was bound to appeal to him. He issued directives to historians and writers and, if Stalin called the Soviet writers "engineers of the soul," Zhdanov could well have been considered chief engineer.[16]

The creation of a uniform Central Administration for Propaganda and Agitation in 1938 was Zhdanov's work; it was he who initiated the abolition of restrictions on the admission of members of the intelligentsia to the Party (1939), the abolition of free tuition in the upper grades of the high schools (1940), and the reintroduction of a graduation examination (1944).

In August 1946, Zhdanov's interference in Soviet intellectual life became particularly aggressive. Earlier that year, in a speech on February 9, Stalin had hinted that a significant change of course was to be expected. Not six months had passed since the end of hostilities, and yet the Generalissimo was ready to declare that the Soviet people needed to be prepared for new wars, which would be inevitable as long as any capitalist systems existed. In this connection, he expressed his conviction that Soviet scientists would, in the course of the coming conflicts, catch up with and overtake their colleagues abroad.[17] This speech became the signal for the beginning of a new and tighter state control of cultural life. The Institute for History at the Academy of Sciences, for example, published a five year plan of voluminous composite works.

This was the basis for Zhdanov's intervention in the Soviet Union's cultural life during 1946-48. In his famous speech to the Central Committee in September 1946,[18] he sharply criticized the cultural front. He sounded the battle call against all influences from abroad. It was time, he said, to end the "truckling" to the bourgeois culture of the West, which actually was in a process of decay. The superiority of socialism had to be demonstrated in matters cultural, and Soviet writers had the duty to create a genuine socialist literature. Two Leningrad magazines were severely castigated in this connection, and a well-informed American reporter in Moscow described Zhdanov's attitude, not unjustly, as an "ideological declaration of war" against the West and as "the beginning of the cold war" between East and West.[19] In a speech to Leningrad writers on September 21, Zhdanov again demanded that Soviet culture take the offensive and teach the world new, humanitarian ethics; it could no longer be content to lean on bourgeois culture and play the school child.

Punitive measures and disciplinary proceedings in all areas of science, art, and literature now became the order of the day. The Law Institute at the Academy of Sciences was taken to task for its cosmopolitan attitude, its lassitude regarding questions of Soviet law, and its objectivist tendencies. The poetess A. Akhmatova and the well-known satirist M. Zoshchenko were accused of having drawn a false picture of Soviet life. In a discussion of G. F. Alexandrov's *History of Western European Philosophy* in the summer of 1947, the accusations made three years previously in *Bolshevik* were repeated. In acid words, Zhdanov advocated "aggressive, Bolshevik partisanship" in philosophy, and seemed to fear that the results of modern scientific research might be considered by Soviet philosophers as a refutation of materialism. Another debate concerned a book by the leading Soviet economist Eugene S. Varga, *The Changes in the Capitalist Economy resulting from the Second World War*.[20] The author was censured for doubting that an immediate crisis in the United States was inevitable. (Two years later, however, Varga was rehabilitated, and *Pravda* published a lengthy article by him. In the meantime Stalin himself had realized that hopes for an imminent collapse of the American economy were futile.[21])

In 1948, Zhdanov made the opening of a new Soviet opera (by V. Muradeli) an occasion to criticize the "formalist direction" in Soviet music as "hostile to the people and as a disintegrating element." At a joint meeting of the Central Committee and the representatives of Soviet musical life, he accused not only the composers—among them as outstanding a man as Shostakovich—but also the other artists of tending toward a "homeless cosmopolitanism" instead of rendering homage to "socialist realism."

Toward the end of the war, historical science had returned somewhat noisily to the Leninist line. This was emphasized publicly by replacing the *Historical Review* with a new organ, *Problems of History (Voprosy istorii)*. The first issue renewed the demand that the class struggle be the primary criterion for the analysis of historical events. This did not conflict with the idea of the glorification of the Russian people, which had caused such a sensation in the spring of 1945. Here, too, the dialectic mentality made it possible to ride two horses simultaneously by constantly shifting the balance.

Thus, in the course of the *Zhdanovshchina,* the historian N. Rubinstein was rebuked for not having stressed sufficiently the merits of Russian historians in his *History of Russian Historiography,* which had appeared in 1941. In February 1948, Rubinstein denounced his own work after it had been condemned by a conference of experts in the Ministry of Higher Education and admitted that he had been a victim of formalist and objectivist points of view. Despite his recantation, however, he was again severely attacked early in 1949 in the historical journal *Voprosy istorii.*[22] In addition, a number of other Soviet historians were reprimanded for attributing too much importance to foreign influences on Russian history and neglecting to give sufficient weight to the heroic Russians. One could not help but notice that a large number of those censured were of Jewish origin.

The climax of the *Zhdanovshchina* was reached in the discussion arising out of Lysenko's biological theories, which led to the Academy of Sciences announcement of its official position in the summer of 1948. T. D. Lysenko, the self-educated son of a peasant, had become the leading Soviet biologist by about 1929. In continuing the attempts of botanist I. V. Michurin to influence the evolutionary process of cultivated plants and to control their heredity, Lysenko developed a new process that shortened the ripening period of cultivated plants by temperature influences at the start of germination. This was of great importance for the acclimatization of grain in the far north and the cultivation of potatoes in the south. On this he based his theory that it was possible to change the heredity of plants, to change wheat into rye, and so on.

As early as 1940, scientists criticizing this theory were reprimanded and, in some instances, arrested. Lysenko now submitted his ideas to a congress and in the discussion sharply attacked the biological theories of the West. Zhdanov supported him and accused his critics of seriously deviating from the materialist world concept.

In 1949 and 1950, the psychologists and physiologists also were reminded of the materialist-scientific basis of their respective spheres, as expressed in the theories of the well-known Soviet physiologist and Nobel Prize winner I. P. Pavlov (1849-1936), who, for example, considered all psychological functions purely mechanical processes. L. A. Orbeli, one of his pupils who showed a little too much independence, was accused in 1950 at a joint meeting of the Academy of Sciences and the Academy of Medicine of having trespassed on the field of metaphysics in his research on the sympathetic nerve system and thus to have corrupted Pavlov's theories. Orbeli was relieved of his office but did not recant.[23]

From all this, it was apparent that Soviet science did not permit freedom of research and teaching. This was considered a bourgeois prejudice; research and teaching have to be subservient to the "building of socialism," they are inseparable from their purpose and receive their assignments and directives from the state and the Party. There are no abstract scientific goals based on the discovery of truth. Truth has, after all, already been established—it is contained in dialectical materialism, in Marxist doctrine. Dialectical materialism *(diamat)* is framework, content, and method for the Soviet scientist. Science that is free of practical purposes and dogmatism is condemned as "formalistic" or "objectivistic."

Within these limits are encompassed the achievements and results of Soviet scientific research. They are practical and real. Close bonds between theory and practice, comprehensive planning and collectivist work methods, which in some areas have been successful, have doubtless resulted in achievements serving the practical necessities of life. Here, too, however, the beneficiary is in the first place the state, not the individual or the community; these are always consoled and spurred to further exertions by the prospect of a future classless and blissful Communist society, the great goal of human development.

The progressive isolation of Soviet intellectual life from foreign influences was undoubtedly calamitous. The lack of intellectual contact with the universal cultural currents beyond the borders robbed it of stimulation and of standards of comparison. Nationalist glorification of Russian cultural achievements and chauvinistic arrogance in the face of Western civilization became only too apparent—for example, in the innumerable attempts to prove priority for Russians as inventors or discoverers of scientific laws, from the law of the preservation of matter and the invention of the steam engine to radio and penicillin. By one-sidedly stressing the frequently undisputed Russian share in several inventions, usually not completed at one stroke, further phases of development are overlooked even though they represent perhaps the decisive stage in the realization of the idea in question. In the area of historical research, too, we find, in the very detailed discussions concerning the periodic division of history, the same attempt to claim priority for Russia over the West regarding the influences initiating great historical epochs.

That this stress on the Russian element must not be viewed as a contradiction of the world revolutionary goals of Stalinism, but simply as one of its dialectic phases, was evidenced in the summer of 1950 by Stalin's letters on philological questions. It was a sensation when, in May 1950, *Pravda* opened its columns to an extensive public discussion directed against the hitherto generally accepted philological theories of Professor N. Y. Marr (died 1934). Marr had been the unchallenged authority in the field of Marxist linguistics. According to the Marxist scheme, he had defined language as belonging to the superstructure of human society, similar to philosophy and art. Thus, language was considered as a function of the existing economic and social conditions, as something secondary, dependent on the material foundation. More important, therefore, than the inner linguistic ties between languages was the developmental stage of the peoples in question. On this premise a new supra-national "language of socialism" could be anticipated, which would prevail after the victory of Bolshevism.

This theory in no way fitted the new ideological and political position of the Soviet Union and its satellites. The public discussion was opened on May 9, by an expert, Professor A. S. Chikobava. On June 20, July 4, and August 2, Stalin took part in these debates. The principal concepts in his "Letters on Linguistics" are: (1) language belongs neither to the superstructure of society nor to the basis it is independent; (2) language is not the concern of individual classes, but of the people as a whole; (3) language is not limited in time, but is eternal and lives through many historical periods; (4) when several languages clash, they do not merge to form a new language, but one of them prevails over the rest—the Russian language has always been victorious.[24]

Stalin's theories gained tremendous importance. The most diverse branches of science had to take them into account. Marr and his pupils were condemned in a manner comparable only to the verdict against Pokrovsky in the 1930's. Beyond this, however, Stalin's formulations played a political role in the development of Communist ideology. The new concept of the nature of language, and of the importance of the Russian language in particular, went hand in hand with the development of Soviet patriotism and the bond established with the national Russian past. If the Russian people—in Stalin's words—represent the fundamental strength of the Soviet state, the Russian language inevitably also has a most important function. As the language of the "big brother" among the Soviet peoples and the People's Democracies affiliated with them, it was the common bond of the new empire and became the official language at all political functions.[25]

There was a third ideological factor. It is noteworthy that Stalin —contrary to previous theories—did not consider society's superstructure of secondary importance, but saw in it a tremendous active force. Part of the superstructure is also the state. A far cry from the original concept of the state withering away after the victory of socialism, it is now described as the "leading and guiding force" in the planned development of society. Thus, the Soviet Union as a political entity, with the Soviet Army as the present-day *avant-garde* of world Communism, takes the place of the international proletariat, the original protagonist of the revolutionary struggle. On the one hand there is the thesis of world revolution, on the other the antithesis of the Soviet Union's supremacy; the only logical synthesis, then, is that world Communism can only be achieved through the hegemony of the Soviet Union.

In the light of this, Stalin's surprising new concept of the "revolution from above" also becomes intelligible. Sudden upheavals are unavoidable only in a society divided into hostile classes; they are not necessary in a Soviet society where the revolution from above, emanating from a powerful state, is appropriate.

In this manner, Stalin's letters go to the very roots of Marxist ideology, bringing about a further change on the road from Marxism via Leninism to the newest phase of Stalinism.

Foreign Policy: The Two Camps

The Soviet Union reaped a bumper harvest in the field of international affairs after the Second World War. Its territorial acquisitions in the west and in the east needed the confirmation of peace treaties only in part. Soviet troops were in Berlin and Vienna, had advanced as far as the Elbe, controlled the Danube area and the Balkans, and also occupied Manchuria. The reality of this was underscored by the joint Allied decisions in Teheran, Yalta, and

Potsdam. On this base, the Soviet Union could now consolidate its international position.

Good relations with the Allies, particularly with the United States and the British Empire, were important requisites for the Soviet Union's international position. But other factors were equally or more important. While the military and economic potential of the Soviet Union had certainly been weakened by the enormous efforts of four years of war, and the people's capacity for work and suffering tested to its limits, the Bolshevik regime had other potentials on which it could call. Were not its Marxist ideology and its propaganda machinery tools with which it could unhinge the whole bourgeois world? Was the world beyond the actual Soviet sphere of influence, particularly countries such as France and Italy, but also the Near East and the Asiatic world, not bound to become a fertile field for Communist agitation, until the day when Communism would be strong enough to strike at the actual bastions of the capitalist world?

The immediate post-war period became the great test of the amount of strain the Allies could bear while still continuing to work together and of how far the West was correct in thinking that it merely faced a Russian empire with certain Bolshevik forms and with limited goals of expansion.

In the spring of 1945, when the war in Europe was approaching its end, Soviet policy had been focused, in the main, on Germany and Poland. In the course of the Allied conferences, the Kremlin had also proceeded to fortify its position in the eastern part of Central Europe, from Finland to Greece. When, however, Japan capitulated in the fall of 1945, the focus of Soviet policy could no longer remain exclusively on Europe. Just as its partner in the arena of world politics, the United States, could not afford to neglect its concerns in the Pacific, so too the Kremlin had to turn its attention to Asia. It seemed necessary here, also, to construct a safety belt of sufficient depth beyond which Soviet influence could be carried into the eastern and southeast Asian world.

The question was whether the Anglo-Saxon powers, already having handed over the eastern part of Central Europe and having permitted Russia to take part in the control of Central Europe, would be ready to countenance Soviet aspirations in the Far East as well.

The common forum for the discussion of questions of international policies, particularly the preparation of a peace conference, was the Foreign Ministers' Council. It met for its first session in September 1945 in London. The consequences of Japan's defeat, which prompted the expansionist interests of the Soviet Union, became immediately apparent. Although it was not on the agenda, Molotov demanded that the occupation of Japan also be discussed. The Western powers rejected this. Only after Harriman, at the end of October, had discussed Far Eastern questions with Stalin, was the Foreign Ministers' Conference that met in Moscow in December 1945 able to achieve a compromise solution. The Soviet Union was to be a member of the Far Eastern Commission and the Allied Council for Japan, but it would not be able to exercise the direct influence on Japanese affairs that the Kremlin desired, because the bodies mentioned—in contrast to the Foreign Ministers' Council and the Allied Control Council for Germany—had only advisory functions.

However, North Korea—as far as the 38th parallel—was recognized as a Soviet occupation zone, and the withdrawal of Soviet troops from Manchuria was postponed until February 1946. At the same time the Soviet Union's control over Rumania and Bulgaria was once again confirmed.[26]

A few days after the Moscow Conference, the attention of the world was drawn to Iran, an old field for Russian politics. In northern Iran a revolutionary regime had been established, not uninfluenced by the presence of Russian troops that had marched into the country in 1941. The effects of this could be felt as far away as the provinces of eastern Turkey (inhabited by Kurds) and northern Iraq, and, as a result, Turkish-Russian relations became seriously strained. In March 1945, the Soviet Union had terminated its 1925 pact of friendship with Turkey and proposed a revision of the Convention of Montreux to allow Russia to participate in the defense of the Straits. In addition, Russia had demanded a border revision, which amounted to a return of the provinces of Kars, Ardahan, and Artvin, ceded to Turkey in 1918. In December, the Kremlin reopened the question of changing the status of the Straits. In an extensive exchange of notes, which continued until the end of 1946, it maintained that the defense of the Straits should be shared by the Soviet Union and Turkey.[27] The negotiations were barren, as the proposal was unacceptable both to Turkey and to the Western powers. In the course of the discussions, the Soviet press frequently adopted a very arrogant tone, at times demanding the whole of Anatolian Armenia and the Black Sea coast as far as Trapezunt. At the same time, the Soviet Union backed Bulgaria's demands for Western Thrace, and the Greek Communist insurgents were secretly given Russian support, contrary to the agreement with the Allies.

When in March 1946, according to the 1942 agreement, the time came for Russian troops to withdraw from Iranian territory, the

Soviet Union simply ignored the date. This caused a profound disturbance in the Western countries. It found expression in the speech of Senator Vandenberg in the United States Senate on February 27, and in Churchill's speech in Fulton, Missouri, on March 5, in which he coined the term "Iron Curtain." The former British Prime Minister advocated close military collaboration in the face of Bolshevik expansionist aims. Stalin's reaction was quick and sharp. In a press interview on March 13, he called Churchill "the warmonger of the Third World War" and compared him with Hitler. Further interviews, however, were more conciliatory in tone. The firm attitude adopted by Great Britain, the United States, and the other nations in the UN Security Council prompted him to change his course. Early in May, the last Soviet troops left Iranian territory, after an agreement regarding the mutual use of oil wells had been reached in a direct Iranian-Russian conference on April 4.[28] This agreement was only valid, however, until October 1947. The North Iranian Autonomist Movement was also soon suppressed; its leaders fled to the Soviet Union. Apart from diplomatic protests, there were no further countermeasures.

The Soviet Union's dominant position in Europe was particularly evident in Berlin. Here, Marshal G. K. Zhukov, the conqueror of Berlin, headed the Soviet Military Administration. After he had been replaced by General V. D. Sokolovsky in April 1946, trends toward the bolshevization of the Soviet-occupied zone of Germany became more and more pronounced.[29] They were encouraged particularly by Colonel Tulpanov, the head of the Party machinery of the occupation troops, and also by the civil adviser to the Military Administration, Semyonov. In the spring of that year, the German Communist Party and the German Socialist Party were combined into the Social Unity Party (SED), a political *fait accompli* leaving no room for question.

Peace negotiations had been started with the European allies of Germany—Italy, Finland, Hungary, Bulgaria, and Rumania—that eventually led to a settlement and to the conclusion of treaties in Paris in 1947.[30] In the case of Austria, the Soviet government refused to embark on treaty negotiations before a peace treaty had been concluded with Germany. Like Germany, Austria was divided into zones, of which one was under the Russians; Vienna was administered jointly.

The German question was the most complicated. The Kremlin refused to discuss the problem of a peace treaty with Germany before two major demands were granted—the payment of $10 billion in reparations and the participation of the Soviet Union in four-power control of the Ruhr industries. These terms, however, were unacceptable to the Western powers. It was felt that the payment of reparations out of current production would handicap German economic recovery, which the Western powers had in the meantime decided to promote. In a speech in the House of Commons, in June 1946, Churchill did not hide his consternation that the Western border of the Soviet sphere of influence had been advanced as far as the Luebeck-Trieste line and that Poland was completely dominated by the USSR. In July of that year, Byrnes declared that the United States could no longer be responsible for the chaos that had resulted in Germany because of its division into four zones. In December 1946, the British and American occupation zones were combined. Earlier, in a speech in Stuttgart, Byrnes had demanded the creation of a central administration and the formation of a provisional German government. This was the beginning of the development that led to the formation of the German Federal Republic and to West European integration.

It became more and more obvious that the Soviet Union considered the Polish western border on the Oder and Neisse permanent, and promoted behind it the speedy incorporation of Poland into the Soviet orbit. The result of the Polish elections, in January 1947, ended all hopes of a revival of Poland's independence. When the Foreign Ministers' Council met for a fourth time in Moscow in the spring, the Western powers gained the impression that, on the one hand, the Kremlin aimed to delay the reconstruction of Germany and Western Europe, while, on the other, it pushed ahead with the bolshevization of the eastern part of Central Europe. The Soviet government, on its part, concluded from the opposition to the payment of German reparations that the West was not at all interested in the Soviet Union's reconstruction. Tied in with this were bad feelings resulting from the termination of United States Lend-Lease deliveries in 1945 and the unfulfilled hopes for sizable American credits, on which the Soviet Union had definitely counted. It was a symptom of the times that, coincidentally with the Foreign Ministers' meeting in Moscow in March 1947, a decree was issued forbidding marriages between Soviet citizens and foreigners.[31] Thus the Iron Curtain dropped a little lower, cutting off even personal ties. On the other hand the Western powers, understandably enough, lost their initial desire to continue the unconditional support of the Soviet Union as they watched the bolshevization of Eastern Europe.

When General Marshall became the American Secretary of State in January 1947, the Western powers' attitude toward Moscow stiffened. The British-French alliance of Dunkirk (March 1947), the announcement of the Truman Doctrine—which, necessitated by the critical situation in Greece, was to put a stop to the advance of the Soviets in the Near and Middle East—and, lastly, the Marshall Plan, the goal of which was the reconstruction of both Europe and Japan, were important stages of a process that was to lead away from the policy initiated at Teheran and Yalta. One might almost say that the conference on the Marshall Plan in Paris in the summer of 1947 was the actual turning point in East-West relations. The Soviet Union had also been invited, and Molotov arrived in Paris with more than eighty experts. Marshall Plan aid was offered to Russia and rejected. After using his familiar delaying tactics for some days, Molotov and the whole delegation were suddenly recalled to Moscow. Stalin, listening to Zhdanov's advice, must have decided to call off cooperation with the West and to continue along the Communist path regardless of the consequences.

For some time, the integration of Moscow's satellites had been in progress behind the Iron Curtain. From the time the Red troops marched into a country, playing the role of liberators both from the German occupation and from bourgeois governmental forms, the country's fate followed a pattern consisting of several stages.[32] Insofar as the latter had not already taken place, the military occupation was followed by a political revolution, at the core of which were local Communist groups that were augmented, where necessary, by reinforcements from the Soviet Union. In the name of a National Front against "fascists and collaborators," the bourgeois opposition and the bourgeois administration of justice were paralyzed. Then, by combining the Communists and Socialists into one "unity" party, the last resistance that the churches or the propertied peasantry might put up could be broken. A good guarantee of this development was always the Soviet occupation army; where there had been no occupation by Russian troops or where they had left the country again, as in the case of Yugoslavia, control usually passed into other hands. The numerous military and civil experts from the Soviet Union were also important factors. Apart from serving in an advisory capacity, they were also responsible for making the country in question economically profitable. It soon became apparent that it was more useful to get production going as soon as possible and to have it work for the benefit of the Soviet Union than to carry out wholesale dismantling operations. The Soviet corporation became the standard vehicle of Soviet economic policy in the satellite states; all of them were supervised and directed by a sub-division of the Ministry of Foreign Trade, located in

Berlin. It became clear that the whole Soviet sphere of influence was to be combined into a huge economic entity. This plan would make it possible to coordinate the Upper Silesian coal fields and the Saxonian industrial centers, on the one hand, and the Rumanian oil wells and the Ukrainian ore mines on the other.

The Soviet experts on military and police affairs and on economic planning and collectivization, as well as the Soviet confidential agents in all departments of domestic and foreign politics, formed a web covering a whole country. The Kremlin's official diplomacy was accompanied by the secret diplomacy of the Party, which was far more dangerous than the secret diplomatic machinations of the 18th and 19th centuries because it was far less scrupulous and more successfully conspiratorial. In its expansionist plans, the Soviet Union was thus by no means dependent on its army and its diplomatic corps alone; the Party, with its international organization centered in Moscow, was a powerful third arm.

Although these processes did not take place in public, their final results could not be kept secret from the world, and they occasionally shed a lurid light on the customary semi-darkness behind the Iron Curtain. Thus, for example, the fall of the Nagy Cabinet in Hungary in May 1947 alarmed the world; in September, the Bulgarian and Rumanian opposition leaders, Petkov and Maniu, and by the end of the year the Polish and Hungarian opposition leaders, Mikolajczyk and Pfeiffer, had to flee in order to escape arrest.[33] When A. Y. Vishinski, the Kremlin's special envoy, forced King Michael of Rumania to abdicate, Rumania was ready to become a so-called People's Democratic Republic. The final act in this logical development was a Communist *coup d'état,* which was dramatically carried out in Prague in February 1948, and which led to the death of Jan Masaryk. Masaryk, the son of the founder of the Czechoslovak state, threw himself out of a window when he was hard pressed by his persecutors; the integration of the country into a Bolshevik system followed.[34] A system of pacts considerably strengthened the political and economic ties between the East Central European states and the Soviet Union.[35]

The Hungarian revolt in the autumn of 1956, the return to power of Gomulka in Poland, and reports of disturbances in other Soviet satellites give powerful evidence that the process of sovietization has not been accepted without national opposition.

In the Soviet zone of Germany, the German Economic Commission was created in answer to the formation of a bi-zonal Economic Council in the West. The Second Congress of the Social Unity Party in September 1947 was of basic importance; it committed itself to the unconditional support of Soviet foreign policy. After Soviet hopes for a spontaneous uprising of the German population in the Western zones in favor of a union with the Soviet zone under Communist leadership were buried in the spring of 1947, the Soviet zone was to be incorporated into the Bolshevik system all the more completely.

In Soviet foreign policy, the strong influence and energetic initiative of Leningrad's Party Secretary, A. A. Zhdanov, had made itself more and more felt since 1945. During the war he, as the most able and ambitious among Stalin's young collaborators, and often considered the heir presumptive, had kept in the background,[36] but now he began to become very active in cultural affairs and questions of foreign policy. As chairman of the Allied Control Commission in Finland, he at first kept himself in hand. He was the chief exponent of the doctrine of "two worlds," with which the Russians countered the American concept of "one world," and he soon became identifiable as one of the advocates of an aggressive Soviet foreign policy.

Zhdanov had clearly recognized that, since the beginning of the year, the American "patience with firmness" policy of the Byrnes era had been replaced by another attitude. This was General Marshall's "policy of containment," the theoretical basis of which had been provided by the head of the Planning Division of the State Department, the outstanding American expert on Russia, George F. Kennan, who first defined it in an anonymous article.[37] Zhdanov's reply to this declaration of America's basic Russian policy was a report on the international situation, which he gave at a Communist Congress in Wiliza Gora in Upper Silesia late in September 1947, at which he and Malenkov represented the Soviet Union. Zhdanov's report became a milestone in the history of Communist ideology, and a major part of the official resolutions of the Congress echoed it. It maintained that the world was split into two camps; as the United States had begun to organize the capitalist states for its aggressive plans, it was the duty of the "democratic" countries to unite for countermeasures. In September 1947, at a secret meeting place near Warsaw, the Comintern, which had been buried in 1943, was resurrected in the form of the Communist Information Bureau (Cominform), which was to coordinate world Communism. It was to consist of representatives of nine Communist parties, with its headquarters in Belgrade, and issue an information and news letter. The two Western Communist parties, the French and the Italian, were sharply criticized at this Congress. The leaders were exhorted to prepare the workers for battle and to make every effort to wreck the Marshall Plan and the whole American policy in Western Europe.

The effects of these new directives soon became apparent. In November, a wave of political strikes and social unrest began to flood France and Italy.[38] Even in the Soviet Union, the new policy induced the Party to stress once more the ideological element in a sector where it had been most consciously allowed to lapse during the war, i.e., in the Red Army, which, in 1946, had been renamed the "Soviet Army." New efforts to achieve a more intensive political education of the army and to establish a new disciplinary system[39] went hand in hand with Soviet rearmament.

The most profound consequences of the new course of world Communism, however, appeared in the satellite states, particularly in the Balkans. Here a fierce battle was waged, this time not against bourgeois opposition, but against opponents within the Party, a situation that led to the conflict between Stalin and Tito.

At the fifth meeting of the Foreign Ministers' Council in London in November and December 1947, the German question was re-opened, but again no agreement was achieved. Particularly heated were the debates concerning Soviet reparation demands, which General Marshall again turned down. The conference had to be broken off.

The failure of the London meeting was the last stage in a development that led from the attempt at collaboration between the Western powers and the Soviet Union to a profound estrangement. In the first half of 1948, the West promoted the reconstruction of Western Germany, including the unification of the three zones and the currency reform. In June 1948, the Soviet Union called the states of the Eastern bloc to a big conference of foreign ministers in Warsaw to frighten the satellites with the "German danger," thus pushing them into a closer relationship with Moscow. It is true that the conference set itself the goal of creating a provisional democratic government of a united Germany, which Zhdanov had already spoken of the year before. A peace treaty in accordance with the Potsdam conditions was to be concluded with this government and then the occupation troops were to be withdrawn. However, the interpretation of the word "democratic" was a symbol of the different languages spoken in the West and in the East. The conference also sharply attacked German efforts to bring about a border revision; the Oder-Neisse frontier was described as an immovable "peace border."

In the meantime, the breach in the common policy regarding the German question had already occurred. On March 20, 1948, after a heated debate, Sokolovsky left a meeting of the Allied Control Council in Berlin, thereby breaking it up. This was the end of the four-power government that had ruled Germany since its collapse; the division of Germany, which some months previously had already seemed inevitable, had become a reality.[40] The practical consequences of this fact became apparent in the Berlin blockade.

On March 31 of that year, rail and road communications to West Berlin had been made more difficult by the Soviets; these measures were tightened further in the following months, until they finally assumed the character of a regular blockade. The Cold War had entered a dangerous phase; at any time an accidental or provoked incident could lead to open hostilities.

At the same time, the conflict between the Soviet Union and Yugoslavia, on the one hand, and the aggressive policy that the Kremlin pursued in Korea, on the other, had created a very serious international situation.

Intensification of the Cold War, 1948–52

In the summer of 1948, the Cold War between the West and the East assumed extremely serious forms.

From August 4, the Berlin blockade cut off 2½ million people from the outside world and thus from all their sources of supply. Stalin appeared affable and ready to come to terms, but further discussions were invariably wrecked by Molotov's stubborn inflexibility, which was undoubtedly authorized by Stalin. Moscow held that the adequate provisioning of Berlin by air lift could not possibly be kept up through the whole winter, and it was believed that the population's will to resist would soon be broken and that the Western powers would be forced to give up the city.[41]

When the Western powers submitted the Berlin question to the United Nations Security Council, Stalin abandoned his geniality. He spoke of the Western powers' aggressiveness and again called Churchill the chief instigator of a new war. The Soviet Union had started to rearm some months before. Until then, the Red Army had undergone limited, partial demobilization.[42] In March 1947, General N. A. Bulganin had succeeded Stalin as Minister of the Armed Forces; Marshal I. S. Konev had been Army Commander in Chief since November 1946. Military appropriations claimed an increasingly large share of the budget. The expenditures of the defense ministries had risen from 66.7 billion rubles in 1940 to 137.9 billion rubles in 1944. By 1948, in the course of demobilization, they had fallen again to 66.1 billion, but rose to 79 billion rubles in 1949 and to 96.4 billion in 1951.[43] While the Soviets claimed that this development was caused by the military talks in Washington in the summer of 1948, which resulted in the Atlantic Pact, it should be noted that the latter were, in turn, partly motivated by the Berlin blockade.

Simultaneously with the rearmament of the Soviet Union, the Kremlin ordered the speedy organization of a People's Police in the East Zone of Germany. In the Soviet Union, domestic measures required by the rearmament policy ranged from the reorganization of the armed forces to the extensive tightening up of the Komsomol, the athletic leagues, and the trade unions, and included an administrative reform of the Party. The new industrial and agricultural policies were also strongly influenced by military considerations.

In the whole of Europe, particularly in Germany, nervous tension reached a climax in the late summer; further aggressive acts by the Soviet Union were believed to be forthcoming.[44]

In addition, there was open dissension between the Soviet Union and Yugoslavia. When the Cominform was created, Belgrade had been chosen as its permanent headquarters. Tito was considered the most important Communist leader in the Balkan countries, and Yugoslavia the model state among the satellites. For these reasons and also because of its geographical position in relation to the Communists of Western Europe, Belgrade occupied a key position. In April 1945, the Soviet Union and Yugoslavia signed a twenty-year friendship and alliance treaty. A Soviet military mission and an economic mission had been sent to Yugoslavia to integrate both the army and the national economy into the over-all plans of the Kremlin. Very soon disagreements arose. Tito realized that Stalin had assigned the role of a second-rate agricultural state to Yugoslavia and that there was a tendency to increase dependency on the Soviet Union in all areas. These considerations led to Tito's plan for a Balkan federation, which he discussed with the Bulgarian Communist leader G. Dimitrov, in Bled, in the summer of 1947. The plan had been in the making for some time; as early as 1944, the Communist leaders of Yugoslavia and Bulgaria had held consultations with this end in view. Now a joint communiqué announced their intention to open the border between the countries as soon as possible and to create a customs union. In a speech in Bucharest in January 1948, Dimitrov hinted that the future federation was also to be joined by Rumania, Albania, Hungary, and even Poland, Czechoslovakia, and Greece. This was more than Moscow could stand. A large Southeast European federation under Tito could become a dangerous competitor for the Soviet Union. Dimitrov was induced to dissociate himself publicly from Tito's plans in the Soviet press.

Against this background, the selection of Belgrade as the headquarters of the Cominform gains additional significance. It may be that P. F. Yudin,[45] who was appointed editor of the Cominform newspaper, had also been entrusted with other tasks, which were to test his qualities as keeper of the Marxist ideology in the field of the Kremlin's practical politics as well. Perhaps it was for these very reasons that he was dispatched to the seat of the infection that had to be uncovered.[46]

Tito's domestic policy also aroused suspicion in Moscow. The ruthlessness with which he enforced compulsory collectivization in Yugoslavia indicated that he wanted to forestall any Bolshevik accusations of ideological sluggishness. The Kremlin, however, was perfectly aware of the meaning of these tactics; Tito's course to the Left was proof of his watchfulness and could be taken as a declaration of war. While the Cominform office made attempts to subvert the Yugoslav Communists by organizing a Stalinist faction within the Party, the Moscow Politburo contacted the other Communist parties in order to isolate Tito.[47]

The break came in June 1948. Immediately following the return of the Yugoslav Deputy Premier, Kardelj, from a visit to Moscow —which had yielded no results, as he had refused to submit to Stalin's dictates—the Soviet Union recalled its entire military mission from Yugoslavia with the explanation that it was "surrounded by an atmosphere of hostility." Subsequently all civilian missions left the country as well. On June 29, when the Berlin crisis was nearing its climax, the Cominform paper published its first attack on Tito. Yugoslavia was expelled from the Soviet family of peoples, and the seat of the Cominform was transferred to Bucharest. The preparations that the Cominform paper had made under Yudin's supervision in its theoretical discussions from January to June were now put into effect. In a large-scale campaign, the programs and membership of all East European Communist parties were to be subjected to a thorough investigation.

As early as July, the Polish and Bulgarian parties were asked to revise their doctrine. In Poland, Communist Party Secretary Gomulka confessed his errors, was removed from office, and was arrested. In Bulgaria, Dimitrov and Kostov were played off against one another. After denouncing Kostov in January 1949, Dimitrov left for Moscow on sick leave from which he did not return. In March, Kostov was found guilty of nationalist deviations and removed from office; he was arrested in June 1949. In Albania, Communist leader Koci Xoxe was hanged that same month, a fate that was also meted out to Hungarian Party Secretary Rajk in the fall of that year.[48]

However, efforts to smother Tito's opposition by means of a thorough coordination of all other Communist parties in the satellite states were of no avail. At first, Tito fought a paper war in his notes to the Politburo of the Soviet Union; then he countered Soviet pressure with domestic measures, and, when diplomatic relations between the two countries were broken off, he successfully established contact with the West. In Titoism, Stalinism found an ideologically dangerous opponent, for its example might at any time be followed by others, even if there existed no marked differences of political principle. Stalin himself had, in a sense, pioneered the nationalist Communist authoritarian state. Now that so much real power was at his disposal, he naturally believed that he could thwart a similar development elsewhere.

At times, it appeared that a military expedition might be launched against Tito. At a time when the attention of the world was concentrated on Berlin, the moment seemed opportune. However, in attempting such an action Stalin could not, in the last resort, have relied on the neighboring Balkan states, and the direct military use of Soviet troops would have presented great strategic difficulties, as well as the danger of enlarging the war to an extent he would not have wanted.

In view of the difficulties in the Balkans, the focus of Soviet expansionism shifted in some degree from Europe to Asia toward the end of 1948. A connection has been suspected between this and Zhdanov's sudden death on August 31, 1948, and it has been thought that the heart attack that felled him at the age of 52 was the consequence of violent debates in the Politburo over the Berlin and Yugoslav questions. Zhdanov is said to have favored military operations, if not against Berlin—i.e., against the Western powers—then against Tito, a proposal that was turned down by the majority of the Politburo, including Stalin. It is well known, of course, that Zhdanov was the proponent of an aggressive policy in Europe. However, it is easy to dramatize matters and thereby oversimplify them. The rumors of Zhdanov's violent death[49] were not authenticated; they apparently originated in the differences existing between him and the Malenkov-Beria-Khrushchev "group."[50]

The fact remains that at the end of the year a certain readiness on the part of the Soviet Union to come to an understanding with the West became noticeable. In an interview with Kingsbury Smith, the European head of the International News Service, on January 27,

1949, Stalin said he was prepared to consider a joint declaration of peace with the United States and to meet with President Truman on Polish or Czech territory. However, when the new Secretary of State, Dean Acheson, declared that the solution of the Berlin question was a prerequisite to such a meeting, the Kremlin failed to take concrete steps. Instead, the East European pact system was completed by mutual aid pacts between Rumania and Poland and between Czechoslovakia and Hungary (both signed in 1949), and was further cemented by the establishment of an East European Economic Council.

At the beginning of March 1949, the world was surprised by the unexpected resignation of Molotov, who had been Soviet Foreign Minister for many years. Like his colleagues Mikoyan, Bulganin, and Beria, Molotov was relieved of his office, without, however, losing his influence or prestige, as had been erroneously supposed in the West. The fact that he was replaced by A. Y. Vishinski, formerly a Deputy Foreign Minister, gave the Soviet Union the advantage of being represented at sessions of the United Nations Security Council and in other UN bodies by a man whose vitriolic language and astuteness in negotiations were suited to the increasing international tensions. In reality, there were no fundamental changes, and even the temporary concentration of Soviet attention on the Far East did not mean more than a shifting from the right foot to the left. The change from Zhdanov's policy to that of Molotov and Vishinski simply meant that a strategy of annihilation was replaced by one of attrition.

During 1949, it became apparent that Soviet activities were increasing in the Far East. Soviet troops had evacuated North Korea at the end of 1948. Now, in March 1949, an agreement for economic and cultural cooperation was concluded with the Communist "Korean People's Republic." A new satellite state had been created whose aggressive aims toward non-Communist South Korea were given the necessary backing. At the same time, the Chinese Communists successfully continued their advance, which had begun in October 1948. In April 1949, they crossed the Yangtze and occupied Nanking. At the end of the year, the whole of China was under Mao Tse-tung's influence, with the exception of Formosa and Tibet. The Chinese People's Republic, which had been created in October, was immediately recognized by the Soviet Union and linked to Moscow by a number of agreements.

In December, Mao Tse-tung went to Moscow. He was the world's only top Communist leader who had never been there. He had not always seen eye to eye with the Comintern or with the Politburo, and, as late as 1945, Moscow had not believed that he would manage to overthrow Chiang Kai-shek. Now, however, the number of Russian advisers in Red China grew rapidly. Would the Soviet Union also succeed in taking this country in tow as a satellite? It was the first Communist state that had a larger population than that of the Soviet Union, the dominant power in the proletarian world. This circumstance alone made it advisable for Stalin to take China's special position into account.

On February 14, 1950, a thirty-year pact of friendship, alliance, and mutual aid was concluded in Moscow between the two countries. The Soviet Union relinquished its special privileges in the South Manchurian Railroad and its occupation of Dairen and Port Arthur as of the date of the Japanese peace treaty, but not later than 1952.[51] Stalin tried to explain to the Chinese that he had claimed these privileges in 1945 only because he distrusted Chiang Kai-shek. In reality, Manchuria as a whole remained dependent on Russia. Its exploitation and closer association with the Russian Far Eastern provinces had constantly been striven for; it was undoubtedly one of the crucial touchstones of the friendship between Moscow and Peking. In a second agreement on September 25, 1952, further consolidating Moscow-Peking relations, the Manchurian Railroad was returned to China, but Soviet troops, at China's request, remained in Port Arthur.[52] Beyond that, however, Sinkiang and Inner Mongolia, an ancient province of the Chinese Empire, remained partially within the Soviet sphere of interest.

The significance of the victory of the Chinese Communists was stressed by Malenkov in a speech on November 6, 1949. He referred to Lenin's words of 1923, according to which the outcome of the international struggle between capitalism and Communism depended in the last resort on the latter's victory in Russia, India, and China, whose combined populations represented the overwhelming majority of mankind. After the victory of the Communists in China, the countries of the people's democracies in Europe and Asia, together with the Soviet Union, comprised about 800 million people.[53]

It was no accident that India was mentioned prominently by Malenkov. The transformation of India and Pakistan from British colonies into sovereign republics within the British Commonwealth had been closely watched by Moscow and raised some hopes that, at first, could not be realized in the field of propaganda. These hopes, however—reaching beyond China—caused the Russians to stir up unrest in French Indochina and to cast an attentive eye on Indonesia.

Soviet interest was even more strongly aroused by events in the Middle East. In Iran, Moscow noted with pleasure all the indications of a coming Anglo-Iranian conflict; the same was true in Egypt. During the Arab-Jewish conflict, the Soviet antipathy toward Zionism had been unmistakable. All the more surprising was the rapidity with which it recognized Israel in 1948, but this turned out to be nothing but a passing gesture, which soon gave way to growing hostility, culminating in the Soviet anti-Semitism of the last months of the Stalin era. Bolshevik propaganda was all the time assiduously engaged in finding points of infiltration in the Arab camp. In Syria and Lebanon, Communist parties of some size came into being; they received backing from the Soviet legation in Beirut, which became the propaganda headquarters for the Middle East. Similar footholds for Communist agitation among the native population of Africa were found in Addis Ababa and Johannesburg. On the West Coast, and also in Kenya, movements for autonomy among the Negroes were often skillfully exploited by the Communists for their own purposes.[54]

In addition to agitation by the Party, Soviet propaganda was also versed in the use of other vehicles of expansion. The Greek Orthodox Church had in Czarist times served the state both in its centralizing efforts within the country and by influencing religious dissenters beyond the border. Since peace was made between the Soviet government and the Russian Patriarchate during the Second World War, the increasingly friendly ties between Moscow and the Orthodox religious communities and clerical dignitaries in the Near East were likewise adroitly exploited for Bolshevik ends. Not only did the Moscow Church Assembly of 1948 align itself with the general campaign against the West, but the visits of Russian bishops in the Near East contributed to the growing prestige of the Soviet Union among both Christians and non-Christians. It was, however, not possible in 1948 to prevent the election of the Metropolitan Athenagoras, a pronounced foe of Bolshevism, to the Patriarchate of Constantinople.[55]

Besides the Greek Orthodox Church, the 20 million Muhammadans in the Soviet Union have been permitted to form a religious community with a spiritual leader, the Grand Mufti of Ufa; the Uzbek University in Bukhara was to compete with the Arab University in Cairo as the spiritual center of the Muhammadan world. This opened up ever greater vistas for the expansion of Soviet influence in the Arab countries, Iran, Albania, and Pakistan.[56] Muhammadan dervishes making their pilgrimage to Mecca are frequently Communist agitators, who have been specially trained for this purpose in a school at Tashkent.

Lenin's old dictum concerning the necessity of awakening the colonial and semi-colonial world poses great tasks for Soviet policy in South America, too. With a view to splitting the Western world, Moscow needs to promote not only the growing self-assertion of the indigenous Indian masses against the Spanish-descended ruling class, but also the South American nations' increasing independence from the economic influence of the United States.

Lastly, Soviet activities in the Arctic and Antarctic regions, which have increased considerably since the opening of the northern sea route along the coast of Siberia, complete the survey of the Bolshevik empire's international position. Here economic interests in whaling and Spitsbergen coal coincide with important interests in routes of communication of strategic and trade value.[57]

Meanwhile, the Western powers continued their efforts to integrate the non-Bolshevik world. The signing of the Atlantic Treaty and the merging of the three Western zones of Germany in April 1949 was followed in September by the creation of the West German Federal Republic. The Kremlin reacted with most aggressive language, particularly toward the United States. At the end of the year, the tenor of official speeches in Moscow became more and more menacing. It was noticeable that these threats were accompanied by a feeling of triumphant certainty of an imminent major crisis in America. Thus, on November 7, 1949, Malenkov spoke of 18 million allegedly unemployed in the United States, forecasting the possibility of a more active policy toward a foe disorganized by internal crisis. However, the new year brought disillusionment, and, surprisingly, E. Varga, who had long been in disfavor, was the first to dare write of these false hopes in an article in *Pravda*. Two possibilities were open to the Soviet government to counter the consolidation of the West: through propaganda by means of a general peace offensive or through power politics by means of a strong German policy. The peace offensive started with the "First World Congress of the Partisans of Peace," which met in Paris and Prague in April 1949, and led to the creation of a permanent committee and a secretariat.[58] A similar congress in Warsaw, in November 1950, transformed the committee into a World Peace Council, to which representatives of fifty-eight nations belonged. An extensive collection of signatures for peace, as Moscow defined it, brought 600 million names, among which were those of several more or less unsuspecting prominent personalities in the West. In a long chain of peace congresses in Vienna, Stock-

holm, and elsewhere, appeals were addressed to the United Nations
and to the world at large, advocating the recognition of Communist
China, as well as a solution of the German question according to
the Soviet formula. In December 1952, the Peace Council arranged
a "Congress of Nations for the Maintenance of Peace" in Vienna;
this had been preceded, in October, by a "Peace Congress of the
Peoples of Asia and the Pacific Area" in Peking.

The strong Soviet policy toward Germany followed the concept
that had led, during the war, to the creation of the National
Committee for a Free Germany in Moscow. Its most prominent
advocate in the Politburo was Beria.[59] After Zhdanov's death, this
concept gained even wider acceptance. Other parties were permitted to exist alongside the Socialist Unity Party in East Germany,
and every attempt was made to establish contact with German
nationalist circles. The most important exponent of this trend in
Berlin was the political adviser of Marshal Sokolovsky, Ambassador Semyonov; his opponent, Colonel Tulpanov, was recalled
at the end of 1949.

In direct answer to the creation of the West German Federal
Republic, the Soviet Union set up the East German Democratic
Republic, headed by Wilhelm Pieck and Otto Grotewohl. In a
grandiloquent congratulatory telegram, Stalin celebrated this event
as a "turning point in the history of Europe."[60] In line with this
policy, in November 1949, the Soviet Military Government was
converted into a Control Commission, directed by General
Chuikov. Soviet support for the new satellite, however, did not
include concessions in the border question. Grotewohl's government had publicly to accept the Oder-Neisse line. When the German Democratic Republic was finally included in the Soviet pact
system in May 1950, reparations were reduced by 50%, but the
agreements that the East Berlin government concluded with Poland,
Czechoslovakia, Rumania, Hungary, and Bulgaria, in the summer
of 1950, meant, in fact, both the cession of the East German
territories beyond the Oder and the Neisse and consent to the expulsion of the German populations from these areas.

As regards Poland, its territorial gains were balanced by its
continuously growing integration into the Soviet scheme of things,
to which it was more rigorously subjected than any of the other
East European people's democracies. In November 1949, General
Rokossovsky was appointed Marshal of Poland and Commander
in Chief of the Polish armed forces. This was a step that deeply
wounded Polish national pride, despite the Marshal's Polish origin.
The resulting bolshevization of the country went hand in hand with

an increasing russification. That the nation was not prepared to submit willingly is evidenced by the Polish officers' conspiracy, which was uncovered in the summer of 1951. In a show trial of four generals and other high-ranking officers, the former General Secretary of the Polish Communist Party, Gomulka, was also heavily incriminated. The defendants were accused of espionage on behalf of the Western powers and the Polish government-in-exile, and also of having planned the return of the Polish "Western territories" to Germany.

Apart from the Berlin blockade and the conflict with Tito, the international situation was further endangered in the summer of 1950 by the outbreak of war in Korea. On June 26, 1950, troops of the North Korean People's Army crossed the demarcation line on the 38th parallel and invaded South Korea. The Kremlin's indirect support of the Korean Communists was dictated by the desire to gain in South Korea a substitute for the Chinese ports whose return had been promised for February 14 of that year. At the same time, Moscow hoped once again to divert the attention of the West from Europe and to delay West European integration. Like Czarist policy during the second half of the 19th century, which had almost rhythmically alternated between the Balkans (1854, 1877, 1885, 1912-13, 1914) and Central or East Asia (1860, 1864, 1884, 1895, 1903-4, 1910), Soviet policy aimed its heavy guns of propaganda, diplomacy, and military threats alternately at Central Europe including the Near East, and at the Far East, thus exercising continuous, but subtly evasive, pressure on the Western world. In 1947, in an article that has since become a classic, George Kennan wrote:

> The policy of the Kremlin can be compared to a current of water which steadily moves toward its goal along all the paths open to it. . . . Even the most hidden corners in the river bed of world politics must be infiltrated. However, if insurmountable obstacles present themselves on the one or the other path, they are accepted philosophically. The decisive point is that an uninterrupted, steady pressure is exercised in the direction of the final goal.[61]

The shift of Soviet interest to the Far East was favored by the intervention of Communist China in the Korean War at the end of 1950. However, the expectation that the United States would abandon its plans in Europe, and especially in Germany, as a result of the troubles it faced in the Pacific now that it had committed American troops to fighting in South Korea was not fulfilled. On the contrary, just at that time—toward the end of 1950—French politicians took up and actively promoted American proposals for the integration of Europe's economic and military strength. Only in one regard were Soviet intentions realized: They managed once again to bring the Western powers to the conference table after several exploratory notes and official declarations by both Stalin and Truman had been exchanged.

From March to June 1951, a conference of the Deputy Foreign Ministers of the four Great Powers met in Paris. However, the wearying sessions brought no agreement on the agenda for a proposed Foreign Ministers' Conference in Washington. The preliminary talks were broken off, as the Western powers were not willing to let the Atlantic Pact come under discussion. Furthermore, not being able to torpedo the preparations for the rearmament of Germany, the Kremlin also could not prevent the signing of the peace treaty between the United States and Japan in San Francisco in September, 1951, or the resultant American-Japanese security pact.

As in the spring of 1949, the Russians again produced the supposed trump card of an over-all German policy. In the summer of 1951, Stalin sent Malenkov to Berlin. The result of his talks was an appeal by East Germany to West Germany to join in all German talks on the holding of elections for a national assembly, thus to speed the conclusion of a peace treaty. In the eyes of the West, however, these proposals were devoid of any guarantees for really impartial elections. When the West spelled out what it considered free elections, Russia rejected the Western definition.

The tension between the Soviet Union and the United States was heightened in June 1951, when the American-Soviet trade agreement of 1937—which at first had been renewed annually, but since 1942 was to remain in force permanently—was abrogated. Negotiations regarding Soviet Lend-Lease debts to the United States foundered on Moscow's refusal to pay more than $300 million (Washington had demanded $800 million). American support of the amalgamation of Russian and East Central European emigrant organizations created a lot of bad feeling in Moscow, and George F. Kennan, appointed U.S. Ambassador to the Soviet Union in 1952, was given a very cool reception.

The Soviets were also particularly perturbed about the extension of the Atlantic Community to the Eastern Mediterranean. The admission of Greece and Turkey fortified the Soviet Union in its resolution to create neutral buffer zones in Europe and the Near East between the two power blocs. This new trend became noticeable at the end of 1951, in an exchange of notes on this subject

with Norway, Italy, and Turkey, in Soviet appeals for Swiss and
Swedish neutrality, a New Year message to Japan, and the plan
of an armed neutrality pact of the Scandinavian countries, which
was suggested via Finland. The Soviet note on Germany of March
10, 1952, was also in the same vein.

On March 10, 1952, the Soviet government addressed a note to
the United States, proposing a peace treaty with Germany in accordance with the Potsdam Agreement. Germany was to receive
an all-German government and its own armed forces. Occupation
troops were to be withdrawn. In itself, the Soviet proposal was
nothing new; it had been put forward previously at the eight-power
conference of the Eastern bloc in Prague, in October 1951. The
reference to the Potsdam Agreement meant the maintenance of the
Oder-Neisse line and the participation of the Soviet Union in the
control of the Ruhr. New, however, was the plan for an armed and
neutral Germany that the Kremlin now proposed.[62] This idea was
part of an over-all plan to create a belt of neutral countries from
Scandinavia to the Mediterranean, as a kind of safety zone for the
protection of the Soviet Union against the West.

The Soviet note was shortly followed by three others, all of
which the Western powers answered. Differences of opinion arose
over how the all-German elections were to be carried out, and the
West German Federal Republic objected in particular to a prohibition of alliances for a reunited Germany. On May 26, 1952, a
general treaty with the Western powers was concluded in Bonn,
which meant the end of the occupation and the restoration of freedom of action in foreign affairs. Soviet commentators spoke of this
as the creation of a West German protectorate and the perpetua-
tion of a divided Germany.[63] Moscow was just as much disturbed
by the signing of the European Defense Pact in Paris on May 27
of that year. Now the radical wing of the German Socialist Unity
Party in the Soviet zone attempted to carry out complete socialization. The civil service was reorganized according to the Russian
model and rearmament was speeded up. At the borders with the
Federal Republic a state of emergency was declared.

On the international plane, large-scale propaganda operations
were initiated to thwart Western integration. A World Economic
Conference, which met in Moscow in April 1952, also received
some attention outside the Iron Curtain without, however, having
any concrete results. The same was true of the Moscow Church
Conference of May 1952, which issued an appeal for world peace.

In the Asiatic-Pacific area, the American-Japanese peace treaty
and the Pacific Pact, which went into effect in April, presented an

effective barrier to Soviet expansion in East Asia. Japanese rearmament influenced the Korean War and placed the Communist side
in a more unfavorable position. In view of this, it was understandable that all disarmament discussions, quite apart from the difficult
question of the atom bomb, collapsed. A new proposal by the
Western powers to call a disarmament conference of the five Great
Powers, including China, was turned down by the Kremlin in
August. Here, too, the Soviet drive for security on its own terms,
which arose from both the actual situation and a pathological fear,
was decisive.

In the summer of 1952, American foreign policy reached a great
turning point: "Containment" was replaced by a policy of the "roll-
back" of Russian power. For John Foster Dulles, Eisenhower's
adviser on foreign policy, the theories that Kennan had formulated
and Acheson put into practice were not sufficiently active and dynamic. The new policy hoped to bring about a revolutionary situation in the satellite states by supporting anti-Communist trends;
the word "liberation" entered political discussion. As a result, the
Soviet rulers were faced with the urgent necessity of re-examining
their own foreign policy. This was one of the reasons why, in
October 1952, Stalin convened the Nineteenth Congress of the
Communist Party of the Soviet Union, which had been due for the
last ten years.

The Nineteenth Party Congress and Stalin's Death

The Party congresses of the Communist Party of the Soviet
Union had, during Lenin's lifetime, been one of the unquestioned
events that, like the Soviet congresses, occurred annually and, in
appearance at least, met the democratic needs of the people. In
1926, the Party congress was not held for the first time, and after
that it met only about every three or five years,[64] ceasing to meet
entirely after the Eighteenth Congress in March 1939. For more
than ten years, Party functionaries and members waited in vain
for the convening of a congress, despite the fact that the party
regulations of 1939 provided for a meeting at least every three
years and a conference once a year. The Second World War was
used as an excuse for this omission, even long after it was over.

The last Party conference on the Union level had met in 1941.
Since then, the executive organs of the Party had pursued their
activities without constitutional authority, filling vacant offices by
cooption whenever necessary. During this period, the Party had
changed its structure. Lenin's elite party had become a mass

party.[65] The high war losses—more than 600,000 Party members —were largely replaced by new admissions. The Party lost its predominantly proletarian character. It is significant that, as early as 1934, details concerning the class background of the members were omitted in official publications in order to hide the drop in the number of workers and peasants and the increase in the new class of functionaries.[66] The Party had thus become more and more the special interest organ of the functionaries, the *"apparatchiki."* At the same time, the execution of Party functions had been taken over by an all-powerful Party bureaucracy and its autocratic leadership, against which the old Bolsheviks had sounded the alarm in their time.

Nevertheless, the Party bureaucracy had the advantage over the two other keystones of the Bolshevik state—the police and the armed forces—in that it rested on a broader basis, namely the Party as a whole. Nevertheless, a certain unrest had arisen since the end of the war, which had to be attributed to the natural conflict between the still dynamic forces of the Party and the rigid conservative tendencies of the bureaucracy. It would be incorrect to call this a loss of confidence in the Western sense; yet, it was indisputable that the Party leadership had suffered a certain loss of prestige through its failure to realize the vainglorious ambitions of Zhdanov and the Cominform in foreign affairs and of Khrushchev's agrarian revolution at home. The Party leadership probably was at least sufficiently aware of the discontent to recognize the need for convening a Party congress.

At the end of 1952, at last, the time had come. At home and abroad, great things were expected from this Congress. Its results represented, in some respects, a milestone in the post-war development of the Soviet Union.

The Nineteenth Party Congress met from October 5 to October 15, in Moscow. The prominence given to G. M. Malenkov among the supreme party hierarchy created a considerable stir. Having in the meantime advanced to the position of Deputy General Secretary, he, rather than Molotov, delivered the great report in Stalin's place. Of domestic importance was the change in the Party's name; it shed the term *Bolsheviki,* which had until then always been added to its title. It was argued that the name had arisen in opposition to the *Mensheviki* and was now only of historical significance. The Politburo, which for a long time had enjoyed an odious reputation both at home and abroad, was changed into a Presidium of the Central Committee, and the Organization Bureau (Orgburo) was dissolved. As a result, the Secretariat of the Central Commit-

tee, which Malenkov ruled and which had been increased to ten
members, now occupied the key position in the Party, far more
important than the Presidium of the Central Committee, which,
with twenty-five members and eleven candidates, was in any case
an unwieldy body.

One of the most important tasks of the Nineteenth Party Congress was approval of the Fifth Five Year Plan (1951-55). Stalin's
giant construction plans for the expansion of power output continued to occupy a central position. The hydroelectric works at
Kuibyshev were to be finished by 1955, those at Stalingrad by
1957. These two mammoth power plants were to conclude the
"Greater Volga Project." It had been begun with the construction
of the Volga-Moscow Canal in 1937, and had been continued with
the canal system connecting the Baltic with the White Sea, the construction of the Rybinsk reservoir with the power plant Shcherba-
kov, and the Uglich power plant on the Volga. Apart from producing electric power, these reservoirs were used for the irrigation
of nearly 15 million acres of arid land. The "Greater Volga Project"
was followed by the "Greater Dnieper Project." The hydroelectric
power plant at Kakhovka, not far from the river mouth, was put
into operation in 1956. About 3.7 million acres of steppe land
near the Black Sea and in the Crimea were irrigated by it.[67]

It was obvious that apart from increasing soil fertility in the
south and southeast, the power output was intended to serve the
armament industry; everything was to be done in order to break
the most critical bottleneck in Soviet armaments, the manufacture
of atom bombs. The necessary human labor force was readily available for this "social system based on water power" in the concentration camps and prisoner of war camps.

While these things were barely mentioned in Malenkov's report
to the Nineteenth Party Congress,[68] all the more emphasis was
placed on the concrete achievements of the Soviet economy. There
was surprisingly sharp criticism, disclosing difficulties and obstacles in the production process. Thus, it could not be denied
that the output of consumer goods lagged behind that of machine
tools. As a result of uneven, spasmodic production, due in the main
to mistakes in planning, output was poor in many plants. In agriculture, Khrushchev's plan for the continuous merging of individual
kolkhozes into giant collective farms met with resistance, and in
many instances also led to a falling off in production.

The line followed by the Congress in foreign affairs was closely
connected with the views concerning the international economic
situation, on which Stalin expounded on the eve of the Nineteenth

Party Congress in a special essay concerning the "Economic Problems of Socialism in the Soviet Union."[69] This essay was interpreted as Stalin's political testament, similar to Lenin's last essay in 1922 on the cooperatives.[70] Inevitably, however, the question arose as to how far the dictator, whom death had already marked, was still capable of an intellectual effort that abruptly departed from the line maintained in the letters on language in 1950. Perhaps the essay was a collective effort of the Party theoreticians, who had received instructions for it from the functionaries who were waiting to succeed Stalin.

After 1949, a struggle between two ideological interpretations had been noticeable. One was expressed during the war by N. A. Voznesensky in *"The Economy of the USSR During World War II,* which had been published in 1947 and awarded the Stalin Prize. Its views completely mirrored the emphasis that Stalin had placed, in his letters on language, on the role of the state "as the chief instrument for the development of Communism." However, in July 1949, the Central Committee opposed Voznesensky's view, because he had described the laws of the socialist economy as "subjectivist and voluntaristic." In actual fact, they said, the state could not arbitrarily change the economic laws of socialist society through planning. After that, Voznesensky's name received no further public mention. His execution was confirmed by Khrushchev in February 1956.

The attitude of the Central Committee reflected certain conflicts within the top Party circle, which, in turn, reflected the undeniable oscillations in the power and personal relationships around the aging Stalin, and which had started with the death of Zhdanov. While Stalin himself, supported by the official press (e.g., *Pravda,* on October 5, 1950), was still singing the praises of the strong state, the steam roller of the revolving general line moved on. In Stalin's new essay of 1952, this forward movement was duly taken into account. "The laws of political economy in the case of socialism," it stated, "are objective laws. They reflect the inflexible logic of the processes of economic life, which take their course independently of our will." A warning is expressed against "adventurers who want to create new laws without understanding and considering the objective laws."[71] Thus, the verdict against Voznesensky's theory was now handed down in Stalin's name as well, just as it had previously been pronounced on Pokrovsky's theories. The theory of the "revolution from above" was also officially displaced by emphatic stress on the iron laws of economic determinism. Political action once more became secondary to economic processes as the basis of all social phenomena.

With regard to the international political situation, Stalin termed the disintegration of the homogeneous and all-inclusive world market the most important economic result of the Second World War. This disintegration had led to a shrinking of the economic basis of the great capitalist powers, and would result in deepening the general crisis of the capitalist system. Specifically, this would mean that France and England, as well as Germany, Italy, and Japan, would in due course emerge from their dependence on the United States. There could be no doubt of the resurgence of Germany and Japan, and for that reason wars between capitalist countries were more likely than an anti-Bolshevik crusade against the Soviet Union. These thoughts were underscored in Malenkov's major speech to the Congress and in Stalin's final address on October 14. Interestingly enough, the usual statement about the possibility of peaceful coexistence between the two great world systems was accompanied by the promise that, if the Western powers would give up their offensive posture, the Soviets would refrain from further revolutionary expansion in order to re-establish a uniform world market.

Regarding foreign policy, the Nineteenth Party Congress represented a transition to a defensive strategy. According to Stalin, the world revolution was a lengthy process made up of several phases: Periods of revolutionary flood follow times of revolutionary ebb.[72] From the Kremlin viewpoint, the years from 1939 to 1952 represent a time of flood, which suggested an offensive strategy, supported by the Red Army. The growing resistance of the West, the plans for European integration, and the beginning of rearmament in West Germany and Japan caused the Kremlin to shift its emphasis from nationalist and military expansion to military security. The Soviet Union needed a breathing spell to consolidate its strength and bring its state of military preparedness in line with that of the United States.

By no manner of means, however, did this represent a renunciation of an active foreign policy. For its own basic purposes, the Kremlin would, as an analysis of the Nineteenth Party Congress shows, try by every method to prevent European integration and military consolidation, especially by furthering the differences between the great powers and by increasing their internal difficulties. This means that, as before 1939, the tools of revolutionary propaganda, secret subversion, the popular front, and secret diplomacy would receive priority. For the Western world, this meant in domestic issues an intensification of the Kremlin's efforts to gain the adherence of the liberal and nationalist-isolationist intellectuals, and in foreign affairs an intensified drive to establish Europe as a "Third Force," with the aim of isolating the United States.

The Nineteenth Party Congress was an impressive parade of world Communism, clearly documenting the tremendous accretion of power of the Soviet Union under the leadership of the "Father of Peoples." The many foreign Communist leaders who had gathered in Moscow, in addition to the 1,359 Soviet Communist leaders, probably did not fail to be impressed by the shift of the balance of power from the non-Soviet Communist parties to Stalin's empire, with its concentrated political, economic, and military strength. The question was whether the feeling inspired by the show of Soviet strength was not marred by oppressive undertones. Since the conflict with Tito, every Western Communist leader could be a potential Titoist, and the mere possibility of such a development resulted in an even more undisguised demand on Moscow's part for a uniform alignment of world Communism with the theses of the Congress.

In the period between the Nineteenth Party Congress and Stalin's death, the winter of 1952-53, several events took place that now seem like dark harbingers of the coming change.

The significance of the formation of groups within the party leadership should not be overemphasized; nor should personal differences be dramatized. But it seems, nonetheless, that after the great purge of the 1930's, two groups emerged in the Kremlin— one promoting a nationalist-Russian trend around Zhdanov, the other stressing supranational and Soviet concepts around Beria and Malenkov. From both foreign and domestic Soviet policy, one can deduce the presence of differences between the two groups, which were exacerbated by personal rivalry among their proponents and adherents.[73] This did not rule out cooperation on certain questions, especially unconditional loyalty to Stalin, or shifts and controversies within the groups. It was significant that, at times, Malenkov bowed to Zhdanov's intellectual superiority, primarily in the years 1945-47, when the latter again directed Soviet cultural policy.

Stalin's successor, Georgi Maximilianovich Malenkov, was Stalin's own creature. He was the prototype of the *apparatchik* of the Stalin era and, like his master, he rose not in the glare of the footlights of the political stage, but rather in the background, in the party bureaucracy. Malenkov was born in 1902, in Orenburg (Chkalov); little is known of his origin.[74] His father appears to have been a subaltern Cossack officer.[75] During the Civil War, he won his spurs in the Party as Commissar on the Turkestan front. He attended the Technological Institute in Moscow, which he left with an engineering degree. At that time, he came to Stalin's attention. As a representative of the younger generation, Malenkov was put into Stalin's private secretariat and the Party apparatus. Stalin's private secretariat, which Malenkov headed together with Poskrebyshev, became the basis of his growing power. In the years of the great purge and the establishment of Stalin's unlimited autocracy, Malenkov gained a position of confidence, which secured for him a substantial share in the events of those years. In 1939, he became a Secretary of the Central Committee and member of the Orgburo; at the same time he held the important position of the head of the Personnel Department of the Central Committee. His close, confidential relationship with Beria began at that time. After the Soviet Union became involved in the Second World War, both Malenkov and Beria were appointed to the National Defense Committee, the inner war cabinet. Perhaps it was more than coincidence that in the decisive stage of the Battle of Stalingrad, Malenkov was sent to the endangered front sector as special Party emissary, just as Stalin had been during the Civil War. Subsequently, he was responsible for the successful reorganization of the aircraft industry and, after the end of the war, for reconstruction in the reconquered territories. Together with Beria, Malenkov was made a full member of the Politburo in 1946.

The rivalry between Malenkov and Zhdanov was brought into the open again shortly before the latter's death, since Malenkov advocated a more cautious foreign policy, especially in the conflict with Tito. It is undeniable that Zhdanov's sudden death decisively aided Malenkov's rise to power. Allied with Beria and Khrushchev, he succeeded in regaining his leading position in the Party by purging the apparatus of Zhdanov's followers and limiting the influence of the older Party members. In this connection, even Molotov was occasionally relegated to the background. Of more far-reaching effect was the removal of N. A. Voznesensky; his departure from the Politburo in 1949 sealed his doom. A. A. Andreyev, the opponent of Khrushchev's revolutionary agrarian policy, suffered demotion in 1952. A considerable number of other followers of Zhdanov, of whom the best known were A. A. Kuznetsov and A. N. Kosygin, were shelved or disappeared from the scene.[76] The attention accorded Malenkov's fiftieth birthday on January 8, 1952, by *Pravda* was unusual; it published a large picture of him on the front page—a distinction heretofore reserved for Stalin.

The Nineteenth Party Congress placed Malenkov second in the Party leadership, immediately after Stalin. The group represented by him now gained the upper hand in the Secretariat and in the Presidium of the Central Committee. At the same time, though, the dividing line between the two factions became blurred. What took place during the following winter behind the scenes of the Doctors' Trial almost looks like an attempt of the older members of the Politburo and other foes of the Malenkov-Beria-Khrushchev *troika* to restrict the influence of that group, though it can also be interpreted as heralding Beria's downfall. Whether Malenkov was the moving spirit here or merely went along, must be left undecided.

On January 13, 1953, *Pravda* published an account of an indictment of nine Soviet doctors, who were alleged to have caused the deaths of leading Soviet personages by wrong diagnoses and sabotage in treatment and who were said to have "planned further assassinations" for the future.[77] Among their victims had been Zhdanov. It was significant that the newspaper campaign against the defendants used the fact that six of them were Jews for an irresponsible campaign against "Cosmopolitanism and Zionism," entirely along the line of the cultural policies of the Zhdanov era. The simultaneous trial of the General Secretary of the Czechoslovak Communist Party, Slansky, employed similar anti-Semitic tactics. The upshot was a diplomatic conflict between the State of Israel and the Soviet Union.

The deeper reasons for the growing anti-Semitism of the Bolsheviks[78] must be sought in a situation not dissimilar to that existing during the Czarist era. What then impelled the Jews into the ranks of the revolutionaries made them suspect in the eyes of the Soviets —their opposition to the authoritarian state, their internationalism, their critical minds.[79] But the prime cause for starting the trial of the Soviet physicians without shrinking from the attending embarrassment lay somewhere else—in the rivalry of the two leading groups in the Kremlin, which assumed increasingly bitter forms in the winter of 1952-53. The sudden attack by one faction in January opened a chink in the curtain hiding the internal struggle for power; it was now entering a dangerous phase. The arrest of the doctors seems to have been initiated by S. D. Ignatyev, the recently appointed Minister for State Security, an opponent of Beria. One theory that has been advanced to explain the arrests suggests that, by removing the leading Kremlin physicians, Stalin would be deprived of his accustomed medical guardians and could thus become the victim of new plots.[80] But he himself agreed to the arrests. A much more convincing theory was that the Doctors' Trial was a countermove of Zhdanov's former followers, undertaken with Molotov's knowledge and approval and with the participation of some members of the military. As Stalin's death became more probable, this faction lost more and more ground and may well have desired to make things difficult for Malenkov and Beria. But in his great secret speech, Khrushchev attributed to Stalin sole responsibility for initiating this trial. In the inner circles of the Kremlin, and radiating from there into the outside world, a strange atmosphere of uneasiness and uncertainty made itself felt, such as had not been experienced with the same intensity since the great *Chistka*. Seen from an international viewpoint, the "Doctors' Plot" of January 1953, the increasing fear of espionage and its accompanying calls for watchfulness, and the renewed ideological attacks on Soviet scientists and artists, which grew in number toward the end of the year, were all part of the almost pathological nervousness with which the Soviet Union reacted to Eisenhower's inauguration as President.[81] At times, there were unmistakable signs of collective hysteria. All in all, during the first months of 1953, the Cold War seemed to have intensified. However, the basic direction for it had been laid down by the Nineteenth Party Congress in October, which had, in fact, anticipated the lessening of tension that followed Stalin's death. This turn of events, as well as the nervousness that began with the new year, was overshadowed by the approaching fatal illness of the dictator.

For some time, Stalin had been suffering from high blood pressure, which had developed into a serious arteriosclerosis of the cerebral vessels. At the end of 1946, he had been seriously sick for the first time. This had not, however, become generally known. As is usual in such cases, he underwent a certain change in personality. He became intellectually more rigid in his decisions.[82] His increased need for rest affected his political decisions, both in domestic and foreign affairs. The nervous tension that existed in the Kremlin was caused by his entourage; Stalin's own wishes were expressed in the decisions of the Nineteenth Party Congress.

On the morning of March 4, 1953, Radio Moscow announced that, during the night of March 1-2, Stalin had suffered a stroke, which had affected the vital parts of his brain and had led to the paralysis of his right side. Two medical bulletins the next day announced a further deterioration. Stalin died that evening, on March 5, around 10 p.m., without regaining consciousness. On March 9, he was buried in the mausoleum on Red Square, next to Lenin.

The funeral speeches were made by Malenkov, Beria, and Molotov.

The Central Committee, the Council of Ministers, and the Presidium of the Supreme Soviet announced the decisions regarding his successors on March 7. Malenkov was appointed Chairman of the Council of Ministers; his deputies were to be Beria, Molotov, Bulganin, and Kaganovich. The place of N. M. Shvernik, Chairman of the Presidium of the Supreme Soviet of the USSR, was taken by Marshal Voroshilov, one of the few surviving comrades of Lenin. The number of ministries was halved by means of various mergers. Molotov once again became Foreign Minister, Bulganin was made Minister of War, and Beria became head of a Ministry of Internal Affairs that had been combined with the Ministry of State Security.[83]

Without question, Stalin's death had been a grave loss for the Russian Bolsheviks and for the international prestige of the Soviet Union. No one compared with him in terms of the power he held in his hands, the authority with which he wielded it for thirty years, or the nimbus that Party propaganda had provided. With an unscrupulous disregard for historical facts, he was described as the legitimate heir of Lenin and the sole authorized interpreter of Marxism. Once more, the ancient truth was proven that it is sufficient to proclaim unalterable laws and then to assume the role of their guardian and interpreter in order to achieve complete control over the masses of the people.[84] At this point, the allegedly rational, materialistic world of Communism stumbled drunkenly into the realm of individual and collective irrationality. The celebration of Stalin's seventieth birthday in 1949 was a striking, if perverted, deification of a living person, analogous only to the customs of the ancient oriental world.[85] However, the rational element becomes evident again in the conscious direction of these phenomena and the exploration of their effect in the international field. When Stalin was called the great teacher of the nations and the leader among the scientists, it was more than gross flattery. It bespoke an attempt to use the Stalin myth as a visible symbol of Soviet hegemony and make it effective far beyond the borders of the Soviet Union.

The cult of his personality was accompanied by distortions of historical facts and linguistic usage. Such concepts as freedom, democracy, nation, state, nationalism, cosmopolitanism, internationalism, objectivity, and truth were given special Soviet meanings and propagated with a completely different content. A Soviet concept of history, combining elements of Marxist eschatology and Russian messianism, was juxtaposed with the more customary approach to history centering on European events of the Christian

era. The history of the various nations was considered only in relation to Moscow. The meanings of wars, migrations, frontier
changes, and the birth of new nations were read only from this point
of view, and all the threads of world historical developments were
made to converge on the person of Stalin.

Was it not inevitable that the sudden collapse of such an essential symbol of the eventual fulfillment of the people's hopes this
side of the grave should shake to its foundation the edifice of
Bolshevik ideology, as well as the Soviet state and its power principle?

CHAPTER 10

KHRUSHCHEV AND AFTER

Collective Leadership

Immediately after Stalin's death, there was a return to the principle of collective leadership in place of the recent dictatorial authority of one person. The cult of the individual was attacked, and Stalin was robbed of his halo.

Within the collective leadership of the state and the Party, changes were soon made. As early as March 21, 1953, N. S. Khrushchev took over Malenkov's post in the Secretariat of the Central Committee. This meant that the latter was free to attend to his duties as Premier, and, while he continued to occupy the first place in the Presidium of the Central Committee (reduced to ten members and four candidates)—a kind of revived Politburo—this shift nevertheless indicated the growing demands of a man whose ambitions had not yet been satisfied.

Nikita Sergeyevich Khrushchev was born of proletarian stock in 1894 in the region of Kursk, not far from the Russian-Ukrainian border. Tough-minded and of robust health, he lacked neither ambition nor a brutal desire for power. Possessed of a jovial humor, he knew how to establish a rapport with those around him and, as a result, was not unpopular with the masses. He joined the Party when he was a worker in the Ukrainian coal region, participated in the Civil War, attended a Moscow school of technology from 1929 until 1931, and made his first mark as a faithful follower of Stalin in the Ukrainian Party organization. In 1934, Khrushchev became a member of the Central Committee and, in 1935, First Secretary of the Party organization in Moscow. In the Ukraine in 1937 and 1938, he so satisfactorily carried out the purges ordered by Stalin that, in 1939, he was called to the Politburo. In the Second World War, he led the Ukrainian partisan movement and, at the end of the war, as Presiding Minister and First Secretary of the Ukrainian Party, he took charge of the reconstruction of the Ukraine, which had been enlarged by the annexation of the Carpathian Ukraine and Galicia. Stalin called him to Party headquarters in Moscow after the death of Zhdanov.

The rivalries among the Bolshevik leaders should neither be overrated nor underestimated. Just as personal alliances shifted and changed after the death of Lenin, so the collaboration of Malenkov, Beria, and Khrushchev after the death of Stalin was of only limited duration. Differences arose between Malenkov and Khrushchev, at the end of 1952, over Khrushchev's proposal of agro-cities. Any alliance between Malenkov and Beria that had existed under Stalin did not long survive his death. Stalin's death made all personal situations entirely fluid.

On July 10, 1953, the Moscow morning papers announced the sensational news that Beria had been relieved of his office as Deputy Premier and Minister of Internal Affairs, expelled from the Party, and arrested. Among the manifold accusations against him was the fact that Beria opposed Khrushchev's agrarian policy, seemed to have advocated a more federalist policy for the nationalities within the Soviet Union, and perhaps also favored less stringent direction of the satellite states. The various concessions to Ukrainian autonomy from April to July 1953, which reversed the purge of the summer of 1951, and similar policies followed in other republics of the Union, giving more leeway to local leaders and opposing Great Russian influences, must indeed be considered to have originated with Beria.

However, the events in Moscow immediately after Stalin's death prove that Beria, who had in 1934-38 supported ruthless centralization in his native Georgia, was, in his opposition to the hegemony of Great Russia in the Soviet Union, acting not on principle, but on tactical considerations and personal ambitions.

After Stalin's death, Beria had assembled all the units of the MVD (Ministry of Internal Affairs) with lightning speed in the capital and for some days had held an accumulation of power in his hands that for the moment no one was strong enough to oppose. He did not play his trump card, however. Regardless of what his intentions really were, his colleagues heading the government and the military had seen enough to fear that he was planning a *coup d'état*. It may be that Khrushchev's inclusion in the Party leadership was motivated by this consideration.

Beria was executed on December 23, 1953, together with his codefendants, most of whom were also Georgians.

The fall of Beria brought about sweeping changes in personnel, especially in the union republics. An effort was made, however, particularly in the Ukraine, to avoid disturbing confidence by resuming severe purges. Representatives of the Ukrainian academic and technological intelligentsia continued to hold high positions in the administration and the Party. The ceremonies commemorating the Treaty of Pereyaslav (1654) glorified all that Russia and the Ukraine held in common. It was also significant that, in February 1954, the Crimea, hitherto a part of the RSFSR, was incorporated into the Ukraine. At the same time, however, there was an especially strong propaganda campaign in favor of young Ukrainians going for labor service to Central Asia, a move obviously in line with the policy of loosening the traditional pattern of nationalities, which had been carried out in severe form by the forced deportation of Volga Germans, Kalmuks, Crimean Tatars, and North Caucasians after the Second World War.

In the government of the Union, the consolidation of ministries that had followed the fall of Beria was reversed, with the result that the total number of ministries was returned to the earlier norm.[1] Moreover, after March 1954, the Ministry of Internal Affairs sat side by side in the Council of Ministers with an autonomous State Security Service under I. A. Serov, a man whose name was synonymous with terror without mercy. It was he who had carried out the mass deportations from the newly annexed areas along the western border in 1940. Nonetheless, it cannot be denied that the political climate underwent a fundamental transformation. The forced labor camps, the most flagrant testimony of Stalin's rule of terror, were gradually being liquidated after the uprisings in the Norilsk (1953) and Karaganda (1954) camps.

A significant shift in Soviet domestic policy followed Stalin's death. In a speech on August 8, 1953, Malenkov announced that production of consumer goods for the satisfaction of essential personal needs would be increased sharply, and the standard of living would be raised appreciably within two to three years.[2] At the same time, the distribution system was to be expanded and improved, and energetic measures were to be taken to advance agricultural production, whose retardation in the country's total economic development could no longer be ignored.[3]

These goals constituted a decisive shift in economic policy, a shift that affected the basis of Communist ideology by proposing to end the priority of heavy industry that had prevailed since 1917. Malenkov's policy decision reflected the realization that Soviet society had undergone a marked change in stratification: The new intelligentsia that had emerged after the Second World War was even more sharply delineated than the elite of the 1930's had been. The government thus felt compelled to heed this stratum's expanded cultural needs. For example, both the quantity and quality of food and other consumer goods, which had been more or less acceptable to the predominantly illiterate masses of the largely agrarian country prior to 1928, no longer seemed adequate to satisfy the needs of either the new elite or even the kolkhoz and factory *apparatchiki.* Another consideration was the Soviet people's closer acquaintance with Western standards as a result of the war. This wartime contact had provided not only forced labor deportees and prisoners of war (most of whom were sent to the Soviet Union's Asian territories when they returned), but also members of the fighting forces and of the occupation army, with the opportunity to develop a more critical perspective on Soviet reality.

These factors influenced Malenkov's decision to pursue his program with serious determination. The real question was to what extent these intentions could be combined with the industrialization program set down in the Fifth Five Year Plan, which envisaged a considerably enlarged production base for both agriculture and heavy industry, to be achieved through the construction of mammoth technical projects along Stalinist lines (power stations, irrigation facilities, dams, and the like).

In foreign policy, Malenkov stressed the principle of peaceful coexistence with the West. The Soviet government agreed to a four-power conference on the German question. An insurrection of German workers in East Berlin and several towns of Saxony on June 17, 1953, had demonstrated to the world that the wish for freedom was not dead in a Soviet-controlled area. But the spontaneous uprising quickly collapsed, and the concentration camps and prisons of East Germany were filled with new prisoners. A conference on Germany was mandatory.

The conference was held in Berlin from January 25 to February 18, 1954.[4] It was the first meeting of the foreign ministers of the three Western powers and the Soviet Union in five years. The West insisted on free elections throughout Germany; Molotov demanded the early conclusion of a peace treaty, with representatives of both German governments participating as equals. The difference of approach caused a stalemate. The results of the conference were negligible.

The fruitlessness of the negotiations caused the Western powers to intensify their efforts toward integration. When the EDC (European Defense Community) foundered on the resistance of the

French, Germany was brought into NATO.[5] The Soviet government protested sharply against the rearming of the West German Federal Republic and formally announced the remilitarization of East Germany, actually a *fait accompli* of long standing. To consolidate their position further, the Soviets staged a conference of the Communist bloc at Warsaw from May 11 to May 14, 1955, that resulted in the creation of the Warsaw Pact as a supreme military command for the East European countries and as a counterbalance to NATO.

The great Geneva double conference from April 26 to June 15, 1954, ostensibly concerned with the problems of Korea and Indochina, was actually of greater consequence for the easing of international tensions than the Berlin meeting. The Korean discussions stemmed from the truce concluded at Panmunjon on July 27, 1953. It was decided to withdraw the occupation troops on both sides and hold elections throughout the country. The talks on Indochina were started as the fighting over the last positions held by the French approached its bitter end. The conclusion was to leave North Viet-Nam in Communist hands and South Viet-Nam as a free country, both flanked by neutral Laos and Cambodia.

In the summer of 1953, a surprising cultural "thaw" set in in the Soviet Union. (The name was derived from a novel by Ilya Ehrenburg advocating such a course.) The loosening of controls was soon obvious in the theater, the creative arts, the movies, music, and broadcasting. Much of the credit for this went to G. F. Alexandrov, a professor of philosophy, disciplined under Zhdanov, who served for a short time as Minister of Culture in 1954-55. Moreover, the President of the Academy of Sciences, the well-known professor of chemistry A. N. Nesmeyanov, advocated in *Izvestia* on December 31, 1954, the exchange of scientific experience and research results. Shortly thereafter, for the first time in a quarter-century, Soviet scientists participated in international conferences. In September 1955, Soviet historians appeared at an international congress of historians in Rome.[6]

On February 8, 1955, a shift in the top leadership of the Soviet Union was accomplished in a fashion that also signaled a change in manners, if not in purposes. At the session of the Supreme Soviet, Malenkov announced his resignation as Prime Minister.[7] He was succeeded by Bulganin. Instead of being "liquidated," Malenkov was given a lesser post.

Nikolai Alexandrovich Bulganin was born in 1895, the son of an accountant, and entered the Soviet security service in 1917. From 1931 to 1937, he was chairman of the Moscow City Soviet

and then held in succession various offices in the state adminstration and the economy. He survived the Stalin purges unscathed, by
virtue of his contacts with the Stalin circle. During the Second
World War, he served as a political functionary with the army, and
in 1944 was rewarded by being appointed a general and being given
membership in the State Committee for Defense. While Minister of
the Army in 1947-49, he was made a Marshal. After the death of
Stalin, he became Minister for Defense. In short, Bulganin represented the interests of the economic-technical, administrative, and
military intelligentsia, and, as such, was a natural mediator between
Party, army, and state.[8] On taking over the Prime Ministership, he
assigned the Ministry for Defense to Marshal Zhukov, who had become deputy minister in 1953, when he was rescued from the
oblivion to which he had been assigned by Stalin after the Second
World War.

Malenkov had enumerated his reasons for resigning, citing the
unsatisfactory situation in agriculture and the retardation in the
development of heavy industry.[9] He added that he lacked the administrative experience to deal with the urgent problems the nation
confronted. Actually, what he said meant that his policy of improving the standard of living, when combined with rearmament, was
a strain on the economy. The policy of favoring heavy industry was
to be resumed.

Moreover, the change reflected the struggle for power behind
the scenes. The shift appeared to have benefited Khrushchev. In
September 1953, he had been appointed First Secretary of the
Party. He made several important speeches, and sponsored some
significant decrees in the summer of 1954.[10] In October 1954, he
made a trip to Peking with Bulganin, which, in retrospect, had
decisive significance. The bonds between the two Communist countries were further strengthened. The Soviet Union, however, had to
face up to exacting economic commitments if the extension of
Chinese heavy industry was to succeed. Moreover, there could be
no relief from the pressure of rearmament if the Soviets were to
maintain their international position. The Malenkov program of
favoring light industry to improve living conditions had to give way.

Lurid light was thrown on behind-the-scenes Soviet politics by
the Abakumov trial of December 1954. V. S. Abakumov had been
Minister of Security from 1947 to 1951 and, in this capacity, had
undertaken a purge, after Zhdanov's death in 1948, of the latter's
followers in Leningrad. The action had Stalin's approval, but
whether Malenkov also approved or took any active part in it is
uncertain.[11] At any rate, after the trial, Abakumov was sentenced

to death, together with other functionaries of the security service, in summary proceedings by the Supreme Court of the USSR, and was executed. Even though it may be questionable to talk about an actual group of followers of Zhdanov, Khrushchev may well have earned from this episode the sympathies of circles hostile to Malenkov.

At any rate, the Abakumov trial was soon followed by newspaper articles criticizing Malenkov's economic policy. At the end of January 1955, the Central Committee of the CPSU came out in favor of Khrushchev's program of priority for heavy industry. This was given a theoretical substructure by D. T. Shepilov, chief editor of *Pravda,* on January 24. Mikoyan, who had favored the Malenkov position, resigned as Minister of Trade at about this time, but continued as deputy premier. Khrushchev's speech before the Central Committee, on February 3, stated his position clearly. All of these events were harbingers of the fall of Malenkov.

Thus on February 8, 1955, the two-man team of Malenkov-Khrushchev was replaced by the two-man team of Bulganin-Khrushchev, in which Khrushchev's position was the stronger. While the military was undoubtedly powerful, there was no justification for adding Zhukov to the team to make a triumvirate.

Since February 1955, the foreign policy of the Soviet Union has been marked by the personal activity of the leading statesmen, an approach without parallel in the history of the country. Molotov's decline in influence was shown not only by his absence from important diplomatic missions abroad, but also by the confession of error that he made on September 16, 1955.[12] He had spoken of the task of building a socialist society in the Soviet Union as not yet completed, whereas the correct line is that it was completed in 1937.

A trip to Belgrade by Khrushchev and Bulganin, in May 1955, had great consequences, for it led to a healing of the breach between Yugoslavia and Soviet Russia. The breach was then blamed on the dead Beria, and subsequently on Stalin. The joint Soviet-Yugoslav declaration of June 2, 1955,[13] made it clear that Tito had decisively established considerable freedom of action, as against tight control from Moscow, thus implying that there were three foci of Communist leadership—Belgrade, Peking, and Moscow.

In the same month, the protracted negotiations for a treaty with Austria came to an end, with remarkable speed in the final phases. The treaty was signed on May 15, and led to the departure, shortly thereafter, of all the armies of occupation, including the Soviet. Austria was neutralized.

At the Geneva "summit conference," from July 18 to July 23, where the Western powers were represented by Eisenhower, Eden, and Faure, the Soviet delegation, consisting of Bulganin, Khrushchev, Zhukov, Molotov, and others, was smilingly friendly as if to underline its determination to achieve a relaxation of Cold War tension. While no agreement was reached on Germany, the door was obviously left open for further discussion. President Eisenhower's proposal for mutual air inspection to safeguard against surprise attack was rejected by the Soviets, but at least it was discussed. By and large, the Western powers were able to claim that tensions had been lessened, with no concessions to Moscow as the price.[14] It seemed clear that the Soviets genuinely wanted calmer relations so that they might prosecute their economic program undisturbed by excursions and alarums.

They tried to handle the German question by direct negotiations with the West German Federal Republic. At the Berlin Conference, Molotov had indicated that a resumption of diplomatic relations without a treaty was a possibility. Chancellor Adenauer was now invited to negotiations in Moscow. A large German delegation arrived in the Soviet capital in September 1955, and was received with marked attention. But the net results of the talks were simply the release of some of the German prisoners of war, still interned ten years after the fighting had ceased, and the promised resumption of diplomatic relations. These were, indeed, resumed shortly thereafter, without, however, any progress on the question of German reunification.

Moreover, at a conference of foreign ministers in October and November, it was clearly apparent that the Soviets were not really willing to change their German line. Molotov rejected free elections for Germany and also firmly rejected any move to tie German reunification to the general question of European security.

The Soviet diplomacy of personalities received a strenuous workout in the extended visit to India, Burma, and Afghanistan made by Bulganin and Khrushchev at the end of 1955. The Soviet leaders essayed the role of jolly tourists, but it was quite obvious that their political objective was to gain the friendship of the three countries by indicating that they supported "neutralism," along the lines laid down at the Bandung Conference. That it was a unilateral friendship they had in mind, not a universal one, was indicated by the tasteless attacks the Soviet leaders made on the Western countries. Preceded by Malenkov, who had ostensibly come to study power stations, the Khrushchev-Bulganin team descended on England in April 1956, and rather spoiled their intended effect when Khrushchev provoked an unseemly altercation with the leaders of the Labour Party over the treatment Soviet Russia and its satellites had meted out to socialist opposition leaders. Thousands of words were expended in an effort to weigh the effects of the Russian visits, with no universally accepted results.

At the same time, the tide of visits to the Soviet Union was running high. Nehru, Tito, the Shah of Iran, Sukarno, and the heads of state of North Viet-Nam, Burma, and Afghanistan, as well as leading statesmen from France, Belgium, Canada, Norway, Denmark, and Sweden, all paid formal calls.[15] It seemed like a revival of the situation that existed in the mid-1930's, enlarged to take in visitors from all over the globe.

Moscow attached great importance to the documenting of friendly relations with Finland, although that country had a bourgeois government with only a small minority of Communists in it. In January 1956, Soviet troops withdrew from Porkkala, which they had occupied since the war; in the era of atomic weapons, this base had lost much of its significance. The dissolution of the Karelo-Finnish Soviet Republic in July of that year was another friendly gesture toward free Finland, as was the subsequent visit of the Soviet head of state, Voroshilov. In the summer of 1957, Khrushchev and Bulganin, those tireless travelers, appeared in Helsinki to announce to their startled listeners that Bolshevist ideology—when greased with butter and seasoned with delicious meals—could easily surmount all barriers and iron curtains! This new foreign policy of smiles appeared completely successful when, in June 1956, Molotov, who had already been disciplined once before, had to vacate the Foreign Office permanently in favor of the former editor-in-chief of *Pravda,* D. T. Shepilov. But again the results were ambiguous, for, in December 1955, Khrushchev had made it plain that coexistence did not include any real ideological concessions. These, he said, must await the moment when crayfish learn to whistle, an earthy way of saying "Never."

The Twentieth Party Congress and De-Stalinization

At the Twentieth Party Congress, held in Moscow from February 14 to February 25, 1956, an opportunity arose to assess more precisely the meaning of the inner and outer changes in the Soviet Union. The most spectacular development was the smashing of the Stalin cult, done with reluctance and in significant part with an effort at secrecy, which unexpectedly failed. As late as December 21, 1954, Stalin's birthday had been commemorated with customary devotion. But at the Congress, Mikoyan led off the attack with a speech on February 16, and Khrushchev called for a new party history that would take account of the historical facts and replace the "doctored" work of 1938. These moves seem to have built up pressures for a fuller statement on the Stalin question, and on February 24, in a secret talk lasting seven hours, Khrushchev made an effort to detail Stalin's "crimes" and reduce the "cult of personality" to ruins. The text of this speech was not officially released, but a version of it was "leaked" to a representative of the United States, presumably somewhere in Eastern Europe, and the State Department promptly published a translation of it in Washington.[16] This text has not been repudiated by the Soviet government.

Khrushchev's speech was a thorough accounting with Stalin. His course at the time of Lenin's death, his struggle for power with Zinoviev, Kamenev, and others, and the purges of the 1930's and 1950's were caustically reviewed to illustrate his insatiable greed for power, his liking for despotic procedures, his megalomania, and his reckless use of terrorism against oppositionists, real or fancied. His behavior at the outbreak of the Second World War and during the war was surveyed, the break with Tito was attributed to his arrogance, and failures of policy at home and abroad were cited as evidence of his incompetence. Several letters and documents— some hitherto unknown, others not known verbatim, and some known in the West but hitherto secret in the Soviet Union—were released to back up the Khrushchev story. The net effect of the attack was to establish a catalog of errors, many of which had been pointed out by Westerners during Stalin's lifetime, which not only destroyed the Stalin myth, but also provoked angry questions from Communists abroad.

At the same time, Khrushchev tried to balance the picture by pointing out allegedly constructive achievements of Stalin, insisting on his fundamental greatness as a leader and advocating as a cure for the Stalinist ills a whole-hearted return to the principles of Lenin.[17]

Consistent with the new line, the Central Committee of the CPSU proceeded to rehabilitate some of the victims of the Stalinist reign of terror. No Trotskyites or Bukharinites were so favored, however, and the name of Tukhachevsky was not even mentioned. Some survivors of the purges suddenly came to light, for example, Petrovsky and Bubnov.

The motives for this elaborate smashing of the Stalin myth were probably rooted in the difficulties experienced in directing contemporary Soviet society, especially where the younger generation was involved. The leadership felt compelled to find some means of re-establishing a relationship of trust between the government and the people, which was wholly lost during the Stalin era. This they sought to do by "shock treatment." In this fashion, they hoped to secure their oligarchical rule and preserve the position of the Soviet Union as a world power.[18] Certainly, the praise of Stalin in the Khrushchev speech and the advocacy of a return to Leninism indicate that no really fundamental ideological shift was intended.

The ruling clique took this course partly to establish a legitimacy reaching back to the era of Lenin, appealing to Leninist theory as it allegedly existed before Stalin's falsifications. The actual foundations of Stalin's dictatorship were left untouched, for the later, degenerated Stalin was confronted with an earlier Stalin who was credited with being a "good" Marxist. The Western world knows, or should know, that a return to Leninism is a return to the principle of Party unity and one-party rule, to limited freedom of opinion and bureaucratic centralism, to elections with the candidates all selected by the Party central office. These principles of Bolshevist state practice were laid down at the Tenth Party Congress in March 1921.[19]

With regard to the methods to be used in the transition from capitalism to socialism (or from a democratic to a Communist order), Khrushchev made several revealing remarks. He stated that it is not absolutely necessary that the transition involve civil war, since various alternatives are imaginable, although not all of them have yet appeared in history. But he added that this did not bridge the gulf between the revolutionary Marxists and the "opportunistic reformists," such as the parliamentary Marxists of the West. "The overthrow by force of the dictatorship of the bourgeoisie and the sharp aggravation of the class struggle entailed thereby is unavoidable in a series of capitalist countries." "The application or non-application of force in the transition to socialism depends not as much upon the proletariat as upon the resistance of the exploiters, upon the application of force and violence on the part of the exploiting classes themselves."[20] This is a familiar and traditional position.

By admitting that there were different roads to socialism, Khrushchev attempted to build a bridge between the Soviet Union and the right-wing socialist parties of Western Europe in order to provide a theoretical foundation for a renewal of the united, or popular, front tactic and also to assist in splitting off the left wings of the socialist parties, as had been done in the Leninist era. At the same time, and on the same reasoning, a bridge was to be built to the Asian and African nationalist movements. On the other hand,

Khrushchev made it clear that his group still considered it inevitable that the overthrow of capitalism "in a series of capitalist countries" would be accomplished only through violence, even though he attempted to push off the responsibility for this violence on the capitalist states.

However, the various attempts to approach the Western socialists after the Twentieth Party Congress resulted in failure, often marked by explicit rejection of Moscow's proffered hand. Nor did the dissolution of the Cominform, in April 1956, improve Moscow's chances. Khrushchev's explosion at his meeting with the Labour Party leaders in London reflected his chagrin at this situation.

Also emanating from the Twentieth Party Congress was the decision to submit to the next Congress the draft of a new Party program and a Sixth Five Year Plan. This new Plan provided for the increase of industrial and agricultural production by a change in the over-all technical level—or a drive for increased productivity. A third industrial center was planned in central and eastern Siberia around Krasnoyarsk and Bratsk on the Angara River.[21]

The Soviet government in its desire to document to the world its willingness to promote a relaxation of tensions in all areas did not ignore the military implications of such a policy. Soviet expenditures for arms had more than doubled since 1948 (from 66 billion rubles in 1948 to 162 billion rubles in 1955) and amounted to 21.6 per cent of total state expenditures in 1955. Thus, the Soviet Union now declared its readiness to engage in international negotiations concerning reductions in conventional weapons, as well as in troop levels. Consequently, disarmament negotiations were begun. They did not, however, lead to any effective agreement.

The Soviet government could afford to display this posture because of its substantial progress in developing nuclear weapons; atomic research and development had been given priority since the Second World War. Most of the credit for the development of nuclear weapons belongs to the physicist P. L. Kapitsa, who returned to his Russian homeland in 1934 after a prolonged sojourn in England. As early as August 9, 1953, Malenkov was able to inform the Supreme Soviet that Soviet technicians had produced a hydrogen bomb. Intercontinental missiles soon followed. The Soviet physicist L. I. Sedov and his collaborators succeeded in developing the first earth satellite, "Sputnik." This was an achievement that strengthened not only the self-confidence of the Bolshevik leadership, but also that of broad segments of the population.

Manned space flights and successful moon probes have provided the Soviet Union with additional experience in outer space.

In March 1965, a Soviet cosmonaut, Lieutenant Colonel Aleksei A. Leonov, became the first man to walk in outer space. At the beginning of February 1966, the Soviet Union accomplished the first soft landing on the moon by an unmanned space probe. In April 1966, Soviet scientists placed the first man-made moon satellite in orbit.

Khrushchev's Ascendancy

Two steps taken by Khrushchev in the summer of 1957 caused changes of paramount importance in conditions within the Soviet Union. The direct control from Moscow of all industrial production had led to the development of an extremely bloated and wasteful administrative apparatus. On March 30, the Party Secretary published in *Pravda* proposals for the reorganization of the entire industrial administration system. These proposals were submitted to the Supreme Soviet in May. The result has been called the greatest upheaval within the Soviet Union since 1928. The entire economic apparatus was decentralized. Local economic councils (*sovnarkhozy*) were formed in each economic region to take the place of the thirty-odd centralized economic ministries. The State Planning Committee (*Gosplan*) became responsible for basic policy only.

In the social structure of the Soviet Union, this change meant that power had been shifted from the top state bureaucrats to lower functionaries. One of Khrushchev's motives in taking this step appears to have been his desire to break up the united front of the technological intelligentsia, the Soviet "management" class, which for some time had been the power behind the throne. The crises in the Communist bloc countries, in October 1956, may well have opened Khrushchev's eyes to the danger of this class some day developing into a real threat to the party leadership.

Not all Party leaders saw these things in quite the same light. Malenkov, for one, had always been considered an exponent of the technological intelligentsia. Khrushchev's new plan met with resistance from the Central Committee. He solved this problem, on June 29, by removing Molotov, Malenkov, and Kaganovich from the Central Committee and the Presidium, and Shepilov from the Central Committee as well as from his post as its secretary. The charges made against the expelled members concerned both domestic and foreign issues: plotting and factionalism within the Central Committee, resistance against the policy of coexistence, sabotage of the new economic plans, and dogmatic adherence to outdated methods. No proceedings were initiated against the expelled men, but they were transferred to subordinate positions in remote regions. Shepilov was replaced as Foreign Minister by A. A. Gromyko in February 1957. Malenkov was accused of instigating, with Beria, the persecution of the Zhdanov group in Leningrad in 1949. Khrushchev could never have succeeded in removing these men if he had not been sure of the backing of a powerful group whose importance was steadily increasing—the Red Army, led by Marshal Zhukov.

Marshal Zhukov moved more and more into the limelight after the fall of Beria (which would not have been possible without Zhukov's compliance and collaboration). At the Twentieth Party Congress the Marshal became once more a full member of the Central Committee and a candidate for the Presidium. Georgi Konstantinovich Zhukov was born of peasant stock in 1896 in the province of Kaluga. As a sergeant-major in the cavalry, he joined the Revolution in 1917, participated in the Civil War as an officer, became a member of the Party in 1919, and attended the War Academy. The fall of Tukhachevsky drew him temporarily into the whirlpool of purges; together with Rokossovsky he was banished to Siberia, but was reinstated when the Japanese marched into Mongolia, his military knowledge having proved indispensable. His great military rise during the Second World War earned for him a degree of popularity that Stalin resented. In November 1946, he was dismissed as Supreme Commander of the Army and exiled to a remote army post in the Urals. Only after Stalin's death did he re-emerge.

In a surprise move on October 26, 1957, Marshal Zhukov was removed as Minister of Defense and as Commander of the Army while he was on an official visit to Yugoslavia, and was replaced by Marshal R. J. Malinovsky, a man of no political importance. The main accusations against Zhukov were that he aspired to be the sole leader of the Army and that he attempted to eliminate the Party's influence over the military. He was also faced with a "cult-of-personality" charge. Undoubtedly some friction had previously existed between the Marshal and the political administration of the Army; but what was probably of greater importance was a basic difference of political interpretation: Zhukov was more concerned with the state and with patriotism than he was with Marxist ideology. This does not mean that the Marshal was not a good Communist. It was Zhukov who had ordered the use of Soviet tanks in Hungary; but the worsening of Soviet-Turkish relations in the autumn of 1957 was also considered Zhukov's work, and, as far as domestic policies were concerned, it seems that Zhukov opposed

Khrushchev's attempts to combine the office of Party Chief with that of Premier. Perhaps he himself aspired to become Bulganin's successor. On the occasion of his removal from office, however, it became plain that the leadership of the Army stood solidly behind the Party.

When, on November 7, 1957, the fortieth anniversary of the October Revolution was celebrated in Moscow in the presence of Mao Tse-tung and all the prominent leaders of world Communism except Marshal Tito, the Soviet Union's hegemony, which had been threatened the year before, appeared to be completely restored. Talks with the Chinese statesmen, which followed the festivities, showed a readiness on both sides to renew and strengthen the coordination of their common policies. Since China was still dependent on the Soviet imports, it was in its interest to support the rulers in the Kremlin.

During the anniversary celebrations, Bulganin, together with Khrushchev, received the ovation of the people, but it soon became clear that Bulganin's position was a questionable one. Rumors about his resignation would not be silenced. At the meeting of the Supreme Soviet on March 26, 1958, he was released from his position as Premier in order to resume management of the State Bank. His position was taken over by Khrushchev. Thus, for the first time since Stalin's death, the leadership of the government and of the Party was combined in the hands of one man.

The assumption of governmental power by Khrushchev seemed to complete the rise of the man who succeeded in outdistancing all other prominent Soviet leaders. One-man rule again took the place of collective leadership, but the nature of that rule was quite different from what it had previously been. Whereas Stalin had systematically accumulated the leadership of Party, state, and economy, Khrushchev relaxed economic control by decentralizing its management. Furthermore, a different disposition of power existed. While Stalin could rely on a pliable Party apparatus, Khrushchev had to contend with the Central Committee, which did not consist solely of unconditional supporters. Neither did he have at his disposal such police forces as the former GPU or MVD.

Finally, Khrushchev's personality was not at all like that of the mistrustful, cunning, obstinate Stalin, whose ability to retain contact with his immediate surroundings, with the people, and with the changing political situation gradually diminished. The uncouth but lively and jovial Khrushchev enjoyed a certain measure of popularity. He was flexible and had the ability to scent out changes and new possibilities in the political situation. However, it is important to realize that his easy grasp of political realities was based on a burning optimism, a firm conviction that the Communist idea would triumph.

The changes in the social background from the 1920's and 1930's to the 1950's must not be overlooked. This period saw the rise of a new ruling class, the Soviet intellectuals, often called the Bolshevik bourgeoisie. A certain amount of tension existed between this class and the Party leadership; but this tension should not be overestimated. The Party leadership fully realized that it could not handle the governmental and economic machinery of such a vast country without the help of highly skilled workers and specialists. One of the most difficult tasks confronting the leaders was the necessity to satisfy the demands of this upper class for comfort, legality, and peace without relaxing the continuous efforts to raise production of heavy industry and armaments.

In this connection, the relationship between the leadership and the masses is very important. Can one lump together the political leadership and the intelligentsia under the name "the new class" that exploits the masses? Even without direct ownership and control of the means of production, the close relations of the intelligentsia with those in power give it the upper hand. For this reason, it stands out above the gray masses. How much importance ought to be given to the expressions of indignation, criticism, and scorn—especially when they appear in the field of literature? Can one truly speak of a "divided society" in the Soviet Union when anyone who has the proper professional training and who does not oppose the political leadership can advance into the ruling class?

There was much discontent with the harshness of the regime, especially among the kolkhoz peasants. But the efficiency of the state machinery insured the regime against organized opposition. Differences in wages split the working class, which lacked true class consciousness and revolutionary initiative because it was without intellectual leadership (in the sense of the old intelligentsia). No libertarian unrest leading to a revolutionary explosion could be expected from the new intelligentsia, either. Both the labor aristocracy and the intellectuals in the technical, administrative, and military fields were fairly well off, and minor demands for improvements in the living standard were readily met, so that a certain bourgeois comfort stifled critical incentive. The abolition of the drastic punishments and severe restrictions in choosing employment that prevailed during the Stalin era further appeased many workers. The position of the unions was also strengthened.

The intellectual elite—university professors, scientists, writers, and artists—had a handsome share in the nation's economy and therefore—financially, at least—benefited by the system. Could one hope that the inflammatory spirit would prevail against state regimentation, after the depressing spectacle of the action taken against Boris Pasternak (when he was forbidden to accept the Nobel Prize)? Could one really hope that the spontaneous urge for freedom that was awakened by the "thaw" in teachers, researchers, and artists would not come to rest? That it would, perhaps, become an element of progressive unrest that would permeate the ruling class and force the Party and the state into an evolutionary development? The school reform of December 1958, which was intended to bridge the gap between intellectual and manual labor and provide industry with new blood, proved that Khrushchev recognized the danger and tried to keep Soviet youth from becoming more and more bourgeois. It was typical of the program that a certain amount of unrest caused Khrushchev to change the first, much more radical draft. This unrest has not abated, but increased; the young Soviet poets Yevtushenko and Voznesensky are impressive proof.

Another important measure was the surrender of MTS inventories to the kolkhozes in March 1958. What was being interpreted as a governmental concession to the kolkhozes and as a sign of progressive liberalization of the Soviet economy was, in reality, a mere stage on the road to total nationalization of agriculture. The objective was to remove gradually the distinction between the sovkhoz worker and the kolkhoz peasant, who had but a share of the net profit and the income from his small private plot. Khrushchev's 1950 proposal to create agro-cities remained on the agenda. In 1954, Khrushchev promoted a large-scale land reclamation project in Kazakhstan; the work force was recruited primarily from the youth of the Ukraine. The first results were promising. As early as January 1965, cultivation of 33 million hectares (an area the size of Italy) could be reported; by 1961, this figure had risen to 48 million hectares. The year 1958 brought a record harvest, a success Khrushchev considered his personal accomplishment.

The official Party history of the Soviet Union has always considered the Party congresses as important landmarks. With the strengthening of the international position of the Communist bloc, the Party congresses have gained international importance as well. The period between the Twenty-first and Twenty-second Party congresses—January 1959 to October 1961—opened new vistas on the domestic scene. In the field of foreign policy, this period saw an intensification of the Cold War and a more far-reaching global strategy of world Communism.

The Twenty-first Party Congress (January-February 1959) had to deal with the problems inherent in the failure of the Sixth Five Year Plan. The decision was made to interrupt the regular rhythm of the Five Year plans in favor of a Seven Year Plan designed to last from 1959 to 1965. During that time, industrial output was to be increased by 80 per cent; steel production was to increase from 55 million tons in 1958 to approximately 90 million tons. (In 1960, Soviet Russia produced 65 million tons, the European Economic Community 75 million tons, the United States 90 million tons.) The economic development of Soviet Asia was to be speeded up by building a third metallurgical base in Siberia; the industrial production process was to be further modernized through automatization.

It soon became obvious that it was difficult for the Soviet economy to increase the output of heavy industry and step up the exploitation of raw materials, while at the same time raising or even maintaining the standard of living. The obvious reasons for these growth difficulties were a shortage of both capital and labor and disproportionate allocations to the various branches of the economy. Whether the Soviet leadership would be able to reconcile the Malenkov course of increased consumer goods with the ideological priority of heavy industry remained to be seen. Khrushchev's economic gamble became evident when he announced a Twenty Year Plan in 1960, before the Seven Year Plan had gone into effect.

Even more obvious were the difficulties encountered in agrarian production and policies. The 1959 harvest was bad, and the harvests of 1960 and 1961 only mediocre. The new territories in Central Asia were plagued by erosion and faulty planning. In January 1961, the plenary meeting of the Party Central Committee dealt with these problems. In northern Kazakhstan, a separate district was carved out (apparently the most Slavic part of that Soviet Republic), with Akmolinsk as its center. A tour of inspection Khrushchev made through the farmlands of the Ukraine, Siberia, and Kazakhstan, resulted in various personnel changes. In northern Caucasia, dust storms necessitated special measures in order to utilize the dry lands on both sides of the Caspian Sea. In view of these troubles, it was a source of great satisfaction to the Soviet Union that the Volga Power Works, the biggest of its kind in the world, could be opened on December 9, 1960, earlier than had been anticipated. An even larger hydropower station, with a capacity of 4.8 million kilowatts, was scheduled to be completed in 1963, at Bratsk, on the Angara River in Siberia.

After the Twenty-first Party Congress, some changes were made in the upper echelons of the Party leadership, and several of

the younger Party leaders were promoted. One of them was Frol
Romanovich Kozlov (born 1908). A former Party Secretary of
Leningrad, and close to the circle around Zhdanov, he had played
a decisive role in the consolidation of Khrushchev's position during
the summer of 1957. He later became President of the Russian
Republic, and, in March 1958, was named First Deputy Premier
of the USSR, achieving the same rank as Mikoyan. In May 1960,
he exchanged that position for a seat in the Secretariat of the Central Committee, the most important command center of the Party
and the state. After that he was—on and off—considered the second man in the Kremlin. His place in the Presidium was taken by
Aleksei Nikolayevich Kosygin (born 1904). Dmitri Stepanovich
Polyansky (born 1917), who had been President of the Russian
Republic since 1958, advanced to a seat in the Presidium of the
Central Committee. Equally important was the chief ideologist of
the Kremlin, Mikhail Andreyevich Suslov (born 1902). He played
an important part in the Soviet intervention in Hungary in 1956
and became a member of the Secretariat in January 1957.

In May 1960, changes were also made among the highest repre-
sentatives of the state. Voroshilov resigned as chairman of the
Presidium of the Supreme Soviet and was succeeded by Leonid
Ilyich Brezhnev (born 1906), a Ukrainian and a member of the
Party apparatus.

These personnel changes—which can be considered a preliminary round in the struggle for the succession to Khrushchev—
strengthened and rejuvenated the Party leadership. Changes were
also made in the military command. About 300 new generals were
appointed, all of them younger men.

Two important publications show the ideological changes during this period and the Party's endeavor to adapt to them. In 1959,
the *History of the Communist Party of the Soviet Union* was published to take the place of the *Short Course* of 1938. Twice as long
as the earlier volume (744 pages), the new book was not really a
history but a handbook for future action, and it did not eschew
violence. Certain shifts in emphasis showed how the situation had
changed, both sociologically and politically. The treatment of some
ideological questions and the new evaluation of some phases of
historical development also proved the adoption of a new course.
Great consideration was given to the nationalistic tendencies of the
underdeveloped countries, and the possibility that these countries
might reach the socialist goal without going through a capitalistic
phase was stressed. This new textbook was written from the point
of view of an expanding Communism, certain of victory.

The second document was the draft of the new Party program, which promised that by 1970 Soviet production would be greater than that of the U.S., and that the Soviet Union would have the highest living standard in the world. It warned, however, that lower prices and shorter working hours could be achieved only through greater voluntary participation in the administrative apparatus by all circles of Soviet society. It is interesting to note that the official view concerning the transition to Communism did not include provisions for greater economic, political, or personal freedom. This can be seen in the revision of the penal code in July 1961, which threatened stiff punishment for all "parasitical manifestations," that is, bourgeois symptoms. These were the circumstances under which the Twenty-second Party Congress met from October 17 to October 31, 1961.

The primary task of the Twenty-second Party Congress was the ratification of the draft of the new Party program, which it adopted with only minor revisions. But the Congress was by no means exclusively preoccupied with the future of Communism. Even more melodramatically than in 1956, the crimes of the Stalin era were raked up. This was done as much to speed the course of a bloodless Party purge as to clarify the changed structure of Communism

Both Khrushchev and the Minister of State Security, A. N. Shelepin, revealed new details about Kirov's murder, the execution of Tukhachevsky, and the fate of other victims of the great purge. Thus, new material was added to Khrushchev's revelations in his secret speech at the Twentieth Party Congress, and provided the basis for a more thorough removal of the remnants of Stalinism. Three measures can be cited.

For the first time, the Congress heard details about the resistance of the "anti-Party group"—led by Molotov, Malenkov, Kaganovich, and Shepilov—against Khrushchev's new course in June 1957. It became known that not only Bulganin, Pervukhin, and Saburov, but also Voroshilov, had belonged to that group, thus giving it a majority in the Presidium. Khrushchev had managed to save the situation only by quickly calling a full plenary meeting of the Central Committee. He had not deemed it advisable to make this fact known at the Twenty-first Party Congress or to expose all concerned, but he did so now—and in a way that was especially painful for Voroshilov—in public, with full confession and absolution, according to the well-established ritual, although in a slightly milder form.

The second measure was a melodramatic gesture in grand style. After a female survivor of the purges had created the proper psychological climate by describing her sufferings, the Congress resolved to remove Stalin's embalmed body from the Lenin Mausoleum and bury it outside the Kremlin wall, next to lesser Soviet leaders. This decision was implemented without delay, and in full view of the public. Only then was the Stalin cult finally laid to rest.

The third measure concerned foreign policy. The Albanian delegation to the Twenty-second Party Congress was conspicuous by its absence. Khrushchev launched a strong attack against Enver Hoxha, the head of the Albanian Communist Party, branding him as a recalcitrant Stalinist. What followed was quite sensational. Chou En-lai not only defended Albania, he publicly reproached Khrushchev for his accusations, then laid a wreath at the Lenin Mausoleoum—before Stalin's body had been removed—and left the Congress prematurely. Khrushchev, unimpressed, attacked Albania even more sharply in his closing speech.

As a result of all this, Khrushchev's position as head of the Party was strengthened. The measures taken against the "anti-Party group" served as a warning for all potential future opposition. At the same time, more changes were made in the Party leadership, making it possible to remove certain people and to bring in more young talent.

Since 1962, the world has witnessed the Soviet Union's attempt to adapt the Communist political system to the conditions of an industrial society in the second half of the twentieth century. This attempt has run into two difficulties. The first is how to do justice to the growing needs of "the revolution of expectations" of the population without renouncing fundamental ideological principles of Communist rule—especially the dictatorship of the Party. The second is how to maintain the priority of heavy industry without giving up the gains of a living standard that is still modest, in Western terms. Because of the enormous costs of armaments, space probes, and atomic energy exploitation, such a balance of the nation's economy requires a reasonably prosperous agricultural sector.

But agriculture is precisely the worst bottleneck of the Soviet economy, as the following statistics indicate. Per capita wheat production still has not reached its 1913 level, that is, it has not kept pace with population growth. Land privately owned by kolkhoz farmers, which represents only 3.6 per cent of all arable land, is responsible for 50 per cent of the increase in cattle and for 66 per cent of the total production of potatoes and vegetables. Under these circumstances, Khrushchev's optimistic forecast of 1962, that Soviet agricultural production would outstrip that of the U.S.A. by 1982, seemed hardly more believable than his prediction of 1960, which had set 1970 as the target date. Hence, agriculture remains the problem child of the Soviet economy. Evidence of the efforts to find personal scapegoats for the failure of the system was shown by the dismissal of the Ministers of Agriculture in 1961 and again in 1962. At a plenary session of the Central Committee in March 1962, Khrushchev openly complained about the backwardness of Soviet agriculture; the plan targets had not been achieved, and there were shortages of meat and butter in some localities. At the plenary session, it was decided to reorganize the agricultural administration system at both the local and central levels. Two leading Soviet agricultural experts were vehemently criticized and expelled from the Academy of Agriculture.

A few months later, a lively discussion arose regarding the overall planning of the Soviet economy—in itself a remarkable occurrence. It was set off by an article in *Pravda* by Professor Libermann of Kharkov University, who reinterpreted the concept of productiveness and suggested that each enterprise establish its own plans.

These proposals were rejected by a plenary session of the Central Committee in November 1962, which pointed out that the goal of Soviet production was not profit, but the satisfaction of needs. However, a "guided" liberalization of economic policy was gradually introduced—although central regulation as well as the priority of heavy industry was, of course, retained. One very important result of this session was the reorganization of the entire administrative apparatus to such an extent that one could speak of a new relationship between Party, economy, and state. The reorganization of the planning and administration of industry and construction went hand in hand with a reorganization of the Party. Henceforth, below the republic level, the Party was organized not on a territorial basis, but according to the production process; two parallel hierarchies were set up, one dealing with industry and the other with agriculture. The Party and state control agencies were consolidated under a new chief, A. N. Shelepin. This process was completed in March 1963, with the creation of the Supreme Economic Council of the Soviet Union as the top agency for industry and construction. *Gosplan* was renamed the State Planning Committee and placed under the Supreme Economic Council.

This reform of the organizational structure of the CPSU represented its most profound transformation since the October Revolution. The Party no longer confined itself to guidance—it took charge of adminstration. The solution of economic problems became the main task of Party activity. As a result, Party, state, and economy became more integrated.

This reorganization was accompanied by certain changes in personnel, which had also become necessary because of Kozlov's sudden illness. In addition to Shelepin, the following joined the ranks of important Party officials: N. V. Podgorny, as representative of the Party Presidium of the Ukraine; V. I. Polyakov, as agricultural expert; A. P. Rudakov, as expert on heavy industry; G. I. Voronov, as President of the Russian Soviet Republic; and several others. Next to Khrushchev, the most important Soviet official became L. I. Brezhnev, who was appointed Secretary of the Central Committee of the CPSU in June 1963, while retaining his high state office. A year later, however, in July 1964, Mikoyan took over the chairmanship of the Presidium of the Supreme Soviet to permit Brezhnev to devote his full attention to Party affairs.

Liberalization within the Bloc

The wave of de-Stalinization engendered by the Twentieth Party Congress produced strong ripples in the other countries of the Soviet bloc. Poland's striving for freedom, especially, gained new momentum. The Poznan workers' riots, in June 1956, were forcefully suppressed with much loss of life, but the Communist regime in Poland was lenient in meting out punishment to the offenders. The persistence of great tension and of much anti-Russian feeling in Poland led to the reinstatement of Wladyslaw Gomulka—who had been removed from the Central Committee in 1949 for "Titoism"—to a position of primacy in the leadership of the Polish United Workers (Communist) Party. More significantly, it resulted in the refusal of the Central Committee to re-elect Soviet Marshal Konstantin Rokossovsky, Polish Defense Minister, to the Politburo. A sudden, unplanned visit to Warsaw by Khrushchev, Molotov, and other Soviet leaders, and their somewhat veiled threat to use force, merely stiffened Polish resistance. By some highly skillful maneuvering, Gomulka succeeded in retaining ties with Moscow while still gaining a certain measure of freedom of action for Poland.

In Hungary, what began as a slight relaxation of tensions following the ouster of Matyas Rakosi from the Party leadership, in the summer of 1956, quickly developed into a rebellion against Stalinism and Soviet control, spearheaded by students and intellectuals and aided by the passivity of the Hungarian troops. On October 23, what started out as a student demonstration in support of the revolutionary events in Poland turned into a mass rally with demands for greater freedom. The new government, which was headed by Imre Nagy—who had served as premier from 1953 to

1955, when he was unseated by Rakosi—attempted to assume the form of a coalition. Its willingness to meet the needs of the Hungarian masses and its demand that the Soviet Union withdraw its troops from Hungary led to the brutal intervention of Soviet armed forces following the employment of a ruse designed to weaken the rebels. A Communist regime more acceptable to Moscow, under Janos Kadar, was proclaimed following seizure of the parliament building in Budapest by Soviet troops early on Sunday morning, November 4, 1956. A renewed wave of strikes, which clearly proved that what took place was not a "fascist-reactionary" intervention from abroad, but a battle for freedom fought by the Hungarian workers and the young intellectuals, was suppressed by the most brutal means.[22]

These events illustrate well the dilemma that confronts the Soviet rulers. Attempts to meet, in part, the needs of their subjects lead to demands for genuine freedom with which Communism is incompatible; attempts to suppress the desire for freedom lead, in time, to a malignancy that can only undermine government.

During the events in both Poland and Hungary, the increasing importance of China on the European scene became clear. Even on the eve of the October demonstrations, the Chinese Communist leaders encouraged the Polish Communists in their attempts to emancipate themselves from Moscow. In Hungary, however, the Chinese sympathy toward similar developments in that country was suddenly reversed—possibly after a Soviet appeal—when Nagy renounced the Warsaw Pact. On December 29, 1956, the Chinese Central Committee made an important declaration of basic ideological principles, and also approved the Soviet intervention in Hungary. In January 1957, Chou En-lai traveled to Moscow and then to Warsaw and Budapest, thus emphasizing the extent of Chinese arbitration in East European affairs. The joint Soviet-Chinese declaration of January 18, 1957, could not conceal the fact that Peking did not really disapprove of some relaxing of Poland's dependency on Moscow—and Warsaw, through direct contacts with Communist China, tried to secure a measure of protection for itself similar to its former alliance with France, which had bypassed neighboring Germany.

In his "Hundred Flowers" speech on February 27, 1957, Mao Tse-tung said that, even in a socialist state, contradictions may exist between collective and individual interests, but these are the dynamic, dialectic element of progress and can be resolved peacefully and without terror. Nowhere was this speech received more eagerly than in Poland, where it was taken as an attempt to advance and develop socialist theory on the basis of the experiences of recent years.

Tito's behavior during the October crisis was not altogether unambiguous. Undoubtedly, the Yugoslav example had influenced developments in Warsaw and Budapest. In September, Tito and Khrushchev had met in Brioni and in Yalta for intensive discussion, which touched on Soviet foreign and domestic policies. But Hungary's complete defection from the Eastern bloc was not acceptable to Tito. To be sure, in his speech in Pola on November 11, Tito did criticize the continued influence of Stalinist elements in the Soviet Union and in the Eastern European countries, but he approved the action of the Soviet Army in Hungary.

A further focal point of international tensions in November 1956 was provided by the conflict between the Western powers and Egypt over the Suez Canal. This led to a brief military action by Israeli, British, and French troops, which temporarily diverted the attention of the world from the Soviet intervention in Hungary. The Soviet Union threatened to take military measures against England and to send volunteers to the Near East—a threat with which China agreed. Thus, the influence of the Soviets, who encourage Arab nationalism, especially in Egypt and Syria—not only with propaganda and economic aid, but also with the delivery of arms —gained greatly in that region. To this state of affairs, the Eisenhower Doctrine of January 5, 1957, provided a certain counterbalance.

The era of Sovietization and assimilation, as well as of Moscow's regimentation of Party policy and economic matters throughout the bloc, had come to an end; it would be misleading to speak of Kremlin "satellites" after 1956. Since then, all the East European countries (with the exception of East Germany) have been able, albeit cautiously and in varying degrees, to achieve a greater measure of independence and to make gradual progress in applying their own initiatives, especially in economic matters. Most significant in this respect has been Rumania's effort since 1964 to extricate itself from Soviet tutelage in economic and Party affairs. In the domain of culture, the drive for liberalization has been especially lively among the Poles, who have been, however, the captives of a pendular swing between alternate periods of cultural "thaw" and cultural "frost," in the form of relaxed and then renewed regulation. The individual East European Communist parties, too, have made noticeable efforts to develop their own national patterns, following the example of Yugoslavia since 1948.

There can be no doubt that the monolithic nature of the Soviet bloc has been transformed by increasing polycentrism.

"Peaceful Coexistence"

The formula "peaceful coexistence" was not Khrushchev's invention. It can be traced to Lenin's time, although it had less ideological and more practical and tactical significance in those days. The Treaty of Rapallo with Germany, in 1922, reflected this kind of cooperation between states that had different political and social systems. Even Stalin, after he had entered into a state of "military coexistence" with the Western powers, through his wartime alliance, occasionally addressed himself to the fundamentals of coexistence—for example, in his interview with American publishers on April 2, 1952.

The term "coexistence" assumed a programmatic quality for the first time in Malenkov's speech of August 6, 1953. Three years later, at the Twentieth Party Congress, Khrushchev adopted the formula and developed it further, to the point where he had revised Lenin's thesis of the inevitability of war in the period of capitalism. Khrushchev's journeys abroad in 1955 turned this new ideological position into practical politics. His engaging candor signified a change in methods. The Soviet Union had by no means renounced its prerogative of spreading Communism throughout the world, however. But now Moscow was pursuing this goal by peaceful means—at least initially—as long as there was no threat to any established Soviet position that would require military intervention, as during the Hungarian uprising.

Yet, as far as the German question was concerned, Moscow was not ready to narrow the limits of its influence. In November 1958, the Soviet Union informed the Western nations, through a series of notes, that it no longer felt bound by any treaties concerning the status of Berlin. In an ultimatum, the Soviet government declared that, unless an understanding could be reached within six months, it would hand over all authority to the government of East Germany. The main purpose of this ultimatum was to strengthen the hand of Walter Ulbricht. During this controversy, Khrushchev repeatedly threatened a separate peace treaty with East Germany.

Neither Prime Minister Macmillan's Moscow visit early in 1959 nor the Foreign Ministers' Conference in Geneva in the summer of the same year provided a solution; but Khrushchev, evidently, did not think it advisable to carry out the threats of the ultimatum.

His spectacular visit to the United States, in September 1959, and his personal talks with President Eisenhower at Camp David seemed to promise a relaxation of tension. During his visit with President de Gaulle in Paris, in March 1960, however, he sharply criticized the West German Federal Republic.

A deterioration of East-West relations occurred in May 1960, triggered by the U-2 incident, when a U.S. air reconnaissance plane was shot down over Soviet territory, on May 1, and the pilot was captured alive. Khrushchev used this incident for a complete about-face. He dynamited the long-prepared summit conference in Paris, on May 19, by unleashing a rude attack on President Eisenhower. The disarmament conference, which had been meeting in Geneva since March, broke up in June, without having achieved any results. The climax of this phase of Khrushchev's personal participation was reached at a meeting of the UN General Assembly in October 1960. The Assembly dealt with the disturbances that had broken out in the Congo after independence and had led to UN intervention on June 30, 1960. The enormous importance of Africa in Soviet foreign policy became clear. Until then, Moscow had concentrated its attention on the Arab countries. Now the independence of former French and British colonies offered new possibilities for intervention and influence—this was the motive behind all offers of diplomatic and economic aid. The Soviet Union opposed the UN action in the Congo and used this opposition for attacks on Secretary General Dag Hammarskjöld, coupled with suggestions for the reorganization of the office of Secretary General. Khrushchev tried to force acceptance of his views in drastic, uninhibited fashion, but he was unsuccessful. A much milder resolution against colonialism than he had proposed was adopted in December, and Hammarskjöld's position remained unassailed. The Soviet Union's interest in Africa came to the fore again in February 1961, when Patrice Lumumba was assassinated and the Congo crisis took a turn for the worse. The chairman of the Presidium of the Supreme Soviet, Brezhnev, visited Morocco, Guinea, and Ghana.

At the same time, Moscow's attention focused on Cuba, where Fidel Castro had seized power. As early as February 1960, Mikoyan had visited Cuba, and, at the end of the same year, a Cuban delegation had been received in Moscow. Castro's anti-American attacks gave the Soviet Union the opportunity to gain a foothold in Latin America.

With the election of President John F. Kennedy, a new chapter in Soviet-American relations began. Moscow remained quietly watchful, but tried to influence public opinion by releasing the

American pilots whose plane had been shot down over the Barents Sea in July 1960. The personal meeting between Kennedy and Khrushchev in Vienna, in June 1961, enabled them to assess their respective positions; but the basic differences concerning the Congo and the reorganization of the UN smoldered in the background. The situation was not improved by the fact that the fighting that had broken out in Laos, in December 1960, between the Western-oriented government and the neutralist and communist factions was followed by Chinese and North Vietnamese intervention.

In August 1961—strengthened by the propagandistic success of the space flights and anticipating discussions of the Central Committee on the eve of the Twenty-second Party Congress—Khrushchev thought the time ripe to bring up once again the question of Berlin and recognition of East Germany through a unilateral peace treaty. Ulbricht received permission to cut the connection between East and West Berlin, using force if necessary. During the night of August 12-13, the East Germans put up the Berlin Wall.

Thus, the question of Berlin and of free access to the city was re-opened—and with it the entire German question. In view of the brutal form this action took and the intensity of the war of nerves that accompanied it, this could be called the most serious world crisis since the end of the Second World War.

In the autumn of 1961, the Soviet Union unilaterally ended the moratorium on nuclear testing with a series of tests in Central Asia that had a terrorizing effect —especially on the conference of uncommitted nations that met in Belgrade. The Soviets did not seem to mind this effect; on the contrary, they probably intended it.

The meeting of Kennedy and Khrushchev in Vienna by no means resulted in the *détente* that had been expected in some capitals. In addition to Berlin, where a meeting of COMECON (Council for Mutual Economic Assistance), in June 1962, again called for the creation of a free city and a peace treaty with East Germany, Cuba became a trouble spot. Several visits to Moscow by leading associates of Fidel Castro and the inauguration of direct flights between Moscow and Havana helped to strengthen Soviet-Cuban contacts. Finally, in September 1962, Khrushchev promised to send Cuba arms, technicians, and other specialists, and to help build a fishing port.

On October 22, President Kennedy announced on television that American intelligence services had conclusive evidence of the construction of launching pads for medium- and intermediate-range ballistic missiles on Cuban soil by Soviet specialists; as a countermeasure, a quarantine of Cuban waters was announced for October 24. Proof of the construction of the missile bases submitted by the United States to the UN Security Council evoked flat denials by the Soviet representative. But, in fact, world Communism had succeeded in establishing a beachhead in the Western hemisphere from which the United States could be put under sudden pressure. On October 23, Soviet Defense Minister Malinovsky canceled all military leaves, and Marshal Andrei Grechko, Supreme Military Commander of the Warsaw Pact nations, put the general staffs of these countries on alert. Moscow, meanwhile, refused to accept a note in which Washington advised it of the Cuban blockade.

At this critical point, UN Secretary General U Thant intervened with a suggestion that led to an exchange of letters between him, Kennedy, and Khrushchev, and between Kennedy and Khrushchev directly. Khrushchev's first letter to Kennedy (October 26) has not been made public, but it seems to have shown a certain willingness to compromise. The following day, however, in his second letter, Khrushchev—pressed perhaps by advocates of a harder line among the Soviet leaders—declared that the dismantling of the missile bases in Cuba depended on the withdrawal of U.S. missiles from Turkey. The White House at once categorically rejected such an exchange. In the meantime, work proceeded on the missile bases in Cuba. During the night of October 27, paratroop reservists were called up in the United States. The crisis was at its height.

Around noon on October 28, Radio Moscow broadcast a third letter from Khrushchev to Kennedy, in which—without referring to his proposed exchange of bases—he promised to dismantle the Cuban missile installations. During the night of October 27-28, the Soviet government had evidently come to the conclusion that the U.S. government had both the military capacity to confront any Soviet threat and the necessary determination to stand fast. Under these conditions, the Soviet government thought it best to give in.

By November 21, the crisis had so far abated that the state of increased military readiness and the ban on military leave could be canceled. The dismantling of the missile bases was witnessed by UN representatives. The Russian people were told that the Soviet concessions in Cuba had prevented a U.S.-directed imperialist invasion of the island.

Viewed in a larger framework, it appears that the Cuban crisis was a historical turning point. The East Wind no longer prevailed over the West Wind, as Mao Tse-tung used to say; the wind seemed to have turned. The temporary superiority of Soviet missiles during 1960 and 1961, as well as several other factors, had led Moscow to misjudge the balance of power between East and West—hence, the self-confidence of the Soviet Union and its provocative foreign policy during those years. In October 1962, Khrushchev became aware of the increased military strength of the United States and of the determination of its President. The further spread of Communism suffered other reverses too. Important Soviet agents were arrested in the United States, England, Sweden, and West Germany. There were occasional stirrings of mistrust and opposition to Communist infiltration in the young African states. After 1962, the aggressive élan of Khrushchev's global political strategy slackened.

The Sino-Soviet Dispute

The dissolution of the monolithic unity of world Communism is also reflected in the growing tensions between Moscow and Peking. To the ideological differences of the two countries has been added rivalry in the arena of power politics.

In the beginning, the Soviet Union was greatly impressed by the dynamism of Communist China, whose industrialization had grown at a far more rapid pace after the announcement of its First Five Year Plan in 1953 than had Russia's after 1930. Chinese steel production alone increased from 0.5 million tons in 1939 to 10.7 million tons in 1958. When communes were established in Chinese villages in the fall of 1958, it seemed that Chinese Communism was trying to overtake Soviet Russia's development from socialism to Communism in one "great leap." This was too much for Moscow. The Soviet Party periodicals declared categorically that there could be no doubt that the European countries would be the first to reach the goal of Communism. China was, however, still as dependent on Soviet consumer goods and arms as on Soviet specialists in many fields. Internal considerations soon compelled the Chinese to lower their goals. The village communes proved unsuited to the building up of heavy industry, and in December, 1958, the Chinese slowed down the tempo of their development. Yet the feeling remained that they had been left in the lurch by the Russians.

China watched Khrushchev's coexistence politics with deep mistrust. The hard line that Moscow took in its relations with the West between the end of 1958 and the end of 1960—and even into 1962—can be explained in part by the consideration Khrushchev thought he owed to China, which was not a member of the United Nations and had only limited relations with the West. After his visit to the United States, Khrushchev did not neglect to report back to his Chinese partner immediately and in person. Nevertheless, after 1959, an estrangement could not be denied. The differences were not merely strategical and tactical; there were latent ideological differences, as well.

Peking did not hesitate to launch a sharp ideological polemic against Moscow in 1960. The main subject of the controversy was Khrushchev's revision of Lenin's thesis concerning the inevitability of war, which was considered sacrosanct in Peking. In Moscow, at the celebration of Lenin's ninetieth birthday, the old-guard Bolshevik Kuusinen, citing the master, countered these accusations with an avowal of coexistence and a rebuttal of "dogmatism." Khrushchev used the conference of the twenty-eight Communist parties in Bucharest, in June 1960, for similar pronouncements. *Pravda* accused China of "left deviationism" and "sectarian errors."

Besides these ideological controversies, there were obviously tactical differences in the two countries' efforts to expand their respective spheres of influence. Khrushchev hoped for agreements with bourgeois-nationalist forces, which he would eventually change into Communist dictatorships. Mao Tse-tung, on the other hand, relied on a "united front from below"—a spontaneous peasant movement and collaboration with the masses—a reliance based on his experiences during the 1920's. The common ideological platform, however, remained for some time sufficiently broad to serve as a base for both Communist systems and to permit continued solidarity in their external relations.

In November 1960, the delegates of eighty-seven Communist parties—representing 36 million members—met in Moscow. This meeting lasted several weeks. The minutes of the December 6 session show a certain compromise. There was no mention of "people's communes" or of a "leap forward," although peaceful coexistence was defined as a form of "class struggle between socialism and capitalism." Khrushchev clarified the question of the inevitability of war by stating—in his speech on January 6, 1961—that world wars and even local wars could and should be avoided, whereas "peoples' uprisings" and "wars of national independence" were unavoidable.

During the Cuban missile crisis, Sino-Soviet tension reached such a pitch that China's full-scale attack on India at the Chinese-Indian border in the Himalayas—the culmination of repeated minor border skirmishes over a considerable period of time prior to the crisis—received no Soviet support. On the contrary, Khrushchev competed with the West in assuring India of his readiness to help. The Chinese were also angered by the pointedly friendly relations between the Soviet Union and Yugoslavia. In late summer 1962, they ordered all Russian consulates in China closed. In November 1962, Peking referred to Khrushchev's decision to withdraw Soviet missiles from Cuba as a new "Munich." At Communist Party congresses in the East European satellite countries and in Rome, the Chinese representatives, though invited, were always kept at arm's length. On March 1, 1963, a Peking newspaper referred for the first time to border regions lost by the Chinese empire in the nineteenth century that were now to be reclaimed. This reference could only apply to Russia's Far Eastern province, the Amur region, and East Turkestan. In November 1963, there were incidents along the Sino-Soviet border in Siberia.

In the summer of 1963, relations between Moscow and Peking grew still worse. In a letter to the CPSU, dated June 14, the Central Committee of the Chinese Communist Party challenged the fundamentals of Khrushchev's foreign policy—peaceful coexistence, economic competition, and disarmament negotiations—as a violation of the revolutionary principles that China and the USSR had jointly agreed upon in 1957 and 1960. Indirectly, though unmistakably, the CPSU was accused of having become a party of the workers' aristocracy and not of the people, a party that took a negative attitude toward the oppressed peoples of the world and sabotaged the onward march of the revolution. The twenty-five point document amounted to a radical commitment to the uncompromising doctrine of revolution and, at the same time, appealed to the non-European Communist movements, with their "storm centers" in Asia, Africa, and Latin America, whose leaders were eventually to inherit the leadership of world Communism. One month later, on July 14, the CPSU sharply rebutted these accusations in an open letter in *Pravda*.

Under these conditions, it is hardly surprising that the Sino-Soviet negotiations on ideological differences, begun on July 5, ended in failure two weeks later, although the talks were supposedly to be resumed in the future. This failure assumes even greater significance in view of the negotiations that took place at the same time between Khrushchev and American and British representatives concerning prohibition of above-ground nuclear weapons tests. On May 21, an American-Soviet agreement on the peaceful uses of atomic energy had been signed. On July 20, agreement was reached on the installation of a "hot line" between the White House and the Kremlin; this project was implemented on August 31. The negotiations on limitation of nuclear weapons tests ended successfully on August 5, 1963. U.S. Secretary of State Dean Rusk and British Foreign Secretary Lord Home, as well as UN Secretary

General U Thant, journeyed to Moscow to affix their signatures to the multilateral document. Although more than a hundred nations signed the treaty (France was a notable exception), the Chinese People's Republic, which had demanded total prohibition of nuclear weapons instead of a limitation of weapons tests, withheld its consent. Regardless of the limited gains that could be expected, the agreement marked a continuation of the policy of relaxation that Khrushchev seemed determined to pursue despite Chinese criticism. Perhaps the Soviet government intended, among other things, to indict eventual Chinese nuclear tests in advance, so as to incriminate China in the eyes of the world.

The profound changes that the Communist world had been undergoing had, meanwhile, become much more noticeable. The Soviet Union had been forced to accept Yugoslavia's independent course after Stalin's death. After the revolt of October, 1956, Poland expressed its national spirit in an independent choice of methods, if not policies. Thus, Moscow's control over all the other Communist parties had to be relaxed. Apart from the growing demand of the Chinese Communist Party—the largest in the world —to be treated as an equal partner, rather than as Moscow's most important satellite, a certain spirit of willfulness among the Communist parties of the Western world was observable. This spirit was most evident in the Italian Communist Party, led by Palmiro Togliatti, undoubtedly one of the most distinctive and intelligent figures of world Communism. It was Togliatti who first put forth the concept of polycentrism, thereby ending forever the erstwhile ideal of a "monolithic bloc" under Soviet leadership.

Once Sino-Soviet differences had become public, the non-European Communist parties felt pressed to choose between Moscow and Peking. Inevitably, this choice became more complex, as considerations of power politics and race were added to the ideological issues of the dispute. The Chinese Communist Party Central Committee's denunciatory memorandum of June 14, 1963, quite clearly suggested that the international class struggle had assumed the character of a confrontation between the colored and white peoples of the world. Yet, despite China's growing domestic and external consolidation—the latter enhanced by French diplomatic recognition and the first successful Chinese nuclear explosion in October of that year—there were limits to Chinese Communist influence in Southeast Asia. Indonesia's anti-Communist shift was but one example.

At the beginning of 1964, Sino-Soviet rivalry assumed a quality of personal animosity. Mao Tse-tung's letter to Khrushchev, on

February 5, was particularly pointed. Subsequently, the Soviet government and Party leaders weighed the idea of convening a world Communist Party conference to condemn China's point of view. In sounding out the other Communist parties, however, the Soviet Union encountered opposition—particularly from the Rumanian and Italian parties—to what would amount to a calculated division of world Communism. When invitations to a preparatory meeting were nonetheless sent out, Togliatti himself hastened to Moscow to declare his personal doubts. Togliatti's views on the future development of Communism, formulated in the so-called Yalta Memorandum, were given wide prominence in the Western press and were also published in *Pravda* on September 10, after his death in the Crimea on August 21, 1964.

The Soviet Union under Brezhnev and Kosygin

On April 17, 1964, Khrushchev was honored by both Party and state as a "Hero of the Soviet Union," on the occasion of his seventieth birthday. A mere six months later, the world was stunned by the news of his ouster.

At a meeting of the Party Presidium on October 13, Khrushchev was confronted with certain accusations; he had been forced to cut short his vacation in Sochi to account for his errors. His attempt to justify his conduct before the Central Committee, on October 14, failed. In addition to the premiership, he also lost all the Party offices he had held. He was replaced by A. N. Kosygin as Premier, and by I. I. Brezhnev as First Secretary of the Party. Thus, the two highest offices in the land were again placed in separate hands, as after Stalin's death.

In reassigning the eleven places on the Party Presidium, the plenary meeting of the Central Committee, in the middle of November 1964, moved up, in their prevailing order of rank, the existing members (Brezhnev, Kosygin, Mikoyan, Suslov, Podgorny, Voronov, Polyansky, Kirilenko, and Shvernik) and appointed at the lowest level two new members—Ukrainian Party First Secretary P. Ye. Shelest (born 1908) and Secretary of the Central Committee Presidium A. N. Shelepin (born 1918), a former chairman of the State Security Committee and the Party-State Control Committee.

Khrushchev's fall from power has been attributed to his conduct of both domestic and foreign affairs. His political style was criticized as a reversion to the cult of personality; he was also charged with nepotism, boastfulness, and willfulness. In domestic affairs, he was held responsible for economic failure caused by his erratic policies. In the sphere of foreign policy, Khrushchev was presented with the grave charge that his emphasis on the relaxation of tensions vis-à-vis the West was finally threatening the unity of the world Communist movement. That Chou En-lai, the Chinese Premier, personally attended the anniversary celebrations of the October Revolution on November 7, 1964, immediately after Khrushchev's removal, suggests that a review of the Sino-Soviet conflict might have been undertaken by the Chinese.

It would, however, be incorrect to hold China or the Chinese Communist Party responsible for Khrushchev's ouster. The hectic activity that seemed an inseparable feature of Khrushchev's policy of coexistence and of his general conduct of foreign affairs—one need only remember his numerous journeys abroad—was distasteful to many Soviet leaders because of its spontaneous nature. Admittedly, his three-week visit to Egypt in May 1964, which was intended to offset Chou En-lai's African tour in 1963-64, had contributed greatly to the restoration of Soviet prestige in that part of the world. But when Khrushchev in June 1964—after a postponement since 1959—visited Sweden, Denmark, and Norway, he offended Soviet leaders because he took his entire family along, not to mention that the visit was neither a political nor a propagandistic success.

There was, moreover, Khrushchev's striking preoccupation with West Germany. The visit by Aleksei Adzhubei, Khrushchev's son-in-law and editor-in-chief of *Izvestia,* had the purpose of laying the ground for a visit by Khrushchev himself. The flavor of *Izvestia*'s editorials on the visit displayed a marked departure from the customary Soviet emphasis on a multitude of facts and pointed polemics. This may have indicated an approaching shift in Khrushchev's German policy, similar to Beria's plans just before his fall from power.

Soviet military circles had for some time been opposed to Khrushchev's disarmament and coexistence policies. Their doubts were shared by the managers of heavy industry, particularly in view of Khrushchev's decision, in September 1964, to increase consumer goods production further. The Soviet security apparatus was apparently also resuming its initiative and hampered his efforts to achieve a relaxation of international tensions.

The most decisive factor in Khrushchev's downfall was his dilettantism in economic policy, particularly in agriculture. Despite a 17 per cent increase in the sown acreage between 1960 and 1963, the "virgin lands" campaign in Kazakhstan had once again proved a failure. Only massive wheat imports from Canada, in September

1963, prevented a major famine—an embarrassing demonstration of Soviet dependence on capitalist production that cost Khrushchev much of his popularity. Industrial production, moreover, had been in a recession since 1959; in the first half of 1964, the annual rate of growth had dropped to 7.5 per cent. Even if this could not be attributed entirely to Khrushchev's improvisations, it contributed to the animosity felt toward him in economic circles.

Khrushchev could no longer counter this catalog of domestic and foreign policy failures with the kind of special appeal to "Party democracy" that he had successfully launched at the Central Committee plenary meeting in 1957. He was even less in a position to turn to the masses, a step he threatened at the Central Committee meeting in October 1964. In short, the Khrushchev era, which had officially come into being in 1958, had come to an end.

The dual leadership of Brezhnev and Kosygin, after October 1964, proved itself stable. They developed a collegial style of governing, which, because it was less colorful and more impersonal, was also less erratic than Khrushchev's.

Leonid Ilyich Brezhnev was born in the Ukraine in 1906, the son of a worker. He completed his technical education in 1935 with a degree in engineering. Thereafter, he successfully held various Party positions in the Ukraine, in the Moldavian Republic, and in Kazakhstan. From 1960 to 1964, as chairman of the Presidium of the Supreme Soviet, he was President of the USSR.

Aleksei Nikolayevich Kosygin, also the son of a worker, was born in Leningrad in 1904 and completed his technical education with a degree in textile engineering. From 1938 on he was an industrial administrator, Mayor of Leningrad, held several positions in the Ministry of Economic Affairs, rose in the Party ranks to membership in the Politburo, was made chief of *Gosplan* in 1959, and, in 1960, became a member of the Presidium of the Central Committee and First Deputy Premier of the USSR.

In December 1965, Mikoyan retired as President of the USSR. He was replaced by Nikolai Viktorovich Podgorny (born 1903). At the same time, to represent the younger generation (as did Shelepin), the Ukrainian Dmitri Stepanovich Polyansky (born 1917) was promoted to First Deputy Premier of the USSR.

In November 1964, Brezhnev embarked on a reorganization of the Party, reversing Khrushchev's decentralization measures of 1957 and resuming where Bulganin's reforms of 1955 had left off. In March 1965, an agricultural plan was formulated that laid down the basis for overcoming the obstacles to agricultural expansion. The plan provided for increased investment and aimed at countering dissatisfaction among agricultural workers by lowering delivery quotas, canceling kolkhoz debts, and promising both higher prices for surplus production and higher wages. Kosygin's industrial reforms, announced in September 1965, eliminated the regional economic councils. Yet, despite central planning and guidance, individual enterprises were given more independence. The planning of the consumer goods industry, in particular, was to take into account demand and productivity along the lines of the Libermann proposals. The most important consideration was that the Party and state leadership, rather than the bureaucracy, held the power of decision-making.

The Twenty-third Party Congress, which met from March 29 to April 28, 1966, scrapped the Seven Year Plan and introduced a new Five Year Plan (1966-70). Moreover, the former Politburo was reinstated, taking the place of the Central Committee Presidium. The Politburo had a rejuvenated membership, since K. T. Mazurov (the former Belorussian Party First Secretary and First Deputy Premier of the USSR) and A. Ya. Pelshe (the Latvian Party First Secretary) displaced Mikoyan and Shvernik.

Within the councils of the Party leadership, the simultaneous pursuit of a hard and a soft line continued. Just as the soft line expressed itself in economic measures, so the hard line was also evident, as in Brezhnev's demand for stepped up rearmament in a speech on July 4, 1965—a demand that the Twenty-third Party Congress ratified. And even while some of the victims of Stalinism were being rehabilitated, some of Stalin's achievements were given their proper recognition in the Soviet press, particularly in the spring of 1966. In September 1965, two writers—Andrei Sinyavsky and Yuli Daniel—were arrested for having published articles in a Paris-based Polish periodical. Their trial and subsequent sentences to hard labor aroused the indignation of the Western world, and evoked protests from a number of Soviet intellectuals.

In foreign affairs, the current Soviet leadership has essentially maintained Khrushchev's policy of coexistence. These efforts bore fruit in the U.S.–Soviet agreement on cultural and technical exchanges, signed in March 1966. But, as could be expected, U.S.–Soviet relations cooled with the progressive escalation of the war in Viet-Nam. De Gaulle, in the wake of his gradual withdrawal from NATO, made skillful use of this development. His visit to the Soviet Union from June 20 to July 1, 1966, which resulted in the publication of a joint Soviet-French communiqué, undoubtedly contributed much to a relaxation of East-West tensions. But as far as the German question is concerned, the Soviet Union has been even more inflexible than during Khrushchev's tenure. The suicide of Erich Apel, head of the East German State Planning Commission, on December 3, 1965, was a macabre consequence of the burden that has been imposed on East Germany's economic development by its new economic ties to the Soviet Union.

A policy of coexistence today means that the Soviet Union has to renounce the thought of resurrecting the unity of world Communism. Only the sacrifice of this principle, the condemnation of Yugoslav revisionism, and the unequivocal rehabilitation of Stalin could have ended the dispute with China after Khrushchev's ouster. Kosygin's visit to Peking, in February 1965, while en route to Hanoi, resulted in no improvement; he could not even persuade the Chinese to let Soviet war materials for North Viet-Nam pass through their country.

When only nineteen of twenty-six invited Communist Party representatives arrived in Moscow, in March 1965, it became clear that polycentrism had become a reality. That same month, there were further quarrels with China. Chinese student demonstrations in front of the American Embassy in Moscow were followed by Chinese demonstrations at the gates of the Soviet Embassy in Peking.

In 1965 and 1966, China suffered new defeats in the competition for influence in the developing countries. Moreover, thanks to Soviet mediation, the Kashmir dispute between India and Pakistan was resolved, at least temporarily, with a peace treaty signed in Tashkent. This achievement, followed by mutual official visits, led to closer contacts between India and the Soviet Union.

In the winter of 1965-66, the press war between China and the Soviet Union was again stepped up. While a Chinese publication placed the CPSU at the "left wing of imperialism," a Soviet letter to all the Communist parties of the world drew attention to China's "chauvinistic great-power politics." The Twenty-third Party Congress was the first to which the Chinese refused to send representatives. At a conference of Warsaw Pact nations held in Bucharest in July 1966, the Soviet Union failed to gain support for a resolution condemning the Chinese Communists. Relations between the two countries have been further aggravated by the so-called Chinese cultural revolution and the provocations of the Red Guard. The detonation of the first Chinese hydrogen bomb in June 1967 adds considerable strength both to Chinese self-assertiveness and to their polemic with Moscow.

The occasion of the fiftieth anniversary of the October Revolution, in November 1967, will give the Soviet Union an opportunity to look back on both internal gains and the successful spread of world Communism. Within the Soviet Union in the last decade, there have been important technical and scientific successes, as well as the first signs of improvement in the standard of living of the people and a certain relaxation in the individual sphere. According to a survey published in *Pravda* on January 20, 1967, there has been a world-wide growth in Communist Party membership from 400,000 in 1917 to 50 million in 1967. In the non-Communist countries alone, there are seventy-four Communist parties. This has been matched by an increasing differentiation among the Communist countries: There is no longer only a Soviet model of government, there are also Yugoslav, Chinese, Polish, and Rumanian models. Initiative is also growing among the Communist parties in the free world. Polycentrism, by taking national considerations into account, may actually encourage, rather than weaken, the forces of world Communism.

The bitterness with which the Chinese fight the Soviet policy of coexistence tends to obscure the fact that the concept advocated by both Khrushchev and his successors excludes ideological coexistence. In this arena, the competition has never ceased. The Soviet concept of "peaceful coexistence" is the Leninist one that peace will be achieved when Communism has triumphed throughout the world. All appeals to the "forces for peace" that come from Moscow must be understood in this sense.

Yet the peoples of the Communist countries undoubtedly feel a genuine desire for peace. One should therefore warn against a dogmatic anti-Communist stance by the free world and instead encourage communication on many levels, including that of personal contact. At the national level, these efforts have been expressed in the formula "peaceful engagement"—a policy that must combine steadfastness and flexibility, realism and imagination, if peace and freedom are to be maintained.

Perhaps it will turn out that the recognition of universal, common tasks for both East and West—the peaceful application of atomic energy, the control of nuclear weapons or the prohibition of their use in outer space, and the fight against hunger, disease, and human need under the shadow of the world population explosion—are more compelling than the adherence to class and race prejudices, the clinging to obsolete ideas of national prestige and ideological zeal, and the desire to impose one's mode of life on others, even in the well-meant conviction that it would redound to mankind's benefit.

The beginnings of the Civil War

The map shows the events that took place between February and August of 1918. The advance of the Central Powers fell into two phases: The starting situation prior to the seizure of the northern Baltic states and the intervention in the Ukrainian Civil War and the situation at the end of these movements in May 1918. In the North, in the region of Murmansk and Arkhangel'sk and in the Southeast, in the Trans-Caspian region, the landings of British and other Allied interventionist forces are shown. The Eastern border line of the areas under bolshevist control, against the Czechoslovak and White forces that were pushing forward from Siberia, is drawn as it was prior to the decisive turning point in August 1918.

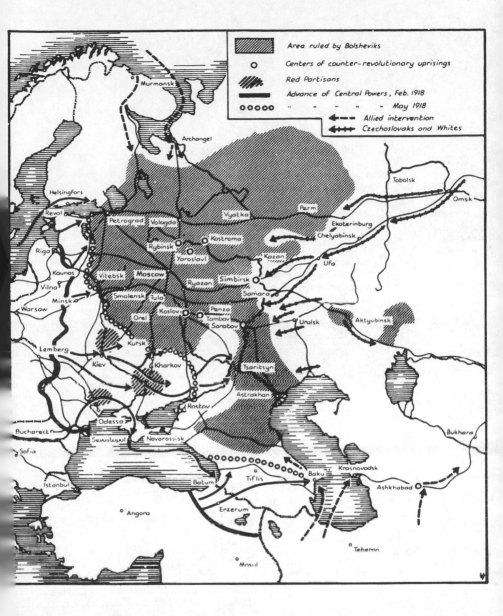

The Civil War during the summer of 1919

During the winter of 1918/19 the area controlled by the Bolsheviks was extended to include the Ukraine, but they had been pushed back from the Baltic states and from Finland. The map shows the position at the start of the operations of Yudenich against Petersburg and of Denikin in the direction of Moscow, which reached their highest point in October 1919. Prior to this, the retreat of Kolchak's Army had already begun in the East. The activities of the Allied interventionist troops and fleet units were concentrated in four areas: the White Sea, the Baltic Sea, the Black Sea and the Trans-Caspian region.

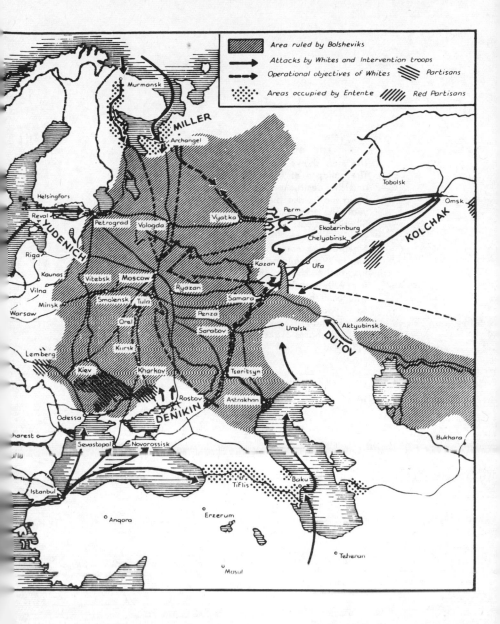

	Area ruled by Bolsheviks
	Attacks by Whites and Intervention troops
	Operational objectives of Whites
	Areas occupied by Entente
	Partisans
	Red Partisans

Murmansk

MILLER

Archangel

Tobolsk

Helsingfors

Omsk

Reval

YUDENICH

Petrograd

Vologda

Vyatka

Perm

Riga

Ekaterinburg

KOLCHAK

Kaunas

Chelyabinsk

Vilna

Vitebsk

Moscow

Kazan

Ufa

Minsk

Ryazan

Warsaw

Smolensk

Tula

Samara

Oral

Penza

DUTOV

Lember

Kursk

Saratov

Uralsk

Aktyubinsk

Kiev

Kharkov

Tsaritsyn

Odessa

Rostov

Astrakhan

DENIKIN

Bukhara

harest

Sevastopol

Novorossisk

Istanbul

Baku

TiFlis

Angora

Erzerum

Teheran

Mosul

The end of the Civil War

The map shows the events of the year 1920. The collapse of Denikin's forces in the South and the destruction of Kolchak's Army in Siberia took place during the first months of the year. The arrows in the Ukraine and in Western Siberia indicate the various stages of the Bolshevist advance. The arrow pointing toward Novorossiysk corresponds to the Allied supply line to Wrangel's army. Wrangel launched the last anti-bolshevist offensive from the Crimea in 1920, but it collapsed in the area from whence it had started toward the end of the same year. The Polish attack from the West, in the direction of Kiev, is shown, though the subsequent phases of the Polish-Soviet war are not indicated.

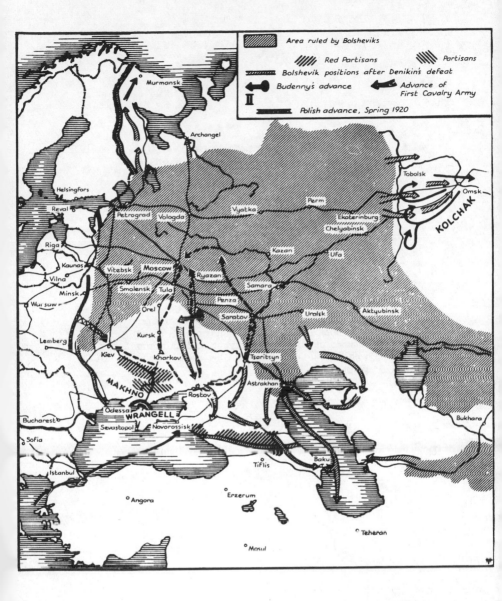

	Area ruled by Bolsheviks
	Red Partisans		Partisans
	Bolshevik positions after Denikin's defeat
	Budenny's advance		Advance of First Cavalry Army
II	
	Polish advance, Spring 1920

Murmansk
Archangel
Helsingfors
Reval
Riga
Kaunas
Vilna
Minsk
Warsaw
Lemberg
Bucharest
Sofia
Istanbul

Petrograd
Vologda
Vitebsk
Moscow
Smolensk
Tula
Orel
Kursk
Kiev
Kharkov
MAKHNO
Rostov
Odessa
WRANGELL
Sevastopol
Novorossisk

Vyatka
Perm
Ekaterinburg
Chelyabinsk
Kazan
Ryazan
Samara
Penza
Saratov
Uralsk
Tsaritsyn
Astrakhan

Tobolsk
Omsk
KOLCHAK
Ufa
Aktyubinsk
Bukhara

Angora
Erzerum
Mosul
Tiflis
Baku
Teheran

The turning point in World War II

The map shows the various stages of the German advance into Russia during 1942 and 1943, from the Soviet counter-stroke near Moscow to the turning point at Stalingrad and up to the Teheran Conference. The edge of the black area is the extreme limit of the German advance on Soviet soil in 1942. The German retreat started in the North at the beginning of the year, while the advance in the South, to the gates of Stalingrad and into the North Caucasus, continued until the end of 1942. On the central front, in the region of Kursk, the dent in the German lines in the summer of 1943 is clearly visible. The irregular front line of December 1943 shows the gains of the Soviet summer offensive of that year and coincides with the starting position for the decisive campaigns of 1944/45.

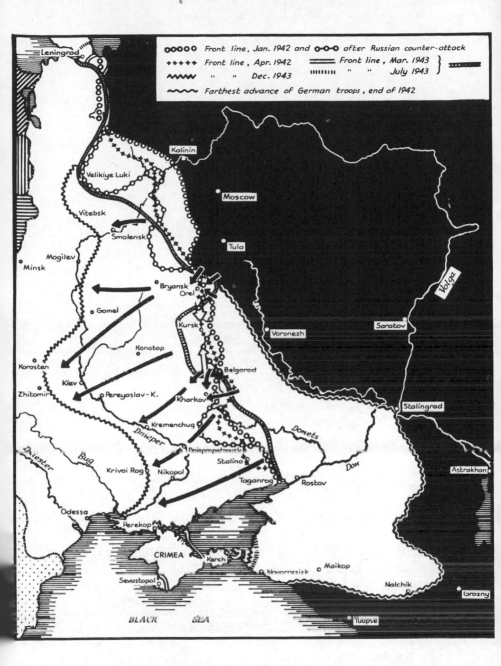

NOTES

Prologue

1. A terrorist conspirator whom Dostoevsky used as model for Verkhovensky in *The Possessed.*
2. Thus the Minister of Culture, Count Dimitri Tolstoy, according to Prince B. von Buelow's memoirs, 1931, Vol. IV, p. 573. Cf. similar views held by K. Leontyev.
3. One *pud* = 35.2 lbs.
4. F. Borkenau, "Zwei Revolutionaere," *Der Monat*, 1950, No. 25.
5. *Ibid.*
6. N. Berdyaev, *The Russian Idea.* London, 1947, p. 119.
7. L. Trotsky, *My Life.* New York, 1930, Chapter 12.
8. L. Trotsky, *My Life.* New York, 1930.
9. After the Russian initials of the "Constitutional Democrats."
10. In Bolshevik terminology the Mensheviks aiming at dissolution of the party and collaboration with the Liberals are called *liquidators;* the Bolshevik "idealists" who were finally condemned by a Party Commission in 1909, were termed *otzovtsi* (from *otzyv* = recall).

Chapter 1

1. The statement that the Bolsheviks started the February Revolution with their call for demonstrations is one of the many historical falsifications of Stalinism. It finds its climax in the following statement from the textbook, *History of the USSR*, Moscow, 1947: "The Bureau of the Central Committee, headed by Molotov, led the insurrection." In actual fact, district committees of the party had opposed the first strikes. Cf. *Der Monat*, 1952/42 (D. Shub) and 1952/44 (N. Hurwitz).
2. F. Borkenau in *Der Monat*, Nov. 1952.
3. L. Trotsky, *The Stalin School of Falsification.* New York, 1937, p. 238ff.
4. This conference is not mentioned in any Stalinist account. A record of it was later given by Kamenev to Trotsky who subsequently published it. *The Stalin School of Falsification*, pp. 231-301.
5. Cf. N. Sukhanov, *Zapiski o Revolyutzii.* Berlin, 1922, Vol. III, p. 10ff.
6. Lenin, *Sochinenia*, 2d. ed., Vol. XX, pp. 87-90.
7. Sukhanov, *op. cit.*, Vol. III, p. 26ff.
8. F. Stepun, *Vergangenes und Unvergaengliches* Munich, 1949, II, p. 188ff.
9. W. Gurian, "Lenins Methoden der Machtergreifung im Jahre 1917" in *Deutschland und Europa. Festschrift fuer H. Rothfels.* Duesseldorf, 1951, p. 278ff., p. 286ff.

477

10. The tribute which Lenin paid Trotsky for his part in bringing in the "Mezhrayontsy" (*Sochinenia,* 2d. ed., Vol. XXI, p. 289) has been omitted in the fourth edition of his works.
11. 150 delegates belonged to smaller groups, 45 had no party affiliation.
12. Cf. his speech of June 4, 1917, *Sochinenia,* 2d. ed., Vol. XX, p 403ff.
13. *Illustrièrte Geschichte der russischen Revolution,* p. 233.
13a. Led until the beginning of the summer of 1919 by the German colonel, Fletcher; subsequently by an English colonel, Sir H. Alexander, a Field Marshal in World War II, and afterwards Governor General of Canada.
14. *History of the Communist Party of the USSR, Short Course,* New York, 1939, p. 194.
15. Cf. F. Borkenau, "Das Jahr 1917. Wirklichkeit und Legends der russischen Revolution," *Der Monat,* 1952.
16. Stalin, *Sochinenia.* Moscow, 1946, Vol. III, p. 156.
17. Deutscher, *Stalin: A Political Biography.* New York, 1949.
18. Stalin, *op. cit.,* III, p. 187.
18a. G. Rhode, *Osteuropa* 1955, No. 2.
19. Cf. W. Gurian, *loc. cit.,* p. 281ff.
20. As V. Ropshin, e.g., "The Pale Horse" (1908) among others.
21. Cf. Lenin, *Saemtliche Werke,* Vol. XXI, p. 76.
22. As the paper money was popularly called. (Tr. note).
23. Cf. Stepun, *op cit,* II, p. 230ff.
24. Of importance also is his September article, "Will the Bolsheviks Gain Mastery of the State?", *Sochinenia,* Vol. XXI, p. 247ff., and his article, "Heroes of Falsification," Sept. 24, *ibid.,* p. 211ff.
25. Antonov-Ovseyenko was later Soviet Consul General in Barcelona during the Spanish Civil War. He was arrested and liquidated in the course of the purge of Trotskyists.
26. The name of the Russian capital had been changed to Petrograd during the first year of the war.
27. The record of this is contained in Lenin's *Sochinenia,* 2d. ed., Vol. XXI, pp. 499-507.
28. Cf. his letters, *Sochinenia,* 2d. ed., Vol. XXI, pp. 334-356.
29. L. Trotsky, *The History of the Russian Revolution.* New York, 1936, III, p. 311.
30. Trotsky, *My Life,* p. 337.
31. *Vergangenes und Unvergaengliches,* II, pp. 184, 204 and elsewhere.
32. F. Stepun, *loc. cit.*
33. More exactly, *Vserossiiskaya Chrezvychainaya Komissiya;* properly speaking, the various local offices were the Chekas.
34. Cf. N. Zubov, *F. Dzierzynski.* Moscow, 1933.
35. Cf. L. Trotsky, *The Stalin School of Falsification,* p. 103ff.
36. Cf. O. H. Radkey, *The Election to the Russian Constituent Assembly of 1917.* Cambridge, Mass., 1950.
37. Trotsky, *Ueber Lenin; Material fuer einen Biographen.* Berlin, 1924, p. 94.
38. Plekhanov, *Ein Jahr in der Heimat.* Berlin, 1921, Vol. II, p. 267.
39. Lenin, *Sobranie Sochinenii,* 1st. ed., Vol. XVI, p. 336. Lenin made this statement in a "Greeting to Italian, French and German Communists" which was published in October, 1919.
40. See E. H. Carr, *A History of Soviet Russia,* Vol. I, p. 121.
41. W. Gurian, *op. cit.,* p. 288.

42. *Ibid.*, pp. 290-291.
43. F. Borkenau, *Der Monat*, 1952.
44. *Ibid.*
45. Cf. *Soviet Documents on Foreign Policy*, ed. J. Degras. Oxford University Press, 1951, Vol. I, p. 1.
46. *Ibid.*, p. 4ff.
47. *Ibid.*, p. 14.
48. In December 1917 a German delegation was in St. Petersburg in order to establish contact with rightist groups. It is not widely known that on this occasion a high official of the former Foreign Ministry explored the possibilities of a general peace with the Allied representatives in St. Petersburg. See *Baltische Monatshefte*, Riga, 1928. Also the diaries of Field Marshal Wilson.
49. On February 1 (14), 1918 the Gregorian Calendar was officially introduced in Russia.
50. *Soviet Documents*, p. 43.
51. Cf. his famous speech at the VII Party Congress on March 7, 1918. *Asugewaehlte Werke* II, p. 330ff.
52. Thus also in his famous appeal of March 12, 1918, *Ausgewaehlte Werke*, Berlin, 1951, II, p. 352, and also on November 26, 1920, *Sochinenia*, 2d. ed., Vol. XXV, p. 500.
53. *Sochinenia*, 2d. ed., Vol XXII.
54. Regarding the supplementary agreement of August 27 which added to the conditions the payment of reparations of 6 billion gold marks, see below.
55. Against acceptance voted, apart from Bukharin: Bubnov, Uritsky and Lomov; Trotsky, Krestinsky, Dzierzynski and Joffe abstained.
56. *Soviet Documents, op. cit.*, I, p. 46.
57. *Ibid.*, p. 50.
58. *Ibid.*, p. 63
59. In his speech of March 7 and his article of March 12. *Sochinenia*, 2d. ed., XII, pp. 327-377.

Chapter 3

1. A few Polish delegates represented the Polish minority in the Ukraine.
2. B. Denewitz and B. Meissner, *Die Verfassungen der modernen Staaten*. Hamburg, 1947, Vol. I, p. 122.
3. Significantly, this declaration is not contained in the most recent edition of Stalin's Collected Works, which in general contains all decrees issued by him in chronological order. Cf. *Sochinenia*, Moscow, Vols. I-VII (16 volumes were planned) and *Der Monat*, 1949, No. 4. Prior to Stalin's Death in 1953 only 13 volumes had been published.
4. B. Krupnickyj, *Die Geschichte der Ukraine*. Leipzig, 1939, p. 283. Cf. C. A. Manning, *The Story of the Ukraine*. New York, 1947, p. 216ff; and J. S. Reshetar, *The Ukrainian Revolution, 1917-1920*. Princeton, N. J., 1952.
5. A. v. Taube, *Die Entstehung der estnischen Eigenstaatlichkeit*. Iomsburg, III, 1939.
6. Stalin, *Sochinenia*, IV, pp. 1 and 9.
7. See the description in K. Tiander, *Das Erwachen Osteuropas. Die Nationalitatenbewegung in Russland under der Weltkrieg*. Wien-Liepzig, 1934, p. 93ff.

8. Stalin, *Sochinenia,* Vol. V, p. 265
9. Cf. E. v. Dellingshausen, *Im Dienste der Heimat.* Stuttgart, 1930, Beilage XI. See also Rosa Luxemburg, *Die russische Revolution.* Hamburg, 1948.
10. *The Revolution and the Nationality Question, Documents and Materials* (in Russian), ed. S. M. Dimanshtein. Moscow, 1930, Vol. III, p. xxii.
10a. Cf. I. Steinberg, *Spiridonova.* London, 1935.
11. *Sochinenia,* Vol. 29, p. 489.
12. Bruce Lockhart, *Memoirs of a British Agent.* London, 1932. Sidney Reilly also described his experiences in *Britain's Master Spy.* London, 1933.
13. R. Wittram,*Baltische Lande,* IV, 1, p. 27.
14. L. Trotsky, *Stalin.* (German edition: Cologne-Berlin, 1952), p. 429.
15. Cf. Deutscher, *Stalin; A Political Biography.* New York, 1949, p. 211.
16. A comparison between the official Stalinist account in the *History of the Communist Party of the Soviet Union (Short Course)* and the critical analysis of the campaign plans given by Trotsky in his Stalin biography (p. 434ff.), lays bare the mutations of the Stalinist evaluation of the campaign, according to whichever political needs were paramount at the moment. Because Stalin later agreed with Trotsky's plan, it is described as his own, while the actually unsuitable plan of the High Command, i.e. Kamenev's, is now ascribed to Trotsky.
17. Trotsky was more interested in the European theatres of war where the Polish invasion in the West was already beginning to take shape. Stalin considered the Siberian hinterland more important. It was clear that by the beginning of the year Kolchak had ceased to represent a serious threat.
18. Makhno held out with his partisans in the Ukraine until the summer of 1921; on August 28 he crossed the Rumanian frontier.
18a. Named after the Englishman, Lord Curzon.
19. K. Zetkin, *Reminiscences of Lenin.* London, 1935, p. 19ff.
20. Lockhart, *op. cit.* Penguin edition, p. 307.
21 Sir George Buchanan, *My Mission to Russia.* London, 1923, II, p. 258.
22. *World Crisis,* p. 244ff.
23. Lenin, *Sochinenia,* 2d. ed., Vol. 25, p. 23.

Chapter 3

1. Cf. E. Goldman, *My Further Disillusionment in Russia.* New York, 1924.
2. A. Beckman, "Der Aufstand in Kronstadt," *Der Monat,* Berlin, 1951, No. 30.
3. Gosudarstvennaya planovaya komissiya.
4. Novaya ekonomicheskaya politika.
4a. Latterly Soviet historiography denied the humanitarian motives of the Hoover effort and alleged intentions of a subversive character.
5. He died in the United States in 1952.
6. Gosudarstvennoye politicheskoye upravlenniye.
7. L. Trotsky, *The Revolution Betrayed.* New York, 1937, p. 96.
8. See above, p.
9. Deutscher, *Stalin.*
10. See my book *Russland, staatliche Einheit, nationale Vielfalt.* Munich, 1953.

11. B. Dennewitz and B. Meissner, *op. cit.*, p. 129.
12. Created from the Soviet republics Khiva and Bokhara, the former Khanates which were protectorates of the Czarist empire
13. Two further Soviet republics evolved out of the RSFSR in Northern Turkestan: Kazakhstan and Kirghizistan.
14. Stalin, *Sochinenia*, Vol. IV, p. 171ff.
15. The First International was founded in 1864 in London as an association of Social Democratic workers; its statutes were prepared by Karl Marx in 1866. After its demise, a new Second International was set up in 1889, with its headquarters first in Brussels, then in Amsterdam, finally in London.
16. *Egelhaags Geschichtskalender*, 1920, p. 66.
17. Lenin, *Sochinenia*, 2d. ed., Vol. 25, p. 279ff.
18. Ruth Fischer, *Stalin und der deutsche Kommunismus*. Frankfurt, 1948, p. 156.
19. Lenin, *Ausgewaehlte Werke*. Moscow, 1947, Vol. 2, p. 770ff.
20. It is interesting to note that this letter is not contained in Stalin's *Collected Works*. It is, however, to be found in Lenin's *Collected Works*, in the unexpurgated second and third editions (Russian), Vol. 25, p. 624, in a note. Cf. B. D. Wolfe, "Tito and Stalin," *Vital Speeches of the Day*. New York, December 1, 1952.
21. Cf. Stampfer, *Die ersten vierzehn Jahre der Deutschen Republik*. Offenbach, 1947, p. 213ff.
22. Cf. E. Wollenberg, *The Red Army*. London, 1938, p. 235ff.
23. On the same day the Treaty of Friendship with Turkey was concluded (see above).
24. Cf. H. Speidel in *Vierteljahrshefte fuer Zeitgeschichte*, 1953/1.
25. In connection with these problems, see G. Hallgarten, *Journal of Modern History*, March, 1949; W. von Bluecher, *Deutschlands Weg nach Rapallo*, Wiesbaden, 1951; E. H. Carr, *German-Soviet Relations between the Two World Wars, 1919-1939*, Baltimore, 1951.

Chapter 4

1. I: 1922-24 in 20 volumes; II: 1926-29 in 32 volumes; III: 1932 without change; IV 1941-1952, 35 volumes, revised.
2. Besides *My Life*, New York, 1930, see also, *Stalin, A Biography*, New York, 1948.
3. Cf. D. Shub, *Lenin*, New York, 1948, and the literature quoted and referred to there.
4. Deutscher, *Stalin*, p. 234.
4a. Printed in *The New York Times*, July 7, 1956.
5. For complete text see R. Fischer, *op. cit.*, p. 293ff.
6. According to L. Trotsky, *The Real Situation in Russia*. London, n.d., p. 320ff.
7. While this concept may actually not have been advocated as frankly as the Georgian Joseph Iremashvili maintains, whom Trotsky quotes in his Stalin biography on p. 360 (English edition), these tendencies are at any rate anticipatory of Titoist leanings.
7a. See document in *The New York Times*, July 7, 1956.
8. Trotsky, *My Life*, p. 485.
9. Cf. the somewhat different explanation by Ruth Fischer, p. 437ff.
10. Trotsky, *My Life*, p. 508ff.

11. Deutscher, *Stalin*, p. 270; Stalin, *Sochinenia*, Vol. VI, pp. 46-51.
12. B. Bazhanov, *Stalin, der Rote Diktator*, p. 32ff; Carr, III, p. 259ff.
13. On October 18, 1926. Also contained in Max Eastman's book, *Since Lenin Died*. New York, 1925. At that time Trotsky still denied the authenticity of the document. Later he himself published details. (*The Suppressed Testament of Lenin*. New York, 1946). In his controversy with Bukharin in 1929, Stalin, too, referred to the testament and quoted from it. (*Selected Writings*. New York, 1942, p. 116).
14. Trotsky, *My Life*, Chapter 40.
15. Cf. Ruth Fischer, *op. cit.*, p. 487ff.
16. Trotsky, *My Life*, p. 512.
17. New York, 1948.
18. J. Stalin, *Problems of Leninism*. Moscow, 1947 German ed., p. 157.
19. Stalin, *Sochinenia*, Vol. VI, p 358ff.
20. A clear distinction must be made between Party Conference and Party Congress. The Conference served as preparation for the Party Congress, and usually met six months before it. The 14th Party Congress took place in December 1925.
21. On March 26 (April 8) 1917, Lenin wrote the Swiss workers as follows: "to the Russian proletariat has fallen the honor to start the series of revolutions which with objective necessity grow out of imperialist wars. But far be it from us to look upon the Russian proletariat as the chosen revolutionary proletariat among the workers of the world." *Sochinenia*, 2d. ed., Vol. XX, p. 88.
22. However, Lenin never as explicitly formulated the thesis of the victory of Socialism in one country and the impossiblity of a simultaneous success of the revolution in all countries as Stalin did in his letter to comrade Kholopov on July 28, 1950, during the linguistics controversy.
23. *Sochinenia*, Vol. VII, p. 21.
24. Deutscher, *Stalin*, p. 299.
25. In addition to Trotsky, see R. Fischer, p. 597.
26. Deutscher arrived at the conclusion, after an analysis of the official text of the protocol of the Congress, that a repentant though stubborn heretic faced the assembly, but we are in no way of this opinion.
27. Cf. N. Popov, *Outline History of the CPSU*. London, n.d., Vol. II, p. 249
28 Trotsky, *My Life*, Chapter 42.
29. R. Fischer, *op. cit.*, p. 687.
29a. See his final letter to Trotsky in Max Eastman's *The Real Situation in the Soviet Union*.
30. The idea of such total planning of the national economy is said to be based on a book by V. I. Grinevetsky, *Post-War Prospects of Russian Industry*, (in Russian) published in 1919.
31. Confirmed by Deutscher, *Stalin*, pp. 313, 318ff.
32. *Problems of Leninism* (English translation). Moscow, 1945, p. 221.
33. *Ibid.*, p. 267.
34. *Ibid.*, p. 325.
35. L. Trotsky, *The Real Situation in Russia*, p. 64ff., and Stalin, *Problems of Leninism*, p. 206ff.
36. Deutscher, *Stalin*, Chapter 8.
37. *Problems of Leninism*, p. 363.
38. *Ibid.*, p. 371.
39. *Ibid.*, p. 480.

40. J. Scott, *Behind the Urals*. Boston, 1942.
41. *Problems of Leninism*, p. 391ff.
42. *Ibid.*, p. 399.
43. Cf. Ruth Fischer, *op. cit.*, p. 691ff.
44. Boris Souvarine, *Stalin*. New York, 1939, p. 495.
45. Trotsky, *My Life*, p 556.

Chapter 5

1. Cf. in this connection E. H. Carr, *German-Soviet Relations Between the Two World Wars, 1919-1939*. Baltimore, 1951.
2. Cf. his important memorandum of July 15, 1922 and his polemic against General von Seeckt. *Der Monat*, 1948, No. 2; G. Hallgarten, *Journal of Modern History*, March 1949.
3. Ruth Rischer, *op cit.*, p. 329.
4. *Ibid.*, p. 368.
5. Curiously enough a sizable portion of these amounts, ca. 250,000 Goldmarks, came from a secret fund of the Reichswehr earmarked for the training of special German army units in the Soviet Union! Now the same money was in part used for the revolutionary infiltration of the Reichswehr. Cf. E. Wollenberg, "Der Apparat, Stalin's Fuenfte Kolonne," *Ostprobleme*, 1951, No. 19, p. 576.
6. Ruth Fischer, *op. cit.*, p. 384.
7. *Ibid.*, p. 388; cf. also W. G. Krivitsky, *In Stalin's Secret Service*. New York, 1939, p. 51ff.
8. Otdel mezhdunarodnoi svyazi.
9. A high officer of the GPU, native Latvian, also known as Gorev and Rose.
10. Ruth Fischer; Seton-Watson, *From Lenin to Malenkov*, p. 95.
11. Cf. G. Cleinow, *Die deutsch-russischen Rechts- und Wirtschaftsvertraege*. Berlin, 1926.
11a. See Hilger and Meyer, *The Incompatible Allies*, New York, 1953.
12. G. Stresemann, *Vermaechtnis*, Vol. II, p. 554; cf. also p. 528; see Gatzke, *Stresemann and the Rearmament of Germany*. Baltimore, 1954.
13. *Ibid.*
14. An observation regarding June 15, 1927. See G. Stresemann, *Vermaechtnis*, Vol. III, p. 151.
15. *History of Diplomacy*, (in Russian) ed. by V. P. Potemkin. Moscow, 1947, III, p. 392ff.
16. *Ibid.*, p. 408ff.
17. Cf. H. Speidel, "Reichswehr und Rote Armee," *Vierteljahrshefte fuer Zeitgeschichte*, 1953, No. 1.
18. Cf. here—with some caution—W. P. Coates, *A History of Anglo-Soviet Relations*, London, 1943, and L. Fischer, *The Soviets in World Affairs*, 2 vols., London, 1930, and Princeton, N. J., 1951.
19. Their mothers had been sisters.
20. After an anonymous brochure, "Aus diplomatischen Faelscherwerkstaetten," published in Berlin, 1926, quoted from Ruth Fischer, *op. cit.*, p. 561.
21. Ruth Fischer, pp. 562-566.
22. All-Russian Cooperative Society.
23. G. Stresemann, *Vermaechtnis*, Vol. III, p. 150ff. With regard to the international agitation of the Comintern in 1928 there is interesting

data in the papers of Jean Herbette, French Ambassador to Moscow, which has received far too little attention.

23a. See G. v. Rauch, "Die baltischen Staaten und Sowjetrussland, 1919-1939," *Europa Archiv*, Frankfurt, 1954, p. 122.

24. This is openly admitted in the official Soviet *History of Diplomacy*, Vol. III, p. 206.

25. W. G. Krivitsky, *In Stalin's Secret Service*. p. 48.

26. Ruth Fischer, p. 567

27. M. Ojamaa-A. Varmas, *Eesti ajalugu*, Stockholm, 1946, p. 347ff.

28. Cf. A. Bilmanis, *A History of Latvia* Princeton, 1951, p. 384.

29. Cf. Hu Shih, "China in Stalin's Grand Strategy," *Foreign Affairs*, October 1950.

30. *Foreign Affairs, loc. cit.* As for Trotsky's opinions regarding the China policy, cf. F. Borkenau, *The Communist International*, London, 1938, p. 306.

31. David J. Dallin, *Soviet Russia and the Far East*. New Haven, 1948, p. 111ff.

32. Cf. E. Hanisch, p. 113.

33. F. R. Dulles, *The Road to Teheran*. New York, 1944, p. 186.

34. Cf. his own account: *The Transport of Weapons to Russia* (in Russian), Moscow, 1934.

Chapter 6

1. See the account by J. Semenow, *Oeseuropa*, Vol. 7, p. 521.

2. Of which at least three million were in the Ukraine.

3. Cf. Deutscher, p. 347ff.

4. Deutscher says the writer was I. N. Smirnov.

5. Cf. R. Smal-Stock, *The Nationality Problem of the Soviet Union and Russian Communist Imperialism*. Milwaukee, 1952, p. 105ff.

6. A. Barmine, *One Who Survived*. New York, 1945, p. 264.

7. *Portrait de Staline*, Paris, 1940, p. 94ff. A. W. Just, *Stalin und seine Epoche*, Munich, 1953, p. 19, doubts the political motive for the suicide without adducing reasons for this view. The allegation that Stalin shot his wife, current after the 20th Congress, is credible but unsubstantiated.

8. According to Weissberg (German edition: Frankfurt am Main, 1951), p. 478.

9. Stalin, *Sochinenia*, Vol. XIII, p. 245 ff. and p. 256.

10. *Ibid.*, p. 161ff.

11. *Ibid.*, p. 216ff.

12 Torgsin = Trade with Foreigners.

13. L. Zaizeff, "Das Rechtverhaeltnis. . . ." *Osteuropa*, Vol. VI, p. 566.

14. Cf. K. Mehnert, *Weltrevolution durch Weltgeschichte. Die Geschichtslehren des Stalinismus*. Kitzingen, 1950. Also the author's articles: "Die Grundlinien der sowjetischen Geschichtsschreibung im Zeichen des Stalinismus," *Europa-Archiv*, 1950, 19-21, and: "Die sowjetische Geschichtsschreibung heute," *Die Welt als Geschichte*, 1951/1.

15. Among them Professor Eugene Tarle, author of books on the Napoleonic invasion of 1812 and on the Crimean War, who had fallen into disgrace in 1931.

16. Weissberg, *op. cit.* (German edition), p. 709.

17. This line was also adhered to during the war: a decree of July 8, 1944 created more rigorous divorce laws and provided awards for mothers

with many children. Cf. B. Meissner, *Die Verfassungsentwicklung der Sowjet Union*, Part II, p. 786; further literature *ibid*.

18. Cf. Meissner, *Russland im Umbruch*. Frankfurt am Main, 1951, p. 36ff.

19. Meissner, *loc. cit.*, pp. 8-9.

20. Meissner, *Europa-Archiv*, 1950/9, p. 2989ff; Achminow, *Die Macht im Hintergrunde*, Ulm, 1950, p. 142; *Russland im Umbruch*, p. 10ff.

21. A. Ouralov, *Staline au pouvoir*. Paris, 1951.

22. N. Basseches, *Stalin*. Bern, 1950. Cf Meissner, *Osteuropa*, 1952/53.

22a. See "Crimes of the Stalin Era, Khrushchev's Speech, Annotated" by B. I. Nicolaevsky, *The New Leader*, Section 2, July 16, 1956, p. 22.

23. Cf. Deutscher, *Stalin* p. 373.

24. Cf. A. Y. Vishinski, *Gerichtsreden*, Berlin, 1951. These speeches require no comment. Joseph E. Davies, who was U. S. Ambassador in Moscow from 1936 to 1938, showed little understanding of people when he speaks of the "admirable moderation" of the public prosecutor (p. 29) and calls him "calm, dispassionate and wise" (p. 51-2, Swiss edition).

25. It is significant of the spiritual relationship of both totalitarian systems that the National Socialist prosecutor in the trial of the insurgents of July 20, 1944 in Berlin uttered very similar insults of the accused.

26. Cf. Davies' description of his conduct, *Mission to Moscow* (Swiss edition: Zurich, 1943), p. 31ff.

26a. Rakovsky was, according to Trotsky, "one of the international figures of the European revolutionary movement." Born in Bulgaria, he grew up as a Rumanian citizen, became a doctor in France, and placed himself at the service of the October revolution. He first became chairman of the Ukrainian Soviet of People's Commissars, later a diplomat. Long close to Trotsky, he had been disciplined in 1928-29.

26b. B. Wolfe, *Saturday Review*, New York, May 26, 1951.

27. Weissberg (German edition), pp. 362, 420, 434.

28. Davies reports an instance where the Public Prosecutor had to "warn" a defendant against straying from the subject and embroidering his testimony with additional crimes (p. 31).

29. Of the 27 members of the Politburo who belonged to it prior to or immediately following World War II, one was exiled (and then murdered), one was murdered in office, 7 were executed, 3 disappeared, 7 died (as far as we know, of natural causes) and one committed suicide. Today only 7 are alive: Andreyev, Molotov, Voroshilov, Kaganovich, Mikoyan, Malenkov, and Khrushchev. Khrushchev gave information about Rudzutak and Eiche in his 1956 speech and said they had been posthumously rehabilitated the previous year, as well as Kosior, Postyshev, Chubar and others. G. I. Petrovsky, the Ukrainian who disappeared in 1938, is still alive and was rehabilitated in 1953. An early member of the Secretariat of the Central Committee, E. D. Stasova, reappeared in 1956. See *Ogonek*, (Moscow), No 9, February 1956, p. 4.

29a. Bela Kun was posthumously rehabilitated, probably for its effect on the Hungarian Communist party.

30. Weissberg (German edition), pp. 409, 562ff, and Deutscher pp. 335ff.

31. D. J. Dallin and B. Nicolaevsky, *Forced Labor in Soviet Russia*. Yale University Press, 1947, where the data are supported in great detail.

32. Deutscher, *Stalin*, p. 379.

33. Davies, *op. cit.* (Swiss edition), p. 149.

34. Krivitsky believes that Stalin had decided in December 1936 to extend the purge to the Red Army.

35. Barmine, *One Who Survived*, p. 306.
36. Deutscher, *Stalin*, p. 379ff.
37. In his famous anti-Stalin speech at the 20th Soviet Party Congress, Khrushchev did not mention the Tukhachevsky's case.
38. Cf. E. Crankshaw, "Beria, Russia's Mystery of Mysteries," *The New York Times Magazine*, April 2, 1950.
39. Since the death of Stalin, missing without a trace.
40. Cf. the exchange of notes of the autumn of 1930, *Soviet Documents*, III, p. 204ff.
41. Deutscher, *Stalin*, p. 385. Trotsky's biography of Stalin was published in New York in 1948. A considerable literature on Trotsky's assassination has accumulated.
42. Meissner, *Russland im Umbruch*, p. 41.
43. For both texts see Meissner, p. 39ff.
44. According to B. Meissner, "Der Wandel im sozialen Gefuege der Sowjetunion," *Europa-Archiv* V, 1950, p. 2998ff; H. Falk, "Die neue sowjetische Oberschicht," *Stimmen der Zeit*, Munich 1951, Vol. 148, No. 8, p. 142ff.; H. Achminow, 1.c. p. 139.
45. Figures according to D. Dallin, *Das Wirkliche Sowjetrussland*. Hamburg, 1948.
46. Achminow mentions suicides, p. 16.
47. B. Meissner, *Russland im Umbruch*, p. 66ff.
48. This is the thesis on which G. F. Achminow based his book, *Die Macht im Hintergrunde, Totengraeber des Kommunismus*. Ulm, 1950.

Chapter 7

1. Dallin, *Russia and Post-War Europe*, New Haven, 1943, p. 61.
   1943, p. 61.
2. *Soviet Documents*, III, p. 75 (Communiqué of *Pravda*, February 16, 1934).
3. In April 1934 the non-aggression pacts with the Baltic states were extended for ten years (*Soviet Documents*, III, p. 78ff.); in July the Estonian, and in August the Lithuanian Foreign Minister visited Moscow.
4. For the Soviet reply to the German rejection see *Soviet Documents*, III, p. 79ff.
5. *Ibid.*, III, p. 96.
6. *Ibid.*, III, p. 36ff.
7. Cf. L. Fischer, *The Soviets in World Affairs*, I, p. 29.
8. For Litvinov's speech, see *Soviet Documents*, III, p. 89.
9. *Slavonic Review* (London), Vol. XIV.
10. For excerpts from this article, see *Soviet Documents*, III, p. 124.
11. *Ostprobleme*, 1950/42.
12. *Soviet Documents*, III, p. 122, 126ff.
13. *Ibid.*, p. 130ff.
14. *Ibid.*, p. 129ff.
15. *Ibid.*, p. 134ff.
16. A. Rossi, *Deux ans d'alliance germano-sovietique*. Paris, 1949.
17. Cf. *Der Monat*, IV, No. 40, p. 351; M. Beloff, I, 1, p. 34; G. Brenan, *The Spainsh Labyrinth*, p. 324. Also *Soviet Documents* III, p. 229.
18. *Soviet Documents*, III, p. 203.
19. *Ibid.*, p. 228.

20. *Ibid.*, p. 234 and 248ff.

21. Verbatim report see Martens, *Nouveau recueil général des traités* II Series, Vol. 36, p. 24.

22. Newspaper reports that Daladier had been authorized to speak for the Soviet Union in Munich and that the French and British governments had consulted Russia on the Czech question, were denied on October 2nd and 4th. *Soviet Documents*, III, p. 307.

23. Coulondre,*Von Moskau nach Berlin, 1936-1939*. Bonn, 1950, p. 240; cf. *Soviet Documents*, III, p. 312.

24. For extracts from this speech see *Soviet Documents*, III, p. 315

24a. J. Lettrich, *History of Modern Slovakia*, New York, 1955.

25. Cf. Meissner, *Osteuropa*, 1952/4.

26. Deutscher, *Stalin*, p. 450ff.

27. Beck, *Denkschriften*, Paris, 1951.

28. E.g., General Fuller, *loc. cit.*, p. 18.

29. According to the memoirs of the French Ambassador in Warsaw, L. Noel, *The German Attack on Poland*, p. 317. Cf. J. G. Leithauser, *Der Monat*, 1953, no. 51, and the letter to the editor in No. 55, p. 101.

30. B. Meissner, "Shdanov," *Osteuropa*, 1952/2, p. 95. The article in *Soviet Documents*, III, p. 352.

31. Carroll-Epstein, *Deutschland und die Sowjetunion, 1939-1941*, Washington, 1948, No. 33.

32. Cf. Meissner, *Osteuropa*, 1952, No. 4-5; see also B. Meissner, *Die Sowjetunion, die Baltischen Staaten, und das Voelkerrecht*, Cologne, 1956.

33. Cf. *Soviet Documents*, III, p. 349ff, 356.

34. This was Hitler's only personal letter to Stalin. Carroll-Epstein, No. 44; Stalin's answer—No. 48; see G. L. Weinberg, *Germany and the Soviet Union 1939-1941*, Leiden, 1954.

35. Carroll-Epstein, No. 55.

36. Churchill, I, p. 305.

37. Rossi, *Der Monat*, 1949/11 p. 90.

38. *Soviet Documents*, III, p. 372.

39. J. F. C. Fuller, *Die Geschichte des zweiten Weltkrieges, 1939-1945*, Vienna, 1950.

40. Rossi, p.92; cf. *Soviet Documents*, III, pp. 374-377.

41. Only the Mariampol territory in Lithuania remained in German hands; cf. Carroll-Epstein, No. 87 and *Soviet Documents*, III, p. 377ff.

42. Cf. Kleist, p. 105ff.

43 Rossi, p. 40.

44. Ciano, p. 456.

45. Poole in *Foreign Affairs*, October 1946.

46. *Soviet Documents*, III, p. 40ff., including Molotov's radio address of November 29th.

47. Churchill, *The Gathering Storm*, p. 543.

48. *Soviet Documents*, III,p. 421. Cf. C. A. Colliard, *Le Droit international et la diplomatie*, Paris, 1950, 2d. ed. p. 581ff.

49. German White Book, issued by the German Foreign Office, *Die Geheimakten des franzoesischen Generalstubes* (Berlin). 1939/41, Vol. 6; General Gamelin, *Servir*, Vol. 3, pp. 206f; P. G. Bourget, *De Beyrouth à Bordeaux; La Guerre 1939-40 vue du P. C. Weygand*, Paris, 1946.

50. Cf. Meissner, *Osteuropa*, 1952, Nos. 4-5.

51. *Soviet Documents*, III, p. 453ff.

52. Cf. B. Meissner, "Die Verfassungsentwicklung der Sowjetunion seit dem II. Weltkriege," *Jahrbuch fuer internationales und auslaendisches oeffentliches Recht*, Hamburg, 1949, pp. 766ff.
53. Carroll-Epstein, No. 158.
54. It is not true that through Russian pressure regarding Bessarabia, Hitler developed a form of "paranoia" and therefore attacked Russia in 1941. (Crankshaw, p. 194). The fact is that Russia's activities in the Balkans beyond the Bessarabian border were as annoying to him as were the German activities to the Russians.
55. According to *Nazi Conspiracy and Aggression*, III, pp. 403-407. For the text of the first secret codicil and the Soviet counter-proposals, see also Kleist, p. 118ff.
56. The information is based chiefly on General Halder's Diary as quoted by G. L. Weinberg, "Der deutsche Entschluss zum Angriff auf die Sowjetunion," *Vierteljahrsshefte fuer Zeitgeschichte*, 1953/54, p. 310ff.
57. *Soviet Documents*, III, p. 484.
58. See W. Schule in *Christ und Welt*, 1951/25.
59. *Soviet Documents*, III, p. 486, and Martens, III Series, Vol. 39, p. 401.
59a. In his secret speech Khrushchev details the warnings Stalin ignored.
60. H. G. Seraphim, *Die deutsch-russischen Beziehungen 1939-41*, Hamburg, 1949; also C. L. Weinberg, *loc. cit.*
61. Cf., the map with positions of April 23 and June 1, 1941 in Seraphim's book, pp. 70/71 and testimony before the Nuremberg War Crimes Court, especially that of General Halder on September 9, 1948.
62. A similar view is voiced by A. J. Thorwald, *Wen sie verderben wollen*, Stuttgart, 1952; also by General A. A. Vlasov.

Chapter 8

1. Hitler's statement of June 22, 1941; see Kleist, p. 297.
2. Printed verbatim in Kleist, p. 298.
3. H. J. Mette, *Russische Geschichte*. Bonn, 1949, p. 160ff.
4. See D. J. Dallin, *Soviet Russia's Foreign Policy 1939-42*. New Haven, 1945, p. 375.
5. Carroll-Epstein, *Deutschland und die sowjetunion, 1939-1941*. Washington 1948, No. 258.
6. Churchill, *The Second World War* (American edition), III, p. 367.
7. *Soviet Documents*, III, p. 490 (extracts).
8. In 1942 Mikoyan and Voznesensky were also included and somewhat later Kaganovich. In 1944 Bulganin succeeded Voroshilov. Meissner, *Russland im Umbruch*, p. 41.
9. Extracts in *Soviet Documents*, III, p. 491.
10. He was replaced in April 1943 by General Vassilievsky.
11. Churchill, *The Grand Alliance*, p. 370 (Am. Ed.).
12. Sherwood, *Roosevelt and Hopkins*. New York, 1948, p. 236ff. Ribbentrop himself gave Russia eight weeks.
13. *Ibid.*, p. 238ff.
14. According to the report of the U. S. Ambassador in Moscow, Steinhardt; Sherwood, p. 272.
15. Cf. J. R. Deane, *Ein Seltsames Buendnis*. Vienna, n.d., p. 84ff.
16. *Ibid.*, pp 86-7.
17. According to the statement of N. Voznesensky, the Director of the State Planning Commission—in *Voyennaya Ekonomika*, p. 42.

18. Churchill, IV, p. 334.
19. Cf. H. Koch, "Staat und Kirche in Osteuropa," *Zeitschrift fuer Geopolitik*, 1952/12, p. 727ff.
20. Cf. also J. Thorwald, *Wen sie verderben wollen*. Stuttgart, 1952.
21. On this subject one finds a great deal of material in the book by Thorwald,*Wen sie verderben wollen* (Stuttgart, 1952), a book more serious than its title might indicate.
22. Contained in Kleist, p. 311ff.
23. *Ibid.*, p. 317ff.
24. For details of the text, see Mette, p. 171ff., and *Europa-Archiv*, 1947, p. 1044. This treaty was voided by the U.S.S.R. in 1955.
25. IV, pp. 341-342.
26. *Ibid.*, Chap. 19.
27. Cf. Meissner, *Osteuropa*, II/5, p. 34.
28. Sherwood, p. 709. Eden to Roosevelt in March 1943 (Am. ed.).
29. Churchill, IV, p. 332.
30. Cf. Churchill, IV, pp. 756-761
31. Cf. Churchill's views IV, p. 760-761., which leave no doubt about his real opinion.
32. Cf. the privately printed publication of the Polish government-in-exile, "Report on the Massacre of Polish Officers in Katyn Forest," against whose submission at Nuremberg the Soviet Representative, Rudenko, protested. Cf. *Der Monat*, 1952/40.
33. Churchill, IV, p. 477.
34. *Ibid.*, p. 478.
35. *Ibid.* p. 498.
36. Sherwood, p. 571.
37. J. Thorwald, *Wen sie verderben wollen;* G. Fischer, *Soviet Opposition to Stalin, A Case Study in World War II*, Cambridge, Mass., 1952; A. Kasanzew, *The Third Force, Account of an Experiment* (in Russian), Frankfurt/Main, 1953.
38. For full text see Kleist, p. 318ff.
39. For full text see Kleist, p. 323.
40. Cf. N. Shnevliskl, *Smersh.* New York, 1950. During the war the entire NKVD comprised about 600,000 men; regarded as indispensable, they were not employed in military operations.
41. First by Rundstedt, and later by Halder.
42. German Press Agency (DPA) report from New York, February 28, 1948.
43. Understandably enough, as many rumors circulated in the West regarding German-Russian feelers as did suspicions in Moscow about Western attempts to make contact with Germany, especially after Rudolf Hess had landed in England. An especially preposterous rumor after Churchill's Moscow visit in 1942 had it that Molotov and Ribbentrop had met in Stalino in the Ukraine!
43a. A suprising confirmation of these somewhat incredible statements by Kleist is given in the book *Die Revolution entlaesst ihre Kinder*, Cologne, 1956, by the German Communist Leonhard who observed the events at first-hand in Moscow.
44. Sherwood, p. 705.
45. Churchill, IV, p. 750ff.
46. *Ibid.*, p. 751ff.
47. *Ibid.*, p. 754ff.

48. Sherwood, p. 733ff.
49. *Ibid.*, p. 734.
50. W. Hagen, *Die Geheime Front*. Vienna, 1950, p. 262ff.
51. Sherwood, p. 734.
52. Cf. Sherwood, p. 748ff.
53. Hull, *The Memoirs of Cordell Hull*. New York, 1948, II, p. 1294.
54. Deane, p. 138.
55. Churchill Vol. V, p. 396; cf. Meissner, *Russland im Umbruch*, p. 29.
56. *Das Ostpakt-System*, I, p. 16.
57 Cf. B. Meissner, *Russland die Westmaechte und Deutschland*, p. 27ff.
58. Cf. Churchill, III.
59. As pointed out by B. Meissner, *Osteuropa*, October 1952, p. 345, and *Russland, die Westmaechte und Deutschland*, p. 31.
60. *Ibid.*, p. 31ff.
61. See Churchill's opinion, Vol. V, p. 361.
62. Deutscher, *Stalin*, p. 508.
63. Deane, *op. cit.*, p. 44ff.
64. He promised this to Hull for the first time in October 1943.
65. Cf. Meissner, *Russland, die Westmaechte und Deutschland*, p.35.
66. Sherwood, p. 793.
67. Cf. Fuller, p. 331.
68. As Fuller maintains, p. 331.
69. Fuller, p. 339.
70. Deutscher, p. 512.
71. Golikov,*Vydayushchiesya pobedy sovetskoi armii v velikoi otechestvennoi voine*. Moscow, 1952, p. 112ff.
72. Cf G. Mannerheim, *Memoirs*, Zuerich-Freiburg, 1952; V. Tanner, *Vaegen till fred 1943-44*, Helsingfors, 1952; W. Erfuhrt, *Der finnische Krieg 1941-44*, Wiesbaden, 1950; W. v. Bluecher, *Gesandter zwischen Diktatur und Demokratie, Erinnerungen 1935-1944*, Wiesbaden, 1951; J. H. Wuorinen, *Finland and World War II*, New York, 1948.
72a. See General Bor-Komarowski, *The Secret Army*. London, 1950.
73. Cf. Hull, II, p. 1573.
74. Deutscher, p. 513.
75. Cf. Borkenau, *Der europaeische Kommunismus*, Munich, 1952.
76. Sherwood, p. 785.
77. Cf. his correspondence with Chester Wilmot.
78. Hull, II, p. 1451ff.
79. *Ibid.*, p. 1458.
80. Byrnes, *Speaking Frankly*. New York, 1947, p. 53.
81. Deutscher, p. 523.
82. Meissner, *Russland im Umbruch*, p. 53.
82a. As shown by Himmler's speech in Poznan on August 3, 1944. See *Vierteljahrshefte fuer Zeitgeschichte*, 1953.
83. For details regarding membership of the Committee, speeches and manifesto of the act of state, see Kleist, p. 326ff.
84. The report according to which a copy of this agreement was offered by Japanese agents to the Soviet Ambassador, Mme. Kollontai, in Stockholm with the semi-official proposal to hand Vlasov over to the Soviet government, if a separate peace was concluded, seems to have been an invention.
85. Kleist, p. 220.
86. Cf. literature mentioned in footnote No. 37.

87. Literature: H. Rothfels, *The German Opposition to Hitler*, Chicago, 1948; A. W. Dulles, *Germany's Underground*, New York, 1947.

88. N. v. Horthy, *Ein Leben fuer Ungarn*, Bonn, 1953.

89. E. R. Stettinius, *Roosevelt and the Russians, The Yalta Conference*, London, 1950, which contains a more reliable and detailed account than those of Byrnes and Sherwood. Cf. also Chester Wilmot, *loc. cit.* and— of less importance—M. W. Clauss, *Der Weg nach Jalta*, Heidelberg, 1952.

90. Sherwood, p. 857 (Am. ed.).

91. See B. Meissner, *Russland, Deutschland und die Westmaechte*. Hamburg, 1953, pp. 38-53.

91a. See W. Wagner, *Die Entstehung der Oder-Neisselinie*. Stuttgart, 1953.

92. This was due less to the influence of Admiral King, as is sometimes suggested (Chester Wilmot), as to that of Harry Hopkins. Cf. *Fleet Admiral King*, edited by W. M. Whitehill, New York, 1953.

93. The text of this agreement is given in *Das Ostpaktsystem*, Vol. II, Hamburg, 1951, p. 15.

94. Cf. Sherwood, p. 864ff.

95. Cf. Liddell Hart and Chester Wilmot.

96. This was, e.g., Marshal Foch's opinion in 1919 when he said that unless the Western powers could solve the Russian question satisfactorily they would in effect forfeit their victory. That his solution was not the right one has been mentioned above, but this is not the important factor here.

97. For an excerpt from this speech see Crankshaw, *Cracks in the Kremlin Wall*, New York, 1951, p. 130.

98. Meissner, *Russland, Deutschland und die Westmaechte*, p. 60ff.

99. Winston Churchill, Vol. II, confuses the rivers. Only in Vol. VI does he emphasize that under his leadership the government would never have recognized the extension of Poland to the *Western* Neisse.

100. At the Yalta Conference the Western Neisse was expressly mentioned. Meissner, p. 40. See also W. Wagner, *loc. cit.*

101. *Ibid.*, p. 69.

102. For details see Meissner, p. 76.

103. For example, Golikov, p. 239ff.

104. Cf. *Der Monat*, 1948-49, No. 5, p. 79; and Georg von Rauch, "Grundlinien der sowjetischen Geschichtsschreibung im Zeichen des Stalinismus," *Europa-Archiv*, 1950, pp. 19-21.

105. Lenin, *Sochinenia*, 4th ed., Vol. 8, p. 32.

Chapter 9

1. H. Klocke, "Der Weg der Sowjetunion zur Industriemacht," *Zeitschrift fuer Geopolitik*, 1952, No. 4.

2. G. M. Werner, "Die Ostwanderung der Sowjetindustrie," *Osteuropa*, 1952, No. 2. Also, N. Voznesensky, *The Economy of the USSR During World War II* (in Russian), Moscow, 1947; published in English in 1949.

3. Miners and other workers in heavy industry had to change from a six-hour to a seven-hour day.

4. N. Jasny, "Close-up of the Soviet Fourth Five-Year Plan," *The Quarterly Journal of Economics*, Cambridge, Mass., May 1952.

5. In 1939 it was on the average five square meters per season, i.e., one-

third to one-fifth of the West European average. In 1947, 5 million people lived in Moscow in space intended for 2 million (1 million were not even registered!) Crankshaw, *op. cit.*, p. 157.

6. Economic survey of Europe in 1951, issued by the UN, Geneva, 1952, according to *Ostprobleme*, 1952, No. 17, p. 518ff.
7. Cf. F. Lorimer, *The Population of the Soviet Union*, Geneva, 1948. The total population of the Soviet Union in 1956 was about 200 million.
8. Capacity 2.2 million kilowatts (Boulder Dam, 1.25 million).
9. Klocke, *op. cit.*, p. 217. Crankshaw has the following figures: 1938, 18 million tons; 1945, 9 million tons; 1950, 25 million tons; *op. cit.*, p. 234.
10. *Ostprobleme*, 1952, No. 17, p. 520ff. Of the total rolled-steel production of the Soviet Union, only 9% was used for thin-plate (automobile construction and household equipment) in 1939 as compared to 39% used in the USA. *Ostprobleme*, 1952, No. 31, p. 1003.
11. In 1950, the number of tractors in the Soviet Union was estimated at 600,000 (England, 260,000; USA, 3 million).
12. Such as Lysenko's method, which envisages "nests of oak trees" among rye and sunflower fields.
13. Cf. B. Nicolaevsky, "Neuer Feldzug gegen das Dorf," *Ostprobleme*, 1951, No. 13, p. 390ff., and F. Loewenthal, "Materialien ueber Gross-Kolchosen," *Ostprobleme*, 1951, No. 23, p. 713ff.
14. K. Mehnert, *Weltrevolution durch Weltgeschichte*, p. 29ff.
15. Following the precedent of the Pugachev revolt (Pugachovshchina) and the Yezhovshchina.
16. Cf. B. Meissner, "Shdanov," *Osteuropa*, 1952, No. 1/2.
17. *Bolshevik*, 1946, No. 3, pp. 1-11. Cf. A. G. Mazour and H. E. Bateman, "Recent Conflicts in Soviet Historiography," *The Journal of Modern History*, March 1952.
18. *Bolshevik* 1946, No. 17/18, pp. 4-19.
19. H. Cassidy, "Shdanov am Werk," *Die Russische Sphinx*, ed. R. B. Considine, Hanover, 1951, p. 9.
20. W. Meder, "Materialien zur sowjetischen Kulturpolitik," *Europa-Archiv*, 1948, pp. 135ff.; also Varga, *Osteuropa*, 1955, No. 2, pp. 100, 125ff.
21. Cf. *Neue Zuercher Zeitung*, May 23, 1950.
22. *Ibid.*
23. A. Buchholz, "Grundzuege und Entwicklungstendenzen der sowjetischen Naturwissenschaft," *Osteuropa*, 1952, No. 3/4.
24. *Problems of Linguistics in the Light of the Works of J. V. Stalin* (in Russian), Moscow, 1952. Cf. "The Stalin-Marr Philological Controversy in the USSR," *World Today*, Chatham House Review, 1952.
25. K. Mehnert, *op. cit.*, p. 41ff., and L. Laurat; *Staline: La linguistique et l'imperialisme russe*, Paris, 1951. Cf. also Crankshaw's detailed account, *op. cit.*, pp. 131-43.
26. See particularly B. Meissner, *Russland, die Westmaechte und Deutschland*, p. 77ff.
27. Particularly in the note of August 7, 1946. See *Ostprobleme*, 1952, No. 34, p. 1103.
28. Cf. *The Foreign Policy of the USSR. Documents and Data, January-1946* (in Russian), Moscow, 1952. Also, *A Decade of American Foreign Policy. Basic Documents 1941-49*, New York, 1950.
29. Cf. G. Klimov, *Berliner Kreml*, Cologne, 1951.

30. *Die Friedensvertraege von 1947 mit Italien, Ungarn, Bulgarien, Rumaenien und Finnland,* ed. E. Menzel. *Quellen fuer Politik und Voelkerrecht,* Vol. 1, Frankfurt, 1948.

31. Decree of February 15, 1947, allegedly annulled in November 1953.

32. Cf. the report by B. Bruegel, "Methods of Soviet Domination in the Satellite States," *International Affairs,* London, 1951, No. 1. For conditions in the newly annexed areas within the borders of the Soviet Union, cf. "La situation dans les pays Baltes," *Bulletin de l'association d'études et d'informations politiques internationales,* Paris, January 1-15, 1951, according to *Ostprobleme,* 1951, No. 12, p. 363ff. Also, Y. Gluckstein, *Stalin's Satellites in Europe,* London, 1952.

33. S. Mikolajczyk, *Der Krieg gegen die Freiheit,* Berlin, 1948.

34. See the expressive and moving report by Sir Bruce Lockhart, *My Europe,* London, 1952, in which the role played by V. A. Zorin in this matter is clearly shown.

35. Cf. B. Meissner, *Das Ostpakt-System. Dokumenten-Zusammenstellung 1-2,* Hamburg, 1951.

36. Meissner, "Shdanov," pp. 98ff.

37. "X" [George F. Kennan], "The Sources of Soviet Conduct," *Foreign Affairs,* July 1947, pp. 566-82.

38. General strikes took place in Italy and France on November 12 and November 18, respectively.

39. Meissner, *Russland im Umbruch,* p. 43.

40. According to L. D. Clay, *Entscheidung in Deutschland,* Frankfurt, 1950, p. 395ff.

41. Cf. Bedell Smith, p. 352ff. One should perhaps also mention the view that the aggravation of the situation in Berlin was designed to divert attention from Communist aggression in Korea and the final victory of Mao Tse-tung in China. Perhaps Zhdanov wanted to concentrate on Europe, whereas his opponents favored the Far East.

42. Meissner, *Russland im Umbruch,* p. 43.

43. *Ibid.,* p. 56. Cf. "The Red Army Quickens Steps," *Economist,* London, March 15, 1952.

44. B. D. Wolfe mentions a plan of operations that the Soviet General Staff (until November 12, Marshall A. M. Vasilevsky was Chief of the General Staff, from that date General S. M. Shtemenko) is supposed to have worked out in the event of war. It envisaged an advance west through Germany followed by a frontal attack on France and a breakthrough to the Atlantic coast, while at the same time another wedge was to be driven into Yugoslavia and Northern Italy in order to reach the French Alpine passes from there. B. D. Wolfe, *Vital Speeches of the Day,* New York, December 1, 1952.

45. Pavel Fedorovich Yudin, born 1899 in Gorky, was professor or dialectical materialism in Moscow, member of the Academy of Sciences, director of the state publishing house, and editor of the trade union paper *Trud.* He was considered one of the foremost experts on Marxist theory.

46. F. Borkenau, *European Communism,* New York, 1953.

47. For additional material regarding the conflict with Tito, see F. Borkenau, *Der europaeische Kommunismus, Seine Geschichte von 1917 bis zur Gegenwart,* Munich, 1952; B. Mlinaric, *Tito der rote Rebell,*

Zurich, 1948; V. Dedijer, *Tito,* New York, 1953; and N. J. Lasky, "Balkan-Tagebuch," *Der Monat,* 1951-52 No. 39/40.

48. Cf. "Die Entwicklung der Kominform von 1947-1950," *Ostprobleme,* 1950, No. 27, according to *The World Today,* London, May 1950.

49. As was officially alleged early in 1953 in connection with the "Doctors' Plot."

50. The fact that Zhdanov was actually sick is corroborated by W. Bedell Smith, pp. 101, 319. Cf. Meissner, "Shdanov," p. 17.

51. Cf. C. M. Chang, "Communism and Nationalism in China," *Foreign Affairs,* New York, July 1950.

52. The treaties of February 14, 1950, were supplemented by an agreement of September 25, 1952, which meant a further strengthening of the Moscow-Peking axis. The return of the Manchurian Railroad to China was set for December 31, 1952, according to the agreement of February 14, 1950; in exchange, however, Port Arthur was to remain a Russian naval base indefinitely. In October 1954, the restitution of Port Arthur was fixed for May 31, 1955.

53. G.Malenkov, "Die Sowjetunion verteidigt die Sache des Friedens," *Neue Welt,* Berlin, 1949, No. 22. For further material regarding Chinese Communism, see C. Brandt, B. Schwartz, J. K. Fairbank, *A Documentary History of Chinese Communism,* Cambridge, Mass., 1952; also W. Z. Laqueur, *Communism and Nationalism in the Middle East,* New York, 1956.

54. Cf. "Rote Umtriebe im Schwarzen Erdteil," *Ostprobleme,* 1952, No. 4, according to the *Times,* London, November 23 and 27, 1951.

55. B. Spuler, "Moskaus kirchenpolitische Offensive in Vorderen Orient," *Ostprobleme,* 1951, No. 22.

56. "Tentativi de penetrazione sovietica," *Relazioni Internazionali,* Milan, July 19, 1952.

57. Cf. L. S. Berg, *Russian Discoveries in the Antarctic and Modern Interest in the Area* (in Russian), Moscow, 1949; also, "Stalins noerdlicher Seeweg," *Neue Zuercher Zeitung,* September 30, 1951.

58. Cf. J. v. Hehn, "Die Weltfriedensbewegung im Atomzeitalter," *Europa-Archiv,* Frankfurt, 1954, No. 16.

59. Cf. Meissner, *Russland, die Westmaechte und Deutschland,* p. 183.

60. For the complete text see Meissner, *ibid.,* p. 216.

61. "X" [G. Kennan], "The Sources of Soviet Conduct," p. 566ff.

62. Cf. Meissner, *Russland, die Westmaechte und Deutschland,* p. 290; also, Meissner, "Die Deutschlandnote des Kreml," *Zeitschrift fuer Geopolitik,* 1952, No. 4.

63. E.g., Professor E. Tarle, *Neue Zeit,* Berlin, 1952, Nos. 21, 25.

64. Fifteenth Party Congress, December 1927; Sixteenth, June 1930; Seventeenth, January 1934; Eighteenth, March 1939.

65. Number of party members (including candidates): January 1, 1939— 2.3 million; January 1, 1940—3.4 million ;1942—4.6 million; 1944—5 million; January 1, 1945—5.7 million; 1952—about 7 million.

66. Cf. B. Meissner, "Der Wandel im sozialen Gefuege der Sowjetunion," *Europa-Archiv,* 1950; G. F. Achminow, *Die Macht im Hintergrunde,* Ulm, 1950; J. Burnham, *The Managerial Revolution,* New York, 1941; D. Dallin, *The Changing World of Soviet Russia,* New Haven, 1956.

67. Cf. A. Sieger, "Stand und Entwicklung der Grundstoffindustrie und die

Energiebilanz der Sowjetunion in der Nachkriegszeit," *Europa-Archiv,* 1952, p. 5296ff.
68. G. M. Malenkov, "Rechenschaftsbericht des Zentralkomitees der KPdSU an den XIX. Parteitag," published by the presidium of the KPD, Stuttgart, n.d.; cf. L. Gruliow (ed.), *Current Soviet Policies I: The Documentary Record of the 19th Communist Party Congress and the Reorganization After Stalin's Death,* New York, 1953.
69. Published in *Bolshevik,* No. 18, September 1952, and in *Pravda,* October 3, 1952; cf. Gruliow, *op. cit.,* pp. 1-20.
70. R. Loewenthal, "Stalins Vermaechtnis," *Der Monat,* 1953, No. 55, p. 16ff.
71. Translated in *Ostprobleme,* 1952, No. 42, p. 1394ff.
72. Cf. Historicus, "Stalin on Revolution," *Foreign Affairs,* 1949, pp. 175ff.; Diplomaticus, "Stalinist Theory and Soviet Foreign Policy," *Review of Politics,* 1952, p. 468ff.
73. See various articles by Boris Nicolaevsky regarding these cleavages.
74. B. Meissner, "Der Nachfolger G. A. Malenkow," *Osteuropa,* 1953, No. 2; cf. the biographical sketch in *Time,* New York, March 3, 1950; L. M. Pistrak, *Ostprobleme,* 1953, No. 13; and B. Nicolaevsky, *Le Figaro,* Paris, September 3, 1953.
75. B. Svanidze, *Im engsten Kreis,* Stuttgart, 1953, p. 137.
76. After the Eighteenth Party Congress in 1939, nineteen full members and forty-eight candidates were removed from the Central Committee, the majority subsequent to 1948. Kuznetsov was a member of the Secretariat of the Central Committee until 1947; Kosygin was Premier of the RSFSR until 1946. That Kuznetsov was executed together with Voznesensky was admitted by Khrushchev in February 1956.
77. Gruliow, *op. cit.,* p. 244ff.
78. Cf. *The Red Anti-Semitism,* ed. E. E. Cohen, Boston, 1953; and Solomon Schwartz, *The Jews in the Soviet Union,* Syracuse, N.Y., 1951.
79. Cf. K. Mehnert, in *Osteuropa,* 1953, No. 2, p. 103.
80. F. Borkenau, *Neues Abendland,* April 1953.
81. *Osteuropa,* 1953, No. 2, p. 103ff.
82. Cf. F. Heni, *Osteuropa,* 1952, No. 2, p. 137ff.
83. Cf. Gruliow, *op. cit.,* p. 255ff.
84. Cf. K. Mehnert, *Osteuropa,* 1952, No. 4, p. 409.
85. The phenomenon of Hitler shows these elements only embryonically.

Chapter 10

1. In 1952, 51 ministries; in 1953, 25; in 1954, 45. According to B. Meissner, *Osteuropa,* 1954, No. 3, p. 213.
2. K. Mehnert, "Moskaus neuer Dreijahresplan des Konsums," *Osteuropa,* 1954, No. 1.
3. O. Schiller, "Der neue Kurs der sowjetischen Agrarpolitik," *Osteuropa,* 1963, No. 6.
4. *Die Viererkonferenz in Berlin 1954, Reden und Dokumente,* Berlin, 1954.
5. *Europa-Archiv,* 1955, p. 7923.
6. Cf. G. von Rauch, "Intellectual Freedom in the USSR?," in *Science and Freedom,* A Bulletin of the Committee on Science and Freedom, Manchester, 1955, No. 4.

7. *Osteuropa,* 1955, No. 2, p. 129.
8. B. Meissner, *Sowjetrussland zwischen Revolution und Rerstauration,* Cologne, 1956, pp. 121-22. Meissner designated Bulganin as a possible successor of Stalin as long ago as 1951 (*Russland im Umbruch,* p. 6).
9. *Ibid.,* p. 107ff.
10. E.g., the aggressively anti-Western speech in Prague in the summer of 1954 and the decree on policy with regard to religion on November 10, 1954.
11. F. Borkenau, *Der Monat,* 1955, No. 78, p. 566.
12. Cf. *Kommunist,* 1955, No. 14, p. 127.
13. C. G. Strohm, *Osteuropa,* 1955, No. 4, p. 287.
14. K. Mehnert, *Osteuropa,* 1955, No. 5, p. 363ff.
15. The interviews granted to the press by Canadian Foreign Minister Pearson after his visit to Moscow analyze the trends of Soviet foreign policy better than do any other reports published at that time.
16. Cf., apart from the State Department release, *The New York Times,* June 5, 1956; *The New Leader,* New York, Sec. 2, July 16, 1956, with annotations by B. Nicolaevsky; and B. D. Wolfe, *Khrushchev and Stalin's Ghost: The Text, Background, Motives and Meaning of Khrushchev's Secret Address,* New York, 1956.
17. B. Meissner, "Die Erlebnisse des 20. Parteikongresses der KPSU," *Europa-Archiv,* 1956, Nos. 9-10; and "The Twentieth Congress of the Communist Party of the Soviet Union," issued by the Free Trade Union Committee, June 1, 1956.
18. Meissner, "Die Erlebnisse des 20. Parteikongresses der KPSU," p. 8869.
19. L. Schapiro, *The Origin of the Communist Autocracy,* London, 1955.
20. *Pravda,* February 15, 1956; *Ostprobleme,* 1956, No. 10.
21. For the text of the Plan, see *Ostprobleme,* 1956, Nos. 8-10, 12.
22. *Report of the Special Committee on the Problem of Hungary,* UN Document A/3592.

BIBLIOGRAPHY

Achminow, G. F. *Die Macht im Hintergrunde: Totengraeber des Kommunismus.* Ulm, 1950.

Adamheit, Theodor. *Rote Armee, rote Weltrevolution, roter Imperialismus.* Berlin, 1935.

Agabekov, Georgii A. *OGPU: The Russian Secret Terror.* New York, 1931.

Albrecht, K. *Der verratene Sozialismus.* Berlin, 1939.

Aleksandrov, Georgii F. *The Pattern of Soviet Democracy.* Washington, 1948.

Anders, Wladyslaw. *Hitler's Defeat in Russia.* Chicago, 1953.

Anderson, Paul B. *People, Church and State in Modern Russia.* New York, 1944.

Araklian, A. *Industrial Management in the U.S.S.R.,* Washington, 1950.

Armstrong, John A. *Ukrainian Nationalism, 1939-1945.* New York, 1955.

Ashby, Eric. *Scientist in Russia.* Harmondsworth, Middlesex and New York, 1947.

Bailey, Thomas Andrew. *American Faces Russia. Russian-American Relations from Early Times to Our Day.* Ithaca, N.Y., 1950.

Balabanov, M. *Istoriya revolyutsionogo dvizhenya v Rossii.* Kharkov, 1925.

Baldwin, Hanson W. *Great Mistakes of the War.* New York, 1950.

Ball, W. Macmahon. *Nationalism and Communism in East Asia.* Cambridge, Mass., 1953.

Barghoorn, Frederick C. *The Soviet Image of the United States.* New York, 1950.

————. *Soviet Russian Nationalism.* New York, 1956.

Barmine, Alexander. *One Who Survived: The Life Story of A Russian Under the Soviets.* New York, 1945.

Basily, Nikolai de. *Russia Under Soviet Rule.* London, 1938.

Basseches, Nikolaus. *Stalin: Das Schicksal eines Erfolges.* Bern, 1950.

————. *Die unbekannte Armee.* Zuerich, 1942.

Bauer, Raymond A. *The New Man in Soviet Psychology.* Cambridge, Mass., 1952.

Baykov, Alexander. *Soviet Foreign Trade.* Princeton, 1946.

Beck, F. and Godin W. (pseud.). *Russian Purge and the Extraction of Confession.* New York, 1951.

Beloff, Max. *The Foreign Policy of Soviet Russia, 1929-1941.* 2 vols. London and New York, 1947-1949.

————. *Soviet Policy in the Far East, 1944-1951.* London and New York, 1953.

Benes, Edvard. *Memoirs: from Munich to New War and New Victory.* London, 1954.

Berdyaev, Nicolas. *The Origin of Russian Communism*. London, 1937.
———. *The Russian Idea*. London, 1947.
Berdyaev, Nikolai A. (Nicolas). *Wahrheit und Luege des Kommunismus*. Darmstadt, 1953.
Bergson, Abram (Ed.). *Soviet Economic Growth: Conditions and Perspectives*. Evanston, Ill., 1953.
Berman, Harold, J. *Justice in Russia: An Interpretation of Soviet Law*. Cambridge, Mass., 1950.
———. *The Russians in Focus*. Boston, 1953.
Bilmanis, A. *A History of Latvia*. Princeton, 1951.
Biografii chlenov politbyuro VKP(b). Leningrad, 1927.
Black, Cyril E. (Ed.). *Rewriting Russian History: Soviet Interpretations of Russia's Past*. New York, 1956.
Bochenski, Innocentius M. *Der sowjetrussische dialektische Materialismus (Diamat)*. Bern, 1950.
Bonnet, George E. *De Washington au Quai d'Orsay*. Genève, 1946.
Borkenau, Franz. *The Communist International*. London, 1938.
———. *European Communism*. New York, 1953.
———. *World Communism: A History of the Communist International*. New York, 1939.
Braun, M. *Russische Dichtung im 19. Jahrhundert*. Hanover, 1947.
Browder, Robert Paul. *The Origins of Soviet-American Diplomacy*. Princeton, 1953.
Brown, John (pseud.). *Who's Next? The Lesson of Czechoslovakia*. London and New York, 1951.
Brzezinski, Zbigniew. *The Permanent Purge*. Cambridge, Mass., 1956.
———. *Political Controls in the Soviet Army*. New York, 1954.
Buber, Margaret. *Under Two Dictators*. New York, 1951.
Buchanan, Sir George William. *My Mission to Russia and Other Diplomatic Memories*. 2 vols., London and New York, 1923.
Budenz, Louis F. *The Cry Is Peace*. Chicago, 1952.
Bunyan, James. *Intervention, Civil War and Communism in Russia, April-December, 1918. Documents and Materials*. Baltimore, 1936.
Bunyan, James, and H. H. Fisher. *The Bolshevik Revolution, 1917-1918*. Stanford, Cal., 1934.
Butler, Ewan. *City Divided: Berlin 1955*. New York, 1955.
Byrnes, James F. *Speaking Frankly*. New York, 1947.

Carr, Edward H. *The Bolshevik Revolution, 1917-1923 (History of Soviet Russia)*. 3 vols. London and New York, 1950-1953.
———. *Germany and the Soviet Union, 1919-1939*. Oxford, n.d.
———. *The Interregnum, 1923-1924*. London and New York, 1954.
———. *The Soviet Impact on the Western World*. New York, 1947.
———. *Studies in Revolution*. London, 1950.
Carroll, E. M. and Epstein, F. T. (Eds.). *Deutschland und die Sowjetunion, 1939-1941*. Washington, 1948.
Carson, George Barr. *Electoral Practices in the U.S.S.R.* New York, 1955.
Casey, Robert Pierce. *Religion in Russia*. New York, 1946.
Cassidy, Henry C. *Moscow Dateline, 1941-1943*. Boston, 1943.
Chamberlin, William H. *America's Second Crusade*. Chicago, 1950.
———. *Beyond Containment*. Chicago, 1953.
———. *Blueprint for World Conquest; As Outlined by the Communist International*. Washington and Chicago, 1946.

————. *The Russian Enigma: An Interpretation.* New York, 1943.
————. *The Ukraine, a Submerged Nation.* New York, 1944.
————. *The Russian Revolution, 1917-1921.* 2 vols. New York, 1935.
————. *Russia's Iron Age.* Boston, 1934.
Chernov, Victor M. *The Great Russian Revolution.* New Haven, 1936.
Churchill, Sir Winston. *The Second World War.* 6 vols., Boston, 1948-1953.
Ciano, Galeazzo. *The Ciano Diaries.* New York, 1946.
Ciliga, Anton. *The Russian Enigma.* London, 1940.
Clauss, M. W. *Der Weg nach Yalta.* Heidelberg, 1952.
Cleinow, G. *Die deutsch-russischen Rechts-und Wirtschaftsvertraege.* Berlin, 1926.
Coates, W. P. *A History of the Anglo-Soviet Relations.* London, 1943.
Coates, W. P. and Coates, Z. *Armed Intervention in Russia, 1918-1922.* London, 1935.
Coulondre, Robert. *De Staline à Hitler: Souvenirs de deux ambassades, 1936-1939.* Paris, 1950.
Counts, George S. *The Country of the Blind: The Soviet System of Mind Control.* Boston, 1949.
Crankshaw, Edward. *Cracks in the Kremlin Wall.* New York, 1951.
————. *Russia and the Russians.* New York, 1948.
Cressey, George B. *The Basis of Soviet Strength.* New York, 1945.
————. *How Strong Is Russia. A Geographical Appraisal.* Syracuse, N.Y., 1954.
Crossman, Richard H. S. (Ed.). *The God that Failed.* By Arthur Koestler and others. New York, 1950.

Dallin, David J. *The Changing World of Soviet Russia.* New Haven, 1956.
————. *The New Soviet Empire.* New Haven, 1951.
————. *The Real Soviet Russia.* New Haven, 1947.
————. *The Rise of Russia in Asia.* New Haven, 1949.
————. *Soviet Russia and the Far East.* New Haven, 1948.
————. *Soviet Russia's Foreign Policy, 1939-1942.* New Haven, 1942
Dallin, David J. and Nicolaevsky, B. I. *Forced Labor in Soviet Russia.* New Haven, 1947.
Dan, F. *Dva goda skitaniya.* Berlin, 1922.
————. *Proiskhozhdeniye bolshevisma.* New York, 1948.
Davies, Joseph E. *Mission to Moscow.* New York, 1941.
Deane, John R. *The Strange Alliance. The Story of our Efforts at Wartime Cooperation with Russia.* New York, 1947.
Degras, Jane (Ed.). *Soviet Documents on Foreign Policy. I, 1917-1924; II, 1925-1932; III, 1933-1941.* London, 1951-1953.
De Huszar, George B., and associates. *Soviet Power and Policy.* New York, 1955.
Dellingshausen, Freiherr E. *Im Dienste der Heimat.* Stuttgart, 1930.
Denikin, Anton I. *La décomposition de l'armée et du pouvoir, février-septembre 1917.* Paris, 1921.
————. *The Russian Turmoil; Memoirs, Military, Social, and Political.* London, 1922.
————. *The White Army.* London, 1930.
————. *World Events and the Russian Problem.* Paris, 1939.
Dennett, Raymond, and Johnson Joseph E. (Eds.) *Negotiating with the Russians.* Boston, 1951.

Dennewitz, B. und Meissner B. *Die Verfassungen der modernen Staaten.* Hamburg, 1947.

Dennis, Alfred L. P. *The Foreign Policy of Soviet Russia.* New York, 1924.

Deutscher, Isaac. *The Prophet Armed: Trotsky, 1879-1921.* New York, 1954.

————. *Stalin, A Political Biography.* London and New York, 1949.

De Vries, A. *Die Sowjetunion nach dem Tode Lenins.* Berlin, 1925.

Dewey, John. *The Case of Leon Trotsky: Report of Hearings on the Charges Made Against Him in the Moscow Trials by the Preliminary Commission of Inquiry.* New York and London, 1937.

Dimanshtein, S. M. *Revolyutsia i natsyonalnyi vopros. Dokumenty i materialy.* 3 vols. Moscow, 1930.

Dixon, C. Aubrey, and Heilbrunn, Otto. *Communist Guerilla Warfare.* New York, 1954.

Dobb, Maurice H. *Soviet Economic Development since 1917.* New York, 1948.

Duchacek, Ivo. *The Strategy of Communist Infiltration: The Case of Czechoslovakia.* New Haven, 1949.

Dulles, Allen W. *Germany's Underground.* New York, 1947.

Dulles, Foster R. *The Road to Teheran; The Story of Russia and America, 1781-1943.* Princeton, 1944.

————. *Russia and America: Pacific Neighbors.* New York, 1946

Duranty, Walter. *Stalin and Co., the Politburo, the Men Who Run Russia.* New York, 1949.

Eastman, Max. *The End of Socialism in Russia.* Boston, 1937

————. *Since Lenin Died.* London and New York, 1925.

————. *Stalin's Russia and the Crisis in Socialism.* New York, 1940.

Ebon, Martin. *Malenkov, Stalin's Successor.* New York, 1953.

————. *World Communism Today.* New York, 1948.

Eisenhower, Dwight D. *Crusade in Europe.* Garden City, N.Y., 1948.

Ely, Col. Louis B. *The Red Army Today.* Harrisburg, Pa., 1953.

Erfurth, W. *Der finnische Krieg 1941-1944.* Wiesbaden, 1950.

Fainsod, Merle. *How Russia Is Ruled.* Cambridge, Mass., 1953.

Fischer, George. *Soviet Opposition to Stalin, A Case Study in World War II.* Cambridge, Mass., 1952.

Fischer, John. *Why They Behave Like Russians.* New York, 1947.

Fischer, Louis. *The Life and Death of Stalin.* New York, 1952.

————. *Men and Politics: An Autobiography.* New York, 1941.

————. *The Soviets in World Affairs. A History of the Relations Between the Soviet Union and the Rest of the World, 1917-1929.* 2nd ed., 2 vols. Princeton, 1951.

Fischer, Ruth. *Stalin and German Communism: A Study in the Origins of the State Party.* Cambridge, Mass., 1948.

Fisher, Harold H. *America and Russia in the World Community.* Claremont, Cal., 1946.

Fitzgerald, Charles P. *Revolution in China.* London and New York, 1952.

Flandin, Pierre Etienne. *Politique française 1919-1940.* Paris, 1947.

Florinsky, Michael T. *Russia: A History and an Interpretation.* 2 vols. New York, 1953.

————. *The End of the Russian Empire.* New Haven, 1931.

————. *Towards an Understanding of the U.S.S.R. A Study in Government, Politics and Economic Planning.* New York,1951.

————. *World Revolution and the U.S.S.R.* New York, 1933.

Foote, Alexander. *Handbook for Spies.* New York, 1949.

Forrestal, James V. *Forrestal Diaries.* New York, 1951.

Freund, Heinrich. *Russia from A to Z: Revolution, State and Party, Foreign Relations, Economic System, Social Principles, General Knowledge.* Sidney and London, 1945.

Fuller, John F. C. *How to Defeat Russia.* London, 1951.

————. *The Second World War, 1939-1945. A Strategical and Tactical History.* London, 1948.

Gafencu, Grigore. *The Last Days of Europe.* London, 1947.

————. *Prelude to the Russian Campaign.* London, 1945.

Gamelin, G. M. *Servir.* 3 vols. Paris, 1946-1947.

Gankin. Olga H. and Fisher, Harold H. *The Bolsheviks and the World War. The Origin of the Third International.* Stanford, Cal., 1940.

Garbutt, P. E. *The Russian Railways.* London, 1949.

Garthoff, Raymond L. *Soviet Military Doctrine.* Glencoe, Ill., 1953.

Gide, Andre. *Return from the U.S.S.R.* New York, 1937.

Gitermann, V. *Geschichte Russlands.* 3 vols. Hamburg, 1949.

Gluckstein, Ygael. *Stalin's Satellites in Europe.* Boston, 1952.

Golikov, S. *Vydayushchiesya pobyedy sovyetskoi armii v velikoy otechestvennoy voine.* Moscow, 1952.

Gorer, Geoffrey, and Rickman, John. *The People of Great Russia: A Psychological Study.* New York, 1950.

Gouzenko, Igor. *The Fall of A Titan.* New York, 1954.

————. *The Iron Curtain.* New York, 1948.

Gruber, Karl. *Between Liberation and Liberty: Austria in the Post-War World.* New York, 1955.

Gruilow, Leo (Ed.) *Current Soviet Policies. A Documentary Record of the 19th Party Congress and the Reorganization After Stalin's Death.* New York, 1953.

————, *Current Soviet Policies II: A Documentary Record, 1953-1956.* New York, 1957.

Gsovski, Vladimir (Ed.). *Church and State in Satellite Europe.* New York, 1955.

————. *Soviet Civil Law.* 2 vols. Ann Arbor, Mich., 1948-1949.

Guillaume, Gen. Augustin. *Soviet Arms and Soviet Power.* Washington, 1949.

Gunther, John. *Behind the Curtain.* New York, 1949.

Gurian, Waldemar. *Bolshevism: An Introduction to Soviet Communism.* Notre Dame, Ind., 1952.

Gurian, Waldemar (Ed.). *Soviet Imperialism: Its Origins and Tactics.* Notre Dame, Ind., 1953.

————. *The Soviet Union: Background, Ideology, Reality. A Symposium.* Notre Dame, Ind., 1951.

Hoettl, Wilhelm. *The Secret Front.* New York, 1954.

Haines, Charles G. (Ed.). *The Threat of Soviet Imperialism.* Baltimore, 1954.

Hanisch, E. *Geschichte Sowjetrusslands, 1917-1941.* Freiburg, 1951.

Hare, R. *Pioneers of Russian Social Thought.* Oxford, 1951.

Harper, Samuel N. *The Russia I Believe In. The Memoirs of Samuel N. Harper, 1902-1941*. Chicago, 1945.
———. (Ed.). *The Soviet Union and World Problems*. Chicago, 1935.
———. and Thompson, Ronald. *The Government of the Soviet Union*. New York, 1949.
Harsch, Joseph C. *The Curtain Isn't Iron*. Garden City, N. Y., 1950.
Hartlieb, W. W. *Das politische Vertragssystem der Sowjetunion, 1920-1935*. Leipzig, 1935.
Hassman, Heinrich. *Oil in the Soviet Union*. Princeton, 1954.
Hazard, John N. *Law and Social Change in the U.S.S.R.* London, 1953
Herling, Albert K. *The Soviet Slave Empire*. New York, 1951.
Herzen, Alexander J. *Polnoye sobraniye sochinenii i pisem*. 22 vols. Petrograd, 1919-1925.
Hindus, Maurice G. *Mother Russia*. Garden City, N.Y., 1943.
History of the Communist Party of the Soviet Union (Bolsheviks). Short Course. Published by the Central Committee of the Communist Party of the U.S.S.R., Moscow, 1952.
Hoare, Samuel. *The Fourth Seal: The End of a Russian Chapter*. London, 1930.
Hodgkinson, Harry. *Challenge to the Kremlin*. New York, 1952.
Horthy, Miklos. *Ein Leben fuer Ungarn*. Bonn, 1953.
Hull, Cordell. *The Memoirs of Cordell Hull*. 2 vols. New York, 1948.
Hunt, R. N. Carew. *The Theory and Practice of Communism*. New York, 1950.
Hurwicz, E. *Geschichte des russischen Buergerkrieges*. Berlin, 1927.
———. *Staatsmaenner und Abenteurer. Russische Portraits von Witte bis Trotski*. Leipzig, 1925.

Inkeles, Alex. *Public Opinion in Soviet Russia. A Study in Mass Persuasion*. Cambridge, Mass., 1950.
Istoriya grazhdanskoy voyny, 1917-1922. Edited by Gorki, Molotov, Voroshilov, Kirov, Zhdanov and Stalin. 2 vols. 2nd ed. Moscow, 1938-1948.

James, Cyril L. R. *World Revolution, 1917-1936: The Rise and Fall of the Communist International*. London, 1937.
Jasny, Naum. *The Socialized Agriculture of the U.S.S.R. Plans and Performance*. Stanford, Cal., 1949.
———. *The Soviet Economy During the Plan Era*. Stanford, Cal., 1951.
Just, A. W. *Militaermacht Sowjetunion*. Breslau, 1935.
———. *Dis Sowjetunion. Staat, Wirtschaft, Heer*. Berlin, 1940.

Kalinow, K. D. *Sowjetmarshaelle haben das Wort*. Hamburg, 1950.
Kazantsev, A. *Tretya sila*. Limburg a. Lahn, 1952.
Kelsen, Hans. *The Communist Theory of Law*. New York, 1954.
———. *The Political Theory of Bolshevism: A Critical Analysis*. Berkeley, Cal., 1948.
Kennan, George F. *American Diplomacy 1900-1950*. Chicago, 1951.
Kerensky, Alexander F. *The Catastrophe: Kerensky's Own Story of the Russian Revolution*. New York and London, 1927.
———. *The Crucifixion of Liberty*. New York, 1934.
———. *Erinnerungen vom Sturz des Zarentums bis zu Lenins Staatsstreich*. Dresden, 1928.

King, Beatrice. *Russia Goes to School: A Guide to Soviet Education.* London, 1948.

Kleist, P. *Zwischen Hitler und Stalin, 1939-1945.* Bonn, 1950.

Klimov, Gregory. *The Terror Machine. New York, 1953.*

Knickerbocker, H. R. *The Red Trade Menace.* New York, 1931.

Kochan, Lionel. *Russia and the Weimar Republic.* New York, 1955.

Koestler, Arthur. *Darkness at Noon.* New York, 1941.

———. *The Yogi and the Commissar and Other Essays.* New York, 1945.

Kohn, Hans. *Pan-Slavism Its History and Ideology.* Notre Dame, Ind., 1953.

Kolarz, Walter. *Russia and Her Colonies.* New York, 1953.

———. *The Peoples of the Soviet Far East.* New York, 1954.

Konstantinovsky, Boris A. *Soviet Law in Action: The Recollected Cases of a Soviet Lawyer.* Cambridge, Mass., 1953.

Kravchenko, Victor A. *I Chose Freedom. The Personal and Political Life of a Soviet Official.* New York, 1946.

Krivitsky, Walter G. *In Stalin's Secret Service. An Expose of Russia's Secret Policies by the Former Chief of the Soviet Intelligence in Western Europe.* New York and London, 1939.

Kropotkin, Peter A. *Memoirs of a Revolutionist.* Boston, 1899.

Krupnickyj, B. *Geschichte der Ukraine.* Leipzig, 1939.

Krypton, Constantine. *The Northern Sea Route and the Economy of the Soviet North.* New York, 1956.

Kulischer, J. *Russische Wirtschaftsgeschichte.* Jena, 1925.

Kulski, W. W. *The Soviet Regime: Communism in Practice.* Syracuse, N. Y., 1954.

Laserson, Max M. *The Development of Soviet Foreign Policy in Europe 1917-1942. A Selection of Documents.* New York, 1943.

Laski, Harold J. *Communism.* New York, 1927.

Lasswell, Harold D. *World Politics Faces Economics, with Special Reference to the Future Relations of the United States and Russia.* New York and London, 1945.

Lasswell, Harold D. and Blumenstock, Dorothy. *World Revolutionary Propaganda.* New York, 1939.

Lazitsch, B. *Lenine et la III. internationale.* Neufchatel, 1951.

Lee, Asher. *The Soviet Air Force.* New York, 1950.

Lehrman, Harold A. *Russia's Europe.* New York, 1947.

Leimbach, W. *Natur, Volk und Wirtschaft der Sowjetunion.* Stuttgart, 1950.

Leites, Nathan C. *A Study of Bolshevism.* Glencoe, Ill., 1953.

———. *The Operational Code of the Politburo.* New York, 1951.

Leites, Nathan C. and Bernaut Elsa. *Ritual of Liquidation: The Case of the Moscow Trials.* Glencoe, Ill., 1954.

Lenczowski, George. *Russia and the West in Iran: A study in Big Power Rivalry, 1918-1948.* Ithaca, N. Y., 1949.

Lenin, Vladimir I. *The Communist International. X. Selected Works.* London, 1936-1939.

———. *Imperialism, the Highest Stage of Capitalism: A Popular Outline.* New York, 1934.

———. *Left Wing Communism: An Infantile Disorder. An Attempt at a Popular Discussion on Marxist Strategy and Tactics.* New York, 1937.

———. *Selected Works.* New York, 1943.

————. *The Revolution of 1917. XX. Collected Works of V. I. Lenin.* Ed. Alexander Tractenberg. New York, 1929.

————. *Sochinenia (Works).* 32 vols., 2nd ed. Moscow and Leningrad, 1926-1929.

————. *State and the Revolution: Marxist Teaching About the Theory of :'ie State and the Task of the Proletariat in the Revolution.* New York, 1935.

————. *Toward the Seizure of Power. The Revolution of 1917: From the July Days to the October Revolution.* New York, 1932.

LeRossignol, James E. *From Marx to Stalin: A Critique of Communism.* New York, 1940.

Lettrich, Jozef. *History of Modern Slovakia.* New York, 1955.

Liddell Hart, B. H. *The Other Side of the Hill.* London, 1948.

Lieb, F. *Russland unterwegs.* Bern, 1945.

Lipper, Elinor. *Eleven Years in Soviet Prison Camps.* Chicago, 1951.

Littlepage, John D. and Bess, Demaree. *In Search of Soviet Gold.* New York, 1938.

Lockhart, Robert H. B. *British Agent.* New York and London, 1933.

Loeber, D. *Das Eherecht der Sowjetunion und seine Anwendung im internationalen Privatrecht Deutschlands.* Marburg, 1950.

Lorimer, Frank. *The Population of the Soviet Union: History and Prospects.* Geneva, 1946.

Lossky, Nikolai O. *History of Russian Philosophy.* New York, 1951.

Lyashchenko, P. L. *Istoriya narodnogo khozaistva SSSR.* 2nd ed. Moscow, 1948.

Lyaschenko, P. J. *Ocherki agrarnoy revolutsii Rossii.* 2nd ed. Petrograd, 1925.

Lyons, Eugene. *Assignment in Utopia.* New York, 1937.

MacEoin, Gary. *The Communist War on Religion.* New York, 1951.

Magidoff, Robert. *In Anger and Pity: A Report on Russia.* New York, 1949.

————. *The Kremlin vs the People: The Story of the Cold Civil War in Stalin's Russia.* Garden City, N. Y., 1953.

Majstrenko, Iwan. *Borot'bism: A Chapter in the History of Ukrainian Communism.* New York, 1954.

Mannerheim, Carl. *Memoirs.* London, 1953.

Manning, Clarence A. *The Story of the Ukraine.* New York, 1947.

————. *Ukraine under the Soviets.* New York, 1953.

Martow, J. and Dan, Th. *Geschichte der russischen Sozialdemokratie.* Berlin, 1926.

Maynard, Sir John. *Russia in Flux.* New York, 1948.

Mazour, Anatole G. *An Outline of Modern Russian Historiography.* Berkeley, Cal., 1939.

————. *Russia: Past and Present.* New York, 1951.

Mead, Margaret. *Soviet Attitudes Towards Authority; An Interdisciplinary Approach to Problems of Soviet Character.* New York, 1951.

Medynsky, Y. N. *Public Education in the U.S.S.R.* Moscow, 1950.

Mehnert, Klaus. *Die Jugend in Sowjetrussland.* Berlin, 1932.

————. *Die Sowjetunion: Bibliographie 1917-1932.* Koenigsberg, 1933.

————. *Stalin Versus Marx: The Stalinist Historical Doctrine.* London, 1952.

Meisel, James Hans and Kozera, Edward S. (Eds.). *Materials for the Study of the Soviet System: State and Party Constitutions, Laws, Decrees,*

Decisions, and Official Statements of the Leaders, in Translation. Ann Arbor, Mich., 1953.

Meissner, Boris. *The Communist Party of the Soviet Union.* New York, 1956.

——. *Russland, die Westmaechte und Deutschland. Die sowjetische Deutschlandpolitik 1943-1953.* Hamburg, 1953.

——. *Russland im Umbruch. Der Wandel in der Herrschaftsordnung und sozialen Struktur der Sowjetunion.* Frankfurt a.M., 1951.

——. *Die Sowjetunion, die baltischen Staaten, und das Voelkerrecht.* Cologne, 1956.

Menzel, E. *Die Friedensvertraege von 1947 mit Italien, Ungarn, Bulgarien, Rumaenien und Finnland.* Frankfort, a.M., 1948.

Mikhailov, Nicholas. *Land of the Soviets.* New York, 1939.

Mikhailov, Nicholas and Pokshishevsky,V. *Soviet Russia: The Land and Its People.* New York, 1948.

Mikolayczyk, Stanislaw. *The Rape of Poland: Pattern of Soviet Aggression.* London, 1947.

Miller, Harry. *The Communist Menace in Malaya.* New York, 1954.

Milioukov, P. *Histoire de la seconde révolution russe.* 3 vols. Sofia, 1921-1924.

Mitchell, Mairin. *The Maritime History of Russia, 1848-1948.* New York, 1950.

Moneta, J. *Kommentar zum kurzen Lehrgang der Geschichte der Kommunistischen Partei der Sowjetunion: Aufgang und Niergang des Stalinismus.* Cologne, 1953.

Monnerot, Jules. *Sociology and Psychology of Communism.* Boston, 1953.

Moore, Barrington. *Soviet Politics: The Dilemma of Power. The Role of Ideas in Social Change.* Cambridge, Mass., 1950.

——. *Terror and Progress U.S.S.R.: Some Sources of Change and Stability in the Soviet Dictatorship.* Cambridge, Mass., 1954.

Moore, Harriet L. *Soviet Far Eastern Policy, 1931-1945.* Princeton, 1945.

Mosely, Philip E. (Ed.). *Face to Face with Russia.* New York, 1948.

——. *The Soviet Union since World War II. Annals, American Academy of Political and Social Science, Vol 263.* Philadelphia, 1949.

Murphy, John T. *Russia on the March: A Study of Soviet Foreign Policy.* London, 1941.

——. *Stalin, 1879-1944.* London, 1945.

Nagy, Ferenc. *The Struggle Behind the Iron Curtain.* New York, 1948.

Nechkina, M. V. *Istorya SSSR.* 2 vols. 2nd ed. Moscow, 1949.

Nettl, J. P. *The Eastern Zone and Soviet Policy in Germany, 1945-1950.* London and New York, 1951.

Newman, Bernard. *The Captured Archives: The Story of the Nazi-Soviet Documents.* London, 1948.

——. *The Red Spider: The Story of Russian Spying in Canada.* London, 1947.

——. *Report on Indo-China.* London and New York, 1953.

Niemeyer, Gerhart with the assistance of John S. Reshetar, Jr. *An Inquiry into Soviet Mentality.* New York, 1956.

North, Robert C. *Moscow and Chinese Communists.* Stanford, Cal., 1953.

Olkhovsky, Andrey. *Music Under the Soviets: The Agony of An Art.* New York, 1955.

Ouralov, A. *Staline au pouvoir.* Paris, 1951.

Owen, L. A. *The Russian Peasant Movement, 1906-1917.* London, 1936.

Paléologue, Maurice. *La Russie des tsars pendant la Grande Guerre*. 3 vols. Paris, 1923.

Pares, Sir Bernard. *A History of Russia*. New York, 1953.

———. *My Russian Memoirs*. London, 1931.

Passfield, Sidney James Webb, Baron, and Webb, Beatrice. *Soviet Communism: A New Civilization?* London and New York, 1935.

Pavlovsky, Michael N. *Chinese-Russian Relations*. New York, 1949.

Payne, Pierre S. R. *Red Storm over Asia*. New York, 1951.

Philipov, Alexander. *Logic and Dialectic in the Soviet Union*. New York, 1953.

Pierre, André. *Malenkov, ou le nouveau destin de la Russie*. Paris, 1953.

Pipes, Richard. *The Formation of the Soviet Union: Communism and Nationalism, 1917-1923*. Cambridge, Mass., 1954.

Plekhanov, Georgi V. *Ein Jahr in der Heimat*. Berlin, 1919.

———. *Russky rabochy klass v revolutsyonnom dvizhenyi*. Moscow, 1940.

Pokrowski, M. *Geschichte Russlands*. Leipzig, 1929.

Pope, Arthur U. *Maxim Litvinoff*. New York, 1943.

Possony, Stephan T. *A Century of Conflict: Communist Techniques of World Revolution*. Chicago, 1953.

Propopovicz, S. N. *Russlands Volkswirtschaft unter den Sowjets*. Zuerich, 1944.

Rabinovich, S. *Kratkaya istoria grazhdanskoy voiny*. Moscow, 1935.

Radkey, O. H. *The Election to the Russian Constituent Assembly of 1917*. Cambridge, Mass., 1950.

Ravines, Eudocio. *The Yenan Way*. New York, 1951.

Reilly, S. *Britain's Master Spy*. London, 1933.

Reshetar, John S., Jr. *Problems of Analyzing and Predicting Soviet Behavior*. New York, 1955.

———. *The Ukrainian Revolution, 1917-1920: A Study in Nationalism*. Princeton, 1952.

Ripka, Hubert. *Czechoslovakia Enslaved: The Story of the Communist Coup d'Etat*. London, 1950.

Rogers, Edward. *A Christian Commentary on Communism*. New York, 1952.

Rosenberg, Arthur. *A History of Bolshevism from Marx to the First Five Years' Plan*. London, 1934.

Rostow, Walt W. and others. *The Dynamics of Soviet Society*. Cambridge, Mass., 1952.

Rothfels, H. *The German Opposition to Hitler*. Chicago, 1948.

Roucek, Joseph E. (Ed.). *Moscow's European Satellites, Annals, American Academy of Political and Social Science, Vol. 271*. Philadelphia, 1950.

Rounds. Frank, Jr. *A Window on Red Square*. New York, 1953.

Roy, Manabendra N. *The Russian Revolution*. Calcutta, 1949.

Salvadori, Massimo. *The Rise of Modern Communism: A Brief History of the Communist Movement in the Twentieth Century*. New York, 1952.

Salazar, L. A. Sanchez. *Mord in Mexiko: Die Ermordung Leo Trotzkis*. Frankfurt a.M., 1952.

Schlesinger, Rudolf (Ed.). *Changing Attitudes in Soviet Russia. Documents and Readings*. London, 1949.

Schlesinger, Rudolf. *Soviet Legal Theory, Its Social Background and Development*. New York, 1945.

──────. *The Spirit of Post-War Russia: Soviet Ideology, 1917-1946*. London, 1947.

Schmidt, P. *Als Statist auf diplomatischer Buehne*. Bonn, 1949.

Schuman, Frederick L. *Soviet Politics at Home and Abroad*. New York, 1946.

Schwartz, Harry. *Russia's Soviet Economy*. 2d. ed. New York, 1955.

Schwarz, Solomon M. *Jews in the Soviet Union*. Syracuse, N. Y., 1951.

──────. *Labor in the Soviet Union*. New York, 1952.

Scott, John. *Behind the Urals. An American Worker in Russia's City of Steel*. Boston, 1942.

Selznik, Philip. *The Organizational Weapon. A Study of Bolshevik Strategy and Tactics*. Santa Monica, Cal., 1952.

Seraphim, H. G. *Die deutsch-russischen Beziehungen 1939-1941*. Hamburg, 1949.

Serge, Victor. *From Lenin to Stalin*. London, 1937.

──────. *Russia, Twenty Years After*. New York, 1937.

Seton-Watson, Hugh. *The East European Revolution*. New York, 1952.

──────. *From Lenin to Malenkov: The History of World Communism*. New York, 1953.

Shabad,Theodore. *Geography of the U.S.S.R.* New York, 1951.

Shepherd, Gordon. *Russia's Danubian Empire*. New York, 1954.

Sherwood, Robert E. *Roosevelt and Hopkins*. New York, 1948.

Shtein, B. E. *Burzhuazniye falsifikatory istorii, 1919-1938*. Moscow, 1951.

Shub, David. *Lenin*. Garden City, N. Y., 1948.

Simmons, Ernest J. (Ed.). *Through the Glass of Soviet Literature: Views of Russian Society*. New York, 1953.

──────. *U.S.S.R., A Concise Handbook*. Ithaca, N. Y., 1947

Sinevirskii, Nikolai. *Smersh*. New York, 1950.

Smal-Stocki, R. *The Nationality Problem of the Soviet Union and Russian Communist Imperialism*. Milwaukee, 1952.

Smilg-Benario, N. *Der Zusammenbruch der Zarenmonarchie*. Zuerich, 1927.

──────. *Von Kerenski zu Lenin*. Zuerich, 1929.

Smith, Walter B. *My Three Years in Moscow*. Philadelphia, 1950.

Snow, Edgar. *The Pattern of Soviet Power*. New York, 1945.

Somerville, John. *Soviet Philosophy: A Study of Theory and Practice*. New York, 1946.

Sontag, R. J. and Beddie J. S. (Eds.). *Nazi-Soviet Relations, 1939-1941. Documents from the Archives of the German Foreign Office*. Washington, 1948.

Souvarine, Boris. *Stalin. A Critical Survey of Bolshevism*. New York, 1939.

Spinka, Matthew. *The Church in Soviet Russia*. New York, 1956.

Staehlin, K. *Geschichte Russlands*. 3 vols. Stuttgart, 1923-1930.

Stalin, J. V. *Economic Problems of Socialism in the U.S.S.R.*, New York, 1952.

──────. *The Great Patriotic War of the Soviet Union. A Selection of Speeches*. New York, 1945.

──────. *The History of the Communist Party of the Soviet Union*. Moscow, 1938.

————. *Foundations of Leninism.* New York, 1934.

————. *Leninism, Selected Writings.* New York, 1942.

————. *The October Revolution. A Collection of Articles and Speeches.* London, 1934.

————. *Problems of Leninism.* Moscow, 1947.

————. *Sochinenia (Works), 13 vols.* Moscow, 1946-1952.

Steinberg, J. *Spiridonova: Revolutionary Terrorist.* London, 1935.

Stettinius, Edward R. *Roosevelt and the Russians.* New York, 1949.

Stevens, Edmund. *This Is Russia, Uncensored.* New York, 1950.

Stevens, Leslie Clark. *Russian Assignment.* Boston, 1953.

Stowe, Leland. *Conquest by Terror.* New York, 1952.

————. *While Time Remains.* New York, 1946.

Stresemann, Gustav. *His Diaries, Letters and Papers.* 3 vols. London, 1935-1940.

Strong, A. L. *This Soviet World.* New York, 1936.

Struve, Gleb. *Soviet Russian Literature (1917-1950)* Norman, Oklahoma, 1951.

Sukhanov, N. *Zapisky o revolutsii.* 7 vols. Berlin, 1922.

Sumner, Benedict H. *A Short History of Russia.* Rev. ed. New York, 1949.

Swettenham, J. A. *The Tragedy of the Baltic States.* New York, 1954.

Taracouzio, Timothy A. *The Soviet Union and International Law. A Study Based on the Legislation, Treaties and Foreign Relations of the Union of Socialist Soviet Republics.* New York, 1935.

————. *War and Peace in Soviet Diplomacy.* New York, 1940.

Theimer, W. *Der Marxismus: Lehre, Wirkung, Kritik.* Bern, 1950.

Thorwald, J. *Wen sie verderben wollen.* Stuttgart, 1952.

Tiander, K. *Das Erwachen Europas Ost: Die Nationalitaetenbewegung in Russland and der Weltkrieg.* Wien, 1934.

Tiedemann, H. *Sowjetrussland und die Revolutionierung Deutschlands, 1917-1919.* Berlin, 1936.

Timasheff, Nicholas S. *The Great Retreat. The Growth and Decline of Communism in Russia.* New York, 1936.

————. *Religion in Soviet Russia, 1917-1942.* New York, 1942.

Tomasic, Dinko A. *The Impact of Russian Culture on Soviet Communism.* Glecoe, Ill., 1953.

Towster, Julian. *Political Power in the U.S.S.R., 1917-1947.* New York, 1948.

Trotsky, Lev. *The History of the Russian Revolution.* New York, 1936.

————. *My Life: An Attempt at an Autobiography.* New York, 1930.

————. *The Permanent Revolution.* New York, 1931.

————. *The Revolution Betrayed. What is the Soviet Union and Where Is It Going?* Garden City, N. Y., 1937.

————. *Selected Writings.* New York, 1942.

————. *Sochinenia (Works).* 3 vols. Moscow, 1924.

————. *Stalin, An Appraisal of the Man and His Influence.* New York and London, 1948.

————. *The Stalin School of Falsification.* New York, 1937.

————. *The Suppressed Testament of Lenin.* New York, 1946.

Truman, Harry S. *Year of Decision.* New York, 1955.

Tugan-Baranowsky, M. *Geschichte der russischen Fabrik.* Berlin, 1900.

Turin, S. P. *The U.S.S.R., An Economic and Social Survey.* London, 1948.

Ulam, Adam B. *Titoism and the Cominform.* Cambridge, Mass., 1952.

Utley, Freda. *The Dream We Lost: Soviet Russia Then and Now.* New York, 1940.

Varneck, Elena and Fisher, Harold H. *The Testimony of Kolchak and Other Siberian Materials.* Stanford, Cal., 1935.
Vernadsky, G. *Lenin: Red Dictator.* New Haven, 1931.
Veselovsky, B. *Istoriya zemstva za sorok let.* 4 vols. St. Petersburg, 1909-1911.
Von Bluecher, W. *Deutschlands Weg nach Rapallo.* Wiesbaden, 1951.
————. *Gesandter zwischen Diktatur und Demokratie. Erinnerungen, 1935-1940.* Wiesbaden, 1951.
Von Freytagh-Loringhoven, A. *Geschichte der russischen Revolution.* Muenchen, 1919.
Von Rauch, Georg. *Die Grundlinien der sowjetischen Geschichtsschreibung im Zeichen des Stalinismus.* Europa-Archiv, Frankfurt a.M., 1950. Heft 19-21.
————. *Russland, staatliche Einheit und nationale Vielfalt. Foederalistische Kraefte und Ideen in der russischen Geschichte.* Muenchen, 1953.
————. "Die sowjetische Geschichtsschreibung heute." (*Die Welt als Geschichte,* 1951, Heft 1).
Von Rimscha, H. *Der russische Buergerkrieg und die russische Emigration, 1917-1922.* Stuttgart, 1924.
Von Sakharov, K. *Die verratene Armee* Berlin, 1938.
Voroshilov, Klimenti J. *Statyi i rechi.* Moscow, 1937.
Voznesenski, Nikolai A. *Economy of the U.S.S.R. During World War II.* Washington, 1948.
Vucinich, Alexander S. *Soviet Economic Institutions: The Social Structure of Production Units.* Stanford, Cal., 1952.
Vyshinsky, Andrey Y. *J. V. Stalin's Doctrine of the Socialist State.* Moscow, 1951.
————. *The Law of the Soviet State.* New York, 1948.
————. *Trotskyism in the Service of Fascism against Socialism and Peace. From the Court Proceedings in the Case of the Trotsky-Zinoviev Center.* New York, 1936.

Walsh, E. A. *Total Empire: The Roots and Progress of World Communism.* Milwaukee, 1951.
Walter, Gerard. *Histoire de la Revolution Russe.* Paris, 1953.
Warth, Robert D. *The Allies and the Russian Revolution, from the Fall of the Monarchy to the Peace of Brest-Litovsk.* Durham, N. C., 1954.
Weinberg, Gerhard L. *Germany and the Soviet Union, 1930-1931.* Leiden, 1954.
Weissberg, Alexander. *The Accused.* New York, 1951.
Werth, Alexander. *Year of Stalingrad.* London, 1946.
Wetter, Gustav A., SJ. *Der dialektische Materialismus. Seine Geschichte und sein System in der Sowjetunion.* Wien, 1952.
White, D. Fedotoff. *The Growth of the Red Army.* Princeton, 1944.
White, J. A. *The Siberian Intervention.* Princeton, 1950
Williams, William A. *American-Russian Relations, 1781-1947.* New York, 1952.
Wilmot, Chester. *The Struggle for Europe.* London, 1952.
Wilson, Edmund. *To the Finland Station: A Study in the Writing and Acting of History.* Garden City, N. Y., 1953.

Wilson, Sir Henry H.   *His Life and Diaries*. Ed. by Sir Charles E. Caldwell. New York, 1927.

Wolfe, Bertram D.   *Khrushchev and Stalin's Ghost: The Text, Background, Motives and Meaning of Khrushchev's Secret Address*. New York, 1956.

———. *Three Who Made a Revolution. A Biographical History*. New York, 1948.

Wolin, Simon and Slusser Robert M. (Eds.).   *The Soviet Secret Police*. New York, 1957.

Wollenberg, Erich.   *The Red Army*. 2nd ed., London, 1940.

Wuorinen, J. H.   *Finland and World War II*. New York, 1948.

Yakhontoff, Victor A.   *Russia and the Soviet Union in the Far East*. New York, 1931.

———. *U.S.S.R. Foreign Policy*. New York, 1945.

Yanson, J. D.   *Foreign Trade in the U.S.S.R.* London, 1935.

Yaroslavsky, E.   *Karl Marx i revolutsionoye narodnichestvo*. Moscow, 1939.

Zavalani, Tajar.   *How Strong Is Russia: Propaganda and Reality of the Five-Year Plans*. New York, 1952.

Zetkin, Klara.   *Reminiscences of Lenin*. London, 1929.

Zhdanov, Andrey A.   *Essays on Literature, Philosophy and Music*. New York, 1950.

———. *Kritische Bermerkungen zu dem Buch A.F. Alexandrows "Geschichte der westeuropaeischen Philosophie."* Berlin, 1950.

Ziff, William B.   *Two Worlds*. New York, 1946.

Zilliacus, K.   *Revolution und Gegenrevolution in Russland und Finnland*. Muenchen, 1912.

Zirkle, Conway.   *Death of a Science in Russia*. Philadelphia, 1949.

Zubov, N.   *Dzierzinski*. Moscow, 1933.

CHRONOLOGY 1855-1966

Reign of Alexander II	1855-1881
G. V. Plekhanov	1857-1918
V. I. Lenin	1870-1924
L. D. Trotsky	1879-1940
J. V. Stalin	1879-1953
Reign of Alexander III	1881-1894
"Liberation of Labor" group founded	**1883**
Reign of Nicholas II	1894-1917
"Union of Struggle for the Liberation of the Working Class"	1895
South Russian Workers' Alliance	1897
I. Social Democratic Congress in Minsk	**1898**
Social Revolutionary Party founded	**1902**
II. Party Congress in London. Split between Bolsheviks and Mensheviks	**1903**
Russo-Japanese War	1904-1905
Bloody Sunday	January 9 (22), 1905
III. Party Congress in London	**1905**
First Soviet in St. Petersburg	**1905**
October Manifesto	**1905**
IV. Party Congress in Stockholm	**1906**
First Duma	**1906**
Second Duma	**1907**
Third Duma	1907-1912
V. Party Congress in London	1907
"Pravda" founded	April 1912
Fourth Duma	1912-1917
Socialist Conference in Zimmerwald	September 1915
Socialist Conference in Kienthal	April 1916
February Revolution	February 27 (March 12), 1917
"Order No. 1"	March 1 (14), 1917
Abdication of Nicholas II	March 2 (15), 1917
Lenin's Return	April 3 (16), 1917
I. All-Russian Congress of Soviets	June 3 (16), 1917
VI. Party Congress	July-August 1917
July uprising	July 1917
Kerensky's offensive	July 1917
Kornilov's revolt	August (September) 1917
Congress of Nationalities in Kiev	September 1917
Russia proclaimed a Republic	September 1 (14), 1917
II. All-Russian Congress of Soviets	October 25 (November 7), 1917
October Revolution	October 25 (November 7), 1917
Period of War Communism	1917-1921
Decree on Confiscation of Land	October 26 (November 8), 1917

Declaration of Peace	October 26 (November 8), 1917
Declaration on the Rights of Nationalities	November 2 (15), 1917
Trans-Caucasian Federation founded	November 2 (15), 1917
Diet of Estonia proclaims sovereignty	November 15 (28), 1917
Finland proclaims independence	November 23 (December 6), 1917
Brest-Litovsk Armistice	December 2 (15), 1917
III. All-Russian Congress of Soviets	January 1918
Constituent Assembly opens	January 5 (18), 1918
Declaration of Independence by Ukrainian Rada	January 9 (22), 1918
Declaration of Independence by the Baltic Knighthoods	January 15 (28), 1918
"Bread Peace" between the Central Powers and the Ukraine	January 27 (February 9), 1918
Ultimatum of the Central Powers	January 27 (February 9), 1918
Introduction of the Gregorian Calendar	February 1 (14), 1918
Estonia's Declaration of Independence	February 24, 1918
Peace of Brest-Litovsk	March 3, 1918
VII. Party Congress	March 1918
Ratification of the Peace Treaty of Brest-Litovsk	March 15, 1918
IV. All-Russian Congress of Soviets	March 1918
Byelorussian Declaration of Independence	March 25, 1918
Trans-Caucasian Federation proclaims independence	April 22, 1918
German-Ukrainian Trade Agreement	April 23, 1918
North Caucasian Federal Republic founded	May 11, 1918
Helsingfors (Helsinki) liberated	May 16, 1918
Georgia proclaims independence	May 26, 1918
Armenia proclaims independence	May 28, 1918
Azerbaijan proclaims independence	May 28, 1918
V. All-Russian Congress of Soviets	July 1918
Assassination of the Czar and his family in Ekaterinburg	July 1918
Social-Revolutionary uprising	July 1918
Constitution of the R.S.F.S.R.	July 10, 1918
First crisis in the Civil War at the Volga	August 1918
Supplementary Peace Agreement of Brest-Litovsk	August 27, 1918
VI. All-Russian Congress of Soviets	November 1918
England and France mark their spheres of interest in Russia	November 13, 1918
Petlura takes the place of Skoropadsky	November 15, 1918
Latvia proclaims independence	November 17, 1918
Kolchak's coup d'état in Omsk	November 18, 1918
Byelorussian Soviet Republic	January 1, 1919
Red Army occupies Kiev	February 3, 1919
VIII. Party Congress	March 1919
First Congress of the Comintern: Foundation of the Comintern	March 2, 1919
Allied Supreme Council reject Foch's plan of an anti-Bolshevik crusade	March 27, 1919
Ukrainian Soviet Republic	April 8, 1919

Riga liberated	May 22, 1919
Second crisis in Civil War (Petrograd)	October 1919
VII. All-Russian Congress of Soviets	December 1919
Red Army occupies Rostov	January 8, 1920
Peace Treaty with Estonia in Dorpat	February 2, 1920
Kolchak executed	February 7, 1920
IX. Party Congress	March-April 1920
Far-Eastern Republic founded	April 6, 1920
German-Russian Treaty on Prisoners of War	April 19, 1920
Pilsudski conquers Kiev	May 7, 1920
Wrangel's Agrarian Law	June 7, 1920
Second Congress of the Comintern	July-August 1920
Peace Treaty with Lithuania in Moscow	July 12, 1920
Peace Treaty with Latvia in Riga	August 11, 1920
"Miracle on the Vistula"	August 15-16, 1920
Polish-Russian Armistice at Riga	October 12, 1920
Peace Treaty with Finland signed in Dorpat	October 14, 1920
Breakthrough of the Red Army at Perekop	November 7-8, 1920
VIII. All-Russian Congress of Soviets	December 1920
Treaties with Iran and Afghanistan	February 1921
Adoption of Gosplan	February 22, 1921
End of the independence of Georgia	February 25, 1921
Kronstadt Mutiny	March 1-18, 1921
Period of NEP (New Economic Policy)	1921-1927
Treaty of Peace and Friendship with Turkey	March 16, 1921
Trade Agreement with Great Britain	March 16, 1921
X. Party Congress	March 1921
Trade Agreement with Germany	May 6, 1921
Third Congress of the Comintern	June 22-July 12, 1921
Treaty with Mongolian People's Republic	November 5, 1921
IX. All-Russian Congress of Soviets	December 1921
Cheka reorganized as GPU	February 1922
XI. Party Congress	March-April 1922
Stalin Secretary General of the Party	April 3, 1922
Dissolution of the Holy Synod, arrest of Patriarch Tikhon	1922
Treaty of Rapallo with Germany	April 16, 1922
Trial of the Social Revolutionaries	Summer 1922
Fourth Congress of the Comintern	November 1922
Annexation of the Far-Eastern Republic	November 10, 1922
X. All-Russian Congress of Soviets becomes I Congress of Soviets of the USSR	December 1922
Establishment of the Union of Soviet Socialist Republics (USSR)	December 27, 1922
XII. Party Congress	April 1923
Constitution of the USSR	July 6, 1923
Communist riots in Germany	October-November 1923
Lenin's death	January 21, 1924
II. Congress of Soviets of the USSR	January-February 1924
De jure recognition of USSR by Great Britain	February 2, 1924
XIII. Party Congress	May 1924
Fifth Congress of the Comintern	June-July 1924

De jure recognition of USSR by France	October 28, 1924
Zinoviev Affair in England	October 1924
Communist uprising in Reval	December 1, 1924
Trotsky dismissed as Commissar of War	January 1925
XIV. Party Conference: Stalin's thesis of "Socialism in one country"	April 1925
III. Congress of Soviets of the USSR	May 1925
Union of Godless founded	1925
Office of Political Commissars abolished in Red Army	1925
Frunze dies, Voroshilov becomes Commissar of War	October 1925
Trade Agreement with Germany	October 12, 1925
XIV. Party Congress adopts program of industrialization	December 1925
S. M. Kirov Party Secretary in Leningrad	January 1926
Treaty of Berlin with Germany	April 26, 1926
Dzierzynski dies, Menzhinsky appointed his successor	July 20, 1926
Treaty with Lithuania	September 28, 1926
Trotsky dismissed from Politburo	October 1926
IV. Congress of Soviets of the USSR	April 1927
Arcos raid, break of diplomatic relations with England	May 1927 (until July 1929)
Trotsky and Zinoviev dropped from Central Committee	October 1927
Trotsky and Zinoviev expelled from Party	November 14, 1927
XV. Party Congress	December 1927
Diplomatic relations with China broken off	December 1927 (until December 1929)
First Five Year Plan	1928-1932
Trotsky exiled to Alma-Ata	January 1928
Start of collectivization	January 1928
Shakhty Trial	May 1928
VI. Congress of the Comintern	July-August 1928
Trotsky expelled from territory of USSR	January 1929
Litvinov Protocol to Kellogg-Briand Pact	February 9, 1929
V. Congress of Soviets of the USSR	May 1929
Bukharin dropped from Politburo	November 1929
Liquidation of the Kulaks begins	end of 1929
XVI. Party Congress	June-July 1930
V. M. Molotov Chairman of the Council of People's Commissars	1930
M. M. Litvinov Commissar for Foreign Affairs	July 1930
Opening of Turksib Railroad	1930
Stalin's speech on industrialization	February 4, 1931
VI. Congress of Soviets of the USSR	March 1931
Trial of "Industrial Party"	1931
Non-Aggression Pact with Finland	January 21, 1932
Japanese invasion of Manchuria	February 1932
Non-Aggression Pact with Latvia	February 5, 1932
" " " " Estonia	May 4, 1932

Non-Aggression Pact with China	June 29, 1932
" " " " Poland	July 25, 1932
" " " " France	November 29, 1932
Opening of Dnieprostroi Dam	1932
The great crisis of the Stalin regime	**end of 1932**
Second Five Year Plan	1933-1937
Opening of the White Sea Canal	August 2, 1933
De jure recognition extended by U.S.A.	November 1933
XVII. Party Congress	January-February 1934
'Chelyuskin"-Papanin polar expedition	Spring 1934
New "patriotic" conception of history	since May 1934
USSR enters League of Nations	September 18, 1934
Assassination of Kirov	December 1, 1934
VII. Congress of Soviets of the USSR	January 1935
Agreement with Japan	January 22, 1935
Eden in Moscow	March 1935
Trade Agreement with **Germany**	**April 9, 1935**
Assistance Pact with France	May 2, 1935
Assistance Pact with Czechoslovakia	May 16, 1935
Laval in Moscow	May 1935
Benes in Moscow	June 1935
VII. Comintern Congress	July-August 1935
Introduction of "Stakhanovism"	**August 1935**
Introduction of ranks in the Red Army	**September 22, 1935**
Death of Kuibyshev	1935
New Family Law	June 27, 1936
Trial of Zinoviev, Kamenev and others	August 1936
Proclamation of non-intervention in the Spanish Civil War	August 1936
Death of Tomsky (suicide)	1936
Yagoda dismissed, Yezhov his successor	September 26, 1936
Zhdanov's threatening speech against the Baltic States	November 1936
Death of Maxim Gorky	1936
The Stalin Constitution	November 1936
VIII. Congress of Soviets of the USSR	November 1936
Trial of Radek	January 1937
Tukhachevsky dismissed as Chief of Staff	May 11, 1937
Re-introduction of Political Commissars in the Red Army	May 1937
Death of Ordjonikidze	1937
I. Supreme Soviet after adoption of Stalin Constitution	1937
Trial of Tukhachevsky	June 1937
Trial of Rykov, Krestinsky, Yagoda, Bukharin and Rakovsky	March 1938
Third Five Year Plan	1938-1942
History of CPSU ("Short Course") published	1938
Frontier incidents with Japan	Summer 1938
Yezhov dismissed, Beria his successor	December 1938
New military oath	January 3, 1939
XVIII. Party Congress	March 1939

Stalin's speech	March 10, 1939
Negotiations with the Western Powers	April-August 1939
Molotov Commissar for Foreign Affairs	May 2, 1939
Beginning of Russo-German conversations	May 20, 1939
Renewed frontier incidents with Japan	May 1939
Trade Agreement with Germany	August 19, 1939
Ribbentrop in Moscow, Non-Aggression Pact with Germany	August 23, 1939
Neutrality Agreement with Japan	September 15, 1939
Soviet intervention in Poland	September 17, 1939
Frontier and Friendship Treaty with Germany	September 28, 1939
Assistance Pact with Estonia	September 28, 1939
" " with Latvia	October 5, 1939
" " with Lithuania	October 10, 1939
War with Finland	November 30, 1939-March 12, 1940
Renewed Trade Agreement with Germany	February 10, 1940
Katyn Forest Massacre	Spring 1940
Annexation of Baltic States	June 1940
Annexation of Bessarabia and the Bukovina	July 1940
Hitler's decision to attack the USSR	July 31, 1940
Assassination of Trotsky in Mexico	August 20, 1940
End of free education in secondary schools	October 1940
Hitler issues directives for plan "Barbarossa"	November 12, 1940
Molotov in Berlin	November 12-13, 1940
Hitler orders troop concentration in the East	December 18, 1940
Coup d'état in Belgrade	March 26-27, 1941
Matsuoka in Moscow	March-April 1941
Pact of Friendship with Yugoslavia	April 4, 1941
Neutrality Pact with Japan	April 13, 1941
Stalin Chairman of Council of Peoples' Commissars	May 6, 1941
Hitler's attack on the USSR	June 22, 1941
Declaration of war by Finland	June 25, 1941
Declaration of war by Hungary	June 27, 1941
State Committee for Defense	June 30, 1941
Military Pact with Great Britain	July 12, 1941
Agreement with Czechoslovak Government-in-Exile	July 18, 1941
Stalin Commissar of Defense and Supreme Commander	July 19, 1941
Agreement with Polish Government-in-Exile	July 30, 1941
Constitution of All-Slav Committee	Summer 1941
British-Soviet invasion of Iran	August 25, 1941
Stalin, for the first time, urges a second front	September 4, 1941
Battle of Moscow	October-December 1941
State of siege in Moscow	October 19, 1941
Attack on Moscow beaten back	December 8, 1941
Molotov in London and Washington	Spring 1942
Treaty of Alliance with Great Britain	May 26, 1942
German offensive near Kursk	July 1942
Churchill in Moscow	August 1942
Battle of Stalingrad	September 1942-February 2, 1943

Stalin Marshal of USSR	March 6, 1943
Dissolution of the Comintern	May 1943
Vlasov's open letter	Spring 1943
Crisis in Soviet-Allied relations	Spring 1943
Metropolitan Sergius elected Patriarch	September 8, 1943
Conference of Allied foreign ministers in Moscow	October 15-30, 1943
Conference of Teheran	November 28-December 1, 1943
Soviet Spring offensive	March 4-May 9, 1944
Allied invasion of France	June 6, 1944
Red Army crosses Polish frontier	July 4, 1944
Warsaw Uprising	August 1, 1944
Armistice with Rumania and Bulgaria	August-September 1944
Armistice with Finland in Moscow	September 19, 1944
Churchill and Eden in Moscow	October 1944
Founding of Committee for Liberation of Russia in Prague	November 14, 1944
Treaty of Alliance with France	December 10, 1944
Yalta Conference	February 1945
Vienna captured	April 13, 1945
Berlin captured	May 2, 1945
Potsdam Conference	July 17-August 2, 1945
Declaration of war against Japan	August 8, 1945
Fourth Five Year Plan	1946-1950
II. Supreme Soviet	1946
Beginning of "Zhdanovshchina"	August 1946
Peace Treaties with Italy, Hungary, Bulgaria, Rumania, Finland	February 1947
Constitution of the Cominform	September 1947
Overthrow of monarchy in Rumania	December 1947
Communist putsch in Prague	February 1948
End of Allied Control Commission in Berlin	March 1948
Break with Tito	June 1948
Conference of foreign ministers of Eastern Bloc in Warsaw	June 1948
Berlin Blockade	from August 4, 1948
Zhdanov's death	August 31, 1948
A. Y. Vishinski Foreign Minister	March 1949
Treaty with Korea	March 1949
Constitution of Soviet Control Commission in Berlin	November 1949
Marshal Rokossovsky Supreme Commander in Poland	November 1949-November 1956
Treaty of Friendship with China	February 14, 1950
III. Supreme Soviet	1950
Stalin's letters on linguistics	Summer 1950
Korean War	June 25, 1950-July 27, 1953
Fifth Five Year Plan	1951-1955
Soviet note on Germany	March 10, 1952
XIX. Party Congress	October 5-15, 1952
Stalin's paper on "Economic Problems of Socialism"	October 1952

Doctors' trial in Moscow	January 1953
Stalin's death	**March 5, 1953**
Malenkov Prime Minister, Molotov Foreign Minister	March 1953
Beria's fall from power	July 9, 1953
Four-Power Conference in Berlin	January 25-February 18, 1954
IV. Supreme Soviet	April 1954
Conference on East Asia in Geneva	April 26-June 15, 1954
Soviet Union joins UNESCO and ILO	**April 1954**
Khrushchev and Bulganin visit Peking	October 1954
Vishinski dies in New York	November 22, 1954
The Abakumov Trial	December 1954
Bulganin succeeds Malenkov as Premier	February 8, 1955
The Warsaw Pact concluded	May 14, 1955
Bulganin and Khrushchev visit Belgrade seeking reconciliation with Tito	May 27-June 2, 1955
Nehru visits Soviet Union	June 1955
Geneva "Summit" Meeting of Eisenhower, Bulganin, Eden and Faure	July 18-23, 1955
Austrian State Treaty comes into force	July 27, 1955
Adenauer in Moscow, diplomatic relations with West Germany	September 1955
Khrushchev and Bulganin visit Southeast Asia	November-December 1955
Porkkala returned to Finland	January 1956
XX. Congress of the Soviet Communist Party	February 14-25, 1956
Riots in Tbilisi (Tiflis) Georgia	March 1956
Khrushchev and Bulganin in England	April 1956
D. T. Shepilov succeeds Molotov as Foreign Minister	June 2, 1956
Workers' riots in Poznan, Poland	June 1956
Karelo-Finnish S.S.R. reduced to status of an autonomous republic leaving 15 instead of 16 union republics within the USSR	July 1956
Gomulka in Poland	October 21, 1956
Riots in Hungary leading to collapse of Communist regime and brutal intervention by Soviet occupation forces and reestablishment of Communist rule	October-November 1956
Demonstrations in Budapest	October 23, 1956
Nagy government in Budapest	October 24, 1956
Soviet troops attack Budapest	November 4, 1956
Reshuffling of Polish government	November 11, 1956
Chou En-lai in Moscow, Warsaw, and Budapest	January 1957
Shepilov replaced by Gromyko	February 16, 1957
Mao Tse-tung's "Hundred Flowers" speech	February 27, 1957
Khrushchev's economic proposals	March 1957
Directives regarding decentralization of the economy	April 1957
Removal from office of Molotov, Malenkov, Kaganovich, and Shepilov	June 29, 1957

First Soviet earth satellite	October 4, 1957
Zhukov replaced by Malinovsky	October 26, 1957
Fortieth anniversary of the October Revolution	November 7, 1957
Kozlov named President of the R.S.F.S.R.	March 1958
Bulganin replaced by Khrushchev as Prime Minister	March 26, 1958
Nasser visits Moscow	April 1958
Pasternak affair	October 1958
First Berlin ultimatum	November 1958
Seven Year Plan	1959-1965
History of the Communist Party of the Soviet Union published	1959
XXI. Party Congress	January-February 1959
Macmillan visits Moscow	February 1959
Foreign Ministers' Conference in Geneva	Summer 1959
Khrushchev visits U.S.A.	September 1959
Russian rocket to the moon	September 1959
Twenty Year Plan	1960-1980
Mikoyan visits Cuba	February 1960
Khrushchev visits de Gaulle in Paris	March 1960
Kozlov elected to Secretariat of Central Committee	May 1960
Voroshilov replaced by Brezhnev as chairman of the Presidium of the Supreme Soviet	May 1960
Marshal Sacharev named Chief of General Staff	May 1960
U-2 incident	May 1960
Paris "Summit" Conference	May 1960
Paris Disarmament Conference	May 1960
Russian rocket sent into orbit	May 1960
U.N. intervention in the Congo	June 30, 1960
U.S. plane shot down over Barents Sea	July 1960
Cuban delegation visits Moscow	December 1960
Volga Power Works opened	December 9, 1960
U.S. pilots of plane shot down in July, 1960, released	January 25, 1961
Plenary meeting of the Central Committee	January 1961
Yuri Gagarin successfully completes first manned space flight	April 12, 1961
Kennedy and Khrushchev meet in Vienna	June 1961
Revision of Penal Code	July 1961
Draft Program announced	July 29, 1961
Soviet Union resumes nuclear testing	August 1961
Gherman Titov's space flight	August 6-7, 1961
Berlin wall put up	August 13, 1961
Conference of nonaligned nations in Belgrade	September 1961
XXII. Party Congress	October 17-31, 1961
Stalin's body removed from Lenin Memorial	October 30, 1961
Khrushchev criticizes Soviet agriculture	March 1962

COMECON meeting in Berlin	June 1962
Outbreak of Sino-Indian border war	October 1962
Cuban missile crisis	October-November 1962
Reorganization of Soviet administrative apparatus	November 1962-March 1963
Valentina Tereshkova becomes first woman cosmonaut	June 1963
Brezhnev becomes Secretary of the Central Committee	June 1963
Chinese Communist Party attacks Soviet policies in letter to CPSU	June 14, 1963
Sino-Soviet talks in Moscow	July 5-19, 1963
CPSU counters Chinese accusations	July 14, 1963
Nuclear test-ban treaty signed	August 5, 1963
U.S.-Soviet "Hot Line" installed	August 31, 1963
Incidents along the Sino-Soviet border in Siberia	November 1963
Khrushchev in Egypt and Scandinavia	May-June 1964
Mikoyan becomes chairman of the Presidium of the Supreme Soviet	July 1964
Khrushchev decides to increase consumer goods production	September 1964
Khrushchev's ouster: L. I. Brezhnev becomes Party First Secretary; and A. N. Kosygin, Premier of the USSR	October 13-14, 1964
Party reorganization	November 1964
Kosygin visits Peking	February 1965
Leonov, the first man to walk in space	March 1965
World Communist conference in Moscow	March 1965
Agricultural reforms	March 1965
Industrial reforms	September 1965
N. V. Podgorny replaces Mikoyan as President of the USSR	December 1965
USSR mediates Indian-Pakistani dispute over Kashmir at Tashkent	January 3-11, 1966
First soft landing on the moon	February 1966
Trial of Sinyavsky and Daniel	February 10-14, 1966
U.S.-Soviet agreement on cultural and technical exchanges	March 1966
XXIII. Party Congress	March-April 1966
Five Year Plan	1966-1970
Presidium renamed Politburo	April 1966
De Gaulle visits the USSR	June 20-July 1, 1966
Warsaw Pact conference in Bucharest	July 1966
Further deterioration in Sino-Soviet relations	end of 1966

INDEX OF NAMES